"STAND TO IT AND GIVE THEM HELL"

Gettysburg as the Soldiers Experienced it from
Cemetery Ridge to Little Round Top,
July 2, 1863

John Michael Priest

S̶B

Savas Beatie
California

The Library of Congress has cataloged the hardcover edition as follows:

Priest, John M., 1949-
"Stand to it and give them hell": Gettysburg as the Soldiers Experienced it from Cemetery Ridge to Little Round Top, July 2, 1863 / John Michael Priest.—First edition.
pages cm
Includes bibliographical references.
ISBN 978-1-61121-176-4
1. Gettysburg, Battle of, Gettysburg, Pa., 1863—Sources. 2. Gettysburg, Battle of, Gettysburg, Pa., 1863—Personal narratives. I. Title.
E475.53.P94 2014
973.7'349—dc23
2014020155

First paperback edition, first printing
ISBN: 978-1-61121-324-9

SB

Published by
Savas Beatie LLC
989 Governor Drive, Suite 102
El Dorado Hills, CA 95762

Phone: 916-941-6896 / (web) www.savasbeatie.com / (E-mail) sales@savasbeatie.com

Unless otherwise indicated, all photographs are from the Library of Congress.

Savas Beatie titles are available at special discounts for bulk purchases in the United States by corporations, institutions, and other organizations. For more details, please contact Special Sales, Savas Beatie LLC, 989 Governor Drive, Suite 102, El Dorado Hills, CA 95762, or you may e-mail us at sales@savasbeatie.com, or visit our website at www.savasbeatie.com for additional information.

Proudly published, printed, and warehoused in the United States of America.

To my mother-in-law and father-in-law,
Margaret M. Whitacre and Elwood Whitacre,
Who have always treated me as one of their family
And To my identical twin, William Lee Priest,

With all my love.

Table of Contents (continued)

Table of Contents

List of Maps

List of Maps (continued)

List of Maps (continued)

Introduction

"Stand to It and Give Them Hell" is the story of what happened from Cemetery Ridge to the Round Tops on July 2, 1863, from the perspective of the men who fought there. As with all of my writing projects, I began with no specific goal or thesis in mind except to learn more about the action as seen through the eyes of the men who were there.

The men whose stories comprise this book wrote it in their pain, suffering, and blood. I merely organized what they did into a readable narrative. The result is a rendition of the battle somewhat different from traditional accounts of the most written about military action in history. I will let readers identify those differences for themselves.

Each of these accounts is a precious firsthand jewel that adds to our knowledge of Gettysburg. For example, after sifting through hundreds of accounts, I discovered more than I ever anticipated I might about what happened at Sickles's Salient, and in some respects it was different than what I had been taught in my youth. Much of this might not be "new" to Gettysburg aficionados, but a lot of it was new to me. Indeed, in several significant ways it changed my perception of the battle. My sincere hope is that readers close this book and feel the same way.

I have no proverbial "axe to grind," no cause to defend, and no underlying agenda unless presenting a battle as realistically as I am capable of doing is an agenda. In weaving this tapestry of accounts, I have gathered information from literally hundreds of primary sources. I have reconstructed the events as I understand them to have occurred, but make no claim to infallibility. I do not take any of my fellow authors to task because my findings might disagree with theirs. I don't question anyone's personal motivations in their use of particular sources or their academic credibility. I have not weighed down the content of the narrative with unnecessary biographical data or extensive sidebars within the text. Instead, I inserted most of that type of information into the footnotes, where I believe it belongs.

To the men and boys who fought and died on that hallowed ground, thank you for the gift of knowledge you have bequeathed to us all.

John Michael Priest
Clear Spring, MD
July, 2014

Acknowledgments

I could never have completed this book without the support and assistance of a host of people and institutions. I am sure I have left someone out, and if so I apologize in advance. You know who you are, and please know I appreciate your help.

Kent Masterson Brown and Dr. Richard A. Sauers graciously read my manuscript and contributed valuable comments and detailed editorial suggestions to clean up my writing. John Heiser, Gettysburg National Military Park, opened the library to me and provided a great deal of generous assistance. Craig Dunne, the author of *Harvestfields of Death*, one of the finest regimental histories I have ever read, graciously loaned me his entire collection of *Gettysburg Magazine*. Special thanks to Dr. David G. Martin, co-author of *Regimental Strengths and Losses at Gettysburg*, for giving me permission to use his material in the Order of Battle.

I used resources from the Vermont Historical Society, Montpelier, VT; Goodhue County Historical Society, Red Wing, MN; Library of Congress, Washington, D.C.; Yale University, New Haven, CT; University of North Carolina, Chapel Hill, NC; Detroit Public Library, Detroit, MI; National Archives, Washington, D.C.; Virginia Historical Society, Richmond, VA; New York State Library, Albany, NY; Ontario County Historical Society, Canadaigua, NY; Bowdoin College Library, Bowdoin College, Brunswick, ME; Queen's University at Kingston, Kingston, Ontario, Canada; Indiana University, Bloomington, IN; Pennsylvania Historical Society, Philadelphia, PA; Indiana State Library, Indianapolis, IN; MOLLUS Civil War Library and Museum, Philadelphia, PA; Bentley Historical Library, University of Michigan, Ann Arbor, MI; William Clements Library, University of Michigan, Ann Arbor, MI; Central Michigan University, Mount Pleasant, MI.

Dr. Richard Sommers (now retired) and the incredible staff at the Unites States Army Heritage and Education Center in Carlisle, Pennsylvania, helped me scour the institution's tremendous collection of documents and manuscripts and were always available to answer my questions.

Morris M. Penny, co-author with J. Gary Laine of *Law's Alabama Brigade in the War Between the Union and the Confederacy* and *Struggle for the Round Tops: Law's Alabama Brigade at the Battle of Gettysburg, July 2-3, 1863* sent me his large collection of research material on the fighting on the southern end of the field, which included materials from Hillsboro College and the Alabama State Archives. Andrew J. DeCusati loaned me copies of materials from his collection on the 27th Connecticut.

Steven Stanley, cartographer, Gettysburg, Pennsylvania, granted me permission to use his base maps of the July 2 battlefield and explained to me the mysteries of using a map program that came without any instructions. Jim Woods, Gillette, New Jersey, generously loaned me his tremendous manuscript on maps of the Battle of Gettysburg to assist with the issues concerning troop positions and time during the battle.

My heartfelt thanks go to my publisher, Savas Beatie, and its managing director, Theodore P. Savas, for publishing this work. Ted, who is a good cartographer in his own right, spent hours helping me learn the craft and carefully proofed many of the maps to save me from mistakes. His staff is also outstanding. Production manager Lee Merideth and developmental editor Tom Schott deserve particular thanks for their patience in helping me prepare my manuscript for publication.

Finally, I thank my wife, Rhonda, for her more than patient support and encouragement.

Chapter 1

July 1, 1863

"I am going to whip them or they are going to whip me."

—*Robert E. Lee, Army of Northern Virginia*

Daylight, II Army Corps Headquarters, Army of the Potomac
Unionville, Maryland, 25 miles south of Gettysburg

Lieutenant Colonel Charles H. Morgan, assistant adjutant general and chief of staff, II Corps, received two dispatches from Headquarters, Army of the Potomac, before breakfast. The first order commanded the corps to march. The second admonished the corps commanders not to lose any dispatches. Absentmindedly, he placed the fragile tissue paper on his field desk, and walked outside his tent to the quartermaster's office to instruct him about managing the supply train.

When he returned to his quarters, he found his black servant packing up his bedding. Morgan's eyes shot to his desk. The orders were not there. He panicked. The servant had not seen the papers. The two rifled the tent but to no avail. With his heart pounding, Morgan finally caught sight of a yellowing paper under the valet's foot. Stuck to the sole, thoroughly soaked by the wet grass, the colonel found the now illegible command to march to Taneytown.

Relieved, Morgan verbally relayed the directive to Maj. Gen. Winfield Scott Hancock, commander of II Corps. Passing up breakfast, he rode off for army headquarters at Taneytown, 10 miles distant, to get another copy of the orders.[1]

---

1   David L. Ladd and Audrey J. Ladd, *The Bachelder Papers*, 3 vols. (Dayton, 1994), vol. 3, 1,349.

V Army Corps, Army of the Potomac
Union Mills, Maryland, 18 miles southeast of Gettysburg

The V Corps broke camp at the Littlestown-Westminster intersection before dawn and took to the road in the dark. Private Robert G. Carter (Company H, 22nd Massachusetts) and the rest of Col. William S. Tilton's 1st brigade in the First Division did not have time to boil their morning coffee. With their uniforms still damp from the long grass, the men formed ranks. Carter gnawed on a hard cracker and washed down each mouthful with a swig of day-old cold sugared coffee from his canteen.[2]

The First Division, which led the corps the day before, rotated to the back of the column. This moved Tilton's brigade to the back of the division, which in turn pushed the 118th Pennsylvania to the tail end of the entire column. Captain Francis A. Donaldson (Company K), too exhausted for active duty, remained with the brigade, under the care of the regimental surgeon, who decided to revive his run-down system with an opium pill and a shot of whiskey. The young captain awakened to the "Assembly" "feeling as tight as a musket" and ready to move on.

Before each regiment stepped off, the regimental commanders bluntly forbade straggling under any circumstances. They instructed all officers, under the penalty of arrest and court martial, to round up all skulkers, regardless of their unit and herd them forward. Everyone, including cooks and the accompanying black "contraband," had to join the advance. They expected officers to summarily shoot anyone who refused to comply. Donaldson, erroneously assuming the commanding general would give the men more than a few hours respite, did not like eating dust at the tail of the column.[3]

Private Carter recalled seeing barefooted and severely chafed men limping along the route of march. Many wore varied colored handkerchiefs tied over their heads or around their necks and a considerable number stumbled forward in their muslin or cotton drawers. The enervating heat increased in intensity as

---

2   Robert G. Carter, "Reminiscences of the Campaign and Battle of Gettysburg," in *War Papers Read Before the Commandery of the State of Maine, Military Order of the Loyal Legion of the United States*, 4 vols. (Wilmington, 1992), vol. 2, 159.

3   J. Gregory Aiken, (ed.), *Inside the Army of the Potomac, the Civil War Experience of Captain Francis Adams Donaldson* (Mechanicsburg, 1998), 295. The Survivors' Association of the 118th Pennsylvania liberally plagiarized Donaldson's letters in the regimental history.

the morning wore away. Companies and regiments sprawled along the roadside, some of the men downed by heat stroke.[4]

It took the rear of the corps until 10:00 a.m. to reach the bivouac of the 118th Pennsylvania. Not very long after Captain Donaldson and his rear guard took to the road, they happened upon Pvt. James Godfrey (Company K) whom the captain described as a stout "poor, miserable, weak minded fellow, utterly unable to stand fire." Godfrey, the headquarters' packhorse driver, with his face downcast, begged for his freedom. He insisted he had to take care of the officers' animals. Donaldson turned the pack train over to a wandering black man and ordered his men to herd the dejected private forward at bayonet point. Shortly thereafter, they provided Godfrey with a weapon and accoutrements. An obstinate Irishman from a New York regiment deliberately straggled behind the detail, forcing it to slow down. Donaldson, believing the man to be more a victim of fatigue than cowardice, did not want to drop him with a pistol shot. He placed two men with leveled bayonets behind the fellow with orders to kill him if he would not budge. Major General George Sykes (V Corps commander) startled him from behind. "Go ahead captain," he shouted, "and leave this man to me. I'll get him along." The general slapped the man several sharp blows with his riding crop while ordering him to "double-quick." The unflappable Irishman fixed his eyes on Sykes and sincerely asked, "I say Gineral, 'ave ye any tobacky about ye?" Everyone burst into uncontrollable laughter. Urging his horse forward, Sykes said to Donaldson, as he passed, "Captain, let the man go, I'll be responsible for him." Before the captain's party crossed the Pennsylvania line, he commandeered the regimental barber, whom he personally loathed, and strong-armed him into the column.[5]

At 11:00 a.m. as the head of the division staggered into Pennsylvania, the regiments unfurled their flags. Cheers rippled along the entire length of the corps, steadily increasing in volume as it progressed down the road.

Brigadier General Samuel Crawford halted his Pennsylvania Reserve division 100 yards short of the Mason-Dixon Line. The soldiers stood in ranks, while each regimental officer read a general order requiring every loyal Pennsylvanian to drive the Rebel's from their native soil. Three resounding "huzzahs" rent the air, which the men thought resonated all the way to

4 Carter, "Reminiscences," *War Papers*, vol. 2, 158-159.

5 Aiken, *Inside the Army of the Potomac*, 295-296, quote on 296.

"Rebeldom." Hurled kepis and slouch hats danced sporadically in the bright morning sky.

The soldiers resumed their march. When the lead regiment crossed into Pennsylvania, someone shouted, "Three cheers for the Keystone." Again, the "manly" Union cheer surged along the column from regiment to regiment like a succession of waves crashing ashore.[6]

Caked with road dust, their faces streaked with sweat, the men of the 22nd Massachusetts heard bugles blaring faintly in the distance along a parallel road, followed immediately by the long rolls of drums. Brigadier General James Barnes' First Division musicians picked up the strain and then Brig. Gen. Romeyn B. Ayres' buglers and drummers, in his Second Division, continued it across the Pennsylvania countryside, the martial music acting like a tonic.

For the better part of the morning, in an effort to stay awake, the exhausted men in Brig. Gen. Samuel Crawford's Third Division sang while the bands played. The moment Col. William McCandless' 1st brigade crossed into its native state the band blared out "Home Again," to which the veterans joined in the heartfelt refrain, many with tears etching salty trails down their dirty faces.[7]

The weary, filthy, and footsore men of the V Corps picked up their feet and plodded in step toward their afternoon bivouacs. "It was dry, dusty, and sultry. The heat was terrible," Pvt. William H. Brown (Company D, 44th New York) recalled. Near Hanover Junction, destroyed fencerows lined both sides of the road. Dead horses, many of them branded "C.S.A.," lay scattered everywhere. Brown latched his eyes onto a severely wounded but "fine horse" leaning in a fence corner. Badly torn up fields, indicative of the presence of large bodies of moving troops indicated to the veteran Donaldson of the 118th Pennsylvania that an extremely "hot" cavalry engagement had occurred there recently. A local told Pvt. Thomas Scott (Battery D, 5th U.S. Artillery), "They [the Rebels] went through here flying."[8]

Captain Frank J. Bell (Company I, 13th Pennsylvania Reserves), along the way, watched the men from Company K, 1st Pennsylvania Reserves, break by

---

6   "Vox Populi" to [Editor], July 8, 1863, in *Daily Evening Express*, September 13, 1863.

7   Captain Frank J. Bell, "The Bucktails at Gettysburg," Vertical Files, GNMP.

8   Carter, "Reminiscences," *War Papers*, vol. 2, 159-160; Aiken, *Inside the Army of the Potomac*, 296-297; Thomas Scott, "On Little Round Top," *National Tribune*, August 2, 1894; William H. Brown, "A View From Little Round Top During the Progress of the Battle," *Philadelphia Weekly Times*, March 17, 1882, quoted.

files from the column to briefly visit relatives as they trudged along. The hometown boys from Adams County hurriedly gulped cups of water or milk then hugged their fathers, mothers, sisters, and brothers, before scampering back to their company. "Goodbye all, I will be back when the battle is over," one fellow shouted behind him. "God Speed to you," wafted over his back.[9]

The corps stopped marching at Mudville—a small cluster of houses on Frederick Street, near the brickyard and the tannery, on the west side of Hanover. It was 4:00 p.m. Private Carter noticed that many stragglers had already rejoined their commands. The men pitched their tents and settled down for what they believed would be a long restful evening.[10]

With two hours between his regiment and the Pennsylvania border, Pvt. William P. Lamson, Jr. (Company B, 20th Maine) recalled how rapidly the pacifist German Baptist Brethren and Mennonites descended upon Colonel Tilton's 1st brigade. Upon examining the men's weapons and accoutrements, one fellow scoffed that the soldiers were "walking arsenals, licensed to do murder at their chieftain's bidding." The ladies wanted to know about the men's provisions and their culinary skills.[11]

Private Henry Clay McCauley (Company B, 1st Pennsylvania Reserves), having gotten permission to throw his knapsack upon the company wagon so he could keep up with the column, wheezed to a halt in a nearby woods with his regiment. The commissary wagon stopped among the trees, and the sergeant began distributing rations. When they played out, and the wagon headed back to the supply train to get some more, McCauley hitched a ride to retrieve his knapsack. Much to his chagrin, "Some damd theaven rascal" had stolen his knapsack. Returning empty handed, he munched his hard crackers and fumed over his loss.[12]

9   Bell, "The Bucktails at Gettysburg," GNMP.

10 Carter, "Reminiscences," *War Papers*, vol. 2 159-160; Aiken, *Inside the Army of the Potomac*, 296-297; Scott, "On Little Round Top," *National Tribune*, August 2, 1894; George Lockley Diary, July 2, 1863, Bentley Historical Library, University of Michigan, Ann Arbor, MI. Hereafter cited as UMI.

11 Aiken, *Inside the Army of the Potomac*, 297; Survivors' Association, *History of the Corn Exchange Regiment, 118th Pennsylvania Volunteers* (Philadelphia, 1888), 236; Roderick M. Engert, (ed.), *Maine to the Wilderness: The Civil War Letters of Pvt. William Lamson, 20th Maine Infantry* (Orange, 1993), 70, quoted.

12 Henry C. McCauley to Father, July 31, 1863, Vertical Files, GNMP.

II Army Corps, Army of the Potomac
Uniontown, Maryland, 20 miles southeast of Gettysburg

Brigadier General John G. Caldwell's First Division of the II Corps arrived in Uniontown early in the morning. He assigned Brig. Gen. Samuel K. Zook's 3rd brigade to march behind the supply train as the corps's rearguard. While the rest of the corps trudged ahead, Zook's people slogged along behind the lurching wagons. A short distance into the advance, however, headquarters countermanded the directive. The 145th Pennsylvania from Col. John R. Brooke's 4th brigade relieved them. The brigade slowly walked back to Uniontown, where the wagons went into park, and Zook's regiments countermarched in an effort to catch up with the division. A death premonition overshadowed Lt. James J. Purman (Company A, 140th Pennsylvania). Turning to his orderly sergeant, John A. Burns, he asked him to act as his executor upon his demise. The sergeant laughed the matter aside, but Purman could not shake his sense of eminent doom.[13]

Shortly before noon, Brig. Gen. John Gibbon's Second Division took its place in the column. From his bivouac southeast of Uniontown Lt. William Lochren (Company K, 1st Minnesota) listened apprehensively to the dull booming to the north as the brigade took to the road back to town. Once they reached the village, the column turned right toward Gettysburg. The reverberations of the artillery fire intensified the closer they got to the town.[14]

III Army Corps, Army of the Potomac
Emmitsburg, Maryland, 10 miles southwest of Gettysburg, Pennsylvania

Farther to the west, it rained. The wet morning found Maj. Gen. Daniel Sickles' III Corps bivouacked in the vicinity of Emmitsburg, Maryland, apparently to protect the flanks and the rear of the army, the lead elements of which were headed north toward Gettysburg, Pennsylvania. Part of Maj. Gen.

---

13 Robert L. Stewart, *History of the One Hundred and Fortieth Regiment Pennsylvania Volunteers* (Regimental Association, 1912), 420, 428-429; *The War of the Rebellion: A Compilation of the Official Records of the Union and the Confederate Armies*, 128 vols. (Washington, 1880-1901), Series 1, vol. 27, pt. 1, 413. Hereafter cited as: OR. All references are to Series 1 unless otherwise stated.

14 Lt. William Lochren, "The 1st Minnesota at Gettysburg," in *Glimpses of the Nation's Struggle. A Series of Papers Read Before the Minnesota Commandery of the Military Order of the Loyal Legion of the United States, 1888-1909*, 6 vols., (Wilmington, 1992), vol. 3, 46.

David Birney's First Division had moved northwest along the road to Waynesboro, Pennsylvania, to cover the Fairfield Road, which branched north about five miles beyond the town. The men of the 105th Pennsylvania never forgot the terribly mucky roads, created by the heavy rain. The division was strung out from Taneytown to Emmitsburg with the 57th Pennsylvania bivouacked at Bridgeport, midway between the two towns.[15]

Brigadier General J. H. Hobart Ward's 2nd brigade had halted within two miles of Emmitsburg. The beautiful Maryland countryside completely captivated Adj. Peter B. Ayars (99th Pennsylvania). Unmolested by warfare, the verdant farms with well-maintained outbuildings and intact fences were so completely different from the devastated homesteads he had seen throughout Virginia. Around noon, a mud-spattered officer raced up on horseback to Capt. George Winslow, commanding Battery D, 1st New York, as he stood alongside the railroad line, which ran into the village from the north. The man asked for General Sickles, and the captain pointed him in the right direction.[16]

Simultaneously, the adjutant of the 110th Pennsylvania, which belonged to Col. P. Regis De Trobriand's 3rd brigade, formed the regiment for its monthly muster, which he should have done the day before. While the company first sergeants called the rolls, the staff officer galloped past the regiment frantically asking for Sickles. The general was not with his corps. Having ridden forward to reconnoiter the South Mountain gap with his two division commanders, Birney and Brig. Gen. Andrew A. Humphreys (Second Division), he had left Brig. Gen. Joseph B. Carr (1st brigade, Second Division) in charge. The aide reported the situation at the front to Carr. Major General John Reynolds, the commander of I Corps, had been killed and a terrible battle was occurring above Gettysburg, some 12 miles distant. Carr immediately ordered the "long roll." Buglers sounded the "Assembly." Sickles and Birney heard the commotion and returned to the corps. Humphreys had gone on a separate reconnaissance with his adjutant and inspector general, Capt. Adolfo F. Cavada. At the same time, Maj. Charles Hamlin, assistant adjutant general of the Second Division, III

15 James M. Martin, et al., *History of the 57th Regiment Pennsylvania Veteran Volunteer Infantry* (Meadville, 1904), 86; *OR* 27, pt. 1, 482; Kate M. Scott, *History of the 105th Regiment, Pennsylvania Volunteers* (Baltimore, 1993), 81.

16 George B. Winslow, "Battery D at Gettysburg," *Philadelphia Weekly Times*, July 26, 1879; Ladd and Ladd, *The Bachelder Papers*, vol. 3, 590; Peter B. Ayars, "The 99th Pennsylvania," *National Tribune*, February 4, 1886.

Corps, detached Col. George Burling's 3rd brigade to cover the Hagerstown Road with Capt. James E. Smith's 4th New York Independent Battery.[17]

Sometime before 1 p.m., Sickles received his orders to proceed to Gettysburg. The men began breaking up their bivouacs. Birney received his formal marching orders at 2:00 p.m. The men of the 99th Pennsylvania had just begun to boil their coffee when they heard the distant thudding boom of artillery fire to the north. The regimental bugler blared "pack up." The brigade stepped out in a heavy shower, churning the muddy road into slimy muck as they headed north toward Gettysburg.[18]

Birney's division struck the Emmitsburg Road, with Brig. Gen. Charles K. Graham's 1st brigade in the lead, marching along one side of the road parallel to Humphreys' division along the opposite bank. The artillery and the ammunition train lumbered along between them. One mile down the pike, Humphreys and his staff came across Lt. Col. Julius Hayden, the III Corps adjutant and inspector general, who was waiting with several guides. Hayden directed the division onto a tortuous "country wagon road" west of the Emmitsburg Road.[19]

After struggling two miles through the mud toward Gettysburg, Sickles received orders to send De Trobriand's brigade with Winslow's Battery D, 1st New York, back to Emmitsburg to protect the South Mountain passes from any possible Confederate flank movement behind the III Corps along the Frederick Road. Sickles was to proceed immediately with his remaining two divisions and three of the corps' five batteries to Gettysburg and report to Maj. Gen. Oliver Otis Howard, commanding the XI Corps. A great many of the men, in typical understatement, referred to the advance as "very hard." Adjutant Ayars (99th Pennsylvania), noting that the temperature seemed to be

---

17 *OR* 27, pt. 1, 530, 570; Captain J. C. Hamilton, "Recollections," 116, Military Order of the Loyal Legion of the United States (MOLLUS) Civil War Library and Museum, Philadelphia, PA. Hereinafter cited as CWL.

18 Henry M. Howell to "Mother," July 5 1863, in "The 124th at Gettysburg," *Middletown, Whig Press*, July 22, 1863; *OR* 27, pt. 1, 482, 497, 500, 502; John P. Nicholson, (ed.), *Pennsylvania at Gettysburg, Ceremonies at the Dedication of the Monuments Erected by the Commonwealth of Pennsylvania*, 3 vols., (Harrisburg, 1904), vol. 1, 355; George R. Large, (comp.), *Battle of Gettysburg*, (Shippensburg, 1999), 81-82; Ayars, "99th Pennsylvania," *National Tribune*, February 4, 1886: Colonel Craig said the regiment moved east of Emmitsburg around 1:15 p.m. and received orders to move at 4:00 p.m.

19 Hamilton, "Recollections," 117; CWL; Captain Adolfo Fernandez Cavada Diary, July 2, 1863, FSNMP Vertical Files; *OR* 27, pt. 1, 531.

above the 90 degree mark, watched squads of soldiers collapse along the roadside from heat prostration. He recalled the column stopping once for a mere 15 minutes during the entire 12-mile trek. The intense heat made the water in their canteens almost too hot to drink. Graham's regiments did not stop to replenish their water supply at Marsh Creek, the only stream they passed en route to the field.[20]

A number of the heavily clad 114th Pennsylvania soldiers decided to rid themselves of their oppressive overcoats. When Sgt. Alexander W. Given and Cpl. Robert Kenderdine (both Company F) encountered a farmer and his family heading south along the Pike in an open farm wagon, the sergeant asked the fellow if he wanted an overcoat. The farmer said he did not want it, but he would keep theirs for them. At that, both of the men threw their greatcoats into the man's lap, knowing full well they would never see them again.[21]

Lieutenant General James Longstreet's Headquarters
Longstreet's Corps, Army of Northern Virginia
Greenwood, Pennsylvania–
About six miles east of Chambersburg
Noon-4:00 p.m.

Longstreet, with his staff, and Col. Arthur J. L. Fremantle of the Coldstream Guards left headquarters at noon and headed east along the Chambersburg Pike. Riding alongside of Lt. Gen. Ambrose P. Hill's Third Corps, they soon came abreast of the "Florida Brigade" near the crest of the gap over South Mountain. Fremantle noted little difference between the renowned brigade and the rest of the Confederate army except the soldiers in the ranks seemed older than the ones he had previously seen. A number of them haled Fremantle and asked if the general riding in front was Longstreet. When he answered, "Yes," a large number of them broke ranks and ran forward, about 100 yards, to gape at the man whose solid reputation in battle they

---

20 Large, *Battle of Gettysburg*, 81-82; OR 27, pt. 1, 519; George B. Winslow, "Battery D" *Philadelphia Weekly Times*, July 26, 1879. Ladd and Ladd, *The Bachelder Papers*, vol. 3, 590; Francis A. Osbourn, "The 20th Indiana Infantry," Francis A. Osbourn Collection, Indiana State Library. Hereinafter cited as ISL. Ayars, "99th Pennsylvania"; *National Tribune*, February 4, 1886; Scott, *105th Pennsylvania*, 81; Nicholson, *Pennsylvania at Gettysburg*, vol. 1, 355. I used the Park Commission time references to determine the sequence of events upon the battlefield.

21 Kenderdine, *A California Tramp* 330. Typescript copy, 3, Vertical Files.

acknowledged. An "immense compliment" to an officer, Fremantle mused. Two hours down the Pike, the sounds of battle drifted over the officers' heads. While it increased in volume as they continued east, it did not alarm Fremantle. He dismissed it as "not very heavy."

Riding next to the colonel, Henry T. Harrison, Longstreet's "spy," regaled him with his folksy observations about what they were marching up against. "A pretty tidy bunch of blue-bellies in or near Gettysburg," the filthy scout warned him before adding he had spent time among their ranks not three days before. Fremantle politely listened to Harrison's bantering. Presently the officers rode upon Col. David Lang's Florida brigade. Having served under Longstreet earlier in the war, they immediately recognized him. Behind his back, they shouted among themselves, "Look out for work now, boys, for here's the old bull-dog again."

By 3:00 p.m., Longstreet and his entourage had reached the northwestern side of the battlefield, about an hour and a half west of Seminary Ridge. Wounded men staggered and hobbled around them, heading away from the battle. Fremantle quietly studied the wounded on stretchers and the occasional ambulances, which rocked past them. A large number of the injured had been horribly mangled but the hardened veterans by whom they passed took little note of them. "This is the effect of two years' almost uninterrupted fighting," he later explained. Yankee prisoners also sprayed around their advance—a colonel with a nasty facial wound, a Confederate carrying a recently captured Pennsylvania regimental flag.[22]

III Army Corps, Army of the Potomac
The Emmitsburg Road
Several miles south of Gettysburg

Fleeing civilians clogged the pike, making progress even more difficult for the III Corps. Corporal William E. Loring (Company E, 141st Pennsylvania) carefully noted how the frightened people used every type of vehicle they could to escape the battle. They flowed around Graham's regiments in a human stream. Some of the women wrung their hands in distress. The Union troops were too late, they blubbered. The Rebs had already whipped the Federals.

---

22 Arthur J. L. Fremantle, *Three Months in the Southern States* (Edinburgh, 1863), 252-253, quote on 253.

Others waved their handkerchiefs at the panting veterans and urged them on with cheers of "God bless you all." Farmers blocked the 2nd U. S. Sharpshooters' column. Fearing the Confederates would steal everything they owned, they had stacked their wagons as high as they could with their children on top of the precarious loads. The soldiers, also called "Berdans," repeatedly asked the frantic civilians about the progress of the battle. Amid the sounds of the fighting echoing lowly over the column from the north, 1st Sgt. Wyman S. White (Company F, 2nd U.S. Sharpshooters) encountered a nearly hysterical woman who sobbed, "Yes, they are fighting terribly up there. There's two men killed in our back pasture." The veterans chuckled at her distress. Having seen thousands of corpses since the war began, becoming completely unstrung at the sight of two dead men seemed absolutely ludicrous to them.[23]

Humphreys' Division, III Corps, Army of the Potomac
On a back road
About one and one half miles west of the Emmitsburg Road

Six miles southwest of Gettysburg, Capt. John G. McBlair, an aide-de-camp of the III Corps, intercepted Humphreys' column with a communiqué from Howard to Sickles, warning him to guard his left flank as he neared Gettysburg. Moments later, a black civilian guide, who had taken the I Corps onto the field earlier that day, approached Humphreys and advised him that no other Federal troops were west of the Emmitsburg Road. "The road is full of 'em, heaps of Rebels!" he warned, but, as it turned out, to no avail to the men of the III Corps.[24]

II Army Corps Army of the Potomac
Taneytown, Maryland, 12 miles southeast of Gettysburg

The 1st Volunteer Brigade had spent the entire day awaiting orders. That morning, the individual battery commissary staffs issued a three-day supply of coffee to their respective commands along with a ration of fresh, raw beef. Later on, as the rumors of the death of General Reynolds and the capture of a

23 William E. Loring, "Gettysburg," *National Tribune,* July 9, 1885; Russell C. White, (ed.), *The Civil War Diary of Wyman S. White, First Sergeant of Company F, 2nd United States Sharpshooter Regiment, 1861-1865* (Baltimore, 1991), 162. Hereinafter cited as *Wyman S. White,* quoted.

24 Henry N. Blake, *Three Years in the Army of the Potomac* (Boston, 1864), 203.

Rebel brigade reached their bivouac, the artillerymen prepared for battle. The extra wagons went to the rear as they waited to move out.[25]

The infantry was not far behind them. Caldwell's division began passing through the town in the forenoon. Brooke's 4th brigade led the division with the 53rd Pennsylvania at the head of the column. Second Lieutenant Charles A. Hale (Company H, 5th New Hampshire), Col. Edward Cross's aide, still chafed over the tongue lashing the colonel had given him the day before when he openly criticized Cross for mentioning his death premonition for the second time in as many days. Today, since the colonel behaved more like his normal cheerful self, Hale concluded that Cross had put the entire affair out of his mind. The veteran 19-year-old Hale, who had risen from the ranks and had survived wounds at Fredericksburg and Chancellorsville, put no stock in such mystic phenomenon. A man died when his time was up and nothing more.[26]

Cross had thoroughly angered the men of the 148th Pennsylvania the night before when he relieved their commander, Lt. Col. Robert McFarlane, and arbitrarily handed the regiment over to Col. Henry B. McKeen (81st Pennsylvania). Adjutant Joseph W. Muffly later wrote, "This act of Colonel Cross was wholly unjustifiable, the culmination of a series of insults and indignities, which, taking advantage of [Col. James A.] Beaver's absence, he had inflicted on the Regiment." The demotion left the rank and file in an ugly, defiant mood. The exhausted 145th Pennsylvania, having not left Uniontown until noon behind the lumbering II Corps wagon train, had been relieved from its onerous duty one mile to the east of the village. It ran the rest of the way to Taneytown, where it rejoined its own brigade.[27]

By then Lt. Col. Charles H. Morgan, chief of staff, II Corps, his stomach growling and his back end sore from a great deal of riding, went to the hotel and ordered lunch. Just as he stuffed the first bite into his mouth, an orderly came with a directive for him to report to army headquarters.

He walked in on a conference between Maj. Gen. George G. Meade, the recently appointed commander of the Army of the Potomac, and major

---

25 Regimental Committee, *History of the 5th Massachusetts Battery* (Boston, 1902), 622.

26 Charles A. Hale, "With Colonel Cross in the Gettysburg Campaign," in John Rutter Brooke Papers, Miscellaneous Papers, Pennsylvania Historical Society, Philadelphia, PA, 3; Hereinafter cited as PHS.

27 Joseph W. Muffly, (ed.), *The Story of Our Regiment, A History of the 148th Pennsylvania Vols.* (Des Moines, 1904), 244, quoted; *OR* 27, pt. 1, 413.

generals Daniel Butterfield and Hancock. Meade ordered Hancock, in the event of General Reynolds' wounding, to take command of the forces in the field. Butterfield quickly informed him that Howard (XI Corps) had seniority and should assume field command. Meade gruffly replied he did not know Howard very well, but he knew Hancock and he needed an officer he knew and trusted in charge. Morgan, at the time, could not understand why Meade did not go to the front, rather than Hancock. (He later learned that Meade had decided to defend the Pipe Creek Line and that by staying in Taneytown he was within easy riding distance of the II, V, and VI corps.) At 12:50 p.m., Hancock and Morgan set off toward Gettysburg in the general's ambulance with their horses in tow and the staff following behind. Despite the driver making the best speed he could, about four miles down the road Hancock decided he and Morgan would mount up and hurry to the town on their own.[28]

They caught up with the head of Brooke's brigade. Lieutenant Charles P. Hatch, Brooke's acting assistant adjutant general, riding up front with Brooke and Hancock, reined to a halt as a mounted orderly spurred to a clattering stop next to the general and handed him a note. Hancock turned to Brooke, informed him of Reynolds' death, spat some directives at him, and galloped toward Gettysburg with his staff close behind. Five miles south of town, they intercepted an ambulance with a blanket-covered corpse inside. Whose body was it? Hancock asked the officer riding alongside. "General Reynolds, sir."[29]

The Taneytown Road
Gettysburg, Pennsylvania
4:45 p.m.

Hancock and his officers rode in silence for several miles, the bitter memory of Reynolds' corpse, lingering in their minds. Supply wagons choked the road near the town. Hancock, discovering they belonged to the XI Corps, vehemently ordered the pike cleared. While the pack animals and wagons struggled south away from the town, the popping staccato of skirmishing reverberated in the distance.

Once the general and his officers cleared the trains, they stumbled into demoralized remnants of the I Corps south of the town cemetery. Lieutenant

28 Ladd and Ladd, *The Bachelder Papers*, vol. 3, 1,349-1,350, quote on 1,352.

29 Nicholson, *Pennsylvania at Gettysburg*, vol. 1, 330.

Colonel Morgan swore the mob, despite its appearance, consisted of regiments rather than the disorganized squads typical of shattered commands. The officers bolted into the throng and shoved the men into regimental lines on the western side of the pike behind a stonewall.

They rounded the point where the Taneytown Road intersected the Emmitsburg Road and continued to the Baltimore Pike. Turning southeast in the road, Hancock spied the one-armed Major General Howard on foot near the cemetery gatehouse. Riding up to him, Hancock said, "General, I have been ordered here to take command of all troops on the field, until General Slocum arrives." He offered to show Howard the written order he carried in his pocket, but Howard declined, stating he was glad that Hancock had arrived. Brigadier General Gouverneur K. Warren, chief engineer of the army, soon came up and also energetically pitched in to restore order to what Morgan described as the "entirely unreliable and quite unmanageable" XI Corps.

With the fields to the north and northwest secured by Brig. Gen. John Buford's cavalrymen, Hancock turned his attention toward Culp's Hill and its defense. He sent Morgan to order Maj. Gen. Abner Doubleday, who had assumed command of the I Corps, to dispatch a brigade to stymie a Confederate battle line, which was assembling to attack it. As demoralized as his men, Doubleday protested. He had no ammunition. His men were too exhausted. Hancock, riding behind Morgan, bellowed, "General . . . I want you to understand that I am in command here, send every man you have." Doubleday complied.[30]

XII Army Corps, Army of the Potomac
Cemetery Ridge and Little Round Top
Two miles south of Gettysburg
5:00 p.m.

Brigadier General John W. Geary's Second Division, XII Corps, was also on the move, northwest along the Baltimore Pike. Near the point where Rock Creek crossed the road, Geary pulled his 1st and 3rd brigades away from the rest of the corps and directed them toward Cemetery Ridge to bolster the left of the I Corps' overextended line. Brigadier General George S. Greene's five regiments of the 3rd brigade connected with the left of the I Corps north of the

---

30 Ladd and Ladd, *The Bachelder Papers*, vol. 3, 1,350-1,352, quote on 1,352.

George Weikert farm, while the five regiments of Col. Charles Candy's 1st brigade continued the line south to the northern base of Little Round Top. Candy detached the 5th Ohio and the 147th Pennsylvania to form a skirmish outpost on top of the hill.[31]

Back on Cemetery Hill, Hancock, received word of the XII Corps' arrival and dispatched Morgan to inspect its placement upon the field. Morgan soon encountered the XII Corps' commander Maj. Gen. Henry W. Slocum. The general, having encountered so many XI Corps refugees—his provost guard had rounded up hundreds of them, he said—thought another Chancellorsville rout had occurred. Believing the Rebels were close on Howard's tail, he had decided to secure the area along their line of retreat.

Morgan told him to assume command of the field, but Slocum declined. Headquarters had specifically picked Hancock for the job, he insisted, and he did not want to take command in a situation in which he did not have real control. When Morgan informed him that Hancock, under orders, transferred the command of the field to him, he readily accepted the responsibility to command the field. With that, Morgan turned his horse about and returned to the cemetery. A staffer informed him that Hancock had departed for Taneytown to confer with Meade. The colonel wheeled his exhausted mount about and spurred after him.[32]

Robert E. Lee's Headquarters, Army of Northern Virginia
In the vicinity of the Lutheran Seminary
Seminary Ridge, Gettysburg, Pennsylvania
4:30 p.m.

Longstreet and his officers arrived at the crest of Seminary Ridge, north of the Lutheran Seminary, in time to see the Yankees retreating to the next large hill south of the town. He dismounted and strode to Lee, who quickly informed him of the Federal position across from them. Longstreet patiently followed Lee's pointing finger as he defined the Yankee lines. "Old Pete" spent about 10 minutes examining their reorganizing troops through his field glasses. He then turned to the commanding general.

---

31 Large, *Battle of Gettysburg*, 120-122.

32 Ladd and Ladd, *The Bachelder Papers*, vol. 3, 1,352-1,353.

"If we could have chosen a point to meet our plans of operation, I do not think we could have found a better one than that upon which they are now concentrating." Growing bolder, he continued:

All we have to do is throw our army around by their left, and we shall interpose between the Federal army and Washington. We can get a strong position and wait, and if they fail to attack us we shall have everything in condition to move back to-morrow night in the direction of Washington, selecting beforehand a good position into which we can place our troops to receive battle next day. Finding our object is Washington or that army, the Federals will be sure to attack us. When they attack, we shall beat them, as we proposed to do before we left Fredericksburg, and the probabilities of our success will be great.

"No," Lee emphatically answered, "the enemy is there, and I am going to attack him there."

Longstreet protested. His plan would put the roads to Baltimore and Washington under Lee's control. He bluntly reminded Lee that his original orders would have placed the Army of Northern Virginia behind Meade and put him on the offensive rather than on the defensive.

"No," Lee insisted, "They are there in position, and I am going to whip them or they are going to whip me."

Longstreet sensed he had piqued the commanding general. Rather than beat a dead horse, he resignedly dropped the matter and walked away, intent upon renewing his argument in the morning.[33]

The III Corps, Army of the Potomac
Emmitsburg Road-Millerstown Road
One and three-fourths miles southwest of Gettysburg
6:00 p.m.

Despite the terrible marching conditions, the exhausted men from Graham's brigade reached the intersection of the Emmitsburg Road and the Millerstown Road around 6:00 p.m. As the men filed right onto the Millerstown Road, they passed by John Wentz's log cabin. Sergeant Alexander Given

---

33 James Longstreet, "Lee's Right Wing at Gettysburg," in Robert Underwood Johnson and Clarence Clough Buel, (eds.), *Battles and Leaders of the Civil War*, 4 Vols. (New York, 1884-88), vol. 3, 339-340, quote on 339.

(Company F, 114th Pennsylvania) noticed a man sitting in the doorway of the single story house, cradling a baby in his arms. He soon would be getting out of there, he thought to himself. Turning east on the lane, the regiment staggered along in the fading light, seeking some much needed respite for the night.[34]

II Corps, Army of the Potomac
On the Taneytown Road, South of Cemetery Hill
Just Before Dark

At the rear of Caldwell's column, 1st Lt. Josiah Favill (Company H, 57th New York), Zook's aide, noted how the sweating soldiers churned up the fine, suffocating dust in the road as they shuffled along. At times, it seemed knee deep. In the distance, he thought he heard the "the music of the distant guns."[35]

The II Corps' march devolved into a persistent, exhausting "stop and go." Zook's brigade briefly halted at 8:00 p.m. to sup upon hard crackers and coffee then pushed on again into the darkness. Along the way the 148th Pennsylvania shuffled by a bunch of very badly shaken young women who told the veterans the Rebels were close by and they "hoped to God" the Union army would whip them.[36]

V Army Corps, Army of the Potomac
Hanover, Pennsylvania
13 miles southeast of Gettysburg
9:00 p.m.

The fatigued soldiers of the V Corps had hardly finished drinking their coffee. Some had already succumbed to the deep sleep of exhaustion when a messenger clattered down Frederick Street headed toward headquarters. Minutes later, the regimental buglers blared out: "Pack-up" and the "Assembly." Captain Francis Donaldson (118th Pennsylvania) glanced at his watch in the bright moonlight. It was 9:00 p.m. The begrimed veterans struck

34 Large, *Battle of Gettysburg*, 84; Kenderdine, "A California Tramp," 4, GNMP; Scott, *105th Pennsylvania*, 82; Martin, *57th Pennsylvania*, 86. Given probably got the Rose house confused with Sherfy's. In the history of the 2nd New Hampshire, the author referred to a cabin (Wentz's) in the corner of the Peach Orchard. The column had to have turned down the Emmitsburg Road.

35 Favill, Josiah Marshall, *Diary of a Young Officer* (Chicago, 1909), 242.

36 Muffly, *148th Pennsylvania*, 534; Stewart, *140th Pennsylvania*, 420.

their tents, packed up their blanket rolls, and assembled in the road. In the moonlight, the corps shuffled into the village and turned northwest toward Gettysburg. Women and children lined the route, passing food and water to the dirty soldiers. "Don't let them come any further, boys," a Michigander heard someone say in the night. "We will not, we will not," the Wolverines replied. Barnes' division left the village in a dejected silence. No one spoke. The monotonous tramping of feet, punctuated occasionally by the clatter of an officer's horse, was all that Donaldson heard in the night.

A few miles north of Hanover, the column passed through McSherreystown and turned west. The bands and the regimental drummers struck up patriotic airs to keep the men moving. Civilians lined the darkened streets wishing the soldiers "God-speed" only to have a number of the hardened grousers shout back, "Fall in! Take a rifle, and defend your own firesides!" Others greeted the exhausted veterans of the 83rd Pennsylvania with refreshing water and reassuring choruses of "The Star Spangled Banner."[37]

III Army Corps, Army of the Potomac
The George Weikert Farm
One and one half miles south of Gettysburg
6:30 p.m.

Graham's regiments, intent upon bivouacking for the night and giving their tired bodies some rest, filed into the field south of the farmhouse between the wood lot and the farm lane. The brigade camped in column of regiments, facing west. The 63rd Pennsylvania formed the head of the formation, followed respectively by the 105th, 57th, 114th, 68th, and 141st Pennsylvania regiments. Dinner fires soon glimmered in the encroaching darkness. The men nestled down on the marshy ground amid the rocks and brush to sleep. "Alas! Before the setting of another sun many of our number were sleeping the long last sleep, only to be broken by the sound of the archangel's trumpet," Sgt. John D. Bloodgood (141st Pennsylvania) recollected. He marveled how men like he, who faced a 50 percent chance of being killed or wounded in the impending

---

37 Carter, "Reminiscences," *War Papers*, vol. 2, 161; Aiken, *Inside the Army of the Potomac*, 298; Survivors' Association, *Corn Exchange Regiment*, n. 236-237; George Lockley Diary, July 2, 1863, UMI, quoted; Scott, "On Little Round Top," *National Tribune*, August 2, 1894; Francis J. Parker, *The Story of the Thirty-Second Regiment Massachusetts Infantry* (Boston, 1886), 164; D. R. Rodgers to "Julia," July 6, 1863, Vertical Files, GNMP.

battle, could sleep as soundly and as heedless of the dangers of the next day as he did that evening.[38]

Between 6:30–7:00 p.m., Ward's Second brigade went into camp a short distance southwest of Graham's men along a stone fence on the eastern border of the first belt of woods east of John T. Weikert's house. The men of the 124th New York bedded down with their weapons and accoutrements. Being the professionals they were, they groused about their meager rations while complying with the order. The officers of the 2nd U.S. Sharpshooters allowed the men to make coffee fires as long as they kept them small. As the left flank of the brigade, they covered the valley along the Millerstown Road from the eastern side of the Wheatfield to the base of Little Round Top's northern slope.[39]

Disconcerting news arrived in the 4th Maine, the Army of the Potomac had been defeated and was rallying on a hill to the north. Colonel Elijah Walker sadly looked up through the smoky haze, which had settled over the battlefield, and noticed how the stars still dimly shown through it. They were on free soil he reminded himself, and they were determined to defend it at the expense of their lives.[40]

At 8:30 p.m., Capt. John M. Cooney (40th New York), Ward's assistant adjutant general, rode into Ward's bivouac, asking for Colonel Walker. Recognizing his friend's voice, the colonel responded, "I am here, captain. Is it our turn to establish a picket line?" " Yes, it is the order of General Sickles that your regiment establish a picket line," Cooney replied, "the right to connect with the I Corps' pickets on the left with those of the II Corps." Depressed and exhausted, Walker reluctantly ordered his men to fall in. They quietly marched

38 David Craft, *History of the One Hundred Forty-first Regiment, Pennsylvania Volunteers, 1862-1865* (Towanda, 1885), 118; Edward R. Bowen, "Collis' Zouaves: The 114th Pennsylvania Infantry at Gettysburg," *Philadelphia Weekly Times*, June 22, 1887; Nicholson, *Pennsylvania at Gettysburg*, vol. 1, 355; Scott, *105th Pennsylvania*, 82; *OR 27*, pt. 1, 497-498; John D. Bloodgood, *Reminiscences of the War* (New York, 1893), 131-132, quoted on 132; Nicholson, *Pennsylvania at Gettysburg*, vol. 1, 387.

39 Osbourn, "20th Indiana," ISL; Craft, "141st Pennsylvania," 118; The Executive Committee, *Maine at Gettysburg, Report of the Maine Commissioners* (Gettysburg, 1994), 159, 349; Albert A. Tucker, "Orange Blossoms: Services of the 124th New York at Gettysburg," *National Tribune*, January 24, 1886; Harvey Hanford, "Hanford, J. Harvey, The Experience of a Private in the 124th New York in the Battle," *National Tribune*, September 21, 1885; White, *Wyman S. White*, 162.

40 Executive Committee, *Maine at Gettysburg*, 179-180; Ladd and Ladd, *The Bachelder Papers*, vol. 2, 1,093.

west. Crossing the Emmitsburg Road near Codori's farm the men pushed another 150 to 200 yards farther west and settled down behind the rail fence along the crest of the ridge, prepared to spend an anxious but quiet night there. While he did connect with the I Corps pickets on his right, Walker failed to find any II Corps troops. Instead, he discovered a few of Brigadier General Buford's cavalry videttes.[41]

Around 10:00 p.m., the 63rd Pennsylvania from Graham's 1st brigade received orders to pack up and follow a guide out for picket duty. The picket reserves nestled down under the cover of the banks of the Emmitsburg Road immediately west of the Peach Orchard, while the forward pickets edged 300 yards west and north of the Millerstown-Emmitsburg Road intersection for an uneasy night. Their left flank rested on the Sherfy house and barn. Back in the brigade bivouac, the night passed without incident other than the appearance of the 105th Pennsylvania's three stragglers who wandered into the regiment sometime during the evening.[42]

Meanwhile, about two miles farther to the west, a III Corps staff officer found Humphreys' Second Division meandering along a side road toward Sach's covered bridge which crossed Marsh Creek about three-fourths of a mile southeast of Black Horse Tavern. He told the general to go into position to the left of Gettysburg when he arrived on the field. Humphreys interpreted the directive to mean that he should change his course east toward the Emmitsburg Road and gave instructions accordingly. Lieutenant Colonel Julius Hayden, III Corps adjutant and inspector general, however, insisted he take the division onto the field by way of Black Horse Tavern to the Fairfield Road. Rather than argue with Hayden, whose instructions came directly from Sickles, Humphreys directed the division to cross to the north side of Marsh Creek.

First Lieutenant Henry N. Blake (Company K, 11th Massachusetts) bitterly recollected how the generals and their staffs laughed at the rank and file as they slogged through Marsh Creek, rather than use the bridge. Once across, the column turned left along the creek bank until it intercepted a road, which

---

41   Executive Committee, *Maine at Gettysburg*, 159, 189; Edmund J. Raus, *A Generation on the March–The Union Army at Gettysburg* (Lynchburg, 1987), 22; Ladd and Ladd, *The Bachelder Papers*, vol. 2, 1,093, quoted.

42   Thomas Rafferty, "Gettysburg," in *Personal Recollections of the War of the Rebellion Read Before the Commandery of the State of New York*, 4 vols. (New York, 1891), vol. 4, 5; *OR* 27, pt. 1, 482, 498, 500; Raus, *A Generation on the March*, 119; Loring, "Gettysburg," *National Tribune*, July 9, 1885; Nicholson, *Pennsylvania at Gettysburg*, vol. 1, 355, 387.

branched to the right going northwest. Half a mile or so later, the guide, fearing they had gone the wrong direction, halted the column. Humphreys, rather than risk precipitating a firefight in the dark, quietly passed the order through the ranks for no one to make any noise. The general and Hayden dismounted and gingerly treaded their way up the ascending road toward Black Horse Tavern, which they assumed was in front of them. The sounds of a Rebel picket outpost emanating from the nearby field turned the two officers around. They stole back to the head of the division to discover that a couple of men from the 73rd New York, who left the column to scrounge for food, had stumbled undetected upon a Confederate artillery crew enjoying their dinner. They bagged one of the Rebel sentinels who had mistaken the Yankees for reinforcements. The New Yorkers told him it was all right—making such a mistake as that in the dark. They returned him to the column. When brought before Humphreys, the captive wasted no time in telling the general and Hayden that they came very close to the 30 or more guns posted on the ridge in front of them.

An order rippled along the division to neither talk nor light matches. The Yankees, with their solitary prisoner, quickly and quietly about-faced and retraced their steps back to the covered bridge. Picking up the road at that point, the division continued east and crossed Willoughby Run about 1,400 feet south of the school house on the Millerstown Road. Hayden took the column north to the school then turned northeast along the road. A short distance beyond the school Humphreys brought his command to a halt. The general and his staff dragged the Rebel into John Flaharty's small house to interrogate him some more. Flaharty further told Humphreys that rebel cavalry pickets were in the woods beyond his house. If he went any further, he admonished the general, he would end up in a fight. A company of infantry preceded the division when it resumed its march, and the Yankees could see the Rebels' campfires flickering through the trees.[43]

---

43 Cavada, Diary, July 2, 1863, FSNMP; OR 27, pt. 1, 531; Blake, *Three Years in the Army*, 203-204; Henri LeFevre Brown, *History of the Third Regiment, Excelsior Brigade, 72nd New York Volunteer Infantry, 1861-1865* (Jamestown, 1902), 104; "Gladiator," to [Editor], August 3, 1863, *New York Sunday Mercury*, August 9, 1863.

De Trobriand's Brigade, III Army Corps, Army of the Potomac
Near Emmitsburg, Maryland
Evening

The newly commissioned 1st Lt. Edwin B. Houghton (Company H, 17th Maine) awoke with the first light of July 1 and noticed the overcast threatening sky. De Trobriand's 3rd brigade, to whom his regiment belonged, had enjoyed a leisurely morning until 9:00 a.m. when the men struck camp and within the hour fell into column, ready to march. The brigade still remained in formation at noon when the sky opened up and it began to pour. Finally, at 2:00 p.m., the regiments got under way. Two miles down the road, De Trobriand halted his command and ordered the brigade to pitch their tents.[44] They camped in a meadow on the grounds of St. Joseph's Academy, completely unaware of the day's fateful events at Gettysburg.

Father Francis Burlando and the Mother Superior of the girls' school took De Trobriand, his staff, and Houghton on a grand tour of the institution. The lieutenant thoroughly admired the varied architecture of the place, with its well-kept lawns and covered passageways between the buildings. He paid particular attention to a few of the young ladies who had not gone home for the summer break yet. The interior walls of a few of the buildings boasted a number of works which he assumed were done by the "masters," and the library, in particular, was one of the finest he had ever seen.[45]

The brigade posted its pickets. Early in the evening, the singing which had rolled through the camp ceased, and the men bedded down for the night. Major Solomon S. Matthews (5th Michigan), the acting brigade officer of the day, posted himself in a grove of trees near the college garden. With the sweet perfume of the flowers wafting through the trees on the evening breeze, he stood there at midnight in its glorious serenity and could not believe that war had come to such a tranquil land.[46]

---

44 Edwin B. Houghton, *The Campaigns of the 17th Maine* (Portland, 1866), 84.

45 Ibid., 84-87.

46 Monument Commission, *Michigan at Gettysburg* (Detroit, 1889), 99-100.

Army of the Potomac Headquarters
Taneytown, Maryland
13 miles southeast of Gettysburg
Midnight

The exhausted Colonel Morgan eventually arrived at Taneytown. During his tedious night ride, his equally fatigued mount had thrown two shoes. The sight of one of Hancock's aides down in the road, alongside his dying mount, dogged him as he dismounted and reported as required before finding a place to sleep.[47]

47 Ladd and Ladd, *The Bachelder Papers*, vol. 3, 1,353.

Chapter 2

July 2, 1863

1:00 a.m.-9:00 a.m.

"... order the instant death of any soldier who fails in his duty on this day."

—*Major General George G. Meade, Army of the Potomac*

III Army Corps, Army of the Potomac
Emmitsburg, Maryland
10 miles southwest of Gettysburg
1:00 a.m.

The III Corps troops at Emmitsburg received their orders to move out. It took Col. George Burling almost three hours to recall his scattered brigade from its outpost duty. He got his regiments going sometime before 4:00 a.m. Colonel De Trobriand's brigade, however, had hardly prepared its bivouac for the evening. The men had not yet pitched their tents or posted pickets. Sickles expected them to arrive at Gettysburg by daylight. De Trobriand, despite being senior in rank and belonging to the First Division, commanded both his 3rd brigade and Burling's. According to Pvt. John Haley (Company I), the 17th Maine turned out around 3:00 a.m. and prepared breakfast, which, for the fortunate, consisted of coffee. By daylight—4:27 a.m.—the two brigades were prepared to advance, three hours behind schedule.[1]

The 110th Pennsylvania drew rear guard again, and as luck would have it, Capt. Isaac T. Hamilton's Company C brought up the rear of the rear guard.

---

1   G. W. W. to [Editor?], July 5, 1863, *New York Tribune*, July 3, 1863; OR 27, pt. 1, 519, 522-523, 570; Ruth L. Silliker, (ed.), *The Rebel Yell & the Yankee Hurrah: The Civil War Journal of a Maine Volunteer* (Camden, 1985), 100; Martin A. Haynes, *A History of the Second Regiment, New Hampshire Volunteer Infantry in the War of the Rebellion* (Lakeport, 1896), 167. Lieutenant Houghton (Company B, 17th Maine) places the arrival of the order at 2:00 a.m. and the departure at 5:00 a.m., Edwin B. Houghton, *17th Maine*, 90.

While the rest of the regiment stayed at the back of the brigade, Company C had to march some distance behind the regiment. Unlike the preceding day, both brigades took to the mucky road.[2]

II Army Corps, Army of the Potomac
Powers' Hill on the Taneytown Road
One and a half miles southeast of Gettysburg
1:30 a.m.

The II Corps wheezed to a halt in the Taneytown Road along the eastern side of Cemetery Ridge. First Lieutenant Josiah M. Favill (Company H, 57th New York) watched his exhausted men collapse where they stood, many of them asleep the moment they hit the ground. The regiment broke from the column in squads to find firewood and water. Private Jacob H. Cole (Company A) sat down in the road and slipped off into a deep sleep, oblivious to everything going on around him. No one bothered to wake him up to eat either. Brigadier General Samuel K. Zook ordered Lt. Josiah Favill to establish a picket line. He and the designated officer in charge of the detachment, however, could not rouse the exhausted soldiers to their feet. Zook dispatched Favill with this information to Brigadier General Caldwell, the First Division commander, who allowed his snoring men to sleep in the road.

Following a briefing on the morning's action, the officers dismounted along the roadside. Wrapped up in their own blankets, side by side, next to a "large friendly boulder," Favill nestled closer to the generals to keep warm. The 148th Pennsylvania, rather than bivouac, moved across the Taneytown Road in a battle line. The men slept on their arms. Lemuel Osmon (Company C) lay alongside his captain, Robert M. Forster. Having lost his shoes in fording a stream, he had walked barefoot since the regiment left Virginia. With bleeding and sore feet, he reclined in the darkness and watched Forster kneel to pray. Osmon listened intently to his earnest supplications that God be with him and his men on the morrow.[3]

The 64th New York received orders to entrench across the Taneytown Road. One of the enlisted men noted that for a regiment "with one ax and two

2   Hamilton, "Recollections," 117; CWL.

3   Favill, *Diary of a Young Officer*, 242-243; Jacob H. Cole, *Under Five Commanders* (Patterson, 1906), 191; Muffly, *148th Pennsylvania*, 244, 602.

Shovels [it] was rather tedious." They had nearly finished their assignment when new orders arrived.[4]

Two hours later, at 3:30 a.m., an hour before daylight, the regimental officers got the men to their feet. Every regiment in Zook's brigade, except the 140th Pennsylvania, managed to breakfast on coffee and hard crackers. In Cross's brigade, Osmon asked Captain Forster what they were having for breakfast. Digging some meat and soft bread out of his haversack, Forster told Osmon to find some water while he made a fire. On the way to a nearby stream, Osmon had the good fortune to encounter a man returning from a hospital, a man with two pair of shoes. After a quick explanation, and with profuse thanks to his benefactor, Osmon hurriedly slipped his size-seven feet his new No. 10 shoes. Getting the water, he reported back to the captain.

Brigadier General Alexander Hays' Third Division would deploy first, followed by Brigadier General Gibbon's Second and Caldwell's First Divisions, respectively. Hays' men breakfasted at dawn over smoldering twig fires. To his dismay, Capt. Benjamin W. Thompson (Company F, 111th New York), who had lost his precious haversack the day before, reconciled himself to a couple of hard crackers and coffee.

By 6:00 a.m., after weapons inspections, Caldwell's brigades got under way. Hapless Private Cole (Company A, 57th New York) did not awaken in time for his morning meal. Throngs of frightened civilians clogged the road. Corporal Thomas P. Meyer (Company A, 148th Pennsylvania), a pioneer, noticed an old man dragging two little girls along on either side of him. "Good morning, father," Meyer told the old man. "Fine morning," he added. "Yes, fully," the old man cried back, his eyes flooding with tears, "but so full of terror and sorrow. "God bless and spare you all." He started running again. Simultaneously, two young women, carrying bandboxes and another with a child running alongside her also passed him. Without warning, a 20-pounder shell screamed in on top of the civilians and burst. The sergeant automatically looked back. The two young ladies with the bandboxes lay along the side of the road. For a moment, he

---

4   *"Diary 1861-1864 of Martin Sigman, Co. C, 64th N.Y.V.,"* U.S. History mss., Manuscripts Department, Lilly Library, Indiana University, Bloomington, IN, 47. Hereinafter cited as IUB.

thought they had died, but presently, they struggled to their feet and stumbled away—concussed but otherwise unhurt.[5]

Coffee-coolers and skulkers had also worked themselves into the refugees. When queried about the front, they generally replied, "all cut to pieces . . . the Johnnies were just whipping the earth" with the Army of the Potomac. Presently, a fully equipped enlisted man stumbled among the ranks of the 145th Pennsylvania. His mangled left hand hung limply by a piece of skin from his bloodied wrist. One of the Pennsylvanians asked him about the condition of things at the front. "Oh, it's all right, we're just knocking seven kinds out of the butternuts," he said, "but look here boys what they did to me." He raised his battered arm with its amputated hand toward their faces. "Go in boys," he continued, "and give them what they gave me."[6]

Shortly after stepping off, Col. Edward Cross, in his customary serious demeanor, told Lt. Charles A. Hale, his aide, to take care of his box in the headquarters wagon. Taking charge of the colonel's personal papers and effects disturbed Hale. Cross never mentioned the box again, but his sense of impending doom had not abandoned him. While passing to the right into the woods north of Solomon Cassatt's farm along the east side of the Taneytown Road, Lt. Charles A. Fuller (61st New York), took the time to shake the surgeons' hands who had established a hospital there and playfully banter with them. "We'll see you again," he quipped, while trying to mask his deep personal fear. His veteran regiment numbered less than 100 soldiers in four ad hoc consecutively designated companies. Fuller was the second in command of the 4th Company. Caldwell's division formed in the woods by regiment on division (two-company) front.[7]

5 Favill, *Diary of a Young Officer*, 244; Charles A. Fuller, *Personal Recollections of the War of 1861* (Hamilton, 1990), 92; Muffly, *148th Pennsylvania*, 460, 534, quoted on 460; Cole, *Under Five Commanders*, 191.

6 Christopher B. Calvin, (ed.), "Recollections of Army Life in the Civil War by Steven Allen Osborn, Company G, 145th Pennsylvania Volunteer Infantry," *Shenango Valley News*, Greenville, PA, April 2, 1915.

7 Fuller, *Personal Recollections*, 92; *OR* 27, pt. 1, 414, quoted; Hale, "With Colonel Cross," 2-3, PHS; Isaac Plumb to Miles W. Bullock, July 24, 1863, Clarke Historical Library, Central Michigan University, Mount Pleasant, MI; Sigman, Diary, 47. Hereinafter cited as CMU.

Barnes' Division, V Corps, Army of the Potomac
On the Road from McSherrystown
2:00 a.m.

Private Robert Carter (Company H, 22nd Massachusetts) heard the sounds of a mounted orderly struggling along the center of the column between the artillery on one side and the infantry on the other. Carter thought he bore more distressing news. Farther to the front, Capt. Francis A. Donaldson (Company K, 118th Pennsylvania) watched the officer as he reined in alongside Lt. Col. James Gwyn. He pulled a note from his inside pocket and, raising his lantern, announced that Maj. Gen. George B. McClellan had assumed command of the army and would lead it in battle the next day.

The regiment burst into wild cheers and acclamations of joy, as did the 1st Michigan. The 32nd Massachusetts enthusiastically repeated the "huzzahs" of the Federal army's "manly cheer" for their beloved general. In Vincent's brigade, the exhausted soldiers of the 16th Michigan briefly broke their glum silence and spiked their morale. The news temporarily relieved Jacklin, the adjutant, who was not pleased with Meade and all of his forced marches and doubted whether the general and the army were "up to snuff" for another major battle.[8]

The cheering resounded along the brigade until it reached the 22nd Massachusetts. In the bright moonlight Carter saw the man push his horse past, with distinct but halfhearted cheers echoing off his back. By the time the message reached his regiment, McClellan had come on board with an additional 60,000 men. The 22nd, however, had lost its love of "Little Mac." A few men cheered, but the majority plodded onward in abject silence and disgust. The regiment grew sullen and uncommonly quiet.[9]

Carter, his feet blistered and bleeding from the undersized government brogans, which he had received in Frederick earlier that week, hobbled as far as he could stand it. With his toes curled under his foot and his blisters rubbed raw by sweat and sand, he and two other men climbed a fence along the road and

8 Aiken, *Inside the Army of the Potomac*, 298; Lockley, Diary, July 2, UMI; Parker, *32nd Massachusetts*, 165; Account of Adjutant Rufus Jacklin, 9, Vertical Files, GNMP.

9 Carter, "Reminiscences," *War Papers*, vol. 2, 161; Survivors' Association, *Corn Exchange Regiment*, 237.

stole a short distance into the woods. Throwing himself upon the forest floor, he sank into a deep sleep, oblivious of both his pain or his friends.[10]

As Brig. Gen. James Barnes' veterans tramped into the night, he ordered the regimental drummers to tap out the cadence. The rhythm of the drums, usually restricted to daily calls while in camp, quickened the pace for several minutes until an officer from V Corps headquarters had them silenced lest they betray the corps' position to the Confederates.[11]

1st Volunteer Brigade, Artillery Reserve, Army of the Potomac
Taneytown, Maryland
12 miles southeast of Gettysburg
2:00 a.m.

The buglers awakened the men at 2:00 a.m. Two hours later, Battery E, 5th Massachusetts, got underway. As luck would have it, the battery had reached the far side of the town when orders came for it to turn around and take the road toward Gettysburg with the rest of the division. The 2nd Volunteer Brigade led the advance.[12]

At about the same time, Hancock and his tired entourage took the road toward Gettysburg. Lieutenant Colonel Morgan shook off his short respite of a couple of hours, mounted his worn out horse, and trotted after the general. The hard riding killed nearly every mount the general and his staff possessed.[13]

Second Division, III Corps, Army of the Potomac
The Millerstown Road, Gettysburg
2:30 a.m.

In a steady rain, Humphreys and his meandering Second Division stumbled into the Federal cavalry videttes in the Emmitsburg Road near the Millerstown Road intersection. The column trudged north along the pike to the lane leading to the Trostle farm. Turning east, the exhausted Yankees staggered into the

10 Carter, ibid., 162.

11 Parker, *32nd Massachusetts*, 165.

12 Regimental Committee, *5th Massachusetts Battery*, 623, 629; Levi W. Baker, *History of the 9th Massachusetts Battery* (Lancaster, 1996), 55.

13 Ladd and Ladd, *The Bachelder Papers*, vol. 3, 1,353.

fields northeast of Trostle's buildings. Cuban born Capt. Adolfo Cavada glanced southeast at the cook-fires of the First Division snapping and crackling in the heavy night air. Completely worn out, he threw himself onto the soaked grass under a nearby tree and quickly blacked out. First Lieutenant Henry N. Blake (Company K, 11th Massachusetts) noted the time—2:30 a.m.

A little more than two hours later, in the predawn twilight made darker by the steady rain, another officer shook the slumbering Cavada into semi-consciousness and said, "Arise." The groggy captain instinctively flexed his sore and stiffened legs and arms, and with his empty stomach pleading loudly for food, leaped to his feet. In the shadowy light, he could see the darker bodies of the general and his staff lying about him, wrapped cocoon-like in their overcoats. The startled captain, having not completely gained his senses, distinctly heard the rain pattering in the ghostlike silence. Looking about he saw their horses, reins on the ground, and heads down, quietly ambling about in the field. Nearby the huddled orderlies slept around their dying campfires.

"Cavada, are you awake?" the other officer whispered. "Yes," he stuttered. "The General wishes you to ascertain the position of the regiment on picket that is to be relieved by one from our Division." "Who am I to ask?" Cavada sleepily queried. "I don't know." "What regiment am I to relieve?" the captain yawned. "I don't know," the officer replied. Cavada correctly interpreted that to mean he was to find his own answers. He shuffled toward his horse when Humphreys, from beneath his poncho directed him to ferret out Major General Birney to answer his questions. Pulling "Brick-Bat," his lethargic and dull horse, from the nearby briars, Cavada mounted and turned in the direction he thought he should have been heading, leaving in his wake a prolific string of mumbled epithets directed at the army, the generals, and everyone else.[14]

Cavada completed his assignment and returned within an hour and noted the sun bathing the surrounding hills and woods in comforting brightness. In the distance, the clarion notes of a solitary bugle echoed melodiously upon the still air, followed within seconds by a dozen or more, all of them kept in time by the steady rattling of drums. As the men awakened, Cavada splashed water on his face then drank a cup of coffee.[15]

---

14 Cavada, Diary, July 2, 1863, quoted, FSNMP; OR 27, pt 1, 531; Blake, *Three Years in the Army*, 204.

15 Cavada, ibid.; Raus, *A Generation on the March*, 51; Ladd and Ladd, *The Bachelder Papers*, vol. 1, 192. This is my conclusion based upon Lieutenant Colonel Baldwin's statement.

V Army Corps, Army of the Potomac
Boneauville (Bonneville), Pennsylvania
Two miles east of Gettysburg on the Hanover Road
3:30 a.m.

The V Corps finally halted around 3:30 a.m., in the woods at the crossroads village of Boneauville. The men stacked their weapons and lit coffee fires. For the first time in a grueling six-and-a-half hours, it looked like they were finally going to get some badly needed rest. Captain Donaldson (Company K, 118th Pennsylvania) curled up in his overcoat and fell asleep on the forest floor. Private James Houghton (Company K, 4th Michigan) in Sweitzer's brigade griped in his journal, "we were too tired to cook any Supper so we ate a cold lunch which consisted of raw pork hardtack and sun cooked coffee."[16]

Having almost literally marched in their sleep, many men in the 13th Pennsylvania Reserves collapsed in place. Their numbed bodies completely blocked the line of march, forcing couriers and orderlies to tear down fence sections to detour around them. An hour later, Donaldson awoke to the sight of his men bending over cooking fires, whose smoke delicately curled into the treetops. They were solemnly preparing to move out again. He thought that 37 miles in 24 hours had been trying enough. Houghton and the men in the 4th Michigan had not slept well either what with officers' shouts, the tramping of the heavy feet, and the rattling of canteens and accoutrements as more troops stumbled into the bivouac.[17]

At 4:30 a.m. Pvt. Oliver W. Norton, Vincent's bugler, sounded "Reveille." Colonel Vincent, at Norton's side, noticed a national flag unfurled in the early morning breeze, doffed his kepi, and bowed his head. "What more glorious death can any man desire than to die on the soil of old Pennsylvania fighting for that flag?" he sighed. "Reform to march," the officers shouted in the ranks.[18]

The corps shifted by divisions into the large open field adjacent to the woods. Tilton's brigade held the right of the line. The 118th Pennsylvania had

16 James Houghton Journal, in Michigan Historical Collections, Bentley Historical Library, University of Michigan, Ann Arbor, MI.

17 Bell, "The Bucktails at Gettysburg," GNMP; Aiken, *Inside the Army of the Potomac*, 298; Survivors' Association, *The Corn Exchange Regiment*, 238; Houghton, ibid.

18 Sgt. John G. Berry Diary, July 2, 1863, in *CWTI* Collection, USAHEC, Carlisle Barracks, PA; Nicholson, *Pennsylvania at Gettysburg*, vol. 1, 462, quoted.

the right of the brigade line with the 1st Michigan and the 22nd Massachusetts falling in on its left without the 18th Massachusetts, which had gone out on detached service before daylight. Sweitzer's and Vincent's brigades completed the line to the left. The Second Division then the Third Division went in on the First Division's left.

All of the regiments formed on battalion front, doubled on center, closed en masse. Each regimental front consisted of the two center companies with the colors, followed in column by the next two companies from either flank, then the next two companies, with the ranks very close together until the regiment looked like a rectangle two companies wide and five battle lines deep. With the colors unfurled and the alignments almost parade ground perfect, Donaldson recalled that it looked more like the corps was preparing for a grand review than for an advance into battle. The quartermaster of the 1st Michigan issued the regulation 40 rounds of ammunition per man. "All filled up and ready," Capt. George Lockley (Company A, 1st Michigan) wrote in his diary.[19]

The corps received orders to proceed toward Gettysburg. With daylight glinting through the clouds over them from the east and warming their backs, the men heard the ominous boom of artillery fire reverberating from the west. Skirmishers sprayed out from each brigade to chase off any Confederates and to tear down fences along the route. The massive formation stepped out, crushing every stalk of grain and every blade of grass along its front. Before long, the refreshing mint fragrance of pennyroyal wafted over the 118th Pennsylvania, reminding Donaldson of previous marches. Sergeant John G. Berry (Company A, 16th Michigan) noted the cloudy sky overhead, which pelted the dirty men with intermittent showers as they marched west. Lieutenant Jacklin, the 16th's adjutant, found the morning pleasant and the air calm. The infantry, as usual, marched without the corps artillery. The artillerymen remained behind until 6 a.m. to tend to their horses.[20]

19 Aiken, *Inside the Army of the Potomac*, 298; Survivors' Association, *The Corn Exchange Regiment*, 238; Lockley, Diary, July 2, 1863, UMI.

20 Carter, "Reminiscences," *War Papers*, vol. 2, 162; Aiken, *Inside the Army of the Potomac*, 298-299; Survivors' Association, *The Corn Exchange Regiment*, 237; Berry, Diary, July 2, 1863, USAHEC; Jacklin, "Account," 8, GNMP; Scott, "On Little Round Top," *National Tribune*, August 2, 1894.

The Federal Line, Army of the Potomac
East of Plum Run, north of Trostle's Lane
From the Emmitsburg Road to Little Round Top
Before 4:30 a.m.

Elsewhere, troops were on the move. Meade decided to extend his front from Cemetery Hill south to the rocky hill at the southern end of the ridge and to reinforce his extreme right at Culp's Hill. Brigadier General John Buford's battered cavalry division, having been heavily engaged on July 1, now patrolled the Emmitsburg Road from the southern edge of town to Warfield Ridge, with his brigades bivouacked near the Peach Orchard.[21]

Daylight brought with it sporadic rifle fire across the fields between the 63rd Pennsylvania's skirmishers and their Confederate counterparts in the woods along the southern end of Seminary Ridge. Farther to the north, the Rebel skirmishers advanced against the 4th Maine. Several times, they ventured into the open only to scurry back to the cover of the woods. Colonel Elijah Walker, realizing Confederates were in force along his front and that an attack seemed imminent, reported his concerns to the III Corps and First Division staff officers and requested reinforcements. They insisted he had no significant forces in front of him, that the main Confederate force had withdrawn from his front. Twice Walker received orders to move out and drive the Rebels from the woods, and twice he refused to execute such a reconnaissance.[22]

Sickles sent Major H. E. Tremain, his aide-de-camp, to Meade's head-quarters requesting he be allowed to secure the Emmitsburg Road because it seemed evident that Lee would not lose the opportunity to take it. The major found Meade sitting at a table in Lydia Leister's house with a large map of Adams County laid out in front of him. Automatically assuming the general was studying the tactical feasibility of whether to keep the road open or not, Tremain requested cavalry to block any Confederate approach from the south,

---

21 OR 27, pt. 1, 939; Large, *Battle of Gettysburg*, 28-32.

22 Nicholson, *Pennsylvania at Gettysburg*, vol. 1, 387, 393; Ladd and Ladd, *The Bachelder Papers*, vol. 2, 1,093-1,094; Executive Committee, *Maine at Gettysburg*, 180. Major Danks (63rd Pennsylvania) said that the Confederates along his front fired at intervals until around 9:00 a.m., at which time a Maine regiment (3rd Maine) made a reconnaissance in force against the woods. It had to have been very light because Pvt. Alfred J. Craighead (Company K, 68th Pennsylvania), whose regiment was farther to the rear, noted that the skirmishing began around 9:00 a.m. and gradually increased until the battle really got under way. Had the rifle fire been more serious before 9:00 a.m., it would have drawn more attention.

thus protecting the III Corps' supply trains, which had not yet arrived. Meade's refusal to give a definitive response Tremain interpreted as a refusal to deny the Rebels access to it.[23] He returned to Sickles without an answer.

Lee's Headquarters,
Army of Northern Virginia
Near the Lutheran Seminary
Around 4:30 a.m.

Before daylight, Lee's headquarters had moved to the crest of Seminary Ridge near the Lutheran Seminary. Lieutenant General Ambrose Powell Hill, the commander of the Third Corps, along with the slightly wounded division commander Maj. Gen. Henry Heth, stayed by Lee on the crest. Longstreet joined them there shortly before 4:35 a.m. Flanked by Longstreet and Hill, Lee set up his "office" on a fallen tree in a small woodlot south of the Seminary's cemetery near the Fairfield Road. Almost immediately, the two corps commanders each picked up a stick and began whittling while Lee talked.

Within a few minutes, Maj. Gen. John Bell Hood arrived with his division from Chambersburg. He joined the generals on the hill, overlooking the town in the low ground to the east. Lee seemed restive to Hood. With his coat buttoned to the throat, his sword and field glasses dangling by his side, he nervously paced back and forth under the big shade trees in the grove, stopping intermittently to stare toward the Federal position on Cemetery Hill, on the southern side of the town.[24]

Hood's exhausted soldiers, having had only two hours of rest since the evening of the day before, filed off to both sides of the Chambersburg Road into the hollow on the western side of McPherson's Ridge. Brigadier General George T. Anderson's Georgians went to the north side of the pike and lay down with their left flank near the railroad cut. Brigadier General Henry L. Benning's Georgia brigade moved south of the road, leaving enough front for Brig. Gen. Jerome B. Robertson's famous Texas Brigade to complete the

23 Ladd and Ladd, *The Bachelder Papers*, vol. 1, 670.

24 Lafayette McLaws, "Gettysburg," in *Southern Historical Society Papers*, vol. 7, 67-69, hereinafter cited as *SHSP*; John B. Hood to James Longstreet, June 28, 1875, in *SHSP*, vol. 4, 147-148.

formation north to the road. Some of them stacked their weapons and reclined upon the trampled grass.

Benning's Georgians did not even bother with that. According to William T. Fluker (Company D, 15th Georgia), the men in his regiment dropped where they stood and were asleep in short order. As they went to ground, Pvt. A. C. Sims (Company F, 1st Texas) could still see in his mind the "bloody shirts"—the walking wounded of the previous day's fight—who had greeted them along the Chambersburg Road as the regiment approached Gettysburg. A verse from the Scriptures rolled through his mind: "Every battle of the warrior is with confused noise and garments rolled in blood."

At 5:00 a.m., the Army of Northern Virginia's foreign contingent—several officers and at least one British correspondent—reined in nearby. They made an impressive entourage: the Honorable Francis Lawley, MP and correspondent for the *London Times*, still suffering from a protracted illness, weakly dismounted. Colonel G. Moxley Sorrel, Longstreet's aide-de-camp, directed the others to the crest of the ridge. Captain Fitzgerald Ross, an Austrian cavalryman, remained on foot, while Sir Arthur Fremantle of the Coldstream Guards and Capt. Justus Scheibert, a Prussian engineer, ensconced themselves in the fork of a tree above the officers. With his spyglass fixed on Cemetery Hill, Fremantle occasionally glanced down to see what was going on. He noted Heth and his bandaged head. Hill's and Longstreet's whittling amused him.

Just as Hood joined the group, Longstreet renewed his argument with Lee to flank around the southern end of the Federal line and to fight on ground more advantageous to the Confederates. The commanding general refused to consider it.[25]

"The enemy is here, and if we do not whip him, he will whip us," Lee blurted to Hood, but loud enough for the others to hear. Longstreet drew away from the cluster of officers and sat down under a tree. Hood walked over to him. "The General," Longstreet told him, "is a little nervous this morning; he

---

25 James Longstreet, *From Manassas to Appomattox*, (New York, 1992), 362. James Longstreet, "Lee's Right Flank at Gettysburg," in *Battles and Leaders*, vol. 3, 340; Fremantle, *Three Months in the Confederate States*, 261; "Recollections of A.C. Sims (Co. F, 1st Texas) at the Battle of Gettysburg," in the Robert L. Brake Collection, USAHEC, quote; Robert M. Willingham, Jr., *No Jubilee: The Story of Confederate Wilkes* (Washington, 1976), 34. George Hillyer, "Battle of Gettysburg," *Georgia Troops at Gettysburg*, in *Walton Tribune* (Monroe, Georgia, 1904), 2; Account of Capt. Benton H. Miller (Company D, 59th Georgia). The last two in Vertical Files, GNMP.

wishes me to attack; I do not wish to do so without Pickett. I never like going into battle with one boot off."[26]

Walking away from Hill, Lee encountered Col. John L. Black, for whom he had sent before daylight. Black, still suffering from a bad head wound he had received during the June 21 skirmish at Goose Creek Bridge (Upperville, Virginia), smartly saluted. Lee warmly grasped his hand and called Longstreet over to them. After formally introducing the colonel, Lee said, "General, Colonel Black has an improvised command of cavalry and a battery of artillery. I turn him over to you to explore your ground, watch your flanks and rear. I commend Colonel Black to you as once a cadet under me at West Point."

Lee bowed to which the two responded in kind. Exactly what did the colonel command? Longstreet asked. Black replied that he had Capt. James F. Hart's excellent South Carolina battery—"as good as there was in the army"—several detachments of good cavalry, and a mix of "strays" from a number of outfits, none of whom he knew. Longstreet curtly told him to send his orderly back for the cavalry and to leave Hart at the rear of the corps until further notice.[27]

At 6 a.m., Maj. Gen. Lafayette McLaws arrived with his division from the vicinity of Marsh Creek. Brigadier General Joseph B. Kershaw's brigade, in the lead, wheezed to a halt about 100 yards from the commanding general's tent. Almost immediately, an aide requested McLaws' presence before the general. He found Lee seated alone on the fallen tree with a map lying across the trunk. "General," Lee began, "I wish you to place your division across this road." He pointed to the Millerstown Road, where it cut across Seminary Ridge, before directing McLaws' attention toward the southeast. "And I wish you to get there if possible without being seen by the enemy." McLaws noted that his line was to form west of and perpendicular to the Emmitsburg Road. Lee concluded with, "Can you get there?" McLaws said he knew of nothing to stop him, but he requested to make a personal reconnaissance with skirmishers. "Captain Johnston, of my staff, has been ordered to reconnoiter the ground, and I expect he is about ready." "I will go with him," McLaws interjected. Longstreet, who

26 William C. Oates, *The War Between the Union and the Confederacy and Its Lost Opportunities*, (New York, 1905), 209.

27 E. D. McSwain, "Crumbling Defenses: Or Memories And Reminiscences of John Logan Black, Col., C.S.A.," 37-38, in Brake Collection, Box 8, Manuscripts Department, USAHEC, Carlisle Barracks, PA.

had been anxiously pacing nearby, immediately shot back, "No, sir, I do not wish you to leave your division."

Rudely stepping between McLaws and Lee, the irritated Longstreet traced a line parallel to the Emmitsburg Road and said, "I wish your division placed so." Lee immediately retorted, "No, General, I wish it placed just perpendicular to that."

Again, McLaws asked to accompany Capt. Samuel R. Johnston but Longstreet again forbade him to do so. Lee remained silent as McLaws returned to his division. He ordered his regiments to the western side of McPherson's Ridge, under the cover of the woods. Simultaneously, he directed his own engineer officer, Lt. Thomas J. Moncure, to go with Johnston. McLaws, on his own accord, stole away from his command to see the ground for himself.[28]

In the meantime, Longstreet told Hood to dispatch his best scouts south toward the Federal left. Hood gave the assignment to John M. Pinckney and two other enlisted men from Company H, 4th Texas. In addition, three men from the 1st Texas—Sgt. Charles H. Kingsley, Pvts. William H. Barbee, (both Company L) and James Deering (Company E) joined the party. They immediately loped south. Simultaneously, Johnston, with Maj. John J. G. Clarke, an engineer officer on Longstreet's staff, and a couple of other scouts started out.[29]

---

28 Lafayette McLaws, "Gettysburg," in *SHSP*, vol. 7, 67-69, quoted on 68; Ladd and Ladd, *The Bachelder Papers*, vol. 1, 453; Longstreet, *From Manassas to Appomattox*, 362.

29 *Congressional Record–House*, 1906, 6,095; E. M. Law, "The Struggle for 'Round Top," in *Battles and Leaders*, vol. 3, 321-322; William Youngblood, "Unwritten History of the Gettysburg Campaign," in *SHSP*, vol. 38, 314-315; John O. Scott, "The Texans at Gettysburg," *Sherman Register*, March 31, 1897; J. O. Bradfield, "At Gettysburg, July 3," *Confederate Veteran*, 40 vols. (Nashville, 1893-1932), vol. 30, 225; S. R. Johnston to Fitz Lee, Feb. 16, 1878, to Lafayette McLaws, June 17, 1892, to Rev. George Peterkin, Dec., 18??, all in *Virginia Historical Society*; Longstreet, *From Manassas to Appomattox*, 363, 365.

A great deal of confusion exists as to what reconnaissances occurred and when. I tend to believe that the scouts from the 4th Texas left "in the early morning" as reported in the *Congressional Record* and that a couple of them returned by 3:00 p.m., just as Longstreet was placing Hood onto the field. Two more scouts—Kingsley and Barbee—reported to Hood just before he sent his division into action. Hood made no mention of Law's scouts, but Law's description dovetails with Hood's account. Based upon a statement from Lt. Col. Phillip A. Work (1st Texas) and J. O. Bradfield (1st Texas), I believe three of the scouts with the 4th Texas came from the 1st Texas.

Longstreet, however, ordered to move out at 11:00 a.m., delayed until noon to await Law's arrival. That means that Johnston's time was off by about two hours.

Johnston's schedule of events was: 4:00 a.m. (daylight)-7:00 a.m., reconnaissance; 7:00-8:00 a.m., conference with Lee; 9:00 a.m., joins Longstreet. His adjusted times are as follows:

III Army Corps, Army of the Potomac
The George Weikert Farm
5:00 a.m.

The Federal troops east of Trostle's house began stirring at 5:00 a.m. In Graham's brigade, William E. Loring (Company E, 141st Pennsylvania) walked among the men of Companies F, C, and I, as well as his own. They sat around their fires, quietly, glumly nursing their fresh tin cups of coffee. In the waning darkness, with impending peril looming once the sun broke over the horizon, Loring astutely noted how personal animosities and private feuds, which had plagued that wing of the regiment, had mellowed or completely dissipated. A "kind of camaraderie" seemed to prevail among the rank and file.

Sergeant John D. Bloodgood (Company I), and his messmates, Jimmy Lunger and Oliver Morse, decided to enjoy a first rate meal to celebrate their return to Pennsylvania. Morse wandered off toward the Trostle house in search of flour. Lunger fetched some water from Plum Run in his tin pail. Bloodgood produced a mess plate propped on a forked stick for their skillet. Sergeants Joseph DeHaven and Alexander Given (both Company F, 114th Pennsylvania) assembled their small group of Christians together for their morning prayer and Scripture reading. When they finished, DeHaven matter-of-factly announced, "Boys, this is the last time we will pray together." The men of the 20th Indiana in Ward's brigade, bugled awake, immediately noticed how wet the morning dew had made the ground upon which they slept.[30]

6:35-9:35 a.m., reconnaissance; 9:35 a.m.-10:35 a.m., confers with Lee; 11:35 a.m., joins Longstreet. At noon, Law arrives and Longstreet moves out.

Longstreet's times: Around 9:00 a.m., Lee rides to Ewell; around 10:00 a.m., Lee returns, but Johnston not back yet; 11:00 a.m. Lee issues order to advance; 11:30 a.m. Law arrives and the advance begins.

30 Loring, "Gettysburg," *National Tribune*, July 9, 1885; Bloodgood, "Reminiscences," 132; Edward J. Hagerty, *Collis' Zouaves: The 114th Pennsylvania Volunteers in the Civil War* (Baton Rouge, 1997), 239, quoted; Osbourn, *The 20th Indiana*, ISL. In Loring's article, the ink blotted making "Company I" look like "Company L." The regiment had no Company L.

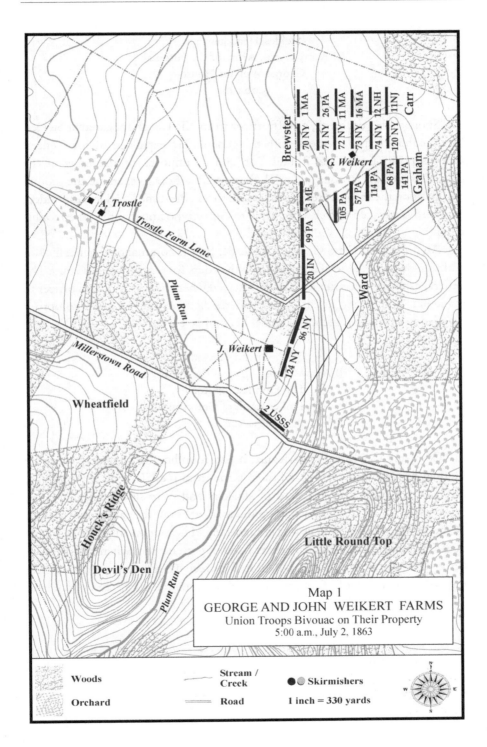

Map 1
GEORGE AND JOHN WEIKERT FARMS
Union Troops Bivouac on Their Property
5:00 a.m., July 2, 1863

Woods

Orchard

Stream / Creek

Road

Skirmishers

1 inch = 330 yards

Sickles' Headquarters,
III Army Corps, Army of the Potomac
George Weikert House
5:00 a.m.

Shortly after daybreak, a staff officer from XII Corps appeared at Sickles' headquarters asking to speak with the general. He explained Major General Geary's position at Little Round Top and its importance and asked if the general could send troops and a III Corps staff officer to examine the ground and position the troops. He would "attend to it in due time," Sickles responded, and the discouraged staffer so reported to Geary, who impatiently waited for his relief.

An hour later, Capt. George G. Meade, Jr., the commanding general's son and aide-de-camp, reported to Sickles with orders for him to relieve Geary. The general listened, and, after the aide left, stayed where he was. With no officer to guide him to the spot, he disingenuously recalled, he was not about to uproot his men to occupy an inconsequential hill on his left flank.[31]

De Trobriand's Brigade,
III Army Corps, Army of the Potomac
The Emmitsburg Road
Three miles south of Gettysburg
6:30 a.m.

Company C, 110th Pennsylvania, began rounding up stragglers from the first day's battle. The majority of them came from the XI Corps. Before long, they had collected a sizable herd of skulkers and were slowly pushing them north toward Gettysburg. Farther up the road, at about the same time, the rest of the brigade halted, and almost immediately, the veterans in the 17th Maine began kindling coffee fires. The water had not gotten warm when an aide from Birney galloped up and ordered them to their feet. They had to get moving lest the Rebs cut them off from the rest of the army, a disgusted John Haley (Company I) recalled.[32]

---

31 Francis A. Walker, "Meade at Gettysburg," in *Battles and Leaders*, vol. 3, 409, quoted; Craft, "141st Pennsylvania," 118.

32 Hamilton, "Recollections," CWL, 118; Silliker, *Rebel Yell*, 100; Ladd and Ladd, *The Bachelder Papers*, vol. 2, 839.

II Army Corps, Army of the Potomac
Cemetery Ridge
One and a quarter miles south of Gettysburg
7:00 a.m.

The II Corps stayed in Cassatt's Woods until around 7:00 a.m. when the brigades "saddled up" and moved west. The 145th Pennsylvania ran into a solid, newly built post and rail fence on the west side of the Taneytown Road. The men in the front rank passed their weapons to the rear rank. Facing the fence, they grabbed the top rails of each section and, at the command, uprooted the entire length of it along their front and dropped it to the ground at their feet. With the obstruction out of their way, they continued beyond the Taneytown Road where they shifted into columns of regiments, halted, and stacked arms.[33]

Within the hour, Caldwell's First Division and Gibbon's Second, (leaving Hays' Third Division on its own), flanked west toward the former right flank of Sickles' III Corps near Jacob Hummelbaugh's house. Caldwell halted in the low ground on the eastern side of Cemetery Ridge near the Cassatt farm and arranged his division by brigades in column of regiments, closed en masse. Colonel Edward Cross's four regiments anchored the left, with the 61st New York—104 effectives—at the head of the column, followed respectively by the 135 men of the 81st Pennsylvania. The 148th Pennsylvania, the largest regiment in the brigade with 518 effectives, came next, formed in column of wings. The 5th New Hampshire with its 182 officers and men finished the formation. Colonel Patrick Kelly's 2nd brigade was to his right with Zook's 3rd brigade next in formation to the north and Brooke's 4th brigade anchoring the right of the division. For reasons known only to God or perhaps an officer of higher authority, someone ordered the 148th Pennsylvania, on the left of Caldwell's Division to construct earthworks. Assistant Surgeon Alfred T. Hamilton, the regimental surgeon, immediately established a temporary field hospital in Hummelbaugh's house and quickly appropriated a half-barrel of flour, which he found in the attic. His assistant, Davy McIlhattan (Company G), and the other attendants began grilling "dapjacks" for themselves and the doctor.[34]

33 OR 27, pt. 1, 414; Calvin, "Recollections of Army Life," 88.

34 Muffly, *148th Pennsylvania*, 172, 590; Hale, "With Colonel Cross," PSH, 3; Cole, *Under Five Commanders*, 193, 195; Sigman, Diary, IUB,47; *New York at Gettysburg*, 3 vols. (Albany, 1900), vol. 1, 460; Ladd and Ladd, *The Bachelder Papers*, vol. 3, 1,984-1,985; William Child, *A History of the 5th*

From his position along the front of Zook's column, 1st Lt. Josiah M. Favill, (Company H, 57th New York), carefully studied the Confederate position along Seminary Ridge and the wide expanse of rolling open ground between the opposing armies. To the left front of the brigade, Capt. James McKay Rorty's Battery B, 1st New York went into park. From where he stood William S. Shallenberger, the 140th Pennsylvania's adjutant, could see battery after battery in position along the crest of the ridge with the entire II Corps massed behind them in support. Orders passed through the regiments to stack arms and to rest with their accoutrements strapped on. Lieutenant James J. Purman (Company A) swapped his broad straw hat for Drummer James A. Woods's forage cap. Believing he would not survive the day, he did not want to accommodate "Death" by making himself a conspicuous target.[35]

Jacob Cole (Company A, 57th New York) confided in his friend, Andrew J. Wilson, that he knew he was going to "catch it." They mutually agreed to write to each other's mothers should either one of them die in the coming engagement. Cole, having a large sum of cash with him, decided to ask General Zook to take care of it for him. When he approached the general with his proposition, Zook's response startled him. "My boy," he said calmly, "you must not have such feelings, but if you are afraid, I will give you a pass to go into the ambulance corps." "No, general," Cole protested, "I have never yet deserted my comrades in battle and I do not intend to desert them now. If I am killed, I shall be doing my duty." Zook took his cash and sent him away. Shortly after he returned to his company, Cole received orders to report to the general. Zook returned his cash with, "My boy, I have the same sensation you have—that I will be killed—and you had better take the money and give it to someone else." Cole took the money to the captain of Company I, Henry H. Mott, who issued him a receipt for it.[36]

Colonel Cross, after briefly studying the front, trotted forward into the Federal bivouacs in the swale between his men and the Emmitsburg Road. A few minutes later, he returned to his aide Lt. Charles Hale and said, "Give my compliments to Colonel McKeen, and say that I will be away for twenty minutes or so." He disappeared into the bivouacs along the front for a second

---

New Hampshire Volunteers, in the American Civil War, 1861-1865 (Gaithersburg, 1988), 215; OR 27, pt. 1, 384; Fuller, *Personal Recollections*, 93.

35 Favill, *Diary of a Young Officer*, 244-245; Stewart, *140th Pennsylvania*, 420, 429.

36 Cole, *Under Five Commanders*, quotations on 193-194.

time and returned within the allotted time. In galloping back, he passed the front of the diminutive 61st New York, to whom he shouted, "Boys, you know what's before you. Give 'em hell!" A number of the men hallooed back, "We will, Colonel!" Dismounting, he cheerfully greeted Hale and Col. Henry B. McKeen (81st Pennsylvania) with, "That is the Third Corps out there." To Hale, Cross seemed like his old impetuous self. "The Second New Hampshire is over there beyond those buildings. The I Corps fought a tremendous battle away to the right yesterday, and were defeated. General Howard and his XI Corps were again driven back." With some emphasis, he concluded, "Gentlemen, it looks as though the whole of Lee's Rebel army is right here in Pennsylvania. There will be a great battle fought today." Colonel McKeen stared at him, a puzzled expression upon his face.

Cross took McKeen by the arm and quietly walked away from his staff. Hale watched them turn, shake hands, and walk back to the brigade officers. Cross gathered his staff around him and bluntly reaffirmed his previous decision on the 148th Pennsylvania. "Gentlemen, Colonel McKeen will command the 148th Pennsylvania today. Before night, he will probably be commanding the brigade." With that, the regiment's 37-year old Lt. Col. Robert McFarlane officially surrendered command of his regiment to the younger but more experienced McKeen. Forty-two year old Lt. Col. Amos Stoh advanced to the command of his 81st Pennsylvania. Loosening the saddle girths on their mounts, the staff officers anxiously waited for the order to advance. It never came, despite the nasty peppering of skirmish fire, rattling in from the west. Gibbon's troops filled in the line to the right of Caldwell, while newly promoted Brig. Gen. Alexander Webb placed his brigade to the right. The 69th Pennsylvania took cover behind the stone wall west of the copse of trees. The remaining three regiments of the brigade went to ground on the reverse slope immediately to the east.[37]

Colonel Norman Hall's 3rd brigade connected Webb with Caldwell. Seventy-five yards to their rear, Col. George H. Ward's four regiments went into formation on the division's center. They fell into close column of regiment, to make them available for easy dispersal to either flank if needed. The 19th Maine stacked its arms and went to ground at the head of the column. The 15th

37 Hale, "With Colonel Cross," 3-4 PHS; Fuller, *Personal Recollections*, 93; *New York at Gettysburg*, vol. 3, 1,602; Nicholson, *Pennsylvania at Gettysburg*, vol. 1, 550; Joseph R. C. Ward, *History of the One Hundred and Sixth Regiment Pennsylvania Volunteers* (Philadelphia, 1906), 399.

Massachusetts and 82nd New York followed suit. The 1st Minnesota hunkered down behind the rest of the brigade.[38]

Hays' three brigades, at the front of the column, moved west of the Taneytown Road as they came abreast of the Catherine Guinn house. Leading the division, Col. Thomas A. Smyth's veterans formed by column of regiment behind the stone wall on the eastern side of Zeigler's Grove to support 1st Lt. George A. Woodruff's Battery I, 1st U.S. Artillery. The 108th New York, followed by the 1st Delaware, 12th New Jersey, and the 14th Connecticut fell in on the gently sloping hill between the fence and the road, with orders to stay below the crest of the hill.

Colonel Samuel S. Carroll's four regiments went into column of regiment behind the 14th Connecticut. Hays posted Col. George L. Willard's unfortunate brigade to the left of Smyth with an easterly running rail fence separating the two commands. Willard's men had just returned to the army from parole. Captured in the ignominious surrender at Harpers Ferry nine months earlier, they had come into the Army of the Potomac as the "Harpers Ferry Cowards" and had to prove themselves. The 125th, followed by the 126th and the 111th New York regiments went to ground behind the Brien orchard. Orders traveled through the ranks for no one—officers included—to go onto the hill. The officers, however, being officers, clustered in the orchard on the crest heedless of the occasional Rebel shells, which sailed overhead. Assistant Surgeon Francis M. Wafer of the 108th New York carefully studied a thin line of butternut clad Confederate skirmishers belonging to Company K, 3rd Georgia cautiously steal down the eastern slope of Cemetery Ridge into the low ground west of the William Bliss orchard.[39]

At one point, a rifleman from the 1st U.S. Sharpshooters nestled down behind a stump not far from the 111th New York and began plying his grisly trade. Captain Benjamin W. Thompson (Company F), having never seen a telescopic scope before, ventured over to the fellow with several other officers for a look and plied the rifleman with questions about his special weapon and

---

38 Official Report of Captain Emil A. Burger, Company L, 1st Minnesota Volunteers, 2nd Minnesota Company, U.S. Sharpshooters, July 5, 1863, Vertical Files, GNMP; Raus, *A Generation on the March*, 47; John Day Smith, *The History of the Nineteenth Regiment of Maine Volunteer Infantry 1862-1865* (Gaithersburg, 1988), 69.

39 OR 27, pt. 2, 627; Diary of Francis Moses Wafer, Archives, Douglas Library, Queen's University at Kingston, Kingston, Ontario, Canada, 38, hereinafter cited as QU; Michael Bacarella, *Lincoln's Foreign Legion* (Shippensburg, 1996), 136.

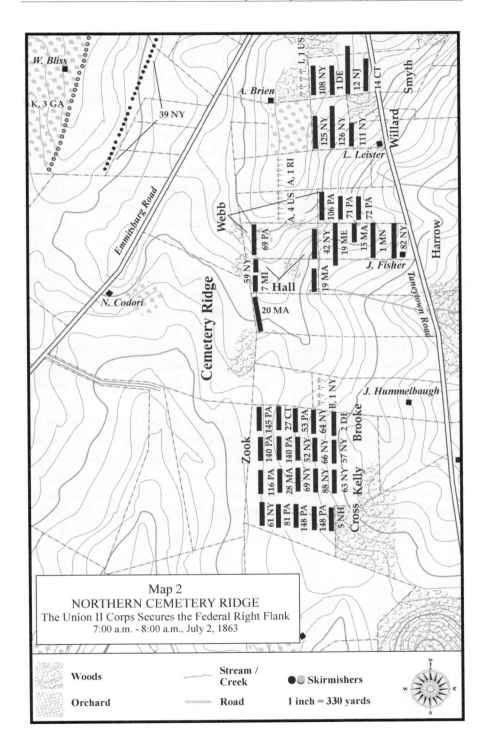

Map 2
NORTHERN CEMETERY RIDGE
The Union II Corps Secures the Federal Right Flank
7:00 a.m. - 8:00 a.m., July 2, 1863

Woods

Orchard

Stream / Creek

Road

Skirmishers

1 inch = 330 yards

the scope. "Put your field glasses to your eyes," he said. While they complied, he peered through the scope. "Do you see that single horseman just coming out of the woods which covers the enemy?" They saw him. "Well, keep your eyes on him." The heavy barreled rifle cracked. Seconds later, the horseman toppled to the ground.

Almost instantly, a shell screamed in on top of the 111th New York. Zeroing through the regimental bass drum, it completely shredded a knapsack and lay, unexploded, on the ground. Nevertheless, the men kept to their posts.[40]

The Rebels used the intervals between rounds to return fire. Captain Richard S. Thompson, acting major of the 12th New Jersey, marveled at the Berdans' innovative solution to the problem. Instead of working in pairs with their heavy rifles, which allowed the Rebs to dodge at the flash of both rifle shots, they formed three man squads. The Number One shooter rested his rifle upon its tripod and methodically sighted in on one of the openings in the Bliss barn. Shooters Two and Three, from nearby, also zeroed in on the same spot. The moment a Reb appeared in Number One's sights, the Berdan squeezed off his round, while his two comrades counted "one, two, three."

The Reb, seeing the flash, dodged the first shot then instinctively popped into the paths of the two shots fired simultaneously from the other rifles. "Alas!" Thompson later recalled, "How little we thought human life was the stake for which this game was being played."[41]

The colorful 39th New York, "The Garibaldi Guard," arrived behind the rest of Willard's brigade, and so fell in along the stone wall to the left of the 108th New York. Seconds later, 1st Lt. Heinrich Dietrich (Company A) heard Willard bellow, "Bayonets, forward march, charge!" The motley regiment of foreigners sprang over the wall, deployed into skirmish order, and advanced. They quickly reached the Bliss farm buildings and orchard and settled down to their grim work.[42]

---

40 The Berdans, according to witnesses, used their telescopic target rifles with great effect on that morning.

41 Richard S. Thompson, "A Scrap of Gettysburg," in *Military Essays and Recollections, Read Before the Commandery of the State of Illinois, Military Order of the Loyal Legion of the United States*, 8 vols. (Wilmington, 1992) vol. 3, 98.

42 Wafer, Diary, 38, QU; Bacarella, *Lincoln's Foreign Legion*, 136.

Longstreet's Corps, Army of Northern Virginia
Seminary Ridge
7:00 a.m.

Sir Arthur Fremantle mounted up and followed Longstreet back to McPherson's Woods, where he found McLaws' and Hood's Divisions, which the general promptly redeployed. Kershaw's South Carolinians led the countermarch onto the Chambersburg Road and back toward Herr's Ridge overlooking Willoughby Run. Along the way, Sgt. D. Augustus Dickert (Company H, 3rd South Carolina) noticed Longstreet riding with his eyes focused on the ground and his face downcast and forlorn, something he had never seen in "Old Pete" before.[43]

At Herr's Tavern, the column turned left along the road and continued south about one mile to the intersection with another back road. Branching left, the head of the corps marched 610 feet to the next intersection, where it took the road south another couple of hundred yards to the lane that led to the Alfred Haas house. It halted there. From the mouth of the farm lane, McLaws, with Kershaw, commanding his lead brigade, by his side, fixed his eyes on the southern end of the Emmitsburg Road, and observed Federal troops maneuvering into position. With the divisions in place, Longstreet, McLaws, and Hood rode back toward Lee's headquarters.[44]

V Army Corps, Army of the Potomac
East of Benner's Hill,
Around one and three-quarter miles east of Gettysburg,
South of the Hanover Road
7:00 a.m.–8:00 a.m.

Three-quarters of a mile east of Benner's Hill, the V Corps veered off the Hanover Road onto the E. Deodorf farm. The three divisions moved half a mile south, to the eastern side of Wolf's Hill, and faced north. The First

---

43 Fremantle, *Three Months in the Southern States*, 257; D. Augustus Dickert, *History of Kershaw's Brigade* (Dayton, 1976), 235.

44 S. R. Johnston to Fitz Lee, Feb. 16, 1878, Virginia Historical Society, hereinafter cited as VHS; Fremantle, *Three Months in the Southern States*, 257; McLaws, "Gettysburg," *SHSP*, vol. 7, 68-69; Ladd and Ladd, *The Bachelder Papers*, vol. 1, 453; E. M. Law, "The Struggle for 'Round Top," in *Battles and Leaders*, vol. 3, 319.

Division held the left of the line with the Second Division, then the Third to its right. Brigadier General James Barnes detailed the 32nd Massachusetts from Col. Jacob B. Sweitzer's's 2nd brigade for skirmish duty on the extreme left flank of the army. Colonel George L. Prescott asked him not to deploy the regiment because it had never served as skirmishers, so Barnes agreed and sent the 9th Massachusetts out instead.[45]

Shortly thereafter, the First Division changed front to rear to cover the western flank of the corps. The regiments had hardly completed the maneuver when the corps flanked to the left. Crossing Rock Creek by the bridge southeast of the Baltimore Pike, it crossed the road and marched another half mile north. Sometime between 7:00-8:00 a.m. Barnes' division finally halted in the orchard on the northeast side of Powers Hill, where the men finally got some rest. Colonel Jacob Sweitzer, commanding the 2nd brigade, did not believe the division would see any action that day.[46]

Neither did Donaldson, nor several other men from the 118th Pennsylvania. Artillery fire roared unceasingly overhead, with the rounds passing well above the regimental line. Donaldson assumed the V Corps was going to spend the day in reserve. While the enlisted men stripped down and went skinny-dipping in Rock Creek, Donaldson quickly shed his clothing and took off in a straight line for a pond, which he had spied not too far behind the regimental line. Diving in, he began splashing and ducking under like a child. Several minutes later, realizing he had picked up an impressive amount of creek bottom weeds, he stopped frolicking long enough to swim to the bank to free himself. The he discovered to his dismay that his "weeds" were leeches. After pulling the blood suckers off, he returned to his company, more embarrassed than injured.

For a while he listened to shells whining overhead and the crash of riflery from nearby Culp's Hill, then he, along with hundreds of other bored and exhausted soldiers, drifted off to sleep, paying no attention to the wispy showers, which periodically moistened the ground and evaporated just as quickly as they arrived. From where he stood with the 16th Michigan, Jacklin

---

45 Parker, *32nd Massachusetts*, 165-166.

46 Carter, "Reminiscences," *War Papers*, vol. 2, 162; OR 27, pt. 1, 610; Jacklin, "Account," 10, GNMP.

heard scattered skirmish fire reverberating across the fields from the west. Every now and then a stray artillery round flew well overhead.[47]

Lieutenant Ziba B. Graham (Company B) left the 16th Michigan and walked toward the front to see the battlefield, while Pvt. George W. Ervay (Company H) used the time to dash a note off to his parents. After casually mentioning harmlessly exploding artillery rounds above him, he wrote about how loyal and generous the Union people had been to the regiment. Everything in Maryland, in particular, the women overwhelmed him with their natural beauty. The Pennsylvania women, while quite numerous, he said, could not match the ladies living south of the Mason-Dixon Line. First Lieutenant Edward Bennett (Company A, 44th New York) had lost all sense of the time during the previous hectic days. Now he soundly slept through all of the surrounding pandemonium. So did the worn out veterans in the 13th Pennsylvania Reserves. Captain Frank J. Bell (Company I) lay on his back with the warm sun bathing his dirty face, its warmth transporting him into complete oblivion.[48]

Meade rode up to Brig. Gen. Romeyn B. Ayres' Second Division 3rd brigade and asked its commander, Brig. Gen. Stephen Weed, to accompany him. Together, with Weed's aide-de-camp, 1st Lt. A. Pierson Case, they started on a tour of the army's artillery positions in the vicinity of Culp's Hill and Stevens' Knoll.[49]

Colonel Patrick Henry O'Rorke (140th New York) remained behind with his adjutant, Porter Farley. Farley, whose admiration for the colonel verged on adoration, noted how resplendent the man looked upon his little brown horse. A West Point graduate, a man of few words and fewer compliments, the colonel looked the part of the beau ideal professional soldier. Farley thought he cut a wondrous figure in his white leather gauntlets, his regulation Army cape, and his floppy felt hat. A courier from headquarters rode up to the two officers and handed the colonel a circular from Army Headquarters. He glanced at it and

---

47 Aiken, *Inside the Army of the Potomac*, 299; Survivors' Association, *The Corn Exchange Regiment*, 239; Jacklin, ibid, 9.

48 Ziba B. Graham, "On to Gettysburg, Ten Days From My Diary," in *War Papers. Read Before the Commandery of the State of Michigan Military Order of the Loyal Legion of the United States*, 2 vols. (Detroit, 1893), vol. 1, 9; George W. Ervay to [parents], July 2, 1863, George W. Ervay, 1845-1863, Civil War Letters, Vertical Files, GNMP, 31; Edward Bennett, "Fighting Them Over," *National Tribune*, May 6, 1886; Bell, "The Bucktails at Gettysburg," GNMP.

49 Norton, *The Attack and Defense of Little Round Top*, 297.

handed it to Farley, while telling him to read it to the troops. The captain called the regiment to its feet. In a loud voice, he announced the following:

Circular
Headquarters Army of the Potomac
June 30, 1863

The commanding general requests that previous to the engagement soon expected with the enemy, corps and all other commanding officers will address their troops, explaining to them briefly the immense issues involved in this struggle. The enemy are on our soil. The whole country now looks anxiously to this army to deliver it from the presence of the foe. Our failure to do so will leave us no such welcome as the swelling of millions of hearts with pride and joy at our success would give to every soldier in the army. Homes, firesides and domestic altars are involved. The army has fought well heretofore. It is believed that it will fight more desperately and bravely than ever, if it is addressed in fitting terms.

Corps and other commanders are authorized to order the instant death of any soldier who fails in his duty at this hour.

By command of Major-General Meade
S. Williams
Assistant Adjutant General

At that, O'Rorke delivered his only formal speech to his regiment. Farley remembered only the conclusion: "I call on the file-closers to do their duty, and if there is a man this day base enough to leave his company, let him die in his tracks—shoot him down like a dog." A murmur of consent rippled through the ranks.[50]

III Corps, Army of the Potomac
The George Weikert Farm
One and a half miles south of Gettysburg
7:30 a.m.

After Ward's brigade finished breakfast, the ammunition wagons came up and the men replenished their cartridge boxes. The officers of the 124th New

---

50 Porter Farley, "Bloody Round Top," *National Tribune*, May 3, 1883.

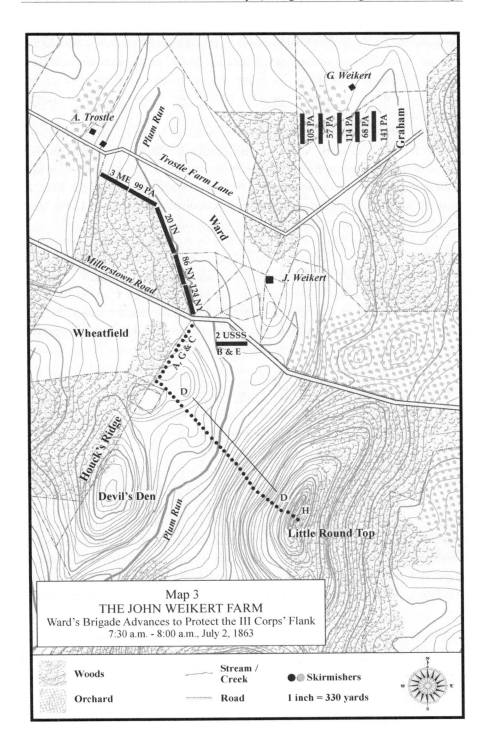

Map 3
THE JOHN WEIKERT FARM
Ward's Brigade Advances to Protect the III Corps' Flank
7:30 a.m. - 8:00 a.m., July 2, 1863

York ordered their men to load themselves down with 80 rounds—double the standard issue. Fearing a rough day, most men picked up an extra 20 cartridges. Albert A. Tucker (Company B) swore that a considerable number of his comrades stuffed an additional 100 rounds or more into their empty haversacks.

Ward maneuvered his brigade out of its bivouac. From the left to the right, the 124th New York, 86th New York, 20th Indiana, 99th Pennsylvania, and 3rd Maine swung facing south, with the three left regiments falling in behind the stone wall on the northern edge of the woods immediately west of the John T. Weikert farm buildings. Sergeant J. Harvey Hanford (Company B, 124th New York) considered it an excellent defensive position.[51]

The 2nd U.S. Sharpshooters under Maj. Homer R. Stoughton fanned out to the south, beyond the left flank of the brigade. Company H covered the crest of Little Round Top with skirmishers on the western slope. Company D spread out across the ravine up to the wood line on Houck's Ridge. Companies A, E, G, and C anchored on the right of Company D and formed a north-south line along the eastern edge of the Wheatfield. Companies B and F stayed in the rear as the reserve.[52]

Smyth's Brigade, II Corps, Army of the Potomac
David Zeigler's Grove,
Northern end of Cemetery Ridge
8:00 a.m.

Without any warning, a large body of Confederate infantry sprang from the cover of Seminary Ridge, heading directly toward their stalled skirmishers in the hollow west of the Bliss orchard. The Garibaldi Guard fired at them from behind the trees and from the Bliss barn and house but could not hold their position. They fled pell-mell for the Emmitsburg Road, abandoning a considerable number of wounded and slow runners to the Rebels. Colonel Thomas A. Smyth, watching this from the crest of Zeigler's Grove with a gaggle of officers, yelled for the 1st Delaware to move to its relief. Lieutenant Colonel

---

51 OR 27, pt. 1, 506, 511, 513; Ayars, "99th Pennsylvania," *National Tribune*, February 4, 1886; "Hanford, J. Harvey, The Experience of a Private," *National Tribune*, September 21, 1885; Tucker, "Orange Blossoms," *National Tribune*, January 24, 1886; Executive Committee, *Maine at Gettysburg*, 127.

52 Executive Committee, *Maine at Gettysburg*, 349-351.

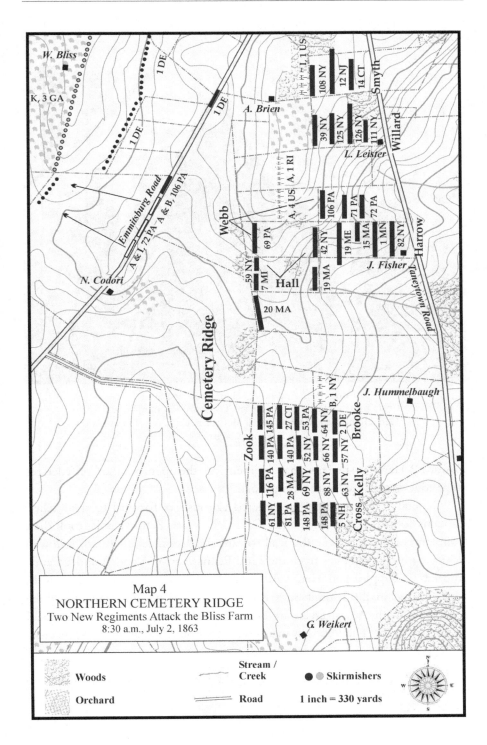

Map 4
NORTHERN CEMETERY RIDGE
Two New Regiments Attack the Bliss Farm
8:30 a.m., July 2, 1863

Brig. Gen. Andrew A . Humphreys and Staff
L to R: Lt. Henry C. Christiancy, Lt. Henry H. Humphreys,
Gen. Humphreys, Capt. Carswell McClellan, Capt. Adolfo Cavada
Library of Congress

Edward P. Harris rushed his small regiment into the open, but the Confederates stopped it cold in the Emmitsburg Road.[53]

General Webb immediately ordered skirmishers forward to their relief. Captains John J. Sperry and James C. Lynch, 106th Pennsylvania, took their Companies A and B over the wall toward the Emmitsburg Road, followed closely by two companies from the 72nd Pennsylvania (A and I) under Capts. Andrew C. Supplee and Henry A. Cook. Loping past Lynch's Company B, which stayed in the Emmitsburg Road, as the reserve, the remaining three companies, with the 1st Delaware on its right, Indian-rushed the wheat field along their front. The Pennsylvanians went to ground along the first fencerow

53 James A. Woods, Manuscript, "The Second Day at Gettysburg," 59-60, Vertical Files, GNMP; Wafer, Diary, 38, QU.

on the ridge west of the Nicholas Codori buildings, while the 1st Delaware drove the Rebs out of the farm buildings and the orchard. The five companies of the small regiment on the left hunkered down in the wheat field south of the barn, keeping their left flank in touch with Company A, 106th Pennsylvania. The right wing advanced onto the high ground in the peach orchard west and north of the barn.[54]

Presently, Meade, the "damned old goggle-eyed snapping turtle" himself, rode into Webb's brigade on the eastern slope of Cemetery Ridge. He wanted a reconnaissance of the Rebel position along Seminary Ridge. The impetuous Webb immediately volunteered to move his entire brigade forward. Meade suggested he deploy one company instead. Webb ordered Company B, 106th Pennsylvania to its feet. Captain James C. Lynch swiftly led his "boys" forward, keeping them low in the tall grass below the line of sight from Bliss' orchard to the northwest. Crawling through the intervening fences, rather than climbing over them, the patrol made it as far as Spangler's Woods. Finding the place swarming with Rebs, the lieutenant silently signaled his men to head back to the Emmitsburg Road. He passed his observations on to Meade and resumed his post under the cover of the road bank.[55]

Skirmishers, III Corps, Army of the Potomac
East of the Daniel Klingle Farm
Around 8:00 a.m.

The escalated skirmishing warranted addition of another regiment from Brig. Gen. Joseph B. Carr's brigade to the line. Captain Adolfo Cavada led the 11th Massachusetts into the boulder strewn creek bottom of Plum Run, north of the Trostle barn. Shots echoed in the morning sky as the Yankees ascended the eastern slope along the Emmitsburg Road. Cavada halted the New Englanders below the brow of the hill and with Lt. Col. Porter B. Tripp galloped over the crest to the Emmitsburg Road in order to determine what was happening there.

54 Nicholson, *Pennsylvania at Gettysburg*, vol. 1, 550; Ward, *106th Pennsylvania*, 399; Ladd and Ladd, *The Bachelder Papers*, vol. 3, 1,388.

55 Nicholson, ibid., 106; Bradley M. Gottfried, *Stopping Pickett: The History of the Philadelphia Brigade* (Shippensburg, 1999), 156.

There they found the 4th Maine's picket reserve. Colonel Elijah Walker warned them that they had ridden into a very exposed position. More rifles cracked as the two men, despite the shouted warnings of the picket officers, bolted onto the ridge about 100 yards west of the pike. Cavada hurriedly commanded Tripp to deploy his skirmishers along the brow of the hill overlooking the apple orchard on the opposite rise in front of Spangler's Woods, about 200 yards distant. The two officers parted—Tripp to his regiment and Cavada to Colonel Walker at the Peter Rodgers house. Cavada and Walker trotted south along the Emmitsburg Road, to acquaint Cavada with the III Corps picket line. From there, the captain reported to Humphreys, who allowed him to reconnoiter the terrain along Cemetery Ridge. The 11th Massachusetts with 286 effectives advanced across Plum Run and up the rise to the eastern side of the Emmitsburg Road opposite the Rodgers house. There it went to ground to support the skirmish line.[56]

III Corps, Army of the Potomac
Sickles' Headquarters at the Trostle House
8:00 a.m.

In the meantime Sickles dispatched Tremain several more times to Meade's headquarters underscoring his concerns about the action along the Emmitsburg Road. Sometime between 8:00 a.m.-9:00 a.m., Capt. George Meade visited Sickles again to find out if the general had obeyed his previous directive. Sickles lied to Meade, saying he had not understood "where" he was to relieve Geary. The general seemed more concerned about the rifle fire echoing across the fields from the west than his quieter left flank toward the foot of Little Round Top.[57]

56 OR 27, pt. 1, 509, 542, 547-548; Elijah Walker, "The 4th Maine at Gettysburg," *The National Tribune*, April 8, 1886; Executive Committee, *Maine at Gettysburg*, 160, 180; Cavada, Diary, July 2, 1863, 3, FSNMP; Ladd and Ladd, *The Bachelder Papers*, vol. 1, 192; Henry N. Blake, "Personal Reminiscences of Gettysburg," 14, Manuscripts Department, USAHEC, Carlisle Barracks, PA; John W. Busey and David G. Martin, *Regimental Strengths at Gettysburg*, (Baltimore, 1982), 52.

57 Ladd and Ladd, *The Bachelder Papers*, vol. 1, 670; Craft, *141st Pennsylvania*, 118.

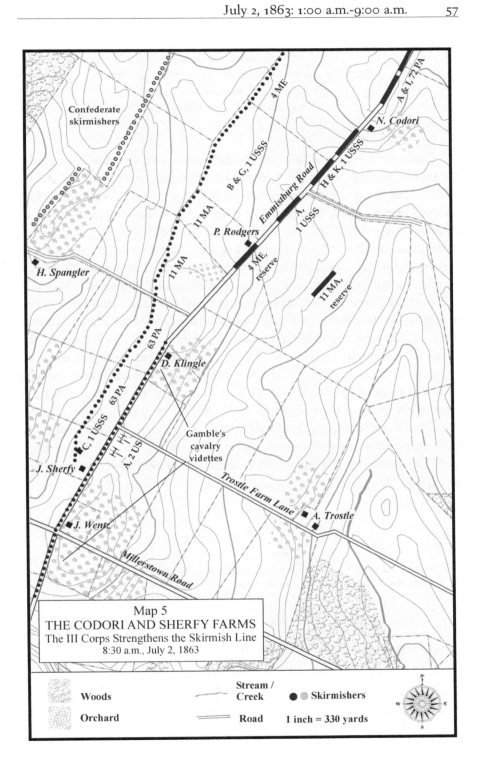

Confederate
skirmishers

4 ME

A. & I. 72 PA

N. Codori

B & C, 1 USSS

Emmitsburg Road

H & K, 1 USSS

11 MA

A,
1 USSS

P. Rodgers

11 MA

4 ME,
reserve

11 MA,
reserve

H. Spangler

63 PA

D. Klingle

63 PA

Gamble's
cavalry
videttes

C, 1 USSS

A, 2 US

J. Sherfy

Trostle Farm Lane

A. Trostle

J. Wentz

Millerstown Road

Map 5
THE CODORI AND SHERFY FARMS
The III Corps Strengthens the Skirmish Line
8:30 a.m., July 2, 1863

Woods

Orchard

Stream /
Creek

Road

Skirmishers

1 inch = 330 yards

N
W   E
S

The Emmitsburg Road
from the Joseph Sherfy Farm to the Rodgers Farm
About one and seven-tenths miles
southwest of Gettysburg
8:30 a.m.

General Birney dispatched Col. Hiram Berdan to the skirmish line to order the 1st U.S. Sharpshooters and Walker's 4th Maine to penetrate the woods and to drive the bothersome Confederate pickets away. Berdan ordered Lt. Col. Casper Trepp to deploy Companies A, B, C, G, H, and K—100 men—forward on line with the 4th Maine. Captain James H. Baker (Company C) held the left of the line at the Sherfy house. Captain Frank E. Marble with Companies B and G went to the right front about 200 yards west of the Emmitsburg Road just past the Rodgers house with the 4th Maine on the right. Companies A, H, and K occupied the Emmitsburg Road between the Rodgers and Codori farms. Their presence pulled the Rebels from the woods north of the Millerstown Road four times. Each time the sniping briefly waxed hot then receded when the Confederates withdrew to the cover of the woods rather than bring on a general engagement. Berdan wanted to go after them. In short order, Walker thought he had convinced Berdan not to do that. A division, he insisted, could not successfully execute the command, and it would be foolish to try. Berdan concurred that the only way to dislodge the Rebs would be to attack their flank. With the promise to report to his superiors what he had seen, Berdan returned to Birney, who did not put much credence in Walker's estimation of the situation.[58]

---

58 Ladd and Ladd, ibid., vol. 2, 1,093-1,094, vol. 3, 1,980; *New York at Gettysburg*, vol. 3, 1,067; A. Stevens, *Berdan's United States Sharpshooters in the Army of the Potomac, 1861–1865.* (Dayton, 1984), 302, 344; OR 27, pt. 1, 517; Nicholson, *Pennsylvania at Gettysburg*, vol. 1, 387, 393; Executive Committee, *Maine at Gettysburg*, 180. Based upon the casualty returns of the three companies, it is evident that A, H, and K suffered the lightest number of losses for the six companies involved along the line. It also seems quite evident that those three companies were in reserve in the Emmitsburg Road, despite the fact that Company K is the only one mentioned in the regimental history as being at that particular spot. Company A reported no losses. Company H had one man hit, while Company K had two men wounded. The three forward companies lost among them 17 men. When Trepp said in the Official Records that he took 100 men, he was evidently referring to three companies on the skirmish line. Companies A, H, and K had a mere 50 men between them.

Chapter 3

July 2, 1863
9:00 a.m.-Noon

"Boys, there are ten thousand men sitting on that one horse."
—*Unidentified Confederate, observing Robert E. Lee*

De Trobriand's Brigade, Army of the Potomac
The Emmitsburg Road, Warfield Ridge,
Two miles southwest of Gettysburg
9:00 a.m.

Having trudged for hours through and over the terribly muddy Emmitsburg Road, De Trobriand halted his brigade around 9:00 a.m. in the shade of the woods where Warfield Ridge crossed the Emmitsburg Road to give them a breather. The men quickly set to making coffee fires, while Burling's brigade continued north. Captain James E. Smith, whose 4th New York Independent Battery traveled ahead of the infantry, searched the surrounding terrain with a veteran's eyes. Small puffs of bluish smoke sporadically rose from the fields to the west, indicative of active skirmishing. All the fences within sight, except along the road, were down. Civilian refugees passed through their ranks. Captain George Winslow's artillerists of Battery D, 1st New York, riding behind Smith's guns, mockingly admonished the men among them for not staying to defend their homes from the Rebel invaders. They had no weapons came the reply, whereupon the soldiers offered to loan them some and press them into the ranks.[1]

---

1   Monument Commission, *Michigan at Gettysburg*, 100; G. W. W. to the [Editor], *New York Tribune*, July 5, 1863; Silliker, *Rebel Yell*, 100; *New York at Gettysburg*, vol. 3, 1,289; James Smith, *A Famous Battery and Its Campaigns, 1861-1864* (Washington, 1892), 101; Winslow, "Battery D," *Philadelphia Weekly Times*, July 26, 1879; Ladd and Ladd, *The Bachelder Papers*, vol. 2, 590.

The thudding of a fast approaching horse snapped Smith's attention to the northeast. He locked his eyes upon a lone aide, madly galloping across the open field and frantically waving his handkerchief above his head. The captain brought his battery to a halt and waited for Lt. Thomas. J. Leigh, an aide-de-camp to Ward, to gallop up. Leigh ordered the guns to follow him toward the Wheatfield. Smith and Winslow peeled away from the road before reaching the Peach Orchard.[2]

The kindling had barely crackled when De Trobriand's buglers sounded "Assembly." The men kicked out their fires and double-quicked north without their coffee, while the civilians quietly, almost ashamedly took to the top fence rails along the road to allow them to pass. Not one word of encouragement or "Godspeed" followed the veterans. Word traveled through the ranks that a Rebel column was closing in on their western flank.[3]

The Skirmish Line, III Corps,
Army of the Potomac
The Millerstown Road from the
Emmitsburg Road to Pitzer's Woods
About one-third of a mile west of the Peach Orchard
Around 9:00 a.m.

Meanwhile, Berdan and Birney had convinced Sickles to strengthen the skirmish line and to probe the woods to the southwest. To that end, he sent an aide to Ward requesting the use of two of his regiments. Consequently, the general dispatched the 3rd Maine and the 99th Pennsylvania from the right of his brigade, with instructions for them to report to General Birney for further directives. At the same time, Colonel Berdan, with Capt. Joseph C. Briscoe from Sickles' staff, and Lieutenant Colonel Trepp brought the remaining four companies of the 1st Sharpshooters (D, E, F, and I) forward to the Emmitsburg Road. Turning north, the 100 men marched to the Millerstown Road

---

2   Smith, *A Famous Battery*, 101; *New York at Gettysburg*, vol. 3, 1,290; *OR* 27, pt. 1, 431, 494.

3   Monument Commission, *Michigan at Gettysburg*, 100; G. W. W., Letter to the Editor, *New York Tribune*, July 5; Silliker, *Rebel Yell*, 100; Winslow, "Battery D," *Philadelphia Weekly Times*, July 26, 1879; Ladd and Ladd, *The Bachelder Papers*, vol. 2, 590. Leigh is listed as T. J. Leigh and S. J. Leigh in the *OR*. His service record shows that at the time of Gettysburg, he was the acting captain of Company C, 71st New York, which is why he referred to as a lieutenant in the reports.

intersection, from which they would begin a half mile sweep to the northwest on the north side of the road.[4]

Everything about the operation alarmed Trepp, who objected to approaching their objective in plain view of the Confederates. The 3rd Maine, with only 14 officers and 196 men, followed the Berdans to the Emmitsburg Road at which point, for reasons unknown to the colonel, the regiment briefly halted before advancing into the field behind the sharpshooters.[5] Meanwhile, the 99th Pennsylvania moved onto the Stony Hill on the western side of the Wheatfield. The Berdans deployed in skirmish order, with six-foot intervals between each man. Company D held the left the line with E, F, and I, respectively, continuing the formation to the right. The Maine men followed in column along the Millerstown Road. Colonel Thomas C. Devin, commanding the cavalry videttes, automatically dismounted two squadrons from his brigade and deployed them in the Emmitsburg Road. At the same time, he ordered a section of 2nd Lt. John H. Calef's Battery A, 2nd U.S. Artillery, into position on the north side of the Peach Orchard just south of Trostle's Lane.[6]

Wilcox's Brigade, Hill's Corps, Army of Northern Virginia
Seminary Ridge, west of Pitzer's Woods
9:15 a.m.-10:00 a.m.

Having been on the move before daylight with Brig. Gen. Cadmus Wilcox's Alabama brigade, Pvt. Baily G. McClelan (Company D, 10th Alabama) believed his regiment had passed behind every regimental bivouac in the Army of Northern Virginia. As the brigade continued its southerly march, toward the right flank, it became clear that Wilcox's veterans were conducting a reconnaissance in force. They had been on the go for more than four hours when the 10th Alabama, which led the brigade, wheezed to a halt on the west

---

4   OR 27, pt. 1, 513;   *New York at Gettysburg*, vol. 3, 1,067; William Y. W. Ripley, *Vermont Riflemen in the War for the Union, 1861-1865, A History of Company F, First United States Sharpshooters* (Rutland, 1883), 115.

5   Hannibal A. Johnson, *The Sword of Honor: A Story of the Civil War* (Hollowell, 1906), 11; OR 27, 1, 516-517. Major Moore's report clearly indicates that he was to support the 3rd Maine; Benjamin W. Thompson, "This Hell of Destruction," *Civil War Times Illustrated*, vol. 12, 16.

6   *New York at Gettysburg*, vol. 3, 1,070; Jonathan Newcomb, Jr., "A Soldier's Story of Personal Experience at the Battle Gettysburg," *Maine Bugle*, Campaign 3, (1896), col. 2, (April), 100; OR 27, pt. 1, 939, 1,032.

2nd Lieutenant John H. Calef
Battery A, 2nd U.S. Artillery
MOLLUS Collection, Library, GNMP

side of the woods between them and the James Warfield and Christian Shefferer farms.

The officers immediately ordered the regiment into line and called for skirmishers. Privates Nathaniel Harrelson and Thomas Mackey (both Company D, 10th Alabama) stepped forward without hesitation. As the skirmishers disappeared into the open wood lot, the rest of the regiment slowly followed then lay down just inside the tree line to see what would happen next.[7]

As Company D of the Berdans fanned around the Shefferer and Warfield farm buildings, a boy came out of the woods on his way home from a visit to a nearby farm. Pointing toward the trees, he blurted: "Look out! There are lots of Rebels in there in rows." Thinking he knew nothing about the army, the veterans ridiculed the boy rather than take him seriously. Within minutes, both commands penetrated the woods along southern Seminary Ridge. Several hundred yards behind the Berdans, the New Englanders extended their line by the left past the southern flank of the sharpshooters.[8]

The Berdans stumbled into the 10th Alabama's skirmishers. A firefight erupted. Private Mackey dropped with a ball through one of his legs. His friend, Nathaniel Harrelson, pulled him to his feet and helped him back toward the regiment. A round brought the "good Samaritan" down, but Mackey managed to hobble to his waiting comrades with the Berdans almost literally on his heels.

7   Baily G. McClelan, "Civil War History of Company D, 10th Alabama Regiment: 'The Alexandria Rifles'" in *Anniston Star*, January 2-March 7, 1901.

8   Newcomb, "A Soldier's Story," in the *Maine Bugle*, vol. 3, 100; *New York at Gettysburg*, vol. 3, 1,067-1,068, quoted on 1,067.

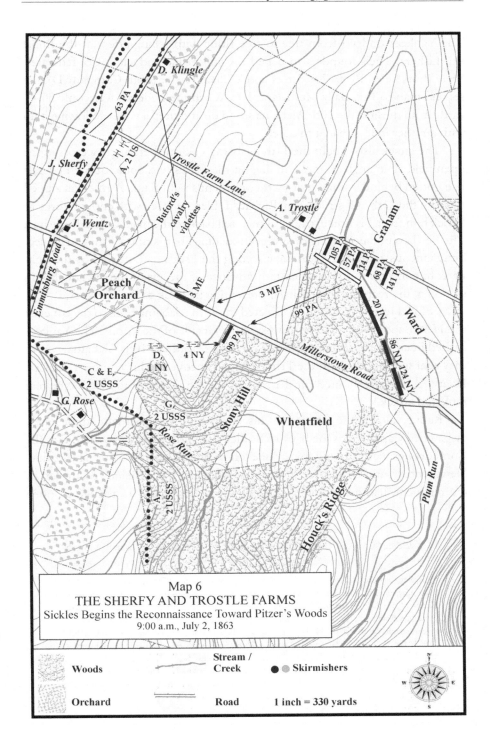

D. Klingle

63 PA

A. 2 US

Trostle Farm Lane

J. Sherfy

J. Wentz

A. Trostle

Graham

Buford's cavalry videttes

105 PA

57 PA

114 PA

68 PA

141 PA

Emmitsburg Road

Peach Orchard

3 ME

3 ME

99 PA

20 IN

Ward

86 NY 124 NY

99 PA

Millerstown Road

4 NY

D, 1 NY

C & E, 2 USSS

G. Rose

G, 2 USSS

Stony Hill

Wheatfield

Rose Run

A, 2 USSS

Houck's Ridge

Plum Run

Map 6
THE SHERFY AND TROSTLE FARMS
Sickles Begins the Reconnaissance Toward Pitzer's Woods
9:00 a.m., July 2, 1863

Woods

Orchard

Stream / Creek

Road

Skirmishers

1 inch = 330 yards

N
W   E
S

The Yankees dodged from tree to tree firing with telling effect at the Rebel skirmishers. Their rounds also pelted the still prone and silent Confederates. Stray shots killed Pvts. Silas Street and William Carter (both Company D), the second man to Pvt. Baily McClelan's left. When the Federals were only 30-40 yards from the line, the 10th Alabama stood up and fired a volley following it up with another in less than a minute.[9]

The attack also caught the 11th Alabama's skirmishers as they crossed the open field at an angle to move in line on the 10th's left. Some of the Federals had gotten behind a stone wall on the regiment's right flank. A rifle ball zipped through the 11th and struck Maj. Richard J. Fletcher's leg with enough force to knock him from his horse, while his men fell back to the main Confederate line. The Berdans pursued, firing their breech-loading Sharps rifles as they advanced. Simultaneously, the 8th Alabama, covering the 11th's rear, moved by the right flank to conform to the northeasterly advance of the left of the brigade. But in so doing, the rear rank found itself presenting its flank to the Yankees.

Colonel John C. C. Sanders directed the 11th Alabama back to the cover of a rail fence about 300 yards northwest of the far side of the woods. The Yankees rushed in and captured a number of prisoners from the 10th Alabama, whom they sent to the rear. With the 11th Alabama uncovering his regiment, Lt. Col. Hilary A. Herbert shouted for the men of the 8th Alabama to face by the rear rank and attack.[10]

Riding along the front of his sharpshooters, Berdan immediately dispatched Captain Briscoe back to Sickles and Birney to advise them that the Confederates were moving toward the left of the III Corps. Corporal Jonathan Newcomb, Jr. and Cpl. John Little (both Company A, 3rd Maine), on the left of the regiment, had just completed extending the company to the left in open

---

9 McClelan, "Civil War History of Company D," in the *Anniston Star*, January 2-March 7, 1901.

10 Ripley, *Vermont Riflemen*, 116; *New York at Gettysburg*, vol. 3, 1,070; Stevens, *Berdan's United States Sharpshooters*, 304, 308-309; George Clark, *A Glance Backward: or Some Events in the Past History of My Life* (Houston, 1914), 35; Hilary A. Herbert, "History of the 8th Alabama Volunteer Regiment, C.S.A.," in the *Alabama Quarterly*, 39 (1911): 114; Fleming W. Thompson to [Sisters and Mother], July 17, 1863, Brake Coll., Box 1, Manuscripts Department, USAHEC, Carlisle Barracks, PA; Hilary A. Herbert, "*A Short History of the 8th Ala. Regiment*," 10, enclosed with ltr, August 8, 1869, McLaws Papers, Vertical Files, GNMP. Ripley, in his account, identifies a rail fence some 300 yards beyond the woods, which would conform to Stevens' statement that they pushed the Rebels 300 yards and came upon the three columns of infantry beyond the woods west of Seminary Ridge at or near Pitzer's Run.

order when firing erupted to the front. The shooting quickly escalated into a lively firefight. With bullets zinging about him, Newcomb noticed Berdan, conspicuous upon his white horse, galloping between the 3rd Maine and the sharpshooters. For half an hour Newcomb held his ground, calmly loading and firing as if at drill. Glancing to his right he discovered that only John Little remained on his flank, and judging by the whiteness of his friend's face, Newcomb surmised that Little was dying. All along the line, the 10th Alabama had been dropping Union soldiers. In the 1st U.S. Sharpshooters, they killed Pvt. Smith Haight (Company D). Farther to the right, Company F lost Sgt. Abraham H. Cooper, killed, and Pvts. George Wooly and William H. Leach, wounded. Lieutenant George W. Sheldon (Company I) did not survive the skirmishing either. The Rebs stripped him down to his underwear before he had gotten cold.[11]

In the same instant, Newcomb spotted a sharpshooter directly in front of him, who had taken cover behind a large tree. Rather than remain a conspicuous target, Newcomb decided to join the Berdan. While darting forward, he suddenly realized that the Federal line had ceased fire. A Confederate regiment, in battle line with its weapons at "charge bayonet," swept into the woods. With both fighting and running obviously suicidal, Newcomb dropped his weapon, stepped away from his cover, and put his hands in the air. More than a dozen of the Rebels, however, had reacted just as quickly. They automatically leveled their muskets and fired. At the muzzle flashes, Newcomb hurled himself to the ground and the sharpshooter, with whom he had shared the tree, crumbled with a bullet through his knee.[12]

With the Confederates closing in on three sides, the 3rd Maine's bugler sounded the retreat, and stubbornly contesting every inch of ground the men retired from the fight. Just before Sgt. Hannibal Johnson (Company B) reached the open field east of the woods, Pvt. Nathan Call caught a musket ball in the hip. "Sergeant," he cried out as he went down, "don't desert me. Help me out of these woods." Private John W. Jones immediately came to Johnson's assistance. Using a musket as a chair between them, they had Call throw his arms around

11 Stevens, *Berdan's U.S. Sharpshooters*, 304; J. J. Renfroe to [Editor], *South Western Baptist*, August 13, 1863; Newcomb, "A Soldier's Story," in the *Maine Bugle*, vol 3, 100-101; *New York at Gettysburg*, vol. 3, 1,068; Ripley, *Vermont Riflemen*, 119; E. A. Wilson, "An Incident at Gettysburg," *National Tribune*, June 10, 1886. Confederate accounts confirm that the action occurred around 9:00 a.m., not noon as traditionally believed.

12 Newcomb, "A Soldier's Story," in the *Maine Bugle*, vol. 3, 100-101.

their necks and they started carrying him away. Bullets zinged about their ears, and the Rebel yell bounced off the backs as they slowly trudged from the field. Then Jones plummeted to the ground with a musket ball in his brain. Before he could free Call's arm from his neck, Johnson found himself surrounded and a prisoner of the 10th Alabama.[13]

By the time the orders to retreat reached Company D on the sharpshooters' left, Pvt. Peter H. Kipp estimated that each man had expended 95 rounds. As he backed out of the woods, he saw Capt. Charles D. McLean collapse. Lieutenant John E. Hetherington, Pvt. Edwin Nelson, and the company first sergeant came to his assistance. As they rolled the captain onto a blanket and started back with him, a bullet cut Nelson down. McLean told them to leave him and save themselves. Laying him down, the three unwounded men kept going. But a short distance later, Lieutenant Hetherington sent Kipp back to stay with their beloved captain.[14]

Kipp (1st U.S. Sharpshooters) reached Captain McLean a moment before the Rebels surrounded him. He told them that he had orders to stay by the officer, but they insisted he go to the rear with them. When he refused to comply, the Rebs lightly poked him in three places with their bayonets. The timely arrival of a Confederate lieutenant sent the enlisted men on their way. The officer assured Kipp that he would get an ambulance for McLean, and that he could remain with him. The New Englanders and the Sharpshooters lost 67 men in half an hour.[15]

Farther to the right, 1st Sgt. Lewis J. Allen (Company F) threw down his rifle after a bullet carried away the hammer. He snatched another from a wounded man who staggered past him on the way to the rear. In the noise of battle, he never heard the bugle call. Looking around, he suddenly realized that his comrades had abandoned the field. With Confederate bullets zipping closely about him, he bolted southeast through the woods.[16]

Some distance to Allen's left, Pvt. Eugene Paine, dove into a gully and continued to fire low at the Confederates who had taken cover behind a stone wall 200 yards from his position. The Rebels returned fire in his direction. Small

---

13 Johnson, *Sword of Honor*, 12.

14 Stevens, *Berdan's 1st U.S. Sharpshooters*, 310.

15 Johnson, *Sword of Honor*, 12; Ripley, *Vermont Riflemen*, 119; Stevens, ibid., 308, 310.

16 Stevens, ibid., 312.

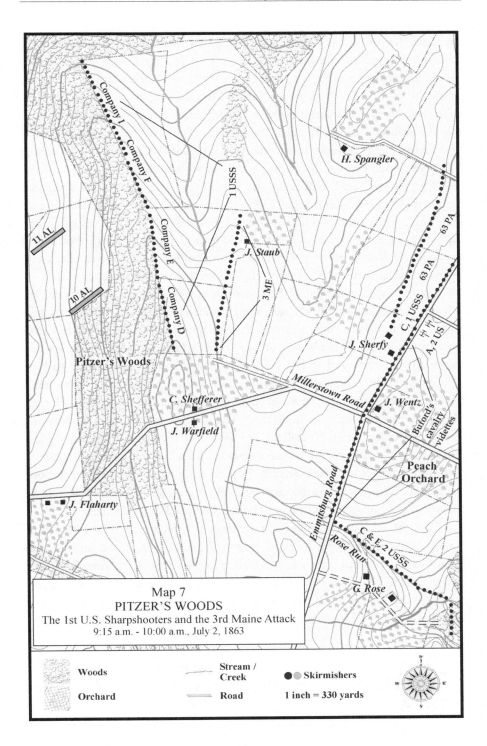

Map 7
PITZER'S WOODS
The 1st U.S. Sharpshooters and the 3rd Maine Attack
9:15 a.m. - 10:00 a.m., July 2, 1863

Company I
Company F
Company E
Company D
1 USSS
11 AL
10 AL
Pitzer's Woods
J. Staub
3 ME
H. Spangler
63 PA
63 PA
C. 1 USSS
A. 2 US
J. Sherfy
C. Shefferer
J. Warfield
Millerstown Road
J. Wentz
Buford's cavalry videttes
Peach Orchard
J. Flaharty
Emmitsburg Road
Rose Run
C & E. 2 USSS
G. Rose

Woods
Stream / Creek
Skirmishers
Orchard
Road
1 inch = 330 yards

branches, leaves, wood slivers, and bark pelted his ears and stung his face, almost blinding him. He fired three more rounds after the bugle call before deciding to make a run for it. Ignoring pleas of the wounded, and mindful only of the fact he could die at any moment, he kept his back to the Rebels, heedless of their screams for him to surrender; he did not stop running until he reached the Wheatfield. The entire affair, he later recalled, had been "reckless" and "foolhardy." He blacked out in front of a shell-riddled barn, unaware that three balls had passed through his clothing without striking him.[17]

The plowed field bordering the eastern side of the woods staggered Sergeant Allen, another fleeing Yankee. Exhausted, with unbelievable pain shooting up through his sides, he found himself winded, unable to run much farther. Staggering several hundred yards toward the John Staub house and expecting to die at every step with a shot from behind, he shoved the back gate open, stumbled a few yards, then collapsed on the grass in the backyard.

Two women rushed out of the house. One, seeing the sergeant grasping his sides and struggling for breath, screamed in an Irish brogue, "Lord save us, he's shot!" As the two of them scurried back to the house, Allen heard the Irish woman shouting, "Where's the butcher knife?" He nearly died of shock when the woman re-appeared with a knife that looked more like a cutlass to him. Dropping by his side, she feverishly cut away his belt, knapsack straps, haversack, and canteen. With the pressure off his chest and waist, Allen blurted, "Don't cut any more, I'm not shot!" The Irish woman stood upright and indignantly yelled at him, "Ye blathering divil ye, ye're making all that divil's fuss and not shot?" Glancing up, he saw a squad of Rebels coming through the back gate and without further ado snatched up his equipment and tore out through the gate, heading south on the farm lane. He veered left onto the Millerstown Road and did not stop running until he reached the Peach Orchard.[18]

The 10th Alabama regrouped in the woods. Wilcox trotted his horse up to William Forney: "Colonel Forney, from my heart I thank you and to your gallant regiment I pull off my hat." Doffing his head cover, he formally bowed to the rank and file, and they cheered him lustily. The nasty skirmish had cost the regiment 10 killed, 28 wounded, and 7 missing. The 11th Alabama in addition to Major Fletcher had 17 wounded enlisted men, half of them severely.

---

17 Ibid.

18 Ibid., 311-312. quoted on 311. I have concluded that the Staub farm was close to Company F's line of retreat.

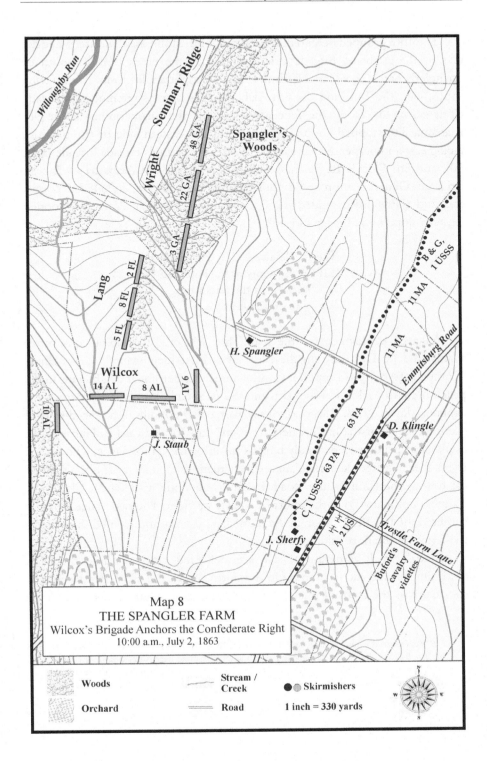

Map 8
THE SPANGLER FARM
Wilcox's Brigade Anchors the Confederate Right
10:00 a.m., July 2, 1863

The 10th grouped behind the fence west of the John Staub house, while the rest of the Alabama brigade extended toward the creek bottom south of Spangler's barn. The 11th Alabama formed at right angles to its front, facing south, with the 14th and the 8th Alabama Regiments stretching the brigade front eastwards, along the fencerow north of the Staub orchard. The 9th Alabama line stopped about 150 feet from the eastern side of the orchard, facing east and perpendicular to the 8th Alabama. Lang's Florida brigade (2nd, 5th, and 8th Florida Regiments) went prone to the 9th Alabama's left rear. Brigadier General Ambrose Wright's Georgia brigade (3rd, 2nd, 48th Georgia, and 2nd Battalion) extended the line another 1,250 feet along the wooded western slope of Seminary Ridge.[19]

The 1st Delaware, Smyth's Brigade,
II Corps, Army of the Potomac
Skirmish at the Bliss Farm
10:00 a.m.-11:00 a.m.

Wilcox's deployment to the south had triggered a simultaneous move against the 1st Delaware on the Bliss farm. First Lieutenant J. Lewis Brady (Company E) noticed a superior Confederate force herding the right wing in the peach orchard back upon the barn and the farm lane. Immediately alerting his captain, Martin W. B. Ellegood, of the worsening condition, he raced toward the lower level of the barn, where he found Lt. Col. Edward P. Harris in his established headquarters. Brady blurted his information to Harris, who leaped to his feet, scurried outside to survey the situation, then shot off like a scalded cat toward the Emmitsburg Road. Brady stood alone with 1st Lt. Charles B. Tanner (Company D) in the midst of a nasty firefight. The two officers hastily gathered the few fleeing men in the immediate vicinity and formed them along the fence on the north side of the lane.

Brady's small gathering of stalwarts delivered a hot fire into the Rebs swarming around the farmhouse to the north. When the Confederates veered south, across the front of the left wing, Tanner started pulling his men out of

---

19 Renfroe to the *South Western Baptist*, August 13, 1863; *OR* 27, pt. 2, 617; George Clark, *A Glance Backward* (Houston, 1914), 36. The formation described here is based upon my own conclusions. The 9th would be in a hollow with its left flank on a creek south of Spangler farm. Being in that position would explain how the 8th Alabama hit the Union line south of the Trostle lane.

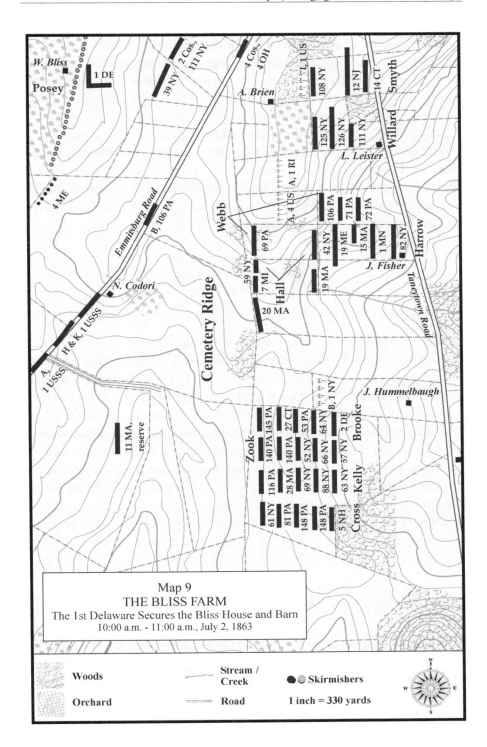

Map 9
THE BLISS FARM
The 1st Delaware Secures the Bliss House and Barn
10:00 a.m. - 11:00 a.m., July 2, 1863

Woods

Orchard

Stream / Creek

Road

Skirmishers

1 inch = 330 yards

the fight when he caught a bullet, his third wound in nine months, that forced him to stagger back toward Cemetery Ridge. The regiment's left companies vainly attempted to "change front to rear" to thwart their envelopment, but the Rebs had them "bagged." Ellegood died in the fighting; Captain Ezechial C. Alexander and several men from his Company H surrendered.[20]

Brady finally stopped in the relative safety of Zeigler's orchard on the crest of Cemetery Ridge, where some wonderfully vehement swearing attracted his attention: General Hancock, standing in the stirrups, was dressing down a dismounted Lieutenant Colonel Harris "in the most choice and forcible language deemed suitable for the occasion." Harris found himself under arrest for "cowardice in the face of the enemy."[21]

Lee's Headquarters,
Army of Northern Virginia
Seminary Ridge near the Lutheran Seminary
10:00 a.m.

Lee, who had left his headquarters an hour earlier to confer with his Second Corps commander, Lt. Gen. Richard S. Ewell, and his generals on the army's left, returned with his secretary, Col. Armistead L. Long, to find that Captain Johnston and his party had not returned from their scouting mission.[22]

Captain George Hillyer (Company C, 9th Georgia), nearby in the clover behind his regiment, watched Lee turn his mount to the right about 60 yards in front of the line. Reining in under a large shade tree, the general focused his glasses upon the hills and fields to the east. His staff remained mounted about 20 yards behind him as he studied the Yankee lines. For a brief moment, Hillyer pondered how wondrous it would be to know what Lee was thinking at that moment. A nearby enlisted man interrupted his reverie with, "Boys, there are ten thousand men sitting on that one horse." At that moment, a large body of

---

20 Ladd and Ladd, *The Bachelder Papers*, vol. 3, 1,389. Brady reported this action as occurring at 8:00 a.m. He had the time off by an hour. It occurred at approximately 9:00 a.m.

21 Ibid.

22 Gary W. Gallagher, *Fighting for the Confederacy*, (Chapel Hill, 1989), 35; "Col. E. P. Alexander's Report of the Battle of Gettysburg," in *SHSP*, vol. 4, 235; Johnston to Lafayette McLaws , June 17, 1892; Johnston to George Peterkin, UHS Dec., 18??; Longstreet, *From Manassas to Appomattox*, 363; A. L. Long to Jubal A. Early, April 5, 1876, in *SHSP*, vol. 4, 68. According to Alexander, Longstreet ordered him forward around 10:00 a.m.

Captain George Hillyer
Company C, 9th Georgia
*Gregory A. Coco Collection
Library, GNMP*

general officers thundered onto the ridge farther south, and Lee nudged his horse toward them.[23]

Johnston had finally arrived and found an impressive gaggle of officers surrounding Lee. The general sat sandwiched between Hill and Longstreet on their "headquarters log," studying a map with Col. E. Porter Alexander. Lee stopped talking and motioned the captain forward. Standing behind the general, he leaned over and traced his route along Seminary Ridge to Warfield Ridge to Big Round Top and the Philip Slyder farm. When Johnston pointed to Big Round Top, Lee turned and asked, "Did you get there?" The captain told Lee he had.

At that, Longstreet spoke over his shoulder to Alexander. Pointing at the map, he informed the colonel that his corps would strike the Yankee flank and he wanted Alexander to assume field command of all of the corps' artillery. He was to leave at once on a reconnaissance, get a detailed concept of the terrain, and then bring his own battalion forward. The Washington Artillery was not to go. Longstreet further admonished Alexander to keep out of sight of the Yankee signal station to the southeast. Saluting, Alexander rushed from the circle, and taking two couriers with him, mounted up and rode off. Turning to Longstreet, Lee said, "I think you had better get on." At that, Longstreet and Hill departed, while Johnston sat down beside the commanding general and explained the topography to him.[24]

23 Hillyer, "Battle of Gettysburg," 3, GNMP.

24 Gallagher, *Fighting for the Confederacy*, 235; "Col. E. P. Alexander's Report," in *SHSP*, vol. 4, 235; Johnston to Lafayette McLaws, June 17, 1892; Johnston to George Peterkin, Dec., 18??,

Meanwhile, Jr. 2nd Lt. Fred Bliss (Company B, 8th Georgia) strolled over to Captain Hillyer. Stretching out in the clover, he rested his head upon the captain's knee. The two quietly lay there, and listened while an enlisted man loudly lectured his "pards." "Now, boys," he said, "we are going to have a great battle and a great victory today. Suppose that, by divine revelation, if it were known in a manner that we all believed it, that some one of us would walk across that valley and up to those batteries and be blown to atoms by one of those cannon, and thus sacrificing one life instead of many, the victory would be ours, is there one of us that could do it?"

The proposal of such a Christ-like act stirred Hillyer's consciousness, but before he could say a thing, young Bliss jumped to his feet and, pointing toward the Yankee guns in the distance, blurted, "Yes, if I could do that, I would walk straight across that valley and put my breast to one of the cannon and myself pull the lanyard."[25]

Colonel Alexander's Reconnaissance
Willoughby Run
Near Pitzer's Woods

Twenty-eight year old Alexander, using the creek bottom for cover, took his horse south in Willoughby Run, across the Fairfield Road, and headed for Pitzer's School House. By sticking close to the woods on Seminary Ridge and cutting into low fields when the road on the east side of the stream rose too high to escape the gaze of the Yankee signal stations on that flank, he safely rode to within about 100 yards of the school. Turning about, he quickly covered the two miles back to his command.[26]

Longstreet's Corps, Army of Northern Virginia
Herr's Ridge near the Hagerstown Road

Black's cavalrymen caught up with Alexander and Longstreet on an open hill overlooking the stone bridge on Willoughby Run. Longstreet immediately

---

VHS, (Richmond, VA); Longstreet, *From Manassas to Appomattox*, 363; A. L. Long to Jubal Early, in *SHSP*, vol. 4, 68.

25 Hillyer, "Battle of Gettysburg," 3-4, quote on 4, GNMP.

26 Gallagher, *Fighting for the Confederacy*, 236.

ordered Black to secure the bridge and to place two reliable officers at his disposal. Black volunteered 1st Lt. Fred Horsey and 3rd Lt. J. Wilson Marshall (both Company I, 1st South Carolina Cavalry). Longstreet directed Horsey to scout three or four miles to the west and Marshall to take off in the opposite direction. Black dispatched some cavalry down to the bridge and sent a courier after Capt. James F. Hart's battered three-gun South Carolina battery.[27]

III Corps, Army of the Potomac
The Emmitsburg Road in the vicinity of the Peach Orchard

Colonel Moses Lakeman rallied as many men as he could find of his 3rd Maine on the eastern side of the Emmitsburg Road in the Peach Orchard and was preparing to take them back to Ward's 2nd brigade when an aide from Birney directed them to the fencerow on its southern side. With its right flank on the road, the regiment marched south and went into line along the fence.[28]

Not too far to the front, in the creek bottom north of the Rose farm, their skirmishers found Company E, 2nd U.S. Sharpshooters. The New Englanders told the Regulars they were looking for Rebs. Corporal Henry C. Congdon and Pvt. Ira Carr volunteered to scout for them and moved out toward the Emmitsburg Road.[29]

De Trobriand's brigade arrived on the field by way of the Emmitsburg Road around 10 a.m. by which time, Burling's 3rd brigade had filed off the road and moved into the low, wooded ground north of Trostle's house. De Trobriand immediately reported his arrival to General Graham, who had ridden out to the Peach Orchard under Birney's directive. Dismounting, Graham climbed onto a fence and perched himself on the top rail to casually observe the fields to the west.[30] As DeTrobriand's regiments passed the Peach Orchard, they came under fire from the over shots of the Confederate skirmishers to the west, who were popping away at the Federal skirmish line. Private John Haley (17th Maine) listened apprehensively to the bullets zipping over his head.

---

27 McSwain, *Crumbling Defenses*, 38-39; Ladd and Ladd, *The Bachelder Papers*, vol. 2, 1,215.

28 Executive Committee, *Maine at Gettysburg*, 130.

29 Ira Carr, "A Sharpshooter at Gettysburg," *National Tribune*, November 25, 1886.

30 *OR* 27, pt. 1, 519, 570; Samuel Toombs, *New Jersey Troops in the Gettysburg Campaign* (Orange, 1888), 207; Hamilton, "Recollections," 117-118, CWL; Ladd and Ladd, *The Bachelder Papers*, vol. 2, 839-840.

Marching north, the column ran headlong into a tremendous crowd of civilians shuffling south out of the town, loaded down with whatever bedding and clothing they could carry. At Trostle's lane, De Trobriand turned his regiments to the right. Passing the house, they crossed Plum Run and moved onto the wooded ridge southeast of the farm house. The regiments formed in column of regiments, facing west. Once the men of the 17th Maine were sure they were going to stay put for a while, they started their coffee fires for the third time that day and within a short while were enjoying the only "meal" they had been able to get within the last 24 hours.[31]

Second Division, III Corps, Army of the Potomac
Plum Run north of the Trostle House

Carr prepared his 1st brigade for an expected advance. His regiments fell into column of regiments. The 1st Massachusetts (321 effectives) held the front. The 26th Pennsylvania (365 officers and men) came next, followed respectively by the 16th Massachusetts (245 men), the 12th New Hampshire (224 effectives), and the 11th New Jersey (275 officers and men).[32] The skirmishers' rounds whistled by the pickets and plunked among Humphreys' staff. For the most part, they fell like pebbles tossed onto the grass around their feet. One, however, zipped low into the huddle of men, and punching through the baggy legs of a sleeping man's trousers, burrowed itself with a resounding slap into his haversack without disturbing him in the least. His comrades' uncontrollable laughter awakened him. What was so funny, he groused. They told him, but he did not believe them until he fingered the holes in his pants, and while rifling his haversack, discovered the round that could have crippled him.[33]

---

31 OR 27, pt. 1, 523, 526; Silliker, *Rebel Yell*, 100-101; Houghton, *17th Maine*, 91; Executive Committee, *Maine at Gettysburg*, 190.

32 John W. Busey and David G. Martin, *Regimental Strengths at Gettysburg* (Baltimore, 1982), 52; Janet B. Hewett, et al., *Supplement to the Official Records of the Union and Confederate Armies*, 100 vols. (Wilmington, 1995), vol. 5, pt. 1, 183; OR 27, pt. 1, 553. I speculate that the 1st Massachusetts was at the head of the column because it was sent forward at 11:00 a.m. and the colonel didn't mention being pulled away from the rear of the column. The 11th New Jersey was at the rear of the column, and I placed the other regiments as they would have deployed in succession when moving by the right into line.

33 Cavada, Diary, July 2, 1863, FSNMP.

Pennsylvania Skirmishers,
South of the Bliss Barn

By the time the bulk of the 1st Delaware had rallied along the stone wall west of Zeigler's Grove, Gen. Carnot Posey's riflemen in the Bliss buildings had wounded 1st Lt. Charles S. Swartz and 2nd Lt. William M. Casey (both Company A, 106th Pennsylvania) and forced the company to peel back toward the reserve in the Emmitsburg Road. Captain James C. Lynch (Company B) immediately ordered his "boys" across the contested field in a beeline toward the Bliss house, but a swarm of minié balls stalled the attack and sent it reeling back to the shelter of the roadbed.[34]

Zeigler's Grove

Hays decided to strengthen the skirmish line in force. Once again, he ordered skirmishers forward. The 39th New York held the left, just north of the Bliss farm lane, with two companies of the 111th New York on center and three companies of the 125th New York on the right. The skirmishers crouched behind the rail fence several hundred yards west of the Emmitsburg Road. Farther north, the 108th New York (Smyth's brigade) hurried Companies A and C forward to extend the line to the right. Colonel Samuel Carroll ordered Lt. Col. Leonard W. Carpenter to reinforce them with four companies from the 4th Ohio, and he immediately sent them out, under Maj. Gordon A. Stewart, to shelter in the Emmitsburg Road. All along the II Corps line regimental commanders hurried skirmishers into the pike. Colonel Paul Joseph Revere (20th Massachusetts) and Col. James Mallon (42nd New York) each ordered two companies forward.[35]

Sickles' Headquarters
The Trostle House

Once again, Major Tremain reported to Meade's headquarters, this time with a request from Sickles to place artillery upon Little Round Top to cover the

---

34 Nicholson, *Pennsylvania at Gettysburg*, vol. 1, 551-552.

35 *OR* 27, pt. 1, 445, 451, 456, 460, and 477; Ladd and Ladd, *The Bachelder Papers,* vol. 1, 314; James Woods, Manuscript of the Second Day at Gettysburg, 71, 75-76.

Emmitsburg Road and to protect the army's left flank. As before, the commanding general did not respond to his suggestion, and, just as previously, the aide returned to Sickles with no directives. Perhaps in anticipation of another rejection, Sickles had decided to take matters into his own hands. He sent word to Ward on the left of the III Corps line to clear any fences in his line of march to the Emmitsburg Road. Ward, in turn, commanded Lt. Col. Benjamin L. Higgins (86th New York) to detach enough men under a commissioned officer to accomplish the task. So Capt. Nathan L. Baker (Company G) and 35 men headed out and completed their work before the end of the hour.[36]

The 1st Volunteer Artillery Brigade, Army of the Potomac
The Taneytown Road
Several miles south of Gettysburg

The 1st Volunteer Brigade rolled quickly on the road north from Taneytown. By 10:00 a.m., shortly after crossing the Mason–Dixon Line, they heard occasional artillery shots reverberating from the front. Suddenly a limber in Capt. Elijah D. Taft's 5th New York Independent Battery from the 2nd Volunteer Brigade, exploded, killing one of its men. First Sergeant Levi W. Baker, who was riding with Capt. John Bigelow's 9th Massachusetts Battery as the gunner on #6, immediately behind the New Yorkers, saw the blast rip off the man's face.

Along the way, Capt. Charles A. Phillips (Battery E, 5th Massachusetts) knew they were heading into a "fight" as he noticed that the surgeons had converted nearly every one of the long Pennsylvania bank barns into hospitals. As the column continued, he saw the inactive Federal infantry formations along the ridges to the west. Within half an hour, shell bursts pocked the sky ahead of them, and the crackle of skirmishing musketry along the Emmitsburg Road, far to the left of the column, echoed overhead. Squads of wounded men, along with Confederate prisoners under guard, occasionally passed around the limbers and caissons.[37]

---

36 Ladd and Ladd, *The Bachelder Papers*, vol. 1, 670; OR 27, pt. 1, 511.

37 *5th Massachusetts Battery*, 623, 629; Baker, *9th Massachusetts Battery*, 55.

The III Corps, Army of the Potomac
Vicinity of the Trostle House
Around 10:30 a.m.

Captain Adoniram J. Clark sent his Battery B, 1st New Jersey Light Artillery, to the destroyed fencerow on the ridge immediately southwest of Trostle's cherry orchard, which was soon picked clean by the artillerymen. Sergeant Bloodgood and his two comrades from Company I, 141st Pennsylvania, having procured some wheat flour, had just settled down to eat their breakfast. Bloodgood and Pvt. Oliver Morse got one large flapjack each and Pvt. James Lunger was about to pour his batter onto the plate when "assembly" sounded. His batter stayed in the pail, while he grabbed his weapon and fell into line with the rest of the company.[38]

Simultaneously, Sickles, just informed that Confederates were in force to his front, shifted General Birney's two brigades farther west and south. With Ward's brigade as the pivot near the base of Little Round Top, he swung Graham's 1st brigade forward, through the woods into the field southeast of the Trostle house, along the eastern side of Plum Run. The narrow front constricted the regimental lines. The 68th Pennsylvania doubled on the center as it moved to the left of the formation. The regiment broke into a column of divisions—two companies on front— closed en masse, as it fell in on the left of the brigade line. The 141st Pennsylvania with the 57th Pennsylvania to its right also deployed doubled on the center, while the 105th Pennsylvania with the 114th Pennsylvania on its left fell in behind them in the same formation. Captain Clark's six 10-pounder Parrotts rolled into position on the ridge east of the Peach Orchard about 650 feet west of the creek.[39]

38 Michael Hanifen, *History of Battery B, 1st New Jersey Artillery* (Ottawa, 1905), 67; Bloodgood, *Reminiscences*, 133.

39 Craft, *141st Pennsylvania*, 118; W. J. Hardee, *Rifle and Light Infantry Tactics*, 2 vols., (Philadelphia, 1861), vol. 2, 172-182; OR 27, pt. 1, 498; See map reference in Raus, *Generation on the March*, and 56-57.

Headquarters, Army of the Potomac
The Leister House
Six-tenths of a mile south of Gettysburg along the Taneytown Road
11:00 a.m.

Having grown impatient with Meade's lax interest in his predicament, Sickles rode to army headquarters himself. Heatedly he argued that he could defend the Emmitsburg Road, but Meade was having none of it. He refused to go inspect the position nor would he dispatch his chief of engineers Brig. Gen. Gouverneur K. Warren to do so. The commanding general insisted that the Rebels intended to strike the army's right rather than its left and rudely dismissed Sickles' concern. Eventually he relented to Sickles' entreaties and allowed Brig. Gen. Henry J. Hunt, chief of artillery, to tour the proposed line with him. Meade, turning to Hunt, who had just come in from a reconnaissance of the entire Federal line from Culp's Hill to Little Round Top, said that Sickles wanted him to inspect his proposed new line. According to Hunt, Sickles "thought that [the position] assigned to him was not a good one, especially that he could not use his artillery there." Being familiar with the "unfavorable character of the ground" near Little Round Top, Hunt accompanied Sickles to the field.[40]

Smyth's Brigade, II Corps, Army of the Potomac
The Bliss Farm

The presence of the strong Yankee skirmish line east of the Bliss orchard and buildings drew a heavy Confederate response. A large body of Rebels rushed down Seminary Ridge from the northwest, temporarily disappearing from view in the hollow then suddenly re-emerging in a swarm in the orchard. Their concentrated fire broke the 39th New York. The Garibaldis bolted from the cover of their fencerow, heading for the Emmitsburg Road. Major Hugo Hildebrandt, who remained in the saddle despite a nasty foot wound, could not stop them. From the east-west leg of the wall, north of the copse of trees, General Hays, with his ever-present adjutant general, Capt. George P. Corts alongside, impetuously leaped his horse into the field heading toward the road,

40 Craft, *141st Pennsylvania*, 119; Favill, *Diary of a Young Officer*, 245; Henry J. Hunt, "The Second Day at Gettysburg," in *Battles and Leaders*, vol. 3, 301-302, quoted on 301.

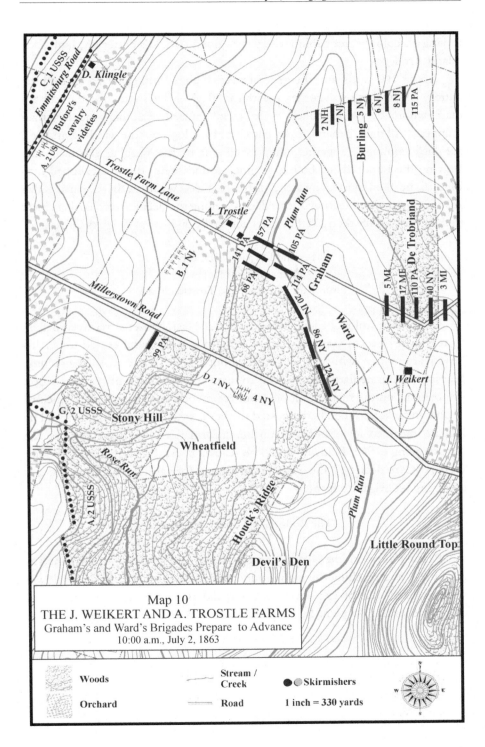

Map 10
THE J. WEIKERT AND A. TROSTLE FARMS
Graham's and Ward's Brigades Prepare to Advance
10:00 a.m., July 2, 1863

leaving his color bearer behind with Capt. Albert Arnold's Battery A, 1st Rhode Island Artillery.

About 100 yards out, the general whirled about and galloped back to the battery. "Why don't you come on with that flag?" Hays shouted at the enlisted man, whom everyone called "Wild Jack." Smartly saluting, the Irishman quipped, "All right, general, if y'ez get's into Hell, look out the window, and ye'll see Jack coming." Together, they raced out to the flagging skirmish line. Braving the hundreds of bullets singing around them, the trio galloped into Bliss' Lane then skirted into the northern field. With the headquarters flag snapping in their wake, they succeeded in turning the fleeing New Yorkers back to their posts. Only then did they trot back to the division at Zeiglers Grove.[41]

Second Division, III Corps,
Army of the Potomac
Plum Run, North of the Trostle House

Lieutenant Colonel Clark B. Baldwin (1st Massachusetts) received orders to report at once to General Humphreys, whom he found seated under his headquarters tree with maps spread about him. After a cordial greeting, Humphreys immediately proceeded to acquaint Baldwin with various troop dispositions on the map. "Colonel, your regiment is detailed to relieve the 3rd Maine on picket." When he requested further instructions, Humphreys said he had no more to give, and that further information would come from the commanding officer Baldwin would be relieving. At the same time, Brigadier General Carr detached the 26th Pennsylvania forward to tear down fences along his 1st brigade's front.[42]

The Rodgers and Spangler Farms

Passing beyond the 11th Massachusetts, and not the 3rd Maine, as instructed, and reaching the high ground around the Rodger's house, Baldwin soon realized that his 321-man regiment did not have enough strength to deploy according to plan. Leaving Companies B and D with the colors just

---

41 Thomas M. Aldrich, *The History of Battery A, First Regiment Rhode Island Light Artillery* (Providence, 1904), 204.

42 Ladd and Ladd, *The Bachelder Papers*, vol. 1, 191-192, quoted on 192; OR 27, pt. 1, 555.

northwest of the house, he sent the rest of the regiment forward by companies, at 50 yard intervals, to the western brow of the ridge. With Maj. Gardner Walker and Adj. Charles E. Mudge, Baldwin posted Companies G, I, and A west, into the open field north of Spangler's lane. The rest of the regiment took cover behind the rail fence west and northwest of the Rodgers house in the following order: C, E, F, H, and K. Ignoring the dangerous Confederate skirmish fire, Baldwin did not leave the line immediately. He directed the company officers to detail five men from each company forward 25 yards as skirmishers with the admonition to keep low and to use as much cover as possible.[43]

The Army Artillery Reserve, Army of the Potomac
Granite School House Road,
one-and-a-quarter miles southeast of Gettysburg,
700 yards east of the Taneytown Road

Neither Meade nor Hunt realized that Sickles had already requested a battery from the Artillery Reserve. While Sickles pressed his case at army headquarters, Capt. Nelson Ames's Battery G, 1st New York, received orders to report to the III Corps. As Hunt and Sickles began their inspection, Ames rode west along the Granite School House Road, with his six Napoleons preparing to follow him.

Once at the Taneytown Road, he swung south to the George Weikert farm lane and followed that south to the Trostle lane, before heading west again. Finding the two generals near the Emmitsburg Road, he reported directly to Sickles, who directed him to go into park in the hollow behind the Trostle barn and to dispatch his battery wagon with the sick to the rear. After placing his guns, Ames allowed his men to refill their canteens from the nearby stream while he mounted up and trotted forward to join the two generals on their reconnaissance.[44]

43 "Where Honor Is Due," *The Sunday Herald*, Boston, July 23, 1899, Robert L. Brake Coll., Manuscripts Div., USAHEC, Carlisle Barracks, PA; Ladd and Ladd, *The Bachelder Papers*, vol. 1, 192.

44 OR 27, pt. 1, 900; Nelson Ames, *History of Battery G, First Regiment New York Light Artillery* (Marshalltown, 1900), 62-63.

III Corps, Army of the Potomac
The Emmitsburg Road
From the Codori Farm to the Peach Orchard

Hunt carefully studied the ground along the Emmitsburg Road to the salient at the Peach Orchard. He agreed with Sickles that while the apex of the line would expose III Corps to enfilades from the south and the west, the high parallel ridges between the western edge of the Wheatfield and the Emmitsburg Road formed natural traverses, which could minimize projected casualties. But he did not believe Sickles' overextended line would hold the ground against any substantial attack. Not realizing Sickles had already probed Seminary Ridge, he advised him to do so. Artillery reverberating from the north diverted Hunt's attention. He told Sickles he could not stay to await the results of the reconnaissance and that he would be returning to army headquarters by way of Little Round Top. As he turned his horse about, Sickles asked him whether he should move his corps forward to which he replied, "Not on my authority; I will report to General Meade for his instructions."[45]

Hunt rode off and Sickles sent an order to General Graham to strengthen the picket line west of the road. Around 11:15 a.m., Graham ordered the 105th Pennsylvania from the right of his brigade to the Emmitsburg Road to support the 63rd Pennsylvania. Companies A, F, D, I, and C splayed across the road into the field northwest of the Sherfy house. Falling prone behind the men of the 63rd, they watched the Rebels pop off rounds at them from the distant wood line while the remainder of the regiment stayed in the road as a reserve. Before too long, one found its mark, hitting Sgt. Robert Doty (Company F) in the skull, killing him instantly.[46]

The Wheatfield
700 Yards east of the Peach Orchard
Around 11:15 a.m.

Just before he reached the Wheatfield, Hunt heard the skirmishing flare up again beyond the Emmitsburg Road. Rather than ride back and personally observe the situation, he assumed the Rebels did occupy the woods west of the

---

45 Hunt, "The Second Day at Gettysburg," in *Battles and Leaders*, vol. 3, 301-302, quote on 302.

46 *OR* 27, pt. 1, 500; Scott, *105th Pennsylvania*, 82. This is my reconstruction of the event.

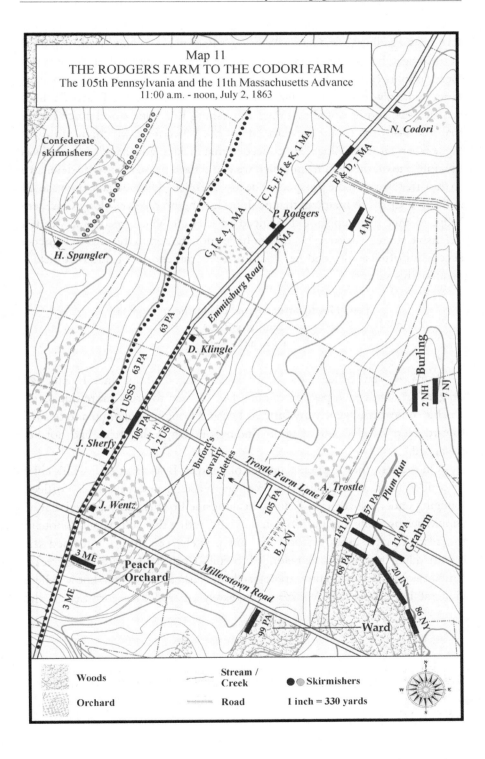

Map 11
THE RODGERS FARM TO THE CODORI FARM
The 105th Pennsylvania and the 11th Massachusetts Advance
11:00 a.m. - noon, July 2, 1863

III Corps. Finding Capt. George Winslow's Battery D, 1st New York, deployed in the wheat, he stopped long enough to voice his disapproval of the battery's location to its captain. As he descended Houck's Ridge into Plum Run Valley, Hunt suddenly realized how far away from the main line the Peach Orchard actually was, and he noted that the Emmitsburg Road line stood much higher than the stony hill on the western side of the Wheatfield, which, in turn, was higher than Houck's Ridge. He conceded that Sickles' advanced position "was the only one on the field from which we could have passed from the defensive to the offensive with the prospect of decisive results." It would take both the III and the V Corps to maintain that position leaving no reserves along Cemetery Ridge to back them up should the need arise. Hunt, who agreed with Meade's defensive strategy because he did not have enough men in the area to launch a successful offense, decided he would not recommend to Meade that Sickles maintain his salient.[47]

Lee's Headquarters, Army of Northern Virginia
Seminary Ridge
11:00 a.m.-Noon

For Lee's staff officer Col. Armistead L. Long, the hour since 11 a.m. had dragged by. With each passing minute, Lee seemed to grow more impatient. Unable to bear the silence any further, Lee and Long mounted up and headed toward Herr's Ridge, intent upon finding out why Longstreet had not yet advanced.

On the way, they happened upon Col. Lindsay B. Walker, A. P. Hill's chief of artillery, and Col. William T. Poague, Walker's reserve artillery officer, lounging under a shade tree. Reining in alongside Poague, Lee snapped that he should be "hurrying into position on the right" rather than lollygagging about in the rear. Poague quickly stood up and politely, yet firmly, informed the commanding general that he belonged to Hill's Corps and not to Longstreet's. Embarrassed, Lee promptly apologized and asked, "Do you know where General Longstreet is?" Walker immediately offered to escort Lee to the

---

47 Hunt, "The Second Day at Gettysburg," in *Battles and Leaders*, vol. 3, 302, quoted; Winslow, "Battery D." *Philadelphia Weekly Times*, July 26, 1879; Ladd and Ladd, *The Bachelder Papers*, vol. 2, 590.

general. Upon reaching Herr's Ridge, Lee found Longstreet awaiting the arrival of Brig. Gen. Evander Law's Alabama brigade.[48]

Colonel E. P. Alexander, having returned from his reconnaissance, had already dispatched Col. Henry C. Cabell's Battalion of McLaws' Division and Maj. Mathias W. Henry's Battalion from Hood's Division back to their respective commands. He then rode into his own battalion and ordered the bugler to call "Boots and Saddles." He led his cannon into the low ground along Willoughby Run and turned south on a direct route to the Pitzer School House.[49]

Longstreet's Corps, Army of Northern Virginia
Herr's Ridge near the Haas Farm
Around 11:00 a.m.

Shortly before 11:00 a.m., Hart's South Carolina Battery rolled into position on the high ground overlooking Willoughby Run. Within a few minutes, Lt. Fred Horsey (1st South Carolina Cavalry) reported to Longstreet that he had seen no Federal activity at all in that sector. As the lieutenant rode back to the regiment, Longstreet turned to Colonel Black and asked if he could rely on Horsey's report. "If there was an officer in the army he could rely on, he could on Horsey," Black told him. Longstreet nodded, and Black trotted down to the stone bridge to check out his detachment.[50]

---

48 A. L. Long to Jubal A. Early, April 5, 1876, B. Lindsay Walker to Fitz Lee, March 5, 1877, both in *SHSP*, vol. 4, 68 and vol. 5, 181, quoted, respectively.

49 Gallagher, *Fighting for the Confederacy*, 236.

50 McSwain, *Crumbling Defenses*, 39, quoted; Ladd and Ladd, *The Bachelder Papers*, vol. 2, 1,215.

Chapter 4

July 2, 1863
Noon-3:00 p.m.

"General, General, do you think we can take those heights?"

—Private James W. Duke (Company C, 17th Mississippi) to General Longstreet

III Army Corps, Army of the Potomac
The Emmitsburg Road
From the Klingle Farm to the Bliss Farm
Noon

At noon, Birney informed Sickles of his disposition, and the corps commander promptly ordered him to swing Ward's brigade 500 yards farther southwest to the vicinity of the Devil's Den and rest his right flank on the Peach Orchard along the Emmitsburg Road. He reassured Birney that two divisions, one from II Corps, the other from V Corps, were under orders to be ready to support his men.[1]

Birney complied. Infantry detachments loped through the oat field northwest of Trostle's house and tore down the fences across their front. With the 57th Pennsylvania on the right front, Graham's brigade moved forward, still doubled on the center across Plum Run. The brigade marched into the field immediately south of the Trostle house, and from there continued west over the destroyed north-south fence to its front into a field of young corn on the slope east of the Peach Orchard. The regiments maneuvered into regimental fronts, and the men stacked arms. Private Lunger (141st Pennsylvania), having held his dough in the pail too long to make it edible, decided to bury his watery batter. With his file closer, Sergeant Bloodgood, watching him, he scooped out

---

1   OR 27, pt. 1, 482; Hanifen, *History of Battery B*, 68.

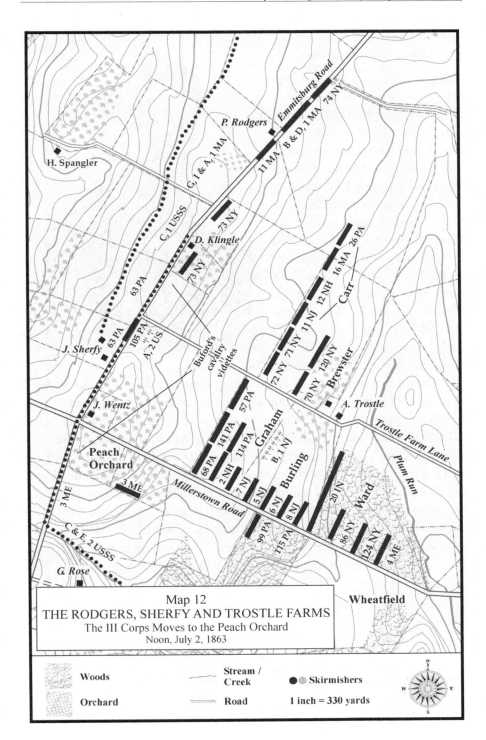

Map 12
THE RODGERS, SHERFY AND TROSTLE FARMS
The III Corps Moves to the Peach Orchard
Noon, July 2, 1863

Woods

Orchard

Stream / Creek

Road

Skirmishers

1 inch = 330 yards

Captain Charles M. Wheeler
(Company K, 126th New York)
Gregory A. Coco Collection, Library, GNMP

a shallow trench with his foot, poured his dough into the small trough and covered it up with a quick scuffle of his toe. Colonel Peter Sides received an order to send 15 handpicked men from the 57th Pennsylvania across the Emmitsburg Road. He handed the assignment to Capt. Alanson H. Nelson (Company K), who, in turn, passed the job to 1st Lt. Thomas J. Crossley. The lieutenant and his detachment promptly darted across the road to the temporary cover of the Sherfy farm buildings.[2]

When small arms fire broke out along Seminary Ridge, Sickles ordered Humphreys to advance his Second Division to the Emmitsburg Road with its right flank anchored on the Codori buildings. Chaplain Joseph H. Twitchell (71st New York), having just returned from visiting acquaintances in the I and XII Corps, absorbed the beauty of the moment as the division stepped off. "It was a splendid sight. Far to the right and left the dark lines of infantry moved on, with the artillery placed at intervals, while the stillness was unbroken save by the scattered fire of skirmishers in front." Carr's 1st brigade—the 26th Pennsylvania had returned to join the column—deployed into line and ascended the first rise of ground to the fencerow 300 yards east of the Klingle farm. The 26th Pennsylvania went to the right of the line with the 16th

---

2   OR 27, pt. 1, 482, 497, 502; Craft, *141st Pennsylvania*, 119, 121; Bloodgood, *Reminiscences*, 133; Alanson H. Nelson, *The Battles of Chancellorsville and Gettysburg* (Minneapolis, 1899), 149-152; Joseph H. Twitchell to Sister, July 5, 1863, Manuscript Department, Yale University Library. Hereinafter cited as YUL.

Massachusetts to its left, followed respectively by the 12th New Hampshire and the 11th New Jersey.[3]

Colonel William R. Brewster's 2nd brigade (the Excelsiors) emerged from the wooded creek bottom to the slope behind Carr. Humphreys immediately ordered Brewster to detach a regiment forward into the orchard around Klingle's log cabin. So the 73rd New York (4th Excelsior), under Maj. Michael W. Burns, advanced 250 yards to the front with orders to hold that position no matter what happened. As the 4th Excelsior with its 349 officers and men moved to the front, Brewster formed his brigade. The 72nd New York (3rd Excelsior), followed by the 71st New York (2nd Excelsior), fell in on the left of Carr's brigade and rested its left flank on the Trostle farm lane to the immediate right of Graham's 1st brigade. The 74th New York (5th Excelsior) trotted into position on Carr's right flank in the Emmitsburg Road. The regiment took cover behind the road bank to the left front of the 26th Pennsylvania. The 70th New York (1st Excelsior) with the 120th New York to its right supported both brigades.[4]

To protect Humphreys' right front from the nettlesome snipers in the Bliss barn, Hays ordered three companies from the 126th New York across the Emmitsburg Road to dislodge them. Captain Charles M. Wheeler (Company K) responded immediately with his own men and the two adjoining companies. Bolting over the road banks, they charged wildly toward the barn and house, and to everyone's amazement, quickly burst into the barn's lower level and bagged several prisoners.[5]

Burling's Brigade, III Corps, Army of the Potomac
Cemetery Ridge Northwest of the George Weikert Farm

Sickles ordered Humphreys to send a brigade south to Birney's division. He directed Captain Cavada to take Burling's regiments (2nd New Hampshire, 5th, 6th, 7th, and 8th New Jersey, and the 115th Pennsylvania) to the right rear of Birney's First Division. The captain quickly marched the regiments to the southeast into the western end of Trostle's woods, north of the Millerstown

---

3 *Supplement to the OR* 5, pt. 1, 183; Craft, *141st Pennsylvania*, 119; Twitchell to Sister, ibid, quoted.

4 OR 27, pt. 1, 532, 558; Charles W. Hardeen, *A Little Fifer's War Diary* (Syracuse, 1910), 219.

5 Ladd and Ladd, *The Bachelder Papers*, vol. 1, 315.

Road, and placed them behind the deteriorating three-foot-high stone wall. By the time he got back to headquarters, the firing along the Emmitsburg Road had intensified. He found the remaining two brigades of the division lying under cover of the eastern slope of the Emmitsburg Road ridge. Occasional minié balls zipped over the crest, and one of them, coming in quite low, struck the canteen of a man using it as a pillow, with hammer-like force. The shot splattered everyone around him with water but, miraculously, injured no one.[6]

Burling's brigade, in close column of battalion, left the cover of the woods below the Trostle house, into the open ground south of the orchard and marched as far as the destroyed fence line on the crest to the west. Burling stood behind a lone apple tree near the southwest corner of the orchard.[7]

Ward's brigade, on the left of Birney's division, now joined by the 4th Maine on its left, moved out at approximately the same time. His men stood up in regimental line, faced to the right, and calmly marched west until the 124th New York's left flank cleared the stone wall behind which they had been resting. At that point the regiments deployed on regimental front into the woods southeast of the Trostle house. The column halted when the lead regiment, the 20th Indiana, entered the field on the western edge of the woods on the north side of the Millerstown Road directly above the Wheatfield.[8] Birney then directed the brigade to move into the wheat.

The regiments executed the command "change front to the rear, on the first company," a complicated maneuver in which each regiment ended up on a new line of advance perpendicular to its original formation and facing south. The regiments then maneuvered into battalion front before the brigade crossed over the fence bordering the Millerstown Road and entered the Wheatfield. Private Albert A. Tucker (Company B, 124th New York) marveled at the pristine beauty of the chest high wheat, brightly glowing in the afternoon sun and sadly recalled how his comrades had trampled it all underfoot. Second Sergeant J. Harvey Hanford (Company B), likewise, detested destroying one of the "finest" crops he had ever seen. The brigade rested in the middle of the field

6   OR 27, pt. 1, 531, 570; Cavada, Diary, July 2, 1863, FSNMP.

7   Report of Maj. John P. Dunne (115th Pennsylvania) to Adjutant General, State of Pennsylvania, July 29, 1863, Vertical Files, GNMP; Ladd and Ladd, *The Bachelder Papers*, vol. 2, 1,006-1,007.

8   OR 27, pt. 1, 511, 513; Tucker, "Orange Blossoms," *National Tribune*, January 24, 1886; Hanford, "The Experience of a Private," *National Tribune*, September 21, 1885.

for about half an hour before the orders came for it to move by the left flank toward the Devil's Den.

The 4th Maine planted its left on Plum Run at the northern base of the Devil's Den. The 124th New York cleared the eastern face of the woods on Houck's Ridge just north of the end of the woods near the Den and deployed on a southeasterly running line in conformity with the crest of the ridge. Colonel Van Horne Ellis carefully kept the regiment below the top of the hill and out of the Rebels' possible line of sight. The leftmost company of the 86th New York followed the 124th onto the slope and went prone with its right flank resting on the fencerow along the front of the woods. The rest of the regiment, with the remainder of the brigade, lay down along the western side of the fence, inside the tree line at right angles to Ellis' men. They left behind Capt. James E. Smith's parked 4th New York Independent Battery, which had been resting in the Wheatfield since around 10 a.m.[9]

With Ward's men clear of Trostle's Woods, De Trobriand's brigade occupied them. Second Lieutenant George W. Verrill (Company E, 17th Maine) scrawled in his diary; "Expect every moment to 'go in,' skirmishing is going on in front." De Trobriand detached the 5th Michigan from the front of his brigade line, with orders to support Calef's section of U.S. artillery north of the Peach Orchard. Colonel John Pulford double-quicked his regiment. Crossing Trostle's lane, the Michiganders went prone to the guns' right.[10]

---

9   OR 27, pt. 1, 511, 513; Hardee, *Tactics*, vol. 2, 169-172; Smith, *A Famous Battery*, 101, 136; Tucker, "Orange Blossoms," *National Tribune*, January 24, 1886; Hanford, "The Experience of a Private," *National Tribune*, September 21, 1885; Ladd and Ladd, *The Bachelder Papers*, vol. 2, 1,023; Executive Committee, *Maine at Gettysburg*, 194, 251. Major Moore (99th Pennsylvania) said that the brigade came upon his right, therefore, it had to have been facing west. To change front as he said the brigade did, each regiment would have had to execute the command cited as described in Hardee's *Rifle and Light Infantry Tactics* under "change of front perpendicularly to the rear." This is my reconstruction of the maneuver. The brigade on battalion front could not have effectively executed "front to rear on the first company" on battalion front. For the entire brigade to fit in the Wheatfield in line of battle, the regiments had to have formed on battalion front.

10   OR 27, pt. 1, 525-526, 528; Ladd and Ladd, *The Bachelder Papers*, vol. 1, 46 and vol. 2, 995, 1,032, 1,059, quote on 1,059; Silliker, *Rebel Yell*, 101. Major Rogers (110th Pennsylvania) said he was sent forward into the woods at 1:00 p.m.

Bigelow's and Phillips' Batteries,
Artillery Reserve, Army of the Potomac
Granite School House Road
A half-mile from the Taneytown Road

Swinging west onto the Granite School House Road, the batteries of the 2nd Volunteer Brigade wheeled into a field a half-mile from the Taneytown Road, with Bigelow's 9th Massachusetts and Phillips' Battery E, 5th Massachusetts, just west of the Spangler barn in the southwest corner of a field. While the artillerists maneuvered into close intervals and prepared for action, one of them shortly noted how damp and cloudy the day had become. The men welcomed the halt after their hard 12-mile march. With occasional hostile artillery rounds bursting over their position, most of the enlisted men bellied down next to the horses and limbers.

Corporal Benjamin Graham, the gunner on Phillips' #1 piece, felt rather secure behind the boulders, which sheltered the guns and limbers. His lead driver, despite wearing a steel vest under his tunic, suddenly fell into the dirt next to his horse. A shell fragment had struck his unshielded buttocks and forced him to quit the field. First Lieutenant Henry D. Scott looked at his watch: it was noon. The surgeons had established a hospital in the Spangler barn for the wounded Confederate prisoners from the previous day's battle. A few of the men from Bigelow's battery, none of whom had ever seen a Confederate, wandered over to look at them. In the brigade, the artillerymen unhitched one or two of the battery's teams at a time to water the horses. The men cooked their lunches and watched the increasing artillery fire to the west with keen interest.[11]

Longstreet's Corps, Army of Northern Virginia
Herr's Ridge, Near the Alfred Haas Farm
South of the Chambersburg Road

Law's Confederate brigade, after an exhausting 25-mile march, finally came to a halt on the western side of the ridge. Colonel William C. Oates (15th Alabama) spied Lee and Longstreet atop the nearest crest carefully studying the Federal position through their field glasses. Colonel Black (1st South Carolina

---

11 *5th Massachusetts Battery*, 623, 629, 639, 655; Baker, *9th Massachusetts Battery*, 56.

Cavalry) reined up alongside Longstreet and told him that he had secured the whiskey and the house. "I suppose you saved some for yourself and me," the general quipped. "Excuse me, General," came the indignant reply, "as I do not drink, I forgot to do so." At that, he requested orders and Longstreet told him to stay at headquarters and await orders, thereby effectually removing him from any further action.[12] Captain Johnston, riding over with Lee, joined McLaws at the head of his column. Johnston would guide the division onto the field, Lee informed the general.

Brigadier General Law's frazzled infantrymen swore they had not rested more than a few minutes when the order came down the line to get moving again. Turning south, they trudged toward what Oates assumed was the left of the Federal line. McLaws' Division, escorted by Johnston, headed up Longstreet's Corps followed by Hood's Division with Law's brigade in the rear. As a precaution, McLaws dispatched Brig. Gen. William T. Wofford's sharpshooters ahead of the column to screen its advance. The corps headed southeast along the road, which passed in front of the Haas farm to the next intersection, about a half-mile from the farm lane. There it turned to the right for four-tenths of a mile then followed an intersecting farm lane to the south, which eventually led them along the northern bank of Marsh Creek, directly toward the Black Horse Tavern. As the column halted at each intersection, McLaws asked Johnston which route to take. "There were many *halts*," Maj. James M. Goggin, McLaws' assistant adjutant and inspector general, noted, "the question arising as to the proper route to be pursued, so as to avoid observation of the enemy, as we had no guide." From the outset, it became apparent that Lee's engineer officer had no idea where he was going. McLaws sent Goggin forward to find out what was causing the delays and to check on his scouts.[13]

---

12 "Account of Col. William C. Oates, 15th Alabama," Mss., Bowdoin College Library, Bowdoin College, (Brunswick, ME), 4, hereinafter cited as BC; Longstreet, *From Manassas to Appomattox*, 365; McSwain, *Crumbling Defenses*, 39, quoted.

13 S. R. Johnston to Fitz Lee, Feb. 16, 1878, [same] to McLaws, June 17, 1892, [same] to Rev. George Peterkin, Dec., 18??, VHS; McLaws, "Gettysburg," in *SHSP*, vol. 7, 69; Oates, "15th Alabama," 4, BC; Longstreet, *From Manassas to Appomattox*, 365; James M. Goggin to Longstreet, August 15, 1887, Mss. Div., USAHEC, quoted; Morris M. Penny and J. Gary Laine, *Struggle for the Round Tops: Law's Alabama Brigade at the Battle of Gettysburg* (Shippensburg, 1999), 29. Johnston denied that he directed the column on the line of march. But considering that he had reconnoitered the route, he had no real purpose to be with the column other than to direct it onto the field.

A little more than 30 minutes after leaving the Haas farm, McLaws, with Johnston and an aide, well in advance of his division, ascended the knoll southeast of Black Horse Tavern and stopped cold. Directly ahead, they clearly saw Little Round Top and the Federal signalmen there busily wigwagging a message. McLaws immediately sent his aide racing back to the division to halt it while he and Johnston feverishly scouted the area looking for a concealed alternate route. Finding none, McLaws galloped back to the tavern where he encountered Longstreet, who had ridden forward to see what was happening to his stalled column.

"What is the matter?" Longstreet inquired. "Ride with me and I will show you that we can't go on this route, according to instructions, without being seen by the enemy." Reining to a halt on the top of the hill, Longstreet exclaimed, "Why this won't do. Is there no way to avoid it?" McLaws immediately suggested that the corps follow the route he had chosen during his private scout that morning. "How can we get there?" Longstreet asked impatiently. "Only by going back—by countermarching." "Then all right," Longstreet snapped. A countermarch required the corps to execute a U-turn. The lead brigade would peel back, followed by each of the successive ones until the entire division headed back to where it came from.

The two generals trotted to Kershaw's brigade east of the Black Horse Tavern, and McLaws gave the orders to turn back. The maneuver created a traffic jam when the head of Hood's Division, the "Texas Brigade," collided with the rear of McLaws' column. Longstreet, on the verge of losing patience with the entire affair, spurred alongside McLaws. "General," he yelled, "there is so much confusion, owing to Hood's division being mixed up with yours, suppose you let him countermarch first and lead in the attack." McLaws, equally frustrated, hastily replied, "General, as I started in the lead, let me continue." Longstreet relented and urged his horse back to Hood's column. About a mile and a half lay between the front of the Corps and the Haas farm. To shorten the length of the column, McLaws ordered his brigades to maneuver from column of fours to company front.[14]

14 McLaws, "Gettysburg," in *SHSP*, vol. 7, 69.

III Army Corps, Army of the Potomac
East of the Peach Orchard
1:00 p.m.

Graham began consolidating his 1st brigade at 1:00 p.m. He recalled the riflemen from the 57th Pennsylvania at Joseph Sherfy's back to their regiment and pulled the 105th Pennsylvania from the skirmish line, which he placed in his second line behind the 57th Pennsylvania and to the right of the 114th Pennsylvania.[15]

The Wheatfield
1:30 p.m.

Captain George E. Randolph, chief of artillery, III Corps, galloped into the Wheatfield to Smith's battery with orders for him to move his guns to the far left of the Federal line. Smith hurriedly roused his men and his six guns wheeled about and moved east to the western side Plum Run where they turned south under the cover of Houck's Ridge. As soon as Smith vacated the Wheatfield, De Trobriand detached the 110th Pennsylvania from his line into the woods on the Stony Hill on the western side of the field, facing west.[16]

Arriving in the deep hollow behind the 124th New York at the Devil's Den, Smith turned south and rode to the crest to reconnoiter the ground on which he was to place his six 10-pounder Parrotts. He had barely 50 yards of open ground between the southern edge of the woods to his right front and the rock ledge on the southern and the eastern side of the Den. He decided to deploy four of his pieces along a level stretch of the ridge about 70 feet east of the upper side of what the soldiers later called "the Triangular Field." First Sergeant Thomas W. Bradley (Company H, 124th New York) watched the artillerymen manhandle the four guns and their limbers to the crest of the Den.[17]

---

15 OR 27, pt. 1, 500, 502.

16 Smith, A Famous Battery, 101; New York at Gettysburg, vol. 3, 1,290; OR 27, pt. 1,528.

17 Thomas W. Bradley, "At Gettysburg," National Tribune, February 4, 1886; Smith, A Famous Battery, 102, 135-136. When measuring the distance between the woods and the declivity, which Smith mentions in his regimental history, I found upon Bachelder's map that his front was actually 150 feet. Maps on file by Robert A. Braun in December 1982 confirm this. In his regimental history, Smith asserted that he did not put his limbers on the ridge because there was no room for them there, which is quite true. The ridge dropped too sharply to place limbers or

The left gun rolled into battery, facing south, immediately next to a large flat rock, with a higher, but narrower boulder to its right. He faced the remaining pieces by the left oblique to its right rear. Smith's last section, with its limbers and the battery's caissons, went into position along the eastern side of Houck's Ridge on a hillock about 150 yards to the northeast of his other guns. From there they could cover Plum Run Valley to the south, thereby effectively protecting his left flank and rear.[18]

Ward's Brigade, III Corps, Army of the Potomac
Plum Run
South of the Devil Den
2:00 p.m.

At 2:00 p.m., Ward told Maj. Homer R. Stoughton to push his 2nd U.S. Sharpshooters south, through Plum Run Valley, to cover the left flank of the III Corps. With Company D on the right, the four left companies moved out with their right flank along the eastern base of Houck's Ridge. Penetrating the woods, they struck the road, which ran west to the Emmitsburg Road on Warfield Ridge, and swung west, using the road as their right guide. Company D halted a short distance beyond the John Slyder house and hunkered down to allow the left wing to swing around and come on line with it. Once the other companies came up, the regiment settled down to await developments.[19]

---

caissons on the crest. He did say he placed the limbers [not the caissons] as near to the guns as the "declivity" [on the eastern slope] allowed. In the *OR* 27, pt. 1, 588, he wrote: "I placed two sections of my battery on a hill, leaving one section, together with [the] caissons and horses [for the battery], 150 yards in the rear." I inserted the material in the brackets to clarify what I believe he implied.

18 *OR* 27, pt. 1, 58; J. E. Smith, "The Devil's Den–Defense of It at Gettysburg by Smith's Battery and Its Supports," *National Tribune*, March 4, 1886; Raus, *Generation on the March*, Map V; Bradley, "At Gettysburg."

19 The Executive Committee, *Maine at Gettysburg*, 350; Stevens, *Berdan's U.S. Sharpshooters*, 325.

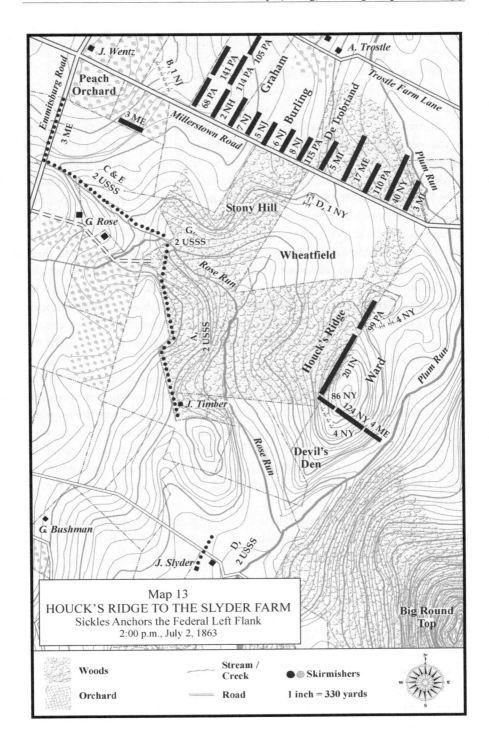

Map 13
HOUCK'S RIDGE TO THE SLYDER FARM
Sickles Anchors the Federal Left Flank
2:00 p.m., July 2, 1863

Company C, 110th Pennsylvania,
DeTrobriand's Brigade, III Corps, Army of the Potomac
The Emmitsburg Road,
About 1.1 miles southwest of the Peach Orchard

Meanwhile, the hapless Company C, 110th Pennsylvania had gotten as far as the Alexander Currens farm. Loaded down with a literal "barn full" of stragglers whom they had actually picked up in a barn on the Pennsylvania border some three miles back, they finally came upon a full field of timothy grass bordering the Phillip Snyder farm. Hundreds of Federals' heads popped up above the grass like ground hogs, spied the rear guard, and instantly dove for cover. Captain Isaac T. Hamilton sent a sergeant with a squad into the meadow to get them. Passing around the house, they discovered an old lady and three young women plucking chickens. Without a moment's hesitation, the women tied the birds together by their feet in pairs and handed them to the squad who slung them over their haversacks. Rather than chase the deserters, they stopped to chat with the ladies, one of whom seemed quite scared. Suddenly a courier dashed up and told the men to forget about the stragglers and to get down the road as quickly as possible.

Returning to the company, the men rushed their captives north on the Emmitsburg Road. To their right they saw Smith's battery on the hilltop a short distance above the Devil's Den. To their left, they heard small arms fire popping in the woods along Seminary Ridge. Presently they encountered their own skirmishers as they neared the George Rose farm. At the Peach Orchard, they ran into a mob of several hundred civilians, many of whom were mounted, which had come out to get a look at the Rebels, making excellent targets for the Confederate artillery.[20]

With Sickles' corps moving on line, Buford decided to pull his cavalry out while the getting was good. His troopers, along with Calef's Regular battery, mounted up and headed south along the Emmitsburg Road.[21]

20 Hamilton, "Recollections," 119, 126, CWL.

21 OR 27, pt. 1, 939, 1,032.

Longstreet's Corps, Army of Northern Virginia
Pitzer's School House
Three-quarters of a mile southwest of the Peach Orchard

Longstreet's column, having increased its pace, back tracked to Haas' farm, turned east at the intersection just north of the lane and took the road over Herr's Ridge, south, to Peter Stallsmith's place. From there the column marched south along the road and crossed the Fairfield Road. At that point, fencerows on both sides of the road forced McLaws to break his regiments from company front by the rear into column of fours.

Lee, having discovered that Longstreet had not yet arrived at his jump off point, rode down the Fairfield Road and intercepted him and Hood's Division. The column continued south, parallel to Willoughby Run until it arrived at Pitzer's School House, where Porter Alexander and his artillery battalion patiently awaited its arrival.

McLaws halted to change his formation. Longstreet trotted forward to investigate the problem. "How are you going in?" he impatiently asked. "That will be determined when I can see what is on my front." "There is nothing in your front," Longstreet replied, "You will be entirely on the flank of the enemy." "Then I will continue my march in column of companies, and after arriving on the flank as far as is necessary will face to the left and march on the enemy." "That suits me," Longstreet said.

Riding up to Kershaw, Longstreet told him to advance his brigade to the front, attack the enemy, turn his flank and move north with his left on the Emmitsburg Road. Reining his horse about, the general rode back to Hood's Division, and McLaws initiated his advance.[22]

McLaws' Division, Longstreet's Corps, Army of Northern Virginia
John Flaharty Farm
2:00 p.m. to 2:30 p.m.

To the southwest Kershaw's skirmishers under Maj. William Wallace (2nd South Carolina), pushing the Federal skirmishers before them, emerged from the woods south of Flaharty's and right into sights of Clark's New Jersey gunners. Methodically, as if on drill, each crew loaded its piece with shell, aimed,

---

22 McLaws, "Gettysburg," in *SHSP*, vol. 7, 70, quotes on 69; A. L. Long to Jubal A. Early, in *SHSP*, vol. 4, 69; Longstreet, *From Manassas to Appomattox*, 366; OR 27, pt. 2, 367.

and fired. Quickly scanning the ridge to the east, a startled McLaws suddenly realized that the Federal line overlapped his right. He had not hit the flank at all. He shouted at Kershaw to form line of battle. Kershaw immediately ordered his companies to deploy by the right into line.[23]

The lead company of the 15th South Carolina pushed through the woods at the right oblique and crossed over the stone wall on the eastern side east of Snyder's and formed a line of battle to anchor the right of the brigade. The 7th South Carolina came next, followed by the 3rd, 2nd, 3rd Battalion, and the 8th Regiments.[24] Knowing he could not keep his men exposed to the guns at the Peach Orchard and the Devil's Den, Kershaw immediately sent them rearwards to shelter behind the stone wall and sped a courier to Longstreet with a description of the field to his front.

Within 10 minutes, at the expenditure of about three dozen rounds, the New Jersey artillerymen successfully forced the Rebels to the cover of the woods west of the road. From where he stood, Pvt. Michael Hanifen thought his battery's shots had taken good effect. As the smoke drifted away from the last rounds, Clark's men limbered up and fell into double column.[25]

Coming up behind Kershaw, Brigadier General William Barksdale flanked his Mississippi brigade into line on Kershaw's left, filling the void between Kershaw's and Wilcox's brigades.[26] The 18th Mississippi (242 effectives) took the left of the formation, followed respectively on the right by the 13th (481 effectives) and the 17th (with 469 present). The 21st Mississippi (424 officers and men) went on line on the south side of the Millerstown Road. Brigadier General William Wofford's Georgia brigade fell in behind Barksdale at the base of the wooded slope within supporting distance.

Brigadier General Paul J. Semmes's Georgians continued the formation on Wofford's right in the woods on the slope behind Kershaw and the artillery. The 50th Georgia (302 men) covered the left center of Kershaw's brigade with the 10th Georgia (303 officers and men) to its right. The 51st Georgia (422

---

23 Dickert, *Kershaw's Brigade*, 237; McLaws, "Gettysburg," in *SHSP*, vol. 7, 70.

24 Mac Wycoff, *A History of the Second South Carolina Infantry: 1861-65* (Fredericksburg, 1995), 79.

25 Hanifen, *Battery B*, 68. Clark's time is correct. Kershaw's men were on the field by 2:00 p.m. because Manly said that his North Carolina battery went into action at 2:30 p.m. and Kershaw stated that the artillery arrived after he had gotten behind the stone wall.

26 McLaws, "Gettysburg," in *SHSP*, vol. 7, 70; Dickert, *Kershaw's Brigade*, 237.

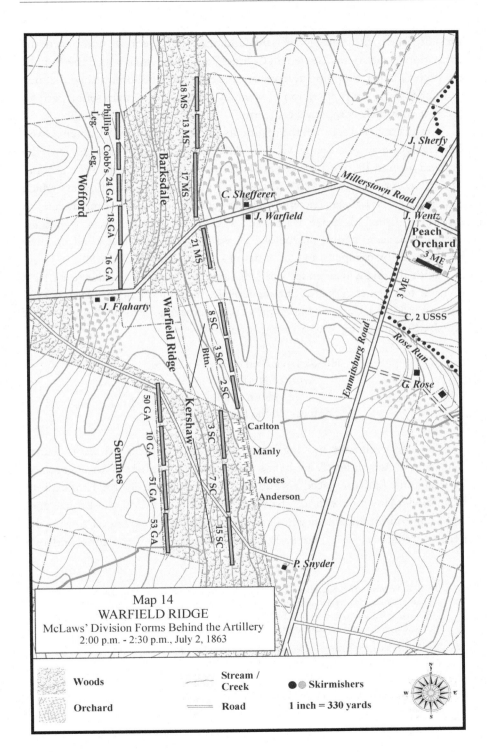

Map 14
WARFIELD RIDGE
McLaws' Division Forms Behind the Artillery
2:00 p.m. - 2:30 p.m., July 2, 1863

Woods

Orchard

Stream /
Creek

Road

Skirmishers

1 inch = 330 yards

present), the same size as the 10th and the 53rd Georgia, completed the formation to the south. Lieutenant Colonel Francis Kearse trooped the front of the 50th Georgia. Stopping in front of each company, he admonished the men to fight and win. In preparation of what lay ahead, each captain sent a party to the rear with their company's canteens.[27]

Orders traveled through the regiments to "strip for a fight." Captain Gwen Reynalds Cherry (Company C, 17th Mississippi) sprang forward into the orchard around the Christopher Shefferer house and flopped to the ground. Major George B. Gerald (18th Mississippi) pursuant to general orders which required all field officers (except brigadier generals or brigade commanders) to dismount, turned his horse, watch, and a few personal belongings over to his servant. Glancing about, he ruefully noted how the men had piled up their blanket rolls by company and left a man to guard each one.[28]

With the maneuver under way, McLaws galloped toward the rear of his division to push it forward. Simultaneously, he sent for his artillery, parked about a mile and a half to the rear, to come up and go into position south of Kershaw to draw fire away from the infantry.[29]

Hood's Division, Longstreet's Corps,
Army of Northern Virginia
The Woods on Warfield Ridge
Southeast of the Emmitsburg Road

With his regiments moving into position, Hood deployed Capts. James Reilly's and Alexander C. Latham's North Carolina batteries to engage the Federal guns. Latham placed his guns 100 yards northeast of the Emmitsburg Road-Slyder lane intersection. The three Napoleons, a 6-Pounder bronze gun, and a 12-Pounder howitzer wheeled into battery facing northeast toward the Peach Orchard. Reilly's two 10-Pounder Parrotts, two Napoleons, and two

---

27 E. P. Harman to W. S. Decker, August 16, 1886, Charles A. Richardson Papers, Ontario County Historical Society, Ontario County, NY, hereinafter cited as OCHS; Busey and Martin, *Regimental Strengths at Gettysburg*, 140-141; Bachelder Map, "Second Day's Battle"; Constance Pendleton, (ed.), *Confederate Memoirs* (Bryn Athyn, 1958), 35.

28 G. B. Gerald, "The Battle of Gettysburg," *Waco Daily Times-Herald*, July 3, 1913; J. W. Duke, "Mississippians at Gettysburg," in *Confederate Veteran*, 40 vols., (Nashville, 1893-1932), vol. 14, 216.

29 McLaws, "Gettysburg," in *SHSP*, vol. 7, 70; Dickert, *Kershaw's Brigade*, 237.

3-inch ordnance rifles rolled into position one-third of a mile southeast of the Slyder farm lane, also facing northeast.[30]

Having ridden back to the left of Kershaw's brigade, McLaws dismounted and stole into a stand of trees along the stone wall. The Yankee position overlapped both his flanks. Longstreet, in an effort to speed up the advance, double-quicked Hood's Division in column of fours forward, south and parallel to McLaws' Division.[31] Hood sent detachments ahead to tear down fences along the line of march. Yankee artillery rounds whined overhead and landed close to his column.

As Anderson's Georgians passed behind Motes' section of the Troup Artillery, Captain Hillyer (9th Georgia) strained his neck to catch a glimpse of his kinfolk, Pvts. Anderson W. Reese and William A. Hemphill, who served with the battery.[32]

Lieutenant Colonel Osmun Latrobe, Longstreet's assistant adjutant general, galloped up to McLaws inquiring why he had not charged the enemy. Only one Yankee regiment and a battery stood to his front. McLaws curtly responded that he would charge when his men were in formation, that the Yankees were in great force along his front, and their "numerous" guns extended well beyond his right flank. Latrobe spurred away, only to quickly return with the same directive.

McLaws pointedly repeated that the strength of the enemy to his front required "careful preparation for the assault, or it necessarily would be a failure." The Yankees had a great many guns, he contended, and he needed the corps' artillery to suppress them. As soon as the artillery opened fire and his men had come on line, he would advance to the charge. He strongly suggested that Longstreet come to the front and personally evaluate the situation.

Again, Latrobe dashed off and returned a short time later with a direct command to advance. Lee, having met with Longstreet, the aide blurted, had issued the order to attack. At that, McLaws climbed into the saddle and growled that he would advance within five minutes. As he rounded up his staff and ordered them to move the division forward in a simultaneous advance, a courier

30 David G. Martin, *Confederate Monuments at Gettysburg*, (Highstown, 1986), 81-82, 84.

31 Longstreet, *From Manassas to Appomattox*, 367; Longstreet, "Lee's Right Wing," in *Battles and Leaders*, vol. 3, 340.

32 Oates, *The War Between the Union and the Confederacy*, 208-209; Hillyer, "Battle of Gettysburg," 4, GNMP.

from Longstreet galloped in with orders to wait until Hood got in position. McLaws dismounted and sent an aide to Hood to coordinate the assault.

Unannounced, Longstreet dashed to McLaws' side. "Why is not a battery placed here?" he angrily demanded, pointing to the spot where the lane from Pitzer's School House turned toward Snyder's house. "General, if a battery is placed there it will draw the enemy's artillery right among my lines formed for the charge and will of itself be in the way of the charge, and tend to demoralize my men." Longstreet shot back that he wanted a battery placed there, no questions asked. Needless to say, McLaws was displeased. "I consider him a humbug," he later wrote his wife, "a man of small capacity, very obstinate, not at all chivalrous, exceedingly conceited and totally selfish. If I can, it is my intention to get away from his command."[33]

Impatient, Longstreet dismounted and ran out to the skirmish line. Finding Captain Cherry (17th Mississippi), he ordered him to rush two unarmed "volunteers" to Sherfy's to tear down the picket fence surrounding the house and the garden. The company first sergeant immediately shouted at the two nearest men. They remained silent, not acknowledging him. He yelled for the next pair and they likewise would not budge. Infuriated by the insubordination, the captain growled, "I will make the detail. Jim Duke and 'Woods' Mears, they will go," he spat.

The two privates, leaving their weapons on the ground, stripped off their accoutrements and got to their feet. Sprinting toward the house, Duke lowly gasped to his friend, "We will be killed." To their amazement, they encountered no Yankee skirmishers, and in clear sight of three lines of III Corps infantry in the Peach Orchard, not to mention their artillery supports behind them, they knocked the fence to pieces and raced back to their own company.

General Longstreet halted Duke when he got back to the lines. "Buddie, what did you see there?" The heaving private quickly rasped out what he had observed along the ridge. Fearful of what would happen and seeking reassurance of some sort, Duke breathlessly panted, "General, General do you think we can take those heights?" "I don't know," the general replied, "Do you?" Before Duke could respond, Longstreet grumbled, "This is not my fight," and walked back to the main line.

---

33 McLaws, "Gettysburg," in *SHSP*, vol. 7, 70-72, quote on 72; McLaws to his wife, July 7, 1863, Vertical Files, GNMP.

Discouraged by Longstreet's negative response, Duke bellied down into the grass, recalling a brief conversation he had had with his brother, Archibald, just before daylight. Arch asked Jim to write home after the battle. Jim retorted that he had penned the last letter, and that it was Arch's turn. In the darkness, Jim noticed tears streaking down his brother's face. "Something is going to happen today," Arch whispered. And no more was said about the matter.[34]

By then Major Goggin, McLaws' assistant adjutant and inspector general, had ridden back from the front. Once again, the division halted. Both officers and men were in ugly moods: Hood's Division would be going in ahead of the rest of McLaws', a slight upon their integrity and manhood, they thought. Another officer pointed toward the rear, where Goggin saw Longstreet and McLaws "engaged, it appeared, in *very earnest* conversation."[35]

Under direct orders, Capt. Basil C. Manly rushed his North Carolina battery of two 12-pounder Napoleons and two ordnance rifles through the woods on the farm lane running southeast from Flaharty's. Heading toward the sounds of the firing, he wheeled his battery onto the rocky knoll in the northeast corner of the woods on Kershaw's center.

By 2:30 p.m., his battery was hurling rounds toward the Peach Orchard. Unknown to Manly, Colonel Alexander had decided to mass Col. Henry C. Cabell's entire battalion as a single battery. Kershaw detached the 15th South Carolina to the right to protect Manly's flank until more help arrived. Almost immediately, Capt. Edward S. McCarthy rushed Lt. Robert M. Anderson with his pair of 3-inch ordnance rifles into the woods about 50 yards to Manly's right. The Troup Artillery under Capt. Henry W. Carlton came up close behind. Carlton took the section of 12-pounder howitzers in on Manly's left. Lieutenant Motes unlimbered his two 10-pounder Parrotts along the stone wall between Manly and McCarthy.[36]

As McLaws had predicted, the Confederate artillery drew deadly responses from the Yankees. The first round from the Peach Orchard burst in Company F, 21st Mississippi. Private J. T. Worley died instantly. It shredded the legs of

---

34 Duke, "Mississippians at Gettysburg," in *Confederate Veteran*, vol. 14, 216.

35 James M. Goggin to Longstreet, August 15, 1887, USAHEC.

36 Bachelder, *Map, July 2, 1863*; Hanifen, *Battery B*, 68; *Supplement to the OR* 5, pt. 1, 380; Gallagher, *Fighting for the Confederacy*, 238; *OR* 27, pt. 2, 379, 384; Martin, *Confederate Monuments*, 111-112. According to Martin, McCarthy was in reserve at 2:30 p.m. It makes sense that he went into battery at that time. Motes opened fire at 3:00 p.m., so he had to be on line between 2:00-3:00 p.m.

Capt. Henry H. Simmons, Pvts. John N. Thompson and John F. Neely. The explosion jarred Pvt. James B. Booth so badly he could not remember the names of the casualties in Company E, to his right. Tree bursts sent branches and limbs falling upon his comrades' heads. Within minutes, the company lost a number of men. Sensing his brigades might break, McLaws mounted up and rode among the ranks, calming the soldiers' frayed nerves.

Barksdale impetuously ran up to McLaws, begging, "General, let me go; General, let me charge!" McLaws declined, insisting he had to await Longstreet's directive. Wait until the Yankees moved half way across the open ground to the east, he advised Barksdale, and then they could meet them "on more equal terms."[37]

Longstreet directed McLaws to advance as soon as Hood engaged the Yankees. Cabell's Battalion, after briefly firing, would cease, after which three pieces would cut loose in rapid succession. While connecting on the right with Hood, Kershaw was to swing north toward the Peach Orchard with Barksdale conforming to his movement on the left. Semmes and Wofford, in the second line would move to their support.[38]

The III Corps, Army of the Potomac
The Peach Orchard
2:30 p.m.

Artillery rounds were falling among or bursting over the civilians in the road next to the Peach Orchard. Frenzied horses reared and pitched their riders. The veterans in Company C, 110th Pennsylvania, laughed at the terrified civilians, who scattered screaming and yelling in every direction. Many of the panic-stricken men tossed away their hats and jackets. Company C rushed down the Millerstown Road with the sky exploding above them, not waiting to see if fragments hit any of the curious noncombatants or not.

"Cover!" reverberated along the 141st Pennsylvania's line. The regiment threw itself to the ground behind its rifle stacks. The corporal in front of Private Lunger (Company I) landed squarely on top of his buried pancake batter. As

37 McLaws, "Gettysburg," in *SHSP*, vol. 7, 72-73; J. S. McNeily, "Barksdale's Mississippi Brigade at Gettysburg," in Franklin L. Riley (ed.), *Publications of the Mississippi Historical Society* (University, MS), vol. 14, 238.

38 *OR* 27, pt. 2, 367; J. B. Kershaw, "Kershaw's Brigade at Gettysburg," in *Battles and Leaders*, vol. 3, 334.

each round that whined overhead, the corporal squirmed his belly over the dough, unknowingly spreading it down his front.[39] When Graham called his brigade to its feet, the corporal suddenly discovered himself covered in muddy wheat batter. Not given to swearing, he pulled out his knife and scraped as much of the muck off himself as he could. The regiment advanced over the next downed fencerow into the oat field and lied down behind Clark's guns, which had begun moving toward the Wentz house.[40]

Brewster's 2nd brigade of Humphreys' division redeployed. Three of the Excelsior regiments flanked left and occupied Graham's former position on the eastern side of the Peach Orchard. The 72nd New York held the left of the line, followed to the right by the 71st New York. The 70th New York stayed in reserve to the right rear of the 72nd. Drum Maj. William H. Bullard (70th New York) found the relative silence "painful" as he lay in the tall grass waiting for something to happen. The 120th New York continued west and went prone on the hillside immediately north of the Trostle farm lane about 150 yards east of the Emmitsburg Road. Meanwhile, Hunt, when he realized the Rebels posed no real threat to Cemetery Hill or the army's right flank, headed to the Peach Orchard, knowing that he would have to deploy his artillery reserve there.[41]

De Trobriand's Brigade, III Corps, Army of the Potomac
The Wheatfield
2:30–3:00 p.m.

To protect his men from any more incoming rounds, De Trobriand repositioned his brigade. The 17th Maine moved into the wooded thicket on the ridge along the west side of the Wheatfield, and went prone, facing south.

---

39 Hamilton, "Recollections," 119, 121, CWL; Bloodgood, *Reminiscences*, 134, quoted.

40 OR 27, pt. 1, 498-499; Bloodgood, ibid.

41 Raus, *A Generation on the March*, Map IV; OR 27, pt. 1,566. Cornelius D. Westbrook, "On the Firing Line," *National Tribune*, September 20, 1900; William H. Bullard to Sickles, September 13, 1897; Hunt, "The Second Day," in *Battles and Leaders*, vol. 3, 303. The monuments on the field show the order of the brigade from left to right as: 70th, 71st, 72nd, and 74th New York. Austin's OR account clearly says that his regiment held the left of the brigade, with its left on a crossroad (the Millerstown Road), east of the Peach Orchard. The 70th, therefore, must have been in reserve and the 71st had to be to the right of the 72nd. According to Lt. Col. Cornelius D. Westbrook (120th New York), the regiment was in an open field about 350 yards north of the cross roads at the Peach Orchard and 150 yards east of the Emmitsburg Road. The battlefield monument places Brewster's brigade behind Graham's men.

Company D held the left of the line, followed to the right by Companies I, F, A, E, G, B, H, K, and C, respectively.[42] The 110th Pennsylvania lay at right angles to the New Englanders, looking west. The 40th New York formed on its right with the 3rd Michigan completing the formation to the right.

Out along the Emmitsburg Road, near the Rose farm lane, the adjutant of the 2nd U.S. Sharpshooters clattered up to Corporal Congdon and Private Carr (both Company E). The two reported that they had seen Rebs massing in the woods to the right front. The adjutant told them he would report their information to General Birney and rode away. Congdon trotted after the aide telling Carr he would follow the adjutant in case the Rebs captured him.[43]

Before the guns had ceased fire, Sickles told De Trobriand to deploy the 3rd Michigan as skirmishers. Colonel Byron R. Pierce marched his regiment into the southern edge of the Peach Orchard. Leaving seven of his 10 companies on the line, he advanced his three left companies (F, I, and K, respectively) until they connected with the left of the 3rd Maine and the point of woods northeast of the Rose Farm. Discovering Confederate skirmishers in the distance to the south, Pierce sent his brother, Lt. Col. Edwin S. Pierce, back to Sickles with that information. Before long, De Trobriand pulled Company A away from the regiment and sent it across the Emmitsburg Road to form a skirmish line near the Sherfy house. With the 3rd Michigan pushing the Confederates back beyond the Emmitsburg Road, De Trobriand committed the small 110th Pennsylvania into the fray. The regiment followed the skirmishers of the 3rd Michigan to within 50 paces of the Emmitsburg Road.

An artillery shell exploded to the left of Company G, directly over the color guard. A shell fragment ripped into Cpl. Orion Wade's back, directly below his right shoulder blade. Severing his spine, the searing hot fragment lodged in his left lung. Private Charles A. Price (Company G) ran over to his mortally wounded friend. Wade spoke frankly about dying, gasping that he could not live long and that the news of his death would kill his mother. He was willing to die, he told Price, if that was his fate, and requested Price to write his family and send his memorandum book home. Price helped place his body on a stretcher

---

42 Ladd and Ladd, *The Bachelder Papers*, vol. 2, 840, 1,011-1,012; The Executive Committee, *Maine at Gettysburg*, 195.

43 Carr, "A Sharpshooter at Gettysburg," *National Tribune*, November 25, 1886.

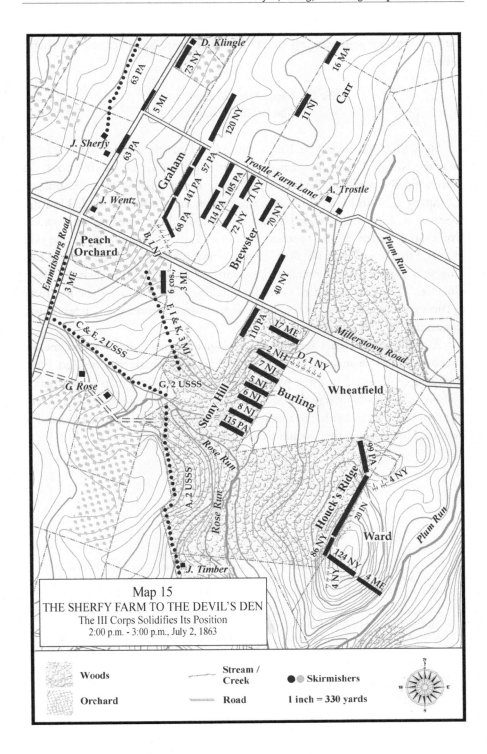

Map 15
THE SHERFY FARM TO THE DEVIL'S DEN
The III Corps Solidifies Its Position
2:00 p.m. - 3:00 p.m., July 2, 1863

Woods

Orchard

Stream / Creek

Road

Skirmishers

1 inch = 330 yards

but forgot about retrieving his book. To his chagrin, he never saw his friend again.[44]

The III Corps, Army of the Potomac
The Peach Orchard

Sickles headed toward the Emmitsburg Road on a personal reconnaissance. Near the Klingle house, he warned the 73rd New York: "Be careful, boys; we must whip them to-day." Around 2:30 p.m., Drum Maj. William H. Bullard (Company C, 70th New York) saw Sickles trotting conspicuously behind the regiment on his white horse, as a courier from Meade galloped up and handed him a slip of paper. Sickles scanned the note. "Say to General Meade," he said bluntly, "that it will be impossible for me to report at his Head Quarters at this time as the battle will be precipitated upon us before I could reach his Head Quarters." The courier denied his request, telling Sickles to turn the corps over to Birney and to report at once. As the aide spurred toward the Leister house, Sickles trailed after him.[45]

A shell unexpectedly screamed over Bullard's head and burst in the air above Burling's unsuspecting regiments. The blast shattered the 2nd New Hampshire's flagstaff in three places and wounded several men in the ranks. Bullard, who was in charge of the regiment's stretcher-bearers, got to his feet and proceeded to gather in the remaining regimental musicians in the Excelsior Brigade. He expected they would be very busy, very soon.[46]

44 OR 27, pt. 1, 520, 524, 526, 528; G. W. W. to the Editor, *New York Tribune*, July 5, 1863; Ladd and Ladd, *The Bachelder Papers*, vol. 1, 47; C. A. Price to his brother, July 30, 1863, Michigan Historical Collections, Bentley Historical Library, UMI; Hamilton, "Recollections," 121, CWL.

45 "Gladiator" to [Editor], *The New York Sunday Mercury*, August 3, 1863; William H. Bullard to Sickles, September 13, 1897, Sickles Papers, New York Historical Society, Vertical Files, GNMP, quoted; Craft, *141st Pennsylvania*, 120; "Comment by Daniel E. Sickles, Major-General, U.S.A." in "The Meade-Sickles Controversy" in *Battles and Leaders*, vol. 3, 416. Sickles said that he reported as ordered to headquarters, and at 3:00 p.m. the artillery fire broke out.

46 William H. Bullard to Sickles, September 13, 1897, GNMP; Haynes, *2nd New Hampshire*, (1896), 169.

Chapter 5

July 2, 1863
3:00 p.m.-4:00 p.m.

"Hood, go where you are ordered. General Lee directs me to attack here."

—*General James Longstreet, Army of Northern Virginia*

Longstreet's Corps, Army of Northern Virginia
Warfield Ridge
3:00 p.m.

Hood's division continued passing behind McLaws' regiments, which Colonel Oates (15th Alabama) interpreted as an attempt to flank the southern end of the Federal line undetected.[1] More Confederate artillery rolled into battery along the eastern face of the woods. Captain John C. Fraser pushed his guns into battery on the right of McCarthy behind an unstable section of the stone wall in the vicinity of the Snyder house. Unobserved by the Federals, he masked his battery behind a large cattle shed. Knocking several holes through the northern side of the building to create gun ports, the crew of his left section rolled two pieces into the shed and opened fire upon the Federal guns along the Millerstown Road. The right section focused its attention upon the Devil's Den.

Captain George V. Moody whipped his Louisiana battery onto an open rocky ledge about 200 yards to the left of Carlton's section of howitzers, an exposed position on an extremely hard surface. His Napoleons and howitzers would recoil wildly with every discharge.[2]

---

1   Oates, "15th Alabama," 4-5, BCL.

2   *OR* 27, pt. 2, 375, 382; Ames, *Battery G*, 67.

U.S. Signal Station, Army of the Potomac
Little Round Top

Captain James S. Hall's signal station on Little Round Top detected the Rebels' maneuvering and wigwagged the station at the Leister house the following:

> Gen. Meade[:] One regt. of the enemy's troops reported massing on Sickles left has moved back to their old position on his center. The rest were still moving to the left.[3]

Upon receiving this, the commanding general went to the front door of the Leister house, where he encountered Sickles reining up in front of him. Do not dismount, he told him, and return immediately to the III Corps. He would be following immediately, Meade said. And he did: he and his staff mounted and clattered toward the III Corps behind Sickles. Cutting southwest, they galloped directly along the front of Humphreys' division and received a rousing cheer from the enlisted men.[4]

Ward's Brigade, III Corps Army of the Potomac
The Devil's Den

Ward placed the 4th Maine on the far left of the brigade immediately behind Smith's New York battery, with its right wing perpendicular to the 124th New York's left flank. The 124th had gone prone on the northern side of the crest, facing south, perpendicular to the 4th Maine's right. The 86th New York, 20th Indiana, and the 99th Pennsylvania, respectively, had entered in the woods to the northwest, with the Pennsylvanians' right flank on the southern edge of the Wheatfield. Colonel Walker's New Englanders, who had subsisted only on water for the last 24 hours, latched their eyes upon the big herd of cattle grazing in Plum Run behind them. Coffee fires quickly sprang up behind the regimental

---

3 OR 27, pt. 1, 202; James S. Hall to Meade 3:00 p.m. Round Top July 2, G. K. Warren Papers, New York State Library, Albany, NY, hereinafter cited as NYSL. Norton said the message went out at 3:30 p.m.; the records show the time as 3:00 p.m.

4 "Statement of Daniel E. Sickles, Major-General, U.S.A." in "The Meade-Sickles Controversy," in *Battles and Leaders*, vol. 3, 416; Craft, *141st Pennsylvania*, 120; Ladd and Ladd, *The Bachelder Papers*, vol. 1, 671-672; Cavada, Diary, July 2, 1863, 4, FSNMP. Sickles said that he reported to headquarters under orders and the artillery fire broke out at 3:00 p.m.

line. While someone killed a young heifer, Col. Augustus Van Horne Ellis (124th New York) had his men drive in several cows as well. Before long, the smell of roasting meat mingled with the aroma of freshly boiled coffee. Most of the ravenous Maine troops did not wait for the meat to cook. Powdering the raw chunks of beef with whatever salt they could scrounge, they devoured it in short order. The smoke had hardly cleared the treetops when an artillery round sailed overhead, followed immediately by a horrendous barrage. The infantrymen dove for cover.[5]

Birney's Division, III Corps, Army of the Potomac
The Peach Orchard and the Millerstown Road
3:00 p.m.-3:15 p.m.

At the Orchard, Brigadier General Hunt intercepted Capt. George Randolph, chief of artillery, III Corps, who immediately informed him that he deployed his batteries along the new line under orders. Glancing up, Hunt saw Meade and Sickles conversing a short distance away and mistakenly assumed that Meade had authorized Sickles' advance. So he sent word to the Artillery Reserve to send more guns and issued orders for the generals on the field to use the batteries, as they needed them.[6]

Warren, noting how poorly Sickles had disposed his corps, approached Meade, who was totally absorbed in what was going on around him, and suggested that he and his aides leave immediately to investigate the situation around Little Round Top. Meade, having already anticipated such a move suddenly spoke up: "Warren, I hear a little peppering going on in the direction of that little hill off yonder. I wish you would ride over and if anything serious is going on, attend to it." Warren and his three staff officers, 1st Lt. Ranald S. Mackenzie, Lt. Washington Roebling, and Capt. Chauncey Reese, spurred east down the Millerstown Road.[7]

5 Walker, "The 4th Maine," *National Tribune*, April 8, 1886; OR 27, pt. 1, 588; Ladd and Ladd, *The Bachelder Papers*, vol. 2, 1,094-1,095; Smith, *A Famous Battery*, 109; Executive Committee, *Maine at Gettysburg*, 160, 181; "Account of the War Record of Lt. Henry P. Ramsdell," GNMP.

6 Hunt, "The Second Day," in *Battles and Leaders*, vol. 3, 303-304.

7 Norton, *The Attack and Defense of Little Round Top* 309; Washington A. Roebling to Smith, July 5, 1913, "Washington Roebling's War," The Gouverneur K. Warren Papers, NYSL, quoted. Warren said that he suggested to Meade while on the field near Sickles that he go and

Clark's battery creaked into the Peach Orchard immediately behind Wentz's house. Private Hanifen saw Hunt, Birney, Meade, Sickles, and their staffs conferring among the trees. The commanding general, within earshot of Major Tremain, advised Sickles of the weakness of his line to which the corps commander promptly offered to fall back. Not practical, Meade replied. Sickles was too far to the front, and it was too late to change, especially since the fight had already started.[8]

The sound of a battery jangling near Battery B attracted Private Hanifen's attention, and turning he observed Ames' Battery G, 1st New York, clattering across Clark's former position. Cabell's Battalion along the face of the woods on Warfield Ridge saw them too. Within seconds, the Rebs loosed a salvo at the New Yorkers. With shells whining into his guns, the diminutive Ames coolly led his six Napoleons toward the rise of ground on the western side of the Peach Orchard immediately south of the Millerstown-Emmitsburg Road intersection. On the way, he halted twice to tear down the rail fences, which the infantry had failed to remove and, in the process, lost two horses to the barrage.[9]

Meade's words had barely left his mouth when the Rebel artillery barrage abruptly terminated the interview and prompted the generals to vacate the immediate premises. Hunt turned east before the smoke cleared and headed toward Smith's battery at the Devil's Den, all the while wondering why his guns had not opened on the oblique at the Confederates.[10]

Randolph immediately ordered Clark to wheel about and respond to the noisome batteries. "Right reverse, trot," Clark shouted. As the guns swung from column into a line facing south near its former position, a round toppled Pvt. Rensalaer Casselman from his horse, killing him. "Action right!" The battery unlimbered its guns and the men rolled the pieces by hand onto the crest

---

investigate the situation at Little Round Top. Roebling in 1913 said he found Warren at Meade's headquarters, and that Meade suddenly spoke up and sent Warren to go to the hill.

8   Hanifen, *Battery B*, 68; Craft, *141st Pennsylvania*, 120; Ladd and Ladd, *The Bachelder Papers*, vol. 1, 671-672. Craft said that the Meade-Sickles' interview took place between 3:30-4:00 p.m.

9   Raus, *A Generation on the March*, 87; Ames, *Battery G*, 64; *OR* 27, pt. 1, 900, pt. 2, 384.

10 Craft, *141st Pennsylvania*, 120; Ladd and Ladd, *The Bachelder Papers*, vol. 1, 671-672; Nicholson, *Pennsylvania at Gettysburg*, vol. 1, 393; Hanifen, *Battery B*, 68; Hunt, "The Second Day," in *Battles and Leaders*, vol. 3, 304-305. Lieutenant Columbus W. Motes said that at 3:00 p.m. Captain Carlton ordered him to fire upon a battery going in on the left of the Peach Orchard and that he drove them back. This fits descriptions and timeframes from both Ames and Hanifen.

of the ridge north of the Millerstown Road. Graham refused the left of his line by placing the 68th Pennsylvania behind the left rear of Clark's guns. The Pennsylvanians lied down to protect themselves from return fire. Sickles rode into the battery. "Hold this position while you have shot in your limbers or a man to work your guns," he commanded Clark.[11]

Simultaneously, Randolph sent 1st Lt. John K. Bucklyn's Battery E, 1st Rhode Island Artillery, into line to the right front of the Wentz house toward the western edge of the Peach Orchard. His center section went into position west of the front door of the house. He detached his right section across the Emmitsburg Road into the Sherfy flower garden north of the house. His left section rolled into battery on the crest of the ridge in the northwest corner of the orchard at the Millerstown-Emmitsburg Road intersection. A heavy projectile screamed harmlessly overhead, but within less than a minute, a second round crashed in on top of one of the caissons and exploded, killing five of the six horses and two of the artillerists. Almost immediately, Bucklyn opened fire on a battery along the east face of the woods on Seminary Ridge.[12]

For over 20 minutes, Graham's brigade remained a stationery target on the eastern side of the Peach Orchard. Finally, Lt. Charles H. Graves, acting assistant adjutant general for Graham, arrived with orders for the 141st Pennsylvania to pass through Bucklyn's guns into the Peach Orchard itself. The Pennsylvanians stood up and moved forward around the guns, going prone in front of them along the Emmitsburg Road.[13]

With occasional shells and case shot hissing above him, Corporal Loring (141st Pennsylvania pushed himself lower to the ground as it pitched and thumped with the discharge of every piece. He felt very uncomfortable, even

11 OR 27, pt. 1, 498-499; Hanifen, *Battery B*, 68, quoted. In his report, Colonel Tippin says that the regiment was on the left of the brigade line, and that it laid down in the rear of Clark's battery and stayed there for two hours. That was around 3:00 p.m.

12 Scott, *105th Pennsylvania*, 270; OR 27, pt. 1, 573, 584; Ladd and Ladd, *The Bachelder Papers*, vol. 1, 72, vol. 3, 1,971; Craft, *141st Pennsylvania*, 121, 271; Raus, *Generation on the March*, 87. Private Edwin Cleveland (Company A, 141st Pennsylvania), who was on detached service with Bucklyn's battery, said the right gun was in the dooryard of the Wentz house. He had to have been referring to the right gun of his section. The right section of the battery was to the right of the house in the garden. The center section (Cleveland's) was at the Wentz house. The left section had to have been in the Peach Orchard to the right of Ames' west facing section. It was that section which Col. Edward L. Bailey (2nd New Hampshire) saw in the Orchard next to Ames' battery.

13 Craft, *141st Pennsylvania*, 121, 271; Bloodgood, *Reminiscences*, 134-135; OR 27, pt. 1, 588.

though the regiment had field pieces to the right of it, field pieces to the front of it, and field pieces behind it, all bellowing and booming. The Pennsylvanians lay there for several minutes while Bucklyn's guns roared over them, at which point the colonel countermanded the order and the regiment retired to a position several yards in the rear of the battery.[14]

Ames personally planted his two left sections on the ridge in the Peach Orchard, facing south, because their two commanders, 2nd Lts. Frederick F. Goff and James B. Hazleton, had never been in combat. He left the experienced 1st Lt. Samuel A. McClellan on his own to bring his right section into play.[15]

The left and center sections the battery opened a deliberate, slow, well-aimed fire against a Confederate battery with case and shell. Sergeant Jessie Burdick, chief of #1 gun, ran up to Ames and exclaimed: "For God's sake come and tell us where to place our guns; we have been running them up and down all over this field; no place is satisfactory to the lieutenant; all my men and Sergeant [James] Hutchinson are tired out." Fuming, Ames raced to the Emmitsburg Road and ordered the guns to the road bank to the right of the battery. While the two sergeants manned their pieces and carefully placed each round into the Rebel batteries, McClellan loudly protested his section's placement. The captain should see to it that close-set trees along the battery's front be cut down to clear a better field of fire, he groused. Ames shouted back. If the lieutenant said one more word, Ames retorted, he would surrender his sword and go to the rear under arrest. Dumbfounded, McClellan, who had not fully recovered from a narrow escape with a passing shell, shut up and returned to his duties. Before Ames departed to the battery's left, he told Burdick to report to him immediately if "there was any special need."[16]

The 141st Pennsylvania had hardly settled down when Col. Henry J. Madill bellowed, "Attention! Forward!" The regiment left wheeled and lay down in the Millerstown Road with its right wing sheltered by the eastern running leg of the Peach Orchard and the slight road bank on the south side of the road. De Trobriand detached the 40th New York southwest to the cover of the Millerstown Road, just east of the 141st Pennsylvania. Presently, the 5th Michigan, having been relieved from its post north of Trostle's Lane, returned

---

14 Loring, "Gettysburg," *National Tribune,* July 9, 1885; Craft, *141st Pennsylvania,* 121, 271.

15 Ames, *Battery G,* 64-65, quoted.

16 Ames, *Battery G,* 64-65; *OR* 27, pt. 1, 900.

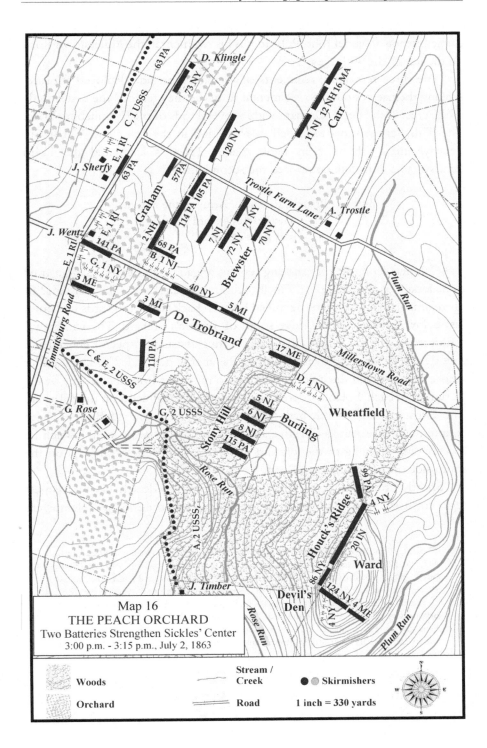

Map 16
THE PEACH ORCHARD
Two Batteries Strengthen Sickles' Center
3:00 p.m. - 3:15 p.m., July 2, 1863

Woods

Orchard

Stream /
Creek

Road

Skirmishers

1 inch = 330 yards

to the brigade. Colonel John Pulford put his regiment in the Millerstown Road on the left of the 40th New York.[17]

The three remaining regiments of Graham's brigade deployed forward, shaking themselves out into regimental fronts as they reached the eastern side of the crest in the Peach Orchard within several rods of the Emmitsburg Road. The 57th Pennsylvania remained in formation in the front line. The 105th Pennsylvania, with its right flank against Trostle's lane, and the 114th Pennsylvania to its left, comprised the second line.[18]

Burling's Brigade, III Corps, Army of the Potomac
The Peach Orchard
3:15 p.m.-4:00 p.m.

Colonel George Burling, having kept his brigade on the exposed ridge, tried to maintain his assigned post. Finally, without orders, and at the insistence of his regimental commanders, he pulled his men back about 100 yards to a point just below the crest of the ridge south of Trostle's orchard. The withdrawal infuriated Capt. John S. Poland, Sickles' acting assistant inspector general and aide-de-camp. Spurring over to Burling, he angrily demanded to know under whose authority did the colonel presume to move his brigade. "By my own," Burling shot back. Poland ordered him to march his regiments up the hill again. The brigade's retro-march had scarcely begun when one of Birney's aides countermanded Poland's directive and told Burling to swing south, which he quickly did, wheeling to the left and marching it onto the Stony Hill on the south side of the Millerstown Road.[19]

Shortly after 3:00 p.m., Birney told Burling to detach his two largest regiments to General Graham's support. Burling sent the 2nd New Hampshire

---

17 Scott, *105th Pennsylvania*, 82; Nicholson, *Pennsylvania at Gettysburg*, vol. 1, 356; OR 27, pt. 1, 497, 500, 520, 526; Craft, *141st Pennsylvania*, 119, 121; Loring, "Gettysburg," *National Tribune*, July 9, 1885, quoted; Hamilton, "Recollections," 121, CWL; Ladd and Ladd, *The Bachelder Papers*, vol. 1, 46. This is my reconstruction of the event based upon Egan's report in the *ORs*, J. C. Hamilton's recollections of the 110th Pennsylvania, and Pulford's description of the two brigade lines when he arrived on the field. Toombs said the 5th New Jersey relieved the 63rd Pennsylvania. The regimental monument indicates that it had to have been near Turnbull's battery and nowhere near the 63rd Pennsylvania. The placement of the regiment at this time is my interpretation of what transpired.

18 Nicholson, *Pennsylvania at Gettysburg*, vol. 1, 356.

19 OR 27, pt. 1, 570; Haynes, *2nd New Hampshire*, (1896), 169, quoted.

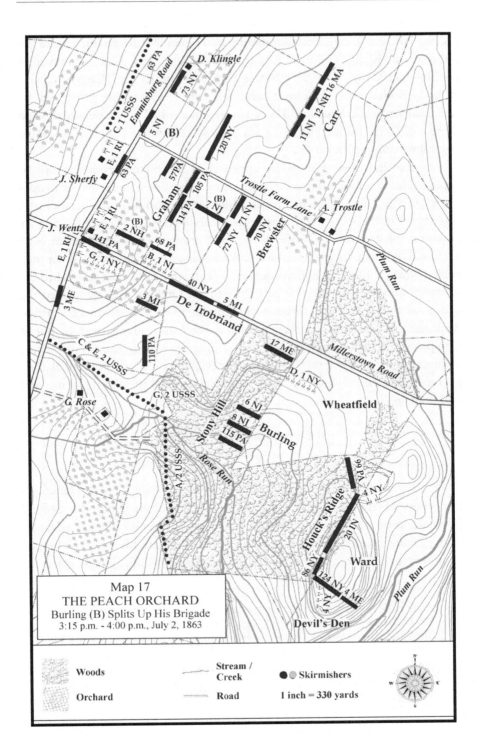

Map 17
THE PEACH ORCHARD
Burling (B) Splits Up His Brigade
3:15 p.m. - 4:00 p.m., July 2, 1863

Woods

Orchard

Stream / Creek

Road

Skirmishers

1 inch = 330 yards

and the 7th New Jersey, both numbering more than 300 effectives, toward the Millerstown Road. Colonel Edward L. Bailey (2nd New Hampshire) double-quicked his New Englanders forward, toward the Peach Orchard. Nobody noticed the eight men who fell out of the ranks, prostrated by sunstroke or heat exhaustion. Those two regiments had barely departed when Birney ordered Burling to send his largest remaining regiment to assist Humphreys on the picket line.[20]

As the 2nd New Hampshire approached the hilltop from the east, it deployed from column of fours into company front. From there, the companies moved forward into regimental front. Bailey reported to Birney in person, who placed him in the second line along the Millerstown Road. The right wing lay down on the crest of the ridge, facing the Emmitsburg Road. The left wing anchored its left on the right of the 68th Pennsylvania, facing south. As the men bellied down, with the right flank near the Wentz house, the colonel studied the situation along the southern edge of the Peach Orchard and recognized the colors of the 3rd Maine through the smoke from the skirmishers' rifles. Realizing that his right flank lay exposed at the Emmitsburg Road, he pulled Company B, armed with Sharps breech loading rifles, from the left of the line and hurried them to the rear of Lieutenant Bucklyn's center section of Battery E, 1st Rhode Island Artillery. They quickly occupied the Wentz house and outbuildings.[21]

II Corps, Army of the Potomac
Cemetery Ridge

Sickles' western movement abruptly terminated Major General Hancock's inspection of the II Corps' position. Gibbon, commanding the Second Division, captivated by the martial splendor of the III Corps' advance, inadvertently blurted, "Yes, but it is not war." From his position behind Humphreys' division north of Trostle's lane, Capt. Adolfo Cavada spied the

---

20 OR 27, pt. 1, 570-571; Ladd and Ladd, *The Bachelder Papers*, vol. 2, 1,007-1,008, vol. 3, 1,979; Haynes, *2nd New Hampshire* (1896), 170; Toombs, *New Jersey Troops*, 205; Martin A. Haynes, *A History of the Second Regiment New Hampshire Volunteers: Its Camps, Marches And Battles* (Manchester, 1865), 138-139.

21 Haynes, *2nd New Hampshire* (1865), 139; Haynes, ibid., 170. Bailey mistook the 68th Pennsylvania for the 63rd Pennsylvania in the *Official Records*. The 63rd Pennsylvania was still on the skirmish line.

snappy zouave uniforms of his brother's 114th Pennsylvania as it moved forward with Graham's brigade. The brigade's military precision thrilled him. Involuntarily flushing, he shivered at the grandeur of the moment.[22]

The activity ended a brief visit between Private Cole (1st U.S. Cavalry)—a dispatch rider, who had been carrying messages from cavalryman Brig. Gen. Judson Kilpatrick to Meade's headquarters—and his brother Jacob, who was in the 57th New York Infantry. With the small arms fire echoing in the distance, Jacob said, "The enemy seems to be moving and I think you had better get back to your quarters." They shook hands, and Jacob watched his brother ride away.[23]

From the southwest, Confederate battery opened upon the II Corps position. The initial round detonated over Company G, 66th New York (Zook's brigade) slaying Capt. Elijah F. Munn. Zook pulled the regiments a short distance back to get them out of the gunners' lines of sight. Another shell exploded above Company C, 148th Pennsylvania (Cross's brigade). One of its fragments struck Pvt. Lemuel Osmon's uncle, Pvt. George Osmon, on the cartridge box as he slept; the concussion killed him instantly. Another shard struck Sgt. Robert H. Patterson (Company G) in the arm. Cross, hands clenched together behind his back, paced anxiously back and forth. He had just deployed the 5th New Hampshire southeast to the Taneytown Road for picket duty. Abruptly stopping near Lieutenant Hale, he jerked a black silk bandana from the inside pocket of his tunic. He meticulously folded it over his one knee, and then handed his hat to the lieutenant while he wrapped it around his head and tied it in the back. Customarily Cross wore a red bandanna into action, and the ominous change of color disturbed Hale greatly. All morning, ever since Cross had reassigned McKeen to the 148th Pennsylvania, his fellow officers had been pestering Hale about the colonel's death premonition. The colonel impatiently put his hat on then tore it off. "Please, tie it tighter, Mister Hale." While the aide's unsteady hands fidgeted with the knot, Cross snapped at him to "Draw it tighter still." As small arms fire reverberated from the southwest and the south, Hale finally got the bandana the way the colonel wanted it.[24]

22 Stewart, *140th Pennsylvania*, 421; Cavada, Diary, July 2, 1863, 4, FSNMP, quoted.

23 Cole, *Under Five Commanders*, 194, quoted; Stewart, *140th Pennsylvania*, 421.

24 *OR 27*, pt. 1, 397-398; Stewart, *140th Pennsylvania*, 421; Muffly, *148th Pennsylvania*, 602, 703; Hale, "With Colonel Cross," 3, PHS, quoted.

III Army Corps, Army of the Potomac
The Peach Orchard
3:15 p.m.

Graham's brigade immediately drew fire, once in the line of sight of Confederate artillery in the fields to the west and southwest. It was about 3:15 p.m. Private Michael Hanifen, the wheel driver on Clark's #1 caisson, estimated. The suddenness and the fury of the fire caught Sgt. Ellis C. Strouss (Company K, 57th Pennsylvania) off guard. He watched several rounds sail harmlessly overhead, while some dropped into the 105th Pennsylvania to his right rear, wounding a few men. The order rippled from regiment to regiment to lie down. Meanwhile, a considerable number of the infantrymen volunteered to run ammunition to the guns.[25]

Colonel Bailey faced the 2nd New Hampshire south, ordering the right wing to change front forward on the color company, which placed the right flank in the garden behind the Wentz house. A far larger proportion of deadly rounds fell among the regiments in and near the Millerstown Road. Unexploded projectiles skipped through the ranks of the prone regiments taking out half a dozen men at a time. Private Martin A. Haynes (Company I, 2nd New Hampshire) helplessly watched the .58 caliber case balls pock up little jets of dirt wherever they hit. Peach leaves, blown loose by shell concussions, blanketed the prone New Englanders. One of the rounds exploded directly above Haynes' section of the line. Private Jonathan Merrill, on his immediate right, curled up, his thigh torn away. Another wounded Pvt. Lyndon B. Woods, but missed the man next to him, Sgt. James M. House. "I came through all right," Haynes wrote later. "I don't know how I did it. I never had a scratch. Talk about luck." Another round shattered the flagstaff in three places.[26]

The 7th New Jersey filed into the middle field east of the Peach Orchard, on the north side of the Millerstown Road less than 50 yards behind Clark's line of caissons. It went prone, facing southwest, with its right flank behind the

---

25 Nicholson, *Pennsylvania at Gettysburg*, vol. 1, 356, 393; Hanifen, *Battery B*, 70; *OR* 27, pt. 1, 498-500.

26 Haynes, *2nd New Hampshire* (1865), 139; Haynes, *2nd New Hampshire* (1896), 171; Martin A. Haynes, *A Minor Raw History, Compiled From a Soldier Boy's Letters to "The Girl I Left Behind Me" 1861-1864* (Lakeport, 1916), 107, quoted. Major Cooper erred when he said the time was around 4:00 p.m. He stated the regiment came under severe artillery fire soon after getting behind the battery. That barrage was the one preceding the infantry attack.

remnants of the north-south fence, which traversed the field from the Millerstown Road to Trostle's lane. Rebel artillery plastered the regiment. A spherical case ball struck Cpl. Eugene Pollard (Company K) in the back of the neck while he lay in formation, knocking him unconscious. His file mate and older brother, Pvt. Francis Pollard, believing him dead, carried him back into the woods on the north side of the road and laid him down among the rocks where he could be found once the regiment left the field. Another round, screaming in from the left, burst in the ranks of Company E, killing two and wounding 2nd Lt. Stanley Gaines, the new company commander who had been transferred from Company K. In Company G, a shell fragment tore Pvt. James Fletcher's buttocks off.[27] In the face of such carnage, Col. Louis R. Francine, got the regiment to its feet and began retiring it from the field rather than allow the continued slaughter of his men.

One of Graham's aides rode up and reminded Francine that he had to support the battery at all costs. "I will support the battery," he retorted, "I was only trying to get a better position for my men, who I am losing very fast." He moved the regiment approximately 200 yards northeast to the destroyed fencerow in front where it lay down perpendicular to the Excelsiors' line and had his men wait there.[28]

By deliberately discharging but one shot per minute, Ames' gunnery sergeants forced the Confederates to shift their batteries to safer locations. The New Yorkers thoroughly enjoyed watching their projectiles bound through the Confederate ranks from the relative safety of their elevated position. The Rebel counter battery fire, while occasionally causing the New Yorkers to duck, did not seriously damage the guns. Most of the incoming rounds ricocheted off the southern slope of the orchard and harmlessly sizzled over the Yankees' heads and fell behind them.[29]

27 OR 27, pt. 1, 578; John Hayward, *Give It To Them, Jersey Blues!* (Highstown, 1998), 115; Paul J. Lader, "The 7th New Jersey in the Gettysburg Campaign," *Gettysburg Magazine*, No. 16, 58; Toombs, *New Jersey Troops*, 222.

28 Hanifen, *Battery B*, 77; Samuel Toombs, *New Jersey Troops in the Gettysburg Campaign* (Orange, 1888), 222; Hayward, *Give It to Them Jersey Blues!* 115, quoted. Hanifen stated that Clark's battery, during its retreat, found the 7th New Jersey 200 yards behind it. That would be very near the position I described; I assume it faced south since it was protecting the guns.

29 Ames, *Battery G*, 66-67; OR 27, pt. 1, 901.

The III Corps, Army of the Potomac
From the Sherfy Farm to the Codori Farm
3:30 p.m.

Out along the skirmish line to the northwest, the fire from the 63rd Pennsylvania slackened perceptibly. The company officers found Maj. John A. Danks (63rd Pennsylvania) and reported the men dangerously low on ammunition: if the Rebels attacked they would have only bayonets with which to defend themselves. Danks hurried a courier back to Birney requesting assistance.[30]

Colonel William J. Sewell double-quicked the 5th New Jersey by the right flank into the road to relieve the 63rd Pennsylvania, south of Spangler's Lane. Sewell immediately deployed his small regiment forward several hundred yards west and south as skirmishers.[31]

Moments later, Birney commanded Burling to take what was left of his brigade and march it southeast over the crest, through the Wheatfield to the stone wall on the low ground at the southern side of the field. Burling had not yet executed the command when Birney told him to detach the largest of his three remaining regiments to reinforce Ward.

So with the 6th New Jersey from the left of his line, Burling passed through the Wheatfield across the front of Winslow's battery (D, 1st New York), while the 8th New Jersey continued its advance to the stone wall. The movement created a hole in the line, which Birney filled by moving the 8th New Jersey by the right flank into the wooded swampy hollow south of the Stony Hill. In short order, Burling and his staff rode to the 115th Pennsylvania, staying long enough to determine that he had no brigade left to command before departing with his officers to rejoin Humphreys on his end of the line.[32]

---

30 Nicholson, *Pennsylvania at Gettysburg*, vol. 1, 387; *OR* 27, pt. 1, 498. Danks' time reference to 5:30 p.m. is probably an error in transcription from the handwritten report to the printed copy of the *OR*. More than likely the regiment pulled back around 3:30 p.m.

31 Raus, *A Generation on the March*, 51-52; *OR* 27, pt. 1, 575.

32 Toombs, *New Jersey Troops*, 206, 219; *OR* 27, pt. 1, 570-571; Ladd and Ladd, *The Bachelder Papers*, vol. 2, 1,007-1,008 and vol. 3, 1,979; Gilbert V. Riddle, "Gettysburg and the Eighth New Jersey Volunteer Regiment," 52-B1, Vertical Files, GNMP. (This article came word for word from Toombs' work.) Burling's 1884 letter does not agree completely with his August 20, 1863 after action report. It appears Ward ordered him forward to reinforce his right flank, and Birney directed him to detach a regiment to Ward's left. When he got back, the 8th New Jersey was already detached and apparently the 115th Pennsylvania with it.

Abandoned without any directives, Maj. John P. Dunne (115th Pennsylvania) sent his "boys" south over the hill to support the 8th New Jersey. The regiment took cover behind the rocks and boulders on the southern slope of the Stony Hill, west of the Wheatfield, while the 179 Jerseymen crawled forward to the right front up to the rail fence along the north side of the stream in the hollow. Private Henry Hartford (Company C) and his comrades found themselves protected by only two rails, which the men piled on top of each other.[33]

Farther to the left, Lt. Col. Stephen R. Gilkyson (6th New Jersey) could not find anyone to tell him what to do. With no one to guide him, he took his regiment east to the far side of the Wheatfield and took cover behind the fence along the ridge overlooking the valley.[34]

Gouverneur K. Warren,
Chief of Engineers, Army of the Potomac
Little Round Top

Minutes after leaving Meade, Warren and his staff dismounted on the wooded eastern slope of Little Round Top and struggled to the boulder strewn open summit. There they found only the U.S. Signal Corps detachment from the II Corps—Captains Hall and Peter A. Taylor (Company D, 49th New York) and an enlisted man. Standing on one of the large boulders, Warren studied the Emmitsburg Road line with his field glasses and saw nothing, despite Hall's insistence that Confederate infantry had flanked Sickles on the left. Warren sent Capt. Chauncey Reese down the hillside toward Smith's battery with orders for it to send one round sailing over the woods along the pike.[35]

33 Toombs, *New Jersey Troops*, 214; Henry Hartford, "At Gettysburg: My Most Vivid Recollection," *The Kansas City Star*, June 29, 1913, Vertical Files, GNMP; Ladd and Ladd, *The Bachelder Papers*, vol. 2, 1,049, 1,053, vol. 3, 590; Winslow, "Battery D," Philadelphia *Weekly Times*, July 26, 1879.

34 OR 27, pt. 1, 577. Colonel Gilkyson leaves the impression that his regiment opened fire as soon as he occupied the position behind the fence, but he did not engage the Confederates for at least 45 minutes. Contrary to the account from Toombs, *New Jersey Troops*, 213, the regiment did not deploy at the same time as the 40th New York.

35 Norton, *The Attack and Defense of Little Round Top* 308; J. Willard Brown, *The Signal Corps, U.S.A. in the War of the Rebellion* (Boston, 1896), 367. Warren noticed the Confederates in the woods along Seminary Ridge when he had Smith fire a round over their heads. Willard Brown in his history of the Signal Corps said that Hall had a difficult time trying to convince Warren

Simultaneously, Hunt, turning south along the western bank Plum Run, rode as far as the Devil's Den, so deeply entrenched in thought that he passed through the large herd of cattle in the valley without noticing any of them. Dismounting, he tied his horse to a tree and climbed the steep hillside into the rear of Smith's two left sections. He heartily approved of the captain's "excellent" position. Pointing at the infantry maneuvering along lower Seminary Ridge in the distance, Smith commanded his gunners to open fire before Warren's messenger ever reached him. After frankly telling the captain he would probably lose his guns, Hunt turned to scrounge up infantry supports.[36]

Meanwhile, Birney, having observed columns of Confederate infantry to the west, maneuvering toward his left flank, ordered his artillery to open fire. Clark's Battery B, 1st New Jersey, responded as soon as the order reached them. Birney glanced at his watch: 3:30 p.m. With every round that gouged a hole in the Confederate ranks, Captain Ames (Battery G, 1st New York) admiringly noted how quickly the line flowed back together.[37]

Longstreet's Corps, Army of Northern Virginia
Warfield Ridge, southeast of the Emmitsburg Road

Keeping in the trees behind the fencerow parallel to the Emmitsburg Road, Law's Alabamians stood on the division's extreme right. Oates had his 15th Alabama lie down, and then ordered the 11 company commanders to detail two men each from their companies to gather up and fill the regiment's drained canteens from the well on the Currens farm, on the northwest side of the Emmitsburg Road, about 100 yards behind the troops. Oates then walked over to his younger brother, 1st Lt. John A. Oates and found him lying behind his Company G, obviously still quite ill from whatever had plagued him during the march toward Gettysburg. The colonel insisted he not go into the fray.

---

that the Rebels had gotten around Sickles' flank. While he did not mention the aide by name, it had to have been Reese, because Mackenzie was sent to get the infantry shortly thereafter, and Roebling apparently stayed with Warren because he never mentioned leaving him for any other errand until the 140th New York came on the field.

36 Hunt, "The Second Day" in *Battles and Leaders*, vol. 3, 305.

37 OR 27, pt. 1, 483, 588; Ames, *Battery G*, 67.

Hood directed General Robertson to keep the left of his brigade anchored on the Emmitsburg Road and his right tight against Law's left. Being unable to do both, Robertson decided to follow Law into the fight. The 3rd Arkansas, leading Robertson's brigade, marched "on the left by file into line," with the 1st Texas followed by the 4th and the 5th Texas regiments to the right. The two Texas regiments moved south in column of fours and stood under the cover of the southwestern face of the woods, with their masked flanks toward the Yankee gunners in the Peach Orchard and the Devil's Den.[38]

Lieutenant Colonel Phillip A. Work ordered the 1st Texas a few paces into the woods, halted them and gave the order to load their weapons. As the regiment maneuvered along the northeastern face of the woods, its flank fully exposed to Yankee artillerists, he had the men cap their pieces.

A Yankee battery pummeled the 4th Texas. As his regiment passed behind Latham's battery, Pvt. James O. Bradfield (Company E, 1st Texas) helplessly watched a shell whistle into the 4th Texas from the crest of the Devil's Den and take out 15 men. A second later, another shell ricocheted along the 1st Texas' left flank. Bouncing into Company E, it struck Pvt. Dick Childers, the company's voracious forager, on his overstuffed haversack. Fresh biscuits flew in every direction. Childers stiffened and collapsed like a felled tree to the ground. As he lay there, unable to move, his passing comrades speculated that the loss of his Pennsylvania Dutch biscuits had paralyzed him and not the shell. The regiment covered another quarter mile before deploying.

---

38 A.C. Jones, "Longstreet at Gettysburg," in *Confederate Veteran*, vol. 33, 552; "Report of Brigadier General Robertson," in *SHSP*, vol. 4, 161; Ladd and Ladd, *The Bachelder Papers*, vol. 2, 860. Robertson's official explanation of his deployment is questionable. He begins by saying he had not had time to reconnoiter the field before deploying. The move created too wide of a gap for him to fill and, therefore, he closed on Law to leave the area between the road and his left for McLaws' Division to occupy. In reality, his brigade did have enough men to cover the ground between Law's left and the Emmitsburg Road. When the attack started, the 4th and the 5th Texas executed the command to close on the right, but the 1st Texas responded to the guns at the Devil's Den and split the attack. Robertson stayed with the 3rd Arkansas and the 1st Texas and in effect lost control of his brigade.

Robertson implies that he got his orders from Hood before starting the charge: "In starting the advance, my orders were to let my right connect with Law's left and my left to rest on the Emmitsburg Road." Hood, his division commander, would have told him to close on Law. He traveled to the right rear of the 1st Texas near Hood and his staff when his brigade committed to action. Six years later, Robertson drastically changed his story by saying that Hood ordered him to keep his left on the Emmitsburg Road "and in no event was I to leave it unless the exigency of the battle made it necessary to do so."

Private William A. Fletcher
(Company F, 5th Texas)
Vallie Taylor Collection, Library, GNMP

A solid shot bounced off the ground about 60 feet to the left of Pvt. John C. West (Company E, 4th Texas), pelting his company with dirt and clods before harmlessly sailing overhead. A second round ploughed into the earth about 60 feet beyond his right. The third barreled through Company E about eight feet in front of him, decapitating one man and cutting another one in half. Their blood splattered him and every man around him. The command of, "Front," echoed through the ranks. Texans wheeled by files to the left into regimental line, with Reilly's battery to their right front. The officers shouted at the men to lie down to better protect them from enemy fire. A private from Company A, 5th Texas, quickly stepped in front of his prone regiment and began praying when an officer ordered him back to the ranks. Within seconds, a shell burst wounded three of his comrades, way too close for Pvt. William A. Fletcher's liking.[39]

From where he stood, Capt. Alexander C. Jones (Company G) studied the batteries at the Devil's Den and Little Round Top. The top of the hill literally swarmed with Yankees. The 3rd Arkansas, on the left of the brigade, rushed into a maelstrom of projectiles. The Yankees "hit our line every time," Pvt. John

---

39 Oates, *The War Between the Union and the Confederacy*, 212, 216; J. B. Polley, *Hood's Texas Brigade: Its Marches, Its Battle, Its Achievements* (Dayton, 1976), 162-163, 167-168, 176-77; John Purifoy, "Longstreet's Attack at Gettysburg, July 2, 1863," in *Confederate Veteran*, vol. 31, 292; Law, "The Struggle for 'Round Top'," in *Battles and Leaders*, vol. 3, 320; "Report of General H. L. Benning," in *SHSP*, vol. 8, 167-168; OR 27, pt. 2, 420; A. C. Sims, *Recollections*, USAHEC, Carlisle Barracks, PA, 1; William Andrew Fletcher, *Rebel Private Front and Rear* (Washington, 1985), 59.

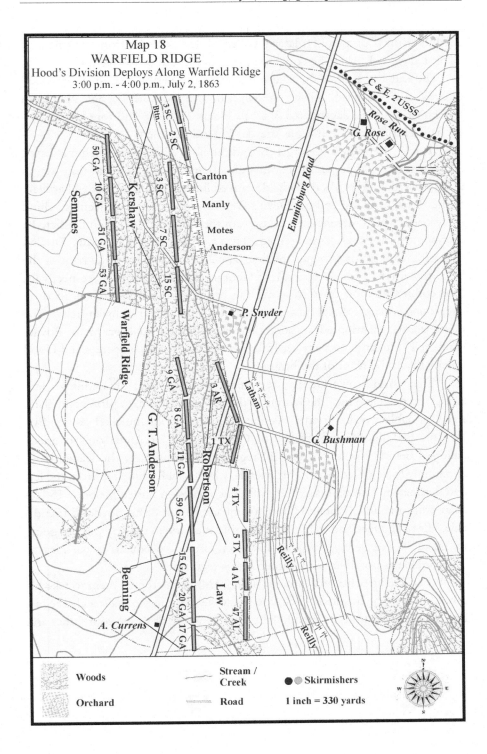

Map 18
WARFIELD RIDGE
Hood's Division Deploys Along Warfield Ridge
3:00 p.m. - 4:00 p.m., July 2, 1863

C & E, 2 USSS

Rose Run

G. Rose

3 SC
Bttn.

2 SC

Carlton

Manly

Motes

Anderson

Kershaw

3 SC

7 SC

15 SC

50 GA

10 GA

51 GA

53 GA

Semmes

Warfield Ridge

Emmitsburg Road

P. Snyder

9 GA

8 GA

11 GA

59 GA

15 GA

20 GA

17 GA

G. T. Anderson

Robertson

3 AR

1 TX

Latham

G. Bushman

4 TX

5 TX

4 AL

47 AL

Law

Reilly

Reilly

Benning

A. Currens

Woods

Orchard

Stream /
Creek

Road

Skirmishers

1 inch = 330 yards

A. Wilkerson (Company H) later recollected. Lying in the front rank next to Capt. Lafayette J. Allen, he could see the entire length of the regiment.

The artillery seemed to take out men with every hit. A shell exploded directly over his head. Killing the captain, it ripped off 1st Sgt. Napoleon Tshear's right arm, decapitated 3rd Sgt. Henry R. King, and tore up 4th Sgt. Richard H. Brashear's left leg as they lay behind the line.[40]

"Rock" Benning's Georgia brigade fell in 200 yards behind Law's Alabamians. Hood personally commanded Benning to follow Law into action at a 400-yard interval. As the brigade moved into position, the Federal artillery at the Peach Orchard and the Devil's Den dropped several projectiles behind the woods, which screened the guns from the Georgians' view and inflicted a number of casualties, among them 1st Lt. J. C. Sapp (Company D, 2nd Georgia), who refused to quit the line. The 2nd Georgia took the right of the brigade, with the 17th, 20th, and 15th Georgia regiments to its left, respectively. The command soon traveled along the brigade for the Georgians to drop everything except their canteens, cartridge boxes, and haversacks. The quartermaster distributed an additional 50 cartridges to every man. Private William T. Fluker (Company D, 15th Georgia) watched Longstreet and Hood quietly troop the front of the brigade.[41]

"Tige" Anderson's Georgia regiments went into line on Benning's left. Anderson detached the 7th Georgia to the A. Currens farm to protect the flank from possible cavalry forays. As the regiment double-quicked south, Pvt. Jackson B. Giles (Company C, 9th Georgia), one of Anderson's couriers, galloped behind the left of his old regiment. Dismounting, he leaned over, apparently to lie down next to his friends, when a shell whined in from the left and detonated. Tearing his left leg off, the concussion hurled his body 15 feet away from the line. Captain Hillyer (Company C) ran to his boyhood friend's side. His paling face and trembling body told the captain the boy was not going to make it. He gently arranged his dying friend's body to make him as comfortable as possible and returned to his regiment.

When the litter bearers came for Giles, Hillyer instructed them to take his schoolmate to the hospital. "Jack, you know we are going to make a charge in a few minutes," he told his friend, "but if I ever get back to see your father and

40 Diary of John A. Wilkerson, "*Experiences of 'Seven Pines'* at Gettysburg," Vertical Files, GNMP, quoted; Jones, "Longstreet at Gettysburg," in *Confederate Veteran*, vol. 23, 552.

41 Willingham, *No Jubilee*, 34; "Report of General H. L. Benning," in *SHSP*, vol. 4, 168.

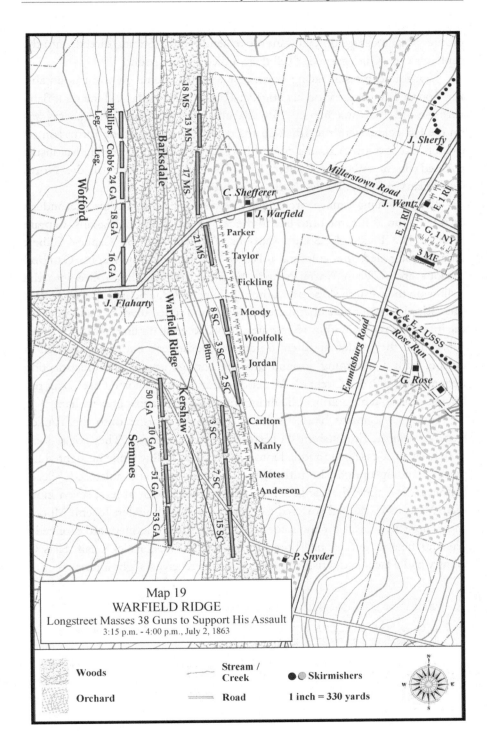

Map 19
WARFIELD RIDGE
Longstreet Masses 38 Guns to Support His Assault
3:15 p.m. – 4:00 p.m., July 2, 1863

Woods

Orchard

Stream / Creek

Road

Skirmishers

1 inch = 330 yards

mother what message do you want me to send them?" Staring directly into the captain's eyes, Giles gasped, "Tell them I died for my country."[42]

Law found himself facing northwest with the seemingly insurmountable Big Round Top centered on his brigade. The 48th Alabama held the right flank with the 44th Alabama then the 15th Alabama to its left. The 47th Alabama was on the left center with the 4th Alabama completing the brigade formation on the left. As the 4th Alabama passed by Reilly's battery, the artillerists lustily cheered them. Adjutant Robert T. Coles noted that one of the North Carolinians' 3-inch rifles had burst at the breech.[43]

The incoming Yankee fire caught the rest of Col. E. Porter Alexander's own battalion as it came onto line to the left of Moody's Louisianans. Captain William W. Fickling's South Carolina Artillery, Lt. S. Capers Gilbert commanding, led the column, followed respectively, by Capts. Osmond Taylor's and William Watts Parker's Virginia artillery. They rolled into the hollow on the western slope of southern Seminary Ridge behind the prone 21st Mississippi. The gunners unlimbered the guns and rolled them by hand through the infantry's ranks. Within 15 minutes, they had gone on line to Moody's left. Altogether, they added another 16 guns to Alexander's line. They opened in unison, with a deafening, ground quaking barrage against the unsuspecting Federals at the Peach Orchard. An acrid, sulfuric cloud billowed back over the Mississippians, temporarily obliterating the sunlight in a in a ghostly haze.[44]

Taylor's Virginians blasted spherical case and canister onto the Yankee batteries near the Emmitsburg-Millerstown road intersection. They got as good as they gave. A case ball thudded into Cpl. William P. Ray while he sighted his piece. Standing upright, he turned, took several steps and collapsed—dead. Within a short time, the Yankees had reduced the crew by at least seven more men. Vincent F. Buford suffered a severely bruised shoulder; Joseph Moody ended up with a facial cut and a contused back; Edward J. Sheppard received a grievous heel wound. A ball bored through Byrd McCormick's calf. Silas C. Gentry had a lacerated wrist, and several others received slight injuries.[45]

---

42 *OR* 27, pt. 2, 397; George Hillyer, "Battle of Gettysburg," 5, GNMP, quoted.

43 Oates, "15th Alabama," 5, BCL; Jeffrey D. Stocker, (ed.), *From Huntsville to Appomattox* (Knoxville, 1996), 103; *OR* 27, pt. 2, 428.

44 *OR* 27, pt. 2, 432; Bachelder Map, July 2, 1863; J. S. McNeily, "Barksdale's Mississippi Brigade at Gettysburg," (Gaithersburg, 1987), 236.

45 "Report of Captain O. B. Taylor," in *SHSP*, vol. 13, 214.

V Corps, Army of the Potomac
Powers' Hill
3:00 p.m.-4:00 p.m.

The V Corps deployed forward at the first reports of the artillery fire. On the top of Powers' Hill, 1st Lt. Edward Bennett (Company A, 44th New York), trying to shake off the effects of a sound nap, quietly studied the surrounding terrain. To the west, he noted how silent Cemetery Ridge seemed. He latched his eyes upon a mounted officer, an aide, he assumed, spurring hard toward the Baltimore Pike. The messenger wheeled to the left as he neared Powers' Hill and suddenly turned into the small grove and the cluster of horses at the northern base of the hill. Bennett, who instinctively started down the slope to his regiment, mumbled to himself, "There comes orders to move." The lieutenant saw the aide hand off some papers to Barnes, before rushing north toward the Second Division.

The bugler sounded "The Assembly." An artillery crew materialized from the grass around their guns on Cemetery Ridge. They began firing their pieces and within seconds, the entire line seemed to ignite into sulfur and flame as battery after battery cut loose on the enemy. Bennett found his brigade deploying without him.[46]

First Lieutenant Graham (Company B, 16th Michigan), having just returned from his "tour" of the front, glanced east and saw the Third Division of the VI Corps rushing onto the field. "Fall in!" echoed through the ranks of Tilton's brigade, rousing the weary Private Carter, (22nd Massachusetts). Having caught up with the regiment around noon, he had plopped down on the ground paying no heed to his crippled feet. Now, with his undersized shoes draped by their strings over the barrel of his weapon, and his body shot through with adrenalin, he ignored his personal discomfort, intent upon doing his duty. At the command "Load at will, load!" thousands of ramrods metallically clattered in the afternoon air. The quartermaster of the 4th Michigan issued 20 extra rounds to the men, which they shoved into their haversacks.[47]

---

46 Bennett, "Fighting Them Over," *National Tribune*, May 6, 1886.

47 Carter, "Reminiscences," *War Papers*, vol. 2, 165, quoted; Large, *Battle of Gettysburg*, 90-91; Aiken, *Inside the Army of the Potomac*, 299; Lockley Diary, July 2, 1863, UMI; Graham, "On to Gettysburg," in *War Papers*, vol. 1, 9; Theodore Gerrish, "The Battle of Gettysburg," *National Tribune*, November 23, 1882; Survivors Association, *The Corn Exchange Regiment*, 240; Houghton, Journal, 13, UMI. According to Carter, the column moved out around 4:00 p.m.

Sykes moved to the front of the column with Vincent's 3rd brigade immediately behind him. Sweitzer's 2nd and Tilton's 1st brigade, respectively, fell in behind Vincent.[48] Tilton's brigade, having been reinforced by the 18th Massachusetts, which had just returned from detached duty, had four regiments, while Sweitzer's had been reduced to three, the 9th Massachusetts being on picket duty.[49]

The brigades shifted from regimental front to march by the left flank.[50] Captain Augustus P. Martin, chief of artillery, V Corps, deployed his batteries in customary formation. Three batteries (D and I, 5th U.S., and C, 3rd Massachusetts Battery) followed Barnes' First Division.[51]

Ayres' Second Division marched in parallel columns in reverse order. Brigadier General Stephen Weed's 3rd brigade led the division, followed, respectively, by Col. Sidney Burbank's 2nd brigade of U.S. Regulars and Col. Hannibal Day's 1st brigade of Regulars. Martin's remaining two batteries—L, 1st Ohio and C, 1st New York—trailed behind the infantry.[52]

Martin specifically requested Lt. Charles E. Hazlett follow behind Barnes with his Battery D, 5th U.S. Artillery. Hazlett, who had served under the captain for at least a year, did not want to go in. "I have just received bad news from home and I would rather someone else lead off to-day. Besides I have a premonition that this will be my last battle." Martin, who had heard the young officer say repeatedly that if he were to die he would rather it be in a big battle than in a little scrap, tried to reassure Hazlett. The captain said he had great confidence in the lieutenant and he preferred to have him accompany him onto

---

The battlefield plaques state the V Corps departure times for the three brigades of the divisions as follows: Barnes—"After 4:00 p.m." (Vincent and Tilton); and "After 2:00 p.m." (Sweitzer); Ayres—"about 3:00 p.m.—preceded by the First Division." Barnes' Division, to have led the Corps onto the field, had to have departed between 2:00 p.m.-4:00 p.m. According to Capt. Francis A. Donaldson (Company K, 118th Pennsylvania), the command flanked left at 3:30 p.m. He noted this time on his watch. George Lockley (1st Michigan) made his notation of the flanking movement at 3:00 p.m.

48 Large, *Battle of Gettysburg*, 91; Norton, *The Attack and Defense of Little Round Top*, 297.

49 Survivors' Association, *The Corn Exchange Regiment*, 238.

50 Aiken, *Inside the Army of the Potomac*, 299.

51 A.P. Martin, "Little Round Top," *The Gettysburg Compiler*, October 12, 1899; OR 27, pt. 1, 659. Martin's OR account, written on July 31, 1863, differs from the later account about the battery dispositions. The 1899 account has two batteries behind the First Division, two batteries behind the Second, and one behind the Third.

52 OR 27, pt. 1, 634.

the field. Resigned to his fate Hazlett assumed his place with his battery.[53] Lieutenant Benjamin Rittenhouse, the battery's second in command, feared for his beloved Hazlett's life because he sported a white slouch hat that day.[54]

The First and the Second Divisions initially followed the Granite School House Road westward in parallel columns to the Taneytown Road. Vincent's brigade marched across from Weed's. A man from the 140th New York, walking alongside Color Cpl. William N. Colestock (Company K, 16th Michigan) collapsed, complaining of exhaustion. A shell screamed in and crashed with a thud onto the ground next to him, its fuse still sputtering: a dud. Colestock got a callous laugh in at the cringing fellow, who lay on the ground bemoaning his fate.[55]

As the First Division turned south by column of fours onto the Taneytown Road, Ayres' Second Division fell in behind it. Vincent's brigade struck the eastern end of George Weikert's farm lane which, branching west, followed the lane beyond the farmhouse to the brush covered woods north of the John Weikert place. At that point, the lane veered south through the woods and narrowed into a corduroyed track. The corps' route followed the spine of a boulder-strewn ridge, which sloped off to the east and the west.[56]

Martin rode forward to Sykes and asked him if he had any specific orders for the V Corps' artillery deployment. The general, who was marching blindly to the left of the Federal line, completely unaware that the III Corps had moved forward, was almost literally feeling his way onto the field. "No, sir," the general emphatically responded, "I hold you responsible that the artillery does its work." Along the way, Captain Donaldson, whose 118th Pennsylvania led the advance of Tilton's brigade, noted how far the line of bloodied ambulances seemed to stretch along the line of march.[57]

---

53 Martin, "Little Round Top," *The Gettysburg Compiler*, October 12, 1899, quoted; OR 27, pt. 1, 659.

54 B. F. Rittenhouse, "The Battle of Gettysburg as Seen from Little Round Top," in *Military Essays and Recollections, Read Before the Commandery of the District of Columbia, Military Order of the Loyal Legion of the United States* 4 vols., (Wilmington, 1993), vol. 1, 40.

55 W. W. Colestock, "The 16th Michigan at Little Round Top," National Tribune, March 26, 1914.

56 Martin D. Hardin, *History of the Twelfth Regiment Pennsylvania Reserve Volunteer Corps* (New York, 1890), 153; Aiken, *Inside the Army of the Potomac*, 299.

57 Martin, "Little Round Top," *The Gettysburg Compiler*, October 12, 1899; Norton, *The Attack and Defense of Little Round Top*, 294; Aiken, *Inside the Army of the Potomac*, 299.

III Army Corps, Army of the Potomac
The Peach Orchard
3:30 p.m.

Clark and his New Jersey men calmly and coolly manned the guns as if at drill. Clark had each piece load case or shell then fire independently so he could observe the effect of each round. George W. Bonnell, the #4 man on Sgt. William H. Clairville's gun, loosed the first round. Then Clark had the pieces fire by section. From there the Parrotts cut loose by half battery. He then followed up with one or two salvos by battery. Cognizant of the smallest detail, he strode from gun to gun supervising the sighting, choosing the projectile type, and personally checking each fuse setting. Finally, when he was sure of the battery's effectiveness, he bellowed above the battle noise, "Fire at will." Within seconds, his men poured shells and case into the flank of the Rebels along their front. Each shot seemed to gouge holes in the Confederate lines.[58]

Longstreet's Corps, Army of Northern Virginia
Warfield Ridge at the Emmitsburg Road
3:30 p.m.

The counter battery fire showed Hood what he needed to know. The Federal infantry extended toward the Emmitsburg Road in a concave position with the flanks anchored at Little Round Top and the Peach Orchard. It was obvious to Hood that if he attacked as ordered, with his left flank on the Emmitsburg road, the frontal and flank fire across the open fields would slaughter his men as they traversed the open field in front of them. So he dispatched an officer to Longstreet requesting he be allowed to flank Big Round Top and take the Yankees from the rear. The reply came back quickly: "General Lee's orders are to attack up the Emmitsburg Road."

Hood immediately sent another officer to Longstreet. Before receiving this latest order, Hood watched helplessly as his men absorbed the deadly Federal artillery fire. By the time the second aide returned with the identical reply, 1st Sgt. Charles H. Kingsley (1st Texas) with Pvts. William H. Barbee and Jim Deering had returned to Hood from the Pinckney reconnaissance. Within earshot of their lieutenant colonel, they excitedly reported that they had been on

---

58 Hanifen, *Battery B*, 69, quoted; Ladd and Ladd, *The Bachelder Papers*, vol. 2, 844.

Little Round Top and found it unoccupied. From its summit they could observe the entire Yankee line: a mass of artillery and infantry arrayed along the eastern side of a two and half mile stretch of Cemetery Ridge.

Hood immediately turned to his adjutant general, Maj. Harry Sellers, and blurted: "Go as fast as your horse will carry you and explain all this to General Longstreet and ask to permit me to move by the right flank so as to envelop that knoll." Hood pointed toward Little Round Top. As Sellers clattered away, Gen. Law approached Hood, formally protesting his attack orders. The Yankees had too strong a position to strike frontally, he argued. If an attack succeeded, his force would be too depleted and exhausted for any successful exploitation of a break through. Obviously a frontal assault was not necessary because Hood's men could easily gain and turn the Federal flank from the south, thus compelling the Federals to abandon their strongly held front. Hood haled Maj. Tilford A. Hamilton from his staff and told Law to repeat everything in front of him. Search out Longstreet as quickly as possible, Hood told Hamilton, and deliver Law's protest with Hood's endorsement. The major departed at a gallop. Within 10 minutes, Sellers came back with the emphatic message: "You will execute the orders you have already received." "Very well," the disgusted Hood retorted, "when we get under fire I will have a discretion." Standing in the ranks of Company L, 1st Texas, Capt. William Bedell, Pvts. Charles Vidor, Augustus Wakellee, William Schadt, and William Von Hutton overheard everything.

Sellers had barely finished when Hamilton along with Maj. John W. Fairfax, one of Longstreet's staffers, reined alongside. One of the "boys" in Company G, 4th Alabama, twisted onto his back at the sound of Fairfax's approach. "Boys," he announced, "we are going to have a battle. There is old Fairfax, Longstreet's fighting adjutant, and we never see him that we do not have a fight." Fairfax seemed very agitated to Pvt. William C. Ward, who watched the major feverishly trace with his hand the Yankee position to the officers gathered around him.

"General Longstreet orders that you begin the attack at once." Fairfax bluntly informed Hood, despite his continued protestations. As Fairfax wheeled about, Hood turned to Law and asked, "You hear the order?" Without responding, Law pulled his horse about and raced back to his brigade.[59] But

59 Oates, *The War Between the Union and the Confederacy*, 209-210; Law, "The Struggle for 'Round Top'," in *Battles and Leaders*, vol. 3, 322-323; John O. Scott, "The Texans at Gettysburg," *Sherman Register*, March 31, 1897; Bradfield, "At Gettysburg, July 3," in *Confederate Veteran*, vol.

Fairfax was convinced that Hood's original proposal would work, and said so when he rode back to Longstreet. Infuriated, Longstreet pushed through the ranks of the 3rd Arkansas to a spot about 50 yards to its front.

Hood spied Longstreet. Reining alongside the commander and his aide, not knowing that Fairfax had argued on his behalf, he insisted that he take his men to the right. Fed up, Longstreet was preemptory: "Hood, go where you are ordered. General Lee directs me to attack here." Wheeling his horse about, Hood called back over his shoulder, "Very well, General, but I'll get all my people killed." He spurred back to the center of his old brigade.[60]

Law's pioneers double-quicked to the left of the brigade line and began clearing a small wood to the right front of the 5th Texas. Their activity drew artillery fire from Smith's battery at the Devil's Den. Several shells whined through the air, one bursting in the rightmost company of the prone Texans, killing three men. Before the smoke had cleared, a section from Reilly's battery rolled into position on the far right of the brigade and quickly opened fire. The 2nd U.S. Sharpshooters at Slyder's helplessly watched the two field pieces pull onto the open crest to the their left front, well beyond the range of their rifles. Major Homer Stoughton quickly detached several men into the woods on his left flank. A short time later, they had stolen up on the gunners and chased them away from the piece on the right.[61]

Hood ordered some men in the 1st Texas to throw down the fence section in front of his horse. As the rails hit the ground, Hood pushed his mount through the gap into the open ground and ordered the regiments forward. The entire brigade sprang to its feet, stepped forward, and, to a man, tore the fence apart. The general trotted to Col. Robert M. Powell, behind the 5th Texas, and, pointing toward Big Round Top, directed him to take his regiment in that direction.[62]

30, 225; W. C. Ward, "Incidents and Personal Experiences in the Battlefield at Gettysburg," in *Confederate Veteran*, vol. 8, 347. Quotes were drawn from all of the sources cited.

60 A. C. Jones, "Longstreet at Gettysburg," in *Confederate Veteran*, vol. 23, quote on 552; Jeffrey D. Wert, *General James Longstreet: The Confederacy's Most Controversial Soldier* (New York, 1993), 273.

61 W. C. Ward, "Incidents and Personal Experiences on the Battlefield at Gettysburg," in *Confederate Veteran*, vol. 8, 347; Executive Committee, *Maine at Gettysburg*, 352.

62 Sims, "Battle of Gettysburg," 2, USAHEC; Ward, "Incidents and Personal Experiences," in *Confederate Veteran*, vol. 8, 347; Scott, "The Texans at Gettysburg," *Sherman* [TX] *Register*, March 31, 1897.

III Corps Artillery, Army of the Potomac
The Peach Orchard
3:45 p.m.

Clark's New Jersey artillery- men were not faring well. Privates Leopold Smalley and Joseph M. Morris went down wounded running ammunition. Despite his excruciating injury, Morris re- mained on the field to service his gun. Shrapnel disabled Privates Anthony Collier, Hiram Tierney, Stephen McGowan, and Patrick F. Castillo. The drivers replaced them at their posts. Eventually 17-year-old 1st Sgt. Aurelius J. Adams (Company K) and a number of other volunteers from the 141st Pennsylvania began running ammunition for the battery.[63]

The Confederate artillery mercilessly pounded the Pennsylvanians. Sergeant John Bloodgood (Company I) believed every projectile had his name on it. A shell exploded over the prone regiment, knocking Capt. Joseph H. Horton (Company A) unconscious. He regained his senses as a couple of men began hauling him away. Stunned and wobbly, he staggered back to his company. Sergeant Edwin G. Owen (Company I) hugged the earth, grateful for the slight rise of ground, which sheltered the regiment in the roadbed. Sergeant David C. Palmer (Company D) who had bragged that he intended to win his shoulder straps that day, kept deliberately rising up to look around, trying to impress his superiors. When a shell fragment killed him instantly, some black humorist in the company cried out: "Sergeant Palmer has got his shoulder straps!" Private Gilbert Corwin, who had gone AWOL from the hospital in Frederick, stripped the dead Palmer of his equipment. "I told the Colonel I would get a gun," he snapped.[64]

Ward's Brigade and Smith's Battery,
III Corps, Army of the Potomac
The Devil's Den

About 20 minutes into the action, Captain Smith, noticed the Confederates rolling Reilly's section of light 12-Pounders toward some high ground to his left

---

63 Hanifen, *Battery B*, 72; Bloodgood, *Reminiscences*, 135; Aurelius J. Adams, "The Fight in the Peach Orchard," *National Tribune*, April 23, 1885.

64 Craft, *141st Pennsylvania*, 121, 132, quoted on 132; Bloodgood, *Reminiscences*, 136.

Colonel Robert M. Powell
(5th Texas)
Gregory A. Coco Collection
Library, GNMP

front southeast of the Emmitsburg Road. Shifting his fire in that direction, his gunners drove the Rebels off before they could open fire.[65]

Colonel Walker (4th Maine) checked the time: 3:45 p.m. The Rebels had just emerged from the woods along Warfield Ridge.[66] He glanced up to see Smith walking toward him. The artillery officer asked him to move his regiment into the rocks of the Den, saying he could protect the front of his battery, but he needed flank protection from the Rebels, who would use the woods to the south to mask their advance upon him. Walker vehemently refused. He would not leave the guns unprotected nor would he descend into the Den unless specifically ordered to do so.

Smith stormed off to find Ward, and he returned in a few minutes with Lt. Thomas J. Leigh, Ward's aide-de-camp, who demanded the colonel obey the order. While Walker profanely protested, Smith heatedly declared he could take care of his own guns and did not need the New Englanders. Leigh reassured Walker that other troops would fill the gap behind the guns, and with that he begrudgingly complied.[67]

Yelling his regiment to its feet, Walker marched it by the left flank toward the creek bottom. From his position on the extreme left of the regiment, on the

65 *OR* 27, pt. 1, 588.

66 Executive Committee, *Maine at Gettysburg*, 181.

67 Walker, "The 4th Maine at Gettysburg," *National Tribune*, April 8, 1886; *OR* 27, pt. 1, 588; Ladd and Ladd, *The Bachelder Papers*, vol. 2, 1,094-1,095; Smith, *A Famous Battery*, 109; Executive Committee, *Maine at Gettysburg*, 181.

top of the hill, 2nd Lt. Nathaniel A. Robbins (Company H) saw the Confederates massing for their assault. And plainly their line extended well beyond the regiment's left. Calling Sgt. Maj. William H. Gardner, he sent him to Walker with the alarm.[68]

Walker immediately responded. He posted Company F's 36 officers and men among the boulders of the Devil's Kitchen on the southern end of the Den, close to the wood line. Simultaneously, he dispatched 1st Lt. Arthur Libby and his 28-man Company B into the thick woods on the eastern side of Plum Run. The rest of the regiment formed a line from the base of the huge boulders at the northern end of the Den across the creek bottom to within 40 rods of the southwestern base of Little Round Top. The shifting of the troops had now created a large gap between the 124th New York and the New Englanders.[69]

Several artillery shots fell on the 124th New York as it lay behind the ridge. Colonel Ellis decided to move the regiment into the woods on his right flank rather than take a horrendous beating in the open. But as the regiment shifted to the right and lay down among the trees, Ellis changed his mind and immediately herded the men back to their original position. Company B, on the right of the line, went to ground within a few yards of Smith's rightmost gun.

Alexander's Artillery Line,
Longstreet's Corps, Army of Northern Virginia
Warfield Ridge

E. P. Alexander's last batteries rolled into position to the right of Moody's battery around 3:45 p.m. Woolfolk was to Moody's immediate right with Jordan between him and Carlton's section. Before the end of the hour, Alexander had 49 pieces in position, most of which were firing. The ground literally rolled and heaved. Several times the thick smoke forced Cabell to order his battalion to cease-fire until it dissipated. The ferocity and the accuracy of the Yankees' counter battery fire surprised Alexander. "I don't believe there was ever in our war a hotter, harder, sharper artillery afternoon than this," he later recalled.

---

68 N. A. Robbins to Selden Connor, December 23, 1892, Records of the Adj. Gen. of Maine, Box 110 (2202-0402), "Material returned for CW history," (Fourth Maine), Vertical Files, GNMP.

69 Walker, "The 4th Maine at Gettysburg," *National Tribune*, April 8, 1886; Executive Committee, *Maine at Gettysburg*, 181.

Both sides had amassed large amounts of artillery quickly, and the gunners stuck tenaciously to their pieces.[70]

III Corps Artillery, Army of the Potomac
The Peach Orchard
3:45 p.m-4:00 p.m.

Three minutes into the action, a solid shot decapitated Pvt. Thomas N. Post, Jr. (Battery B, 1st New Jersey Light). A few rounds fell among the limbers and caissons, killing and wounding several horses and terrifying those which remained. Unsure of the source of the harassing fire, Ames stepped beyond his smoke enshrouded Battery G, 1st New York, into a cleared spot to the left of his guns. And from there he spotted Fraser's section hidden inside Phillip Snyder's shed. Calmly strolling back to his left piece under Sgt. George H. Barse, he told him to set fire to the building. The sergeant methodically trained his gun on the shed, sighted it, and sent a shell whining in its direction. A few bursts later, a direct hit set it ablaze with an explosion that mortally wounded Fraser, killed three men, and wounded Lt. R. H. Cooper. Having exhausted his spherical case, Hazleton ordered his gunners under cover until the Rebs came within canister range.[71]

Fraser's Battery, Longstreet's Corps,
Army of Northern Virginia
Phillip Snyder Farm

Lieutenant William J. Furlong assumed command of the remaining section. Abandoning those two guns, he sent to Cabell for some more men who complied and detached Lieutenant Anderson from his two 3-inch rifles and

---

70 *OR* 27, pt. 2, 375; Tucker, "Orange Blossoms," *National Tribune*, January 24, 1886; Bachelder Map, July 2, 1863; Gallagher, *Fighting for the Confederacy*, 239-240, quote on 239.

71 Hanifen, *Battery B*, 69; *OR* 27, pt. 1, 585, 588, 901. Captain Clark, in his official report, stated the Confederates placed the battery in the field about 1,400 yards to his front in the vicinity of a house along the Emmitsburg Road. That house is the Snyder house. Captain Smith said that about 20 minutes or so into the action he opened fire on a battery that rolled into the field about 1,400 yards to his front. Both officers erred in their estimation of the distance. On the Bachelder map, the Confederate position is about 1,150 yards from Clark's position and about 1,080 yards from Smith's battery.

sent him to Furlong.[72] All along the line, the gunners were taking a severe pounding. Yankee artillery dismounted two of Furlong's four guns and quickly wounded or killed 40 of his 75 artillerists.

Moody's pair of howitzers had lost too many men to even function. The captain asked Alexander for volunteers from Barksdale's brigade. The colonel rushed to Barksdale with the request, and he in turn called on the 17th Mississippi for men. Private William B. Abernathy (Company B) saw Pvts. "Dundy" Gunn and his brother (both Company A), one of the Robertsons with W. D. Mimms (both Company B), and four others instantly respond to the call. By nightfall, only three of them would remain unscathed.[73]

The Stony Hill

With the fire intensifying along the Emmitsburg Road, Birney decided to strengthen the skirmish line south of the Peach Orchard. He dispatched a staff officer to Lt. Col. David M. Jones with instructions for him to advance the 110th Pennsylvania to the Emmitsburg Road and to connect with the 3rd Maine. The Pennsylvanians executed the maneuver, according to Maj. Isaac Rogers "with much coolness."[74]

Smith's Battery, III Corps, Army of the Potomac
The Devil's Den

With typical understatement, Smith later referred to the artillery fight as "a spirited duel." General Hunt might have described a bit differently. For it caught him dismounted and running through a terrified herd of cattle in the valley behind the battery. An incoming shell had blown up one of the cows and splattered it all over the valley floor understandably agitating the others. Carefully picking his way through the terror-stricken bovines, the equally

---

72 Ames, *Battery G*, 68; *OR* 27, pt. 2, 375, 383.

73 Gallagher, *Fighting for the Confederacy*, 240; William M. Abernathy, *Our Mess: Southern Gallantry and Privations* (McKinney, 1977), 31.

74 *OR* 27, pt. 1, 528. While Major Rogers and the OR do not specifically mention the Emmitsburg Road, the men advanced under severe artillery fire and the regiment under orders, connected with "the brigade on the right," which does not mean that it joined with its own brigade but with another. The only brigade near the right flank was Graham's, in particular, the 3rd Maine, which was at the Peach Orchard.

frightened Hunt found his horse still tied where he left it. He wasted little time mounting up and getting out of the valley.[75]

U.S. Signal Station, Army of the Potomac
Little Round Top

The same artillery fire screamed over Little Round Top as well. Warren scribbled a dispatch to Meade, pleading for a division to come to his relief and gave the note to 1st Lt. Mackenzie. While the aide spurred toward the Wheatfield, Captain Hall decided to pack up the station and leave, but Warren "convinced" him to remain and keep signaling.[76]

V Corps, Army of the Potomac
John T. Weikert Farm

Barnes' division had veered southwest, across the low fields south of George Weikert's keeping east of the woods around John T. Weikert's house. As the first men of Vincent's brigade appeared in the eastern end of the Millerstown Road, they came under the same artillery fire that had driven Hunt to safer ground. Private Carter (22nd Massachusetts), near the rear of the column, watched soldiers in front of him instinctively duck when shells burst overhead, and then automatically straighten up before the smoke had cleared. At the head of the brigade, Captain Donaldson (118th Pennsylvania) anxiously watched what seemed like hundreds of projectiles sporadically exploding all around him. They "left an unpleasant feeling upon us," he later wrote with his usual understatement.[77]

Mackenzie, in the meantime, found Sickles near the Peach Orchard. The general refused to send him any of his regiments, insisting he needed them along his own front. At that, the aide clattered down the Millerstown Road, where he ran into Sykes and his staff well in advance of his V Corps near the northwest corner of the Wheatfield. Putting his request to Sykes for assistance,

---

75 OR 27, pt. 1, 588; Hunt, "The Second Day," in *Battles and Leaders*, vol. 3, 305-306.

76 Norton, *The Attack and Defense of Little Round Top*, 309-310; Willard J. Brown, *The Signal Corps, U.S.A. in the War of the Rebellion* (Boston, 1896), 367.

77 OR 27, pt. 1, 610; Carter, "Reminiscences," *War Papers*, vol. 2, 165; Aiken, *Inside the Army of the Potomac*, 301, quoted.

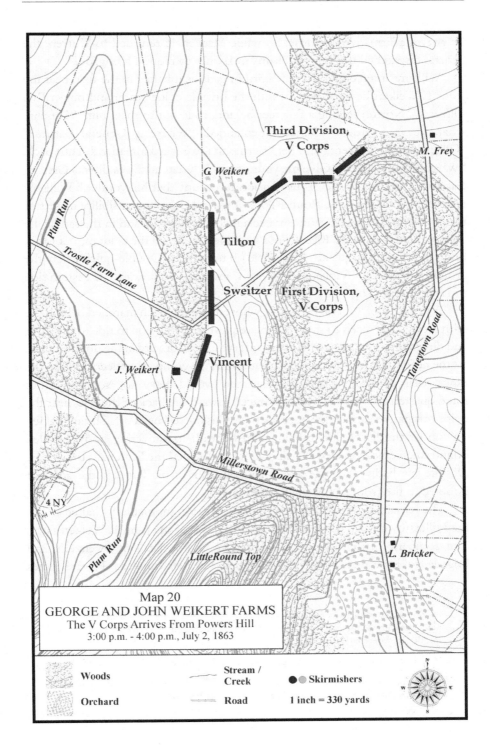

Third Division, V Corps

M. Frey

G. Weikert

Plum Run

Trostle Farm Lane

Tilton

Sweitzer   First Division, V Corps

Taneytown Road

Vincent

J. Weikert

Millerstown Road

4 NY

Plum Run

LittleRound Top

L. Bricker

Map 20
GEORGE AND JOHN WEIKERT FARMS
The V Corps Arrives From Powers Hill
3:00 p.m. - 4:00 p.m., July 2, 1863

Woods

Orchard

Stream / Creek

Road

Skirmishers

1 inch = 330 yards

he got an affirmative response. So while Mackenzie returned to Warren, the general dispatched Capt. Jay Williams to Barnes to request a brigade.[78]

Williams intercepted Vincent's 3rd brigade as it halted in the field near the John T. Weikert house. Vincent, with the brigade color bearer and bugler Pvt. Oliver W. Norton trailing a few feet behind, rode out to meet him. "Captain, what are your orders?" Vincent demanded. "Where is General Barnes?" Williams asked. Vincent, who held Barnes in low regard impatiently shot back: "What are your orders? Give me your orders." "General Sykes directs General Barnes to send a brigade of his division to occupy that hill yonder," Williams retorted, indicating Little Round Top. "I will take the responsibility myself of taking my brigade there," Vincent exclaimed. Turning around in the saddle, he commanded Col. James Rice, whose 44th New York led the column, "Colonel, bring the brigade as quickly as possible on to that hill. Double-quick where the ground will permit." Vincent and Norton spurred away toward the eastern side of Little Round Top.[79]

When Lt. Col. Norval E. Welch, whose 16th Michigan marched behind the 44th New York, received the word, he requested permission to ride to the front and directed Jacklin, the adjutant, to order the men forward at the double quick. At the head of the regiment, Jacklin cautioned the company officers to keep the ranks well closed up because the men would have to trot for about three-quarters of a mile. Then as he raced toward the back of the line, near the color company a cannon ball tore the top of his horse's head off. The animal fell on top of the lieutenant, pinning him beneath its quivering body. Startled infantrymen quickly pulled the animal off and helped the lieutenant to his feet. Despite his badly cut knee and torn ligaments in his left leg, the adjutant hobbled to the front of the small regiment.[80]

The remaining two brigades of Barnes' division momentarily halted where the Millerstown Road passed by the southern end of the John T. Weikert farm. The company officers in the 4th Michigan, at the head of Sweitzer's 2nd brigade, told the men to use the respite to fill their canteens. Private James

78 Norton, *The Attack and Defense of Little Round Top*, 292, 294-295. I based this upon my study of the Bachelder Maps. Carter mentions the column striking the Millerstown Road but does not mention it proceeding west along it.

79 Oliver W. Norton to Frank Huntington, September 22, 1888, Vertical Files 4-10e, GNMP.

80 Jacklin, "Account," 9, GNMP; Amos M. Judson, *History of the Eighty-Third Pennsylvania Volunteers* (Dayton, 1986), 125; Berry, Diary, July 2, 1863, USAHEC.

Houghton (Company K) and a few comrades found a ditch nearby filled with stagnant water. Pushing the green scum on the surface aside with their tin cups and slapping the surface to sink the bugs and "wigglers" to the bottom, they plunged their canteens under to fill them up.[81]

Discovering what he later described as a "gap in the line" Sykes asked Birney if he could fill it with his own men. With Birney's consent, he sent an aide down the Millerstown Road to bring Tilton's and Sweitzer's brigades forward. Within minutes the 4th Michigan reassembled its formation and marched.[82]

III Corps Artillery, Army of the Potomac
The Peach Orchard

A Confederate limber along the lower end of Seminary Ridge burst in an explosion of smoke and flame and simultaneously the Yankees dismounted one of the guns. Bucklyn's six Napoleons silenced the pair of rifled guns to their right front. They then shifted their fire toward a battery a considerable distance to their left. The counter battery action slackened considerably.[83]

Private Billy Riley (Battery B, 1st New Jersey Artillery) straddled the tube of Clairville's gun, cheering lustily. The 141st Pennsylvania joined in the "huzzahs." Within minutes, the "manly cheer" reverberated from the Peach Orchard to the Devil's Den as regiment after regiment picked it up. Moments later, the Confederate guns fell silent and the battery near the Snyder house limbered up and quit the field.[84]

Captain Hall on Little Round Top noted the time as he sent off his last message to Meade—4:00 p.m. It read:

"The only infantry of enemy visible is on extreme left. Some have been seen moving towards Emmitsburg. The battery that just opened on our troops has ceased firing."[85]

81 Houghton, Journal, 13, UMI.

82 Norton, *The Attack and Defense of Little Round Top*, 294; Houghton, ibid.

83 Hanifen, *Battery B*, 69; OR 27, 1, 588; Ladd and Ladd, *The Bachelder Papers*, vol. 1, 72. Captain Smith said about 20 minutes after the Confederate battery rolled into action, their infantry advanced from the woods near the Emmitsburg Road.

84 Hanifen, *Battery B*, 69.

85 James S. Hall to George G. Meade, 4:00 pm, July 2, 1863, G. K. Warren Papers, NYSL.

Chapter 6

July 2, 1863
4:00 p.m.-4:30 p.m.

"Give them shell; give them solid shot; damn them, give them anything!"
—Captain James E. Smith, 4th New York Independent Battery

V Corps, Army of the Potomac
North of the Millerstown Road, At the J. Weikert Farm
4:00 p.m.

At the rear of Barnes' column, Captain Martin twisted about in the saddle and fixed his eyes upon Little Round Top. The summit would be a good place to plant a battery, he suggested to Lieutenant Hazlett. He ordered the remaining two batteries to stay where they were, then turned to Rittenhouse, Hazlett's senior officer, and yelled, "Battery D, this way." While the guns skirted around the northern base of the hill, Martin and Hazlett clattered their mounts up the northern face to the first plateau below the huge boulders on the crest. He could not possibly get his guns to the summit, Hazlett said. "You work them up as far as you can with the horses," Martin retorted, "and I will call for infantry volunteers, and throw them up by hand."[1]

No sooner had Hazlett left Barnes' division than one of Sickles' staff encountered the other two batteries in the Millerstown Road. Finding no one in charge of them, the designated officer having left them to take cover, the staffer

---

1 Scott, "On Little Round Top," *National Tribune*, August 2, 1894; Martin, "Little Round Top" in *The Gettysburg Compiler*, October 12, 1899. Scott said the battery approached Little Round Top from the east on a north-south road, which ran parallel to the eastern side of the hill. This would have to have been the Baltimore Pike. The evidence indicates the battery was on the east-west Millerstown Road.

immediately commandeered them. He insisted he had instructions to take any batteries he could find regardless of who they belonged to. So he detached 1st Lt. Malbone F. Watson's Battery I, 5th U.S. Artillery, to the Peach Orchard and 1st Lt. Aaron F. Walcott's Battery C, 3rd Massachusetts, to a knoll on the eastern side of Weikert's farm lane immediately north of the Millerstown Road.[2]

Ward's Brigade, III Corps, Army of the Potomac
The Devil's Den and Houck's Ridge

With the Confederates herding the Federal skirmishers back upon his position, Ward hurriedly dispatched orderlies to every regiment in his brigade. The 124th New York crawled closer to the brow of the hill on Smith's right flank so that the officers, who remained on foot, could see over the crest. In so doing, the regiment closed to the right up to the tree line, forcing the leftmost company from the 86th New York into the woods, where it assumed its correct facing on the left of its own regiment. From their elevated position along the eastern face of the woods, the New Yorkers had a clear line of sight into the woods to the west and the fields to the southwest. Ward directed the two New York regiments on his left wing not to fire until the Rebels came within 200 yards. On the right wing, the 20th Indiana and 99th Pennsylvania were to hold their fire until the Rebels came clearly into view.[3]

Vincent's Brigade, V Corps, Army of the Potomac
Little Round Top

Vincent and Private Norton reined to a halt on the lower plateau on the southern end of the hill, completely unaware of Warren's or the signal station's presence to their right rear. As they sat there, observing the valley and the low ground along the Emmitsburg Road, a Confederate shell burst dangerously close overhead, followed almost immediately by two others. "They are firing at the flag," Vincent blurted, wheeling toward Norton. "Go behind the rocks with it." Norton turned his horse around and took it down behind the knoll. The overshots fell among the brigade, which was moving through the woods along the eastern slope of the hill. The exhausting pace coupled with the crashing

2   Parker, *32nd Massachusetts*, 313; OR 27, pt. 1, 660.

3   *OR* 27, pt. 1, 493.

projectiles "undid" several of the men in the 20th Maine, who fell out, too frazzled to keep going.[4]

Several minutes later Vincent rode around the southern face of the hill, along a descending ledge and rejoined the private. Dismounting, he left his horse, "Old Jim," with Norton, his sword still in its saddle scabbard. Walking back along the southern side of the crest, he returned a few minutes later just as Col. James Rice (44th New York), riding with his staff and Vincent's two mounted orderlies, several yards in advance of the brigade, came onto the plateau on the southeastern side of the hill.[5]

To the north, completely hidden from Vincent's view, and amidst the ear shattering concussions of exploding projectiles, Warren heard the crash of a battery coming up the hill behind him. He and his aides ran down the slope where they found Hazlett's Battery D straining up a logging trail, which came from the Leonard Bricker farm. Hazlett and Martin, having heard the racket, rode south behind the boulders and found the battery at a standstill below a ledge. A couple of the guns had tipped over in the ascent. The artillerymen righted the pieces and began pushing them by hand up the last 150 feet of the hill. Warren turned to the captain: "Martin, how the hell did you get those guns up here?" He then assisted about two dozen stragglers from Vincent's brigade, who had sheltered behind some of the boulders, manhandle one of the 10-pounder Parrots over a rock outcropping onto the crest. The Confederates wounded three artillerymen during this process, but they refused to go to the rear. Lieutenant Washington Roebling and another officer, taking opposite wheels, helped shoulder one of the guns to the crest. Hazlett and Martin managed to get four pieces in battery on the rocky summit. Three of them were positioned on the flat top of the southern side of the east-west ridge, which divided the hill into distinct northern and southern sections. The #1 gun deployed on the extreme left, followed respectively by guns three and five. Gun six went into position in a flat area below the crest on the southern side of the divide. Almost instantly, a round of some sort killed 18-year-old Pvt. Arthur H. Tibbitts, the #1 man on the first gun. Orderly Sergeant Thomas Broderick

4 Oliver W. Norton to Frank Huntington, September 22, 1888, GNMP; Nicholson, *Pennsylvania at Gettysburg*, vol. 1, 461-462; William B. Styple, (ed.), *With a Flash of His Sword* (Kearny, NJ, 1994), 77.

5 Oliver W. Norton to Frank Huntington, September 22, 1888; Nicholson, *Pennsylvania at Gettysburg*, vol. 1, 461-462.

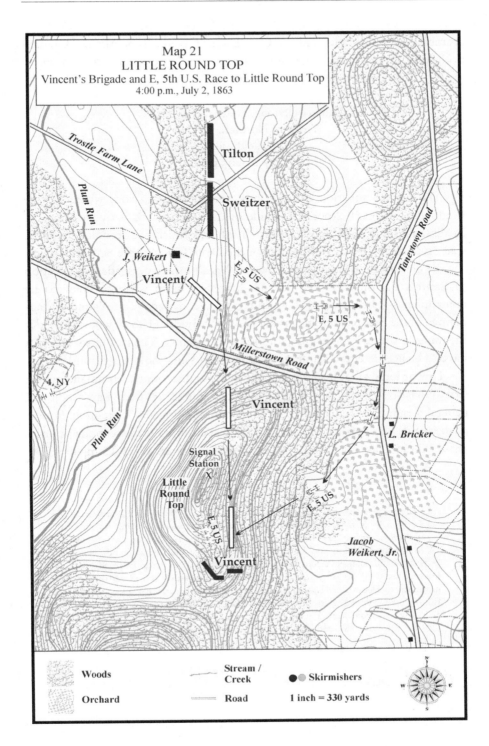

Map 21
LITTLE ROUND TOP
Vincent's Brigade and E, 5th U.S. Race to Little Round Top
4:00 p.m., July 2, 1863

crumbled with a thigh wound and Cpls. Daniel Cavanagh and Michael Graham both went down. The remaining two guns—#'s 2 and 4, having no room to safely go into battery, never made it to the crest.[6]

Hood's Division, Longstreet's Corps
Army of Northern Virginia
Warfield Ridge
4:00 p.m.-4:15 p.m.

The tactical situation did not look very promising from where Private Bradfield (1st Texas) stood just inside of the skirt of woods overlooking the Bushman farm from the west. A heavy Yankee skirmish line occupied the stone wall on the level ground at the base of the Devil's Den, some 800 yards away. On the crest of the Den, he spied part of Ward's infantry brigade and a section of Smith's Parrotts. Farther beyond, he gazed upon what he knew to be unattainable—Little Round Top and Hazlett's battery. The Yankees' flags flapped in the breeze, inviting an assault, which Bradfield knew would be under the muzzles of the Federal guns for the entire distance. The gunners would not have to be accurate to discourage men from crossing the open ground.[7]

Law ordered all of his regimental officers to dismount, a command, which Col. William F. Perry (44th Alabama) thought ill advised. Law's adjutant general, Leigh R. Terrell trotted to the front of the brigade. "Attention, Fourth Alabamians!" he bellowed. The regiment leaped to its feet, weapons at order arms. "O God, just for a half hour's rest," prayed Private Ward (Company G).[8]

---

6 Norton, *The Attack and Defense of Little Round Top*, 310, 313; Washington Roebling to Col. Smith, July 5, 1913, in "Washington Roebling's War," NYSL; Scott, "On Little Round Top;" *National Tribune*, August 2, 1894; Martin, "Little Round Top" in *The Gettysburg Compiler*, October 12, 1899, quoted; Parker, *32nd Massachusetts*, 313. Having studied the ground carefully, and knowing that 10-pounder Parrotts, on hard ground, recoiled about 10 feet with each discharge, I realized that the lower part of the hill, particularly where the 44th New York and the O'Rorke monuments are located, had enough room to place three guns. Interestingly enough, there is an Edwin Forbes painting, which shows three of Hazlett's guns in the area of the O'Rorke and 44th New York monuments. For the painting, see Editors of Time-Life Books, *Echoes of Glory: Civil War Battle Atlas* (Alexandria, 1996), 122.

7 Polley, *Hood's Texas Brigade*, 168.

8 W. F. Perry, "The Devil's Den," in *Confederate Veteran*, vol. 19, 61; W. C. Ward, "Incidents and Personal Experiences on the Battlefield at Gettysburg," in *Confederate Veteran*, vol. 8, 47, quoted.

Very shortly afterwards, Private West (4th Texas) glanced to the left and saw whom he believed to be Hood emerge from the woods on horseback about 300 yards distant. Plucking his hat from his head with his right hand, the general stood in the stirrups about 20 feet in front of the 1st Texas and shouted above the exploding shells, "Forward, My Texans; win the battle or die in the effort!" Company I, 1st Texas, under Lt. John H. Wooters, loped across the open ground, headed for the Devil's Den. The Texas Brigade bolted forward at a run the moment the bugles sounded.

Hood and his staff stayed behind the brigade while he spoke with Longstreet, who had just ridden forward to observe the assault. Once again, Hood voiced his concerns about the attack along the Emmitsburg Road and his desire to flank south of Big Round Top. Longstreet, weary of the wrangling, shot back, "We must obey the orders of General Lee." Hood wheeled about and chased after his division.

At the top of his voice, Terrell hollered, "Shoulder arms!" "Right shoulder; shift arms!" "Forward; guide center; march!" Law's Brigade advanced, leaving the 15th Alabama's water detail back at Currens' well. Companies A and H from the 48th and Capt. Henry C. Lindsey with Companies A, F, and D from the 47th sprang forward as skirmishers into the low ground along the front. The rest of the brigade soon followed. The line stepped off into the valley to the east as the last regiment formed in the line. Almost immediately, with Bushong Hill blocking his right wing, Law had the 44th and the 48th Alabama regiments fall back into a reserve position behind the 15th and the 47th Alabama regiments.

The 4th Alabama splayed around Reilly's six guns. The air zipped, snapped, and bellowed, filled with case shot and minié balls. Men collapsed by the handfuls. A minié ball slapped Private Ward across the left thigh, staggering him, but feeling the wound, he discovered no blood and limped after his company.

Colonel Oates (15th Alabama) vainly tried to convince his sick brother, 1st Lt. John A. Oates (Company G), to leave the ranks. "Brother, I will not do it," he emphatically protested. "If I were to remain here people would say that I did it through cowardice; no, sir, I am an officer and will never disgrace the uniform I wear; I shall go through, unless I am killed, which I think is quite likely." These were the last words Colonel Oates would ever hear from his brother.[9]

9   Oates, *The War Between the Union and the Confederacy*, n. 207 and 210-212, quote on 226; West, *A Texan in Search of a Fight* (Waco, TX, 1901), 94. William C. Oates to Joshua L. Chamberlain,

2nd U.S. Sharpshooters, III Corps, Army of the Potomac
The Slyder Farm

Major Stoughton, having ridden half a mile beyond the Slyder house, ran head-on into Robertson's Texans. With no protection on his right flank, he raced back to his regiment, yelling at them to fall back. The Yankees split up, some taking cover around the farm buildings, and others going to ground along the western base of Big Round Top.[10]

First Sergeant Wyman S. White (Company F) hunkered down in a corner of the stone wall between the house and the barn. With the Rebel skirmishers getting closer and more daring, he expected a major assault from a much stronger force. The 4th Alabama, along with the 5th and 4th Texas, popped into view on the ridge in front of the farm buildings. The sergeant carefully studied the mass of butternut, comparing its color to that of a moving plowed field, as it surged northeast from the Emmitsburg Road, apparently heading toward the Peach Orchard. Colonel Van H. Manning (3rd Arkansas) kept his left flank on the Emmitsburg Road, pursuant to his original orders without realizing that Work had directed the 1st Texas toward the left of the 4th Texas.[11]

In pushing east, Law's charge completely disorganized Robertson's attack, which was supposed to guide on Law's left. The 4th Texas, to the left of the 5th Texas, crashed through the Bushman's peach orchard, destroying the regiment's formation. As it cleared the trees, it rushed headlong into the waiting marksmen of the 2nd U.S. Sharpshooters. One of them cut down Pvt. Zack Landrum (Company H). The minié ball penetrated his left thigh above the knee, exited through the opposite side, and bruised the inner side of his right leg.

Colonel Work shot a hurried glance to the right as his 1st Texas swept north of the orchard. He spied Hood and his staff riding a few steps to the right front of the line having passed around the right flank of the regiment. As the

---

March 8, 1897, Schoff Civil War Collection, William Clements Library, University of Michigan, Ann Arbor, MI, 4; *OR* 27, pt. 2, 392; "A soldier in bivouac near Hagerstown, MD, July 7, 1863" in the *Montgomery Mail*, July 26, 1863; "From the 48th Alabama, July 8, 1863" in the *Daily Huntsville Confederate*, September 11, 1863; Scott, "The Texans at Gettysburg," *Sherman Register*, March 31, 1897; P. A. Work to Tom Langley, May 28, 1908, Vertical Files, GNMP; Ward, "Incidents and Personal Experience," in *Confederate Veteran*, vol. 8, 347.

10 Executive Committee, *Maine at Gettysburg*, 352.

11 Scott, "The Texans at Gettysburg," *Sherman Register*, March 31, 1897; P. A. Work to Tom Langley, May 28, 1908, GNMP.

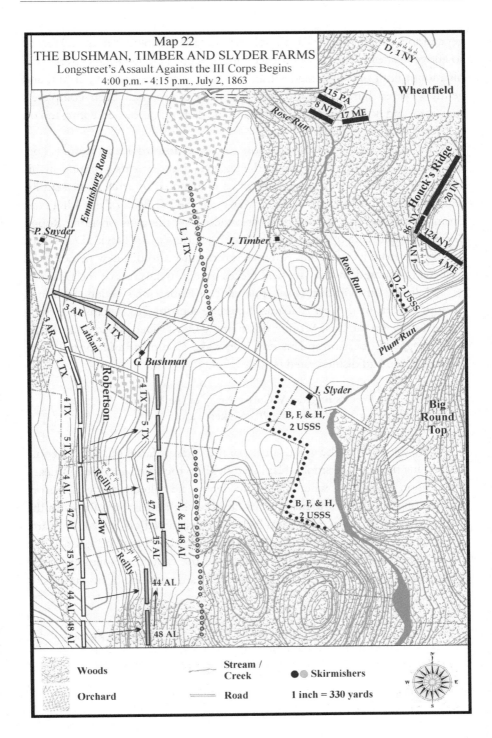

Map 22
THE BUSHMAN, TIMBER AND SLYDER FARMS
Longstreet's Assault Against the III Corps Begins
4:00 p.m. - 4:15 p.m., July 2, 1863

D, 1 NY

Wheatfield

115 PA
8 NJ
17 ME

Rose Run

Houck's Ridge

20 IN

86 NY
124 NY
99 PA
4 ME

P. Snyder

L, 1 TX

Emmitsburg Road

J. Timber

Rose Run

D, 2 USSS

3 AR

3 AR   1 TX

Latham

Plum Run

G. Bushman

Robertson

4 TX

J. Slyder

B, F, & H,
2 USSS

Big
Round
Top

4 TX

5 TX

1 TX

4 AL

4 TX

5 TX

4 AL

A, & H, 48 AL

47 AL

47 AL

Reilly

Law

15 AL

15 AL

44 AL

Reilly

44 AL

48 AL

B, F, & H,
2 USSS

48 AL

Woods	**Stream / Creek**	**Skirmishers**
Orchard	**Road**	**1 inch = 330 yards**

general spurred into the orchard, a spherical case shot exploded about 20 feet or so above his head. The impact rocked him violently and he began teetering off his mount until one of his aides leaped from the saddle and caught him and gently lowered him to the ground. Hood's left arm had been completely shattered, and no longer able to command the division, he passed command on to Brigadier General Law.

The burst drew Work's attention eastward, toward Little Round Top, where to his astonishment he spied Hazlett's four Parrotts pointing in his general direction. As was his custom when confronted by artillery, he sent his regiment toward the guns, pulling it away from the left flank of the 4th Texas. From behind the brigade line, Robertson also saw the guns on Little Round Top just as incoming rounds from the Smith's battery at the Devil's Den struck the brigade from its left front. Robertson turned toward this new nemesis and mistakenly counted another six field pieces on the rocky crest of the Den.

While the 4th and 5th Texas, pursuant to Robertson's orders, remained close to the left of the 4th Alabama, Manning sent the 3rd Arkansas hurtling northeast toward the Rose Woods, north of the Devil's Den. Meanwhile the 1st Texas dragged Robertson and his staff in its wake. Command and control in the Texas Brigade had disintegrated.[12]

Weed's Brigade, V Corps, Army of the Potomac
The John T. Weikert Farm

From the point of the woods north of the Weikert farmhouse Weed could see nothing through the smoke-blanketed fields to the south and the southeast. Intent upon finding out where he was to deploy, he halted his brigade before disappearing in the sulfuric mantle that covered the Millerstown Road. In the murk, he encountered an aide from Sickles, who ordered his brigade forward. Weed returned to his regiments. Before handing the command over to the brigade adjutant, Capt. C. B. Mervine, he told the captain to follow with the column. Weed then turned about and rode forward with one of his staffers.[13]

---

12 Polley, *Hood's Texas Brigade*, 162-163, 168-169, 173; Scott, "The Texans at Gettysburg," *Sherman Register*, March 31, 1897; P. A. Work to Tom Langley, May 28, 1908, GNMP; Zack Landrum to his mother, July 15, August 4, 1863, 4th Texas Infantry Folder, Vertical Files, GNMP.

13 Norton, *The Attack and Defense of Little Round Top*, 294, 295, 298.

V Corps, Army of the Potomac
Little Round Top
4:15 p.m.

With the guns in place on the hill, Warren briefly spoke with Hazlett, who assured the general that his field pieces would bolster the infantry's morale, despite their having minimal effect upon the Confederates. Besides, he added, holding the hill was far more important than the safety of his guns. A case shot blew up overhead, and one of its musket balls grazed Warren in the neck. Captain Hall, preparing to signal another message, saw the general recoil under the impact, and sarcastically called out, "Now do you see them?"[14]

Meanwhile, on the eastern side of the hill, Colonel Welch halted the 16th Michigan on a ledge behind the 44th New York and immediately detached Company A and Brady's Independent Company of Sharpshooters south toward the high ground on Big Round Top. The two small companies bounded into the hollow to the south and disappeared into the thick woods on the mountainside.[15] Rice turned his mount over to one of the orderlies while Private Norton dismounted and handed his reins to the other. Vincent and Rice started toward the open crest with Norton and the brigade flag not too far behind. While they surveyed the valley, Vincent directed Rice to move his regiment around the southern side of the hill toward the western slope.

"Colonel," Rice protested, "in every battle, the 44th has fought by the side of the 83rd; I wish it might be so today." "It shall be so," Vincent replied. "Let the 16th pass behind the 44th." Word went back to the 16th Michigan to proceed to the right of the line. Moving by the flank, the very small regiment reached the southwestern point of the summit, where it abruptly turned northeast. From there they spied Confederate skirmishers swarming along the northern end of Big Round Top near southern end of Plum Run gorge. As the

14 Ibid., 310, 311; Brown, *Signal Corps*, 367; Martin, "Little Round Top." *The Gettysburg Compiler*, October 12, 1899, quoted. Testimony from various sources clearly indicates that Hazlett arrived at the summit of Little Round Top before the 140th New York reached the hill. In his account, Martin said Warren spoke to him *after* the guns were in position, which would contradict Warren's statement that he helped shoulder one of the guns over a boulder.

15 Berry, Diary, July 2, 1863, USAHEC. The 16th Michigan had to have detached Company A before it went into position on the right of the line because the men advanced about half a mile before encountering the Confederates, and the company did not rejoin the regiment until July 3. Had the company gone south from the right of the line, they would have run into the Confederates before getting a half mile from the main line.

Wolverines skittered down the hill, about 60 feet below the huge slab of rock on the southwestern crest of the hill, 1st Lt. Ziba B. Graham (Company B) caught a glimpse of Rittenhouse's left section of Hazlett's guns getting shoved into battery on the higher ground behind the regiment. The Michiganders took cover among the rocks on the highest part of the rock shelf, which descended diagonally from the point at the southwestern corner of the hill into the rocky low ground to the southeast. The 44th New York fell in on its left along the same ledge, with its colors about half of the way down the hillside and its left flank resting among the boulders at the base. Colonel Rice immediately sent Company B, under Capt. Lucius S. Larabee, scrambling down the slope into the heavy woods along the foot of Big Round Top.[16]

From where he stood on the southern slope, Vincent could clearly see the Confederate infantry stepping off from Warfield Ridge in no less than three battle lines, without any skirmishers to their front. Catching the attention of Capt. Eugene A. Nash, brigade adjutant and inspector general, and pointing toward Big Round Top, he shouted at him, "Take a mounted orderly, go up on that bluff and observe the movements of the enemy." Running at full tilt with the orderly alongside, Nash clattered down the southern side of the hill and disappeared into the woods at the base of Big Round Top.[17] Colonel Walker (4th Maine) watched the New Yorkers lope down the hill and recalled Libby and Company B from the woods back to his line in the valley.[18] The command never reached the skirmishers.

The 83rd Pennsylvania continued the brigade formation, facing south, with its center bent forward in front of some massive boulders along the southeastern base of Little Round Top. Captain Orpheus S. Woodward, commanding the regiment, immediately detailed skirmishers forward. With the command, "On the right by file into line," the 20th Maine finished out the formation along the ascending ground to the immediate left of the 83rd Pennsylvania about 20 feet below the crest of the plateau from which the 16th

---

16 Oliver W. Norton to Frank Huntington, September 22, 1888. GNMP, quoted; Graham, "On to Gettysburg," in *War Papers*, vol. 1, 9-10; William H. Brown, "On Gettysburg Field, A View From Little Round Top During the Progress of the Battle," *Philadelphia Weekly Times*, May 26, 1883; Smith, *A Famous Battery*, 142; Report of Lt. Col. Freeman Conner, 44th New York, July 6, 1863, NA.

17 Eugene Arus Nash, *A History of the Forty-Fourth Regiment, New York Volunteer Infantry in the Civil War, 1861-1865* (Chicago, 1911), 144.

18 Executive Committee, *Maine at Gettysburg*, 181.

Michigan had dispatched its skirmishers. Private Gerrish (Company H) carefully studied the boulder-strewn hillside below the regiment where the sparse covering of thin oaks offered nominal protection from incoming rounds. The artillery bursts in the treetops pelted the men with branches and splinters and showered leaves down on top of their heads while the concussions drowned out officers' commands. But the shouts and screams of men in the distance reached the color guard, which, at first, could not distinguish the cries as being either Rebel or Federal. Before the line had completely formed, Col. Joshua L. Chamberlain sent Capt. Walter G. Morrill and his 41-man Company B east as skirmishers into the woods on his left flank.[19]

Tremendous small arms racket rolled toward the regiment from the right. Vincent strode over to Chamberlain and admonished him, "You understand, Colonel, this ground must be held at all costs!" As he walked away, Chamberlain told the men to aim carefully when the Rebels fell upon them. Private Elisha Coan (Company D) in the rear rank of the color guard finally recognized the fearsome "Rebel yell" reverberating above the sounds of the distant fighting. "Once heard it is never to be forgotten," he recollected. Stray rounds snapped off the foliage above his head. Leaves wafted to the ground. Twigs and branches dropped at the men's feet. Coan watched the bullets eat away the tree bark around him in descending increments until several struck a few men in the regiment.[20]

Law's Brigade, Longstreet's Corps, Army of Northern Virginia
Big Round Top
4:15 p.m.-4:30 p.m.

Farther to the south, the five skirmishing companies from Law's Alabama brigade disappeared around the southern and southwestern side of Big Round Top, completely unaware that the brigade had not followed them. The 15th Alabama moved northeast and, while crossing muddy Plum Run, immediately came under rifle fire from the Berdans who had taken cover behind a fence along the wood line on the western foot of the mountain. The green-jacketed

---

19 D. R. Rodgers to Julia, Vertical files, GNMP; Report of Lt. Col. Freeman Conner, July 6, 1863, NA; Report of Capt. O. S. Woodward, 83rd Pa., July 6, 1863, NA; Gerrish, "The Battle of Gettysburg," *National Tribune*, November 23, 1882; Styple, *With a Flash of His Sword*, 82; Theodore Gerrish, *Army Life: A Private's Reminiscences of the Civil War* (Baltimore, 1995), 107.

20 Styple, *With a Flash of His Sword*, 77, 82, 124, quotes on 82, 124.

Captain Walter G. Morrill
Company G, 20th Maine
Maine State Archives, Library, GNMP

riflemen cut down Alabamians like a harvester in a field. The Yankees killed Pvts. Alsey Kennedy (Company B) and William Trimner (Company G), while wounding Pvt. G. E. Spencer (Company D) and Lt. Col. Isaac B. Feagin. The bullet through the colonel's right kneecap would cost him his leg. Oates pushed the regiment forward without halting, then glanced behind to see the 48th Alabama crossing the bottomland, heading directly north.[21]

A second fusillade peppered his regiment. Not knowing whether he faced a company, a regiment, or a brigade, Oates pondered what he should do. He decided to eliminate the opposition to his right front and so wheeled the 15th Alabama to the right, which dragged the 47th Alabama away from the 4th Alabama, to its left, and charged the irksome Berdans.[22]

Law's Alabamians had the Sharpshooters in a bind. The 47th and 15th Alabama, in pursuing some of them up the southwestern face of Big Round Top, had passed the left flank of the Berdans at Slyder's. Simultaneously, the 4th Alabama with Robertson's Texas Brigade hit the farm head on. The incoming small arms and artillery fire completed what the orchard had started. The right wing of the 4th Texas jammed into the left wing of the 5th Texas, shattering the former's alignment, but not the 5th's.

---

21 William C. Oates to Joshua Chamberlain, March 8, 1897, UMI; Oates, *The War Between the Union and the Confederacy*, 210-211; *OR* 27, pt. 2, 392. Contrary to his later account, Oates said the first fire dropped the lieutenant colonel. I decided to go with the earlier account.

22 W. F. Perry, "The Devil's Den," in *Confederate Veteran*, vol. 19, 161; Oates, *The War Between the Union and the Confederacy*, 207 fn, 210-212; William C. Oates to Joshua L. Chamberlain, March 8, 1897, UMI; *OR* 27, pt. 2, 392.

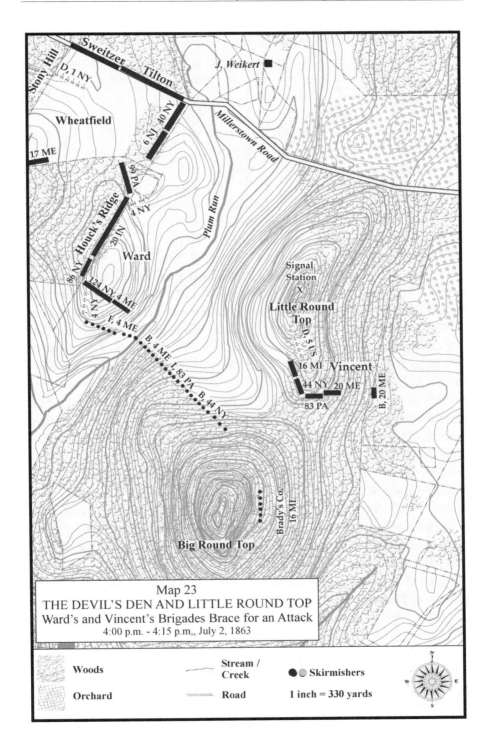

Map 23
THE DEVIL'S DEN AND LITTLE ROUND TOP
Ward's and Vincent's Brigades Brace for an Attack
4:00 p.m. - 4:15 p.m,, July 2, 1863

Woods

Orchard

Stream / Creek

Road

Skirmishers

1 inch = 330 yards

Officers from the 4th Alabama sprang to the front of their companies, screaming for the men to "Come on." Adjutant General Terrell, realizing that the charge was unraveling, frantically attempted to countermand the order. Dashing along the line, he yelled at them to calm down. Look at the 5th Texas on the left, he admonished them. See how well dressed their line is.

Canister crashed over the 4th Alabama in waves. Private Ward (Company G) distinctly heard the zip of a rifle ball to his right. From the corner of his eye saw Company I's orderly sergeant, Taylor Darwin, abruptly halt, tremble, and collapse with a bullet through his brain. At that instant, Pvt. Rufus B. Franks (Company I) darted ahead of the formation. "Come on, boys; come on!" he screamed. "The Fifth Texas will get there before the Fourth! Come on, boys; come on!" A few steps later, a bullet snuffed him out.

The Sharpshooters held their ground, hitting the Confederates so effectively with their breech loading rifles that they forced the two Texas regiments to regroup three times before they could mount a charge. The three Rebel regiments suddenly halted to fall in on front in three distinct battle lines. To the left of the 4th Alabama, the two Texas regiments untangled themselves and opened fire. The 4th Alabama pushed to within 100 yards of the southern side of Slyder's, dragging the 5th Texas with it, while the 4th Texas hammered the Yankees head on. With the Rebels on their flank, the Berdans scattered. Robertson galloped up to Maj. John P. Bane (4th Texas), hollering at him to close the regiment's right wing on the left of the 5th Texas. With the Yankees gone from his front, the major flanked his men to the right and double-quicked after the rest of his brigade.[23]

Part of Company D, 2nd U.S. Sharpshooters, fell back into the rocky southern base of the Devil's Den, and joined forces with Company F, 4th Maine.[24] They caught the 4th Texas and the 5th Texas from the left front as they careened northeast toward the stone fence facing the southern side of the Slyder lane, west of Plum Run. Private Billy O. Marshall (Company G, 4th Alabama), running as fast as he could to keep pace with William Ward, suddenly dropped to his belly along Plum Run. Ward left him there, lapping up the water like a dog. He never saw Billy again.

---

23 *OR* 27, pt. 2, 411; Ward, "Incidents and Personal Experience," in *Confederate Veteran*, vol. 8, 347.

24 Executive Committee, *Maine at Gettysburg*, 350-351.

All the while, the sharpshooters, who had taken to the woods, fired into the Texans and the Alabamians from the front. The wall brought the three regiments to a halt. Prostrated by the heat, Lt. Col. Lawrence H. Scruggs (4th Alabama) transferred command of the regiment to Maj. Thomas Coleman. As a stretcher crew picked Scruggs up and carted him toward the rear, a stray round killed one of them—Pvt. James H. Cooke (Company G). Coleman used the brief halt to send Adj. Robert Coles back toward Warfield Ridge to round up all the stragglers.

Private Ward (Company G) dropped to his left knee behind the wall. Without thinking, he fixed his bayonet and leaped over it, expecting to rush head first into a bullet. To his surprise, the Yankees had fled. His regiment scrambled into line on both sides of him and at the quick step struggled up the rugged slope. Fallen chestnut trees disrupted the formation, breaking the regiment into squads.[25]

Reforming, the Texans scrambled over the wall and careened toward the creek. Colonel John C. G. Key and Lt. Col. Benjamin F. Carter (both 4th Texas) went down. Carter died immediately, riddled with bullets. Panting from exertion, Lt. Joe Smith (Company E) dropped to his knees along the creek. He soaked his handkerchief in the water, twisted it out, and tied it around his head as the company bolted up the rise of ground in front. A minié ball crashed into his forehead and exited out the back, leaving 11 neatly-cut, blood-rimmed holes through the white handkerchief. Private West saw Lieutenant Smith fall and credited his death to wearing such an inviting target for some sharpshooter hiding in the trees.[26]

Clamoring over the large rocks south of the Devil's Den, Pvt. William E. Barry (Company G, 4th Texas) stumbled upon a terrified Yankee crammed in a crevice between two boulders. Covered with white clay, he piteously cried out in a thick German accent for mercy. Barry left him there. On the right of the line, the 5th Texas slammed headlong into a stake and rider fence. "Ten dollars to the first man who gets over that fence!" Capt. John S. Cleveland screamed, immediately prompting Pvts. J. S. Stone (Company H) and H. G. Settle (Company A) to vault over it into the woods. Second Sergeant Madison Ross of the color guard also leaped forward. "Come back to your place, Sergeant Ross,"

25 Stocker, *From Huntsville to Appomattox*, 104; Ward, "Incidents and Personal Experience," in *Confederate Veteran*, vol. 8, 347.

26 OR 27, pt. 2, 411; Polley, *Hood's Texas Brigade*, 177, 186.

the captain yelled, "color file not included." The Texans raced headlong into a large number of formidable rock ledges and formations, which further dispersed their already jumbled regimental formation. Private John W. Stevens (Company C) noted the outcroppings varied in size from that "of a wash pot to that of a wagon bed." With no Yankees or officers in sight, he pushed blindly through the woods, panting from the stifling heat.[27]

Adjutant Coles (4th Alabama) was attempting to prod his weary comrades on. A few of the overheated men did attempt to stagger after the regiment, but many, like one of the men he found and accosted in the field—he thought it was Pvt. Charles T. Halsey (Company F)—refused to respond to his pleas. Fatigue and the heat had overpowered their courage, and they lay about the field too worn out to go any farther. The adjutant had no idea how many of the veterans, after having marched over 20 miles that day and now going into action without water had succumbed to dehydration. Rejoining the regiment as the men passed around and climbed over the boulders on the northwestern base of Big Round Top, Coles, to his amazement, saw Halsey advancing to his immediate right front. "How in the world did you get here?" he asked. "Get here?" Halsey shot back. "I've been here all the time." Coles suddenly realized why the man he found had not responded when he called him by name—it wasn't Halsey at all.[28]

Law's Brigade, Longstreet's Corps
Army of Northern Virginia
The 44th Alabama and the 48th Alabama

Near the bottom of the swale below Slyder's, Law detached the 44th Alabama to the left with orders to take Smith's guns at the Devil's Den because they had a partial enfilade on their line. Colonel Perry halted the regiment, creating a gap between the 15th Alabama and the 48th Alabama. Peeling away from the brigade with a left quarter wheel, he pushed his men at the oblique on a northeasterly route toward the left of the brigade. Studying the ground to the east, he concentrated upon Hazlett's three left guns on Little Round Top then

---

27 Scott, "The Texans at Gettysburg;" *Sherman Register*, March 31, 1897, quoted; John W. Stevens, *Reminiscences of the Civil War* (Hillsboro, 1902), 114. Scott's quote for Cleveland was, "Fifty dollars to the first man who crosses the works at Round Top!"—an apparent misquote because many of the Confederates at the time referred to Little Round Top as Sugar Loaf.

28 Stocker, *From Huntsville to Appomattox*, 104.

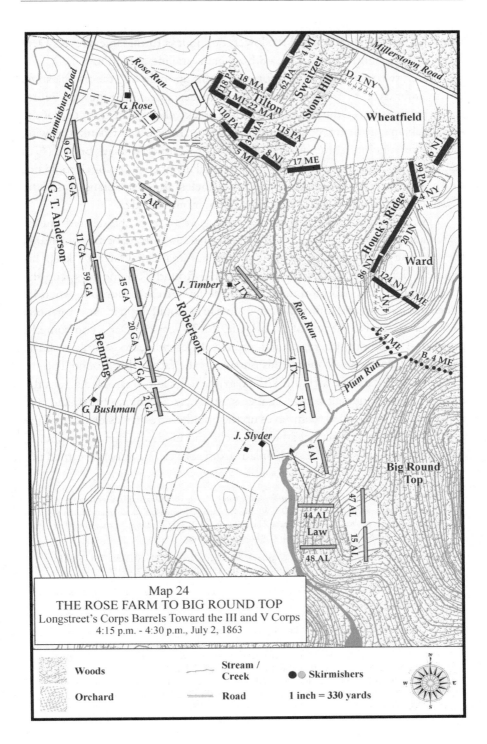

Map 24
THE ROSE FARM TO BIG ROUND TOP
Longstreet's Corps Barrels Toward the III and V Corps
4:15 p.m. - 4:30 p.m., July 2, 1863

Woods

Orchard

Stream /
Creek

Road

Skirmishers

1 inch = 330 yards

moved down the slope toward the lower, but no less formidable, Devil's Den. As an afterthought, Law sent the 48th Alabama trailing behind it.[29]

Oates' two regiments surged forward intent upon driving the troublesome enemy infantry away from its cover. The Yankees abandoned the wall before the Rebel line cleared the eastern side of the creek valley.[30] The right end of the 47th Alabama, however, collided with the 15th Alabama's left flank, throwing both regiments into some disarray. Lieutenant Colonel Michael Bulger (47th Alabama), not realizing that heat exhaustion had dropped his colonel, could not find anyone to help him restore order. Nevertheless the Alabamians chased the Federals away, sending them skittering up the mountainside.

Law observed the two regiments veering away from the desired line of march and rode over to Oates to inform him that his 15th Alabama constituted the extreme right of the brigade line. He commanded Oates to keep his regiment tight along the northern base of Big Round Top and to sweep the valley between the two mountains. Turn the left of the Union line when he struck it, said Law, and inflict all of the damage he could upon it. As the general rode away to tend to the rest of the brigade, the 25-year-old Oates confronted a problem. He did not think he could effectively left wheel to comply with the order, so he decided to continue his pursuit up the face of Big Round Top.[31]

The 15th Alabama, with the 47th Alabama to its left, scrambled across the rugged terrain in pursuit of the Yankee skirmishers. Grabbing brush and tree branches, the men pulled themselves up the boulder-strewn western face of the mountain. Yankees, ensconced behind rocks and hidden under outcroppings, sent rounds zipping over the Alabamians from above. The Rebels returned fire

29 Perry, "The Devil's Den," in *Confederate Veteran*, vol. 19, 161; Oates, *The War Between the Union and the Confederacy*, 207 fn, 210-212; William C. Oates to Joshua L. Chamberlain, March 8, 1897, UMI; A soldier in bivouac near Hagerstown, MD, July 7, 1863; "From the 48th Alabama," July 8, 1863, *Daily Huntsville Confederate*, September 11, 1863.

30 Executive Committee, *Maine at Gettysburg*, 350-351; Oates, "15th Alabama," 6-7; BCL; Perry, "The Devil's Den," in *Confederate Veteran*, vol. 19, 161; OR 27, pt. 2, 411.

31 Perry, "The Devil's Den," in *Confederate Veteran*, vol. 19, 161; Oates, *The War Between the Union and the Confederacy*, 207 fn , 210-212, quote on 226; William C. Oates to Joshua L. Chamberlain, March 8, 1897, UMI; OR 27, pt. 2, 392; John Purifoy, "The Horror of War," in *Confederate Veteran*, vol. 33, 255; White, *Wyman S. White*, 163-164. Oates' subsequent accounts state that Law gave him these instructions before he received the fire from the Berdans and that Law told him that Bulger was to stay in contact with him and to take orders from him, thereby creating a detached command on purpose. The OR says that Law contacted Oates after he drove the Federals away from the wall and that he failed to obey Law's order because he was already in his advance. No mention is made of Bulger being under his command.

only when individual Union soldiers broke from cover to claw higher up the mountainside. Midway up the rugged slope, the Federals unexpectedly ceased fire and split up—one group heading east and the other breaking to the south. When Oates' right flank came under small arms fire, he deployed Company A, under Capt. Francis Key Shaaff as skirmishers to silence them while the rest of the regiment continued climbing. The determined Rebels dragged their way to the top, leaving a number of men on the slope unconscious from overexertion and dehydration.[32]

Anderson's and Benning's Brigades, Longstreet's Corps
Army of Northern Virginia
Warfield Ridge

Pursuant to orders, Benning led his brigade to the eastern side of the woods. Smith's four guns at the Devil's Den caught his attention first. To the right front, he saw Hazlett's four pieces on Little Round Top. Glancing northeast, he saw the right half of Robertson's Brigade descending into the low ground west of the Devil's Den and, mistaking it for Law's command, ordered his Georgians to its assist.

Semmes' voice sounded above the noise. The regiments stood up and upon command, emerged from the trees in parade ground formation at the double-quick. Their heart-stopping Rebel yell rolled over the field.

Colonel Dudley M. DuBose's 15th Georgia, on the left of Benning's line, surged ahead of the rest of the brigade and closed to within 150 yards of the 1st Texas. Benning galloped ahead and brought the regiment to a standstill to allow the rest of the brigade to come on line before racing to the right to preserve the line's integrity. He wanted to bring the maximum number of his muskets to bear at the appropriate time, something a fragmented formation could not do. DuBose waited until the 20th Georgia came up on his right before continuing his advance.[33]

---

32 Oates, "15th Alabama," 7; BCL.

33 "Report of General H. L. Benning," in *SHSP*, vol. 4, 168; *OR* 27, pt. 2, 421; Hillyer, "Battle of Gettysburg," 5, GNMP. Benning counted three guns at the Devil's Den, three more on the higher ground behind it, and five more on the higher mountain to the right (Little Round Top). He also said there were two guns, which swept the gorge (Plum Run Valley)—13 guns in all. What he actually saw was Smith's battery (4 guns), his reserve (2 guns) and Hazlett (4 guns)—10 guns total. The two he encountered in the gorge were Smith's reserve section.

Ward's Brigade and Smith's Battery, V Corps
Army of the Potomac
The Devil's Den

Smith and his guns were being sorely pressed by the Confederate infantry. His four guns opened with case shot at the Rebs descending Warfield Ridge toward the woods at its base. Making every shot tell, his gunners caught "Tige" Anderson's regiments in the open. Men instantaneously went down. The left of the 9th Georgia collided with a stake and rider fence. Captain Hillyer found Pvt. John Stevens from his Company C upright, with his arms dangling over the top rail. Hillyer spied the bullet hole in Stevens' clothing but found no blood. "What's the matter, John?" he asked. "Captain," the private moaned, turning his face toward the officer, "if you will help me over the fence, I will try to go on." His blood-drained pallor told the veteran captain all he needed to know. He advised Stevens to lie down and wait on the stretcher crew, but as he scaled the fence he knew he would probably never see his comrade alive again.[34]

To the right, a shell struck the rear rank of Company K, 8th Georgia, and exploded in acting 1st Sgt. Trev Maxey's chest. It atomized his body, from the chest up, splattering the file closer of Company I—4th Sgt. Jeff Copelan— with gore from head to foot. From the next closed file 1st Lt. John C. Reid gaped at Copelan's red soaked shirt convinced he had incurred a severe wound.[35]

The 9th, 8th, and 11th Georgia regiments with the left wing of the 59th Georgia veered northeast toward the rear of the 3rd Arkansas, which had shifted toward the woods below the Rose farm. The right wing of the 59th Georgia abruptly came up behind the 20th Georgia in approaching the right of the 15th Georgia and veered from the regiment's left wing.[36]

Private Tucker (124th New York) distinctly heard Smith yell at his men by the limbers to cut the fuses for five or six second burns. One of the artillerist shouted that they had no case left. "Give them shell; give them solid shot; damn them, give them anything!" Smith yelled. The gunners slammed several shot into the trees on their left flank until the Confederates burst into the open at the

---

34 Smith, *A Famous Battery*, 103; OR 27, pt. 1, 588; Hillyer, "Battle of Gettysburg," 6-7, GNMP.

35 Diary of 1st Lt. J. C. Reid, 8th Ga., Alabama State Archives, Vertical Files, GNMP, 68.

36 Cross, *The War, Battle of Gettysburg,* Account of Capt. Benton H. Miller both in Vertical Files, GNMP.

creek bottom within 300 yards of Smith's position, drastically changing the situation. At that point, they switched to canister.[37]

Robertson's 3rd Arkansas and 1st Texas had not discharged a weapon until they descended into Rose Run valley. The 3rd Arkansas continued farther to the northeast in pursuit of the skirmishers from the 3rd Michigan, flushing them away from the stone wall on the eastern side of the orchard immediately south of the Rose house, thereby widening the gap between them and the left of the 1st Texas. The Arkansans fired a volley at the Wolverines, startling Pvt. A. C. Sims, who on the far right of the 1st Texas had not seen any Yankees from his end of the line.[38]

But rifle fire suddenly spattered into the Texans' ranks as they loped down the slope into the open ground north of the Berdans and raced across the Timber farm, heading for Rose Run. A loose rock on the top of the stone wall sent Private Sims nose-diving headfirst on the creek bank. His file leader, seeing him fall, turned to check on him and went on ahead when he saw Sims not badly injured. The jarred soldier regained his feet and stumbled back into the company. While the center of the regiment splashed through the creek heading directly for the stone wall at the base of the Triangular Field, the far left of the line dashed toward the woods on its northern end and the far right surged toward the southern end of the Devil's Den. "Forward—Double-quick!" reverberated above the regiment.

The line fragmented into squads, "everyman for himself," Private Bradfield (Company E) recollected. No sooner had he cleared the stream than a minié ball cracked loudly into the Pvt. William Langley's skull. The impact hurled the dead man heavily against Bradfield, who caught him in his arms. Laying his friend on his back, Bradfield went to straighten up when he heard the all too familiar sound of a round striking home. Glancing about he saw Pvt. Bose Perry, shot in the leg, catch himself from falling by planting his weight on his rifle. Refusing to give in, Bose pulled his wounded leg stiffly behind him and fired as he advanced.

The skirmishers of Company I, 1st Texas, went to ground behind the boulders to Smith's front and flank and began pinging rounds off the rocks around his crews. The Texans started taking hits. Second Lieutenant Henry N. Jones and Pvt. Wiley House, both from Crockett, Texas, died in the fighting, as

---

37 Tucker, "Orange Blossoms," *National Tribune*, January 24, 1886; *OR* 27, pt. 1, 588.

38 Sims, *Recollections*, 2, USAHEC.

did Pvt. Mort Murphy. A round zipped by Pvt. H. W. Berryman's right ear and grazed his brother Newt across the forehead, instantly dropping him. H. W. thought him dead, but to his surprise, Newt leaped to his feet and resumed his place on the skirmish line. H. W. tried to get him to leave the field, but Newt refused: "If every man left for a slight wound we would never gain a battle."[39]

With minié balls zipping close about his artillerists, Smith wondered how long he could hold his position. Private Michael Broderick, his battery wagoner, showed up among the guns. Having picked up a discarded weapon, he took cover behind a boulder and began firing away at a Rebel rifleman to his front. Smith accosted him for not remaining with his team. "Let me stay here, Captain," the Irishman pleaded, "sure there are plenty back there to look after the horses." Shifting into the open from one side of the rock to the other, Broderick persistently teased his Confederate counterpart by barking at him to step out and fight him face to face. "Come on now," he hollered, "if you dare, bad luck to you."[40]

Captain Charles Weygant (Company H, 124th New York) positioned himself on the western side of the ridge in front of the regimental colors to the right rear of Smith's battery, and studied the massive Confederate assault. Fierce Rebel yells filled the open hollow in front of the guns. The skirmishers, 1st Texas, 20th Georgia, and the right battalion of the 59th Georgia came on at a rush in four lines, columns of battalion. Glancing along the single brigade line to the right, the captain believed that the Rebs were going to overpower them.[41] Although the battery accelerated its rate of fire, it did not shatter the Rebel lines.

Just before it reached the stone wall at the western edge of the Triangular Field, the 1st Texas abruptly stopped, as if to regain its breath. They had inadvertently rushed into a field of friendly fire. The shells hissing in on top of them from Latham's battery on Warfield Ridge behind them created as much havoc as Smith's gunners. A burst over Company G shot a searing fragment into Capt. John R. W. Woodward's skull. Eager hands quickly hauled him from the field. Major Frederick S. Bass screamed at Pvt. J. C. K. Mullay (Company E) to mount his horse and race back to the battery to make them cease-fire. Four

---

39 Polley, *Hood's Texas Brigade*, 168-169; Sims, *Recollections*, 2, USAHEC; Smith, *A Famous Battery*, 103; P. A. Work to Tom Langley, May 28, 1908; H. W. Berryman to Mother, et al., July 9, 1863, *New York Times*, July 3, 1913, both in GNMP.

40 Smith, *A Famous Battery*, 111.

41 Ibid., 103.

hundred yards behind the 1st Texas, "Rock" Benning had determined that the Texans could not carry Smith's position and accordingly charged his Georgians to their support with the stray wing of the 59th Georgia in tow.[42]

The Rebel yell rose to a shrill crescendo as the front line of the 1st Texas surged forward. On the right of the regiment, Company C ran pell-mell into the face of a seemingly insurmountable boulder. Private Handsom H. Hendrickls, one of the tallest men in the ranks, flattened his back against the rock and, using his cupped hands as a stirrup, lifted each man high enough to get a footing on his shoulders from which they singly scrambled to the top. Once the entire company had scaled the obstacle, a couple of men pulled Hendrickls up. The Yankee skirmishers broke for safer ground at the top of the hill. All the while, the New York gunners hurled canister at the Rebels as fast as they could, without sponging the bores between rounds.[43]

When the 1st Texas got within 100 yards of Smith's guns, Colonel Ellis ordered the men of the 124th New York to fix bayonets and not to open fire until he gave the command.[44] Simultaneously, Lieutenant Colonel Work (1st Texas), discovering that the 3rd Arkansas had moved too far to the left, dispatched Lt. B. A. Campbell and his 40 men in Company G to fill the gap and to protect his left flank and rear from an enfilade. A Yankee bullet in Campbell's heart killed him instantly, but his men pressed the Yankees north.

Smith's guns ceased firing. Sheathing his sword, the distraught captain ran to Colonel Ellis, who was standing behind the center of his prone New Yorkers. With tears streaming down his face he pleaded, "For God's sake, men, don't let them take my guns away from me!" With the Confederates within pistol shot of the pieces, and almost to the rail fence near the crest of the hill, Ellis ordered the New Yorkers to their feet. They stood up and opened fire, cutting huge swaths in the Rebel ranks, staggering them.

---

42 Bradfield, "At Gettysburg, July 3," in *Confederate Veteran*, vol. 30, 225; "Report of General H. L. Benning," in *SHSP*, vol. 4, 168; "Texas Troops at Gettysburg"; Cross, *The War*, Account of Capt. Miller, all three in GNMP.

43 Smith, *A Famous Battery*, 103; Bradfield, "At Gettysburg, July 3," in *Confederate Veteran*, vol. 30, 225; "Report of General H. L. Benning," in *SHSP*, vol. 4, 168; "Texas Troops at Gettysburg," in GNMP. Bradfield erred when he said the regiment attacked Little Round Top. The regiment assaulted the Devil's Den.

44 Tucker, "Orange Blossoms," *National Tribune*, January 24, 1886; Scott, "The Texans at Gettysburg," *Sherman Register*, March 31, 1897.

The volley caught the right of the 1st Texas as it crested the ridge overlooking Plum Run and the southern end of the Devil's Den. A minié ball jerked the rifle from Private Sims' hands, sending it whirling at least 10 feet behind Company F. Stooping down, he plucked a discarded weapon from the ground only to have a second round disable it. Throwing the weapon down, he scooped up a third rifle, and followed his company toward the eastern slope of the hill, which descended into the low ground between Plum Run and the woods.[45]

Simultaneously, the rest of the Ward's brigade fired a volley into the left of the Confederate line in the woods as it topped a ridge about 150 yards from the right of Ward's position. At the first shots, Lieutenant Colonel Higgins (86th New York) glanced at his watch. It was 4:30 p.m.[46]

---

45 Sims, *Recollections*, 2, USAHEC; Hanford, "The Experience of a Private," December 23, 1885, quoted.

46 *OR* 27, pt. 1, 511.

Chapter 7

July 2, 1863
4:30 p.m.-5:00 p.m.

"My God! My God! Your major's down; save him! Save him!"
—*Colonel August Van Horne Ellis, 124th New York*

44th New York, V Corps
Big Round Top
4:30 p.m.

Captain Nash and his orderly had just reached the summit. Throwing the reins to the enlisted man, Nash scurried forward and climbed atop a large boulder glasses in hand to see what was going on. Several rifle balls pinged against the rock. With the 47th Alabama moving directly toward him, he and the enlisted man made tracks for Little Round Top. On the western slope of Big Round Top the Rebels had flushed Brady's Independent Company and Company A, 16th Michigan, farther up the mountainside.[1]

4th Alabama and 5th Texas, Hood's Division
Army of Northern Virginia
Plum Run

Meanwhile, the 4th Alabama, with the 5th Texas to its left, moved through the woods along the western base of Big Round Top toward the sounds of the fighting. A bullet zipping through Company I and clipped off the middle finger

1   Berry, Diary, July 2, 1863, USAHEC; Nash, *44th New York*, 144-145.

of Pvt. John Young's right hand as he dove behind a large boulder. Heading rearward, the former editor quipped, while holding up his wounded hand, "Well, boys, there is one consolation about this loss; I can, when this cruel war is over, set type as well as ever." The "boys" headed northeast into the skirmishers of the 44th New York.[2]

Two hundred yards south of Little Round Top, in the woods east of the Devil's Kitchen, Capt. Lucius S. Larabee and his Company B suddenly found themselves being hard pressed by the heavy body of Rebels. The concealed Yankees opened fire as soon the 4th Alabama's Company G came into sight. Private Ward and two of his comrades fell together. An electric shock reverberated through his lower body. Plummeting, semiconscious to the forest floor, Ward hastily thought, "This is the last of earth." A second later, he blacked out. His comrades returned fire and gave pursuit as the New Yorkers scattered upon command, abandoning their dying Captain Larabee upon the forest floor with a bullet through his body.[3]

Ward's Brigade, V Corps,
Army of the Potomac
Little Round Top

From his position on the hillside behind his 83rd Pennsylvania, Capt. Orpheus S. Woodward watched the skirmishers skitter through the woods along the northern base of Big Round Top, headed in full flight toward the regiment. The flash of sunlight glinting off the Confederates' bayonets as they advanced through the trees told the him that the Rebs were coming in for blood. Many of the Pennsylvanians hunkered down behind the rock outcroppings and boulders along their front while others piled up rudimentary breastworks of loose stones. Private Theodore Gerrish (Company H, 20th Maine) reckoned about 10 minutes had passed between the time the regiment had fallen in to line and the Rebels began driving in the brigade's skirmishers.[4]

---

2   Oates, *15th Alabama*, 8, BSL; Stocker, *From Huntsville to Appomattox*, 110, as quoted; Berry, Diary, July 2, 1863, USAHEC; Nash, *44th New York*, 144-145.

3   Report of Lt. Col. Freeman Conner, July 6, 1863, NA; Ward, "Incidents and Personal Experience," in *Confederate Veteran*, vol. 8, 347, quoted.

4   Report of Capt. O. S. Woodward, 83rd PA, July 6, 1863, NA; Gerrish, *Army Life*, 107.

The 16th Michigan took cover behind the rocks lining the descending rocky ledge along the southwestern face of Little Round Top. Color Sergeant Tommy Morton (Company K) jabbed the flagstaff into the hard ground and threw himself onto his belly, and then discovered that the colors would not stand upright. He began struggling with the staff, trying to keep the flag from falling to the ground. First Lieutenant William Kidd (Company C) nastily accosted Morton, demanding what he was trying to do. Color Corporal William N. Colestock (Company K) who had bellied up next to the struggling color sergeant impertinently shot back at Kidd that he should leave Morton alone because everything was going to be all right.[5]

First Sergeant Wyman S. White (Company F, 2nd U.S. Sharpshooters) took the route through the low swampy ground on the northern base of Big Round Top. Bullets cracked against the granite boulders and ricocheted off the large trees in the saddle between the two Round Tops as the oncoming Rebels spooked the Sharpshooters from cover to cover. While crossing from the woods into the huge rocks along the southern end of the hill, White encountered one of the 16th Michigan's officers. The officer was livid, on his feet screaming, "God Damn you, what are you afraid of? There ain't anything out there." Swearing vehemently, he jumped out towards the fleeing sharpshooters and tried to herd them back the way they had come.

At that moment, a volley from the entangled 4th Alabama and the 5th Texas regiments burst from the woods and sent the officer scurrying back for cover behind one of the rocks. Lieutenant Samuel F. Murry (Company F, 2nd U.S. Sharpshooters), while loading and firing a rifle, stepped up to the cowering officer and tapped him on the shoulder: he dared him to stand up and drive away the "nothing" he had gotten so exercised about moments before.[6]

The Yankees poured a horrendous fire into the 5th Texas as it bolted from the tree line below them and dashed for the boulders along the base of the hill. Private John W. Stevens (Company K) watched in disbelief as the bullets seemed to cut down every line officer but Maj. Jefferson C. Rogers. The bloodied Texans took cover and, using the rocks to steady their aim, they began dropping Yankees, who returned as good as they got. Color bearer T. W.

5 Colestock, "The 16th Michigan at Little Round Top," *National Tribune*, March 26, 1914.

6 White, *Wyman S. White*, 165. White said he fell in with a regiment about 100 feet below the crest which was lying down among the rocks and the trees near the crest. That had to have been the 16th Michigan. The 83rd Pennsylvania was at the bottom of the hill.

Fitzgerald fell, severely wounded. Color Corporal J. A. Howard (Company B) snatched the flag and also fell—killed instantly. The staff pitched forward, striking Private Fletcher (Company F) across the face. He stumbled, muttered an expletive, and headed for cover. Sergeant W. S. Evans picked up the flag and bravely took it forward, while Fletcher crouched down behind a rock, which did not afford him much protection anyway—"with good aim we could have been shot in the top of the head, either standing or kneeling," he later recollected. Captain John Cussons, Jr., Law's volunteer aide-de-camp, suddenly appeared along the line. "Boys," he coolly advised them, "aim well." "Cussons," Fletcher shouted back, "move on; you are drawing fire our way." With a determined look upon his face, the captain stepped aside, indifferent to the incoming rounds. "It was the bravest act I ever saw," Fletcher remembered.[7]

Lieutenant Colonel King Bryan (5th Texas), on the right of the line, having secured his wing, headed toward the center of the regiment to get directions from its commander Col. Robert Powell. He had to avoid great many wounded and dead officers and men athwart his path. Near the center of the line, he found Powell face down upon the rocky ground and, while rushing to his side, Bryan caught a bullet in his left arm. He found his friend alive, but the exit wound in his tunic indicated a fatal wound. Unable to help the colonel, and with blood pumping fast from his own wound, the lieutenant colonel pressed toward the left of the regiment, where he found Major Rogers, to whom he handed over the command.[8]

Sixteen-year-old Sgt. John Mosely (Company G, 4th Alabama) found his messmate Ward crumbled up in a bloody heap behind a boulder. "What are you doing here, John?" Ward feebly asked. Terribly sick, Mosely muttered, "I have fallen behind. What can I do for you?" "You can do nothing," Ward replied. "Your place is with our company. Do you not hear they have joined battle with the enemy?" Thus prodded, Mosely grimly continued forward: he never came back.[9]

---

7   Polley, *Hood's Texas Brigade*, 186; Stevens, *Reminiscences*, 114; Fletcher, *Rebel Private*, 79-80; quote on 79; OR 27, pt. 2, 413. In his memoirs Fletcher referred to Cussons as "Cousins."

8   Polley, *Hood's Texas Brigade*, 186.

9   Ward, "Incidents and Personal Experience," in *Confederate Veteran*, vol. 8, 348.

The Devil's Den

When an order to halt rippled through the 1st Texas, the Yankees had enough time to reload and shoot into them a second time. The 59th Georgia, having gotten to the field ahead of the 20th Georgia, delivered three precise drill manual volleys toward the top of the hill. The two sides exchanged fire for a couple of minutes, then the Rebels bolted forward again. "Without awaiting orders, every man became his own commander," Private Bradfield (Company E, 1st Texas) later recalled. In Rose Run Valley, someone countermanded the order and the right half of the regiment pushed forward with the 59th Georgia going in with it.[10]

This Confederate drive against Smith's New York battery lacked the steam of the first attempt. Canister ripped bloody swaths in the line. "I could hear the bones crash like glass in a hailstorm," Capt. Maston G. Bass (Company E, 59th Georgia) said. The charge devolved into a half-hearted series of lurches, measuring several steps at a time. As canister tore through Company A, one of the cast iron balls gouged a massive hole through 2nd Lt. Elijah Rich's right shoulder, carrying away the shoulder blade as it exited. The impact hurled him, unconscious, to the ground. Private William Hollingsworth pulled Rich to his feet, tossed him over his shoulder like a sack of oats, and ran down the hill to the stone wall.[11]

Smith returned empty handed from his attempt to get assistance from Brigadier General Ward. Instead of relief, Ward had directed him to hold on for another half an hour until help could arrive. With Confederate infantry desperately close to his left flank and skirmishers pressing his front and right, Smith decided to leave three of his guns where they were and to get out. While some men from the 124th New York brought off one of his disabled guns, he yelled at his remaining gunners to take the implements and skedaddle to the limbers in the valley. Then he took off at a run toward the right section. From where he stood beside some large boulders on the southern crest of Little Round Top, Lieutenant Bennett (44th New York) watched Smith abandon his

---

10 Bradfield, "At Gettysburg, July 3," in *Confederate Veteran*, vol. 30, 225.

11 Smith, *A Famous Battery*, 103, 138; Tucker, "Orange Blossoms," *National Tribune*, January 21, 1886; OR 27, pt. 1, 493, 506, 511; Polley, *Hood's Texas Brigade*, 169, 181; Sims, *Recollections* 2, USAHEC; Cross, *The War*, GNMP; Account of Capt. Miller, GNMP, quoted. NB: Sims citation is changed also.

three pieces. At the same time, he observed a number of batteries redeploying near the Peach Orchard.[12]

Plum Run Gorge

As Smith reached his remaining two pieces, he immediately swung them into action firing canister into the left flank of the Confederate troops of the 4th Texas trying to move up the southwestern base of Little Round Top. Three times, he watched their regimental colors go down. When the 4th Texas had materialized along the small pine grove on the left flank of the 4th Maine and to the right front of the 16th Michigan, it surprised all three regiments. In all the smoke and confusion, the Michiganders did not even see the 5th Texas on their right.[13]

To make matters worse for the Rebels, the 4th Texas, like the 1st Texas at the Devil's Den, had bolted into the descending fire of their own batteries along Warfield Ridge. "Confusion reigned supreme everywhere," Fourth Sergeant Val C. Giles (Company B, 4th Texas) remembered, as the regiment swung north into the boulder field at the southwestern base of Little Round Top.[14]

The Yankees had cut the regiment to ribbons during its exhausting charge. Major John P. Bane could not locate any other officers besides himself. Now rifle balls were slamming into them from the left and front. Finding himself in command and unable to take the hill unassisted, Bane screamed for his men to fall back into the pines along the southern foot of the hill. The order traveled to the right into what remained of the 5th Texas, which also fell back. A large number of the Texans took cover behind the large boulders in the northern fringe of the woods; most of the regiment retired about 200 yards. Sergeant Giles and Pvt. John Griffith (Company B) dodged behind the moss covered side of a rock about the size of a 500-pound cotton bale, according to Giles. Confusion reigned, with enlisted men and the few officers remaining bawling orders at one another. Private West (Company E), who had never gotten any

---

12 Smith, *A Famous Battery*, 103-104; OR 27, 1, 588; Ladd and Ladd, *The Bachelder Papers*, vol. 2, 1023; Bennett, "Fighting Them Over," *National Tribune*, May 6, 1886. In the OR Smith said he abandoned three guns and had the disabled one retired from the fighting. The ideal time for that would have to have been when he quit the field to tend to the lone section. Lieutenant Colonel Cummins (124th NY) said his regiment dragged off two of Smith's guns.

13 Smith, *A Famous Battery*, 104-105.

14 Polley, *Hood's Texas Brigade*, 173.

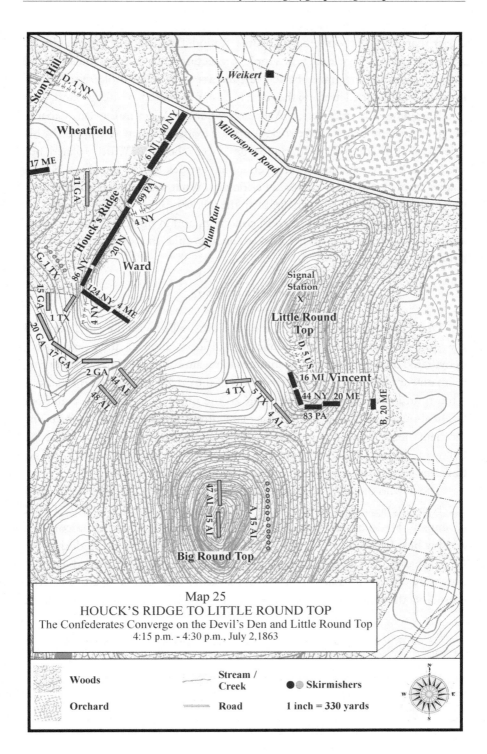

Map 25
HOUCK'S RIDGE TO LITTLE ROUND TOP
The Confederates Converge on the Devil's Den and Little Round Top
4:15 p.m. - 4:30 p.m., July 2, 1863

Woods

Orchard

Stream / Creek

Road

Skirmishers

1 inch = 330 yards

closer than 50 yards to the base of Little Round Top, thought the boulder he sheltered against provided him ample protection. But when a bullet sliced through his beard and grazed his left ear, and a second nearly took off the top of his skull and flattened itself on the rock, he instantly bolted to safer ground.[15]

Regaining consciousness, the severely wounded Ward in the 4th Alabama dragged himself behind a large rock. A private from Company A dropped by his side to ask if he could do anything for him. Go to the front, Ward groaned, but the fellow had barely moved on when a bullet struck him in the chest. Next a soldier from Company E sheltered beside him. What was he doing there? Ward moaned. His weapon had been disabled, the fellow replied. Ward pointed to his own piece: "Take mine; it is in good condition, and in my hands can never be again of service." The soldier picked up the rifle and disappeared in the smoke.[16]

Little Round Top

Upon retiring into the woods, the 4th Texas rallied with the 5th Texas and the 4th Alabama. The few remaining officers allowed their exhausted, dehydrated men to rest for a few minutes to regain some strength before urging them onward again. The bloodied soldiers of the 5th Texas stepped off without a murmur, but as they neared the edge of the timber, a considerable number "right about faced" and headed to the rear ignoring any commands to stop. The moment he wheeled about, Private Fletcher (Company F) heard someone bellowing in pain. It turned out to be a lieutenant with his big toe shot away, hollering louder than any wounded man he had ever heard before.[17]

Those who did leave the wood line opened upon the 44th New York and the 16th Michigan quickly dropping the men around Cpl. Reuben R. Turrill (Company H, 16th Michigan). Private Ervay, standing between the corporal and his best friend, Pvt. Allen A. Young, took a bullet in the head during the first exchange. Young heard a sickening crack and instinctively turned. Ervay's eyes were open, but as he tried to speak, no words came. Young could see the entry and the exit wounds on opposite sides of his comrade's skull. Turrill

---

15 OR 27, pt. 2, 411; Polley, *Hood's Texas Brigade*, 173, 177, 187; Rufus K. Folder to his mother July 9, 1863, in Confederate Research Center, Hill Junior College, Hillsboro, TX.

16 Ward, "Incidents and Personal Experiences," in *Confederate Veteran*, vol. 8, 348.

17 Fletcher, *Rebel Private*, 60.

leaned over him and unpinned the metal V Corps badge from his tunic. With the bullets pinging off the rocks and the Rebels so close, no one could leave the firing line to tend to the wounded.[18]

Sergeant White (2nd U.S. Sharpshooters) recalled he could have seen the proverbial "whites of their eyes" had smoke not obscured his vision. The suddenness of the volley stalled the charge then shattered it. Before the rifle smoke dissipated, Lieutenant Hazlett bellowed at his gunners, "Action Right! Commence firing! Load!" The left section boomed into action, discharging shells over the infantrymen's heads. The gunners were aiming at the Rebels just reaching the Emmitsburg Road. Nash, having safely returned to the 44th New York, said it was the "sweetest music" the men had ever heard and it elicited lusty cheers. Terrified by the noise, a small red fox darted from cover near the section, frantically dancing around the wheels and scurrying down into the Sharpshooters' ranks. They cheered the poor creature as it leaped in the air, twisted, turned, and bolted madly back and forth before breaking into a frantic run over the crest of the hill, heading toward Gettysburg.

Colonel Rice's 44th New York deliberately withheld its fire until the Rebels emerged into the open. At 40 yards, they unleashed a devastating volley into the Alabamians. Despite the deadly hail the Southerners pushed into the boulders part way up the southern face of the hill. Private William H. Brown (Company D) was amazed at their tenacity and effective fire. Within short order, Brown's lieutenant, Eugene L. Dunham lay dead along with Sgt. Sidney S. Skinner and Pvt. Daniel Casey. When a minié ball severely wounded suspenders-hater Sgt. Charles E. Sprague (Company E) in the left shoulder, he unsnapped his military belt before leaving the firing line. Grasping his sagging waistband and his left wrist with his good right hand, he staggered back to 1st Lt. Robert H. McCormic (Company F) and received permission to go to the rear.[19]

On the New Yorkers' right, the Texans closed in for the kill. Some of them surged up the hill into the ranks of the diminutive 16th Michigan. For a few frantic moments, the opposing lines crossed bayonets, which took out what seemed like an appalling number of the Wolverines. During the melee, a bullet

18 Polley, *Hood's Texas Brigade*, 187; R. Turrill to Daniel Ervay, July 28, 1863, Allen A. Young to Daniel Ervay, July 29, 1863, 32-33, GNMP.

19 White, *Wyman S. White*, 166-167; Scott, "On Little Round Top," *National Tribune*, August 2, 1894, as quoted; Nash, *44th New York*, 145; Report of Lt. Col. Freeman Conner, July 6, 1863, NA; William H. Brown to his mother, July 7, 1863, BU; Charles E. Sprague to Oliver W. Norton, January 16, 1910, GNMP.

sent a rock splinter slashing into Lt. Charles H. Salter's cheek, knocking him flat. Several of his men in Company B saw him unconscious and bleeding profusely and automatically assumed him dead. With the left of the 16th Michigan wavering, the badly stunned, semi-delirious Sergeant Sprague pleaded with them to stand their ground. Too stunned to move, most just stared back mutely when Colonel Vincent, his wife's riding crop in his right hand, quietly stepped up and gently tapped Sprague on his good shoulder. "That will do, Sergeant Sprague." He seemed unbelievably cool and self-possessed. "I'll take hold of this." Wading into the confused Michiganders, he began slapping them back into line with the crop, while the sergeant stumbled toward the top of the hill. The left of the line held, but the right broke and headed up the slope toward the massive flat rock on the southwestern point of the plateau behind them. Vincent leaped onto a rock behind the 44th New York. "Don't give an inch, boys, don't give an inch," he screamed. A moment later, a minié ball ripped through his hip and penetrated his groin. His brigade had been on the field about 20 minutes.[20]

Outgunned, the Alabamians and Texans quickly retired to the cover of the woods and the small arms fire in that area gradually petered off. Halting and reforming the 5th Texas in a small clearing about 50 yards south of Little Round Top, Major Rogers sadly discovered he had already lost about two-thirds of his men.[21]

At the Devil's Den the 4th Maine used the lull to drag off one of Smith's abandoned guns. When Hazlett's battery opened fire from the crest of Little Round Top, Smith took it as a signal his guns could safely retire and ordered his remaining section through the Wheatfield.[22]

---

20 Charles H. Salter to Isabella Duffield, July 12, 1863, Burton Historical Collection, Detroit Public Library; Charles E. Sprague, to Oliver W. Norton, January 16, 1910, GNMP; Nash, *44th New York*, 145; White, *Wyman S. White*, 166; Report of Lt. Col. Freeman Conner, July 6, 1863, NA; William H. Brown to his mother, July 7, BU; John P. Vincent to D. McConaughy, November 30, 1863, Vertical Files, GNMP, quoted.

21 Nash, *44th New York*, 166-167; Executive Committee, *Maine at Gettysburg*, 181; Polley, Hood's Texas Brigade, 187.

22 Smith, *A Famous Battery*, 105.

Northern End of Little Round Top

With Hazlett's battery in position, Warren mounted up and, with Reese, galloped down the rocky northern face of the hill, looking for infantry support. At the intersection of Weikert's farm lane and the Millerstown Road, they chanced upon Capt. C. B. Mervine and Col. Patrick O'Rorke and the 140th New York at the head of Weed's Brigade. "Colonel," he ordered, "Take your regiment to the left, up the hill." Not exactly sure what to do, O'Rorke nodded to the west: "General Weed and the rest of the regiments are ahead," he said. "I will take responsibility," Warren shouted back, "follow me." The men, recognizing Warren as their old brigadier, cheered him lustily, and while he trotted with the regiment toward the base of the hill, Mervine headed west along the Millerstown Road with rest of the brigade: the 91st Pennsylvania, 146th New York, and 155th Pennsylvania.

When Warren realized the rest of the brigade was not behind him, he put Reese in command of the 140th New York and spurred back up the road to get the brigade moving. Intercepting the head of the column, he told Mervine to halt and await Weed's return. Leaving Roebling behind while he backtracked to Weikert's farm lane, the general turned north, looking for more infantry. He encountered Burbank's U.S. Regular brigade double-quicking toward the hill. Satisfied that Little Round Top would be secured, Warren trotted north toward Meade's headquarters.[23]

Meanwhile Colonel Burbank had formed his brigade along the eastern side of Weikert's ridge, which he later referred to as the "rocky hill." The 2nd Regulars (201 officers and men) held the right of the line, with the 7th U.S. (116 effectives) to its left. The 10th U.S. (93 men) occupied the center with the 11th (286 on line), and 17th regiments (260 rank and file) finished the formation to the left. Colonel Day's Regular brigade remained in the lane to the north.[24]

A staff officer ordered Burbank south to support Walcott's 3rd Massachusetts Battery. The colonel attempted to relocate his troops but found part of Weed's command in his "assigned" place. About-facing his regiments, he moved back to his first position, halted, and maneuvered them into column of regiments, fronting southwest, north of the Millerstown Road. While Day's Brigade, still in column of fours in the lane, stayed inside the woods north of the

23 Norton, *Attack and Defense of Little Round Top*, 311.

24 Busey and Martin, *Regimental Strengths*, 63; Raus, *A Generation on the March*, Map V.

Major James Cromwell
124th New York
Talley Kirkland, Jr. Collection
Library, GNMP

John Weikert house, Burbank's regiments formed a new line, perpendicular to the battery.[25] The 2nd U.S. anchored the right in the corner of the woods behind the Weikert house. The 17th U.S. held the extreme left in a marshy field at the foot of the knoll, which separated Little Round Top from Cemetery Ridge.

Within a few minutes, Weed and Sykes arrived. Furious with Sickles' interference with his own directives for Weed, Sykes did not hesitate to countermand the III Corps commander's orders. So Weed immediately countermarched his brigade and sent it toward Little Round Top. Lieutenant Roebling led the column east along the Millerstown Road.[26]

---

25 *OR* 27, pt. 1, 644-645.

26 Norton, *Attack and Defense of Little Round Top*, 294, 296, 298, 303, 308, 310, 316, 319, 330. I recreated the account of Weed's arrival on the field by blending Warren's, Sykes', Case's, and Mervine's accounts together into a logical pattern. I believe that Mervine's recollection of the 140th New York being at the head of the column is correct. While Warren did not say that he rode back toward Little Round Top, it makes sense that he did and that he had to return to the head of Weed's column to retrieve it. I believe Warren did not see Weed. He said that had he met Weed, he would have taken the entire brigade, which implies that he had to have gone somewhere before Weed returned with Sykes to the column. According to Oliver Norton, Sykes did not personally order Weed's brigade to Little Round Top. Lieutenant A. P. Case (146th NY) said that Weed returned to the command with Sykes and that Weed sent the regiment toward the hill. Roebling's postwar accounts are confused and, I believe, somewhat exaggerated as to what he actually did there. Warren identified Reese as the officer who took the 140th New York to Little Round Top. Roebling took the rest of Weed's brigade up the hill and not the 140th, as he later asserted.

The Devil's Den
4:45 p.m.

Spoiling for a fight, Maj. James Cromwell rushed over to Ellis, who still remained behind the 124th New York's colors, and begged him to order a charge. The colonel, whom one of the men described as cold, ambitious, and profane, shook his head—"no"—and sent the major back to his post on the left of the line. Once again, the New Yorkers shot the Confederates to a halt, this time within 50 feet of the guns.[27]

Cromwell, with Adj. Henry P. Ramsdell, approached Ellis again, and again the colonel told him to return to his post. As he was complying, he spotted the orderlies bringing up his and the colonel's horses. Ellis mounted his big iron gray. Running over to the colonel, Cromwell also swung into the saddle, despite Capt. Charles Weygant's protests. "The men must see us to-day," Cromwell declared. Walking his horse slowly around the left flank of Company B, Cromwell wheeled to a halt in front of the center of the left wing about 200 yards from the southern point of the Triangular Field. He calmly unsheathed his blade and waited for the colonel's command. Ellis nodded. The major waved his sword twice above his head, and dug his spurs into his horse's flanks. The startled infantrymen stopped shooting and followed him with a cheer. Popping over the ridge and swarming around Smith's silent guns, they promptly shattered the Confederate line and chased them to cover behind the rail fence at the eastern side of the field.[28]

The assault dragged the 86th New York, the 20th Indiana, and the 99th Pennsylvania into the fray. Colonel Higgins (86th New York) again noted the time—4:45 p.m. On the far right of the brigade line, in the 99th Pennsylvania, Adjutant Ayars heard, "Up and charge!" The Pennsylvanians scrambled to their feet and loosed a volley, as someone shrieked above the racket, "Pennsylvania and our homes!" The brigade left quarter wheeled on the 86th New York at the double-quick, pushing the Rebels back over the northwesterly running ridge along Ward's front.[29]

---

27 NYMCBGC *New York at Gettysburg*, vol. 2, 869; Raus, *Generation on the March*, 80.

28 NYMCBGC *New York at Gettysburg*, vol. 2, 869-871; Raus, *Generation on the March*, 80; Tucker, "Orange Blossoms," *National Tribune*, February 4, 1886, quoted.

29 OR 27, pt. 1, 506, 511, 513; Ayars, "The 99th Pennsylvania," *National Tribune*, February 6, 1886, quoted.

Colonel John Wheeler rode along the rear of his 20th Indiana, encouraging his men to make every shot count. At the right of the regiment, a bullet coming in from the hollow to the west drilled through his jugular vein and exited through his right temple sending him careening to the forest floor. As Lt. Col. William C. Taylor immediately assumed command, Adj. John E. Luther barked at the enlisted men to lift the colonel onto a blanket. They hurried his corpse away, the adjutant alongside, without informing any other officer.[30]

At the Devil's Den, Ellis waited until the 124th New York cleared the front of Smith's guns and then bolted forward. Unable to slow down from the descending momentum of their charge, the New Yorkers rushed headlong into a trap. The 15th Georgia overlapped the rock fence on the north side of the field, with part of its left flank in the woods. The 20th Georgia continued the line to the south among the boulders on the southwestern side of the Devil's Den. The 17th Georgia and the 2nd Georgia struck the southern end of the Den, overlapping the rear of the 44th Alabama.

The Texans rallied in the field in front of the 15th Georgia in time to return fire. Their fusillade caught New Yorkers' left wing in the open within 100 yards of the rail fence. Before the smoke cleared no less than a quarter of the Yankees had been shot down. The Rebels admired Cromwell's superb courage: the major and his horse, its ears perked up on the alert, seemed to Private Bradfield (Company E, 1st Texas) "the very impersonation of heroic courage." "Don't shoot at him—don't kill him," he heard men around him cry out. "He is too brave a man to die—shoot his horse and capture the man." Cromwell raised a deep throated cheer and slashed his blade forward a second before a bullet bored through his heart. His right arm fell lifeless by his side and his frenzied horse bolted almost 50 yards ahead of the regiment.[31]

"My God! My God, men!" Ellis yelled above the din, "Your major's down; save him! Save him!" Private Henry M. Howell (Company E) and a handful of his comrades charged after Cromwell as his lifeless body reeled in the saddle and toppled to the ground. They grabbed his corpse and dragged it up the hill. Corporal James "Scotty" Scott (Company B) went berserk. A bullet smashed through his left wrist but even crazed with pain, he continued to load and fire.

---

30 Francis A. Osbourn manuscript, "*The 20th Indiana Infantry*," and Erasmus Gilbreath manuscript, both in Manuscripts Department, ISL; Craig L. Dunn, *Harvestfields of Death* (Carmel, IN, 1999), 183.

31 O. Bradfield, "At Gettysburg, July 3," in *Confederate Veteran*, vol. 30, 225.

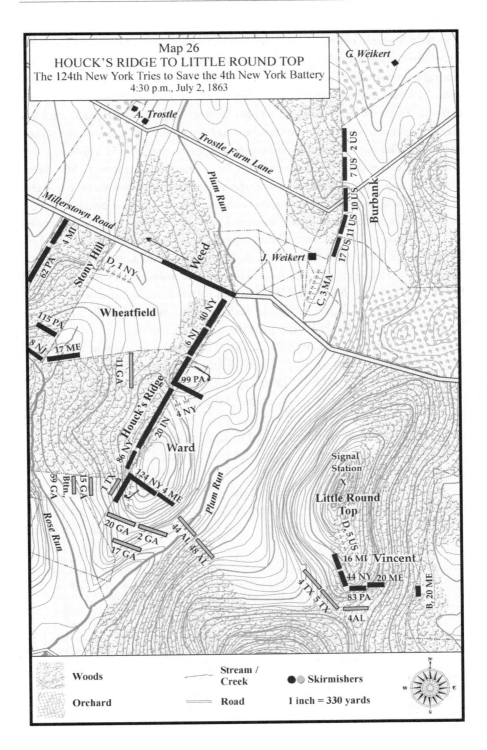

Map 26
HOUCK'S RIDGE TO LITTLE ROUND TOP
The 124th New York Tries to Save the 4th New York Battery
4:30 p.m., July 2, 1863

Woods

Orchard

Stream / Creek

Road

Skirmishers

1 inch = 330 yards

The New Yorkers rallied and surged toward the rail fence. Forcing the second Rebel line to give way, they walked into the killing fire of the third line. The 20th Georgia abruptly opened a flanking fire upon their left from among the rocks near the Den, accidently catching the right wing of the 1st Texas between them and the Yankees. The regiment's color bearer George A. Branard, with no thought for his safety, leapt into the open and waved the Texas state colors back and forth. The Georgians ceased fire and rushed to the Texans' aid.[32]

Despite the deafening turmoil, Lt. Col. Francis Cummins (124th New York), managed to back the remnant of his regiment uphill toward the battery. As he stopped momentarily to catch his breath next to one of Smith's guns, a Rebel shell broadsided the piece, slammed the wheel against him, and knocked him flat. Some of his men carried him unconscious from the field. Ellis, finding himself alone to the right front of the regiment, rose in the stirrups trying to see above the asphyxiating pall of smoke. His sword arm suddenly plummeted and his chin dropped to his chest. His body fell forward, and he pitched face first into the rocks as his frightened horse reared up and galloped wildly toward the Confederates along the rail fence near the top of the hill.[33]

Several members of Company B, 20th Georgia bolted well in advance of their regiment to the crest of the hill near Smith's now silent left Parrott rifle. The sight before Pvt. John W. Lokey took him aback. A solid line of Federal infantry had formed in the woods north of the battery. Lokey and the few men around him, after firing several random shots into the timber, hastily retired down below the brow of the ridge and melted into the regimental line. Unable to sight in on anything from there, the private sidled toward the right and started up the slope again.

Aside a boulder, he spied the mangled corpse of his colonel "Jack" Jones, lying on his back, the top half of his skull completely blown away by a ricocheting shell fragment. Nearby, a prone member of Company K advised

---

32 NYMCBGC *New York at Gettysburg*, vol. 2, 869-671; Tucker, "Orange Blossoms" *National Tribune*, January 21, 1886; Henry M. Howell to "Mother", July 5 1863, in "The 124th at Gettysburg," *Middletown Whig Press*, July 22, 1863, quoted; Polley, *Hood's Texas Brigade*, 171; OR 27, pt. 2, 421, 424-426; Sims, *Recollections*, 2, USAHEC. Bradfield said that his men killed a major and that he was literally within their ranks. The description fits that of Cromwell. Colonel DuBose (15th Georgia) spoke about the right of the brigade attacking across open ground, unprotected by trees which implies that part of his regiment was in a wooded area along the stone wall. The 20th Georgia took the guns, which were to its front while the 17th Georgia's left flank passed to the right of the battery.

33 NYMCBGC *New York at Gettysburg*, vol. 2, 870.

Lokey, "You had better not go up there; you'll get shot." Lokey ignored him. Cresting the ridge, he brought his Enfield to bear upon a Yankee infantryman when a minié ball plowed through his right thigh. Jarred as if struck by lightning, he dropped his weapon and limped back down the hill toward cover.[34]

At about the same time, someone in the 1st Texas yelled: "Here comes Barbee." Glancing over his shoulder, Private Bradfield saw Private Barbee (Company L) careening toward the western base of the Den on his small sorrel and waving his hat wildly in the air. The sorrel suddenly pitched forward onto its neck and face while the unarmed Barbee hit the ground at a run. Snatching up a discarded rifle, he rushed up to the firing line. He headed directly to a huge rock about five feet to Bradfield's left where a number of wounded Texans huddled. Springing to the top of the boulder, Barbee stood up and fired, then passed the rifle down to a wounded man, and immediately picked up a loaded weapon from one of the casualties.

For several minutes, with bullets swarming about him, "Will" Barbee continually "pulled trigger," as the wounded men handed him loaded weapons. A round to his right leg eventually knocked him off the rock, but within moments he had climbed back up and resumed firing until a second ball, in the left leg, knocked him to the ground again. Caught up in the frenzy of combat, Barbee pulled himself onto the rock and again cut loose. Less than two minutes later, seconds after he discharged his 25th round, a third ball struck him in the body and rolled him off the right side of the boulder. Landing on his back, wedged between his rock and Bradfield's, and too badly wounded to extricate himself, he pleaded for someone to help him back to his firing post. No one dared brave the incoming rounds to come to his assistance. Fully exposed to the Yankee's fire, he lay there vehemently swearing his heart out because no one would help him back into the fight.[35]

Once again, the badly-riddled 124th New York rushed forward and chased the Confederates back to the rail fence. Corporal Scott (Company B), looking more like a bloodied fiend than a human, suddenly dropped as a round bored through his chest and out his back. A startled comrade watched his arms go limp and saw his rifle clatter to the ground as he dropped like stone on top of it. The charge suddenly died out, and his comrades left him for dead. On the way back to their original position, they brought in a great many of their wounded

---

34 John W. Lokey, "Wounded at Gettysburg," in *Confederate Veteran*, vol. 22, 400.

35 Polley, *Hood's Texas Brigade*, 171-172, quote on 172; "*Texas Troops at Gettysburg*," GNMP.

and their dead colonel as well. The rest of the brigade did not retire with them. Realizing the Confederates were going to collapse his left flank unless he reinforced it, Brigadier General Ward dispatched an orderly to bring up the 99th Pennsylvania from the right of the brigade.[36]

The Woods on Houck's Ridge
4:45 p.m.–5:00 p.m.

Ward's courier arrived on the right of the brigade and ordered Maj. John Moore to detach his 99th Pennsylvania to the left of the line. As the regiment double-quicked to the rear, Lt. Col. William C. L. Taylor (20th Indiana) pulled Capt. Charles A. Bell and his Company B from the left of the Hoosier position. Double-quicking behind the regiment, Bell passed rapidly north. On the way, he hauled Company H away from the right of the line. The two companies sprayed west into the gap left by the Pennsylvanians. Their right rested on the stone wall east of the 17th Maine. The left overlapped the right front of the regiment.

Shortly thereafter, Taylor rode up to Capt. Erasmus C. Gilbreath, who commanded Company I, the color company. "Gil," he painfully rasped, "You will have to take charge of the line, as I am wounded." With that, he abruptly walked his horse toward the rear, away from the firing. Unable to find Adjutant Luther, Gilbreath seized the colonel's abandoned mount and swung into the saddle. He quickly discovered that he could not control the frightened animal, so he dismounted and turned it loose.

He rapidly trooped the rear of the line on foot, stopping behind Company C. A minié ball slammed into 1st Lt. Ezra B. Robbins, hurling him into the captain's arms. Gilbreath hauled him to the backside of a nearby tree, about 10 feet behind them, and left him there to die from his chest wound.[37]

The Devil's Den

Captain Weygant, the fourth senior captain, found himself in command of a skirmish line-strength 124th New York. He had the major's and the colonel's bodies placed on a large boulder behind the regiment, where everyone could see

---

36 NYMCBGC *New York at Gettysburg*, vol. 2, 870-871; OR 27, pt. 1, 511.

37 E. C. Gilbreath Manuscript, ECL.

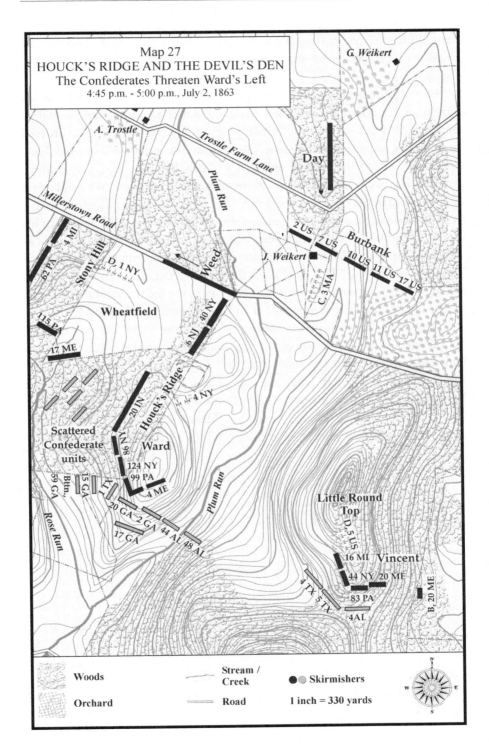

Map 27
HOUCK'S RIDGE AND THE DEVIL'S DEN
The Confederates Threaten Ward's Left
4:45 p.m. - 5:00 p.m., July 2, 1863

them. With a little more than 100 of his 240 souls left, he scattered his men by squads to whatever cover was available to fend off another expected Rebel assault.[38]

With Confederates spilling around his right flank, Walker had quickly withdrawn his outnumbered 4th Maine about 100 yards into a hollow immediately north of Smith's former position. Halting his men, he ordered them to fix bayonets and charge. Moving at the right oblique, the New Englanders scaled the hillside and threw themselves headlong into Smith's abandoned guns, pushing the Rebels down the opposite slope. Walker, having lost his horse in the charge, went down with a hamstrung Achilles tendon in a hand-to-hand fight, while a Reb yanked his sword from his grasp. Several of his men bolted into the fray, rescuing him and his sword. The fighting ebbed just as suddenly as it began. The two sides temporarily untangled themselves. The 4th Maine fell in with the 124th New York, the colors of the two regiments standing side by side. Volunteers from the 86th New York carried the wounded Colonel Higgins. He turned the regiment over to Lt. Col. Jacob H. Lansing.[39]

The 99th Pennsylvania, coming in from the right of the brigade, materialized on the left of the New Englanders. By then the 124th New York had thinly spread itself out more than 200 feet into the woods on Houck's Ridge. Hinging the left wing on the colors, Major Moore refused the Pennsylvanians' line by the left, to face south down the hillside toward Plum Run.[40] Prayers rushed through Color Sgt. Harvey M. Munsell's mind as he stood at the apex with the national colors and his eight-man color guard.[41]

---

38 NYMCBGC *New York at Gettysburg*, vol. 2, 870-872.

39 Executive Committee, *Maine at Gettysburg*, 182, 194; Tucker, "Orange Blossoms;" *National Tribune*, January 21, 1886; OR 27, pt. 1, 511.

40 Executive Committee, *Maine at Gettysburg*, 182; Smith, *A Famous Battery*, 140; J. E. Smith, "From Comrade Tucker," *National Tribune*, February 4, 1886.

41 Theodore F. Rodenbough, (ed.), *Uncle Sam's Medal of Honor* (New York, 1886), 188.

Chapter 8

July 2, 1863
4:00 p.m.–5:00 p.m.

"I am going to have one more shot at them, leg or no leg."

—*Private John Krouse, Battery G, 1st New York Light*

1st Volunteer Brigade, Artillery Reserve, Army of the Potomac
Granite School House Road
4:00 p.m.–4:15 p.m.

Shortly after 4:00 p.m., an aide galloped up to the wall on the left of Bigelow's 9th Massachusetts Battery, calling for Maj. Freeman McGilvery, who was commanding the 1st Volunteer Brigade. "Captain Randolph, Chief of Artillery, Third Corps sends his compliments and wishes you to send him two batteries of light twelves." Turning about, McGilvery called out, "Captain Hart and Captain Bigelow, take your batteries and report to Captain Randolph." As the bugler sounded "Attention," Bigelow's men jumped to their feet, cleared the grain off the limbers and away from the horses, and prepared for action. Hart's 15th New York Battery also readied their teams. First Lieutenant Scott (Battery E, 5th Massachusetts) broke off his conversation with 1st Lt. Christopher Erickson of Bigelow's 9th about the outcome of the battle. Erickson immediately mounted up and trotted away with his section while McGilvery spurred ahead of the batteries to scout the ground.[1]

---

1 Baker, *9th Massachusetts Battery*, 56, quoted; Charles W. Reed to Mother and Sister, July 11, 1863, Robert L. Brake Collection, USAHEC; Eric A. Campbell, *"A Grand Terrible Dramma" From Gettysburg to Petersburg: The Civil War Letters of Charles Wellington Reed* (New York, NY, 2000), 117; Freeman McGilvery, *"Part taken by the 1st Brigade Vol. Div. Arty. Res, et al,"* Freeman McGilvery Papers, GNMP. Reed clearly states that during the battle McGilvery was a major

Within minutes, the major also sent for Phillips' 5th Massachusetts Battery. A staff officer galloped up to Phillips' battery and ordered it forward. Throwing encumbrances aside, the gunners stripped their limbers and caissons for action before climbing into their dangerous perches on top of the ammunition boxes. Leaving the caissons behind, the captain raced ahead with the other officer. Lieutenant Francis W. Seeley's Battery K, 4th U.S. Artillery followed them.[2]

III Corps, Army of the Potomac
The Klingle Farm

Carr's Brigade stepped over the demolished fence along its front and advanced in formation toward the Klingle farm. Part way across the field, Carr detached 100 men from the 16th Massachusetts to secure the Klingle cabin. They burst into the cabin and began knocking the chinking out between the logs to create firing loopholes.[3]

The 73rd New York considered itself relieved and double-quicked from the Klingle house southeast to the right of the 120th New York. The regiment did not stay long. Colonel William Sewell, whose pickets from the 5th New Jersey deployed as far as the Spangler buildings, sent a runner to Brigadier General Humphreys informing him that the Rebels were pushing back his pickets and that two battle lines had formed behind them preparing for an attack. Humphreys, responding to Sickles' request for another regiment to reinforce the Peach Orchard, dispatched the 73rd New York. The regiment ran along the front of the 120th New York, crossing the Trostle lane to Brewster's Brigade line behind the orchard. Brewster immediately sent the regiment forward about 60 yards to the top of the ridge in the orchard to support Graham's Brigade. In the next instant, Humphreys detailed his aide Lt. Henry C. Christiancy to Hancock requesting a II Corps brigade, if at all possible, to assist him.[4]

---

and received a promotion after the fighting. This is why the majority of the official reports refer to him as a major, not as a colonel.

2   Regimental Committee, *Fifth Massachusetts Battery*, 624 and 629; Ladd and Ladd, *The Bachelder Papers*, vol. 1, 166, 607.

3   OR 27, pt. 1, 533, 543; W. Bartlett, *History of the Twelfth Regiment New Hampshire Volunteers in the War of the Rebellion* (Concord, NH, 1897), 121.

4   OR 27, pt. 1, 559; Westbrook, "On the Firing Line," *National Tribune*, September 20, 1900.

Carr's regiments went to ground about 20 feet from the Emmitsburg Road. The 11th New Jersey occupied the small peach orchard south of the barn. The 12th New Hampshire held the apple orchard north of the barn. The 16th Massachusetts lay on the open ground between the apple orchard and the Rodgers house. The 11th Massachusetts was on the road bank immediately east of the Rodgers house with the 74th New York to its right. The 26th Pennsylvania crossed the farm lane to the right of the 74th New York and went prone behind the east bank of the pike.

Fourteen-year-old Josephine Miller, Peter Rodgers' enterprising granddaughter, baked bread for the 11th Massachusetts and also sold chickens to men eager to supplement their rough diets. Her grandfather, who Lieutenant Blake (11th Massachusetts) mistook for her husband, "whiningly said it was strange that they could not fire over his dwelling, and not through it." "What will you do when the battle begins?" Lieutenant Colonel Baldwin asked Josephine. "Is there really going to be a battle? Where shall we go?" she replied. "Yes, we shall have a battle right here," came the reply, "and you will either have to go to the rear or down the cellar, if you have one." Josephine considered: "Yes, we have a small cellar. I think we will stay." Lieutenant Blake momentarily absorbed the beauty of his surroundings. "A herd of thirteen or fourteen cows was quietly grazing upon the field; flocks of tame pigeons sat upon the dovecots and sheds," he later wrote.[5]

Sickles' Artillery Position, III Corps, Army of the Potomac
The Peach Orchard

A spherical case round exploded amidst Clark's battery, to the right of the first caisson and within a few feet of Private Hanifen, who was holding the bridle of the left wheel horse. One animal immediately floundered—dead. Searing hot metal gouged the flank of the right front horse while shrapnel and musket balls bloodied the shoulders of the pair behind it. At the same instant, a fragment gutted the wheel horse and tore off one of its forelegs. The rest of the terrified team broke free of the other two drivers and took off at a frantic gallop.

---

5   Charles Carlton Coffin, *Eyewitness to Gettysburg* (Shippensburg, PA, 1997), 73-74, quote on 73; Thomas D. Marbaker, *History of the 11th New Jersey Volunteers* (Highstown, NJ, 1990), 97; *OR* 27, pt. 1, 543, 553; Blake, *Three Years in the Army*, 206-207; Blake, *"Personal Reminiscences of Gettysburg,"* 9, USAHEC. Coffin claims the quoted conversation came from a personal interview with Josephine Miller.

Executing a "fine 'left about'," they dragged the hapless Hanifen and his maimed animal with them. Fifty yards from the line of caissons, the team abruptly stopped, throwing Hanifen and his now dead horse down in a heap. Corporal Charles Banks with Pvts. George Williams and Peter Vandine helped the shaken Haifen replace the caisson's broken pole and cut the dead horses free of their harnesses. The battery's farrier, Pvt. John Fairchild, brought up spare horses, and the men harnessed a pair of them and hauled the team back into the line.[6]

Colonel Bailey (2nd New Hampshire), probably checking to see if many of his men were among the scores of wounded and demoralized soldiers streaming to the rear, had the company officers take roll: in the midst of which a shell struck Cpl. Thomas Bignall (Company C) square on his back. The impact drove his cartridge box into his body where the heat from the projectile ignited the cartridges. They "popped" like a string of lit firecrackers, Pvt. Martin A. Haynes (Company I) recalled. Within seconds, another shell wounded three more men in his company, likewise setting off Sgt. James M. House's cartridge box. Those rounds also disabled and killed a number of Brewster's New Yorkers behind them.[7]

III Corps, Army of the Potomac
The Emmitsburg Road,
From the Sherfy Farm to the Codori Farm

To the north, while under fire from a Confederate battery on Seminary Ridge, Lt. Francis W. Seeley's six 12–Pounder Napoleons in Battery K, 4th U. S. Artillery, wheeled into line on the east side of the Emmitsburg Road to the immediate right of Klingle's log cabin in front of the 12th New Hampshire. Seeley lucked out when a shell fragment only bruised his left thigh without disabling him. Humphreys, whose division lay behind the house, calmly strode among the pieces, helping direct their fire and hoping that Seeley could knock out some of the guns, which were bloodying his prone regiments. Within about 15 minutes, the artillerists had indeed silenced the Confederate battery.[8]

---

6 Hanifen, *Battery B*, 69, 71-72.

7 *OR* 27, pt. 1, 559, 573-574; Haynes, *2nd New Hampshire* (1896), 172.

8 Raus, *Generation on the March*, 166; Ladd and Ladd, *The Bachelder Papers*, vol. 1, 563, 607; *OR* 27, pt. 1, 590; Cavada, Diary, July 2, 1863, FSNMP.

The men in the 11th Massachusetts held their ground despite the enfilade of solid shot. Blake watched the lethal missiles ricochet across the ground like stones skipping on the water. Several plowed into the Rodgers house, one shattering Josephine Miller's stove, which sent her scurrying into the cellar.[9]

Sickle's Position, III Corps
The Peach Orchard

The Yankees along the southern face of the orchard saw a lengthy line of Confederate skirmishers, followed by Hood's infantry brigades closed en masse, break from the cover along Seminary and Warfield Ridges. Private Alfred J. Craighead (Company K, 68th Pennsylvania) popped his head up at the sound of the guns and saw the Rebels heading for the southern end of the Federal line.[10]

The Rebels also attracted Colonel De Trobriand's attention. He immediately dispatched the 5th Michigan forward to relieve his skirmish line, as the Rebs pushed it back from the Emmitsburg Road. Colonel Pulford herded his men into the Rose Woods. With bullets sweeping through his ranks, he flanked his regiment to the left and formed a line along the northern bank of Rose Run to the right of the 8th New Jersey, facing south. With the bulk the regiment under cover, near the point of the woods closest to the Peach Orchard, he detached one company from each flank and a third one toward the springhouse on the Rose farm to the west.[11]

Simultaneously, Sweitzer halted his 2nd brigade opposite the northwest corner of the stony hill on the Millerstown Road and had the men lie down. From where he lay, Private Houghton (4th Michigan) noticed Battery B, 1st New Jersey, to the northwest and the 17th Maine in the brush along the crest of the Stony Hill. Unable to return fire, the 4th Michigan helplessly lay on its arms and absorbed lead. The man on Houghton's left took a bullet in his right arm which split his sleeve from the wrist to the elbow and splattered Houghton's

---

9   Blake, *Three Years in the Army*, 207; Blake, "*Personal Reminiscences*," 13, USAHEC.

10 OR 27, pt. 1, 483; Nicholson, *Pennsylvania at Gettysburg*, vol. 1, 393.

11 Monument Commission, *Michigan at Gettysburg*, 101-102; G. W. W. to the Tribune, July 5, 1863, GNMP. The monument for the 5th Michigan appears to be a second line position. De Trobriand and J. C. Hamilton (110th Pennsylvania) clearly state that the two regiments served side by side along the creek.

face with fragments of cloth. Wounded men continually staggered through the line, nearly all admonishing the Wolverines to "go in and give them hell."[12]

De Trobriand's Brigade
III Corps, Army of the Potomac
The Wheatfield

Colonel De Trobriand, cognizant of the tremendous gap between Ward's right flank and the Peach Orchard, committed the 17th Maine into the Wheatfield. He instructed Lt. Col. Charles B. Merrill to connect his left with Ward's right. Moving the regiment by the left flank, Merrill maneuvered it into the low ground along a stone wall, which extended almost the entire length of the southern edge of the field. The north-south rail fence, which intersected the wall near the eastern base of the Stony Hill, separated the four right-hand companies from the rest of the regiment as it deployed into line. Lieutenant Verrill's Company C, on the right of the line, found itself in the woods without any cover. With the grassy field in the swampy low ground on the west end of the Wheatfield behind him, he deployed his men in line facing south.[13]

A short time later, under orders, de Trobriand had Capt. Joseph C. Briscoe pull the 40th New York east along the Millerstown Road until it reached the Stony Hill, at which point the regiment veered southeast into the Wheatfield Cutting across the front of Winslow's Battery D, 1st New York, the regiment crossed over the stone wall on the eastern side of the field and went into line on the left of the 6th New Jersey, northwest of Captain Smith's left section of artillery. One of the enlisted men in the 40th New York wondered how well the

---

12 *Houghton Journal*, 13-14, UM. Houghton's narrative contains a sizeable gap. The regiment, which the 4th Michigan relieved in the north end of the strip of woods on the west side of the Wheatfield, had to have been the 17th Maine. At this point, however, Houghton's recollections merge what appears to have been a series of events together. The 17th Maine did evacuate the line from the front of the 4th Michigan but did not go to Little Round Top. Nor did Bigelow's battery move to Little Round Top.

The reference to the artillery unit and the infantry moving toward Little Round Top happened after the 4th Michigan and Sweitzer's brigade evacuated the Rose Woods. Houghton is talking about an action later in the day when the Confederates forced de Trobriand and Winslow's battery from the field. He was present at both actions and appears to have blended them together into one event in his later memories. The next part of his journal refers to the second attack of Sweitzer's brigade, which took the regiment across the Wheatfield into the woods at the southern end of the Stony Hill.

13 OR 27, pt. 1, 522; Ladd and Ladd, *The Bachelder Papers*, vol. 1, 1,011-1,012.

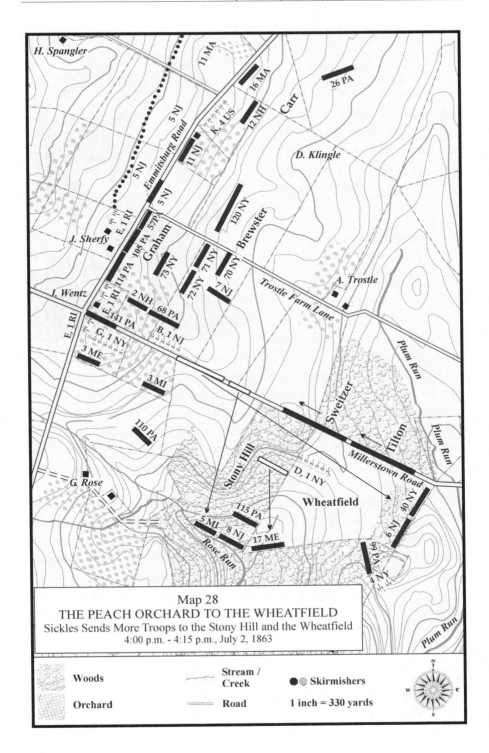

Map 28
THE PEACH ORCHARD TO THE WHEATFIELD
Sickles Sends More Troops to the Stony Hill and the Wheatfield
4:00 p.m. - 4:15 p.m., July 2, 1863

Woods

Orchard

Stream / Creek

Road

Skirmishers

1 inch = 330 yards

Capt. John Bigelow
9th Massachusetts Battery
Library, GNMP

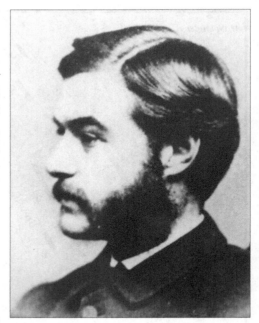

hodge-podge regiment would perform, considering that its 600 men came from the 38th, 55th, 87th, and 101st New York as well as from the original organization.[14]

Bigelow's Battery,
1st Volunteer Brigade
Army of the Potomac
Near the Trostle House
4:15 p.m.

Bigelow halted the 9th Massachusetts Battery in the field southeast of Trostle's and ordered the battery into double column. The battery formed by sections (two guns, limbers, and caissons per section) with the right section at the front, followed respectively, by the middle and the left section. The odd numbered gun crews were the right column and the even on the left. Sergeant Levi Baker believed the captain did that to save time when they renewed the advance. Shells shrieked overhead, and a number of them exploded in front of the teams as they stood there awaiting orders—a trying time for the "green" artillerists.

First Lieutenant Erickson and 2nd Lt. Richard S. Milton asked permission from Bigelow to ride to the line of battle. Bigelow nodded: "They will see enough before night," he remarked to Jr. 1st Lt. Alexander H. Whitaker, and Sergeant Baker, overhearing the conversation, noted how calm everyone seemed although none of them had ever been in battle before.

Many of them, he believed, knew they would never be together again. One of the men approached Sgt. George Murray and asked that if he were killed, "to get my watch and money, and send [it] to my wife; and there's seven dollars that

<hr />

14 OR 27, pt. 1, 526; Ladd and Ladd, *The Bachelder Papers*, vol. 3, 1,980-1,981; File Closer to [editor], August 29, 1863, *New York Sunday Mercury*, September 6, 1863.

[Henry] Fen owes me, get that too." Presently the order came to move forward. The battery pulled a short distance beyond the Trostle house, and then turned left through the gate. The left piece had not gotten into the field before Bigelow shouted, "Forward into line, left oblique. Trot!" And a few feet beyond the fence: "Action front!" The battery swung into line on the run.[15]

Phillips' Battery, 1st Volunteer Brigade
Army of the Potomac
Near the George Weikert House

Phillips and the staff officer quickly out-distanced the rest of Battery E. First Lieutenant Scott had his hands full trying to keep his lead section within sight of the captain. As it neared Trostle's Lane, an officer galloped up to him, shouting, "The Battery is wanted at once on the Round Top." Without stopping, Scott replied: "There is my captain ahead. I know no other," and continued toward the Trostle farm.

Two men in the battery got left behind in the rush. Rumbling onto the rocky farm lane, Cpl. John Agen lost his balance and fell into the road, breaking his arm in two places. Private John Moudorf also ended up in the road but escaped injury. Halfway between the farmhouse and the Emmitsburg Road, the horse teams swung abruptly and cut cross-country toward the Millerstown Road.[16]

Sweitzer's Brigade, V Corps
Army of the Potomac
The Stony Hill

After conferring with both Barnes and Sykes, Colonel Sweitzer followed Barnes' directive to anchor his right flank on the Millerstown Road and to extend his line south. As the 17th Maine flanked south, the 4th Michigan, at the head of the column, initiated the maneuver. At the command, "On the right, by file into line," the regiments, in succession, faced to the left, shifted from four ranks into the required two rank battle line, and wheeled into front, facing west. The extension of the brigade line threw the 32nd Massachusetts on the far left,

15 Baker, *9th Massachusetts Battery*, 56-57.

16 Regimental Committee, *5th Massachusetts Battery*, 629, 630, 637, quote on 629.

down the southern slope of the hill into the open space along the creek bottom to the right rear of the 110th Pennsylvania. The brigade had hardly assumed its post when Tilton's brigade began crossing its front to deploy among the rocks in the descending point of woods facing the Rose farm.[17]

Under a canopy of shellfire, most of which passed overhead, the 118th Pennsylvania led the advance from the Millerstown Road. As the regiment left the road bank, an orderly, leading a beautiful black horse from the field, passed near Donaldson. Whose horse was it? Donaldson asked. It belonged to Capt. John B. Fassett, one of Birney's aides responded, who had switched to another horse to keep this one from being injured. The words had barely escaped his lips when a shell fragment ripped off one of the horse's hooves.

Before Donaldson had time to dispatch the wounded animal, Capt. Lemuel L. Crocker (Company G) approached and asked what he thought of the maneuver. Judging from the successive Rebel yells resounding in the distance and the severe small arms fire to the right front, Donaldson told Crocker, he thought the regiment was going to fill a void in the line or to save part of it from collapse.[18]

Federal Skirmishers, III Corps, Army of the Potomac
The Rose Farm

The 110th Pennsylvania and the skirmishers from the 3rd Michigan did not wait for the 3rd Arkansas' onslaught. The Michiganders fell back until the left flank rested around the Rose farm buildings and the right on the left flank of their regiment at the southeast corner of the Peach Orchard. Simultaneously, the 110th Pennsylvania went into line behind them not attempting to stay on the field. As the skirmishers of the 5th Michigan rushed into the farmyard unobserved by the Pennsylvanians, the 110th executed a "left in front" around a cluster of trees on the edge of the woods behind them and raced into a small open area in the bottom of the ravine on the north side of the creek. Facing south, they anchored their right flank on the left flank of the 5th Michigan's reserves. Sergeant James C. Hamilton (Company C, 110th Pennsylvania) did

---

17 *OR* 27, pt. 1, 607, 610.

18 Survivors' Association, *The Corn Exchange Regiment*, 241; Aiken, *Inside the Army of the Potomac*, 301.

not like the open defile in which Lieutenant Colonel Jones had placed the regiment.[19]

The 3rd Michigan, and its skirmishers, retired to the left flank of the 141st Pennsylvania while the 3rd Maine moved to the right front of the Pennsylvanians. The 5th Michigan's skirmishers occupied the Rose farm and extended their line from the Rose springhouse to the right flank of the Berdan's, north of Slyder's. The men near the buildings poured a galling fire into the flank and the rear of the 3rd Arkansas as it crashed through the orchard south of the house, heading for the woods. The 5th Michigan's skirmishers along the stone wall on the opposite side of the orchard shot the Confederates to a standstill. For a minute or two both sides slugged it out, until, faced with capture by overwhelming numbers, the Yankees abandoned their position for the safety of the woods behind them.[20]

The Confederate attack startled a squad from the 8th New Jersey on the top of the ravine east of the Rose farm, as they gathered up fence rails to protect their line. Screaming the alarm, they bolted into the woods to warn the regiment of the imminent danger. As a Rebel yell rent the air, a herd of panic-stricken pigs and cows thundered into the ravine around the 110th Pennsylvania, which had not yet formed the right wing on the line. From their concealed position in the creek bottom to the right front of the 8th New Jersey, the soldiers of the 110th could see feet and pant legs suddenly appearing near the edge of the woods above them.[21]

From his elevated position on the southern side of the Stony Hill, Private Carter (22nd Massachusetts) saw the Confederates' "usual dirty, grayish, irregular line advance into the woods." Colonel Manning halted the 3rd Arkansas just as it reached the boulders on the ledge overlooking Rose Run. Taking hits on both his left flank and from the fields behind him, he immediately yelled for the regiment to execute a "front to rear on the first company." The horrendous noise of the artillery and musketry drowned out the command. He ran from company to company pulling back the left wing of the

---

19 Hamilton, "Recollections," 121-123, CWL; Ladd and Ladd, *The Bachelder Papers*, vol. 3, 1,981, 1,983. Hamilton said the regiment formed on the left of the 5th Michigan. The monument is in the hollow described by Hamilton.

20 Hamilton, "Recollections," 121, CWL; Ladd and Ladd, *The Bachelder Papers*, vol. 1, 20, vol. 3, 1,981.

21 Toombs, *New Jersey Troops*, 219; Hamilton, "Recollections," 121, CWL.

regiment. Within minutes, he had repelled the skirmishers from the 5th Michigan and had advanced the regiment into the woods to the edge of the precipice above Rose Run. Again the Yankees enfiladed his flank from the Stony Hill and the Rose Woods, and again Manning was forced to withdraw about 75 yards to the stone wall on the eastern side of the orchard, where he continued slugging it out with the obstinate westerners.[22]

The fences along the line of advance had disrupted Anderson's formation, and artillery fire from the Peach Orchard had split the 59th Georgia in half and forced it to realign. The 11th Georgia pressed on well ahead and burst into the Rose Woods, unseen by the hard-pressed 3rd Arkansas. In the process, Col. Francis H. Little's Georgians flushed the skirmishers away from Manning's front. Halting just inside the tree line, the 11th Georgia cut loose, delivering a couple of volleys blindly into the trees. Before the smoke cleared, Little sent his line forward. Sloshing through the marshy, rock strewn bottomland, the 11th Georgia veered east toward Ward's waiting brigade. Manning extended his regiment to double its length by placing the two ranks in skirmish order, instructing the left company to cover his front. Then he charged back to the rock ledge.[23]

The 8th New Jersey
The Wheatfield
4:15 p.m.-4:30 p.m.

As Manning's infantry opened upon their prone line from the top of the hill, the 8th New Jersey found itself in an untenable situation. They could not effectively return fire as the Rebels poured a terrible plunging fire into them. Within 10 minutes, the regiment lost about 40 of its officers and men, most to head, back, and leg wounds. A few men staggered from the line. Lieutenant Robert S. Brown (Company A) watched 2nd Lt. Andrew J. Mandeville, till then trying to keep his Company D in the line, suddenly turn and run. Adjutant

---

22 Carter, *Reminiscences, War Papers*, vol. 2, 167; Ladd and Ladd, *The Bachelder Papers*, vol. 1, 20; *OR 27*, pt. 2, 407. Manning's report said he did not get beyond the ledge just inside the wood line. 1) He drove the Federals from the stone wall at the orchard; 2) refused his left to counter the skirmishers at the Rose buildings; 3) advanced into the woods to the ledge; 4) was driven back to the stone wall; and 5) extended his line, advanced to the ledge again, and was there when Anderson arrived.

23 Silliker, *The Rebel Yell*, 101; Ladd and Ladd, *The Bachelder Papers*, vol. 1, 20; *OR 27*, pt. 2, 407. My explanation of how the 11th Georgia got onto the field ahead of the rest of the brigade.

William B. Mason called to him to stop; so he did. Colonel John Ramsey who finally drew his revolver and forced Mandeville to return to his post.[24]

The Rebels lost no time exploiting the gap. Steadily pushing into the cover of the creek across from the 110th Pennsylvania and the 5th Michigan, they unwittingly walked into a desperate firefight with the Pennsylvanians' waiting line. A dense sulfuric pall blanketed the entire area. Pennsylvanian Benjamin H. Barto dashed to the right of his Company A and took cover behind a flat rock. Propping his weapon to steady it, he took a shot right into his forehead. First Lieutenant David Copelin found him dead with his finger on the trigger.

A Company C sergeant went down with a grazed skull. Glancing up, he saw a Rebel behind a tree across the stream loading his gun. Believing the Reb was going to pick him off, he leaped aside, just as Pvt. John Walker popped up between him and the Rebel; the ball, which would have hit the sergeant in the chest, killed Walker instead, while Lt. Frank B. Stewart (Company H) shot the Reb down before the smoke cleared.

When a rifle shot shattered Lieutenant Colonel Jones's leg, Maj. Isaac Rogers unhesitatingly pulled the colonel up, slung him onto his shoulder, and carried him to the hilltop behind the regiment where he handed the colonel over to the stretcher-bearers. Others fell: Orderly Sgt. Samuel Tobias (Company C) died beside his close friend Sgt. James C. Hamilton, and Capt. Francis Cassidy (Company H), captain for but a single day, also got shot.[25]

Colonel Ramsey shouted orders for the 8th New Jersey to withdraw through the low marshy ground behind the line. As the regiment abandoned its position, a tree snagged the colors, and as Ramsey rallied about 15 men around them, a spent ball hit his shoulder and knocked him off his horse. He turned command over to Capt. John G. Langston (Company K), who wasted no time in pulling what was left of his regiment from the field.[26]

The 17th Maine opened fire at the left wing of the 11th Georgia crossing its front, without perceptibly slowing the Rebels at all. To the 17th's right rear, the 5th Michigan added to the horrific racket. Between the lines, dead and dying cows and pigs lay intermixed with the Rebels' corpses. A stray dog bounded

24 Hartford, "At Gettysburg;" "Nominal List of Casualties," both at GNMP.

25 Hamilton, "Recollections," 116, CWL.

26 Ladd and Ladd, *The Bachelder Papers*, vol. 2, 1,050.

over the hill behind the 17th chasing a rabbit. The rabbit leaped the wall with the dog right behind it. Seconds later, a Rebel bullet killed the dog.[27]

Lieutenant Verrill (Company C) suddenly became aware of bullets zipping over his men from behind. To his rear he found another Federal regiment behind the boulders in the low ground to the right of his company. He walked over to a cluster of soldiers behind one of the rocks and asked them to which regiment they belonged. They were the 115th Pennsylvania. In all likelihood, he gave them a salty piece of his mind, although he left no record of what he said.[28]

To the right front, the Confederate onslaught fell upon the 5th Michigan and the 110th Pennsylvania, whose ranks were thinning by the minute. When company officers told Colonel Pulford (5th Michigan) there were no longer enough men to maintain the regimental alignment, he shouted back: "Close in on the colors, then, we must hold this ground until relieved." At this juncture the men had shot away half their 40 rounds and soldiers were pilfering the cartridge boxes of the fallen. Pulford refused to yield his position despite his dwindling front. Two rifle balls and a shell fragment killed Pulford's mount, and he had taken two bullets himself, which hurt so badly that his men had to hold him up. Major Solomon S. Matthews caught a round also but, like Pulford, refused to leave the field.[29]

"Tige" Anderson, realizing that the 11th Georgia had advanced too far in front of the brigade, brought the left wing of the 59th Georgia into line on the right of the 3rd Arkansas. While the rest of the brigade—the 8th and 9th Georgia—approached on the left, the general spurred into the low ground, raced up to Colonel Little, and ordered him to pull the 11th Georgia back to the edge of the woods. Little complied, losing a number of men in the process.[30]

---

27 Silliker, *Rebel Yell*, 100; ibid., vol. 1, 47, vol. 2, 1,066; Cpt. J. C. M. Hamilton, "The 110th Regiment in the Gettysburg Campaign," accessed April 2, 2014, http://www.gdg.org/Research/Other%20Documents/Newspaper%20Clippings/v6pt2k.html.

28 Ladd and Ladd, *The Bachelder Papers*, vol. 2, 1,059-1,060.

29 Monument Commission, *Michigan at Gettysburg*, 102, quoted; G. W. W. to [Editor], *New York Tribune*, July 5, 1863.

30 *OR* 27, pt. 2, 401.

The Peach Orchard

Anderson's Brigade with the 9th Georgia on the left flank pushed northeast toward the orchard while skirmishers from Tilton's Brigade crossed the field from the point of the Rose Woods to meet them. With the infantry giving way on the left flank, Ames' Battery G, 1st New York, at the most advanced artillery post at the Peach Orchard, became the particular target of the Confederate artillery. Hunt, realizing how crucial the position was to the security of the Federal line, galloped up to Ames: how long could he hold the position? Before Ames could reply, Hunt barked something about staying until he established a new line farther to the rear. Despite his badly depleted supply of ammunition, Ames told the general he could hang on until the action ended.

Seconds after Hunt left, canister clattered into the right flank of the battery, and 1st Lieutenant McClellan frantically rushed up to Ames blurting something about a battery (Fickling's) having opened upon the right section from a stand of timber about 300 yards to the west. The battery could no longer hold out against so many enemy guns, the rattled lieutenant said. The command should fall back. But Ames' blood was up, so he told McClellan to shut up and to return to his section. Should the battery have to retreat, he would certainly "hear of it" at the appropriate time.

However Ames did storm after the lieutenant to assess the situation. He immediately ordered the right section to change "front forward on the right piece" and to respond with shot. The Rebs were using canister, McClellan protested; so should he. As long as his eyes were good, Ames snapped, using solid shot would show the Rebs what they could do with them.

Stepping north of the right gun, clear of the smoke, Ames locked his glasses on the Confederate battery. The first round bounded underneath the axle of one of the Rebel guns. After Ames had the sight adjusted, the second shot passed right above the same axle. Don't worry, the captain told Gunnery Sergeant Burdick: the third round would settle the fate of that piece. He told the sergeant he could fire when ready. Although it seemed to take a long time for the gunner to acquire his target, the third ball struck the piece squarely on the stock, sending the tube as high as the treetops. When the smoke cleared, the gun's entire crew lay about the destroyed carriage.

Congratulating Burdick on his marksmanship, Ames calmly advised it "would be well" to sight in on the next gun. Over at the left piece Ames learned that Sgt. James Hutchinson had moments before knocked a wheel of his target to pieces. The artillerists quickly disabled a third gun and forced the fourth to cover. Unknown to Ames, his gunners had devastated Fickling's gun crews. Ames told Lieutenant McClellan to change his opinion about using canister.

Ames kept watching the well-disciplined, thoroughly drilled Confederate infantry along Warfield and Seminary Ridges as they emerged from the woods and prepared to advance. As they stepped out, he directed Lieutenant Hazleton, in charge of his left section, to bring his pieces to bear upon them. Hazleton scrounged up every spherical case he found in the battery's chests and stockpiled them near the guns. Seconds later, while Lieutenants Goff and McClellan slammed the Confederates to the south with shot, Hazleton raked them with case. The shelling slaughtered the infantry in the rolling wheat field to Ames' left front, gouging large gaps in the Rebel ranks.[31]

Tilton's and Sweitzer's Brigades
The Rose Woods

By now, Tilton's Brigade had gone on line in the point of woods northeast of the Rose farmhouse. The 118th Pennsylvania formed the right of the line, its right wing near the tip of the woods. The 22nd Massachusetts continued the line to the left, facing south, its left flank literally "crossing the 'T'" on Sweitzer's line, cutting off the 32nd Massachusetts from the rest of the brigade. The 1st Michigan took position behind the 22nd Massachusetts with the 18th Massachusetts to its right rear and to the left of the 118th Pennsylvania. The small brigade of less than 425 men had hardly deployed when the 5th Michigan filed into the hollow at its left front. To shore up his right flank, Tilton shifted the center of the 118th Pennsylvania to the right and refused the right wing of the regiment to face west while still keeping within the woods. The 1st Michigan slipped into the space vacated by the New Englanders.[32]

From his position in Company K on the right of the 118th Pennsylvania, Donaldson could see only the regiment's skirmishers in the field a short distance in front of him. He directed his men, who were spoiling for a fight, to withhold fire until the Rebs fell back on the main line. Private Godfrey, the skulker whom Donaldson had coerced into the ranks during the march to the field, stepped up to him and handed over his wallet, watch, and a letter to his

---

31 Ames, *Battery G*, 66, 67, 69-72; "Report of Col. [William W.] White," in *SHSP*, vol. 4, 166; Gallagher, *Fighting for the Confederacy*, 240; *OR* 27, pt. 1, 901.

32 Aiken, *Inside the Army of the Potomac*, 301.

wife. "Here, Captain, take these things," he said, "and if I get killed send them to my wife, I am going to show the boys how to fight today, I have been called coward long enough." The captain grinned broadly as he took the private's hand and vigorously shook it. "Well done, Godfrey! I knew you were sound at heart and I will write to your wife of your conduct this day. Here," he said quietly, reaching for his canteen. "Take a pull at this." Behind a tree, out of sight of the rest, Donaldson handed him his canteen and watched as Godfrey choked down several vigorous chugs of rum. The captain had to pull the canteen away to keep him from draining it. Back with the company a few minutes later, he saw Godfrey standing in front of the line with his sleeves rolled up for serious work.[33]

Sweitzer, in the meantime, having reconnoitered the left of his 2nd brigade, thought the 32nd Massachusetts was in a potentially dangerous situation. Its left flank rested in the open creek bottom perpendicular to the left of the 110th Pennsylvania while its right rested on the crest of the hill perpendicular to the 22nd Massachusetts' left flank. Ordering the regiment to change its "front to rear on the tenth company," he had the line face south and extended Tilton's position along the military crest on the southern face of the Stony Hill.[34]

Corporal Oscar W. West (Company H, 32nd Massachusetts) did not expect to survive the coming fight unscathed, so he volunteered for the dangerous job of fetching water before the battle started. Carrying four canteens, he asked his captain's permission to go. The captain refused, saying: "I don't dare give you permission, for you will likely to be killed, and I shall be blamed for letting you go." Instead, he sent West to Col. George L. Prescott. "There is going to be a battle right away," the colonel said. "I know that," West replied, "and that is why I want the water." "If you go down there you probably will be shot," Prescott said. "Is your captain willing to let you go?" Upon hearing the story, Prescott assented and told West to get back as fast as he could. The private did exactly that and returned to his place in the line unharmed just as the colonel gave the order to lie down.[35]

As Private Carter (22nd Massachusetts) squeezed his blistered, cut feet into his undersized shoes, Lt. Col. Thomas Sherwin, Jr. shouted for his older

33 Ibid., 302.

34 OR 27, pt. 1, 610-611; *Supplement to the OR* 5, pt. 1, 191.

35 Oscar W. West, "On Little Round Top," *National Tribune*, November 22, 1926.

brother Walter, the sergeant major, to recall the skirmishers. Minutes later, sword in hand, Walter Carter led the skirmishers back to the 137-man regiment at a run. At the command "Fix bayonets!" the foreboding sound of steel clinking on steel reverberated through the woods. To the right, Lt. Col. William A. Throop (1st Michigan) saw a Confederate battle line about 200 yards away. These troops also attracted Col. Ira C. Abbott's attention, as he recalled his skirmishers and had the regiment fix bayonets in preparation to receive the Rebel charge.[36]

Battery G, 1st New York
The Peach Orchard

The left of Anderson's Brigade swept past the southern side of the Rose house. Ames and his New York artillerymen spotted them about the same time that Sickles ordered the battery to quit its post. Rather than limber up and risk the Rebels capturing his guns, Ames decided to let them have it. He told his men they had to repel the attack before they could safely make their escape, and his exhausted crews sprang to their work once more.

An incoming round tore off one of Pvt. John Krouse's feet at the ankle as he approached the muzzle to charge the gun. The #2 man, standing opposite him, stepped back, round in hand, awaiting someone to take Krouse's place. "Damn you," Krouse growled. "What are you waiting for? Put your charge in; I am going to have one more shot at them, leg or no leg." Balancing himself on the bloody stump, he rammed the charge home.

Ames noticed what was happening and chided: "Well, John, have they wounded you at last?" "Yes, the damn fools have shot my foot off; that was the best they could do." The captain proffered him a swig of whiskey. "I don't think I ever saw a time in my life when it would be more acceptable," Krouse grimaced. Ames always carried a flask for his wounded soldiers. "Take a good drink; that will brace you up," he said, handing it to Krouse, who proceeded to follow instructions explicitly. After he got his nearly empty flask back, Ames had Krouse placed on a stretcher and evacuated, and in the meantime ignored a

---

36 Carter, Robert G., *Reminiscences: War Papers*, vol. 2, 66; "Col. Troop's [sic] Action Report of the 1st Michigan Infantry at the Battle of Gettysburg," from the *OR*, accessed April 1, 2014, http://www.esthersscrapbook.com/HHawkinsGettysburg.htm.

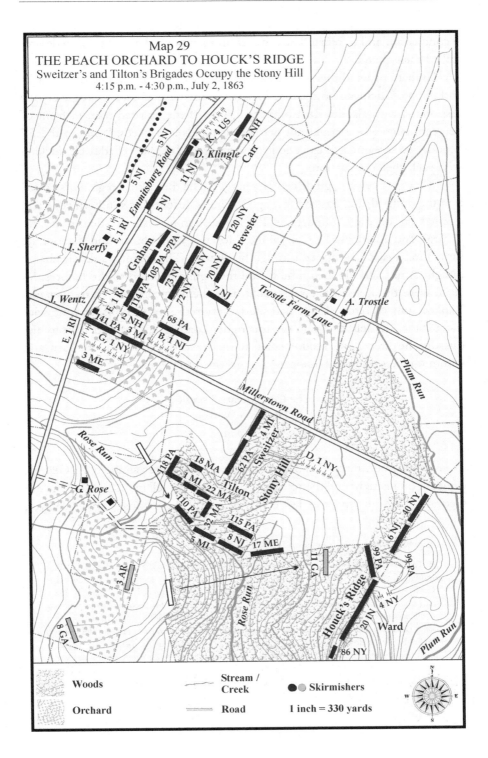

Map 29
THE PEACH ORCHARD TO HOUCK'S RIDGE
Sweitzer's and Tilton's Brigades Occupy the Stony Hill
4:15 p.m. - 4:30 p.m., July 2, 1863

Woods

Orchard

Stream / Creek

Road

Skirmishers

1 inch = 330 yards

second command to retire. The canister his men poured into the Confederates stalled their charge.[37]

Graham ordered the 141st Pennsylvania, with the 3rd Maine on the right and the 3rd Michigan on the left, forward to rescue the battery. Not everyone responded with alacrity. In Company I, one of the enlisted men in front of Sergeant Bloodgood could not get off his hands and knees. "Get up there," Bloodgood screamed. "I can't do it," the frightened soldier yelled back, ducking with each shell concussion.

"Charge! Forward, guide center, charge!" The three small regiments bolted into the orchard, and passing through the guns, reached its southern edge and opened fire on the Confederates' left flank. A minié ball whistled in the 9th Georgia and bored into Lt. Col. John C. Mounger's right breast and at about the same time a case ball ripped through his bowels. The infantry's timely charge bought Ames and his men time to roll their guns by hand to the limbers. So close were the Rebs that Ames could hear them screaming, "Surrender you Yankee sons of bitches!" He had the battery retire by sections, starting with Lieutenant McClellan's guns on the right. Loading his wounded onto the caissons, he directed the section chiefs to rendezvous near the Trostle barn, and within minutes, they had limbered and galloped to the rear.[38]

The Confederate Assault
The Rose Woods
4:30 p.m.

Manning contracted his 3rd Arkansas on the center as the 59th Georgia came up on his right and the retreating 11th Georgia fell in on his left. The 8th Georgia, with the 9th to its left came on line in the woods. Captain Hillyer,

---

37 Ames, *Battery G*, 73-75, quote on 75.

38 Tom and John Mounger to Mrs. John C. Mounger, July 18, 1863, Vertical Files, GNMP; Loring, "Gettysburg," *National Tribune*, July 9, 1885; OR 27, pt. 1, 504-505; Bloodgood, *Reminiscences*, 138; Ames, *Battery G*, 74, 76, quote on 74. This attack preceded the charge by the 68th Pennsylvania, 2nd New Hampshire, and the 3rd Maine. In his account of the action, Madill says that both his flank regiments pulled back and left him alone on the field. Colonel Bailey (2nd New Hampshire) said that his regiment crossed the southeast corner of the Peach Orchard over the downed fence. That was the same position held by the 141st Pennsylvania. The Pennsylvanians could not have charged at the same time as the 2nd New Hampshire and the 68th Pennsylvania. The 3rd Michigan, 141st Pennsylvania, and the 3rd Maine relieved the pressure on Ames' battery. The 3rd Maine, 68th Pennsylvania, and the 2nd New Hampshire saved the guns of Watson's Regular battery.

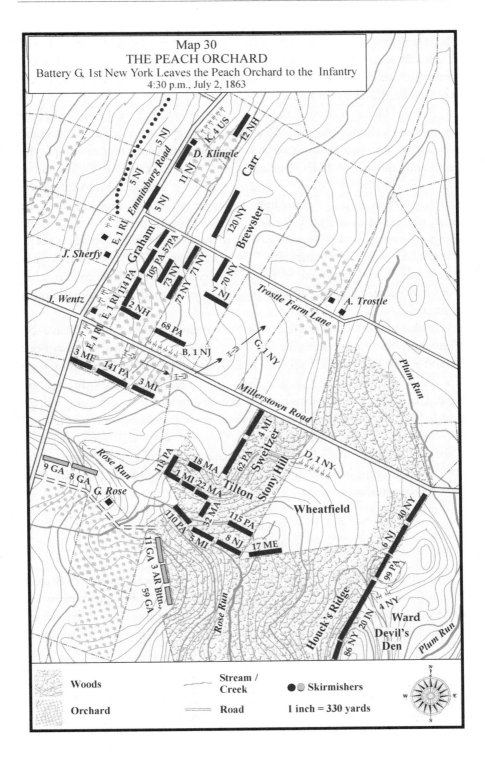

Map 30
THE PEACH ORCHARD
Battery G, 1st New York Leaves the Peach Orchard to the Infantry
4:30 p.m., July 2, 1863

whose Company H occupied a hillside south of Tilton's Brigade, found himself in a deadly box. Tilton's and Sweitzer's Brigades hammered his front and left, while the Yankee regiments on the southern face of the Peach Orchard were shooting up the rear of his line.

Before Hillyer could react to his situation, Adj. William A. Tennille brought his horse to a thundering stop alongside him. Hillyer strained his ears to hear above the din. Lieutenant Colonel Mounger was mortally wounded, the lieutenant reported, and Maj. William M. Jones had also been hit. Hillyer had to take over what was left of the regiment. Anderson directed him to refuse the regiment's three leftmost companies to suppress the harassing fire from the flank. Before the lieutenant had ridden away, Hillyer turned the remains of the company over to 1st Lt. John W. Arnold then screamed at the top of his voice: "Attention, three left companies!" No one responded. The battle's roar completely drowned him out. So Hillyer delivered the message on foot, rushing from man to man, tapping shoulders, and ordering them to refuse the line at right angles.

In the confusion, he missed three men in Company C, 2nd Lt. Daniel N. Easley and Pvts. Ephraim Prince and Warren Rogers, who remained ensconced behind a large rock on the left of the line, banging away at the Yankees on their left and front. Before long, both enlisted men were killed—shot through the head. Unable to retreat because of the extreme incoming fire, the gray haired, grizzled Easley, resplendent in his new uniform, picked up one of the dead men's rifles and continued firing at the Yankees. Not long after Anderson's Georgians came to the 3rd Arkansas' assistance, Manning was concussed by shell fragments to the nose and forehead, and Lt. Col. Robert S. Taylor took over the battered regiment.[39]

Sickles' Position
The Peach Orchard

Incoming small arms fire and artillery rounds pummeled Bucklyn's Battery E, 1st Rhode Island. The Confederates had already killed two gunners on the same piece earlier that afternoon, and he was losing men and horses at an alarming rate. One of the losses was a friend, Pvt. Ernest Simpson, the company

---

39 Ladd and Ladd, *The Bachelder Papers*, vol. 1, 21; Hillyer, "Battle of Gettysburg," 7, quoted.

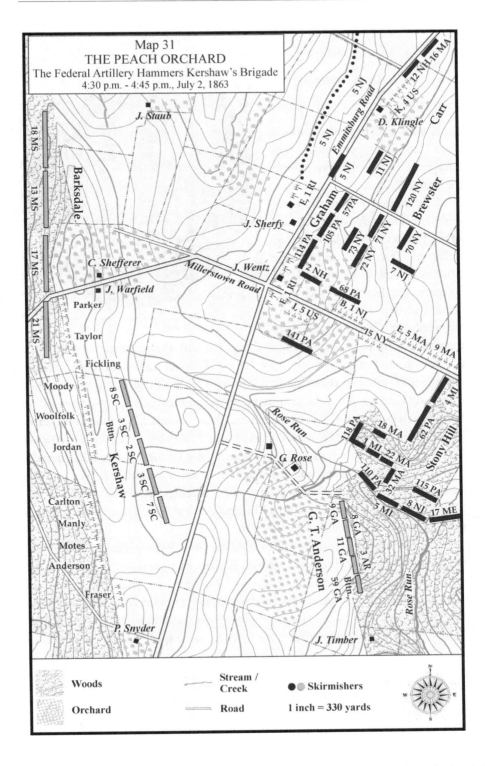

Map 31
THE PEACH ORCHARD
The Federal Artillery Hammers Kershaw's Brigade
4:30 p.m. - 4:45 p.m., July 2, 1863

Woods

Orchard

Stream / Creek

Road

Skirmishers

1 inch = 330 yards

Col. Van H. Manning
3rd Arkansas
*Gregory A. Coco Collection
Library, GNMP*

clerk, who had begged to take a place at the gun and was decapitated by a solid shot shortly thereafter.[40]

The musketry from the three regiments along the southern face of the Peach Orchard kept the 3rd Arkansas' left flank below the Rose buildings. The second Rebel column—Anderson's—had succeeded in deploying west of the Emmitsburg Road and was marching north toward the Federal flank. The 3rd Maine poured a volley into the Rebels and turned them back before Colonel Lakeman attempted to execute a "front to rear on the first company." An unexpected volley caught Company K in the left flank as it maneuvered and forced it to give way. All of the six-man color guard fell, two dead and four wounded. Six rounds hit Capt. John C. Keene, mortally wounding him; 1st Lt. Henry Penniman collapsed with a leg wound. Within minutes, no less than a third of the 150 New Englanders went down in the maelstrom. The regiment could not hold. It broke, and the veterans did not stop running until they reached the north side of the Millerstown Road, where they fell in behind the 2nd New Hampshire. Colonel Bailey checked the time. It was 4:30 p.m.

The 3rd Michigan, on the left of Madill's 141st Pennsylvania, also quit the field, leaving the Pennsylvanians, about 180 men, on their own hook. Before the smoke settled, Lt. Malbone F. Watson's four ordnance rifles (Battery I, 5th U.S.) took over Ames' former position on the ridge overlooking the Rose farm. Private Haynes (2nd New Hampshire), who was watching, later observed that: "The regulars did not serve their guns with the same spirit" as the volunteers of

---

40 Ladd and Ladd, *The Bachelder Papers*, vol. 1, 72; "*Bucklyn's Battery E, 1st Rhode Island Artillery, Report written April 30, 1878*," RG 94, Union Battle Reports, vol. 27, NA.

Ames' battery. Now with fire superiority the Confederate gunners hammered the Union line at the Emmitsburg Road salient. Watson soon went down with a shattered right leg.[41]

Carr's Brigade, III Corps,
Army of the Potomac
The Klingle Farm
4:30 p.m.-4:45 p.m.

To meet the threat from the southwest, Carr shifted his line. The 11th New Jersey flanked left into the open field in front of the 120th New York, while Seeley limbered up his six guns (Battery K, 4th U.S.) and wheeled the battery farther to the left of the Klingle house until his right flank cleared the apple orchard. With the 5th Michigan on his left, he rolled into position along the Emmitsburg Road. The 12th New Hampshire obliqued northwest into the road and went prone to the right front of the Klingle cabin, leaving the 16th Massachusetts by itself. Lieutenant John Graham Turnbull's Batteries F and K, 3rd U.S. Artillery, galloped south from its position on Cemetery Ridge west of the Leister house, and under the direction of Capt. Dunbar R. Ransom (1st Regular Brigade, Artillery Reserve) quickly reoccupied the old position north of the cabin. Ransom, severely wounded, left the field.[42]

Willard's Brigade, II Corps,
Army of the Potomac
The Brien Farm

With the pressure intensifying to the south, Hays had Col. George Willard recall the three companies of the 126th New York from the Bliss farm. Reforming with their regiment on the eastern side of Cemetery Ridge, they shifted south about 200 yards. Smyth, in turn, flanked his 14th Connecticut

---

41 OR 27, pt. 1, 505, 508, 573, 574, 661; Executive Committee, *Maine at Gettysburg*, 131-133; Craft, *141st Pennsylvania*, 121; Raus, *Generation on the March*, 168-169; Haynes, *2nd New Hampshire* (1896), 140.

42 *Supplement to the OR* 5, pt. 1, 183; Bartlett, *12th New Hampshire*, 121; Raus, *A Generation on the March*, 161, 166; OR 27, pt. 1, 532. Langley mistakenly said that he moved to the right of Battery D, 4th U.S. There was no Battery D at Gettysburg. It had to have been Battery K, 4th U.S.

through the apple orchard to the stone wall on its southwestern face. His men hunkered down behind the stacked stones awaiting orders.[43]

Confederate Brig. Gen. Ambrose Wright immediately dispatched Maj. George W. Ross and the 2nd Georgia Battalion to the skirmish line. The small regiment spread out along the entire front of the brigade and loped into the low ground to the east to reinforce Company K, 3rd Georgia. The Georgians went into position along the fence, which ran southeast from the southern end of the orchard; they quickly became involved in a long range fight with the skirmishers from Hancock's II Corps.[44]

Sickles' Artillery Line
The Peach Orchard

At 4:30 p.m., McGilvery personally directed Bigelow's 9th Massachusetts Battery into line east of Battery B, 1st New Jersey. Reaching the destroyed fencerow of the north side of the Millerstown Road, Bigelow's right section unlimbered about 30 feet from the road. The left section ended up in the road where it passed through the band of woods on the west side of the Wheatfield.

When Bigelow rode up to the left section, he discovered it had an obstructed line of fire. "Left section, limber to the rear; by the left flank, march!" he bellowed, and the two left guns wheeled into battery on the right of the right section fixing the gun positions from the right to the left as: five, six, one, two, three, and four. Whitaker commanded the two right guns, with Erickson then Milton in charge of the next two sections of the line. From his position on the far right of the battery, Sergeant Baker saw no supporting infantry to his left.

Confederate artillery raked the New Englanders' front as they unlimbered, wounding a number of men. Bigelow directed his men to sight in on the woods along the southern end of Seminary Ridge to roust those Rebels out. Within short order, the Confederate counter battery fire slackened, at which point

---

43 Charles D. Page, *History of the Fourteenth Regiment, Connecticut Vol. Infantry* (Meriden, CT, 1906), 140-141. Page said the regiment moved into the space occupied by the New York brigade (Willard's). Therefore, the skirmishers of the 126th New York had to have been recalled at this time.

44 *OR* 27, pt. 2, 630.

Bigelow commanded his men to shell Rose's barn to silence the Rebel sharpshooters there.[45]

Cabell's Battalion
South of the Warfield Farm

But Cabell's Artillery Battalion had fallen silent by Longstreet's order and not from Bigelow's suppressive fire. Before the acrid smoke drifted away from the stone wall, behind which Kershaw's South Carolinians lay, three of the guns suddenly discharged, one after the other. With the blasts reverberating west over the ridge Longstreet threw himself into the saddle and spurred toward the high ground with his orderly Pvt. William Youngblood (Company I, 15th Alabama) right at his side.

Without orders the Southerners stood up and climbed over the wall into the open. The 8th South Carolina (300 strong) secured the left with the 203 men of the 3rd South Carolina Battalion to its right. The 2nd South Carolina (412 effectives) held the center while the 3rd South Carolina (406 men) and the 7th South Carolina (408 officers and men) finished the line. The Carolinians silently reformed their lines and waited upon their officers, all of whom had dismounted. The 448-man 15th South Carolina remained on the flank of Cabell's right battery.

Kershaw specifically instructed his regimental officers to guide right on the 7th South Carolina and, when the left struck the Peach Orchard, they were to wheel north. They should pass on the same directives to every company commander and they to the rank and file. Kershaw's center would pass around the Rose buildings, some 500 yards distant, then swing north toward the Stony Hill to flank the Peach Orchard.

While Kershaw yelled for the brigade to advance, Youngblood noticed that he and Longstreet had ridden in front the South Carolinians. They should get behind the line, he warned the general, lest they fall prey to "friendly fire." Longstreet instantly reined his horse aside to allow Kershaw a clear passage. Meanwhile, the regimental officers picked up the command, and the regiments stepped out in fine style at the "common time." Under orders to neither fire nor cheer, they stoically stepped into the hellfire before them. The 7th South Carolina, the regiment of direction on the right, made straight for the Rose

---

45 Baker, *9th Massachusetts Battery*, 57, quoted; McGilvery, "Part taken by the 1st Brigade," GNMP.

farm. The water detail had not returned in time, so Semmes' brigade stepped off without their canteens. Longstreet had dismounted and was walking alongside Kershaw in the advance. Neither general knew that Barksdale's and Wofford's brigades had gotten entangled in Maj. Frank Huger's Artillery Battalion, confusing their ranks and stalling their advance.[46]

Sickles' Artillery Position
The Peach Orchard

Captain Patrick Hart brought his 15th New York Battery onto the field, rolling his four 12-pounder Napoleons into line on the southern bank of the Millerstown Road. Fifteen minutes later, Phillips' guns fell in on Bigelow's right and Hart's left rear. Phillips, who approached from the northeast, maneuvered by the "right oblique" into his part of the line. "On the left into line," Lieutenant Scott yelled. In so doing, his designated right section became the left section of the battery. The #1 gun rolled over the rails of the destroyed fence along the Millerstown Road and unlimbered in the road. The rest of the battery fell in along the road's northern bank. From where he stood on the left of the line, Lieutenant Scott could see no infantry to his front, but in the distance, some 1,200 yards away, he spotted the smoke of the Confederate artillery. When Hart realized he had posted his guns too far to the front, he retired them to the north side of the road on Philips' immediate right.[47]

The three batteries mercilessly pummeled Kershaw's and Semmes' brigades as they headed toward the Emmitsburg Road. Lieutenant William A. Johnson (Company F, 2nd South Carolina) vividly recalled how Capts. George M. McDowell (Company F) and Robert C. Pulliam (Company B) had agreed, just before the charge started, that they fail if their division did not attack in

---

46 Kershaw, "Kershaw's Brigade at Gettysburg," in *Battles and Leaders*, vol. 3, 334; Mac Wyckoff, *A History of the Second South Carolina Infantry 1861-1865* (Fredericksburg, 1994), 79; Ladd and Ladd, *The Bachelder Papers*, vol. 1, 454-455, 471; William A. Johnson, "The Battle of Gettysburg, July 2, 1863," *The Atlanta Journal*, n.d., Vertical Files, GNMP; Youngblood, "Unwritten History," in *Confederate Veteran*, vol. 38, 315; Lafayette McLaws, "Gettysburg," in *SHSP*, vol. 7, 73; Constance Pendleton, (ed.), *Confederate Memoirs* (Bryn Athyn, PA, 1958), 35. Over the years, Youngblood confused Wofford's brigade with Kershaw's. Wofford supported Barksdale from the rear not from the right, and Kershaw was initially to Barksdale's right.

47 Hanifen, *Battery B*, 70-71; Regimental Committee, *5th Massachusetts Battery*, 624, 626, 630, 637, quote on 637; Ladd and Ladd, *The Bachelder Papers*, vol. 1, 167. Hanifen confused Phillips' battery with Bigelow's. He has Bigelow deploying on Philips' right, when the positions were just the opposite.

conjunction with Hood's. Johnson said he felt like a "sightseer" not being allowed to fire, helplessly watching the Yankee artillery "cutting off the arms and heads of our men cutting them down and exploding in their bodies, tearing them into mincemeat."[48]

Second Army Corps, Army of the Potomac
Cemetery Ridge—North of the George Weikert Farm

With the fighting growing more intense to the south, Colonel Cross assumed it would not be long before his brigade went into the fracas. To escape the artillery fire the division had already shifted about a quarter-mile to the south, only to march back. Now, aside a large boulder, the colonel handed Assistant Surgeon William F. Child (5th New Hampshire) a massive gold ring, a pocketbook, and several other personal papers and possessions. "Good-by!" he said. "It will be an awful day. Take care of yourself. I must go into the fight, but I fear I shall be killed. Good-by!"[49]

Hancock and his staff suddenly clattered in from the north. "Colonel Cross," he said, "this day will bring you a star." "No, General," the colonel replied, shaking his head, "this is my last battle. . . . I shall never live to obtain that star." As Hancock rode off, Cross turned his attention to the firing in the Peach Orchard. The general had hardly departed when Cross spied Lieutenant Colonel Morgan, Hancock's chief of staff and inspector general, galloping madly toward him. "Mount, gentlemen," Cross commanded. Within a few minutes, the brigade was up. Caldwell led the division. As he and his staff turned south, Cross dispatched his aide, 1st Lt. Daniel K. Cross (Company G, 5th New Hampshire), to find Sykes.[50]

Three brigades to the north, Fr. William Corby (Chaplain 88th New York) stood on a boulder in front of his brigade and announced he was going to administer a general absolution to everyone present. Reminding the men of their sacred Christian duty as soldiers not to desert, he warned that the Church

---

48 Johnson, "The Battle of Gettysburg, July 2, 1863," GNMP.

49 Child, *5th New Hampshire*, 217.

50 Charles A. Hale, "With Colonel Cross," 6-7, quoted; Ladd and Ladd, *The Bachelder Papers*, vol. 3, 1,355; *OR 27*, pt. 1, 379, 414. Hale identified the officer who relayed the command as a Colonel Wilson. It was actually Lt. Col. Charles Morgan. He said he took in Caldwell's Division until a V Corps officer took over. I blended Hale's account of Cross' response to Hancock with Child's rendition of the same incident.

1st Lieutenant Daniel K. Cross
Company G, 5th New Hampshire
Scott Hann Collection
Library, GNMP

would refuse a Christian burial to anyone who deserted the ranks. At that, he asked everyone to kneel, and all 530 men in the brigade bared their heads and knelt. As Corby finished delivering the general absolution in Latin, the order came for them to move out.[51]

In Zook's brigade, Col. Richard P. Roberts dramatically faced his Pennsylvanians, at the head of the column. "Men of the 140th!" he bellowed. "Recollect that you are now defending your own soil, and are fighting to drive the invader from your homes and firesides. I shall therefore expect you to conduct yourselves as if in the presence of your wives, your sisters, and your sweethearts, and not disgrace the flag you bear or the name of Pennsylvanians." The men's hearty cheers reverb- erated above the clanging and clatter of accoutrements as they faced left and moved out at the double-quick.[52]

The column had not gone far when Lieutenant Cross returned without having found General Sykes. Not long after, however, Lt. Col. Fred T. Locke, Sykes' assistant adjutant general, clat- tered up to Caldwell with orders to direct the division to the front. As the column neared the northern base of Little Round Top, Morgan spurred away from the division to see what was going on.[53]

---

51 Ladd and Ladd, *The Bachelder Papers*, vol. 1, 420-421; St. Clair A. Mulholland, *The Story of the 116th Regiment, Pennsylvania Infantry* (Gaithersburg, MD, 1993), 407.

52 Ibid., 417.

53 OR 27, pt. 1, 379; Ladd and Ladd, *The Bachelder Papers*, vol. 3, 1,355.

Kershaw's Brigade, Longstreet's Corps
Army of Northern Virginia
The Emmitsburg Road

Longstreet parted with Kershaw when his brigade reached the Emmitsburg Road. As the corps commander walked his mount to the rear, Kershaw heard Barksdale's drummers rapping out the "Assembly," and he suddenly realized he was going into action alone with no support on his left flank. Barksdale's troops had gotten tangled up in the guns and had to regroup.[54]

The fences along the Emmitsburg Road and in Rose's southern fields played havoc with Kershaw's and Semmes' advance. Nevertheless, Kershaw's men struck the Rose farm lane exactly as he had intended—150 yards ahead of Semmes' Georgians and his detached 15th South Carolina. The 8th South Carolina planted its left flank on the Emmitsburg Road, north of Rose's farm lane, with the 3rd Battalion and the 2nd to its right. The regiments automatically wheeled left on the 8th going into a ragged line along the worm fence on the crest overlooking the hollow perpendicular to the Emmitsburg Road. At that point, Kershaw sent the 2nd Regiment, 3rd Battalion, and the 8th Regiment toward the Peach Orchard. At the same time, the 7th South Carolina wheeled north, with the 3rd South Carolina, disrupted somewhat by the Rose farm buildings, on its left rear.[55]

III Army Corps, Army of the Potomac
The Peach Orchard

Under the cover of their own artillery fire, Kershaw's three left regiments charged at the oblique against the Peach Orchard. Only the 141st Pennsylvania remained along the southern face to oppose them, and with pressure coming in from the west, Madill swung his regiment toward the Emmitsburg Road. Realizing they were outnumbered and isolated, he gave the order for the 141st to retire. The Pennsylvanians did not stand on ceremony. They bolted north as fast as they could run.[56]

---

54 Kershaw, "Kershaw's Brigade at Gettysburg," in *Battles and Leaders*, vol. 3, 334.

55 Wyckoff, *2nd South Carolina*, 79; Kershaw, ibid., 335; Ladd and Ladd, *The Bachelder Papers*, vol. 1, 455, 474.

56 Craft, *141st Pennsylvania*, 122; *OR* 27, pt. 1, 505.

Second Lieutenant Charles MacConnell (Battery I, 5th U.S.), on the hill behind them, also panicked. The battery had been in action less than five minutes, firing five rounds of canister per piece. Without waiting for the infantry behind him to come to his assistance, he ordered the four guns limbered to withdraw. "The conduct of the officers and men throughout was unexceptional," he later wrote with ironic understatement.[57]

Colonel Bailey, seeing the Rebels dangerously close to the battery, turned to Graham, who was riding behind his 2nd New Hampshire, and requested permission to advance. "Yes, for God's sake, go forward!" Graham screamed back. Bailey gave the command, and the line stood up, hurriedly maneuvering into formation. "Forward, guide center," Bailey shouted. The regiment stepped into the road and scampered up the southern bank. McConnell's remaining operational left gun loosed a final round of double canister into the Carolinians as the regiment came abreast of it. Yelling wildly, the New Englanders dashed into the Peach Orchard on a southwesterly course. Sweeping in front of the guns, the 2nd New Hampshire, with its left wing field east of the Orchard, caught the Confederates in the open. Rather than risk a bloody melee, the Rebels retreated to the creek bank across from the orchard.[58]

Kershaw's Brigade, Longstreet's Corps
Army of Northern Virginia
The Rose Farm and the Peach Orchard
4:45 p.m.–5:00 p.m.

Having gotten into the low ground behind the Rose buildings, Kershaw and his right wing had lost sight of the three left regiments. As the 3rd and the

---

57 Raus, *Generation on the March*, 169; Haynes, *2nd New Hampshire* (1896), 140, 309; OR 27, pt. 1, 505, 661, quoted on 661; Beyer and Keydel, *Deeds of Valor*, vol. 1, 240-241. While just briefly mentioning its action in the Peach Orchard, the monument to Battery I, 5th U.S. Artillery, notes that at the conclusion of the fighting on July 2 its guns were "unserviceable." Private Haynes (2nd New Hampshire) mistakenly noted, "A lieutenant of the battery to our front spiked his guns, expecting they would soon be captured." Lieutenant Samuel Peeples, commanding one of the battery's sections, however, said the guns were still operational by the end of the day. Later, in his "Dedicatory Address" in the regimental history, Haynes mistakenly wrote that the 3rd Maine fell back through the 2nd New Hampshire in great confusion (p. 309), yet in the main text of the book he identifies the men who ran back as just "skirmishers." Based upon Madill's description, I believe that Haynes saw the 141st Pennsylvania coming back through the guns.

58 Ladd and Ladd, *The Bachelder Papers*, vol. 2, 846.

7th South Carolinas neared the refused left wing of the 9th Georgia, the general ordered them toward the Stony Hill. Behind them, Semmes' Georgians struggled over the high post and rail fences along the Emmitsburg Road. Captain William Pendleton (Company B, 50th Georgia) seriously doubted he would get across either of them alive. A cannon ball ripped through the 50th Georgia, which had just executed a right oblique toward the Rose farm, shattering Sergeant William Jones' (Company K) right ankle and crumpling him onto his knees.[59]

As the 2nd New Hampshire cleared the cast aside rails that had once been the fence along the southern face of the Orchard, Bailey quickly realized he had to stop his men or risk losing them in a senseless charge against a determined, well-covered enemy. The bugler sounded the "Recall," and Bailey shifted his entire line to the right until the right rested on the Emmitsburg Road. He ordered his men to lie down behind the demolished fence and to pile up the rails in front of them. Resting their weapons upon their wooden barricade, the New Englanders popped off rounds at the Confederates, who under cover of the creek bank were trying to get into the woods on the Yankees' left front.[60]

The New Englanders shot the daylights out of the Rebel regiments as they approached the marshy creek above the farm lane, the relentless fire forcing them to cover in the creek bed. Meanwhile, the right of the brigade dashed over the rise south of the creek into the security of its banks, below the line of sight of the Yankee gunners. The 7th South Carolina, in passing over the three left companies of the 9th Georgia, crowded the front of the 3rd South Carolina, causing its right company to fall in behind the left of the 7th.[61]

No sooner had Battery I, 5th U.S., left the high ground in the orchard than Capt. James Thompson's Batteries C and F, Pennsylvania Independent Artillery, unlimbered in the vacated position. Battery F's four ordnance rifles faced south against Kershaw, while C's two rifles were pointed west toward Seminary Ridge and Barksdale's line.[62]

59 William Jones, "Wounded and Captured at Gettysburg," Keith, Bohannon (ed.), *Military Images*, May-June, 1988, vol. 9, 14; Pendleton, (ed.), *Confederate Memoirs*, 35.

60 Ladd and Ladd, *The Bachelder Papers*, vol. 2, 846; Haynes, *2nd New Hampshire* (1865), 175-177, and (1896), 140, 308.

61 Ladd and Ladd, *The Bachelder Papers*, vol. 1, 455.

62 Regimental Committee, *Fifth Massachusetts Battery*, 626; Raus, *Generation on March*, 141-142.

Kershaw halted his right wing, temporarily stalling the attack. He ordered Col. D. Wyatt Aiken to shift his 7th South Carolina several steps to the right to allow the 3rd to come on line to its left. In the confusion of the moment, Maj. Robert C. Maffett (3rd South Carolina), following his initial directive to close to the right on the 7th, immediately flanked his regiment toward the woods.[63]

Colonel John D. Kennedy (2nd South Carolina) having misunderstood Kershaw's intentions for him to take the battery at the orchard regardless of what the rest of the brigade did, complied immediately. The 2nd temporarily disappeared from the gunners' sight by descending into the creek bottom, dragging the 3rd Battalion and the 8th South Carolina and along with it.[64]

McGilvery's Artillery Line, Army of the Potomac
The Millerstown Road
4:45 p.m.-5:00 p.m.

McGilvery's gunners spotted the head of Kershaw's brigade as it emerged from the depression where it petered out near the southwestern side of the woods. The major commanded Bigelow and Phillips to cut loose at the Rebels' front as they formed the battle line about 700 yards southwest of the batteries. A nasty shoulder wound knocked down 1st Sergeant Baker on Bigelow's #6 gun. The lieutenant did not think the shells were bursting soon enough and told the man at the ammunition chest to cut the fuses for one and one half seconds. "It will burst before it is half way there," one man protested. But according to Baker, the case shots exploded in front of the Rebel brigade. Corporal Jonas Shackley, the chief of caisson for Phillips' #1 gun, watched canister tear holes in the ranks of the Confederate brigade, moving across the guns' front.[65]

---

63 *OR* 27, pt. 2, 368, 372.

64 Fred E. Gaillard, "*Franklin Gaillard's Civil War Letters*," 36, Gaillard Papers, Vertical Files, GNMP; Ladd and Ladd, *The Bachelder Papers*, vol. 2, 900; Johnson, "The Battle of Gettysburg, July 2, 1863," GNMP.

65 Baker, *9th Massachusetts Battery*, 59, 75, 226, quote on 226; Hanifen, *Battery B*, 70, 71; Ladd and Ladd, *The Bachelder Papers*, vol. 1, 167; Regimental Committee, *5th Massachusetts Artillery*, 624, 626-627. Baker reported he incurred severe wounds in the hip and shoulder. Lieutenant Whitaker reported that the Rebs wounded one of the sergeants as the guns went into action and told him to go to the rear, but he refused, saying he was not disabled. I assume that Baker's first wound was in the shoulder rather than the hip, because a hip wound would have kept him from performing his duty at the gun.

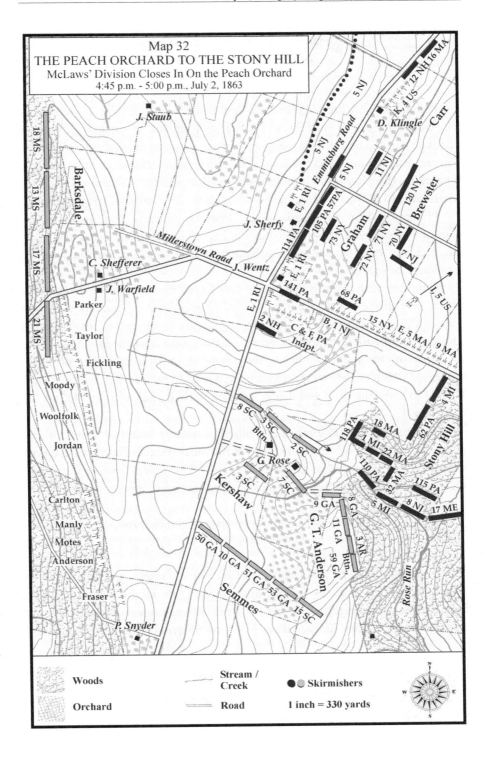

Map 32
THE PEACH ORCHARD TO THE STONY HILL
McLaws' Division Closes In On the Peach Orchard
4:45 p.m. - 5:00 p.m., July 2, 1863

Woods

Orchard

Stream / Creek

Road

Skirmishers

1 inch = 330 yards

Kershaw's Brigade, Longstreet's Corps
Army of Northern Virginia
The Rose Farm

Federal artillery literally blew the 2nd South Carolina away by squads as they came into the open. Second Lieutenant Johnson (Company F), sensing what fate awaited him and his men, kept a wary eye upon the one gun, which the Yankees had trained upon the end of the depression. The moment he saw the #4 man on the piece stretch out the lanyard, the lieutenant froze with his side turned toward the piece. The gun roared and canister whistled through the air.

Private William G. Lomax died instantly. Private Jonathan Fooshe slammed to the ground behind Johnson, his left leg snapped below the knee. His pleading eyes latched on the lieutenant and Johnson handed him his canteen as he gasped for water.

Simultaneously an iron ball grazed and frayed the back of the lieutenant's jacket, as it struck Pvt. R. Elmore "Whig" Chaney in the chest. Another shot pierced Pvt. James H. Casson (Company A) just above the eye. Johnson saw his former schoolmate unsteadily kneeling on the ground, totally incoherent, the front part of his skull completely torn away. A canister shot slammed Pvt. George W. McKenzie's weapon into his chest and knocked him unconscious. Unable to assist the dead and dying, Johnson dashed after what was left of his company.[66]

Lieutenant Colonel Franklin Gaillard helplessly watched the Yankees decimate his 2nd South Carolina. "It was the most shocking battle I have ever witnessed," he later confessed in a letter home. "There were familiar forms and faces with parts of their heads shot away, legs shattered, arms torn off."[67]

Sickles' Artillery Position, Army of the Potomac
The Millerstown Road

To Captain Phillips' disgust, most of Kershaw's brigade got into the Rose Woods unscathed. Semmes' brigade in the second line did not fare as well. The first Yankee shell caught Company K of the 50th Georgia crossing the stone fence along Seminary Ridge, killing Cpl. Jim Alderman and Pvt. Jim Dixon

---

66 Johnson, "The Battle of Gettysburg, July 2, 1863," GNMP.

67 Gaillard, *"Franklin Gaillard's Civil War Letters,"* 36, GNMP.

while wounding Pvts. George Merriman and Jesse Stephens along with several others. Two hundred yards into the open, a case shot killed Lt. Col. Francis Kearse. Captain Peter A. S. McGlashan (Company E) took over the 50th Georgia. The men crossed the Emmitsburg Road and attempted to take cover behind the Rose farmhouse and barn, which stalled its advance long enough for Phillips' artillerists and the other gunners along the line to accurately peg their position. The harried charge across the open fields had cost the regiment almost one third of its men.[68]

The Yankees, having forced the Georgians to cover, inflicted a greater number of casualties upon the second wave than on the first. Part of the Confederate line, rather than stay in the open, swung north into the creek bottom and disappeared from sight. Phillips ordered his men to load canister, but the Rebels never came back into view along his front.[69]

II Army Corps, Army of the Potomac
The George Weikert House

About a quarter-mile south of Brigadier General Zook's original position, Major Tremain, Sickles' senior aide-de-camp, unexpectedly encountered the general and his staff. The brigade halted. Hurriedly introducing himself to Zook, Tremain asked where he could find the division commander, because the III Corps needed immediate assistance. Zook shot back that his orders were to follow the column. Tremain once again requested his help again and promised to secure a written order from Sickles.[70]

"Sir," Zook relented, "if you will give me the order of General Sickles, I will obey it." "Then, General Sickles' order is that you will file your brigade to the right and move into action here." Twisting about in the saddle, the general shouted, "File right!" The brigade deployed by regiment into line, right in front. The 140th Pennsylvania, the largest regiment in the brigade led, followed respectively by the 66th and 52nd New York regiments. Zook detached the

68 Lt. Col. Peter A. S. McGlashan, "McLaws' Division and the Penna. Reserves on the Second Day at Gettysburg," *The Press*, October 20, 1886; Bohannon, (ed.), "Wounded and Captured at Gettysburg." Reminiscences by Sgt. William Jones, 50th Georgia Infantry," *Military Images*, May-June 1988, vol. IX, no. 6, 14.

69 Regimental Committee, *5th Massachusetts Battery*, 624, 626-627, 638.

70 Henry E. Tremain, *Two Days of War: A Gettysburg Narrative and Other Experiences* (New York, 1905), 81-83; OR 27, pt. 1, 398.

57th New York from the rear of the column to form the reserve and marched it parallel to the other three commands. Rushing north, the brigade headed toward the fencerow west of Plum Run. Tremain then galloped to Trostle's and returned with Sickles' written orders, at which point he took lead of the column.[71]

71 J. J. Purman, "Recitals and Reminiscences," *National Tribune*, March 25, 1909; OR 27, pt. 1, 394, 397; Tremain, *Two Days of War*, 84, 85, 86. quote on 84; Henry E. Tremain to St. Clair Mulholland, July 7, 1895, Vertical Files, GNMP.

Chapter 9

July 2, 1863
5:00 p.m.-5:30 p.m.

"Lieutenant, if your hip was shot off like that,
what the bloody hell would you do?"

—*Private Billy Riley, Battery B, 1st New Jersey Light*

The Emmitsburg Road
The Bliss Farm
5:00 p.m.

Mississippians did not hesitate to reoccupy the Bliss farm buildings once the men from the 126th New York abandoned them. Again their sharpshooters nested in the windows on the barn's second floor successfully picking off Yankees on the skirmish line west of the Emmitsburg Road and playing havoc with the II Corps batteries from Ziegler's Grove to the copse of trees at the Angle. Hays, tiring of the harassment, turned to Smyth, and asked, "Have you a regiment that will drive them out?" Wheeling about, Smyth shouted for volunteers, and to his amazement, the entire 12th New Jersey—more than 400 men—stepped forward. "But, I don't want all of you," the colonel exclaimed, "Major Hill, send four companies."[1]

John T. Hill detailed Companies B, E, H, and G under his senior captain, Samuel B. Jobes (Company G), to eradicate the sharpshooter problem. Jobes formed his 150 men for the attack on the run. In column of fours, each company passed just beyond the western face of the Brien barn, before turning

---

1   William P. Haines, *History of the Men of Company F* (Mickeleyon, NJ, 1897), 38-39, quote on 38.

north. Halting at the whitewashed board fence bordering the farm lane, which ran from the north side of the barn west to the Emmitsburg Road, each company faced to the left, in column of company.

Jobes led the attack party in three hearty "hip-hip huzzahs" for Colonel Smyth, followed immediately by three more for New Jersey. Advancing at a trot, each company in turn negotiated the stubborn post and rail fences on both sides of the Emmitsburg Road, reformed on the western side, and charged pell-mell toward the Bliss farm buildings. Confederate riflemen shot down the Yankees along the entire front of the advance. In quick order, Company H absorbed several casualties: killed—Pvt. Daniel Kiernan; mortally wounded with a ball in the head—Pvt. William S. Harker; wounded—Sgts. Clarkson Jennings and Alfred H. Buck, and Cpls. George A. Cobb and Edmund C. Tier. Still the bluecoats surged forward. Reaching the first fence row west of the road, they picked up Company B of the 106th Pennsylvania under Captain Lynch. The Pennsylvanians left 12 men down in the open field as they swarmed toward the ground south of the barn.

Armed with .69 caliber Springfield muskets charged with buck and ball loads, the Jerseymen got to within near spitting distance of the house and barn before stopping. Bringing their weapons to bear upon every opening in the two buildings, they poured a crippling fire into the Rebs. The stricken enemies streamed from the barn, house, and nearby hay-mounds, many of them bleeding from facial wounds, and most pleading for mercy. As they did so, those attackers not occupied with the prisoners and the wounded dashed up the earthen ramp on the north side of the barn into the upper level. Making quick work of the Rebels remaining on that floor, the Yankees hurried down to the lower level and secured it, gathering more prisoners.[2]

A couple of the Confederates used the confusion of the mass surrender to snap off parting shots into the Jersey boys. One of them wounded Company B's acting first sergeant, John W. Mitchell, as he stood next to Pvt. Albert S. Emmell (Company H). Another shot drilled Sgt. George W. Clark of Mitchell's company through the left arm as he attempted to run the man through with his bayonet. The angered Clark subdued the Confederate and herded him outside at bayonet point. "[He] shot me after I entered the barn door," the sergeant

---

2   Thompson, *Military Essays*, vol. 3, 98-99; Christopher Mead to his wife, July 6, 1863, Robert L. Brake Coll., USAHEC; Nicholson, *Pennsylvania at Gettysburg*, vol. 1, 552; Gerry Harder Porriss and Ralph G. Porriss, (eds.), *While My Country is in Danger* (Hamilton, NY, 1994), 76; Edward G. Longacre, *To Gettysburg and Beyond* (Highstown, NJ, 1988), 127, n. 35, 419.

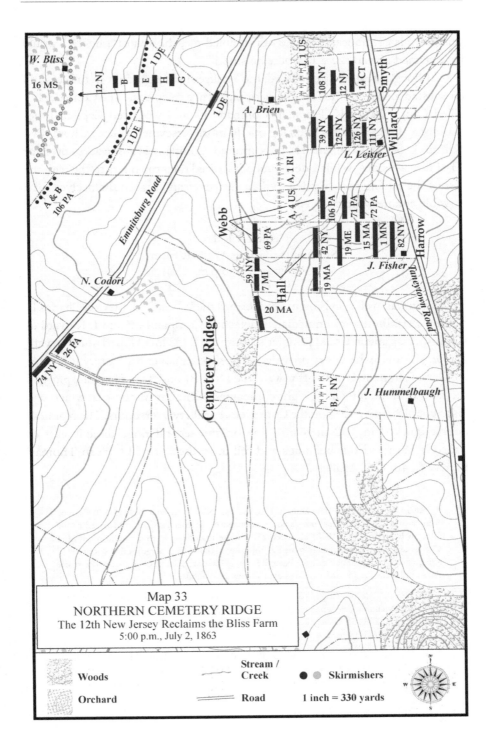

Map 33
NORTHERN CEMETERY RIDGE
The 12th New Jersey Reclaims the Bliss Farm
5:00 p.m., July 2, 1863

Woods

Orchard

Stream / Creek

Road

Skirmishers

1 inch = 330 yards

yelled to his comrades. "Had he not disabled me, the son of a bitch, I would have pinned him to the wall where he stood!"[3]

Although greatly outnumbered, the Yankees had bagged seven officers and 85 enlisted men from the 16th Mississippi, but at a steep cost. The Confederates killed Capt. Charles K. Horsfall (Company E) and wounded Captain Jobes (Company G) in addition to taking out 40 more Jerseymen, one of whom, Pvt. William L. Seran (Company H), got captured. Company H alone accounted for 13 of the casualties. While a detachment escorted their prisoners to the rear, the rest of the raiding party tended to their casualties and braced themselves for a possible counterattack.[4]

Cemetery Ridge
North of the George Weikert Farm
5:00 p.m.–5:30 p.m.

When Caldwell's division moved toward the Wheatfield, Lt. Col. Charles P. Adams (1st Minnesota) immediately detached Companies F and L forward as skirmishers. Captain Emil L. Burger's Company L (32 men) loped north toward Ziegler's Grove, where they provided sharpshooter cover for Battery I, 1st U.S. Artillery. Company F took off toward the Little Round Top. Hancock plugged the hole with the remaining eight companies of the 1st Minnesota, which had lost a couple of men to sporadic Confederate artillery overshoots. The regiment double-quicked its 262 men into line on the second ridge directly east of Trostle's barn and out buildings and fell in to the left of Lt. Evan Thomas' Battery C, 4th U.S. Artillery.[5]

---

3   Albert Stokes Emmell to his aunt, July 16, 1863, in "Now is the time for Buck & Ball," n.p., Vertical files, GNMP. While not listed as wounded in the rosters, Clark transferred to the Veteran Reserve Corps (VCR) in March 1864, more than likely from a wound received at Gettysburg. John W. Mitchell became the company's second First Sergeant on November 3, 1863, which means he had to have been the Acting First Sergeant at Gettysburg. The roster does not list him or any other enlisted man among the wounded.

4   Thompson, *Military Essays*, vol. 3, 98-99; Christopher Mead to his wife, July 6, 1863, USAHEC; Nicholson, *Pennsylvania at Gettysburg*, vol. 1, 552; Gerry Harder Porriss and Ralph G. Porriss, (eds.), *While My Country is in Danger*, 74; Edward G. Longacre, *To Gettysburg and Beyond*, 127, n. 35, 419; *OR* 27, pt. 1, 470.

5   Richard Moe, *The Last Full Measure* (St. Paul, MN, 1993), 267; "Official Report of Captain Burgess [sic], The First Minnesota Sharpshooters at Gettysburg," July 5, 1863, Vertical files, GNMP; Lochren, "1st Minnesota," *Glimpses of the Nation's Struggle*, vol. 3, 48; Smith, *19th Maine*, 69.

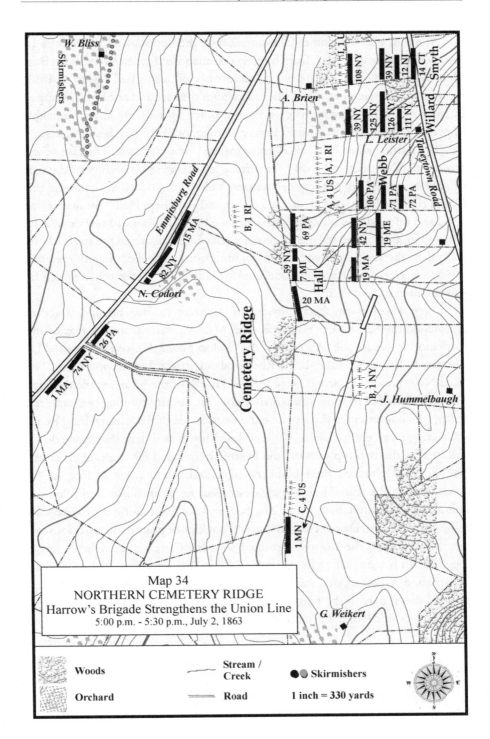

W. Bliss

Skirmishers

A. Brien

108 NY

39 NJ

12 NJ

14 CT

Smyth

39 NY

125 NY

126 NY

111 NY

Willard

L. Leister

A, 1 RI

Webb

Emmitsburg Road

15 MA

B, 1 RI

A, 4 US

106 PA

71 PA

72 PA

Tangtown Road

82 NY

69 PA

42 NY

19 ME

19 MA

59 NY

7 MI

Hall

20 MA

N. Codori

Cemetery Ridge

26 PA

74 NY

B, 1 NY

J. Hummelbaugh

1 MA

C, 4 US

1 MN

Map 34
NORTHERN CEMETERY RIDGE
Harrow's Brigade Strengthens the Union Line
5:00 p.m. - 5:30 p.m., July 2, 1863

G. Weikert

Woods

Stream /
Creek

Skirmishers

Orchard

Road

1 inch = 330 yards

At about the same time, Gibbon relieved the unpopular Col. George H. Ward (15th Massachusetts) from brigade command and replaced him with Brig. Gen. William Harrow.[6] Ward, who had lost his left leg at Ball's Bluff in 1861, returned to his regiment, while Harrow, whom the men did not know, stopped in front of every regiment to give them a brave up talk. He left an indelible impression upon Pvt. Roland E. Bowen (Company B, 15th Massachusetts).

The battle had to be won, Harrow insisted, at all hazards. The fate of the army depended upon it. "Now," he threatened, drawing his revolver, "the first God Damn man I see running or sneaking, I blow him to Hell in an instant, this Damn running is played out, just stand to it and give them Hell." By all that was good and infernal he would kill every son of a bitch that ran without a cause, he concluded, and "if you see me running I want you to kill me on the spot." As he walked to the next regiment in the column, one of the Bay Staters shouted, "Bully for Harrow." Another concurred, "He is tight;" yet another agreed he was the man to lead them.[7]

Once Harrow finished introducing himself to the brigade, Gibbon dispatched the 82nd New York and 15th Massachusetts from the rear of the formation to secure the area around the Codori house. He also dispatched Lt. Thomas F. Brown's Battery B, 1st Rhode Island, forward to support them. The 82nd New York went prone along the road north of the house, while the 15th Massachusetts fell in to its immediate right. An easterly running post and rail fence, which intersected the fence on the eastern side of the Emmitsburg Road, cut through its right battalion. Ward ordered his men to tear that fence down and to take the two top rails off the Emmitsburg Road fence along his front. The veterans chucked their blankets, haversacks, and rifles and broke by companies to the rear. They quickly destroyed the worm fence and piled the rails along the Emmitsburg Road. The post and rail fence along the road posed more of a problem. Discovering they could not kick or pound the posts loose to free the top rails, the troops organized squads of five or six men to heave together and snap the rails in half. Within five minutes, the men had constructed a breastwork measuring 24 to 30 inches high. Private Bowen flopped down behind the rails to catch his wind and quit shaking. Turning to the fellow beside him, he noticed him also quaking uncontrollably. "I thought

---

6   OR 27, pt. 1, 423.

7   Roland Edwin Bowen Journal, Vertical Files, GNMP.

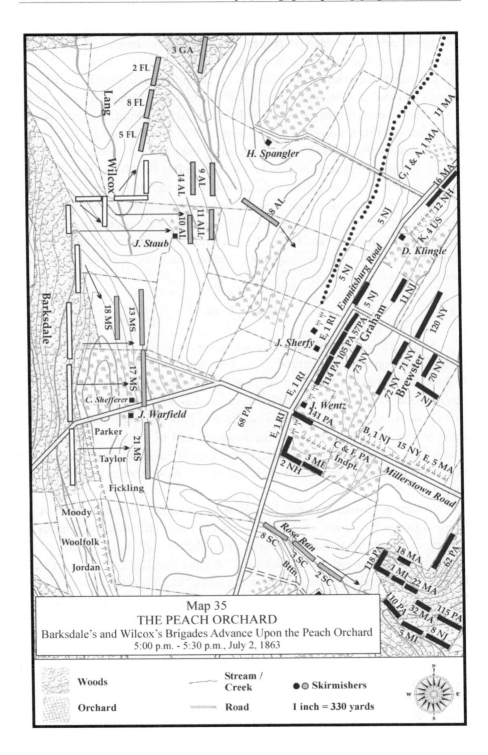

Map 35
THE PEACH ORCHARD
Barksdale's and Wilcox's Brigades Advance Upon the Peach Orchard
5:00 p.m. - 5:30 p.m., July 2, 1863

you never trembled," Bowen chided him. "By God almighty, I never did before," the frightened soldier shot back.[8]

Lieutenant Thomas Frederic Brown's six Napoleons (Battery B, 1st Rhode Island) wheeled into position on a knoll to the 15th's immediate right rear. Bowen rolled onto his back to scan the field behind him. Ward, using his sword as a cane, hobbled along the line, while Lt. Colonel George C. Joslin still remained mounted. "Colonel, for God's sake," the private shouted, "get off the horse." Joslin dismounted and handed the reins to Pvt. Bill Griswold, Company B's cook, who very willingly took the animal to the rear and safety.

With the ridge immediately west of the Emmitsburg Road obscuring their line of sight, neither infantry regiment could adequately protect the Federal pickets who had been sent forward to defend it. Lieutenant Colonel James Huston ordered the two left companies from his 82nd New York to occupy the Codori house.[9]

Barksdale's Brigade

As Brigadier General Barksdale lumbered along the rear of the line, his horse's gait bouncing the rotund general clumsily up and down on its back, Colonel Benjamin G. Humphreys (21st Mississippi) screamed, "Attention!" His regiment sprang to its feet. Rifle balls zipped into the line, thudding heavily as they occasionally dropped men from the line. Barksdale rode around the left flank of the 18th Mississippi, on the northern end of the line, and wheeled south. Centering himself on the front of the 13th Mississippi, his old regiment, he twisted to the right and yelled at Humphreys to move forward and swing to the left.

"Attention, Mississippians! Battalions, Forward!" Barksdale bellowed. Colonel James W. Carter, mounted on a white horse and sporting a red fez, trotted in front of the 13th Mississippi. "Attention!" he shouted. "Fix bayonets!" Steel clinked coldly on steel. "Forward march." The regiment had hardly gone several yards before Carter shouted, "Double quick, march!" The Rebel yell yipped shrilly above the din as the 13th and the 17th regiments surged forward, leaving the 18th and 21st in their wake. The 17th took hits. Private

8   Ibid.; Journal of Roland Edwin Bowen, GNMP, quoted.

9   OR 27, pt. 1, 423, 426; Ladd and Ladd, *The Bachelder Papers*, vol. 3, 1355; "Journal of Roland Edward Bowen," GNMP.

William Abernathy (Company B, 17th Mississippi) helplessly watched his friend Charles "Cul" Cummings go down. Colonel Humphreys (21st Mississippi) picked up the cry, "Double quick, charge!"[10]

As Barksdale's Mississippians stepped off, Wilcox put his own brigade in motion. Riding up to the 8th Alabama, still facing by the rear rank from the morning's fight, he commanded Lt. Col. Hilary A. Herbert to lead his regiment forward by the left flank to form the right of the brigade during the attack. Herbert hurriedly pushed his regiment in column of fours up the rolling hill, inadvertently leaving the rest of the brigade behind to reorganize as it advanced. The 9th Alabama waited for the rest of the brigade to form up; meanwhile, the 8th Alabama all by itself, continued leading a non-existent brigade charge. The 14th Alabama came up behind the 9th, while the 11th Alabama moved into line on the 9th's right, with the 10th falling in 75 yards behind as support.[11] The unavoidable delay destroyed any hopes they had of reinforcing Colonel Herbert's stalwarts. The dense smoke along the Emmitsburg Road completely swallowed up the 8th Alabama, making it impossible to observe its line of advance.

The Peach Orchard

A staff officer galloped up to Clark (Battery B, 1st New Jersey) with instructions for him to redirect his fire against the far left of the Union line to relieve the pressure upon the New Yorkers at the Devil's Den. The gunners switched to solid shot and trained their pieces on the trees above the Confederates' heads.[12]

10 McNeily, "Barksdale's Mississippi Brigade at Gettysburg," 236, 239, quoted on 236; J. F. H. Claiborne Papers, No.151, 29, Southern Historical Collection, University of NC Library, Chapel Hill, NC. Hereinafter cited as UNC; Abernathy, *Our Mess*, 34; "Reminiscences of the Boys in Gray, 1861-1865," 834, Vertical Files, GNMP; William H. Hill Diary, July 2, 1863, State of Mississippi Department of Archives and History, Jackson, MS, Barksdale and Carter quotes. Private William Hill noted that four minié balls struck and killed Carter. I have concluded that it sounds very much like the officer riding the white horse and wearing a fez that the 11th New Jersey cut down.

11 Marian S. Fortin, (ed.), "History of the Eighth Alabama Volunteer Regiment, C.S.A.," by Col. Hilary A. Herbert, *The Alabama Historical Quarterly*, vol. 39, 1977, 115-116; Norman E. Rourke, (ed.), *I Saw the Elephant*, (Shippensburg, PA, 1995), 42.

12 Hanifen, *Battery B*, 70.

Lt. Christopher Erickson
9th Massachusetts Battery
Robert E. Erickson Collection
Library, GNMP

Sergeant Ellis H. Timm and the plucky Pvt. Billy Riley, while swinging the trail of their gun around by the handspike, got hit by a shell, which burrowed into the ground underneath the trail before bursting. The explosion kicked up the rear of the piece, throwing the muzzle downward, and catapulted both men 20 feet into the air. The concussion wounded the #1 man in the knee and knocked out Pvt. George W. Bonnell, the #4 man. Timm and Riley hit the ground as one with Riley on the bottom. Private Hanifen, judging by the amount of dirt and blood covering them, at first thought them both dead. Timm quickly got to his feet, scraping the dirt out of his eyes. Was Riley hurt? he asked. As a matter of fact, he was, and the blood that splattered them was his. "By Jiminey," the Irishman moaned, "I didn't think they could touch me without taking a limb, and now, damn 'em, they have taken half the meat I did have." The shell had ripped all the flesh from his right hip down to the bone.

Unaware of his injury, 1st Lt. Robert Simms shouted at him: "Riley, why the bloody hell don't you roll that gun by hand to the front?" Turning his pulverized hip toward Simms, he yelled back: "Lieutenant, if your hip was shot off like that, what the bloody hell would you do?" Simms ordered him to the hospital.[13]

As the crippled Irishman dragged himself away on his two hands and his good leg, Pvt. Caleb B. Harrison took the place of #1 on the gun. He cursed the Rebs when a solid shot burst the sponge bucket under the muzzle. The crew had to empty their canteens into the replacement bucket, enabling him to

13 Ibid.

sponge the bore. Having regained consciousness and resumed his post, Bonnell pulled the lanyard and a number of the men cried out: "Take that for Riley!" Lieutenant Simms sent Pvt. Michael Hanifen back to Plum Run, near Trostle's, with the crew's empty canteens.[14]

With the wounded already filling the farm yard, it was too dangerous to keep the III Corps field hospital there. As the hospital attendants began packing up to move, a stretcher party brought in Pvt. Timothy Kearns (Company A, 71st New York) with both his legs shot away. Both Kearns and Chaplain Twitchell, who went to his side, knew he did not have long to live. Giving Twitchell his wife's address and commending his soul to the Lord, he died. By then the hospital had relocated to safer ground, and the preacher abandoned his friend's corpse to attend to the other wounded.[15]

While all this was happening, Captain Ames had rendezvoused with his Battery G, 1st New York, in the hollow near the Trostle house from which it had started a few hours earlier. Rounding up his crews, he led them east toward the Baltimore Pike to refit from the ammunition trains and to count their losses.[16]

Confederate artillery rounds continued to pour into the Federal batteries from the front and the right. From the start, the Rebel artillery to the south seemed to have singled out Phillips' guidon, which was posted near his right gun. The first round killed the two wheel horses on his right limber and shattered the carriage pole into splinters. A succession of case shots from the right flank whooshed in among the battery's horses, taking a grisly toll. The drivers had to continually cut dead animals from their harnesses and replace them. The Rebels, however, were killing horses faster than they could be replaced. Despite the annoying flank fire, Phillips continued methodically to exchange shots with the Confederate batteries to his front. He had his men fire slowly, and periodically had them cease altogether.[17]

To his left, Bigelow's 9th Massachusetts Battery began taking hits also. Rebel fire decimated #2's crew in seconds. Private Reuben L. Willis, who was running ammunition on the left piece, watched helplessly as Pvt. Arthur

14 Ibid., 71-73, quote on 73.

15 Joseph H. Twitchell to Sister, July 5, 1863, YU.

16 Ames, *Battery G*, 76.

17 Regimental Committee, *5th Massachusetts Battery*, 635-636; Ladd and Ladd, *The Bachelder Papers*, vol. 1, 166-167.

Murphy collapsed—dead at the trail of the gun before he could pull the lanyard. Private Henry Fenn, temporarily serving as #1 at the muzzle, dropped his rammer and raced around the tail of the piece. Seizing the lanyard, he attempted to fire the gun, but a bullet through the heart killed him before he could snap the friction primer. Seeing Fenn go down, Pvt. John Crosson, the #2 man, stepped back to the trail and was also slain instantly. Private Albert B. Smith, the only crewmember left, leaped over the trail, snatched up the lanyard and discharged the gun.[18] Simultaneously, a piece of spherical case struck Lieutenant Erickson in the chest. Captain Bigelow ordered him to get the wound treated, and the lieutenant rode off toward Trostle's.

A considerable number of the men farther to the rear threw themselves down to escape the bullets and shrapnel whistling about them. Gunner Augustus Hessie, on #5, the far right gun in the line, hurled himself to the ground every time the piece loosed a round. Interpreting his actions as cowardice, Captain Bigelow rode over to reprimand him when he realized that Hessie was merely watching the effects of each round by peering under the voluminous sulfuric cloud that enveloped the gun every time it fired. In the fury of the action, a piece of shrapnel hurtled into the crew from out of nowhere. It struck Pvt. David Brett on the hand and knocked him to the ground just as the gun fired. Before he could recover himself, the wheel recoiled over his foot. Miraculously, he came away with a flesh wound and a bruised foot. Private James T. Gilson, one of that crew's drivers sat up to fill his pipe when a bullet tore through his neck. Spurting blood, he fell over, twitched, and died.[19]

Presently, the 3rd Maine came upon the left flank of the 2nd New Hampshire and joined them in cracking off rounds at the Confederates. No sooner had they gotten there, than the 68th Pennsylvania, under Graham's personal direction, crossed behind the 2nd New Hampshire and went into line on the west side of the Orchard, overlooking the Emmitsburg Road.[20]

With the Confederates to their front under cover, Colonel Bailey (2nd New Hampshire) noticed a Rebel brigade veering toward the Millerstown-Emmitsburg Roads. He immediately ordered the New Englanders to redirect their musketry by the right oblique into that brigade's flank, but to no avail. No

---

18 Baker, *9th Massachusetts Battery*, 76.

19 Ibid., 76, 79, 221; Putnam Deane, (ed.), *"My Dear Wife…" The Civil War Letters of David Brett, 9th Massachusetts Battery, Union Cannoneer* (Little Rock, 1964), 59.

20 Ladd and Ladd, *The Bachelder Papers*, vol. 2, 846.

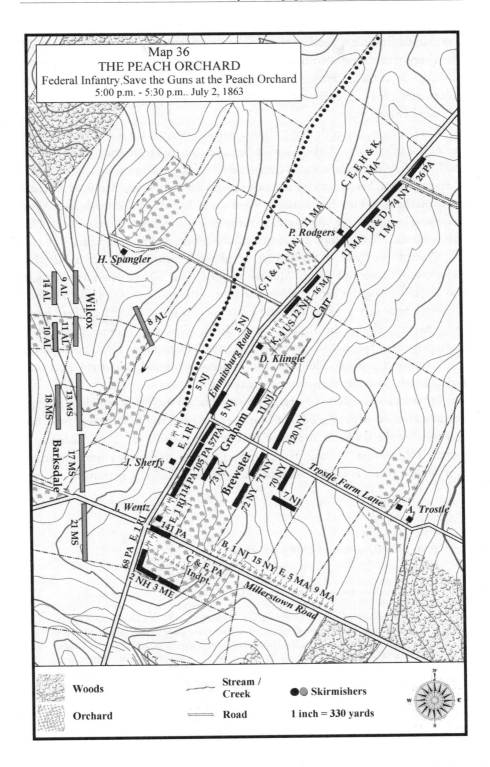

Map 36
THE PEACH ORCHARD
Federal Infantry Save the Guns at the Peach Orchard
5:00 p.m. - 5:30 p.m., July 2, 1863

less than 62 field pieces had opened fire across their position from what seemed like every point of the compass. The air thundered and rolled. The ground quaked. Screaming projectiles whined and screeched overhead, their trajectories crossing each other in midair and trapping the infantry in the orchard beneath them.[21]

On the right, the 68th Pennsylvania patiently waited for the opportunity to get a clear field of fire. As Barksdale's Brigade emerged from the woods behind the J. Warfield farm and entered the first field east of the house, Col. Andrew H. Tippen ordered his men to hold their fire until the Rebels reached the rail fence between them and the Emmitsburg Road. At 250 yards the Pennsylvanians cut loose and knocked a goodly number of the 21st Mississippi to the ground. The Mississippians halted, took cover behind the fence, and returned fire.[22]

The color sergeant of the 68th perished in the exchange. Before the flag hit the ground, Color Cpl. James McLarnon (Company K) snatched up the staff and began waving the banner from one side to the other cheering the men on. Artillery shells tore gaps in the regimental line. As more Federal artillery went into battery along the Millerstown Road, Graham ordered the 68th Pennsylvania to fall back to the rear of the guns. The regiment raced north along the Emmitsburg Road, filed into the Millerstown Road, and went into line facing south, with the Wentz house behind it.[23]

Private Haynes (2nd New Hampshire) watched the Pennsylvanians pulling out, and erroneously assumed that Confederates had driven them away from his regiment's right flank. At the same time, the 3rd Maine left about faced and marched to the rear. Without flank supports, and with rounds coming in from everywhere, Bailey could not maintain his position. The regiment stood up, and

---

21 Haynes, *2nd New Hampshire* (1896), 141, 308-309.

22 *OR* 27, pt. 1, 499.

23 Nicholson, *Pennsylvania At Gettysburg*, vol. 1, 394; *OR* 27, pt. 1, 499; Haynes, *2nd New Hampshire* (1896), 141, 308-309; Hanifen, *Battery B*, 76. Tippen stated that his regiment fell back behind the guns. Haynes noted in the regimental history that the 3rd Maine and the 68th Pennsylvania came to the regiment's support the second time when it reached the crest of the hill, which would have been along the Millerstown Road. To come to that regiment's aid, the 68th Pennsylvania had to have been on the north bank of the road facing south. Tippen does not say how long his regiment was in that position before Graham ordered him to face his regiment to the west. Michael Hanifen, of Clark's battery, mistakenly referred to the 68th as the 63rd.

turning their backs to the Rebs, the line hurriedly retired up the slope. Occasionally, men turned around to snap off rounds to the south.[24]

About 140 yards north of the fence, just under the crest of the hill south of the Millerstown Road, Bailey halted the 2nd New Hampshire and commanded it to "Change front to the rear, on first company." The maneuver brought the regiment onto a new line perpendicular to its old one, with its left company on the low ground and the rest of the regiment on the top of the hill facing west. On the right of the regiment a considerable number of men from Company B, many of them wounded, darted across Millerstown Road, took cover behind the Wentz house, and began sniping at the Confederate color bearers. At that point, with the Rebels about 60 feet away, the New Englanders poured a volley directly into their faces.[25]

The Millerstown Road
5:30 p.m.

Seeing, Clark ordered his gunners to blast the Confederates attempting to flank the orchard from the west. With the battery's ammunition getting dangerously low, he dispatched Orderly Sgt. Benjamin Galbraith to the rear to hurry Pvt. John Cronk forward with the ammunition wagon.[26]

The Woods on the West Side of the Stony Hill

Farther to the east, Captain Donaldson (118th Pennsylvania) could see no Confederate infantry through the smoke, which engulfed the low ground between his men and the Peach Orchard. The artillery fire, now at a deafening crescendo, shook the woods and filled the fields south of the Millerstown Road with billowing sulfuric clouds. To his right, in the distance, Donaldson heard an officer scream for canister. Just then an unexpected volley reverberated in the woods behind him to the left rear. Two others followed in rapid succession until crash of small arms fire merged into a constant roar. The pungent, unmistakable acrid taste of black powder soured the men's stomachs and burned their nostrils and eyes.

24 Haynes, *2nd New Hampshire* (1896), 141, 308-309.

25 *OR* 27, pt. 1, 574; ibid., 309, quoted.

26 Hanifen, *Battery B*, 73-74.

Presently, the regiment's skirmishers raced back into the ranks. Incredulously Donaldson watched as Kershaw's 8th South Carolina, 3rd Battalion, and 2nd South Carolina veered obliquely across his front, heading directly for Bigelow's guns. Many of the Rebels in their shirtsleeves fired as they advanced, while Bigelow's gunners cut loose with spherical case, which burst instantly upon leaving the muzzles of the guns.

Unable to resist such a target of opportunity, the right wing of the 118th Pennsylvania simply fired at will. The men maintained a regimental line, refusing to take cover. Private Godfrey (Company K), still several steps in front of the company, blazed away. "Give them hell boys," he screamed as he rapidly loaded and fired. His enthusiasm carried into the line. Several of the men loaded their weapons and passed them up to Godfrey who kept firing away. While Donaldson paced the line, he noticed a tall, bearded Confederate halt to return several shots before he followed after his men into the smoke at trail arms.[27]

The Rose Woods
South of the Stony Hill

Kershaw pushed the 3rd and 7th South Carolina by the right flank into line toward the wooded low ground immediately south of the Stony Hill, a movement which dragged Anderson's Georgians and the 3rd Arkansas into the fray also. Hillyer straightened out his Company C, 9th Georgia, picked up his stray lieutenant, Daniel N. Easley, and left wheeled his dwindling regiment down over the rocky ledge into the grassy creek bed along the northern base of the hill. Like the South Carolinians on his left flank, he sent his line plunging into the creek, its two- to three-foot high banks offering good protection from incoming rounds.[28]

To the right, loading and firing as they ran, the 8th Georgia charged with a yell into the marshy low ground at a right angle to the 9th. Some of them sloshing into the bog vainly tried to get at the Yankees across from them. Color Sergeant Felix H. King, leading the charge, sank to his hips in the muck. Unable to extricate himself, he waved the flag from one side to the other until a minié ball prostrated him. He sank into the mire, severely wounded, refusing to relinquish the colors until 1st Lt. Melvin A. Dwinnell (Company A) jerked the

---

27 Aiken, *Inside the Army of the Potomac*, 302-303, quoted on 303.

28 Hillyer, "Battle of Gettysburg," 7.

staff from his grasp. Just then a round smashed into the lieutenant's upper left arm. Private Edward Manes, a Jewish fellow from Company H, picked the colors up and brought them to the southern side of the bog. First Lieutenant John C. Reid (Company I) saw several men get cut down in the marsh, including one who had gotten too mired in muck to fall over. On the left of the line, Hillyer noticed that the water flowed red around his feet. Canister and case shot chipped the branches off the trees above his head while bullets gnawed the bark away all around him. Through occasional breaks in the asphyxiating smoke, he distinctly noted how the Federal ranks had drastically thinned in front of him.[29]

The Stony Hill

Rifle fire passing through the ranks of the 5th Michigan and 110th Pennsylvania and over their heads was cutting down men of the 32nd Massachusetts and others along Tilton's left front. As 2nd Lt. William H. Barrows (Company E), one of the most respected officers in the 32nd, fell dead, the enraged regiment instinctively cut loose "at will."[30]

An incoming round zipped into Company H, 22nd Massachusetts, and struck Pvt. Charles Phillips in the head as he stood in the front rank to the left of Private Carter. Carter heard "a thud, a sickening, dull cracking sound" as Phillips whirled to the right with blood rolling down his face, covering his eyes and nose. He gurgled blood as he collapsed, his cracked skull landing on Carter's left shoe. Carter stopped shooting long enough to drag his comrade behind the line and lay him on his back.[31]

Every regiment was getting shot up. As rounds peppered the color company of the 1st Michigan, Color Sgt. Patrick Connors dropped in the first fire; Cpl. John H. Harrington (Company A) immediately snatched the colors from the forest floor. A bullet slammed into Col. Ira C. Abbott's face. Two other officers from the 1st Michigan evacuated him from the fighting. Shortly thereafter three lieutenants went down.[32]

29 John C. Reid, Diary, GNMP; ibid.

30 Parker, *32nd Massachusetts*, 168.

31 Robert G. Carter, *Four Brothers in Blue* (Austin, 1978), 309.

32 George Lockley, Diary, July 2, 1863, UMI; "Col. Troop's [sic] Action Report of the First Michigan," accessed April 6, 2014, http://www.esthersscrapbook.com/HHawkinsGettysburg .htm.

With no targets to his front, Sweitzer ordered the 62nd Pennsylvania and then the 4th Michigan to break their regiments by the left to the rear. As the lines changed facing toward the south, and the two regiments fell into column of regiment behind the 32nd Massachusetts, a stray bullet instantly killed Maj. William G. Lowry (62nd Pennsylvania).[33]

The New Englanders of the 32nd opened fire the moment the Confederates reached the creek bottom. From their position on the hillside, peering down through the smoke-obscured valley, the Yankees saw little if anything of their enemies. They could hear them, and every now and again, a man dropping in their ranks confirmed the uncomfortable reality of the Rebels' presence. The soldier alongside Corporal West (Company H) fell and was carried away from the firing line. His lieutenant, James E. March, contrary to the regulations, picked up his weapon and cartridge box and shot back. Calling to West, he pointed toward a spot in the low ground where muzzle flashes pierced through the sulfuric veil; there had to be men there, he shouted. And West aimed below the sporadic bursts of smoke, hoping to avenge fallen comrades.[34]

Brigadier General Barnes rode up to brigade commander Sweitzer and instructed him to retire through the woods when he finally decided to leave the field. Nearby, Col. George L. Prescott (32nd Massachusetts) overheard the directive and loudly protested that he did not want nor was he ready to retire. "I can hold this place," he averred. Sweitzer immediately calmed him down, assuring him that the regiment would not retire until given specific orders.[35]

The Woods on the West Side of the Stony Hill

From his position along the Millerstown Road, Bigelow of the 9th Massachusetts Battery saw what remained of Kershaw's three left regiments, at that point not much more than a strong skirmish line coming toward him from the Rose farm. Donaldson saw them as well. The 118th Pennsylvania began disintegrating. Gaps appeared momentarily in the right wing as the men stepped back from their ranks to reload. An alarming Rebel Yell rose from the ridge along the Millerstown Road as the Confederate infantry surged toward the battery. With the Rebels now passed beyond his right flank, Donaldson bolted

---

33 *OR* 27, pt. 1, 611.

34 Oscar West, "On Little Round Top," *National Tribune*, November 22, 1906.

35 *Supplement to the OR* 5, pt. 1, 192; *OR* 27, pt. 1, 611, quoted.

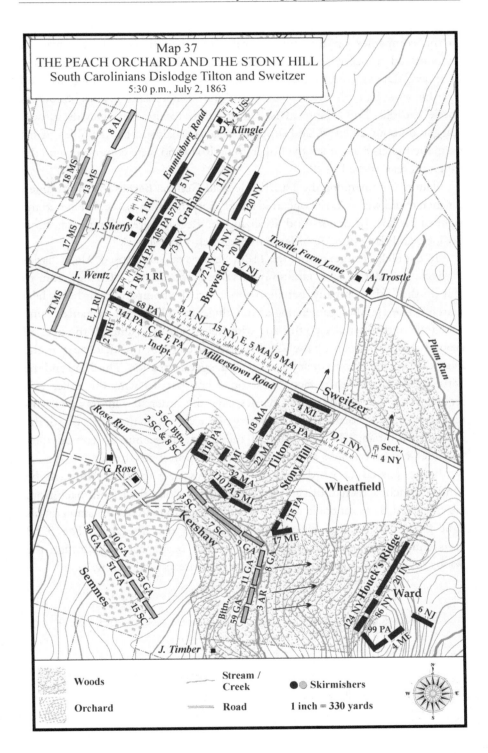

Map 37
THE PEACH ORCHARD AND THE STONY HILL
South Carolinians Dislodge Tilton and Sweitzer
5:30 p.m., July 2, 1863

Woods

Orchard

Stream / Creek

Road

Skirmishers

1 inch = 330 yards

to the companies on the right to calm the men down. On the way he encountered a barely-standing Capt. Richard W. Davids (Company G). "Captain," Davids said, "I am hit." "Where?" Grimacing and holding his hand over his waist belt, his friend said: "Thro' the stomach and bowels." Shouting above the din, Donaldson advised him to go to the rear. Davids turned, staggered about 20 steps, and dropped dead. Donaldson had troubles of his own: the Rebels had gained the Millerstown Road and were coming around the right and rear of the line.[36]

Tilton, commanding the 1st Brigade, told General Barnes that he doubted his men could withstand a concerted attack, and after Barnes reconnoitered the right of his line, he understood. Realizing the Rebels were going to smash his position and flank him, he ordered the regiments to fall back.[37]

In the nick of time: before the 118th Pennsylvania collapsed, Maj. Charles P. Herring, under Lt. Col. James Gwyn's direction, ordered, "Change front to rear on the 10th Company, battalion about face, by company right half wheel march!" The 1st Michigan, acting as the hinge, the 118th Pennsylvania swung back toward the east. Seeing this and with Rebel yells bouncing off the trees all around them, the men of the 22nd Massachusetts quit the field next as the individual soldiers ran to their places in the ragged formation. The 22nd and the 18th Massachusetts then faced west on a line parallel with the other two regiments of the brigade. Now, Barnes gave the order to withdraw. Tilton's regiments flanked north toward the safety of the woods on the north side of the Millerstown Road. The few men of the 22nd Massachusetts carried their wounded out on blankets and brought their weapons with them.[38]

Barnes passed the word along to Colonel Sweitzer to retire. Although the 32nd Massachusetts had driven the Confederates along their front back from the creek bed, Sweitzer could not expect his brigade to fend off an assault on his right flank. He ordered his three regiments to quit the field. The 32nd Massachusetts gathered up their wounded and began backing through the woods toward the Millerstown Road, returning fire as it withdrew.[39]

---

36 Baker, *9th Massachusetts Battery*, 59; Aiken, *Inside the Army of the Potomac*, 303-305, quote on 303.

37 *OR 27*, pt. 1, 607.

38 Aiken, *Inside the Army of the Potomac*, 303-305, quote on 305; Carter, *Four Brothers in Blue*, 309.

39 *OR 27*, pt. 1, 611; Parker, *32nd Massachusetts*, 169.

Near the bottom of the Stony Hill, Capt. Isaac Hamilton (Company C) saw Maj. Isaac Rogers, with a shattered pistol in his right hand, go into the ranks of the 110th Pennsylvania to steady them. He also watched General de Trobriand and his staff ride into the line to steady the 5th Michigan. At that moment, the Pennsylvanians' color bearer staggered under the impact of a hit and tottered away from the line. Hamilton, who miraculously had not been shot from his horse, rode over to the standard bearer, admonishing him to remain steady. "I am wounded," the man choked back. "Where?" the lieutenant demanded. "In the throat." But the fellow was mistaken: the bullet had only glanced off the leather collar of the flag harness. Leaning over the man, the captain reassuringly touched his shoulder. "It is nothing," he said, "I see no blood." With that, the badly dazed soldier staggered back into the ranks.

De Trobriand and his entourage headed east into the Wheatfield. Hearing small arms fire erupting behind him, Maj. Isaac Rogers sent Adjutant Copelin scampering to the crest of the hill to see what was going on. Copelin was soon racing down to the regiment screaming the alarm: the Rebs were behind them. Without further ado, Rogers ordered the 110th to withdraw, leaving their dead in the hands of the enemy.[40]

Kershaw, realizing that the firing had faded to his front, sent the 3rd and 7th South Carolina into the woods and up the hill toward the position formerly held by Sweitzer's Yankees. The right flank of the 7th South Carolina halted upon reaching the rocky brow. The charge across the open fields to the Rose farm had severely whittled the regiment down. The 3rd South Carolina went in line on its left in the edge of the woods Tilton's Brigade had formerly held. While the right wing peppered the backs of the Yankees, the left sighted in on the muzzle flashes of the Yankee batteries, piercing the thick smoke like lightning slashing through billowing thunderheads.[41]

---

40 Hamilton, "Recollections," 117, CWL.

41 OR 27, pt. 2, 372. Various Confederate sources, while not specifically describing the direction which the 7th South Carolina faced, make it clear that the 3rd and the 7th fired at the Yankee batteries—Bigelow's and Phillips'— which had hit them as they approached the field. The 7th got hit on the right flank. A 200-yard gap existed between the 7th's right flank and any other Confederate troops, which indicates that it was facing north, with its right flank on the crest of the hill and not in the hollow to the east. Soldiers do not needlessly expose themselves to fire: the battle line had to have extended west across the face of the Rose Woods.

Chapter 10

July 2, 1863

5:00 p.m.-6:00 p.m.

"A handful of men can't drive the Yankees from that place."
—*Private Rufus Franks, Company I, 4th Alabama*

Big Round Top
5:00 p.m.–5:30 p.m.

With no immediate opposition along their front, the 15th and the 47th Alabama regiments halted in a north-south line across the summit of the hill. Colonel Oates ordered his worn out men to lie down and rest. Barely five minutes later, Law's assistant adjutant general, Captain Terrell, approached the regiment from behind along the trail that meandered down the mountain to the regiment's right rear and asked Oates why his men were not advancing. In his opinion, Oates replied bluntly, he had secured an important position. The colonel was to press forward, Terrell retorted. Oates protested: some of his men had fainted from the heat and needed a rest. Where was Law? Oates queried. Hood was wounded, Terrell said, and Law, the senior brigadier, had assumed division command. And his orders were that Oates turn the Union left and take the lower hill to the north [Little Round Top], if at all possible, and do it quickly.

Oates pressed the matter. His position on the peak, he argued, with a sheer drop off to the south and east, would necessarily funnel any Federal advance to the northern slope, and given half an hour more, he could convert the position into an impregnable Gibraltar from which he could repel 10 times his number. Artillery planted on the crest could command any place on the field from its height. Terrell basically agreed with Oates, but he did not have the authority to alter or create orders. Oates immediately asked to speak with Law and was told he was somewhere to the left, but the general had dispatched him to tell Oates "to lose no time and drive everything" before him as far as he could. Oates could argue no more: inform the general of the situation, he told the staffer, and that against his better judgment, he would obey his orders.[1]

Oates got the 15th and the 47th to their feet. Moving the regiments by the left flank, they filed down the mountain to the north until their right cleared the precipices in front. With the worst piece of terrain out of his line of advance, Oates faced to regiments right and sent them by the left oblique to the northeast toward the valley below. The men stumbled down the rock-strewn slope without encountering Yankees. Upon reaching the level ground south of Little Round Top, Oates peered through the trees into an open field beyond and spotted a large enemy supply train and, not 600 feet further on, the Federal ordnance wagons. With no skirmishers in front, and his men running hard, Oates believed he had found the Yankees' flank. He immediately sent Company A from the right of the line under the fearless Capt. Francis Key Shaaff to surround and capture the wagons.[2]

Ward's Brigade, III Corps, Army of the Potomac
The Devil's Den

Captain Weygant took stock of what remained of his 124th New York. At Company I, two companies to the right of the colors, he didn't see 2nd Lt. Milner Brown. "Where is your plucky new lieutenant?" he asked. "You will find him lying down yonder with four or five of 'I' beside him," one of the enlisted men said. "What!" Charles Weygant exclaimed, "Is he dead?" Yes, came the reply, killed at the head of the company.[3]

Farther left, he stopped behind Company K and learned that some men had evacuated 1st Lt. James Finnegan with two wounds. And at Company G, formerly the largest in the regiment, only a squad under a corporal remained intact. Captain Isaac Nicoll remained down at the rail fence, dead, lodged

---

1   Oates, *The War Between the Union and the Confederacy*, 212-214, quote on 212.

2   Ibid.; William C. Oates to Joshua L. Chamberlain, March 8, 1897, UMI; Ladd and Ladd, *The Bachelder Papers*, vol. 1, 465.

3   Charles H. Weygant, *History of the One hundred and twenty fourth Regiment*, N.Y.S.V. (Newburgh, NY, 1877), 178.

between two rocks. In Company E, only three enlisted men—Pvts. George Godfrey, Adam Miller, and Henry M. Howell—remained around the colors.[4]

Second Sergeant Hanford (Company B) knelt behind a large rock to load his rifle just as 1st Lt. James O. Denniston (Company G) jumped over him from the right to take cover behind another rock. Catching his foot on Hanford's ramrod, the lieutenant clattered to the ground, bending the rod and disabling Hanford's weapon. As Denniston tried to hobble to the rear with an injured leg, a second round cut him down. Several men carried him away. Hanford, despite four slight wounds, remained upon the field.[5]

The regiment's injured and dying remained helplessly strewn about the rough hillside in front of them. Nineteen-year-old 1st Sgt. Thomas W. Bradley (Company H), who fell during the counterattack to recover Cromwell's body lay propped behind a rock. In great pain, he prayed not to die and for a Federal victory. From where he stood at the crest of the ridge, Weygant occasionally observed a bloodied hand rise up among the casualties along the rail fence, feebly wave to and fro, then fall back down. Unknown to him, it was Corporal Scott (Company B).

Scott hardly moved. His comrades had left him unconscious, presumably dead, at the wall. As he lay there, a shell fragment struck him on the left shoulder, and a second bullet hit him in the left side. Breaking two ribs, it glanced downward and exited through his right groin. Another shell exploded over him, leaving a ghastly wound on his lower back. Upon regaining consciousness, Scott found everything paralyzed but his right arm.[6]

The 140th New York, V Corps, Army of the Potomac
The Millerstown Road

Having led the 140th New York east on the Millerstown Road, Colonel O'Rorke with Adj. Porter Farley cleared the northern base of Little Round Top. As the regiment double-quicked through the woods in column of fours toward the sounds of the firing, Farley heard horses crashing through the woods

---

4 NYMCBGC *New York at Gettysburg*, vol. 2, 871; Henry M. Howell to "Mother," July 5, 1863, "The 124th at Gettysburg," Middletown *Whig Press*, July 22, 1863.

5 Smith, *A Famous Battery*, 138-139.

6 Bradley, "At Gettysburg," *National Tribune*, February 4, 1886; NYMCBGC *New York at Gettysburg*, vol. 2, 871.

behind him, and turned to see the center and left sections of Capt. Frank C. Gibbs' Battery L, 1st Ohio Artillery, struggling up the hillside. The drivers lashed their horses and the gunners strained their shoulders at the wheels of the guns. The pieces pushed through the sweating infantrymen and continued west to the top of the hill.[7]

O'Rorke brought the first four companies of 140th toward the crest around Hazlett's left guns. Nobody on the southern face of the hill heard them in the din. The hellish panorama of the chaos in the valley took Farley aback. Riderless horses stampeded to and fro in the smoky creek bottom. The pitiful screams and plaintive mewling of the wounded and the dying, writhing helpless in the surrounding fields, drifted up the hillside. "Dismount," O'Rorke shouted. The adjutant and the colonel leaped from their horses and threw the reins to the sergeant major as the head of the column arrived. There was no time to deploy "On the right by files into line," the colonel cried out, "Down this way, boys. Follow me, my brave boys." With their weapons in their left hands at "trail arms," many of the New Yorkers struggled to "fix bayonets" on the run as they cut to the left then zigged to the right around Rittenhouse's left section.[8]

Confederates to the right front of the New Yorkers were putting a tremendous amount of pressure on Company B, 16th Michigan. Corporal William N. Colestock (Company K) was one of many who stayed at his post, casting aside his powder-choked weapon and snatching up one from a nearby corpse. The wounded lay unattended: Lieutenant Graham would not allow any of the men to leave the line.[9]

The 140th New York rushed down the southern face of the hill into the ranks of the 44th New York and the 16th Michigan. "Here they are, men," O'Rorke yelled, slashing the air with his sword, "Commence firing." The New

---

7 Farley, "Bloody Round Top," *National Tribune*, May 3, 1883. Farley insisted that Hazlett's battery cut through the 140th New York and supported this with an undated letter from Warren, which asserted that Hazlett came up after Warren had left Little Round Top. Oliver Norton in his book on the assault on Little Round Top published a tremendous amount of Warren's correspondence to Farley, which clearly indicates that after Farley badgered him long enough, Warren changed his original account of the action to agree with Farley's. Warren's earlier correspondence clearly located Hazlett on Little Round Top before the 140th New York arrived. So the battery which cut through the regiment had to have been Gibbs'.

8 Scott, "On Little Round Top," and Farley, "Bloody Round Top," *National Tribune*, August 2, 1894, and May 3, 1883, quoted, respectively.

9 Graham, "On to Gettysburg," in *War Papers*, vol. 1, 10; Colestock, "The 16th Michigan at Little Round Top," *National Tribune*, March 26, 1914.

Yorkers' sudden presence may have startled, but it did not panic the Rebels. Their galling fire dropped soldiers like autumn leaves in a gale. Company A returned fire. The Rebs seemed to single out the officers, in particular. Captain Milo L. Starks, at the head of Company A, took four hits but was able to stay with his command; Capt. Perry B. Sibley (Company G), shot through both legs, lay crippled, unable to crawl away; Capt. Christian Spies (Company B) took a bullet through the body and his lieutenant, Charles Klein, fell with a mortal leg wound; Lt. Hugh McGraw (Company K) suffered an identical fate. The regiment dove for cover in the rocks, among the ranks of Vincent's regiments, loaded, and returned fire.

Behind them just below the crest, virtually unnoticed, lay O'Rorke, dead from a bullet through his throat. Not 40 feet away lay the Reb whom the men thought had killed the colonel, his body riddled with 17 rounds. Dazed by the horrendous bloodshed around him, 1st Lieutenant Bennett (44th New York) stared emptily at the colonel's fresh corpse. The newly married Irishman lay at Bennett's feet, a victim of the first volley.[10]

Private William H. Brown (44th New York) shot away 35 rounds before the New Yorkers, the Sharpshooters, and Hazlett's guns slowly forced the Rebels back into the pines below. With the pressure off his front, Colonel Rice directed his regiment's fire by the right oblique into the rocky ground near the point of woods in Plum Run gorge. Once again, the shooting died away. Knowing from experience the Rebels never gave up that easily, the Yankees reassured themselves by solemnly repeating, "We must beat them." When the man next to him asked what had happened to his face, Brown slipped his hand to his cheek. To his astonishment blood flowed down over his fingers. In the excitement, he had never felt the shell fragment strike him. Lieutenant Graham (16th Michigan) used the relative quiet to scrounge cartridges from the fallen.[11]

---

10 Farley, "Bloody Round Top"; Bennett, "Fighting Them Over"; Samuel R. Hazen, "The 140th New York and Its Work on Little Round Top," all in *National Tribune*, May 3, 1883; May 6, 1886; September 13, 1894, respectively, quote from final article.

11 White, *Wyman S. White*, 166; Report of Lt. Col. Freeman Conner, NA; William H. Brown to "Mother," July 7, 1863, BU; Graham, *"On to Gettysburg,"* in *War Papers*, vol. 1, 10; Brown, "A View From Little Round Top, During the Progress of the Battle," *Philadelphia Weekly Times*, March 17, 1882.

Vincent's Spur

On the left wing of the 20th Maine, Private Gerrish (Company H) saw the woods to the southeast swallow up the skirmishers. But then he heard the excited cry: "But look! Look! Look!" Through the trees, the New Englanders saw a Confederate battle line charging through the same woods their skirmishers had been not seconds before. Oates' 15th Alabama and Lieutenant Colonel Bulger's 47th Alabama slammed headlong into Vincent's center and left. The 47th hit the 83rd Pennsylvania and the right flank of the 20th Maine head on. The 15th Alabama approached the 20th Maine's line at the oblique, with its two left companies closest to the New Englanders.

On the extreme left of the 15th, Pvt. William C. Jordan (Company B) deliberately stopped and squeezed off a carefully aimed shot. Expecting to die at any moment, he sidestepped behind a tree and hastily loaded his rifle. Ready again, he found himself alone, the bulk of his company having dashed across the narrow valley to the cover of large boulders at the base of the hill in front of the 20th Maine. Without thinking, he madly raced toward a large rock to his front. Throwing himself to the ground behind it, he glanced over his shoulder to see "Sandy" McMillan, as well as Ben and Sam Kendrick, running from the cover on the hillside to join him. The Yankees dropped McMillan and Ben not 10 yards behind Jordan. Sam, though hit in the foot, managed to make it to Jordan's side. Within a minute, six other Alabamians had piled in behind them.

The 47th Alabama, having lost contact with the 4th on its left, broke from the cover of the woods at the base of Big Round Top right into a shattering crossfire from the 44th New York to its left front and the Pennsylvanians directly across.[12]

Incoming rifle fire peppered the 83rd Pennsylvania on the right. Two rounds nicked 2nd Lt. David R. Rogers (Company A), one above the ear and the other on the arm. Bruised and bleeding, he remained at his post.[13]

Acting Major Ellis Spear (Company G, 20th Maine), behind the regiment's left wing, could see nothing in the thick woods to his left and front. Nor could he see the colors below the slope to his right. Corporal William T. Livermore

---

12 Gerrish, "The Battle of Gettysburg," *National Tribune*, November 23, 1882; Gerrish, *Army Life*, 107, quoted; Oates, "15th Alabama," 11, BCL; Oates, *The War Between the Union and the Confederacy*, 217; OR 27, pt. 2, 393; William C. Jordan, *Incidents During the Civil War* (Montgomery, AL, 1909), 43-44.

13 D. R. Rodgers to Julia, July 6, 1863, GNMP.

Sgt. William T. Livermore
Company B, 20th Maine
Library, GNMP

(Company B) in the color guard sent a round at the first Reb he saw. With that, the entire regiment loosed a volley at the right oblique into the Alabamians, enveloping the line with smoke and flame. "Boys, hold this hill," Chamberlain yelled.[14]

The unexpected volley from less than 50 feet away slashed through the 15th Alabama's left wing with devastating effect. Oates recalled it as "the most destructive fire I ever saw." The blast temporarily stopped the Rebels. They loosed several rounds at the Federals and again attempted an advance.[15]

Private Elisha Coan (Color Guard, 20th Maine) noticed some officers running in from the left behind the line. One of them, Major Spear, shouted at the colonel that the Rebs had them flanked and were getting behind the regiment and requested Chamberlain's permission to refuse the two left companies, which he granted. Spear ran back to the left of the line and pulled Companies G and C onto the ledge at right angles to Company H.

Oates saw the Mainers break ranks in front of his right and fall back through the smoky valley toward the west. But on the left the 47th Alabama was taking a drubbing. Oates determined to alleviate the pressure on Bulger's men by flanking the Federal left. He commanded his right wing to change direction to the left and wheel against the Yankee's exposed flank.

Captain J. Henry Ellison (Company C), having not heard the command, stepped up to Oates from the right. With his hand cupped behind his ear, he shouted above the racket, "What is the order, Colonel?" Oates yelled it back,

14 Styple, *With a Flash of His Sword*, 59-60, 77, quoted on 77; William C. Oates to Joshua L. Chamberlain, March 8, 1897, UMI.

15 Oates, "15th Alabama," 11 quoted, BCL; OR 27, pt. 2, 393.

"Forward, my men; forward!" Ellison cried out, as he faced his part of the line. At that moment, a bullet struck him in the head. Oates watched him thud onto his left shoulder, roll over onto his back, raise his clenched fists skyward, shudder, and die. The colonel thought him the handsomest corpse he had ever seen in battle.[16]

The New Englanders surprised the Alabamians with horrendous rifle fire. Oates recalled that the force of the riflery's effect upon his line was "like a man trying to walk against a strong wind." Captain Henry C. Brainard stepped in front of his Company G. Instantly, he exclaimed, "O God, that I could see my mother!" then fell dead among the trees. His second in command, 1st Lieutenant Oates, the colonel's younger brother, immediately took over, but just as quickly fell, severely wounded by eight bullets that found their mark. Former classmate and friend Lt. Isaac H. Parks (Company I) quickly dragged him behind a large rock for protection. And the moment he laid Oates down, a minié ball tore off one of his little fingers.[17]

The fusillade also cut down a number of other officers, including 18-year-old 2nd Lieutenant Barnett H. Cody, Company G's sole remaining commissioned officer. The impact of the blast drove the Confederates back a short distance. Oates drew his revolver, unsheathed his sword, and ran through his regiment's ranks. Waving the blade and racing ahead of his men, he screamed: "Forward, men, to the ledge!"[18]

A swarm of minié balls stung the 20th Maine from the front before a number of shots zipped in from their left flank. Chamberlain climbed on top of a large rock about 15 feet behind the colors and shouted for the left wing to refuse the flank by executing a backward left wheel, which put it at right angles to the colors. Companies G and C fell in on the left of the formation. At the same time, he shouted for the right wing to double its front by extending in single rank to the left, which pushed the colors to a point southeast of the rock upon which he stood.[19]

16 Oates, *The War Between the Union and the Confederacy*, 227.

17 Ibid., 218.

18 Ibid.

19 Gerrish, "The Battle of Gettysburg," *National Tribune*, November 23, 1882; Gerrish, *Army Life*, 107; Styple, *With a Flash of His Sword*, 82-83, 120-121, 133; Abbott, Spear, et al., (comp.), *The Civil War Recollections of General Ellis Spear* (Orono, ME, 1997), 35; ibid., 218, 226, 227. Spear

The Devil's Den
Smith's Section
East of Houck's Ridge

The fourth time the Rebels came out of the woods east of Plum Run, they did so in seemingly insurmountable strength. Captain Smith (4th New York Battery) ran back to the woods behind his guns and begged for the 6th New Jersey to save them. Stepping into the open, the regiment crossed in front of his section into the valley. As they continued forward, Smith urged Col. Thomas Egan with the 40th New York to save his guns at the Devil's Den. Egan promised he would and double-quicked his regiment in column of fours through the limbers and caissons, towards the Jerseymen's left flank. Soon enough the New Yorkers found themselves plunging knee deep into Plum Run. With the infantry covering his front, Smith had his men tear down the fence behind his section, enabling them to roll the limbers and caissons into the woods and witness the outcome of the chaos in the valley to the south.[20]

The Woods on Houck's Ridge

On the right of Ward's line, Capt. Erasmus C. Gilbreath's 20th Indiana had shot away most of its ammunition. The captain sent a runner to Ward begging for more and informing him of Colonel Wheeler's death. The general sent Lt. Alfred M. Raphall careening back to the Hoosiers. "Hello, Gilbreath," he blurted. "I am sorry Wheeler is gone; but as you are in command, General Ward directs me to say that you must hold the line as long as you can using ammunition of the killed and wounded, and when you can stay no longer, fall back toward the small cabin we passed coming in." At that, a minié ball shattered courier's left arm. Gilbreath eased him to the ground, unrolled his own blanket, and had some men place the lieutenant on it and carry him away.[21]

With his rate of fire dwindling with each passing minute and the Rebels getting too close, the captain ordered the regiment to quit the field. Color Sergeant William I. Horine collapsed with a ball through the right leg. With the

---

stated in his recollections that he got permission to turn back the two left companies to meet the attack. I believe Spear did not stay to hear the command to refuse the left.

20 Smith, *A Famous Battery*, 104-105; OR 27, 1, 526.

21 E. C. Gilbreath Manuscript , 72-74, quote on 73, ISL.

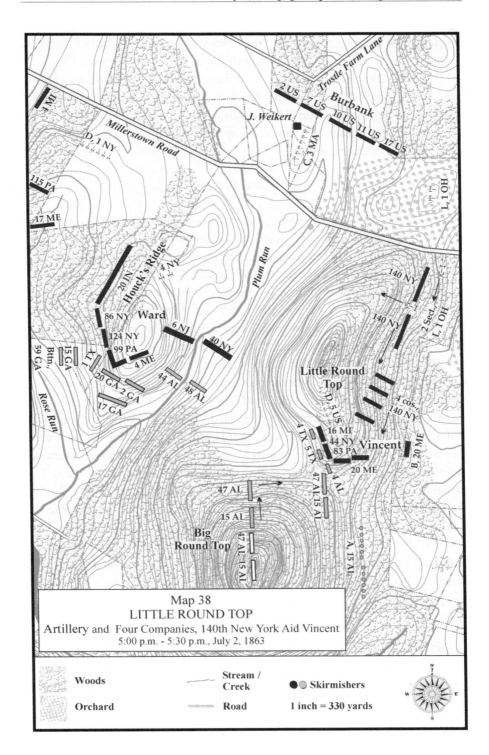

Map 38
LITTLE ROUND TOP
Artillery and Four Companies, 140th New York Aid Vincent
5:00 p.m. - 5:30 p.m., July 2, 1863

Woods

Orchard

Stream /
Creek

Road

●● Skirmishers

1 inch = 330 yards

Confederates taunting them with "they had it"—the flag—a boyish corporal snatched the colors up and backed out of the fight with the regiment.[22]

With the 20th Indiana retiring from the woods, Lt. Col. Jacob H. Lansing commanded his 86th New York to "Cease fire," and the New Yorkers marched back to their original position in the woods to the right of the 124th New York. There they faced about again and cut loose into the Rebels in the trees on the western slope of the ridge.

The Devil's Den

Meanwhile, Adjutant Ramsdell (124th New York) glanced into the valley behind the regiment, relieved to see Col. Thomas W. Egan riding his gray horse at the head of the 40th New York, near the southern end of Little Round Top. Survivors from the 20th Georgia saw him as well. Lieutenant Colonel James D. Waddell watched as Pvt. John F. Jordan (Company G) carefully sighted in on Egan and squeezed off a shot. Egan's mount dropped like a stone to the ground, but the Yankee colonel pried himself free, regained his feet, and swung his sword over his head, shouting, "Come on Fortieth to victory!"[23]

The left wing of the 99th Pennsylvania, protecting Ward's left flank, descended into Plum Run Valley. At the apex of the angle the Rebels thrashed the color guard. Eighteen-year-old Pvt. George Broadbent (Company C), a tall, slender, genteel soldier, whom everyone called "The Lady," had gone into battle with a death premonition. As he was asking Color Sergeant Munsell what were they to do when they ran out of rounds to fire, a minié ball hit him in the temple. He collapsed, blood spurting out the wound covering his grimy face. His messmate, Pvt. Charles W. Herbster (who also believed he would not survive the battle) knelt beside his friend's frail corpse. He gently wiped the gore off Broadbent's boyish face with his handkerchief, and just as tenderly kissed him. "Poor Lady is dead," he sobbed. Recovering and kneeling behind the body, he began calmly and deliberately firing into the Rebs. Color Corporal George W. Setley did likewise.[24]

---

22 Ibid.

23 Account of the War Record of Lt. Henry P. Ramsdell, Vertical Files, GNMP; Ladd and Ladd, *The Bachelder Papers*, vol. 1, 41-42; "File Closer" to Editor, August 29, 1863, New York *Sunday Mercury*, September 6, 1863, quoted.

24 Theodore F. Rodenbough, (ed.), *Uncle Sam's Medal of Honor*, (New York, 1886), 191-192.

The Confederates exploited the situation. As the Federal line melted across their front, they rushed forward to seal the victory. Heading toward the sound of the firing, the 44th Alabama, with the 48th Alabama to its right, burst into Plum Run Valley from the woods on its eastern side. The 6th New Jersey came into line to the left rear of the Pennsylvanians and the 40th New York deployed by files from the right into line and connected with their left, with the colors on the eastern side of Plum Run. They collided head-on with the 48th Alabama, which stood in the rocky swamp on the northern edge of the woods to the south. The colors went down, and the 48th's adjutant, Henry S. Figures, snatched them up.[25]

A few scattered shots zipped through the 44th Alabama's ranks. The veterans instinctively hit the ground as the 4th Maine unleashed a volley from less than 50 yards. The Yankees dropped the Luckie brothers—William and Archie—and killed James Mathews (all Company C). The bullet that killed Archie crashed through his lower jaw from one side to the other, tearing away the tip of his tongue. Litter bearers, believing the unconscious William had also perished, picked up his younger brother and carried him from the field. For a second, only a second, it seemed as if the Yankees had stopped the Alabamians, but their vigorous counterfire soon gouged holes in the Yankee line.

Colonel Perry's (44th Alabama) lightning survey of the field revealed his lack of support. Nonetheless without any hesitation he dashed over his men, screaming, "Forward!" And leaping to their feet, they charged pell-mell toward the eastern face of the Devil's Den. During their scramble over the boulders, Pvt. James Stuart (Company C) disappeared, never to be heard from again.[26]

Two enlisted men from the 4th Maine surrendered to the winded Colonel Perry, while his regiment swarmed past them. Incoming rounds from the 16th Michigan and the 2nd U.S. Sharpshooters from the ledge to the Southerner's right rear unexpectedly slammed into their backs, while at the same time, Hazlett's guns on Little Round Top were delivering a killing enfilade fire.[27]

---

25 Ibid.; Account of the War Record of Lt. Henry P. Ramsdell, GNMP; Raus, *A Generation on the March*, Map V, F-9 and E-7; "From the 48th Alabama, July 8, 1863," in the *Daily Huntsville Confederate*, September 11, 1863.

26 Perry, "The Devil's Den," and Purifoy, "The Horror of War," both in *Confederate Veteran*, vol. 9, 161, quoted, and vol. 33, 254, respectively.

27 Executive Committee, *Maine at Gettysburg*, 181; Purifoy, "The Horror of War," in *Confederate Veteran*, vol. 33, 254; *OR 27*, pt. 2, 394.

Grasping the 44th Alabama's colors, Maj. George W. Cary led the regiment's left wing up the rugged southern face of the rocks, while Perry took them in from the east. Cary's troops came in behind Company B of the 4th Maine and Company D of the 2nd U.S. Sharpshooters, completely cutting them off from any hopes of retreat.[28]

Private John W. Lokey (Company B, 20th Georgia), lying wounded among the bullet-battered rocks, spotted Sgt. Zuinglas C. Gowan (Company E, 4th Maine), isolated from his regiment, also braving the rain of bullets around the rocks. Lokey hailed the Yankee over. Gowan unhesitatingly offered help. "Put your arm around my neck and throw all your weight on me; don't be afraid of me. Hurry up; this is a dangerous place." As the pair headed toward the rear lines, Gowan said: "If you and I had this matter to settle, we would soon settle it, wouldn't we?" Since the Yankee was a prisoner and he himself a wounded man, the Georgian replied, they could come to terms pretty quick. A member of the provost guard picked them up a short distance into the field west of the Devil's Den, asking where they were going. Lokey told him he was wounded and heading back to their own lines. The guard helped them to a spring, and as Lokey laid down underneath some shade trees to rest, he led Gowan away.[29]

The Alabamians' unexpected surge brought the Rebels in the woods at the western base of Little Round Top storming onto the boulder strewn and brush covered slope again. Their Rebel Yells shrilled above the din. As the right end of the 1st Texas rushed down the hill behind the 44th Alabama, an artillery round shattered a monstrous oak on the other side of the creek, and the right of the regiment had to scatter for their lives to avoid getting crushed by its fall. Reforming on the flat below the eastern face of the Devil's Den, just north of the Devil's Kitchen, the front rank of the right wing knelt while the rear rank stood. They fired two volleys into the hard pressed 99th Pennsylvania then advanced, coming up behind Smith's abandoned guns.[30]

With his flank finally protected, Ward decided to retire his bloodied regiments from the battle. When the shooting subsided, Weygant turned

---

28 Executive Committee, *Maine at Gettysburg*, 351.

29 Lokey, "Wounded at Gettysburg," in *Confederate Veteran*, vol. 22, 400, quoted; Executive Committee, *Maine at Gettysburg*, 174. Company E, 4th Maine, held the southern end of the Devil's Den, right in the path of the 20th Georgia. Although Lokey never knew the name of his prisoner, Gowan was the only sergeant listed as captured in Company E.

30 Perry, "The Devil's Den," in *Confederate Veteran*, vol. 9, 161-62; Sims, *Recollections*, 2, USAHEC.

toward the flat boulder behind the left of the 124th New York and stared at Colonel Ellis' brains seeping out the hole in his forehead. The bloodied gold locket glistening on Cromwell's breast, he sadly realized, contained a photograph of the major's young wife. He ordered Ramsdell to take Company A's bugler, Moses P. Ross, and several other unarmed men and evacuate the bodies to the rear lines. He intended to get them North to their families by any means possible. The regiment began withdrawing, carrying most of their wounded away with them.[31]

Someone from the left of the line screamed, "They are advancing." Shooting an anxious glance into Plum Run gorge, Weygant saw the 40th New York retiring under pressure from a Confederate battle line on its left flank, which in turn, forced the shredded 6th New Jersey to pull out. The 99th Pennsylvania also began falling back. In the confusion, Color Sergeant Munsell misunderstood the order. Standing firm with several prone men around him firing, he mistakenly assumed someone had ordered the line to lie down. The regiment, however, had dropped back 60 feet before he realized that the Rebs had cut down five of his eight-man color guard. Private Herbster and Corporal Setley remained kneeling over Private Broadbent's riddled corpse, plugging away at the Rebs. Setley literally foamed at the mouth, while Herbster calmly loaded and fired as if at drill. Munsell pleaded unsuccessfully with them to fall back and then left them.[32]

Corporal James Casey (Company K), the identical twin of the state color bearer Amos Casey, lagged behind to smash up discarded muskets to keep the Confederates from salvaging them. Finding one loaded, he told Major Moore he was going to fire it. The second he discharged the weapon a round mortally wounded him. Moore and Sgt. Robert Graham (Company K) tried to drag him away, but he told them to lay him down and to save themselves. Munsell found himself about 100 yards from the Devil's Den when four shells whizzed in on top of him. Three burst well behind, but the fourth burrowed into the ground at his feet and exploded. The flagstaff landed in some rocks and brush on the edge of the crater with the flag draped down the side of the hole. Munsell collapsed spread-eagled, face first on top of the banner with his legs sticking out the edge

31 Executive Committee, *Maine at Gettysburg*, 166-167; *New York at Gettysburg*, vol. 2, 872; Account of Lt. Henry P. Ramsdell, GNMP; Henry M. Howell to "Mother," July 5, 1863, in "The 124th New York at Gettysburg," *Middletown Whig Press*, July 22, 1863.

32 Theodore F. Rodenbough, (ed.), *Uncle Sam's Medal of Honor*, (New York, 1886), 191-192.

of the shell hole. Stunned but conscious, he played dead, while the battle swirled around him, his greatest fear being that a Reb might bayonet him as he lay there. Presently, both the major and his senior captain, William J. Uhler (Company C), dropped with wounds, and command devolved upon Capt. Peter Fritz, Jr. (Company B).[33]

Captain John M. Cooney, Ward's assistant adjutant general, galloped up to Weygant with orders to withdraw immediately. Weygant hollered at Capt. William Silliman (Company H) to execute the order then ran into the woods on the regiment's right flank to retire the squad of men he had placed among the trees to fill the gap between his regiment and the 86th New York.[34]

Little Round Top

Major Jefferson C. Rogers finally rallied his demoralized 5th Texas. Turning them around, he cried out: "Forward!" The skulkers from the previous "charge" took a few steps and then turned back for better cover, leaving the major and his few stalwarts to attack on their own. Perry's charge dragged the 48th Alabama with it, which in turn pushed the 4th and 5th Texas and the 4th Alabama into the fighting again. This new pressure quickly forced the 40th New York to abandon its position. A couple of volleys burst from the opposing lines melded into a sustained roar with minié balls screeching loudly off of the rocks and bark flying off trees as if hit by mechanical strippers. Private Rufus Franks (Company I, 4th Alabama) drifted rearward from beneath the sulfuric pall enshrouding the regiment and encountered Adjutant Coles. "Adjutant, a handful of men can't drive those Yankees from that place," he shakily observed. "Can't you get Major Coleman to call the boys off before all are killed?" "There goes a soldier whose heart is gone," Coles thought to himself, as he shouted at Franks to come back. Without stopping or turning around, the private called out, "I am wounded." Coles did not pursue the matter, assuming the brave soldier had a slight wound. Franks, however, was gut shot and died later that day in the hospital.[35]

---

33 Nicholson, *Pennsylvania at Gettysburg*, vol. 3, 539-540; ibid., 188, 189, 192.

34 NYMCBGC *New York at Gettysburg*, vol. 2, 872.

35 Fletcher, *Rebel Private*, 60; OR 27, pt. 2, 411; Polley, *Hood's Texas Brigade*, 185, 187; Stocker, *From Huntsville to Appomattox*, 109, quoted.

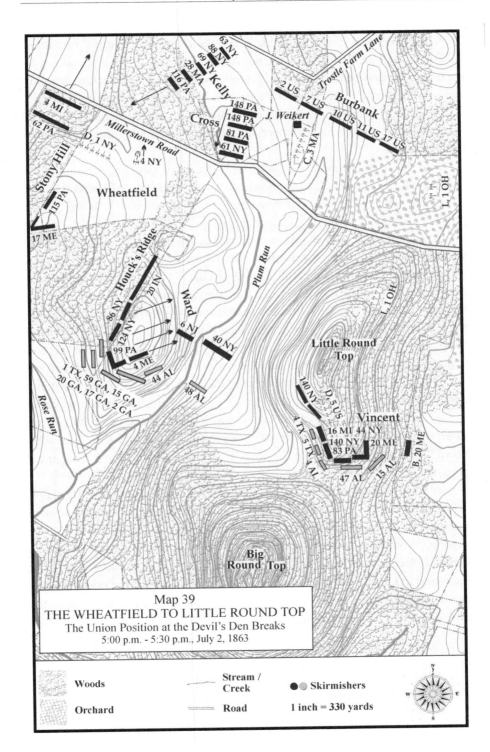

Map 39
THE WHEATFIELD TO LITTLE ROUND TOP
The Union Position at the Devil's Den Breaks
5:00 p.m. - 5:30 p.m., July 2, 1863

Woods

Orchard

Stream / Creek

Road

Skirmishers

1 inch = 330 yards

The Berdans, behind the boulders near the crest, took minimal casualties. As they pushed the Rebels back, the rest of the 140th New York materialized on the higher ground behind them and bounded down the hill in pursuit, dragging the remaining regiments of Weed's Brigade with them. Sergeant Wyman S. White (2nd U.S. Sharpshooters) heard, "Forward into line. Charge." The relief column broke into a run, its cheers jubilantly reverberating down the steep mountainside.[36]

Still sheltered behind his boulder with Pvt. John Griffith, Sergeant Giles (4th Texas) could not pull his ramrod out of his rifle's fouled barrel. He had seated the ball by shoving the rammer against a rock, hopelessly wedging it in. Not one to waste a perfectly good cartridge, he shoved the rifle over the top of the boulder, ducked his head down, and pulled the trigger. The recoil sent the weapon sailing out of his hand, and the barrel cracked Griffith on his left ear. The stunned Griffth vehemently swore at Giles "like a pickpocket for my carelessness." To his left, Giles eyed a straggler from the 3rd Arkansas kneeling down behind a stump calmly firing away as if at drill—and, to Giles' incredulity, singing between rounds: "Now, let the wide world wag as it will, I'll be gay and happy still." The Texan later confessed that he "failed to see where the 'gay and happy' part came in." Bullets ricocheted off the rocks and splattered bark off the trees behind them. Amidst the chaos, Giles saw only two officers standing upright during the fight: the 4th Alabama's Captain Cussons, an aide-de-camp to Law, and Major Rogers of the 5th Texas. Rogers climbed atop an old log close to Giles and began exhorting the men to "stand fast." The few men who heard him had no other choice. To leave the field under such an intense small arms fire invited death.[37]

John Haggerty, an aide to Law, braving the leaden rain, ran up to the major. Saluting, he cried out, "General Law presents his compliments and says to hold the place at all hazards." Rogers straightened and stared at the aide, his eyes blazing. "Compliments, hell!" he shouted. "Who wants compliments in such a damned place as this? Go back and ask General Law if he expects me to hold the world in check with the Fifth Texas regiment." Despite the odds, though, the color bearer of the 5th Texas, Sgt. W. S. Evans (Company F), defiantly bounded on top of a rock, fully exposed to the Yankee riflery and displayed the

36 White, *Wyman S. White*, 166-167, quoted on 167.

37 Polley, *Hood's Texas Brigade*, 174.

flag. Company G had just overtaken Smith's three silenced Parrott rifles at the Devil's Den.[38]

Adjutant Figures (48th Alabama), having urged the men forward, picked up a discarded musket and plugged away at the Yankees above him. Colonel James L. Sheffield assumed command of the brigade, pulled his hat from his head, and, in a moment born of desperation, shouted at anyone who could hear the reminder that they were Alabamians and were never to yield. Three spent balls cut the speech short, jarring but not injuring him.[39]

Captain Robert W. Hubert screamed at his Company K, 5th Texas, to "stand fast." Five enlisted men and two more officers rallied around him. The bullets zipped around them by the "hatfuls," Private Stevens recollected. Presently, twin brothers from Company C, who had strayed from their own men, joined the stalwarts and began shooting. The one brother staggered under the impact of a round. The other caught his lifeless body as he fell and tenderly laid him on the ground. At that instant, a bullet snuffed out his life too. Inseparable in life, the two brothers lay the same way in death. Before long, a private named Fitzgerald, whom Stevens had known his entire life, stepped up to the small knot of men and was immediately killed. Six other men soon joined the determined squad and in short order, they all perished by Stevens' side. Caught up in the deafening frenzy around him, the private never once thought the Yankees would kill him; he feared friendly fire from his own men who had sheltered behind him.[40]

The 4th Alabama, its ammunition expended, fell back 200 yards onto the higher ground south of them among the boulders in the forest. As they gathered around the large rock behind which Private Ward (Company G) lay, he heard a distinct voice call out: "Halt here, boys, and let us make a stand at this place!" It was Maj. Thomas Coleman trying to reorganize the few men of the regiment he could find. Suddenly an officer on Longstreet's staff, bedecked in full regalia, clattered into a nearby squad. Reining in his panting horse, he shouted, "Who is

38 Ibid., 174-175, quote on 174; Scott, "The Texans at Gettysburg," Sherman *Register*, March 31, 1897; *OR* 27, pt. 2, 413; "Pickett and Hood at Gettysburg," *Southern Bivouac*, vol. 3, 77. Scott erroneously reported Pvt. George A. Barnard (Company G, 5th Texas) as the regiment's color bearer. Rogers claims Sgt. W. S. Evans (Company F) carried the flag to the front.

39 Henry S. Figures to "Ma and Pa," July 30, 1863, Figures Collection, Madison County Public Library, Huntsville, AL, hereinafter cited as MCPL; John Dykes Taylor, *History of the 48th Alabama Volunteer Regiment, C.S.A.* (Dayton, 1985), 18.

40 Stevens, *Reminiscences*, 114.

in command of this regiment?" An exhausted soldier, gasping for breath, pointed toward the rear where Coles was attempting to reform the line. The officer spurred up to Adjutant Coles. Leaning out of the saddle, and putting his entire weight on Coles' shoulder, he commanded, "Get your men into line, sir, and charge that position." The man reeked of alcohol; nevertheless, the adjutant politely told him he needed to give the order to the major and pointed him out. The officer, however, changed his mind and crashed through clusters of howling and cursing Alabamians getting out of the way of his plunging horse.[41]

Little Round Top
5:30 p.m.-6:00 p.m.

With the infantry cleared from the front of the guns on the brow of the hill, Hazlett yelled "By hand to the front! Now, boys, give them canister." His guns plastered the Confederates in Plum Run gorge and along Houck's Ridge. As Weed's men poured around the northern part of the hill, Captain Augustus Martin glanced at his watch and estimated that Hazlett and Vincent had been there about half an hour before their arrival.[42]

At the Devil's Den, the severely wounded Colonel Walker ordered his 4th Maine from the field. Sergeant Edgar L. Mowbry (Company B) and Cpl. Freeman M. Roberts (Company F) lifted their hamstrung commander between them and carried him away. Color Sergeant Henry O. Ripley (Company B), the only uninjured member of the color guard, bore the tattered flag on its shattered staff off the field.[43]

Plum Run Gorge

With Confederates swarming over the ground the regiment formerly held, Weygant and his skirmishers from Company A, 124th New York, quickly slipped into the valley. Making their way toward the northern end of Little Round Top, they happened upon Ward. The general had halted the 124th to

---

41 Stocker, *From Huntsville to Appomattox*, 105, quoted; Ward, "Incidents and Personal Experiences," in *Confederate Veteran*, vol. 8, 348.

42 Scott, "On Little Round Top," *National Tribune*, August 2, 1894, quoted; Martin, "Little Round Top," *Gettysburg Compiler*, October 12, 1899.

43 Executive Committee, *Maine at Gettysburg*, 182.

compliment it for its defense of the left of the line. According to Weygant, Ward "expected almost impossible things of his old troops; but that such a heroic, noble resistance as we had made, was beyond anything he had ever dared to hope for, even from them."[44]

With his arms filled with captured swords, Major Cary (44th Alabama) bounded down the eastern face of the Den and found Colonel Perry leaning against a large boulder. Their own artillery as well as the Yankee guns, Cary warned, had them in their sights. He could attest to the effectiveness of the Yankee pieces, the exhausted Perry replied. A case shot detonated, peppering a rock within arm's reach of the colonel. Pull the men back to the shelter of the western and the southern face of the slope, he told Cary. The major had barely gone when he returned with word that a Yankee counterattack was coming that would envelop the regiment. Jumping up Perry collapsed, completely done in by the heat. At that moment someone hollered: "There is Benning; we are all right now." Seconds later, Benning's 2nd and 17th Georgia Regiments swept over Cary's left wing, moving north. Too spent to move, Perry crawled between two boulders and hunkered down, to await his fate. He later recalled, "The incessant roar of small arms, the deadly hiss of minié balls, the shouts of the combatants, the booming of the cannon, the explosion of shells, and the crash of their fragments among the rocks, all blended in one dread chorus whose sublimity and terror no expressing could compass." The Georgians pushed onto the high ground right into a wall of fire. A bullet to the heart killed Col. William T. Harris (2nd Georgia) while he cheered his regiment on. Both regiments went to ground.[45]

Little Round Top

Oates, his Alabamians right behind him, leaped upon the vacated ledge, and fired his pistol at Maj. Spear's Companies G and C as they fell back on the left of Companies H and A and the left wing of Company F, perpendicular to the colors. The stubborn Yankees rallied and charged, but the Rebs drove them back with heavy losses.

44 NYMCBGC *New York At Gettysburg*, vol. 2, 872.

45 Perry, "The Devil's Den," in *Confederate Veteran*, vol. 9, 162, quoted; OR 27, pt. 2, 420; "Report of General H. L. Benning," in *SHSP*, vol. 4, 170.

Farther to the left, Lieutenant Colonel Bulger (47th Alabama) went down in a heap, severely wounded with a minié ball through his lung. Believing the colonel had perished, Maj. James M. Campbell took command, helplessly watching the small arms fire slaughter his men. His line shattered and streamed to the cover of the woods. Unable to find Adj. William H. Keller, Campbell tried to stop them. Oates temporarily abandoned his line and bolted into the 47th's disorganized ranks but also failed to make them stand. He never forgave Campbell or the adjutant for not trying to remain upon the field. While Oates attempted to restore the 47th, the Yankees once again unsuccessfully attacked his right wing, grappling with his Rebels in hand-to-hand combat.[46]

Casualties were escalating in the 20th Maine. Private Gerrish (Company H) watched the ranks rapidly thin around him. One of the casualties, recoiling from a bullet in the chest, was his former messmate and close friend, 1st Sgt. Charles W. Steele. "My God, Sergeant Steele!" Capt. Joseph F. Land blurted. Steele realized his plight: "I am going, captain," he gasped, falling dead at the officer's feet. The giant Sgt. Isaac N. Lathrop collapsed with a mortal wound, as did Pvt. George W. Buck, whom Land promoted to sergeant as he lay dying. Before long the men had expended their allotted rounds and were forced to loot the cartridge boxes of the crippled and slain.[47]

Spear walked toward the east-west ridge which separated the left wing of Company F, the color company, from the rest of the regiment. Color Sergeant Andrew J. Tozier (Company I) held the center with what was left of the guard between the boulders on the southern face of the hill. Jabbing the flagstaff in the ground, he looped his left arm around the staff and with a discarded rifle plugged away at the Rebels. All the while, he chewed on a piece of cartridge paper. The major leaned over Pvt. James A. Knight (Company G), asking where he was hit. "Right through me," he groaned. From there the 20th Maine's line bent at right angles: Companies G, C, A, and H with half of Company F on the top of the plateau formed the left wing. The other half of Company F, with Companies D, K, I, and E, continued the right of the line downhill to the left of the 83rd Pennsylvania. Spear, noting that the colors had given ground and left

46 Oates, "15th Alabama," 11; Oates, *The War Between the Union and the Confederacy*, 217-219; Purifoy, "The Horror of War," in *Confederate Veteran*, vol. 33, 254-255; William C. Oates to Joshua L. Chamberlain, March 8, 1897, UMI; *OR*, vol. 27, pt. 2, 395.

47 Styple, (ed.), *With a Flash of His Sword*, 67-68, quote on 68.

wounded men stranded between the lines, did not return to his assigned position until he felt certain the color guard were holding their own.[48]

Color guard Corporal William T. Livermore could not see the Rebels on the left flank, who had taken cover among the boulders and along the ledge to the east. Every time a Mainer popped his head up to see where the rounds were coming from, he caught a bullet in the skull. One struck Capt. Samuel T. Keene (Company F) in the side, wounding him severely. First Lieutenant Holman Melcher assumed command.

At that point, the eight rightmost companies of the 15th Alabama bolted from their cover. Advancing behind their flag, they got as far as a large rounded boulder, about 40 paces from the ledge, and for the third time the Mainers rushed forward. One of the men lunged at the flag of the 15th Alabama, but Ensign John Archibald stepped aside, and Sgt. Pat O'Connor drove his bayonet into the Yankee's skull, dropping him lifeless to the ground. The sergeant's action stunned even the battle-hardened Colonel Oates, who witnessed the entire incident from less than 10 feet away. His adjutant, Capt. DeBernie B. Waddell, ran in from the right and asked for permission to take 40-50 men from the right of the line and advance them to a ledge from which he could enfilade the Yankees. Oates consented.[49]

Waddell's overshots whistled into the rear rank of the 83rd Pennsylvania in the low ground below the southern slope of the ridge. Captain Orpheus Woodward, commanding the regiment, immediately dispatched his acting adjutant, 1st Lt. Martin V. Gifford, to Chamberlain to inquire if the Rebs had turned the 20th's flank. He pulled the center of the regiment 15 paces north until his men's backs rested against the massive boulders at the base of the hill. With his line molded into a quarter circle, he still directed his men to volley to their front.[50]

Chamberlain got down from the boulder behind the colors as an officer raced in from the left of the line with the distressing news that the Rebs seemed to be outflanking the regiment again. Chamberlain, the professor turned tactician, sent a runner to Capt. Atherton "Pap" Clark, his acting lieutenant

48 Ibid., 60, 68-69, 300; Spear, *The Civil War Recollections of General Ellis Spear*, 34, quoted.

49 Styple, (ed.), *With a Flash of His Sword*, 61-62, 78, 83, 84, 106, 121-123; Executive Committee, *Maine at Gettysburg*, 256; Oates, *The War Between the Union and the Confederacy*, 219, 221; William C. Oates to Joshua L. Chamberlain, March 8, 1897, UMI.

50 Judson, *83rd Pennsylvania*, 128-129.

colonel, to hurry Company E from the right of the line to assist Company G on the left.[51]

He ordered Gifford back to Woodward, asking him to loan him a company to fill the gap created by Company E's departure. Braving a shower of lead, Gifford raced back to his regiment, breathlessly delivering Chamberlain's request; the Rebs had nearly bent the 20th Maine back upon itself, he told Woodward. The hard-pressed captain yelled at the adjutant to kindly inform Colonel Chamberlain that while he could not spare a company, he would extend his line to the left if the colonel would contract his to accommodate the move.[52]

In the meantime, Chamberlain, realizing that his men might misinterpret the maneuver as a retreat, ordered Company E to remain where it was and advised the left wing "to hold on as best it could." Which they did. The New Englanders advanced again. Unable to withstand the musketry at point-blank range, most of the Alabamians retired east to the cover of the ledge, leaving Waddell and his 50 riflemen on their own hook far to the right.

Gifford, nearly totally fagged out, returned to his own regiment with a request to extend the line to the left. From there, he slowly started north, looking for reinforcements. Chamberlain subsequently reformed his bloodied right wing into the standard regimental line.[53]

Oates bellowed at Sgt. Maj. Robert C. Norris to find the 4th Alabama and ask Col. Pickney D. Bowles to come to his assistance. The sergeant returned within a minute with the doleful news that the Yankees had gotten between the regiment's left flank and the rest of the brigade. He could not find friends anywhere to come to the 15th's aid. Simultaneously, Capts. Blanton A. Hill (Company D) and Frank Park (Company I) alerted Oates to the presence of Yankees behind them. Oates sent Park dashing through the open woods to verify the information and without delay he did: two regiments were closing from the rear. Through the woods Oates spied what appeared to be two lines of infantry taking position along a fence row about 200 yards southeast of his position.

51 Styple, *With a Flash of His Sword*, 61-62, 78, 83-84, 106, 121-123; Executive Committee, *Maine at Gettysburg*, 256; Oates, *The War Between the Union and the Confederacy*, 219, 221; William C. Oates to Joshua L. Chamberlain, March 8, 1897, UMI.

52 Judson, *83rd Pennsylvania*, 129.

53 Styple, *With a Flash of His Sword*, 61-62, 78, 83-84, 106, 121-123; Executive Committee, *Maine at Gettysburg*, 256; Oates, *The War Between the Union and the Confederacy*, 219, 221; William C. Oates to Joshua L. Chamberlain, March 8, 1897, UMI; Judson, *83rd Pennsylvania*, 129.

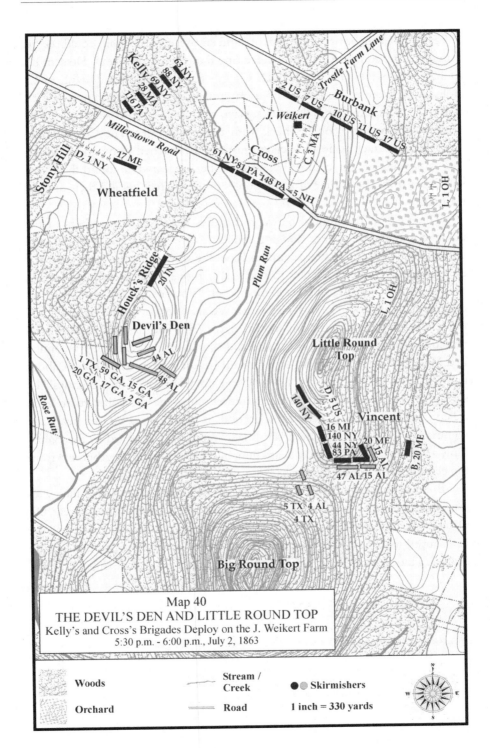

Map 40
THE DEVIL'S DEN AND LITTLE ROUND TOP
Kelly's and Cross's Brigades Deploy on the J. Weikert Farm
5:30 p.m. - 6:00 p.m., July 2, 1863

Woods

Orchard

Stream / Creek

Road

Skirmishers

1 inch = 330 yards

Through a slight rift in the pall of acrid smoke, Chamberlain could see his battered color company valiantly defending the regiment's salient. He sent his younger brother 1st Lt. Thomas D. Chamberlain, the acting adjutant, to Lt. Holman Melcher asking him to hold on until a regiment could come to their assistance. Not expecting Tom to survive the dash, he also sent Sgt. Reuel Thomas (Company I) on his heels with the same order. The Confederates unleashed an attack against the center just as they reached Company F. Flame and smoke masked the colonel's view, but when it cleared he found the colors still flying from the shelter of some boulders several feet behind their original position.

The pleas of the injured between the lines angered the members of the color company. Melcher, dodging bullets, approached the colonel and complained, "It's a damned shame to leave the boys there; let's advance and cover them." Though reluctant to risk such a move, Chamberlain acceded to the opinion of the other officers in the matter. "You shall have the chance," he told them. "I am about to order a charge. We are to make a great right wheel." He sent the order along the line to "Fix bayonets!" The clank of steel on steel rattled along the crest amid the thuds and thunks of the dwindling incoming fire. Melcher, his sword drawn, darted about 10 feet in front of the colors, about half way between the opposing lines. "Come on! Come on! Come on boys!" he screamed, as other company officers joined him. One the color guard even called out "Forward!" but for a few seconds it seemed as if no one heard the command. "Bayonet!" Chamberlain finally bellowed. "Forward to the right!" Only a handful of men actually heard him, but the command reverberated from the center of the line to the flanks.[54]

Bullets swarmed in from every quarter. Oates watched his men falling with stark rapidity. Captains Hill and Park both insisted that the regiment retreat, but Oates, with almost half his command shot down, didn't think he could pull the 15th out of its bad fix and decided to hang on and await reinforcements. With his men's blood lying in puddles on the rocks and the ground oozing with every

---

54 Styple, *With a Flash of His Sword*, 61-62, 69, 78, 83, 84, 106, 121-123, quoted on 69 and 122; Executive Committee, *Maine at Gettysburg*, 256, 257; Oates, *The War Between the Union and the Confederacy*, 219, 221; William C. Oates to Joshua L. Chamberlain, March 8, 1897, UMI. Private Coan mistakenly said that Captain Keene was acting major of the regiment. According to *Maine at Gettysburg*, p. 271, Keene was wounded and not on the staff. Coan attributes Melcher with having asked Chamberlain to move the company forward to retrieve the wounded. Gerrish probably misjudged the distance between Melcher and the Confederates. With the lines so close together, he probably did not step that far to the front.

step, according to Oates, he refused his officers' request and demanded they return to their men and "sell out as dearly as possible." Hill departed without muttering a word, but Park, after smartly saluting, calmly, smilingly replied, "All right, sir." Moments later, Oates changed his mind. He realized he could not stay where he was, and he ordered Sgt. Maj. Robert C. Norris to travel the line and have company officers tell their men to watch for the signal to retreat, at which they were to run back the way they came and not stop until they reached the summit of Big Round Top. No formalities: this was not going to be an orderly withdrawal.

The left wing of the 20th Maine surged forward and quickly got repulsed from the ledge. Seizing his chance, Oates gave the command to retreat. The regiment dashed to the rear—every man for himself. Private John Keils (Company H), blood streaming from a bullet wound which had severed his trachea, shot past the colonel at an astounding run.

Spear had hardly reached the center of the wing when he heard "Forward!" rolling from the center of the 20th toward him. Wheeling about, he saw the tip of the colors bobbing above the ledge. The four left companies quickly picked up the command. Company G on the far left rushed Waddell's startled detachment sheltering behind the boulders directly to its front. Unable to hear the command above the horrendous din, Waddell just happened to glance back toward the regiment to see Oates and all the soldiers around him leaving. He immediately yelled at his boys to pull out. He and the two soldiers closest to him broke into a run. The Yankees dropped the two enlisted men in their tracks, but Waddell did not look back. The rest of his men hurled down their weapons and went prone as the Mainers ran over and around them. "Don't fire! We surrender." Yelling at the Rebels to go to the rear on their own, the Mainers kept on going.[55]

On the 15th Alabama's left, Pvts. Jordan and John W. Hughes (Company B) decided not to hang around. Having determined he would prefer death to capture long before this, Jordan stooped low and cut off at the left oblique to the southwest. A volley whistled about his ears, miraculously missing him. Within 50 yards of the base of Big Round Top, he heard someone shouting his name. It was Pvt. Elisha Lane (Company B) limping toward him with a copiously bleeding thigh wound. As he reached Jordan, Lane threw his right

55 Styple, *With a Flash of His Sword*, 60-61, 78, 84, quoted on 84; Oates, *The War Between the Union and the Confederacy*, 220, 221; Ladd and Ladd, *The Bachelder Papers*, vol. 1, 465.

arm around his friend's shoulders, and they staggered to the safety of the woods. Hughes caught up with them on the hillside and helped drag Lane to the top of the mountain.

The Confederates on the right headed toward the stone wall east of their former line. To their surprise, Captain Morrill and his Company B from the 20th Maine with several stray Berdans materialized from behind the wall and rounded them up.

A captain in the 44th New York found the elderly Lieutenant Colonel Bulger leaning against a tree not too far from the regiment's line. Blood soaked his tunic from his chest to his waist as he sat, sword in hand, wheezing through the hole in his breast. To the demand for surrender of his sword, Bulger, without looking up, arrogantly demanded to know his rank. "I am a captain," the stunned New Yorker replied. "Well, I am a lieutenant colonel and I will not surrender my sword except to an officer of equal rank." "Surrender your sword or I will kill you," the captain demanded. "You may kill me and be damned," Bulger snarled, "I shall never surrender my sword to an officer of lower rank." The officer stormed away and returned with Colonel Rice, who proceeded to relieve Bulger of his blade.[56] By this point Waddell had run into Captain Shaaff and his detached Company A along the northeastern base of Big Round Top. There were Yankee troops in the woods east of the wagons, Shaaff explained, and he feared losing his entire command had he attacked. Waddell took over and retired the errant company a short distance up the hillside, where he decided to make a stand. The Alabamians opened fire upon Morrill's detachment and brought them to a standstill.

Simultaneously, the 20th Maine chased the rest of the Rebels as far as the base of Big Round Top then halted around the colors. Three Union cheers rent the sulfur-laden woods before they began leading their captives back to their old position. They dragged in the Rebel wounded while the Confederate prisoners brought in the Mainers' casualties.[57]

---

56 Oates, *The War Between the Union and the Confederacy*, 217.

57 Styple, *With a Flash of His Sword*, 69, 78; Oates, *The War Between the Union and the Confederacy*, 221; William C. Oates to Joshua L. Chamberlain, March 8, 1897, UMI; Purifoy, "The Horrors of War," in *Confederate Veteran*, vol. 33, 254-255; Jordan, *Incidents*, 44. Oates said that Shaaff returned to the regiment, but later he amended that statement by explaining that during the retreat he had no idea that Shaaf had met up with Waddell and made a stand on Big Round Top. He erred. During the fighting at Little Round Top, Oates remained near the colors and therefore did not have contact with the right of the line, where he assumed Shaaff was.

An officer and two enlisted men, separated from the rest of the regiment, slipped up behind Captain Hubert and his 15-man detachment, from Company K, 5th Texas. The Texans never expected to be captured. Private Stevens, who had fired off about a dozen rounds, started suddenly when the New Englanders' officer slapped him across the back with the flat of his sword. Throw down his weapon and behave himself, the Yankee demanded. Stevens saw blue uniforms flitting through the woods around him and complied.[58] As the detachment reached the hollow between the Round Tops, Hubert asked the Yankee officer where the rest of his men were. They would soon come up came the reply. Hubert soon realized that he had been had. "That is a Yankee trick, sure enough," he spat, "three men to capture fifteen!" Reaching into his haversack, he pulled out a silver cup and gave it to the Yankee officer in admiration of his courage.[59]

As Oates neared the crest of the mountain, he tried unsuccessfully to rally the regiment, but the ranks had gotten too scattered. Overcome by tension, exertion, and heat, he blacked out. Two enlisted men picked him up and pulled him to safety. Oates revived on the top of the mountain with Assistant Surgeon Alexander J. Reeves pouring water over his face; he then turned the regiment over to Capt. Blanton A. Hill (Company D) with instructions to reform it in the field on the western base of the hill.[60]

58 Stevens, *War Reminiscences*, 115; Judson, *83rd Pennsylvania*, 130.

59 Morris M. Penny and J. Gary Laine, *Law's Alabama Brigade in the War Between the Union and the Confederacy* (Shippensburg, PA, 1996), 384. In their superb brigade history, Penny and Laine identified the officer as Joseph R. Breare (Company E, 15th Alabama) because he was the last of four captured officers for whom they had no specific information. I tend to identify him as Capt. Robert W. Hubert (Company K, 5th Texas) based upon Stevens' detailed account and upon Judson's statement that the lieutenant and his two men got separated from the rest of their regiment. Either assumption could be correct. Penny and Lane did not cite Stevens' work because their account focused on the 15th Alabama.

60 Judson, *83rd Pennsylvania*, 130; Stevens, *War Reminiscences*, 115.

Chapter 11

July 2, 1863
5:30 p.m.-6:00 p.m.

"You will be killed too if you don't lie down."

—*Second Lieutenant Columbus Heard, Company I, 8th Georgia*

The Wheatfield

To the southeast, the closer the dense Confederate column approached the stone wall, the larger the holes in their formation appeared to the men of the 17th Maine. From the crest behind the New Englanders, Battery D, 1st New York, hurled shot low over them into the woods. With satisfaction, Private Haley (Company I) watched Rebels collapse by the score. But the 17th Maine began taking serious casualties as well. A bullet slammed into Cpl. Aurelius A. Robertson's forehead, killing him; a rifle ball caught Cpl. Frederick A. Mitchell in the leg; 1st Sgt. Franklin C. Adams lost a finger. Minié balls clipped the heads off the wheat stalks among Winslow's guns, clipping a few of his men and horses too.[1]

As the fire died away from his front, Captain Hillyer (9th Georgia) shifted the regiment's fire to the right oblique into the flanks of the 115th Pennsylvania and the 17th Maine, although dense smoke completely obscured their line of sight.[2] Kershaw's advance up the Stony Hill had flanked both regiments. Using Company B as the hinge, Companies B, H, K, and C of the 17th fell back along with the Pennsylvanians. Scrambling over the rail fence behind them, they

---

1   Silliker, *Rebel Yell*, 101-103; Ladd and Ladd, *The Bachelder Papers*, vol. 2, 1,059, vol. 3, 590; Winslow, "Battery D," *Philadelphia Weekly Times*, July 26, 1879.

2   Hillyer, "Battle of Gettysburg," 8.

Lt. Franklin C. Adams
Co. K, 17th Maine
Maine State Archives
Library, GNMP

reformed at right angles to the rest of the regiment and held their ground. Shot, case, and canister whistled and whooshed overhead in unrelenting cacophony. Suddenly De Trobriand galloped up behind the regiment and shouted at an aide, "What troops are those holding the stone wall so stubbornly?" When he discovered it was the 17th Maine, he ordered: "Fall back, right away!" But the regimental officers disregarded the command. On the right of the line, the companies at the rail fence continued to blast away at the Rebels. "Aim low, boys! Make every shot tell!" their officers commanded. At one point, a bullet killed a Confederate color bearer as he planted his flag on the wall. The New Englanders held on until they were out of ammunition, then they scrounged cartridges from their casualties in order to keep firing.[3]

Coming down through Plum Run Valley from the west, two mounted officers intercepted Cross and his staff, who had halted at the Millerstown Road on the southeastern point of the woods west of the John T. Weikert house. Lieutenant Hale recognized the one as a division aide. The other rode a fractious horse, which, in the noise of battle, violently plunged and kicked, bouncing the rider all over the place and sending Cross's staff dodging about to avoid him. The lieutenant tried to stay by the colonel's side, but only managed to hear him yell something unintelligible about Sykes to which the division

3   OR 27, pt. 1, 522; Silliker, *The Rebel Yell*, 101-103, de Trobriand quote on 101; Executive Committee, *Maine at Gettysburg*, 195, 196, officer's quote on 196; Ladd and Ladd, *The Bachelder Papers*, vol. 2, 1,059; Houghton, *17th Maine*, 92.

officer shouted back, "The enemy is breaking in directly on your right. Strike him quick!"[4]

Cross wheeled his horse about and raced along the southern flank of the column bellowing, "By the right flank! March." The 61st New York (97 men), on the right of the brigade, stepped into the Millerstown Road, with the rest of the brigade falling in on its left. This threw the officers and file closers in front of the regiment. Captain Lee Nutting grimly realized they had maneuvered into a "bad fix." Fronting by facing right would turn their backs to the Rebels. With no time to countermarch, the regimental line faced south. The 81st and the 148th Pennsylvania followed suit. The latter, which had approached the field in parallel wings, completely disrupted its formation deploying. The Company C, the color company, instead of being in the center of the line, led the regiment into the Millerstown Road, with Company A bringing up the rear of the wing. Company B, which was supposed to be on the left flank came next. The regiment was going into action with an inverted company formation and by the rear rank. This placed the taller men in the front rank and deployed the companies contrary to the manual-prescribed formation. But the Pennsylvanians advanced in good order nonetheless.[5]

Cross deployed facing southwest. His line halted a short distance into the field. The regimental "markers" darted to the front to indicate the 61st New York's place in the brigade formation. The right marker halted about 100 yards south of the Millerstown Road, with his counterpart on the left facing southwest. The line officers and file closers professionally aligned the small regiment before stepping behind the formation to their assigned positions. During the maneuver Lieutenant Fuller (4th Company) had not seen any Confederates behind the stone wall to his front, but after stepping behind his men, he noticed a couple of Rebels dash to cover behind the wall. Captain Lee

---

4   Hale, "*With Colonel Cross*," 7-8, quote on 8, PHS.

5   Hale, "*With Colonel Cross*," 7-8, quote on 8, PHS; Sigman, Diary, 49, IU; *New York at Gettysburg*, vol. 2, 460; Muffly, *148th Pennsylvania*, 876; "Account of an Unidentified Soldier of the 64th New York Infantry," Lilly Library, Indiana University, 50. Hale got his directions mixed up in his writing but not on his map. In the text, he said the road was on the eastern edge of the Wheatfield rather than the northern edge. The woods he is talking about are the woods immediately north of the Millerstown Road. The brigade did pass onto the field from the route east of Weikert's Woods. The "unidentified private of the 64th New York" clearly described Brooke's and the division's line of march.

Nutting (3rd Company) saw them too as part of the 11th Georgia crashed through the woods up to the wall.[6]

The 150-man 81st Pennsylvania came on line to the left of the 61st New York, followed by the 148th Pennsylvania. Passing through the thin belt of woods on the eastern side of the Wheatfield into a small corner of standing grain, Pvt. Henry Meyer (Company B) noted how incoming fire knocked the heads off the stems, making them dance dizzily in the air. Then he saw Colonel Cross waving his sword about as he followed the regiment down the gentle slope, blood trickling from under the black bandanna on his head. The seven leftmost companies entered the woods on the Confederates' right flank unobserved. Company B, in the center of the line inside the wood line, opened fire at point-blank range. Private Meyer, who had double charged his weapon, leveled it on two Confederates barely 10 yards away. Just as he was about to fire, the pair waved their handkerchiefs in surrender; Meyer held his fire with some regret. Just before reaching the woods on the southeastern side of the field, Pvt. William C. Meyer popped off a round at a rabbit which had been flushed from cover. Replenishing his haversack meant more at the time than the enemy minié balls zipping around his head.[7]

From where he stood, Private Osmon noticed how the Confederates' rifle barrels glistened like mirrors in the light. The regiment halted on a line running northwesterly, and its three companies on the right exchanged volleys with the Rebels. Private Ezra B. Walter fired his weapon so fast that it fouled. When a round lodged in the barrel while loading it, he asked Captain Forster and to pound the ramrod down with a rock.[8]

The Woods on Houck's Ridge

Lieutenant Colonel Hapgood, having left 1st Lt. Nathaniel F. Lowe (Company D) and the picket detail behind, double-quicked his 5th New Hampshire from the Taneytown Road toward the sound of the fighting.[9] The

6   *New York at Gettysburg*, vol. 2, 460; Fuller, *Personal Recollections*, 93-94.

7   Muffly, *148th Pennsylvania*, 536, 537. Accounts from the 8th and the 9th Georgia regiments indicate they did not get past the creek and the bog. The 11th Georgia, which could have charged to the wall, was the only regiment in the area.

8   Ibid, 591, 877.

9   Hale, "*With Colonel Cross*," 8-9, PHS; Child, *5th New Hampshire*, 204, 206-207.

New Englanders found remnants of the 20th Indiana trying to regroup in the hollow along the eastern face of Houck's Ridge. Captain Charles A. Bell of that regiment's Company B, took the regimental colors from the color corporal's hands while Captain Gilbreath (Company H) tried to call the roll among the survivors. Bell, the senior captain, assumed command and tried to rouse the exhausted men's martial fervor with a truly horrendous rendition of "Rally 'Round the Flag." Racing rearwards to find an appropriate spot to reorganize, Bell halted and frantically waved the flag to and fro. But the men interpreted his bravado as a signal to clear out, which they lost no time doing, breaking ranks and racing past the dismayed captain. By then the majority of Ward's Brigade had left the field.[10]

The 5th New Hampshire wheezed into line on the left of the 148th Pennsylvania. From less than 20 yards away, the Rebel fire punished the New Englanders' front. Color Sergeant Sampson W. Townsend (Company H) caught a bullet in the right thigh and handed the flag off to Cpl. Charles W. Reynold (Company K) before limping toward the rear. Puffs of smoke pocked up the horizon along its entire front.

To Lieutenant Hale, who stood behind the brigade in the Wheatfield, bullets seemed to materialize from everywhere. Officers hastily dismounted to make themselves less inviting targets and turned their horses over to their orderlies. Despite the tumult, Hale noticed the wheat flattened in the dirt. The Confederate skirmishers suddenly ceased fire, seeming to have evaporated before the brigade's speedy advance. The moment a Yankee head jutted above the horizon, the Rebs in the woods along the stone wall opened fire and dropped them from the line. The brigade's center and right professionally closed ranks, moved to the crest, halted, and returned fire.

The Rebel skirmishers, who lay on the opposite slope pinned between the opposing lines, could not escape. Leaving their weapons on the ground, they sprang to their feet and bolted into the right wing of the 148th Pennsylvania. "Get a file of men for a guard and hold them, Mr. Hale," Cross snapped to his aide. "Look sharp, there's more in the edge of the woods by the wall." Hale glanced left towards the stone wall on the southern side of the field as Cross blurted, "There's an officer. Get his sword."[11]

10 E. C. Gilbreath to ??, January 16, 1898, Erasmus Gilbreath mss, ISL, 73.

11 Hale, "*With Colonel Cross*," 9.

As Hale sprinted toward the Confederate officer, he defiantly plunged the tip of the blade into the ground and snapped the weapon off at the guard with his foot. Colonel McKeen (148th Pennsylvania) saw him throw the hilt at the lieutenant's feet and immediately dispatched a sergeant and two privates to Hale's side. The Yankees quickly rounded up 20 prisoners and herded them to the cover of a sassafras outcropping on a rock ledge a short distance behind the center of the regiment.[12]

In the woods on the southeastern side of the field, the 5th New Hampshire and the left of the148th Pennsylvania still held their own against the Confederates along the stone wall. Company D of the 148th Pennsylvania, however, in closing to the left, had crowded the line too much, squeezing men from their places in the ranks. Two companies to the left, on the right of Company B, Pvt. Henry Meyer and a few of his comrades darted about five yards ahead of the regiment and hurled themselves prone on the forest floor. From under the thick smoke, which obscured men standing in the firing line behind them, they could shoot more effectively.

Unfortunately, some of the men behind them went prone also, and their muzzle blasts singed the faces of Meyer and a few of his friends. Meyer never learned whether any of the others with him died from "friendly fire." But once, while rolling over to reload, he spied one of the "boys" behind him sitting upright, loading, and firing his musket into the air as fast as he could. "Why do you shoot in the air?" Meyer yelled at him. "To scare 'em," came the reply. Meyer, who knew about the fellow's religious objections to killing, shrugged it off and went back to his work.[13]

Cross stepped behind the 148th's line where the wood line bisected the regimental formation. Hale was surprised by how informally he spoke to his junior officers. "Boys," he said, "instruct the commanders to be ready to charge when the order is given; wait here for the command, or, if you hear the bugler of the Fifth New Hampshire on the left, move forward on the run." In the woods to the rear of Company G, Cross complimented the men for their cool efficiency. Indicating a large group of boulders to the company's left front to Capt. James J. Patterson, he told him not to permit the Rebels to get a lodgment among them, even if it meant losing contact with the regiment. Patterson ordered his men to volley by the left oblique then charge. Crashing through the

12 Ibid., 8-9; Child, *5th New Hampshire*, 204, 206-207.

13 Muffly, *148th Pennsylvania*, 537.

woods, the Pennsylvanians drove the Rebels away from the boulders. Before the smoke cleared, Pvt. James A. Williams lay dead on the forest floor.[14]

Meanwhile Cross stormed into the 5th New Hampshire. He had just reached his old regiment when a minié ball struck him in the belly, barely missing his navel. It exited near his spine and sent him to the ground. The men hastily carried him away.[15]

Volleying between the Rebels and the 61st New York erupted without orders, and the Confederates decimated the ranks of the company-sized regiment. Captain Willard Keech, acting major, caught one of his lieutenants ducking his head below those of his men. "Stand up!" he bellowed. "What are you crouching for?" "I'm not crouching," the frightened lieutenant yelled back. "Yes, you are! Stand up like a man!" Keech demanded, while slapping him across the small of his back with the flat of his sword. With a grunt, the lieutenant straightened himself. Captain Ike Plumb (3rd Company) suddenly clasped his hands over his stomach and crashed to the ground. Writhing about, he expected to bleed to death. But no blood appeared: all Plumb had suffered was a badly dented belt buckle—and a major embarrassment in front of his company. A moment later, though, a minié ball plowed through Keech's neck. Bullets cut down Lts. Frank Garland and William A. Collins (both 1st Company). Collins took one in the leg, while the one in Garland's breast proved mortal.

Private John Daley also went down with a bullet through the neck. Lieutenant Fuller (4th Company) stepped through the breast-high wheat to pick up Daley's weapon when a ball dully thudded into his left shoulder. The impact staggered him, but feeling no pain, he assumed he had suffered a flesh wound and that the subsequent paralysis would quickly pass. Shortly thereafter a second ball hammered his left leg above the knee. When it gave way, he instinctively knew the ball had snapped it. Still feeling no pain, he turned to hop to the rear when he tangled his good foot in the wheat and thudded to the ground. Helpless, he succumbed to an unbearable panic, fearing he'd be shot yet again.[16]

14 Hale, "*With Colonel Cross*," quote, 10, PHS; ibid., 703-704.

15 Child, *5th New Hampshire*, 204, 208.

16 Fuller, Personal Recollections, 94-95, 99, quote on 94; Isaac Plumb to Miles W. Bullock, July 24, 1863, Clarke Historical Library, Central Michigan University, Mount Pleasant, MI.

As a shell burst over the 148th Pennsylvania and hurled a fragment into Adj. Joseph W. Muffly's leg, he instinctively reached down to see if it was still attached. It was, and he staggered back to a large boulder behind the regiment to inspect his wound. Before he could pull up his pants leg, a sergeant with a terrible shoulder injury hobbled up and asked him to unstrap his knapsack. Then another fellow with blood spurting from his wrist asked Muffly to bandage him up. When he finally managed to look at his calf, Muffly found a bad bruise was all that he had. Rather than show the "white feather" he limped back to his position behind the firing line.[17]

Plum Run

With the troops cleared from his front, Burbank immediately sent his U.S. Regular brigade forward at the double-quick into the spongy marshland around Plum Run. On the left of the brigade, Lt. Louis S. Sanger (Company A, 2nd Battalion, 17th U.S.) irritated his captain, Dudley Chase, by racing back and forth behind his company screeching, "Give 'em Hell! Give 'em Hell!" Chase rebuked Sanger twice, reminding him who was in command and telling him to shut up. It did no good, but as the regiment sank into the ankle deep mud on the eastern side of Plum Run, the lieutenant tripped over his sword scabbard and pitched face first into the muck. As he picked himself up and followed them, blanketed in filth and humiliation, the laughter of his men rang in his ears.

Confederate riflemen at the Devil's Den viciously peppered the 17th U.S. on the left flank as it swung west toward the woods south of the Wheatfield. The men sheltering behind the rocks on the hilltop near Private Fluker (15th Georgia) admired the splendid discipline of the well-drilled Regulars as they came across the valley. Their "manly cheer" of "hip, hip huzzah!" reverberated three times above the noise of battle. But the Georgians and Texans did not budge.[18]

They hit the 11th U.S. as well. A spent round struck Lt. James Pratt over the heart and knocked him off his feet. A soldier dropped by his side and poured water over his face. Bruised and dazed, the officer regained his feet and tottered after his company. The brigade, its formation now ragged, veered west, headed

---

17 Muffly, *148th Pennsylvania*, 245-246.

18 Willingham, *No Jubilee*, 36; Timothy J. Reese, *Sykes' Regular Infantry Division 1861-1864* (Jefferson, NC, 1990), 243, quoted.

directly for the stone wall along the woods on the eastern side of the Wheatfield.[19]

At that point, Day's Brigade filed by the left flank into column of regiments into the field east of the J. Weikert house and marched forward behind Lt. Aaron Walcott's guns. The brigade's lead regiments stepped over the low rail fence along the line of march until they halted temporarily at the Millerstown Road. Toward the rear of the column, the veterans of the 14th U.S. simply kicked the rails down and stepped around them. Second Sergeant M. Reed (Company A) overheard Pvt. Dan Cole, in the rear rank not two paces in front of him, say, "I wish I was in the front rank." Reed, for no logical reason, had always believed the rear rank was more dangerous than the front. Nat Copp, his file leader replied, "Dan, I will change with you. I had rather be in the rear rank." Sergeant Reed, whose job was to keep every man in his assigned place, nodded his okay. As Copp switched places with Cole, a minié ball plowed into Copp's neck. He collapsed on top of the rails—dead.[20]

"Forward! Guide center, march!" The column stepped across the Millerstown Road and advanced across the sloping western base of Little Round Top, following Burbank's 1st brigade into action. From the Stony Hill, Private Carter (22nd Massachusetts) silently lauded their courage as they marched down the hill toward the Wheatfield.[21]

The Wheatfield

Meanwhile, Kelly's 508-man "Irish Brigade" flanked northwest through the cornfield west of John T. Weikert's toward the woods on the north side of the Millerstown Road. The brigade's front barely covered the distance of a

---

19 *Supplement to the OR* 5, pt. 1, 199; Timothy J. Reese, *Sykes' Regular Infantry Division 1861-1864* (Jefferson, N C, 1990), 243; *OR* 27, pt. 1, 645; W. H. Sanderson, "Sykes' Regulars," *National Tribune*, April 2, 1891; *The Soldier of Indiana* (n.d.), 117, J. W. Ames File, 11th U.S. Inf., Greg Coco Collection, USAHEC. According to Colonel Burbank, during the charge, "being perpendicular to the woods in our front," the brigade had to move onto the hill. The brigade was moving south and had to right wheel to get to the stone wall.

20 Laura K. Chapman, *Descendants of John Messer Lowell, Revolutionary Soldier Who Changed His Name to John Reed* (North Syracuse, NY, 1992), 58. According to Reed, the regiment moved by the left flank into a field and advanced to a rail fence across its path. That fence is perpendicular to the ridge on which Walcott had his battery. This would have put the base of Little Round Top across its path.

21 Carter, "Reminiscences," *War Papers*, vol. 2, 170.

single battalion. The 116th Pennsylvania with only 54 officers and men had the right of the line, followed on the left by the much larger 28th Massachusetts (224 effectives). The remaining three regiments, thrown together under the command of Lt. Col. Richard C. Bentley (63rd New York) consisted of two companies from each. The 69th New York (75 men) had the extreme left of the line with the 63rd New York's 75 effectives in the center. The 88th New York (80 men) anchored the right of the combined regiments.[22]

The John Weikert Farm

Kelly's deployment left Brooke's Brigade to cover Cross' regiments. The 145th Pennsylvania (202 officers and men) was on the right of the brigade when the five regiments flanked south along Cemetery Ridge. It led the advance, followed by the tiny 75-man 27th Connecticut, then the 53rd Pennsylvania (120 effectives), the 64th New York (185 rank and file), and the 2nd Delaware (234 officers and men). Marching by the right flank placed the rear rank on the side fronting the Rebels, a maneuver, which one member of the 64th New York noted, "to any but well drilled troops would have been disastrous." Passing through John T. Weikert's woods, the brigade spread out around his white house, crossed over the stone wall in front of it, and bolted across the boulder strewn low land along Plum Run. Passing through the woods north of the Millerstown Road, the brigade fell into line along the stonewall, facing south, and went prone.[23]

The Stony Hill

By the time the Irish Brigade reached the Millerstown Road what remained of De Trobriand's shattered regiments had gathered around Winslow's battery. With their weapons at "right shoulder shift," Kelly's "boys" emerged from the woods on the north side of the Millerstown Road heading southwest and passed around the shot-up 17th Maine. Reaching the base of the Stony Hill relatively unmolested, the 116th Pennsylvania on the right of the brigade,

22 OR 27, pt. 1, 386-390, 392; Ladd and Ladd, *The Bachelder Papers*, vol. 3, 1985, 1986; Affidavit, July 12, 1895, "116th Pennsylvania vs. 140th Pennsylvania," Vertical Files, GNMP.

23 OR 27, pt. 1, 405-406, 409, 413, "Account of an Unidentified Soldier," 51, quoted, IU. McMichael and Bradley described the regiments as facing north (their proper fronts) in their official reports.

crossed the fence, wheeled right, and started up through the woods, weaving around the huge rocks along its line of advance.[24]

Kershaw, having seen both Kelly's and Cross's brigades deploy, immediately reacted. With the Irishmen heading directly for the 7th South Carolina's flank, he yelled at Lt. Col. Elbert Bland to pull the regiment's right wing back. Wheeling his horse about, the general bolted down toward the Rose farm to bring up Semmes' Georgians, who remained hunkered down around the out buildings. The right companies of the 7th fell back at an acute angle to the rest of the line, which placed them on the crest of the ridge, staring down into the Wheatfield.[25]

On the right of the line an Irishmen in the 116th Pennsylvania cried out, "There they are!" Forty feet from the crest of the hill a volley from Kershaw's South Carolinians slammed through the treetops above the Yankees' heads. Adjutant Garrett St. Patrick Nowlen impetuously emptied his revolver at them.[26]

The Rose Woods

Through the smoke-choked woods Captain Hillyer (9th Georgia) saw the Irish Brigade heading directly toward his small regiment. He admired the courageous color guard of the 63rd New York, who, marching the regulation six feet in front of the line, closed to within 40 yards. Hillyer knew what was coming. He passed the word along the line for the men to hold their fire. Ramrods clattered down bores. Weapons went to full cock, virtually unheard in

---

24 Mulholland, *The Story of the 116th Regiment*, 136-137, 373; St. Clair A. Mulholland, "The Irish Brigade. The Battle of Gettysburg," *The Irish American*, August 29, 1863; Silliker, *The Rebel Yell*, 101-103; Ladd and Ladd, *The Bachelder Papers*, vol. 2, 1,059; OR 27, pt. 1, 522. After the war, Mulholland contended that Zook's brigade had gone in ahead of his and had already broken. He later asserted that by the order of a staff officer the 140th Pennsylvania came up on his right rear. Stewart of the 140th Pennsylvania said his regiment came up on the rear of the 116th Pennsylvania as it volleyed. By piecing the two accounts together I had to conclude that: 1) the 116th Pennsylvania had reached the crest of the Stony Hill before Zook; 2) that the 140th Pennsylvania and Zook's regiments arrived after the Irish Brigade had gone in, which explains why Mulholland had not seen any of Zook's men during his advance; 3) that Mulholland erred in assuming that the 140th Pennsylvania was directed into the attack by a staff officer.

25 OR 27, pt. 2, 368, 372.

26 Mulholland, *The Story of the 116th Regiment*, 136-137, 373; Mulholland, "The Irish Brigade," *The Irish American*, August 29, 1863, quoted.

the horrendous din.[27] To the right, 1st Lt. John C. Reid (Company I, 8th Georgia) locked his gaze upon the Irishmen also. From his vantage point, he saw two colors and a battle line extending a considerable distance beyond them on both sides. Their burnished musket barrels glinted in the sun.[28]

Simultaneously, the color guard stepped back into the ranks of the 63rd. The men in the 9th Georgia watched the New Yorkers level their muskets and crouched to the ground just as the volley crashed through the trees over their heads. Hillyer watched the musket balls harmlessly skip and thud into the ground behind them. But in passing over the 9th Georgia, the volley caught the 8th Georgia on the flank. First Lieutenant Reid described it as a "scythe of fire." The air literally "hissed" and "zipped." Ninety feet to Reid's left, 2nd Lt. Benjamin F. Gilham, a file closer in Company K, threw his arms in the air. Slowly sinking to his knees, he dropped back onto his back, the blood flowing copiously from the hole in his forehead. The riflery killed a number of men, including Company C's Capt. C. M. Ballard.

While the Yankees hurriedly reloaded, Hillyer stood up and scanned his line. Satisfied that no one had been hit, he gave the command to return fire. His veterans coolly rested their weapons on the creek bank and volleyed. Stooping down behind them, he peered underneath the veil of smoke blanketing his front. "It seemed that not a bullet went above their heads or below their feet," he observed. The blast had knocked Yankees down like nine pins.[29]

The Stony Hill

For 10 minutes, the opposing sides shot volleys into each other. The South Carolinians took terrible losses from the Irishmen's "buck and ball" loads. Then Kelly ordered the brigade to charge. The 116th Pennsylvania, on the right of the line, under Maj. St. Clair Mulholland, bolted forward and topped the crest before the Rebels could reload. Corporal Jefferson Carl (Company C) killed a Rebel only eight feet away. A hand-to-hand fight ensued, which ended as abruptly as it began, leaving both sides mutely staring at one another. First Sergeant Francis Malin (Company C) collapsed with a bullet through his head. In the drifting smoke, Mulholland gazed down the southern slope littered with

27 Hillyer, "Battle of Gettysburg," 8.

28 John C. Reid, Diary, July 2, GNMP.

29 Hillyer, "Battle of Gettysburg," 8, quoted; John C. Reid, Diary, July 2, 1863, GNMP.

casualties mostly from the 110th Pennsylvania, and saw Pvt. Benjamin H. Barto's lifeless body. He lay on top of a flat rock spread-eagled upon his back, rifle in his hand. Blood still flowed from the hole in the center of his forehead into a gory puddle beneath him. The horrendous number of head and chest wounds among the Rebels indicated how telling the Yankee fire had been. "Confederate troops, lay down your arms and surrender!" Mulholland bellowed. A considerable number of the Rebels to the regiment's right threw down their weapons and ran through the Yankees' ranks.[30]

The Rose Woods

First Lieutenant Reid (Company I) dashed 20 yards to the left of the 8th Georgia, trying to locate a piece of solid ground upon which to cross the bog. Finding none, he returned to his place behind his company and leaned his left shoulder against a two-inch thick hickory sapling, shifting his weight onto his right leg. Second Lieutenant Columbus Heard (Company I) gingerly scooted over to him and listened while Reid calmly informed him of Gilham's death. "You will be killed too if you don't lie down," Heard warned. "No, I shall only get a furlough." Reid nonchalantly answered, expecting that a wound would be the worst that could happen.[31]

The Wheatfield

The 11th Georgia in front of Cross's Brigade melted away from the wall. "They are falling back, boys; forward!" Captain Forster (Company C, 148th Pennsylvania) cried out. Private Osmon asked the captain what he should do with his fouled weapon. Throw it down and get another, the captain snapped. Hurling the piece aside and running along the line to replace it, he returned to find his beloved captain dead. Osmon placed the captain's cap over his bloodied face but never thought of cleaning out his pockets.

Returning to the ranks, he leveled his weapon to shoot when a Rebel apparently intent upon surrendering zipped through the gap between him and the 81st Pennsylvania. Instead, he drew a large revolver and shot down a

---

30 Mulholland, *The Story of the 116th Regiment*, 136-137, 373; Mulholland, "The Irish Brigade," *The Irish American*, August 29, 1863.

31 John C. Reid, Diary, July 2, 1863, GNMP.

sergeant of the 81st. Without thinking, Osmon clubbed the scoundrel down with his rifle butt, and an enraged officer from the 81st rushed over and repeatedly struck him with his sword. Just then, the state color bearer was killed. Osmun picked up the flag, leaped over the small stream at his feet, and planted the staff in the ground.[32]

The Rose Woods

To the 11th Georgia's left rear a number of men from the 8th Georgia surged into the swamp separating the two lines. Rather than try to take cover, they stood in the open taunting the Yankees with, "Stand up and fight fair . . . Stand up and fight for your apple butter!" Their bravery inspired the watching Lieutenant Reid, who snapped out of his trance as Lieutenant Heard screeched when a bullet struck him. Wheeling about, Reid started out to find his friend when a bullet caught him in the back of his right knee. Although jarred, Reid did not fall. His leg had not been broken but was bleeding profusely, and it would not support his weight. Using a discarded rifle as a crutch, he limped toward the western side of the woods.

Alone in his pain, he tuned in on the distinctive patter of the minié balls tearing through the trees around him. Spotting a depression in the ground not 20 yards distant, he painfully headed toward it. "I thought every step would be my last," he later confessed. "Nothing else in the war ever tried my courage as severely as the going those twenty yards."[33]

The Millerstown Road

Double-quicking across the Millerstown Road, Tilton's Brigade, still in two columns, continued north along the stone wall which led to Trostle's lane. Three hundred yards from the road, he halted his regiments to make a stand. The 22nd Massachusetts about faced in a small, irregular line. Pandemonium ruled the field. Private Carter (Company H) could not sort out the officers' individual commands through the cacophony of exploding shells, zipping minie balls, and the shrieks and howls of the wounded. The heart-rending screams of

---

32 Muffly, *148th Pennsylvania*, 603.

33 John C. Reid, Diary, July 2, 1863, GNMP.

wounded horses tore at his nerves as he stood helplessly in the ranks, the maelstrom whirling around him.[34]

Sweitzer's men stopped in the edge of the woods north of the Wheatfield and about-faced. The 4th Michigan held the right, in the northwest corner of the woods, close to Bigelow's battery. The 62nd Pennsylvania stood next to them with the 32nd Massachusetts finishing the line.[35]

The Wheatfield

Lieutenant Fuller (4th Company, 61st New York) hailed over two of his men, as they skirted around him. "Drag me back," he pleaded. Each one grabbed an arm and began pulling him like dead game over the rough ground. Only then did he realize the extent of his injuries. The bullet that apparently had done no harm had actually destroyed his left shoulder at the joint. The pain of being pulled was excruciating. As they cleared the small ridge immediately south of the Millerstown Road, he screamed, "Drop me." The pair left him where he lay and disappeared into the smoke. Feverishly clawing through his haversack with his good hand, Fuller tried to find something to tie off his shattered left leg before he bled to death.[36]

The Emmitsburg Road
The Sherfy Farm

Barksdale's Brigade plowed toward the ridge along the Emmitsburg Road from the south and the west. On the right of the brigade, the 21st Mississippi, unable to keep up with the 17th on its left, dashed toward the Peach Orchard south of the Emmitsburg Road-Millerstown Road intersection. The left of the brigade, with the 8th Alabama trailing behind and northwest of its left flank, drove the skirmishers from the 5th New Jersey back onto their reserve.[37]

Captain Randolph, fearing for the safety of Bucklyn's guns at the Sherfy farm and unable to find Graham, took the initiative. Riding up to the 114th

34 Carter, Reminiscences, *War Papers*, vol. 2, 168-169.

35 *Supplement to the OR 5*, pt. 1, 192.

36 Fuller, *Personal Recollections*, 95.

37 E. P. Harman to W. S. Decker, August 16, 1886, & "Willard's Brigade at Gettysburg," both in Richardson Papers, OCHS. My conclusion.

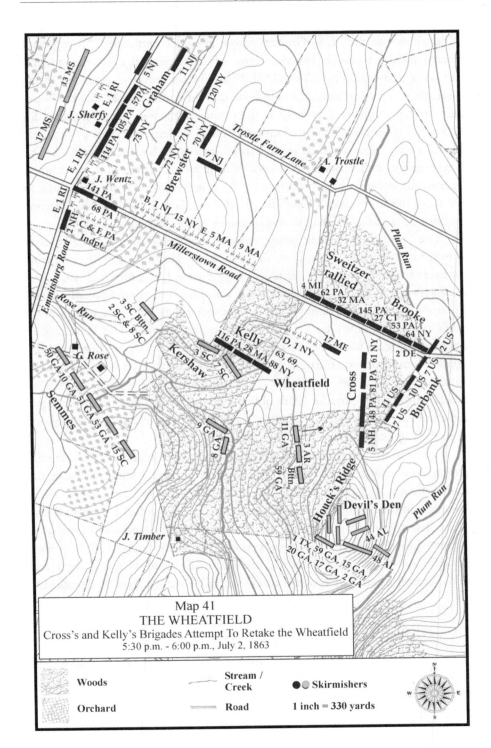

Map 41
THE WHEATFIELD
Cross's and Kelly's Brigades Attempt To Retake the Wheatfield
5:30 p.m. - 6:00 p.m., July 2, 1863

Woods

Orchard

Stream /
Creek

Road

Skirmishers

1 inch = 330 yards

Pennsylvania on the left of Graham's front line, he commanded: "If you want to save my battery, move forward. I cannot find the general. I give the order on my own responsibility." The 57th Pennsylvania, on the brigade's right, immediately crossed the road where some of their number broke into the house and took up sharpshooters' nests in the rooms on the west side. Sergeant Ellis C. Strouss (Company K) posted himself behind a cherry tree on the north side of the house against which quite a few fence rails had been stacked. The Keystoners as well as Bucklyn's section of artillery to the right of the farmhouse opened fire upon Barksdale's Brigade as it came from the cover of the swale to the west. In the confusion which followed, one of the guns slammed a parting 12-pounder solid shot into the cherry tree right above Strauss' head.[38]

The 114th Pennsylvania, being under the command of acting major Capt. Edward R. Bowen, did not move out right away. He first sent the regimental pioneers forward to destroy the fence along the road, and they had hardly laid their axes into the rails on the Pike's east side when the Mississippians opened fire upon them. Private James F. Priest (Company F) nearly "bought it" when a minié ball slapped into the fence post next to him. The detail broke for cover: only a small section of fence row had been torn down. Colonel Calvin Craig's 105th Pennsylvania, on the right of the second line behind the 57th, crossed the Emmitsburg Road into the Sherfy farmyard. Unable to fire because the 57th blocked its line of sight, the 105th obliqued into the open ground to the 57th's right and cut loose into the left flank of the 8th Alabama, which had just popped onto the ridge to its front.[39]

Lieutenant Colonel Herbert immediately halted his regiment, shouting the command to change front forward on the first company. Facing northeast, the lead company right wheeled to the east, followed successively by every company in the regiment. Each company blasted off a volley as it moved into place, hammering the exposed 105th Pennsylvania. Herbert immediately dispatched Adj. Daniel Jones back to the 9th Alabama to ask Col. J. Horace King for assistance. Jones found the rest of the brigade in the low ground west of the Spangler barn and led it due east to where he had last seen his regiment.[40]

---

38 *OR* 27, pt. 1, 497, 502, quoted on 502; Martin, *57th Pennsylvania*, 88-89.

39 Bowen, "Collis' Zouaves: The 114th Pennsylvania Infantry at Gettysburg," *Philadelphia Weekly Times*, June 22, 1887; Kenderdine, "A California Tramp," 4, GNMP.

40 Herbert, "A Short History of the 8th Ala. Regiment," 10, GNMP.

The 114th Pennsylvania had barely cleared the front of the center and left sections when Bucklyn decided to quit the field. The Rebels having managed to close within 40 yards of his position, halted, and delivered a volley into his guns. After unloading a barrage of canister, he ordered the battery to limber up and retire at a walk from the front. Captain Bowen, watching Confederates swarm the field to the west of the barn, ordered the right wing of the 114th to fall in on the left of the 57th Pennsylvania.[41]

Halting in the road to reform, the Pennsylvanians hastily tore down the fence rails for cover. All the while men fell by the score scrambling over the fence under a murderous barrage of lead. As Pvt. David Shively (Company E, 141st Pennsylvania) raised his weapon a minié ball tore through his throat, exited his neck, and penetrated shattered the bone of his right arm. The 17-year-old fell in a bloody heap. Trying to raise himself from the ground, he took a second bullet that gouged out his right eye. Amazingly, he survived to write about it years later.[42]

The Klingle House

An unexpected lull in the Confederates' small arms fire from the left quickly drew Captain Cavada's attention from Seeley's guns toward the elevated ground around Sherfy's. Cavada, who had remained on horseback with many of Humphreys' staff, peered through the drifting sulfuric haze that had settled over the fields, straining to see what had become of his brother's 114th Pennsylvania. The unmistakable "Rebel yell" sounded louder and louder as the Confederates closed in on the farm.

The Second Division's skirmishers opened fire to the west. Cavada compared the sporadic firing to "the first drops of a thunder shower that was to break upon us." An aide from Birney raced up to Humphreys, warning of Rebels massing to the west and advising him to prepare for an assault. Despite the terrible enfilade fire from the south, he and his officers remained mounted, constantly listening for the incoming rounds. Within minutes, the firing reached a crescendo along the skirmish line, and Cavada observed the Yankee

---

41 Ladd and Ladd, *The Bachelder Papers*, vol. 1, 721; "Bucklyn's Battery E, 1st Rhode Island Artillery," NA; *OR* 27, pt. 1, 502, 589.

42 Hagerty, *Collis' Zouaves*, 241-242; David Shively, "A Blighted Career. The Work of Two Bullets at Gettysburg–A Sad Story," *National Tribune*, July 3, 1884; E. P. Harman to W. S. Decker, August 16, 1886, OCHS.

skirmishers gradually falling back. Seeley's and Turnbull's gunners stood silently by their guns, waiting.[43]

The Sherfy Farm

Sergeant Given (Company F, 114th Pennsylvania) leaped the fence ahead of his men and ran into the open space between the house and the barn, followed closely by Col. Federico Cavada, who had finally shown up with the regiment. Kneeling down together, they studied the smoky fields to the southwest. The colonel rather stupidly asked if the Rebs were coming. "You bet your life they are coming," the sergeant retorted, jumping up and racing back to the fence all the while swinging his sword above his head and directing his men to fire between the house and the barn. Captain Frank Mix (Company E) took a round in the right knee; it eventually cost him his life. Clearing the fence into the farmyard, the regiment tried to reform while advancing, at the same time loading and returning fire on the move. The regiment had been reduced to a skirmish line before it reached the barn. Corporal Robert Kenderdine (Company F) died to the left of the farmhouse.[44]

The 17th Mississippi and stray soldiers from the 21st pounced upon the flank of the 114th, capturing a number of hapless men, among them 2nd Lt. Aaron K. Dunkle (Company H) and 1st Lt. Harry C. Rulon (Company B). Captain Bowen ordered Capt. Henry M. Eddy (Company D) to lead the colors of the 114th Pennsylvania out of the fray. In the melee, a bullet snuffed out Capt. Isaac D. Stamps (Company E, 21st Mississippi) not three feet from Company F and Pvt. James B. Booth.[45]

The 73rd New York, having advanced to the crest of the hill in the Peach Orchard, could not fire to the front because the Zouaves were in the way. The moment they took off, north along the Emmitsburg Road, the New Yorkers emptied their rifles into the Rebels at point-blank range. Men dropped to the ground by the handfuls. The Rebels briefly recoiled under the fusillade but

43 Cavada Diary, July 2, 1863, FSNMP.

44 Hagerty, *Collis' Zouaves*, 241-242; Bowen, "Collis' Zouaves," *Philadelphia Weekly Times*, June 22, 1887; ibid.; Kenderdine, "A California Tramp," 4, quoted, GNMP.

45 Nicholson, *Pennsylvania at Gettysburg*, 1, 356; OR 27, pt. 1, 497; Bowen, "Collis' Zouaves," *Philadelphia Weekly Times*, June 22, 1887; McNeily, "Barksdale's Mississippi Brigade at Gettysburg," 238.

quickly reformed at the barn and began slugging it out round for round with the New Yorkers. An impenetrable sulfuric cloud, spasmodically belching flame, enveloped the contending lines.

In rapid order, the Rebels unhorsed all three of the regiment's mounted officers. Major Michael Burns survived but Capt. Eugene C. Shine (Company F) did not. A solid shot bored lengthwise through Capt. Michael D. Purtell's small bay, killing the horse, while miraculously missing its rider. Lieutenant Frank M. Moran (Company H, 73rd New York) found himself in the swirling inferno, unable to hear anything above the incessant concussions of the bursting shells and the deadly whine of minié balls. Amid the tumult, word traveled along the ranks that the regiment was going to charge. Cheers burst out from the Rebels along the 73rd's front when a caisson, to its left rear, part of Lt. Edward M. Knox's section of Hart's 15th New York Battery, exploded in a misshapen plume of smoke and fire. It killed 11 horses and wounded six enlisted men.[46]

Seeing the field and the road behind him filled with fleeing soldiers, Captain Nelson (Company K, 57th Pennsylvania) sprinted to Col. Peter Sides and pointed to the fleeing 114th Pennsylvania: "It looks as though we will soon have to move out of here or be captured." Calmly turning his head, Sides surveyed the situation. "Yes, I think we will go now," he said. Nelson, not anticipating a quick response, suggested that the colonel send a detail to order the officers and men who had taken shelter in the outbuildings and farmhouse to pull out with the regiment.

But Sides remained adamant about withdrawing the regiment immediately. Nelson could stay behind to warn as many of the men as he could. Sergeant Strouss (Company K) and others screamed in vain for the men who had

---

46 Frank M. Moran, "What Was Seen by a Captive Federal Officer from Seminary Ridge," *Philadelphia Weekly Times*, April 22, 1882; W. F. Beyer and O. F. Keydel, (eds.), *Deeds of Valor*, vol. 1, 231; "Gladiator" to the "*New York Sunday Mercury*," August 3, 1863. Moran did not identify which battery lost the caisson. However, he did say that the wounded officer of that battery came over and asked the regiment to save his guns. The wounded Edward Knox lost most of the horses in Hart's battery that day. He also suffered the heaviest number of casualties in the battery, which conforms to Moran's observations about them. Thompson does not mention a subordinate being wounded. By his own testimony, Knox was wounded on both days of the battle; he also had to retire his guns by prolonge, indicating that the Rebels had severely shot up his guns and crew. I've concluded that Knox was the mounted officer Moran saw, and it was his caisson that exploded, wounding seven men, including himself.

Lt. Frank M. Moran
Co. H, 73rd New York
Library, GNMP

occupied the house to get out. Their rifle fire from the windows on the west side drowned out the warnings.[47]

Handing company command over to 2nd Lt. John M. Robinson, the captain took off at a run from building to building. In the infernal noise, he physically shook each man to get his attention. The trip seemed to take an eternity. Finally, Nelson reached the farmhouse. He could see no Rebels within striking distance of the west side of the building and he thought he had enough distance between him and the approaching enemy to search the house thoroughly. Bolting through the front door, he darted upstairs and raced from room to room shooing men out. Thundering to the downstairs hallway, he could see through the front door Mississippians filling the yard not 50 feet away. They yelled at him to surrender, but he bolted out the door as fast as his legs could carry him. With bullets whizzing about his head, he cleared the fence around the yard and did not stop running.[48]

The 13th and the 17th Mississippi swarmed around the farm house, the right flank of the former striking a point immediately south of the house. The Rebels bagged almost 100 Pennsylvanians in the farmyard. The impetus of their attack carried them past the barn and the Yankee riflemen holed up inside of it, who severely shot up the 18th Mississippi as it came up to the support of the 13th. Behind the left center of the line, Maj. George B. Gerald (18th

---

47 Nicholson, *Pennsylvania at Gettysburg*, vol. 1, 356; OR 27, pt. 1, 497; Bowen, "Collis' Zouaves," *Philadelphia Weekly Times*, June 22, 1887. Alanson H. Nelson, *The Battles of Chancellorsville and Gettysburg* (Minneapolis, MN, 1899), 150, quoted.

48 Nelson, *The Battles of Chancellorsville and Gettysburg*, 151.

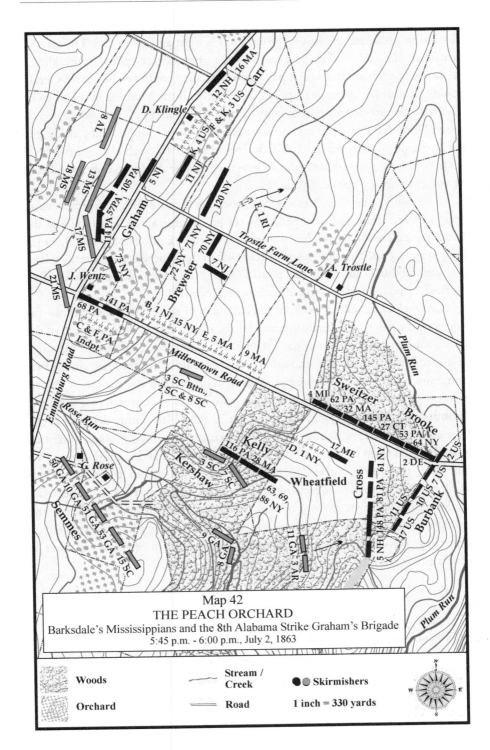

Map 42
THE PEACH ORCHARD
Barksdale's Mississippians and the 8th Alabama Strike Graham's Brigade
5:45 p.m. - 6:00 p.m., July 2, 1863

Woods

Orchard

Stream / Creek

Road

Skirmishers

1 inch = 330 yards

Mississippi) scanned the smoky ground to his right and spied Col. Thomas M. Griffin and Lt. Col. William H. Luse sheltering behind a couple of outbuildings. He hollered at them. But in the pandemonium they could not hear, and Gerald could not wait for them to respond. The barn and the Yankees in it had to be taken, so he decided to take it out on his own. Yelling at a handful of men around him that he would get the door and they were to follow him inside, the small gaggle of determined Confederates charged through the ground level door. Shooting and stabbing blindly into the smokey shadows, they soon killed or wounded every Yankee inside.[49]

The bulk of the 57th Pennsylvania, concerned more with self-preservation than heroics, followed the panicked 114th Pennsylvania north along the Emmitsburg Road. While they pulled out, Captain Eddy (Company D, 114th Pennsylvania) and the handful of officers left in the regiment temporarily rallied a squad of the Zouaves in the road. Halting, they faced about, fired off an ineffective volley and continued their retreat north.[50]

Colonel Craig quickly realized the left flank of the 105th Pennsylvania was uncovered when Confederate infantry fell into battle line in the front yard of the house and emptied a volley into his line. Craig immediately herded his small command north until it had enough room to execute a "front to rear on the first company." Once the 105th refaced itself to meet the enemy threat, a tiny portion of the 57th Pennsylvania fell in with it and anchored its right on the Emmitsburg Road. They did not stay long: as the 114th stampeded past them, they also collapsed and headed into the fields east of the road. Nelson caught up with the men from the 57th whom he had evacuated. Having outdistanced the rifle fire, they now contended with bursting shells from the Confederate artillery. One whined past Nelson barely missing his head. He fully expected it to decapitate the man in front of him. The round missed him, too, but to the captain's astonishment, the man collapsed apparently feigning injury. Walking up to him, Nelson rolled him over and discovered him quite dead—without so much as a scratch or a bruise upon his body.[51]

49 E. P. Harman to W. S. Decker, August 16, 1886, OCHS; McNeily, *Barksdale's Mississippi Brigade at Gettysburg*, 238; G. B. Gerald, "The Battle of Gettysburg," *Waco Daily Times-Herald*, n.d.

50 Bowen, "Collis' Zouaves," *Philadelphia Weekly Times*, June 22, 1887.

51 OR 27, pt. 1, 501; Scott, *105th Pennsylvania*, 82; Nelson, *The Battles of Chancellorsville and Gettysburg*, 151-152.

The 114th Pennsylvania, in their conspicuous red and blue Zouave uniforms ran a deadly gauntlet. A short distance north of Trostle's Lane, what remained of the regiment bolted east into the field. Captain Eddy, still with the colors, dropped to the ground next to Captain Bowen with a chest wound. Thinking he had lost another fine officer, Bowen stopped to assist him only to find that a spent ball had merely winded his friend. While someone helped the bruised captain from the field, Bowen tried to stem the rout by forming a rear guard. Though little more than a color guard, they loaded while withdrawing, halted and fired again, enabling the colors to get to the rear safely.[52]

To the west, Herbert ordered the 8th Alabama to charge. Moving by the right oblique, the regiment widened the gap between it and the 9th Alabama. As the Yankees cleared the off from the east of the Sherfy farm buildings, the survivors of the 8th plowed into the road ahead of Barksdale's men, with the intersection of the Trostle lane to their left.[53]

The Klingle Farm

The Confederate artillery fire from the left flank was increasing, while the "Rebel yell" shrilled demonically along the front of Carr's still prone brigade. The rest of Wilcox's Brigade was coming on line. Skirmishers from 5th New Jersey scurried back into the roadbed on the left of the 11th Massachusetts. First Lieutenant Blake (Company K) checked his watch—5:30 p.m. "Here they come!" someone shouted, and the cry carried along the line. "Steady, boys," admonished another. "Keep cool." "Aim low." "Wait for orders." "Don't be in a hurry." A bullet whacked Captain Cavada's horse in the leg, causing it to dance painfully and wildly about the field.

As the skirmishers melted back to their regimental positions, Battery K, 4th U.S., roared into action. Primers skyrocketed into the air from the vents. The six Napoleons thundered and recoiled, their bronze barrels ringing loudly in the smoke and flame. A rifle ball shattered Seeley's right thigh, slamming him to the

---

52 Bowen, "Collis' Zouaves," *Philadelphia Weekly Times*, June 22, 1887.

53 Herbert, "A Short History of the 8th Ala. Regiment," 10, GNMP; Ladd and Ladd, *The Bachelder Papers*, vol. 2, 1,057. In later accounts Herbert does not mention the 9th Alabama on his left as he did in 1869. He walked the field after he wrote that letter and concluded that his regiment had moved across the Emmitsburg Road south of the Klingle farm while the rest of the brigade had crossed north of the farm. So the 9th Alabama never connected with his left as he originally stated.

ground, but he refused to leave the field. Lying on the ground behind the guns, he continued to direct the gunners. To the north, on the right of the 16th Massachusetts, Turnbull's artillery fired canister into the Rebels at close range.[54]

A frantically screeching kitten shot from the Rodgers' house, and leaped onto the shoulders of one of the prone men in the 11th Massachusetts. A couple of the New Englanders hastily dispatched a snake similarly slithering for safety within the ranks. Blake noticed men who had straggled during the march finally catching up with the regiment and taking their places in the ranks. He could see nothing behind him through the dense smoke. An order came from Carr not to fire to the front for fear of hitting their own men, but the artillerists ignored it.[55]

The Wheatfield

First Lieutenant Albert N. Ames (Battery D, 1st New York), one of Captain Winslow's section officers, reported Confederate infantry in the woods, 60 yards from his piece. The captain hastily confirmed the report and told Ames to change the front of his guns and reply with canister. Leaving Ames to his own devices, the captain galloped up to Birney on the high ground in the Wheatfield's northwestern corner. The general approved the maneuver and sent the captain back to his guns.[56]

Wounded men limped into the woods north of the Wheatfield, among them the allegedly injured 2nd Lt. Mandeville (Company D, 8th New Jersey), whom the regiment's assistant surgeon, James Riddle, spied among the crowd. Hobbling up to the doctor, Mandeville reported himself with a shell-contused thigh that needed treatment. Lacking time to examine the injury, Riddle directed the lieutenant to the rear where someone could examine the thigh. Meanwhile, a large number of Tilton's men encountered Zook's Brigade as it arrived on the northern side of the Millerstown Road. Zook halted the brigade and faced it to the left, while the order to load traveled along the ranks.[57]

---

54 Ladd and Ladd, *The Bachelder Papers*, vol. 1, 231, 608; Blake, "Personal Reminiscences of Gettysburg," 14, quoted, USAHEC.

55 Blake, "Personal Reminiscences," 14, USAHEC.

56 Winslow, "Battery D," *Philadelphia Weekly Times*, July 26, 1879.

57 NJ State Archive Records, Civil War Misc., Vertical Files, GNMP; Robert Laird Stewart, *History of the One Hundred and Fortieth Regiment Pennsylvania Volunteers* (n.p., 1912), 102. A military

The Stony Hill

Rounds plowed into the northern end of the woods from several directions, taking out members of the 22nd Massachusetts so quickly even veterans in the ranks were stunned. Barnes' men hurriedly untangled themselves from the confused mob and descended into the boulder-strewn northwestern corner of the Wheatfield. As the 22nd Massachusetts came out of the woods, Private Carter (Company H) saw his Sgts. James H. Abbott and Charles H. Hazeltine struggling to evacuate Pvt. John Morrison on an improvised litter—a blanket suspended between two rifles. "Oh, let me down to rest," Morrison pleaded. "Oh! I can stand it no longer! Let me die!" They gently lowered the gut shot man to the ground. But as a Rebel yell burst out nearby, Morrison begged: "Oh, take me up, Charlie. Don't let them get me!" They lifted him off the ground and disappeared across the Millerstown Road. Carter never again saw Morrison, a man who had predicted his own death the day before.[58] Meanwhile, Zook's line surged forward, passing through the disorganized ranks of the 22nd. The Stony Hill and Wheatfield were blanketed in smoke.[59]

The Rose Woods

The smoke lifted a bit as firing subsided along the 9th Georgia's front. Hillyer peered toward the Yankee line. He saw no one standing, and the casualties were lying so close together he believed he could have walked along their entire formation without touching the ground. He wanted the Yankee's flag. Telling the men around him not to fire at him, he ran to where he had last seen the color guard. But the flag was gone, and for a second, Hillyer hoped that the brave standard bearer had escaped with his life. Wheeling about, he raced back to his own men.[60]

---

court later acquitted Mandeville of all charges of misconduct and misbehavior upon the field of battle.

58 Carter, *Four Brothers in Blue*, 309-310, quoted.

59 Ibid., 309; Ladd and Ladd, *The Bachelder Papers*, vol. 1, 417; *OR 27*, pt. 1, 395, 396; Favill, *Diary of a Young Officer*, 246.

60 Hillyer, "Battle of Gettysburg," 8.

Chapter 12

July 2, 1863
6:00 p.m.-6:20 p.m.

"Colonel, for God's sake, can't you hold on?"
—*General Daniel E. Sickles, III Corps*

McLaws' Division, Longstreet's Corps,
Army of Northern Virginia
Seminary Ridge
6:00 p.m.-6:20 p.m.

At 6:00 p.m., McLaws started Wofford's, Lang's, and Wright's Brigades toward the Emmitsburg Road.[1] Wright shot over Seminary Ridge to the left rear of Lang's men, trailing behind like a streamer. Farther south, Wofford's Brigade, having reformed after passing through Huger's Artillery Battalion, advanced with the Phillips' Legion, its left regiment, south of the Millerstown Road. To the east, the 21st Mississippi, on Barksdale's right, pressed toward the Peach Orchard.

Graham's Brigade, III Corps, Army of the Potomac
The Peach Orchard

To the 68th Pennsylvania's right rear, Graham, seeing the Rebels closing in from the west, rode up to the regiment's commander Colonel Tippen, and told him to wheel his Pennsylvanians in that direction. The men stood up, faced about, and fired point-blank into the flank of the Confederates, shattering their

---

1   Large, *Gettysburg*, 134, 138-139.

advance.[2] Pursuing them from the field, Tippen left wheeled the regiment toward the Emmitsburg road. Small arms fire quickly dropped Graham's horse beneath him. Prying himself free, Graham refused Tippen's help, turned the brigade over to him, and walked toward the rear. Captain Milton S. Davis (Company F) took over the regiment. Within minutes, he went down wounded. Major Robert E. Winslow assumed command and was also soon wounded and replaced by Capt. Michael Fulmer (Company K). Officers seemed to be dropping faster than enlisted men.[3]

Madill (141st Pennsylvania), having rallied the better part of his regiment in the field east of the Peach Orchard, fell in behind the 68th Pennsylvania as it advanced. Graham commandeered Lt. Charles H. Graves's horse and reined into the regimental line. At his command, "Attention! Forward! Charge!" the Pennsylvanians pressed through the Peach Orchard, already choked with fleeing men from their own brigade. Their approach drove away some Confederates, who were almost on top of Bucklyn's guns, enabling the artillerymen to retrieve their pieces by hand to the limbers.[4]

Bucklyn (Battery E, 1st Rhode Island) barely got away with his life trying to save a caisson, which had lost all of its horses. The lieutenant had two mounts shot out from under him, and before he could make good his escape, a case ball pounded into his left shoulder and ripped through his lung. Severely wounded, he turned the command over to 2nd Lt. Benjamin Freeborn, who retired the battery to a position 200 yards to the rear.[5]

As the 141st Pennsylvania approached the road, the 68th melted away from its front, leaving it alone behind the board fence on the ridge to face the Confederates who were swarming around the Sherfy buildings. First Lieutenant John F. Clark (Company E) stepped alongside of Madill, who stood behind the

2 Hanifen, *Battery B*, 76; OR 27, pt. 1, 499. This is my interpretation. The 68th Pennsylvania retired to the Millerstown Road. The 114th Pennsylvania charged across the road into Sherfy's, was shattered, and left the field, while the Confederates filled the gap and penetrated the Peach Orchard. Graham rode into the 68th to alert them to the situation. After the regiment destroyed the Confederate formation, it wheeled toward the Emmitsburg Road.

3 Ibid., 27, pt. 1, 499; Craft, *141st Pennsylvania*, 137; Nicholson, *Pennsylvania Gettysburg*, vol. 1, 394; W. H. Quay, "Still in Error," *National Tribune*, April 30, 1891.

4 Craft, *141st Pennsylvania*, 121, 137; Loring, "Gettysburg," *National Tribune*, July 9, 1885, quoted.

5 Ladd and Ladd, *The Bachelder Papers*, vol. 1, 72; "Bucklyn's Battery E, 1st Rhode Island Artillery;" OR 27, pt. 1, 502, 589.

Col. Henry J. Madill
141st Pennsylvania
MOLLUS Collection
Library, GNMP

center of the regiment, his mount having been killed, and shouted, "Hadn't we better get out of this?" "I have no orders to get out," the colonel exclaimed. "If I had my old regiment back again, I could whip all of them!"[6]

With its front uncovered, the hapless 141st Pennsylvania walked into the waiting Confederate line. The front erupted into a huge cloud of smoke, slashed with muzzle flashes and the deadly zips of minié balls. The Pennsylvanians closed ranks and blazed back, but no fewer than 30 men went down before the smoke cleared. A bullet in the left leg disabled Adj. Daniel W. Searle; Sgt. Maj. Joseph G. Fell, recipient of the prized Kearney Cross, collapsed with a shattered right thigh. Private Daniel Baumgartner (Company A), whose brother died at Chancellorsville, took a thigh wound. Private Ethiel C. Wood (Company B), the color corporal's cousin, had a minié ball shatter his right leg below the knee. Private Samuel Molyneux (Company K) fell dead next to Pvt. George T. Phillips just as a ball bored through Phillips' arm. He started to the rear, but returned to his place in the ranks where rifle ball hit him in the chest, perforated his lung, and knocked him to the ground. It was his third wound since Chancellorsville, two months before. The 20 minutes Madill and his stalwarts held their ground had to have seemed like an eternity.[7]

Thompson's Battery C and F, Pennsylvania Independent Artillery, stood in the 21st Mississippi's path. While the men feverishly limbered up, the rest of the crew with the remaining five pieces of the battery began to make good their escape. Meanwhile, a deadly burst of small arms fire whistled into the right gun,

6   Craft, *141st Pennsylvania*, 122.

7   Ibid., 121-122, 130-131, 135; *OR* 27, pt. 1, 505.

killing the four lead horses, and terribly wounding a fifth along with the three outriders.[8]

Captain Clark's 1st New Jersey Light still remained in the line. Much to his relief, the eloquently swearing Private Cronk brought his careening ammunition wagon to an abrupt halt behind the guns and steadied his cantankerous mule team. Corporal Charles Banks, with Pvt. Charles Bush and Cpl. Henry E. Buffum and a couple of other enlisted men, piled on board to unload the cartridges. Searing hot iron slapped into the ground around them.

One burst hurled Private Hanifen to the ground as he ran ammunition to the #1 gun. He awoke to find Pvt. Martin Donohoe kneeling over him with his canteen. "Mike," the Irishman sobbed, his salty tears falling on Hanifen's face as he pressed his canteen to his mouth, "shure you're not hit entirely, for I would be lonesome without you." Still numbed, Hanifen slowly got to his feet and wobbled back to his post. "Were you hit hard?" someone asked disingenuously. "No," Hanifen mumbled. "Bully boy! Hurry up the ammunition lively now and we will give them hell yet. You see the devils are gaining ground on our left." Hanifen looked up and noticed a gap in the Federal line some 500 yards to the east.[9]

Hanifen counted six battle flags through the smoke in a Confederate brigade that formed front near the Rose house. The Rebels advanced steadily despite the terrible barrage the artillerists dropped into their ranks. Not 450 yards from the guns the line broke and then regrouped. Clark's men answered their next advance with canister; Sgt. "Old Bill" Timm's first round into the Rebels' front knocked down the color guard and cut a gory hole through their ranks. Clark coolly strode from gun to gun, encouraging and reassuring his sweating men.

Timm notched the stick he carried to record each round the #1 gun expended. Growling at every shot, he told his "boys" to "keep their shirts on" because they were shooting too wildly and could possibly lose "Old Betsy" if not more careful. Hanifen handed off two canister cartridges to Pvt. Elias V. Campbell, #3 on the piece. "Tis good for them," Hanifen called out to the sarge on his way back to the caisson. "Feed it to their bellies, Timm. Mow them down, Timm." Mow them down he did as the double canister literally cut the

8   Benjamin T. Arrington, *The Medal of Honor at Gettysburg*, (Gettysburg, 1996), 11.

9   Hanifen, *Battery B*, 74.

Rebels off at their ankles. "Damn them," Pvt. Caleb H. Harrison spat, "we are paying them off for Riley now."

The crews kept to their pieces despite the hundreds of minié balls cutting through the air and the horrendous screams of the incoming artillery rounds. Smoke and dirt enveloped the guns, cutting visibility to nil. In all of the confusion, both Sgt. Leander McChesney and Pvt. Robert Stuart fell severely wounded. Splinters flew from the gun carriages and the limber wheels. Nevertheless, the gunners had forced the Confederates to the cover of the gradual hillside before they had gotten to within 200 yards of the battery.[10]

The Rebs, however, exploited the gap in the Federal salient and a considerable number of them boxed in McGilvery's two remaining batteries from the orchard to their right rear, the woods to the left, and their front along the Millerstown Road.

Carr's Brigade, III Corps, Army of the Potomac
North of Trostle's Lane

Carr recalled the 11th New Jersey to the right from the front of the 120th New York. He needed it to support Seeley's guns. The Jerseymen went prone in the apple orchard, 50 yards east of the Emmitsburg Road. Too excited to lie down, Col. Robert McAllister stood up to observe the bloody tapestry unfolding around him. Projectiles snapped the branches from the trees above his men's heads, whirling them through the air like grain tossed in the wind.[11]

Lieutenant Colonel Cornelius D. Westbrook moved his 120th New York 50 feet west to the cover of the stone wall on the rise of ground to his front and ordered his men to lie down. It was 6 p.m. Second Lieutenant Edward H. Ketcham (Company A) refused to lie down. His captain, Abram L. Lockwood, warned him not to needlessly put himself in jeopardy, to which the lieutenant defiantly shot back: "A dead man is better than a living coward." Within a breath, he was a dead man: a shell fragment killed him. Not too much later, a solid shot hissed into Company D, carrying away Capt. Lansing Hollister's

---

10 Ibid., 74-75, quoted on both pages.

11 Robert McAllister to Samuel Toombs, January 10, 1888, Rutgers University Library, New Brunswick, NJ; Thomas D. Marbaker, *History of the 11th New Jersey Volunteers* (Highstown, 1990), 104. While the *ORs* do not say exactly when the 11th New Jersey returned to support the battery, it can be assumed that it happened around 6 p.m. when the 120th New York advanced to the stone wall to its front, which apparently had been uncovered.

haversack. While chattering excitedly with several friends about his miraculous escape, a second 12-pounder ball hit him square in the body and completed what the first one had failed to do.[12]

McGilvery's Position, 1st Volunteer Brigade,
Army of the Potomac
The Millerstown Road

Minié balls pinged off Phillips' guns from the east. A musket ball struck one of the sergeants in the chest near a coat button. It miraculously ricocheted, passed around his body between his wool tunic and its liner and exited along the midseam above his waist. Another ball glanced off the top of his gun while he was aiming it and bored through the top of his cap.

It was no less hazardous for the men on the left gun. Before the fighting ended, the left wheel on the gun had taken no less than 22 hits. Bullets and artillery shards had struck 13 of the 14 spokes and each of the seven fellies—the wooden pieces comprising the circumference of the wheel. One piece lodged in a spoke close to the hub. Lead and iron literally pitted the left side of the piece. Nevertheless, Cpl. Benjamin Graham continued to site the gun, all while singing to himself in an effort to steel his nerves. "Hear Ben!" "Hear Ben!" the men shouted throughout the ordeal.[13]

On the right, the vents of Battery B, 1st New Jersey's Parrotts had burned to half an inch in diameter, rendering the guns unsafe to fire. Clark ordered the guns to limber up, but gunfire killed the lead team. Private John Higgens leaped from the pole horse, hastily cut the two dead animals free, and, remounting, took the limber off at a run. Privates Harrison and Edson Sheppard hurled themselves onto opposite sides of #1 and held on for dear life. Although the scalding tube melted all of the skin from his palm and fingers, Harrison stayed latched on to it. Sheppard took a musket ball in the left breast that glanced off a rib and bored a bluish track under his skin completely around his body, exiting

12 Cornelius D. Westbrook, "On the Firing Line," *National Tribune*, September 20, 1900; Cornelius Van Santvoord, *The 120th Regiment New York State Volunteers, A Narrative of Its Services in the War for the Union* (Roundout, NY, 1894), 75, quoted; J. J. Rudolph Tappen, *Seventh Annual Re-Union of the 120th N. Y. V. Regimental Union*, "Lieut. Col. J. J. Rudolph Tappen," February 22, 1875 (Kingston, NY, 1875), 9.

13 Regimental Committee, *5th Massachusetts Battery*, 624, 627, 631, 633-636, 638, 640, 642-643, quote on 643; Ladd and Ladd, *The Bachelder Papers*, vol. 1, 67-68; Baker, *9th Massachusetts Battery*, 60.

Lt. Edward M. Knox
15th New York Battery
Postwar image at the monument
which bears his image.
Library, GNMP

near his breastbone, not three inches from where it entered. "Halt, you Yankee sons of bitches!" a Confederate screamed. We want those guns." "Go to hell!" Pvt. Samuel Ennis retorted, "We want to use them yet awhile."[14]

While Clark's exodus dragged Hart's left section with him, 2nd Lt. Edward M. Knox's right section did not have time to escape. With the Mississippians' ranks reeling under the impact of a blast of double canister, the resourceful lieutenant screamed at his men to lie down and play dead. Galloping up to the 73rd New York, he pleaded with Lieutenant Moran (Company H) to save his guns. Amidst the deafening noise around them, Moran mistakenly believed he had obtained his superior Maj. Michael W. Burns's permission to assist the artillerymen.[15]

Colonel Humphreys and what remained of the 21st Mississippi temporarily "overran" the guns surrounded by the "dead" Yankees. At this point Moran shouted at his men to follow Knox. The line had barely stepped off when a bullet hit Moran, reeling him in the saddle until several of his men helped him to the ground while the charge swept around him. Within seconds, an exploding shell sent him to the ground with a broken ankle and a powder burned left eye. Nevertheless, his men successfully drove the Mississippians from Hart's two

---

14 Ladd and Ladd, *The Bachelder Papers*, vol. 2, 844; Hanifen, *Battery B*, 76, quoted.

15 Beyer and Keydel, *Deeds of Valor*, 231; Arrington, *The Medal of Honor at Gettysburg*, 11, 18; Frank M. Moran, "What Was Seen by a Captive Federal Officer," *Philadelphia Weekly Times*, April 22, 1882. Based upon the various accounts of rescued batteries, it is clear that Knox received aid from Lieutenant Moran and his company of the 73rd New York. That regiment would have been closer to Knox than the 72nd New York.

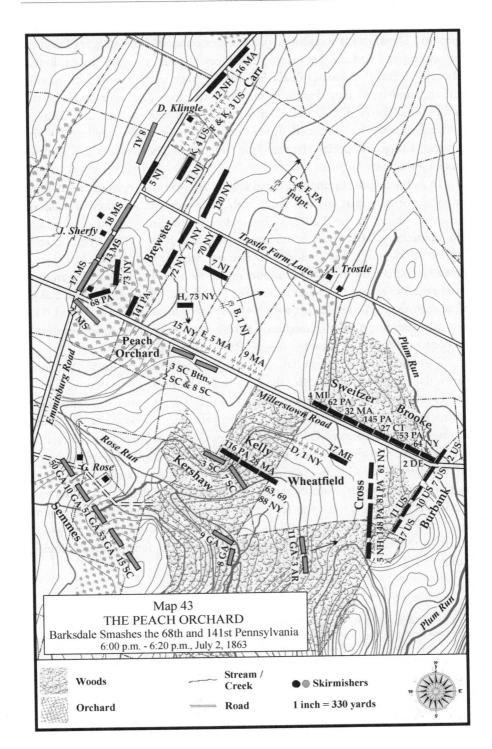

Map 43
THE PEACH ORCHARD
Barksdale Smashes the 68th and 141st Pennsylvania
6:00 p.m. - 6:20 p.m., July 2, 1863

Woods

Orchard

Stream / Creek

Road

Skirmishers

1 inch = 330 yards

guns and Thompson's abandoned piece. The wounded Knox staggered back to his section and ordered his men to their feet to retire the guns by prolonge. Thompson and Pvt. Casper R. Carlisle rushed back to their right gun. As rifle fire engulfed them they frantically cut away the four dead animals from the limber pole. Throwing themselves onto the two remaining horses, they dragged the limber with the wounded drivers on board out of the orchard. In the process, a fragment peeled the skin from the top of Thompson's arm without cracking the bone.[16]

In a short while, Graham noticed a fresh line of infantry in dark uniforms moving north against his left flank with their weapons on their shoulders. Believing them to be Federals, he rode out to bring them to his aid. Simultaneously, Maj. Israel Spaulding, on the left of the 141st Pennsylvania, barked at his wing, "Cease firing, boys; those are our own men." Just then a breeze unexpectedly unfurled Confederate colors over the approaching troops, and Sergeant George L. Forbes (Company I) hollered, "They are Rebels, major! I see their flag." At that, he brought his weapon to his shoulder and fired. The few men standing nearby immediately also started firing. Graham soon realized he confronted a Confederate unit—the 21st Mississippi.

With the Rebels yelling at him to surrender, he wheeled his horse about and spurred back to his own line. But the volley killed his horse and wounded him in the shoulder. While Graham was pinned to the ground under the animal, the advancing Mississippians quickly took him prisoner. The same volley struck Acting Assistant Adjutant General Lieutenant Graves in the hip, knocking him off his horse and dropping 30 Pennsylvanians about him. One of Bucklyn's artillerymen pulled Graves on top of one of the caissons as it hastened away from the fight. Finally, outnumbered, with casualties escalating out of control, Madill decided to get what was left of the 141st Pennsylvania out of the fight. Barksdale's three left regiments—the 13th, 17th, and 18th Mississippi—took cover in the Emmitsburg Road behind the destroyed fence and continuing firing. [17]

---

16 Andrew Humphreys to Lafayette McLaws, January 6, 1878, Vertical Files, GNMP; Beyer and Keydel, *Deeds of Valor*, vol. 1, 231; Arrington, *The Medal of Honor at Gettysburg*, 11, 18; Moran, "What Was Seen by a Captive Federal Officer," *Philadelphia Weekly Times*, April 22, 1882; Freeman McGilvery, "Part taken by the 1st Brigade Vol. Div. Arty. Res.," Freeman McGilvery Papers, Vertical Files, GNMP.

17 Craft, *141st Pennsylvania*, 122, 137; Bloodgood, *Reminiscences*, quote, 140; OR 27, pt. 1, 505.

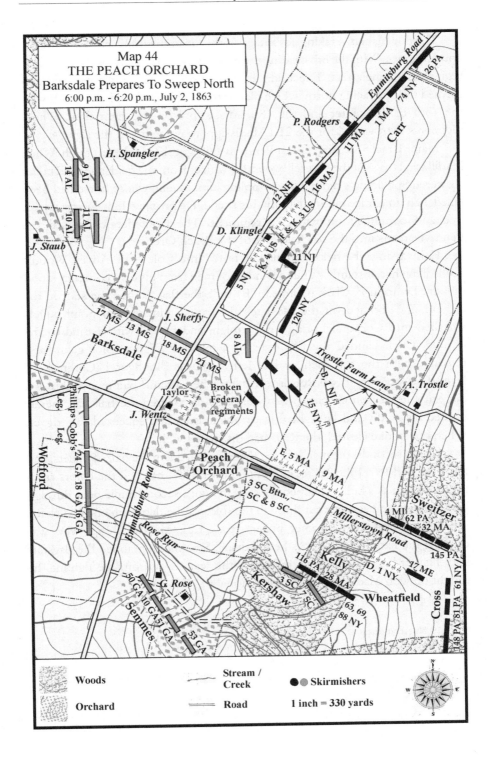

Map 44
THE PEACH ORCHARD
Barksdale Prepares To Sweep North
6:00 p.m. - 6:20 p.m., July 2, 1863

The 8th Alabama, taking advantage of the lull in the firing, closed in for the coup de grace. With the 8th clearing the front, Barksdale's officers shouted their regiments to their feet. Executing an "about face," they right wheeled and formed the line facing north, which placed the 17th Mississippi on the left with the 13th in the center and the 18th Mississippi on the right flank. These regiments then waited for the 21st Mississippi to come up on the right.[18]

Major Israel Spaulding (141st Pennsylvania) got shot in the left thigh. When Madill tried to assist the severely wounded officer from the field, a second bullet shattered Spaulding's right ankle, crippling him. Madill, whose horse had been killed, had no choice but to abandon his friend. He propped him against an ash tree and continued on with the regiment. The Confederates chased the Pennsylvanians into the oat field east of the Peach Orchard.[19]

Halfway into the field, a minié ball bored into Color Cpl. Amasa Wood's skull killing him instantly. While a handful of men from his own company stood by him, Lt. John F. Clark (Company E) took the flag, jabbed the staff in the ground, and shouted for the 141st to rally around him. At this point bullets smashed into Corporal Loring's right thigh, and he fell with a thud to the ground. Clark handed the flag over to a member of the color guard and retreated with the few men he had left. Sergeant Bloodgood (Company I) leveled his weapon at two Rebels to his left when a minié ball tugged through his pants leg. Upon checking his wound, he discovered the ball had merely burned his ankle, and he sighted in on them again and squeezed the trigger. When the smoke cleared, the Rebs had dissipated with it.[20]

Within seconds, the man bearing the state flag fell in the hail of bullets, and the wounded Pvt. John J. Stockholm (Company H) snatched the colors from his hands just as a bullet snapped the staff in two; a second minié bore through his cap brim, and another cut through the folds of the flag from one end to the other.[21] Seconds later another bullet struck Cpl. Morton Berry, who was carrying the national colors. As he fell dying, Stockholm grabbed the flagstaff with his left hand. Bearing both flags to the rear, away from the fighting, he caught up with Madill who took the national flag from him.

---

18 My reconstruction.

19 Craft, *141st Pennsylvania*, 121, 129.

20 Loring, "Gettysburg," *National Tribune*, July 9, 1885; Bloodgood, *Reminiscences*, 141-142.

21 Craft, *141st Pennsylvania*, 121.

On the way, the colonel gathered up his three remaining uninjured officers. Along with Capt. Joseph H. Horton (Company A), 2nd Lt. Elisha B. Brainerd (Company F), 1st Lt. Joseph Atkinson (Company G), and 16 enlisted men, Madill retreated as far as the farmyard west of the Trostle house, where he encountered the frantic Sickles, the corps commander. "Colonel!" the general pleaded, "for God's sake, can't you hold on?" With tears streaming down his cheeks, the exhausted colonel plaintively replied, "Where are my men?" In fact, the regiment was scattered all over the field east of the Peach Orchard. Unable to answer, Sickles rode back to the knoll immediately west of the barn.[22]

Zook's Brigade, II Corps, Army of the Potomac
The Wheatfield

Zook's Brigade, in two lines, with the general and the brigade's inspector general, Capt. James D. Brady, riding behind the center of the 140th Pennsylvania, had just crossed the Millerstown Road onto the northern end of the Stony Hill and the northwestern part of the Wheatfield. The 66th New York held the center of the line with the 52nd New York on its left. The 140th Pennsylvania scrambled over the stone wall to its front into the woods and halted, bringing the brigade to a standstill. Adjutant William S. Shallenberger quickly glanced at his watch—6 p.m.[23]

In the second line, Private Cole (57th New York) felt something slap his right arm, numbing his elbow. Turning to the man to his right, he asked why he hit him. "I did not hit you," the fellow snapped back, "but you have been shot and you had better go to the rear." Cole laughed at him: he was not hurt bad enough to quit the field, he said.[24]

A shell fragment, which Brady mistook for a bullet, ricocheted off a boulder and struck Zook right in the chest just after his horse jumped the stone fence along the road. Captain John F. McCullough (Company A, 140th Pennsylvania), seeing Zook get hit, struck his first lieutenant, James Jackson

---

22 Ibid., 121-122, 132, quote on 122; *OR* 27, pt. 1, 505; Loring, "Gettysburg," *National Tribune*, July 9, 1885.

23 Stewart, *140th Pennsylvania*, 422; Gilbert Frederick, *The Story of a Regiment Being a Record of the Military Services of the Fifty-Seventh New York State Volunteer Infantry in the War of the Rebellion 1861-1864* (Chicago, 1895), 170.

24 Cole, *Under Five Commanders*, 202.

Purman, on the back with the flat of his sword: "There goes poor Zook!" Purman glanced behind in time to see the general reel off his horse into the arms of 1st Lt. Charles H. H. Broom (Company K, 57th New York). Broom quickly eased Zook back into the saddle and, with a mounted orderly, turned the horse about to lead him off the field. Captain Favill (57th New York) rode to their assistance. "It's all up with me, Favill," Zook groaned painfully. Favill told Broom he would rejoin them after he turned the brigade over to Col. Orlando H. Morris (66th New York) and trotted toward the center of the brigade line. Behind him, another shell detonated over Company A, shattering Private Cole's right leg and killing two of his comrades. The man who wasn't hurt enough to leave now lay senseless in the wheat.[25]

Meanwhile, General Birney rode into De Trobriand's line and ordered the men to abandon their position or face imminent capture. Major John P. Dunne (115th Pennsylvania) found his right flank compromised, and having suffered no casualties, he decided to pull the regiment out of the battle. Retiring northeast through the wheat, he encountered Winslow's Battery D, 1st New York. Winslow asked Dunne to have his men to support his battery until he had time to evacuate his guns. Halting his small regiment to the right of the battery, Dunne ordered the men to kneel down in the wheat. From there, his men opened a steady fusillade upon the Confederates in the woods to his right and front.[26]

With their ammunition exhausted, and the 115th Pennsylvania on their right quitting the field, the men of the 17th Maine ceased firing and backed up the hill behind them. On the way, men rifled the cartridge boxes of the fallen. The Confederates immediately occupied the wall, and some boldly crossed over it. De Trobriand, whom Haley referred to as the "old fellow," watching the Rebels getting dangerously close to the crest, trotted into the regiment and commanded it to make a stand. Some of the men yelled back that they had no ammunition. "Then you must hold them with the bayonet," he replied. Under his direction, the 17th Maine halted and reformed, and then De Trobriand rode

25 James D. Brady to St. Clair Mulholland, April 18, 1898, Vertical Files, GNMP; Purman, "Recitals and Reminiscences," *National Tribune*, March 25, 1909; Favill, *Diary of a Young Officer*, 246; Stewart, *140th Pennsylvania*, 422; Cole, *Under Five Commanders*, 202-203.

26 Raus, *A Generation on the March*, 38, 117, 137; Report of Maj. John P. Dunne (115th Pennsylvania) to Adjutant General, State of Pennsylvania, July 29, 1863, Vertical Files, GNMP. According to the monuments of the 32nd Massachusetts, Sweitzer's Brigade, and the 53rd and 145th Pennsylvania, Brooke's brigade, they arrived on the field around 5 p.m.

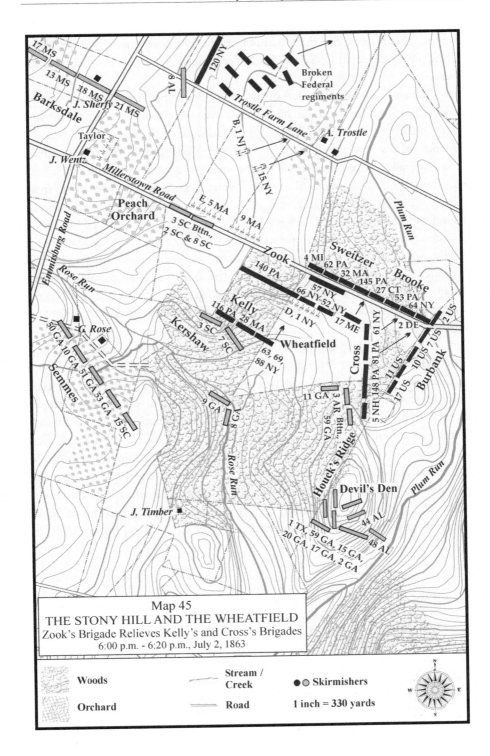

Map 45
THE STONY HILL AND THE WHEATFIELD
Zook's Brigade Relieves Kelly's and Cross's Brigades
6:00 p.m. - 6:20 p.m., July 2, 1863

Woods   Stream /   ●○ Skirmishers
               Creek

Orchard   Road   1 inch = 330 yards

away to superintend the right of his brigade. Every moment, Private Haley (Company I) expected to see a Rebel bullet knock his beloved colonel from his horse.[27]

Quite a few men on the left of the Irish Brigade broke ranks and streamed rearward around the stunned survivors of the 17th Maine, pushing their line back on the front and both flanks. With a number of the men crying over the prospect of being whipped, the 17th Maine fell back around Winslow's battery, which literally blasted the Rebels out of their shoes at point-blank range with canister. "Blood poured out like water," Haley later wrote.[28] A messenger from Birney, coming with the admonition to "Be careful" and not "get cut off," found Winslow, mounted behind his line. The captain kept his battery in position for a few minutes longer when a bullet brought both him and his horse to the ground. Now, without any infantry support—the 17th Maine had retreated to the shelter of the oaks on the north side of the Millerstown Road—he decided it was time to withdraw. With rounds materializing from the front and both flanks, he mounted his orderly's horse and raced to the left of his battery.[29]

As he did so, Captain Smith, having run the gauntlet of small arms fire, wheeled his remaining two guns onto the right of the line. Despite the tumult around him, Smith did not understand why Winslow was preparing to leave until he cast his eyes upon the wood line to the south. The massive line of Rebels on his front also convinced him to get out. A bullet cut down Smith's horse as the first gun entered the woods north of the Millerstown Road. First Lieutenant Thomas Goodman immediately gave the captain his mount. As Smith caught up with his lead gun, one of the men tugged on his right leg, exclaiming, "Captain, you're shot!" Looking down at the white morocco lining of his legging that had rolled down over the top of his boot to the ankle, he suddenly realized that blood saturated his pants leg. Almost immediately, he

27 Silliker, *The Rebel Yell*, 101-103, quote on 102; *OR*, vol. 27, pt. 1, 522; Ladd and Ladd, *The Bachelder Papers*, vol. 2, 840, 1,050; Report of Maj. John P. Dunne (115th Pennsylvania) to Adjutant General, State of Pennsylvania, July 29, 1863, GNMP.

28 Silliker, *The Rebel Yell*, 101-103, quote on 102; Ladd and Ladd, *The Bachelder Papers*, vol. 2, 1,059; *OR* 27, pt. 1, 522.

29 Silliker, *The Rebel Yell*, 101-103; Ladd and Ladd, *The Bachelder Papers*, vol. 1, 590, vol. 2, 1,059; *OR* 27, pt. 1, 522; Winslow, "Battery D," *Philadelphia Weekly Times*, July 21, 1879.

became aware of blood swishing around in his boot and intense pain surging through his leg.[30]

Winslow ordered Lieutenant Ames to retire his guns one piece at a time. The remaining two sections would retreat in the same manner. The Confederates wounded several of the New Yorkers and killed a few horses on the right section during the attempt, disabling a caisson. The five 12-Pounders wheeled to the left, and headed north through an opening in the fence along the Millerstown Road. Rolling through the woods, they passed through the 64th New York, which lay with the rest of Brooke's Brigade on the southern edge of the tree line.[31]

Private Osmon (Company C, 148th Pennsylvania) saw the Rebels massing for another attack. Plucking the state flag free, he handed it to his sergeant, John F. Benner. Standing out in the open ground, Osmon was capping his gun when a shell fragment violently tore the barrel out of the stock, leaving him holding bare wood. Beside him he saw the wounded William David Krebs (Company B) and took his weapon. Orders came to fall back to the east side of the Wheatfield, and during the withdrawal, Color Sergeant Benner quickly removed Captain Forster's sword and belt and took it with him. The three right companies lay down behind the stone wall.[32]

Once Winslow's guns cleared their line, Brooke's five regiments got to their feet. Colonel Hiram L. Brown delivered a cryptic "brave up talk" to his 145th Pennsylvania by reminding his "boys" they were on Northern soil and everyone's eyes were upon them. Private Steven A. Osborn (Company G) noticed tears welling in the eyes of some of his fellow veterans. "That class of men," he proudly recollected, "can be killed, but are hard to whip or conquer."[33]

To the southeast, Lieutenant Hale had watched Cross stride into the woods on the brigade's southern flank and never return. The lieutenant had his hands full with his fractious prisoners. The Confederate officer kept eyeing Hale and the woods, looking for a chance to escape. While the lieutenant and his few

30 Smith, *A Famous Battery*, 105, 109-110, quote on 110.

31 Silliker, *The Rebel Yell*, 101-103; Ladd and Ladd, *The Bachelder Papers*, vol. 1, 590, vol. 2, 1,059; OR 27, pt. 1, 522; Winslow, "Battery D," *Philadelphia Weekly Times*, July 21, 1879; Sigman, Diary, 49, IU.

32 Muffly, *148th Pennsylvania*, 602-603.

33 Calvin, (ed.), "*Recollections of Army Life in the Civil War*," 90.

enlisted men nervously herded their charges north, Brooke's Brigade formed in the Millerstown Road behind them.[34]

With the guns in a relatively safe position, Smith painfully dismounted. Calling over one of his men, he had the fellow pull the boot off his terribly swollen calf and foot, nastily chaffing the fellow for being unnecessarily rough with him. With the boot free, he anxiously looked down at his foot, expecting the worst. Instead, he saw nothing. No wound. No blood. Looking into the enlisted man's broad grin, he sheepishly admonished him: "Let me tell this story first, please." A close inspection showed that Goodman's horse caught a round in the right flank and, in spurring the wounded animal, its blood had soaked into his pants. Smith's vivid imagination and the anxiety of the moment had created the phantom wounding and his embarrassment.[35] Birney and his aide-de-camp, Captain Briscoe, found the 17th Maine sitting down near the road, awaiting ammunition. Placing themselves in front of the line, they led the regiment back into the fighting. The Confederates retreated to the cover of the stone wall. Birney halted the 17th along the crest of the ridge and ordered it to hold the line.

Second Lieutenant Verrill (Company C) got shot in the leg and collapsed. Rifle fire cut down seven of the 10 men in the color guard. Color Sergeant James H. Loring (Company H), carrying the state flag, died instantly. Corporal Joseph F. Lake (Company A), with the national colors, snatched up the blood splattered state flag and quickly handed it off to Cpl. William D. Merrill (Company F). The Rebels shot down and mortally wounded Cpl. Bernard Hogan (Company D), and dropped Cpl. Benjamin F. Huff (Company G). And a bullet mauled Merrill's hand, forcing him to relinquish the flag to Cpl. Edwin A. Duncan (Company K) who came out of the scrape unscathed.[36] But Birney's defense had dissolved.

Farther to the right, De Trobriand pushed what he could find of the 5th Michigan and the 110th Pennsylvania into the fray. They fell in on the right of the 17th Maine. Private Haley (17th Maine) and Cpl. Owen Stacy, whom he was assisting from the field, were nearly surrounded when three huzzahs rent the air above the Confederates' fierce "Rebel Yell" and a volley from the north stopped the assault and hurled the Rebels back to the stone wall. Brooke's

34 Hale, "*With Colonel Cross*," 10, PHS.

35 Smith, *A Famous Battery*, 110.

36 Silliker, *The Rebel Yell*, 101-103; Ladd and Ladd, *The Bachelder Papers*, vol. 1, 46, vol. 2, 1,059; OR 27, pt. 1, 522; Executive Committee, *Maine at Gettysburg*, 197-198, 213-214.

Brigade came to the field and the 17th Maine with the remnants of the brigade retired toward the Taneytown Road.[37]

The seriously wounded Lieutenant Fuller (61st New York) listened to the firing ebb around him. Lying in the trampled wheat, he heard Brooke's men rushing toward him. "Don't step on me, boys," he cried out. Having gotten too far ahead of Zook's regiments on their right, Brooke's line lay down on the brow of the ridge overlooking the corpse-strewn hollow between them and the stone wall. Bullets zipped into the 64th New York. One caught Color Cpl. Chauncey McKoon (Company B) in the left thigh, and he handed the flag over to Cpl. Edward Stone (Company D). First Sergeant Horace French (Company F) fell with a bullet in the right breast and shoulder. Another round hit Capt. Rodney R. Crowley (Company B) in the left leg.[38]

The 121 survivors of the 5th Michigan gathered around their tattered colors in the woods north of the Millerstown Road and broke into a "manly cheer." General Birney rode up to them and removed his hat before paying them his respects.[39]

Zook's Brigade, II Corps, Army of the Potomac
Trostle's Woods
North of the Millerstown Road

Amid a virtual hail of rifle fire from the Stony Hill, the panting soldiers of the 140th Pennsylvania loosed a ragged volley into the trees at the shadows in front of them, and the firing rolled down the brigade to the left. Within the first two minutes, Zook's soldiers had hurled three or four volleys at the distant Confederates. When the color bearer of the 66th New York went down, Colonel Morris picked them up, and immediately he too was shot. He staggered to the rear, never knowing that command of the brigade had devolved upon him. He turned the regiment over to 21-year-old Lt. Col. John Sweeney

---

37 Hamilton, "*Recollections*," 124, CWL; Silliker, *The Rebel Yell*, 101-103; Ladd and Ladd, *The Bachelder Papers*, vol. 2, 1,005, 1,059; OR 27, pt. 1, 522; Executive Committee, *Maine at Gettysburg*, 198. Haley mistakenly believed the relief troops were from the VI Corps. They were actually regiments from the Irish Brigade.

38 Fuller, *Personal Recollections*, 96, quoted; "Unidentified Soldier of the 64th New York Infantry," 50, IU; George Whipple, "Father's own story of his army life in the civil war of 60's," Vertical Files, GNMP, 20; "The Sixty-fourth Regiment," *Philadelphia Public Ledger*, July 18, 1863.

39 G. W. W. to [Editor], July 5, 1863, *New York Tribune*, July 23, 1863.

Hammell, who was immediately wounded and sent to the rear. At that point, Maj. Peter A. Nelson, a man almost twice his age, assumed command.[40]

Unable to find Colonel Morris, Favill quickly passed the command of the brigade to Lt. Col. Charles G. Freudenberg (52nd New York) then departed for safer ground. Freudenberg immediately rode to the left to inform Col. John R. Brooke—whose 4th brigade had gone to the ground—that Zook had left the field wounded and pass command on to him. When Freudenberg spurred back to his regiment, he centered himself in front of it and commanded, "Cease fire!" then "Forward March!" Almost immediately, a rifle ball struck him, hurtling him from his horse. His men passed around him.[41]

Brooke also took charge of Zook's two left regiments and ordered the line forward. The horrendous roar of the musketry, though, completely obliterated his command. It took several minutes for the color bearers to step out from the line. The 53rd Pennsylvania, in the center of the brigade, ceased fire and stood up. The order traveled the brigade to fix bayonets, and bristling steel, the rest of the brigade followed their comrades deeper into the Wheatfield. The 145th Pennsylvania had just gotten to its feet when Colonel Brown went down, wounded above the right elbow. Senior Capt. John W. Reynolds (Company A) assumed command and sent the line forward. As the two combined brigades moved out, the 61st New York, 81st Pennsylvania, and the right wing of the 148th Pennsylvania retired from the battle. In the woods to the left of the line, the 5th New Hampshire and the four left companies of the 148th Pennsylvania pushed forward, firing, to support Brooke's left flank. Company G, already in front of the 148th, also joined in the advance.[42]

Brigadier General John Caldwell (First Division, II Corps) galloped into the woods north of the Millerstown Road where he found Col. Jacob Sweitzer with his brigade (2nd Brigade, V Corps). Pointing toward the woods on the southwest side of the Wheatfield, Caldwell excitedly blurted something about how his division was "driving the enemy like hell." Would the colonel support his division with his brigade? Sweitzer, having no idea who Caldwell was, sent

---

40 Carter, *Four Brothers in Blue*, 309; Ladd and Ladd, *The Bachelder Papers*, vol. 1, 417; OR 27, pt. 1, 395-396, 398; Frederick, *57th New York*, 170; Raus, *A Generation on the March*, 67.

41 Ladd and Ladd, *The Bachelder Papers*, vol. 1, 667.

42 Ibid., vol. 2, 1,140-1,141; "Unidentified Soldier of the 64th New York Infantry," 50, IU; OR 27, pt. 1, 409; Report of Chaplain J. H. W. Stuckenberg, RG 94, NA; Ladd and Ladd, *The Bachelder Papers*, vol. 2, 1,032.

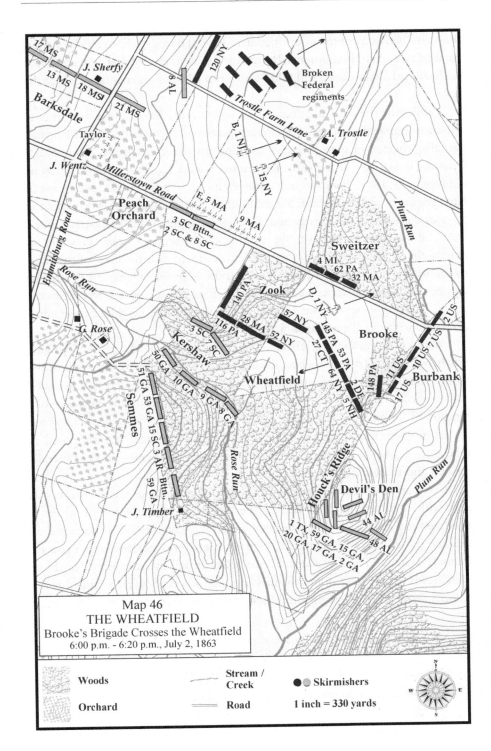

Map 46
THE WHEATFIELD
Brooke's Brigade Crosses the Wheatfield
6:00 p.m. - 6:20 p.m., July 2, 1863

Woods

Orchard

Stream / Creek

Road

● ● Skirmishers

1 inch = 330 yards

him to his division commander Brigadier General Barnes, whom he saw a short distance away. Within moments, Barnes rode over to the colonel, repeated what Caldwell had already said, and told Sweitzer to take his regiments back into the fray.[43]

Guided by the sounds of battle roaring from the fields to the west, the six rightmost companies of the 140th Pennsylvania, on the right of Zook's Brigade, partially wheeled in that direction, heading for the crest of the Stony Hill.[44] Crossing the stone wall along the eastern base of the hill, Pvt. Robert L. Stewart (Company G, 140th Pennsylvania) plunged into a Stygian wooded landscape of large granite boulders, shrouded in a choking pall of acrid smoke. The rocks and trees disrupted the regimental line, forcing the men to tread gingerly around them, all the while trying to avoid treading on the scores of casualties that lay among them. An unexpected burst of flame erupted near the crest of the ridge to the south, silhouetting a Federal line on the Pennsylvanians' left front. The regiment's chaotic advance had dragged the four left companies too far to the south, bringing it behind the 116th Pennsylvania at the height of their initial exchange with the South Carolinians.

With three resounding cheers, the men flanked to the right. Swinging north, behind the Irishmen's line, the 140th fell in along the western face of the woods at a right angles to and slightly to the rear of the 116th. The 140th halted and fronted. "Load and fire at will!" Colonel Roberts bellowed. As the smoke temporarily lifted in the field immediately to the west, Stewart suddenly realized at that moment that the III Corps troops, which his brigade was supposed to relieve, had already left the field. Several rods to the front, the field literally flashed and roared incessantly.[45]

Companies C, F, and G on the right end of the regiment cleared the woods first with their left flank in the northeast corner of the woodlot where it bordered the field east of the Peach Orchard. A determined Roberts, riding quickly toward the right, cautioned: "Steady, men. Fire low. Remember you are Pennsylvanians." The first Confederate volley struck the tree branches above their heads. Their next ones whistled in much lower. Several rounds hit the colonel, knocking him from the saddle. Seconds later, they killed the senior

---

43 Orvey S. Barrett, *Reminiscences, Incidents, Battles, Marches and Camp Life in the Old 4th Michigan Infantry in the War of the Rebellion, 1861-1864* (Detroit, 1888), 22.

44 *OR* 27, pt. 1, 395, Stewart, *140th Pennsylvania*, 104-105, 422.

45 Stewart, *140th Pennsylvania*, 104-105, 422, quote on 104.

Pvt. John McNutt
Co. G, 140th Pennsylvania
George W. Neely Collection
Library, GNMP

captain, David Acheson (Company C), who stood nearby. Other men dropped by the score. Company G, on the right, got severely punished. One bullet struck 1st Sgt. John F. Wilson in the right arm, knocking his musket to the ground; a second one in the other arm turned him about, and he staggered away with his arms dangling limply at his sides. Private John McNutt collapsed, mortally wounded at Stewart's feet. Close by, Stewart watched two of his fellow classmates, Pvt. Hugh Wier and 2nd Lt. Alexander Wilson, bleed to death. Lieutenant Colonel John Fraser, former college professor turned warrior, took over the regiment.[46]

Brooke's charge completely disorganized the 66th and the 52nd New York. During the advance, large contingents of Confederate prisoners, who were making their way to the rear, passed through their ranks. The three regiments on the left of the 140th Pennsylvania merged with the shattered ranks of the Irish Brigade, facing south. With his men inextricably mixed up with the 52nd New York, Major Nelson hurriedly tried to reform his 66th New York. The 57th New York remained in line to the left rear of the brigade. The 7th South Carolina had fought them to a standstill.[47]

46 Purman, "Recitals and Reminiscences," *National Tribune*, March 25, 1909; Raus, *A Generation on the March*, 134-135; John B. Bachelder to Col. John P. Nicholson, July 8, 1889, Vertical Files, GNMP; Stewart, *140th Pennsylvania*, quote on 105.

47 OR 27, pt. 1, 395-396, 398; Stewart, *140th Pennsylvania*, 104; *New York at Gettysburg*, vol. 1, 420; L. E. Estilow, "Doing My Duty, The Wartime Experiences of John S. Hard," 21, Vertical Files, GNMP.

Chapter 13

July 2, 1863
6:20 p.m.-6:30 p.m.

"I don't care what anyone says, those troops in front are running away."
—*First Lieutenant William H. Powell (4th U.S.)*

Kershaw's Brigade, Longstreet's Corps,
Army of Northern Virginia
The Rose Farm

Brigadier General Kershaw reached the rear of Semmes' line as it entered the orchard below the Rose house and intercepted the 15th South Carolina a short distance behind the Georgians. Colonel William De Saussure lay dead in the hedgerow on the west side of the orchard, sword in hand. Major William M. Gist had assumed command. A minié ball passing through Company C creased Pvt. Wesley Nichols' skull. Blinded by the blood, he crawled down behind a large rock. Kershaw yelled at Gist to move into the hollow at the southern base of the Stony Hill and then directed Brigadier General Semmes toward the right and the creek bottom behind Anderson's battered position.[1]

Brooke's Brigade, II Corps, Army of the Potomac
The Wheatfield

Brooke's five small regiments pressed forward, leaving Zook's men behind. The 27th Connecticut lost Lt. Col. Henry Merwin on the crest of the ridge south of the road. Leaving his lifeless body in the wheat, the regiment pressed

---

1 *Autobiography of Wesley Nichols*, n. d., 6, Vertical Files, GNMP; Kershaw, "Kershaw's Brigade at Gettysburg," in *Battles and Leaders*, vol. 3, 336.

forward.[2] The brigade careened south with the right wing rushing over the southeastern side of the Stony Hill. On the far right, the 145th Pennsylvania volleyed through the smoke-filled woods to their front at the presumably hostile shadows flittering through it. Before the haze cleared, they rushed through the woods headlong into the 8th Georgia. Overwhelming the Rebels by the speed of their advance, the Pennsylvanians disarmed around 25 of them and sent them rearward. On the right, the 11th Georgia fell back toward the western side of the woods. Descending into the wooded marsh, Brooke's small brigade herded the Georgians to the top of the rocky ledge to the west.[3]

The 27th Connecticut pressed into the creek bottom, leaving Lt. Jed Chapman (Company H) among the slain on the southern slope of the Stony Hill. They cornered some Rebs behind a clump of trees on the southern bank of Rose Run. Halting briefly to reorganize the company-sized regiment, the 27th then charged, flushing the Confederates into the marsh. It was a charge that cost them over half of their men.[4]

When the 64th New York entered the pasture on the east side of the field, Color Cpl. Edward Stone, Jr. (Company D) collapsed, mortally wounded. Corporal Albin C. Blackmore (Company I) pulled the flag from his hands. Another flag-bearer died when a bullet drilled into the head of Color Cpl. Thomas J. Zibble (Company F), who carried the new state flag. His replacement, Color Cpl. Albert Empey (Company E) took the standard and, seconds later, took hits in the hand and the thigh. Lt. Arnold R. Chase (Company A) carried the colors forward. Across the pasture, the 64th New York collided with the stone wall. Private George Whipple (Company F) stopped behind some bushes to reload when a minié ball cracked Pvt. William E. Owen (Company E) in the forehead and another hit him in the breast. He fell heavily against Whipple, startling him. "Never mind, George," his captain, Henry V. Fuller, calmly told him.[5]

2   Almond E. Clark, "The Stand Made by the Remnant of the 27th Conn.," *National Tribune*, October 10, 1918.

3   Calvin, "Recollections of Army Life," 91; "Unidentified Soldier of the 64th New York Infantry," IU, 50-51.

4   Clark, "The Stand Made by the Remnant of the 27th Conn.," *National Tribune*, October 10, 1918; A. C. Clark, "*The 27th Connecticut at Gettysburg*," Vertical Files, GNPM.

5   Whipple, "Father's own story," Vertical Files, GNMP, 20, quoted; "The Sixty-fourth Regiment," *Philadelphia Public Ledger*, July 18, 1863.

Lt. Col. Henry Merwin
27th Connecticut
*Andrew DeCusati Collection
Library, GNMP*

The regiment struck the wall on a diagonal, which briefly threw its ranks into confusion because they were marching by the rear rank. Despite the obstacles, the men climbed over the wall, stepped across the creek bottom, and continued west, shooting and shouting as they went. The 2nd Delaware, on the left of the brigade, dove to cover at the foot of the declivity and responded with musketry, scattering the Rebels in front of it. The brigade charged up the hill. The 2nd captured two commissioned officers and several enlisted men.[6]

Poking their rifles over the brow of the ledge, the Yankees fired away at their adversaries, who had taken cover behind the stone wall on the east side of the Rose orchard.[7] Fewer than 25 enlisted men of the 27th Connecticut made it to the ledge. Private Almond E. Clark (Company C) frantically looked about for officers and other comrades, but could see none through the smoky woods. Nevertheless, the color bearers defiantly jutted their flags above the crest, several bullets tugging at their folds.[8]

The riflery waned. Despite a severely bruised ankle, and two wounded aides—Capt. H. J. Smith and Lt. C. F. Smith—Col. John R. Brooke hurried a courier to Caldwell asking him for more troops on his right flank and shortly

---

6   Report of Chaplain J. H. W. Stuckenberg, RG 94, NA; OR 27, pt. 1, 403; "The Sixty-fourth Regiment," *Philadelphia Public Ledger*, July 18, 1863.

7   "Unidentified Soldier of the 64th New York Infantry," IU, 51.

8   Clark, "The Stand Made by the Remnant of the 27th Conn.," *National Tribune*, October 10, 1918.

thereafter he sent another rider with a request either for relief or more ammunition.[9]

Anderson's Brigade, Longstreet's Corps,
Army of Northern Virginia
The Stony Hill

The impetuosity of Brooke's assault broke through the center of Anderson's Brigade. The 9th Georgia, in the creek bed, found itself alone. The 145th Pennsylvania, in cutting through the smoke enshrouded valley, completely passed by the regiment's right flank. Above the racket, Captain Hillyer, commanding the 9th, heard another regiment crashing down the hill into the creek on the left. Shooting an anxious glance behind him, he saw Brigadier General Semmes splashing into the bloodied stream, placing men on the line. It was the 10th Georgia under Semmes' own personal direction. Wounded in the thigh, the general feverishly improvised a tourniquet using his handkerchief and sword to staunch the blood flow. Private William R. Stilwell (Company F) and a couple men from the 53rd Georgia came to his assistance. As they lifted Semmes up, he quietly acknowledged Stilwell's faithful service.[10]

By this point Kershaw had returned to the 7th South Carolina which he found nearly doubled back upon itself with the Federals pressing the 3rd South Carolina's front. With no artillery fire coming in from the left of his line, he sent for the 2nd South Carolina to reinforce his right.[11]

Brooke's Brigade, II Corps, Army of the Potomac
The Ledge on the West Side of the Rose Woods

With five rounds per man left, Brooke knew he could not hold the position for long. Finally, he notified his division commander of a Confederate column (Semmes') closing in upon his left flank.[12] The Georgians fell into line with the

---

9   OR 27, pt. 1, 400-401; Ladd and Ladd, *The Bachelder Papers*, vol. 2, 1,141-1,142.

10 Hillyer, "Battle of Gettysburg, Georgia Troops at Gettysburg," *Walton Tribune*, 1904, 7-8; Ladd and Ladd, *The Bachelder Papers*, vol. 1, 474; William Ross Stilwell to "Mollie," July 10, 1863, Vertical Files, GNMP.

11 OR 27, pt. 2, 368-369.

12 OR 27, pt. 1, 400-401; Ladd and Ladd, *The Bachelder Papers*, vol. 2, 1,141-1,142.

3rd Arkansas and the left wing of the 59th Georgia along the stone wall only yards from the Federals.

The Irish Brigade, II Corps, Army of the Potomac
The Stony Hill

To Brooke's right rear, Major Mulholland (116th Pennsylvania) peered across the smoky field behind his line and observed what he believed to be a Confederate column breaking through the eastern side of the Peach Orchard. He ran down the slope to Colonel Kelly, who refused to believe the flankers were Rebels because of the smoke and the distance from the orchard. For his part, Mulholland insisted Kelly relieve him of command of the 116th and grant him permission to take the 140th forward to investigate the situation. Kelly assented to this. Returning to the 116th, Mulholland handed the regiment over to Adj. Garrett Nowlen. Hurrying into the left wing of the 140th Mulholland could not find Maj. Thomas Rogers, so he pointed toward the Confederates and convinced some of the men to follow him.[13]

On the far right of the line Lt. Col. John Fraser (140th Pennsylvania) glanced over his left shoulder into the Wheatfield. The left of the brigade line disintegrated before his eyes. Unaware of Zook's wounding, he immediately rushed a runner to the rear to find out what the general wanted him to do. A flood of soldiers from various commands to his left streamed around the 66th New York's right flank, and completely engulfed the regiment. Major Peter A. Nelson gave the command to retreat.[14] His rout dragged the 52nd New York with him.

In just a matter of minutes, the 140th Pennsylvania sustained horrendous losses. One of the color guard toppled simultaneously along with Color Sgt. Robert Riddle (Company F), who collapsed on top of the regimental colors, gasping from a hole through his left lung. Corporal Joseph Moody (Company H) knelt by his side and rolled the sergeant over. Passing the flag to Cpl. Jesse T. Power (Company E), he tried to make Riddle more comfortable.[15]

The noncommissioned officers bawled at their men to cease firing for fear of cutting down a large body of troops, supposedly friends, which were slipping

---

13 Mulholland, *116th Pennsylvania*, 374.

14 *OR* 27, pt. 1, 395-396, 398.

15 Stewart, *140th Pennsylvania*, 106-108.

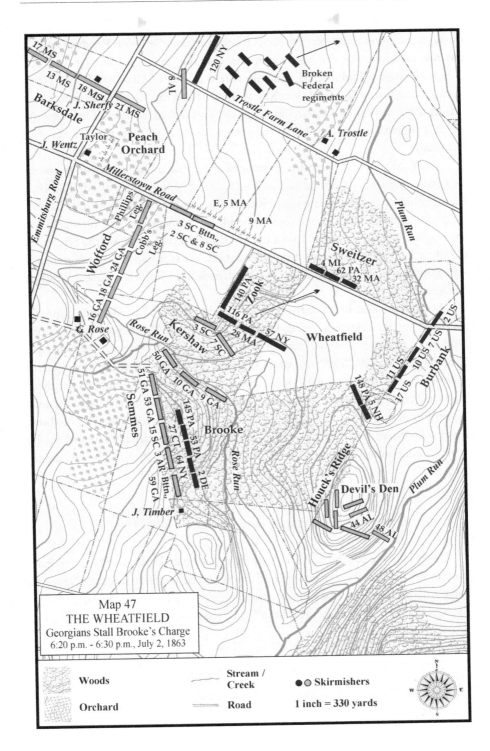

Map 47
THE WHEATFIELD
Georgians Stall Brooke's Charge
6:20 p.m. - 6:30 p.m., July 2, 1863

Woods

Orchard

Stream / Creek

Road

Skirmishers

1 inch = 330 yards

through the smoke between the Federal batteries and the 140th Pennsylvania. It did not take long for the Yankees to see that the ghosts in the fog were the enemy.[16] Major Mulholland, having taken a small portion of the 140th Pennsylvania onto the field, incredulously watched the Confederates halt and unfurl their colors. The Georgians volleyed and bolted forward. Ordering the Pennsylvanians to follow him to the south, he took off at a run for his own command.

Wofford's Georgia brigade, approaching the Peach Orchard from the west, was sweeping east, its left flank just south of the Millerstown Road. The 18th Georgia held the right of the line with the 24th and the 16th to its left. Cobb's Legion and the Phillips' Legion completed the formation to the north. When the brigade moved out, portions of the 3rd Battalion, the 2nd, and the 8th South Carolina regiments followed it into the action. Wofford spurred to Kershaw's left wing, reassuring them that they had "friendlies" on their flank instead of Yankees.[17]

Longstreet and his orderly, Private Youngblood (15th Alabama), quietly followed in the brigade's wake. Glancing northeast, Youngblood noted out loud that the men on the left of the line had not gone far beyond the Emmitsburg Road. "Do you want General Barksdale to halt?" Longstreet snapped his head in Youngblood's direction. "No," the general curtly replied, "Go, and tell him to retake his position in line." Jerking the reins hard to the left, Youngblood dug spurs and clattered across the fields toward the Emmitsburg Road. His horse bolted a fence, throwing the startled orderly forward on its neck. Pulling himself back into the saddle, he continued galloping to the Klingle farm.[18]

Sweitzer's Brigade, V Corps, Army of the Potomac
The Woods North of the Millerstown Road

Caldwell rode south to confer with Ayres, whose division of Regulars had gone to ground on the eastern side of the Wheatfield. Fifth Sergeant Orvey S. Barrett (Company B, 4th Michigan), standing close by Barnes, heard him shout: "Boys, I want you to put in a few licks for Pennsylvania; the Bucktails will go in

---

16 Frederick, *57th New York*, 170-171.

17 Mulholland, *116th Pennsylvania*, 374; *Richmond Daily Enquirer*, August 5, 1863.

18 William Youngblood, "Unwritten History," in *SHSP*, vol. 38, 316.

on your left. Forward. March." Getting his men into line, Sweitzer urged the brigade into the smoke obscured Wheatfield, apparently believing that his right flank remained secure.[19]

Winslow's Battery, III Corps Artillery Brigade, Army of the Potomac
The Wheatfield

Winslow's stranded artillerymen had an incredible stroke of luck by capturing several stray, but fully harnessed artillery horses as they raced across the rear of his battery from the direction of Little Round Top. Hitching them to the unmanned caisson of his right piece, the captain ordered the gun from the field. He had lost touch with the other five guns from his battery in the woods, but he saw Sweitzer's brigade double-quicking into the Wheatfield. He wheeled his lone artillery piece through the fence opening behind Bigelow's battery. Turning right along the stone wall on the west side of the field, he headed north in search of either Birney or Hunt.[20]

140th Pennsylvania, II Corps, Army of the Potomac
The Stony Hill

Sporadic fire spattered the 140th Pennsylvania's Company G. Adjutant William S. Shallenberger, who could not locate a brigade commander anywhere, jogged to Lieutenant Colonel Fraser and warned him of the Rebels on the regiment's flank, at which Fraser yelled for the Pennsylvanians to quit the field. Returning to his post behind the right company, Shallenberger yelled the command and turned to guide the withdrawal when a ball ripped through his right calf. After a few steps toward the rear, his leg buckled under his weight. Using his sword as a cane, Shallenberger pushed himself to his feet and staggered several more feet before a second bullet snapped the blade in half. The impact tore the sword's hilt from his hand and sent him crashing to the ground. Rounds from the front and both flanks cracked and crashed through

---

19 Barrett, Reminiscences, 22, quoted; *Supplement to the* OR 5, pt. 1, 193; OR 27, pt. 1, 379.

20 Silliker, *The Rebel Yell*, 101-103; Ladd and Ladd, *The Bachelder Papers*, vol. 1, 590, vol. 2, 1,059; OR 27, pt. 1, 522; George B. Winslow, "Battery D," *Philadelphia Weekly Times*, July 26, 1879.

the trees like hail pelting a tin roof. A couple of enlisted soldiers pulled the lieutenant to his feet and hauled him away.[21]

In the pandemonium, the men on the far left of the regimental line did not realize the right wing had collapsed. Frantically looking around, Sgt. John A. Burns (Company A) never received the word to retreat. But it was plain that's what he had to do. Chucking his knapsack, he clutched his weapon and took off at a dead run toward the Wheatfield. "Halt, you damned Yank!" echoed over his head from behind, but he kept going as bullets clipped the heads of the wheat around him. He had retreated a short distance with what was left of the regiment, leaving. As the Rebels yelled at him to surrender, Cpl. Jesse T. Power (Company E), who had left Cpl. Joseph Moody (Company H) on his own, high-tailed it toward the regiment in its grand skedaddle for the safety of the eastern side of the Wheatfield. Unable to locate the Rebels through the smoke, Major Rogers and a small portion of the left wing skittered down to the eastern edge of the woods and hurried north toward the Millerstown Road. Emerging from the northern face of the tree line, the major saw three Confederate battle flags race across their front, and, almost immediately, the Pennsylvanians found themselves captured, under guard, and on their way to the rear.[22]

Meanwhile, a staff officer galloped up to Mulholland (116th Pennsylvania), shouting they were surrounded. Mulholland ordered an immediate withdrawal to save whomever they could. Noting that only his regiment and a portion of the 140th Pennsylvania remained upon the field, he ordered Pvt. Samuel D. Hunter (Company C) with Color Sgt. Abraham Detweiler to furl the colors and follow him. The colonel then led the color guard and about half of the regiment in a mad dash into the Wheatfield. Private Thomas Scarlett (Company A) saw Mulholland and the colors break toward the rear but never heard the retreat order and found himself encircled by Rebels. Taking advantage of the chaos, he bolted east to the relative safety of the Wheatfield. Meanwhile the brigade raced pell-mell through a crossfire across the Millerstown Road into the woods.[23]

That same staff officer who had warned Mulholland imparted the same warning to Lt. Col. Alfred Chapman and the 57th New York to retire and

---

21 Stewart, *140th Pennsylvania*, 422.

22 "St. Louisans Among Gettysburg Heroes," *St Louis Globe-Democrat*, March 9, 1913, 15, USAHEC.

23 Mulholland, *116th Pennsylvania*, 374-375; "116th Pennsylvania Vs. 140th Pennsylvania," July 12, 1895, GNMP.

escape capture. Chapman tried to protect the rest of the brigade by ordering the regiment to change front to the right, but the movement fouled as the left of the brigade stampeded through the New Yorkers' ranks. Chapman then unhesitatingly commanded "about face," and the regiment fell back across the small rocky field on the north end of the Stony Hill and re-crossed the Millerstown Road into the corner of the woods on the opposite side. There they regrouped and returned several wild volleys into the Rose Woods, barely missing several of their own men who had stayed behind to give the Rebels a few more rounds.[24]

The 9th and the 10th Georgia pushed north into the trees. Hillyer noticed two New Yorkers at the front of the regiment who refused to retreat. The pair, apparently messmates, stood their ground, and when one of them fell dead, his comrade went to ground behind his body, using it for cover. Within two minutes he was also killed.[25]

From across the road, the men of the 57th New York saw the Confederates coming through the trees in formation, as if on parade, colors flying and weapons at "right shoulder shift." Rather than await capture, the New Yorkers retreated. Private Cole (Company H), awakening in severe pain, realized that someone was standing upon his broken leg. He found himself under a Rebel officer. Cole begged him to get off him to which the officer responded by baring his sword: "You damned, Yankee, I will cut your heart out." As the Rebel raised the sword, a rifle ball drilled through his throat, and he fell lifeless alongside the private.[26]

Brooke's Brigade, II Corps, Army of the Potomac
The Ledge on the West Side of the Rose Woods

For about 20 minutes, Brooke's men, on the left of the brigade line behind the 2nd Delaware, had held their ground until the Rebels got around their right flank. With fire coming from both sides and his own ammunition nearly gone, Brooke ordered the regiments to retire. Captain Henry V. Fuller (Company F, 64th New York), on the company's right, had taken cover between two rocks

---

24 Frederick, *57th New York*, 170-171; Capt. Jedediah C. Paine to St. Clair Mulholland, April 23, 1898, "116th Pennsylvania vs. 140th Pennsylvania," GNMP.

25 Hillyer, "Battle of Gettysburg," 9-10.

26 Frederick, *57th New York*, 170-171; Cole, *Under Five Commanders*, 203, quoted.

Capt. Henry V. Fuller
Co. F, 64th New York
Orton Begner Collection
Library, GNMP

and was emptying his pistol at a Rebel color bearer when the word reached his men. Fuller could not find out who had given the order until suddenly an aide from the Irish Brigade galloped into the company, yelling for them to fall back.

Simultaneously Sergeant Joseph Charlesworth (Company C) dropped with a slight head wound and Pvt. Leroy Shippey had a large chunk of flesh and bone torn from his hand. A bullet through both lungs killed Lt. Alfred H. Lewis (Company D). First Lieutenant Willis G. Babcock (Company G) also succumbed to lung wounds. Two bullets hammered 1st Sgt. Ira S. Thurber (Company I) in the hand and the breast.

Captain Fuller stood up to leave when his legs collapsed and he fell at Pvt. George Whipple's feet. Whipple hauled him upright by his right arm, but his one leg would not support his weight. Private Charles Clock (Company F) grabbed Fuller's left arm. They had dragged the captain only a short distance to the rear when a second round hit him in the back and exited under Whipple's arm. Clock let go of the captain and took off running. Whipple and Fuller could not keep pace. As the captain passed out, Whipple dropped his weapon and dragged him several rods to the creek bank. There Fuller weakly asked to be placed behind a rock.[27]

The Yankees retreated through the pasture behind them under a vicious crossfire. Wounded and unable to walk, Brooke barely escaped: two enlisted men slung his arms around their shoulders and dragged him rearward. Private

---

27 OR 27, pt. 1, 401; Ladd and Ladd, *The Bachelder Papers*, vol. 2, 1,141, 1,143; Whipple, "Father's own story," 20, GNMP.

Clark (27th Connecticut) lost his haversack when a minié ball bored through the gum blanket across his shoulder and cut the strap. His major, James H. Coburn, staggered aimlessly across the field, concussed by a shell burst. Sergeant John F. Sanford (Company C), carrying the national flag, and Sgt. James Brand (Company I), with the State colors, assisted him to the rear.[28]

Near the southern side of Rose Run, Pvt. Steven Osborn and Sgt. James Heckman (both Company G, 145th Pennsylvania) stumbled across a sergeant from Company C with a pulverized kneecap. He pleaded with them to get him out of there. Despite Heckman's small stature, both he and Osborn lifted the sergeant's arms over their shoulders and clumsily began dragging him away. Part way through the pasture Osborn spied a "strapping big" Confederate skulking behind some brush. They shouted at him to help them out, but the Rebel called back he was wounded. Osborn did not believe it and yelled at him that if he refused to help, he would "surely be a wounded or dead man right away." The Rebel dashed to their aid.[29] Captain John W. Reynolds, commander of the 145th Pennsylvania, turned the regiment over to 30-year-old Capt. Moses W. Oliver (Company B) and staggered to the rear with a head wound. Oliver managed to bring out 127 of his 202 effectives.

Lieutenant Colonel Richards McMichael (53rd Pennsylvania) lost 79 of the 135 officers and men whom he took into the fray. The retreat devolved into a rout.[30] On the top of the ridge, Pvt. John A. Wilkerson (Company H, 3rd Arkansas) leaped the wall and, spying smoke rolling from behind a large boulder to his front, ran toward it. Whipping around to the south side of the rock, weapon at the ready, he surprised six enemy soldiers. "Hands up!" he demanded. The Yankees dropped their weapons and marched around to his side. "Young man," one of the prisoners blurted, "where is your troop?" He was it, Wilkerson snapped back, and rushed his prisoners back to the stone wall.

He reached it as the rest of the line sprang into action. Once again, he made for the rock and found it reoccupied by another frightened Yankee who shot wildly at Wilkerson's face. Frantically raising his weapon in the air, he pled for

28 Ladd and Ladd, *The Bachelder Papers*, vol. 2, 1,142; Clark, "The Stand Made by the Remnant of the 27th Conn.," *National Tribune*, October 10, 1918; Affidavits from the Pension File of Major James H. Coburn, 27th Connecticut, Andrew J. DeCusati Collection.

29 Calvin, (ed.), "Recollections of Army Life," [Greenville, PA] *Shenango Valley News*, April 2, 1915, 92-93.

30 "Unidentified Soldier of the 64th New York," IU, 51-52; Report of Chaplain J. H. W. Stuckenberg, RG 94, NA; *OR 27*, pt. 1, 403, 406-407, 410, 414.

his life. The shaken Razorback assured him everything would be alright, and had Wilkerson not quickly intervened, another Reb who came up from behind would have shot him.[31]

As Private Whipple (64th New York) gently laid his beloved Captain Fuller behind the rock, he groaned that he had a fatal wound. "Keep up good courage, George," he sighed. "Surrender, you damn Yankee!" Whipple looked up to find himself cornered by two Confederates. He asked to stay by his captain's body to remove some mementos from his pockets. "Go to the rear[,] you damned Yankee son of a bitch," one of the Rebels threatened, and they prodded him to his feet with their bayonets.[32]

Private Osborn and Sergeant Heckman had almost gotten to the Millerstown Road with their Confederate prisoner and wounded sergeant, when they decided to leave their comrade behind an eight-foot high boulder near the road. As they dropped him and started to run away, their prisoner bolted back to his own men. Osborn heard the distinct hiss of a minié ball and felt his right leg catch fire between his knee and his hip. That was close, Heckman blurted. "Yes, that one was meant for me and got me in the leg," Osborn gasped, still running. "I can feel the blood running down into my shoe, but the bone is all right." Neither man stopped to inspect his wound.[33]

Ayres' U.S. Regular Division, V Corps, Army of the Potomac
Plum Run Between Little Round Top and the Wheatfield

Caldwell, having seen the Regulars go to ground along the stone wall on the eastern side of the Wheatfield, sadly realized that Sweitzer's brigade had gone too far for the Regulars to properly support him. The 5th New Hampshire and the four left companies of the 148th Pennsylvania, which blocked the Regulars' line of fire, held on for an additional 15 minutes until they had shot away all of their ammunition.[34]

This while from the crest of the Devil's Den the Georgians and Texans hammered the left flank of the 17th U.S., which lay in the deep hollow to the

---

31 Wilkerson, "Experiences of 'Seven Pines' at Gettysburg," GNMP.

32 Whipple, "Father's own story," GNMP, 20.

33 Calvin, (ed.), "Recollections of Army Life," *Shenango Valley News*, Greenville, PA, April 2, 1915, 93.

34 *OR* 27, pt. 1, 379; Muffly, *148th Pennsylvania*, 703.

north. Lieutenant Colonel J. Durrell Greene pulled the two left companies back at right angles to the line to cover the flank.[35] The New Englanders and the Pennsylvanians retired through the ranks of the Regulars, leaving Company G of the 148th to fend for itself. Caldwell ordered Ayres to commit his men. The entire brigade rose to its feet and left wheeled bringing the 17th and the 11th Regulars into the woods and the 10th, 7th, and 2nd regiments into the Wheatfield.[36]

While they executed a magnificent quarter left wheel, Day's brigade along Plum Run got to its feet and advanced in with almost parade precision through the muddy creek bottom. A stray bullet struck Lt. Silas A. Miller (12th U.S.) in the chest near the heart. "Oh, God, I am shot," he gasped. Adjutant Bernard P. Mimmack helped him over to the protection of a nearby boulder where, unable to speak, the lieutenant sat, awaiting the inevitable. Day placed each regiment on line as it struggled out of Plum Run. The 6th U.S. (196 effectives) went to the right with the 4th U.S. (173 officers and men). Then the 300-man strong 3rd U.S. completed the formation to the left. The much larger 14th U.S. (490 men) fell in behind those three regiments, while the 12th U.S. (413 effectives) remained in the rear. The first line rushed to the crest of the hill along its front and lay down within 50 yards of the stone wall.[37]

Fronting on the trees, Burbank's regiments closed ranks and volleyed into the woods, which had become eerily silent. At their feet, immediately in front of his company from the 11th U.S., Lt. James Pratt watched a dying staff officer. The man, covered in blood, lay on his side weakly smiling and waving his hand toward the front. "I could not keep my eyes off of him," the lieutenant later wrote home. On the far right of the brigade, Maj. Arthur T. Lee ordered the 2nd U.S. to open fire upon a body of Rebels that he saw moving through the woods toward his right flank.[38]

35 OR 27, pt. 1, 645; Richard Robbins, "The Regular Troops at Gettysburg," *Philadelphia Weekly Times*, January 4, 1879.

36 Muffly, *148th Pennsylvania*, 703; OR 27, pt. 1, 379, 645-650.

37 B. P. Mimmack to C.W. Miller, July 18, 1863, Vertical Files, GNMP, quoted; *OR*, vol. 27, pt. 1, 638-640, 643.

38 OR 27, pt. 1, 645-650; [no author], *The Soldier of Indiana* (n.d.), 116, Greg Coco Collection, USAHEC, quoted.

Lt. Col. Peter A. S. McGlashan
50th Georgia
*Thomas County Museum of History Collection
Library, GNMP*

50th Georgia, Longstreet's Corps,
Army of Northern Virginia
The Stony Hill

Minutes seemed like hours to the South Carolinians and Georgians on the western side of the Wheatfield. Kershaw, spying Sweitzer's men approaching through the smoke, did not think his brave men could absorb this next onslaught, and as the approaching Yankees pushed across the blood-soaked, trampled wheat, Kershaw decided to pull his men out of the fight. He ordered the 7th and the 3rd South Carolina to retreat to the stone wall east of the Rose orchard.[39]

From his position around the Rose buildings, Capt. Peter McGlashan (Company E, 50th Georgia) watched the 7th South Carolina recoil under the shower of lead from incoming musketry. A considerable number of the spooked Southerners fled back into the stalled ranks of his regiment. On his own accord, McGlashan roused the regiment from its cover. The Georgians dashed down into Rose Run, which had turned red from the blood of wounded men who drank from it. It did not deter the thirsty: Capt. William Pendleton (Company B) stopped to lap up some of the water. The 50th charged up the hill into the 7th's former position, closed with maniacal fury on the Irishmen, and literally slugged it out.[40]

---

39 Estilow, "Doing My Duty," GNMP, 21.

40 McGlashan (50th Ga.), "McLaws' Division," *The Press*, October 20, 1886; Pendleton, (ed.), *Confederate Memoirs*, 35.

Sweitzer's Brigade, V Corps, Army of the Potomac
The Wheatfield

As his men neared the eastern side of the Stony Hill, Sweitzer saw what seemed to be two or three Federal regiments—the 116th and 140th Pennsylvania—breaking from the woods on his right front. Believing they had been relieved, he pressed forward to the stone wall. From where he stood on the far left of the line, Colonel Prescott (32nd Massachusetts) spied what appeared to be a Federal brigade fleeing from the Stony Hill. The same group also caught the attention of Col. Harrison H. Jeffords, whose 4th Michigan held the right of the line. The colonel's right wing tramped into the brush and woods on the eastern and southern base of the hill. The Wolverines earnestly blazed away at the few Rebels along their front, Private Houghton (Company K) recollected. Finding no Union regiments on their right flank, and no supports where he had expected them to be, Jeffords haled Lt. Col. James C. Hull (62nd Pennsylvania) and told him that without some help the Rebs would envelop the brigade from the right. Hull bolted off on a search for Sweitzer behind the brigade and when could not find him, continued toward the 32nd Massachusetts on the left of the line.[41]

Sweitzer, a considerable distance behind the right of the 4th Michigan, completely ignored the nasty rifle fire passing over and through his right flank and right rear from the woods on the top of the hill. He thought the fire came from Union troops there trying to shoot over his brigade. Eventually his brigade color bearer, Edward Martin, blurted out, "Colonel, I'll be damned if I don't think we are faced the wrong way; the Rebs are up there in the woods behind us, on the right." In the woods on the southern end of the Stony Hill, Private Houghton, in the right wing of Jeffords' 4th Michigan suddenly became aware of the peculiar, rhythmic rattling of canteens and the distinctive crackling and crunching of well-trained infantry on the march pulsating through the woods behind him. Glancing behind, he saw a substantial body of troops in the distinctive brownish gray garb of veteran Confederates not 50 yards away.[42]

On the eastern end of Sweitzer's line, Colonel Prescott detached Company H into the wheat on the left of the 32nd Massachusetts. Rifle balls from the

41 *Supplement to the* OR 5, pt. 1, 193; Parker, *32nd Massachusetts*, 169, 170; Ladd and Ladd, *The Bachelder Papers*, vol. 3, 867; Houghton, Journal, UMI, 14.

42 Houghton, Journal, UMI, 14.

front clipped off the tops of the stalks around Corporal West as he gathered up a handful of them to put in his haversack.[43]

Taylor's Battery, Longstreet's Corps,
Army of Northern Virginia
The Sherfy Farm

A shell exploded over Capt. Osmond B. Taylor's Virginia battery as it rumbled down the Emmitsburg Road, heading for the Millerstown Road. A fragment took out one of his best gunners, Cpl. Joseph T. V. Lantz, shattering both of his legs above the knees. Taylor ran to his side and cradled him in his arms. "You can do me no good," the corporal muttered in pain, "I am killed; follow your piece." With that Taylor left him where he lay and mounted up.[44]

Captain "Frank" Mix (Company E, 114th Pennsylvania), lying helpless in the Emmitsburg Road, heard Taylor's battery coming toward him and fully expected to be crushed to death. Taylor, however, halted his guns and dismounted his men to assist the Federal casualties. They dragged the dead to the side, out of the way of the wheels, and hauled the wounded to the cellar of the Sherfy house. Leaving their canteens with their wounded enemies, the Rebels promised to return when the action ended.[45]

McGilvery's Artillery Reserve, Army of the Potomac
The Peach Orchard

The Rebel guns rolled into position in Wentz's back yard, as Clark (Battery B, 1st New Jersey) withdrew his #1 gun. Captain Phillips (Battery E, 5th Massachusetts) directed Lt. Frederick A. Lull, commanding the right section, to reverse limbers and be prepared to haul his guns 200 yards to the rear to a knoll between the battery and the Trostle house. At that point, he was to re-form the battery a provide cover fire until the rest of the guns could reach that point. He instructed the remaining two sections to pull out, firing by section. The order

---

43 West, "On Little Round Top," *National Tribune*, November 22, 1906; Ladd and Ladd, *The Bachelder Papers*, vol. 3, 1,867.

44 *OR*, 27, pt. 2, 432.

45 Bowen, "Collis' Zouaves," *Philadelphia Weekly Times*, June 22, 1887.

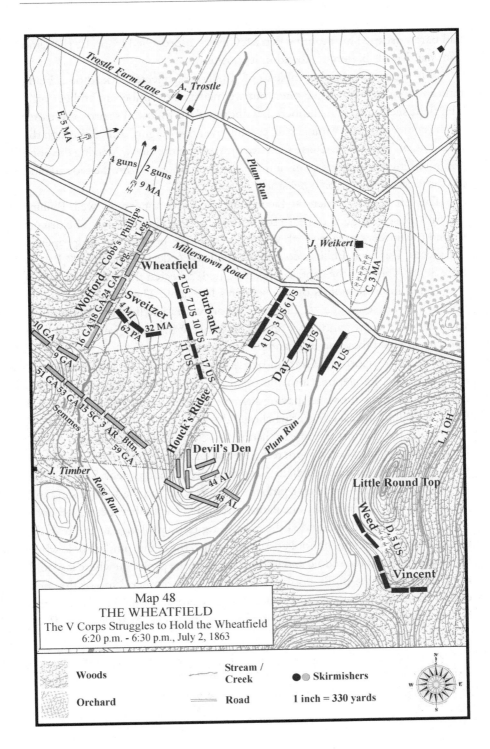

Map 48
THE WHEATFIELD
The V Corps Struggles to Hold the Wheatfield
6:20 p.m. - 6:30 p.m., July 2, 1863

Woods

Orchard

Stream /
Creek

Road

Skirmishers

1 inch = 330 yards

had barely escaped his mouth when McGilvery approached from the right and commanded his battery to abandon its position.[46]

"My horses were rather mixed up," Phillips recollected, "dead ones being rather more plenty then live ones, but we managed to limber up and get off." The right section, already limbered, withdrew first, followed shortly thereafter by the center section. A minié ball, passing over the #2 gun, drilled through the meat of Cpl. Thomas E. Chase's left arm, just above the elbow, grazing the bone and numbing two fingers of his left hand. Blood poured from the wound, and as Chase retreated, his pain became intolerable.[47]

The left section under 1st Lieutenant Scott did not fare as well. Phillips ordered those two guns to retire by prolonge, firing as they went. The drivers turned the limbers to face north while the artillerists hooked the drag ropes to the pieces. But then Phillips countermanded the order: "Limber up!" By the time Scott, who, like the captain, was mounted, repeated the order, the Rebels had gotten into the woods on the section's left flank. They quickly killed the right wheel horse on the #1 limber. The drivers hurriedly freed the harness from the dead animal and put it on Bugler James Winter's mount. But he took two wounds and they had to abandon the animal.

"Drive on," Corporal Graham bawled from behind #1's limber. When it did not budge, he stepped into the open to find only the right swing horse remained standing, the volley having slain his three outriders. Wheeling toward Captain Phillips, he asked what he should do.

"Bring the gun off if you can, if not, leave it," Phillips yelled at Graham. Break the sponge staves, he ordered. They would stay by the gun as long as it stayed by them, Graham replied. Simultaneously, Phillips sent Sgt. William Pattison to the rear to bring up a limber. Graham, who had the sponge staff and worm with him, finding only one canister round in the limber, destroyed both staves. The captain commanded the men to retire by prolonge to the rear. At that, Corporal Graham unhooked the prolonge from the pintle hook while Phillips leapt from the saddle and grabbed hold of the prolonge where it would have attached to the pintle hook on the back of the limber. One of the men caught the captain's horse and returned it to him. Holding onto his horse by the bridle, Phillips along with Corporals Graham and Jonas Shackley, and Pvts.

---

46 Hanifen, *Battery B*, 76; Regimental Committee, *5th Massachusetts Battery*, 624, 627, 631, 633-636, 638, 640, 645; Ladd and Ladd, *The Bachelder Papers*, vol. 2, 167-168.

47 Regimental Committee, *5th Massachusetts Battery*, 627, 645, quote on 627.

Albion K. P. Hayden, James Kay, William L. Purbeck, William H. Wells, and William Barry, shouldered the wheels and manned the prolonge on the other side. They dragged the gun away under a hail of gun fire.[48]

To the west, canister ripped into Adoniram Clark's #3 and #4 caissons, killing all of the latter's horses and four of the former's. The round, which shattered both of Pvt. Richard S. Price's legs and an arm, also wounded Pvts. Hiram Grover, John Truly, and Joseph Baker. Clark immediately abandoned the #4 caisson and cast off the caisson body of #3 from its limber, while Privates Buffum and Daniel W. Laws turned back in their retreat to rescue the crippled Price. The Rebels captured the two rescuers and left Price to die on the field. Private Henry E. Davis temporarily escaped capture near Trostle's by hiding behind a large boulder. Two hundred yards from the Millerstown Road, near the Trostle orchard, the guns passed by the left of the 7th New Jersey.[49]

Daniel Sickles and His Staff, III Corps,
Army of the Potomac
The Trostle House

Captain Winslow (Battery D, 1st New York) found General Sickles on the rise west of the barn. Surprised that both he and his six guns had escaped the Wheatfield unscathed, the general told him to regroup his battery and await

---

48 Regimental Committee, *5th Massachusetts Battery*, 624, 627, 631, 633-636, 638, 640, 645, quote on 640; Ladd and Ladd, *The Bachelder Papers*, vol. 2, 167-168. Graham reported that Shackley brought up the limber but did not credit him with being with the gun during the retreat. According to Phillips' wartime letter to Bachelder, both Shackley and Graham as well as Privates Barry, Kay, Wells, and Hayden helped get the gun off the field. In a letter dated June 8, 1866, he amended the list to include Corporal Graham and Pvts. James Kay, William H. Wells, A. K. P. Hayden, William Berry and William L. Purbeck. "This I think is correct," Phillips wrote. In his 1864 diary, Phillips listed the "Men who brought off the right piece in Gettysburg," a list that included Shackley's name but not Purbeck's. Based upon Phillips' wartime statement that a sergeant went back to get the limber, it had to have been Sergeant Pattison, so Graham erred in his November 12, 1906, recollection of the incident. That Purbeck and Shackley both assisted in bringing the gun off the field is also a reasonable assumption.

49 Hanifen, *Battery B*, 76-77.

further instructions. The captain turned away into the Trostle farm lane and headed east.[50]

Private George W. Bonnell (Battery B, 1st New Jersey), who was staring at the fuses of the Confederate projectiles sputtering across the sky, followed one north as it whirled in on top of a cluster of officers immediately west of the Trostle barn.[51] Drummer Bullard (70th New York), having just returned with the stretcher-bearers from the field hospital, noticed a flurry of activity on the knoll west of the Trostle house and saw aides lower Sickles from the saddle and carry him over to the barn's wall. Without thinking, he ran to offer his assistance. Since he carried a surgical kit, the staffers allowed him access to the general. Sickles had sustained a ghastly wound: his right lower leg was horribly mangled. Using a saddle strap, Bullard applied a tourniquet above the general's knee to stop the bleeding from the compound fracture below it. He also gave the deathly pale general a swig of whiskey from his canteen, which seemed to revive him a bit.

Major Tremain, just arriving, leaped from the saddle and rushed to Sickles. "General, are you hurt?" he asked before seeing the wound. Believing himself dying, Sickles clearly replied: "Tell General Birney he must take command." Promising to fetch an ambulance, the major ordered a nearby enlisted man to find one. He rushed for his horse and was swinging into the saddle when Birney arrived. "Here is General Birney now, sir," the major yelled. Dismounting, he stepped close to Birney. "General Sickles was desperately wounded, and directs me to notify you, sir, to assume command of the corps." Before Birney could respond, Sickles called out, "General Birney, you will take command, sir." Birney acknowledged Sickles' order and quietly asked Tremain if he had sent for an ambulance, and, as he was riding away, one miraculously trundled to a halt in the farm lane near the creek bottom.

Placing the general on a stretcher, Bullard turned to get the ambulance, which had taken shelter behind some nearby boulders. "Before you start, [drum] major," Sickles weakly said, "won't you be kind enough to light a cigar for me?" In blatant violation of standing orders in the Army of the Potomac prohibiting an enlisted man from personally touching an officer, Bullard

---

50 Craft, *141st Pennsylvania*, 121-122, 132; OR 27, pt. 1, 505; Loring, "Gettysburg," *National Tribune*, July 9, 1885; Winslow, "Battery D," *Philadelphia Weekly Times*, July 26, 1879; Ladd and Ladd, *The Bachelder Papers*, vol. 3, 590-591.

51 Ladd and Ladd, *The Bachelder Papers*, vol. 2, 844.

instinctively reached into Sickles' inside coat pocket and took out his cigar case. Removing one of the small cigars, he bit off the end, lighted it, took a drag or two and placed it between the general's lips. "Oh, thank you," Sickles winced. At that point, Bullard suddenly became aware of the staff officers' astonishment at his actions. Sickles reassured him: "It is all right." Walking alongside the general as the stretcher carriers bore him from the field, Bullard passed behind the surging Federal battle line amidst a rain of bullets and artillery projectiles.[52]

Meanwhile, word quickly spread among the men that the general was dying. An orderly raced down the farm lane broadcasting the news of the general's wounding. He found Captain Winslow calmly walking his lone artillery piece toward the rear. With shells bursting everywhere and shot plowing up the ground all around him, Winslow, mustering all of the self-control he could find not to show panic or any semblance of it, refused to increase the team's gait. The sight of a caisson racing to safety could have created a stampede during an already bad situation.[53]

With little thought for his own safety, the indomitable Sickles pushed himself up on one elbow, still puffing away on his smoke, and reassured everyone near him. "No. No. Not as bad as that. I am all right and will be with you in a short time." Bullard recalled Sickles raising his voice and shouting something like: "You must hold your position and win this battle. Don't waver! Stand firm and you will surely win!" Someone close by yelled back: "We will! We will bring you a good report!" "I must go back to the field," Bullard told the general as he placed him into the ambulance. Sickles, however, insisted that Bullard accompany him to the hospital. Bullard also motioned Major Tremain into the ambulance. A little further down the road, with shells bursting everywhere, Fr. Joseph O'Hagan, the 73rd New York's chaplain, joined them.[54]

Once at III Corps Hospital, Chaplain Twitchell (71st New York) helped lift the general from the wagon and carry him to the operating table. As they prepared to chloroform him, Sickles babbled incoherently: "If I die let me die on the field. . . . God bless our noble cause. . . . In a war like this, one man isn't

52 Preceding paragraphs based on W. H. Bullard to Daniel E. Sickles, September 13, 1897; copy in Vertical files, GNMP; Tremain, *Two Days of Battle*, 88-90, quotes on 88 and 89. Bullard's actions were bold: it was strictly forbidden in the Army of the Potomac for an enlisted man to personally touch an officer.

53 Winslow, "Battery D," *Philadelphia Weekly Times*, July 26, 1879.

54 Bullard to Sickles, September 13, 1897, GNMP, quoted; Tremain, *Two Days of Battle*, 88-90.

much," and finally, "My trust is in God." Twitchell later confided to his sister: "I loved him then, as I never did before."[55]

Barnes and His Staff, V Corps, Army of the Potomac
The Millerstown Road

Confederate skirmishers dashed into the woods north of the Wheatfield, forcing Barnes and his staff to vacate the area hastily. The general sent a mounted orderly across the road to tell Sweitzer to retreat, and that was the last anyone saw of the man. As the orderly left, Lt. Charles H. Ross, one of the general's aides, matter-of-factly told Barnes he might as well say goodbye to the 2nd Brigade, which not too long before had disappeared into the low ground to the south. He did not think that any of them would come out of it alive.[56]

Barnes and his officers, barely escaping capture, galloped north until they rendezvoused with Tilton's brigade. They got there just as the Confederates began closing in on the pocket of Federal resistance in the orchard south of the Trostle house. Rifle fire zipped into the cluster of mounted officers. Tilton went down under his horse. Barnes himself got shot, and staff officer Lt. Walter Davis (22nd Massachusetts) nearly lost his head when a searing hot fragment gouged his hat brim.[57]

Bigelow's Battery, McGilvery's Artillery Brigade,
Army of the Potomac
The Millerstown Road East of the Peach Orchard

Meanwhile, Pvt. Reuben L. Willis, the ammunition runner on Bigelow's #4 gun, also saw Kershaw's skirmishers infiltrate the woods on McGilvery's flank. He stood helpless at the limber chest as a Confederate rifleman stepped from behind a tree, deliberately aimed at him, and fired. Willis clinched his teeth so hard he heard his jaw crack as the bullet zipped just above and behind his skull. Instinctively following the track of the ball, he saw Lieutenant Scott (Battery E,

55 Joseph H. Twitchell to [his sister], July 5, 1863, YU.

56 *Supplement to the OR* 5, pt. 1, 194-195.

57 Carter, "Reminiscences," *War Papers*, vol. 2, 169.

5th Massachusetts) fall from his horse and mistakenly assumed the bullet had found its mark.[58]

Actually, at that moment Scott was leaping from the saddle to assist his right gun limber up. The cannoneer immediately abandoned the piece, leaving one of the gunners at the trail. That man helped Scott throw the lunette (the iron ring on the back of the carriage) over the pintle hook. "Drive on!" Scott yelled, just as a bullet killed Pvt. Henry Soule, plucking him from the saddle of the lead horse. Within another second, a shot shattered the arm of pole driver Pvt. John G. Sanford, and a third round struck the lieutenant in the face right as the muzzle of the gun passed by his head. Shattering both his cheeks, it broke the roof of his mouth before exiting. Knocked unconscious, he toppled, seemingly lifeless to the ground. "The blood flew and I was gone," Scott later recollected. Captain Phillips saw him go down and quickly regain consciousness. Gaining his feet and disregarding the corpses of horses and men around him, he unsteadily staggered away. Sergeant Otis B. Smith rode onto the field, dismounted, and put the lieutenant on his own horse and led him to safety near the Trostle house.[59]

Struck in the chest, Pvt. John B. Stowe, gunner on gun #6, staggered to the rear about 20 yards and passed out. He lay there alone and unconscious. Not too long after that, a shell fragment slammed into Sergeant Baker's hip, disabling him. Lieutenant Erickson, a bloody froth bubbling from his mouth with each breath, unexpectedly returned to Bigelow's battery (9th Massachusetts). At Private Willis' limber he stopped and asked for some water, and Willis watched incredulously as the lieutenant nearly drained his canteen. Erickson returned the canteen and then reported to the astonished Bigelow, who never expected to see him again. Assuming the wound not as serious as he originally thought, Bigelow replied, "It is all right."[60]

In front of Bigelow, Kershaw's men with the 50th Georgia lay down to avoid incoming lead, but they were not deterred from attacking the guns. Private William J. Doe, the lead driver of Milton's #4 gun, from his position in the saddle could see them crawling on their hands and knees up the slope toward the guns. McGilvery clattered up to Bigelow on the left of the line and

58 Baker, *9th Massachusetts Battery*, 75.

59 Regimental Committee, *5th Massachusetts Battery*, 630-631, quote on 631; Ladd and Ladd, *The Bachelder Papers*, vol. 1, 167-168.

60 Baker, *9th Massachusetts Battery*, 221.

yelled, "Where is the enemy, Captain?" Private Doe, overhearing him, told him exactly where they were.[61]

"Limber to the rear and get out!" McGilvery demanded. "I shall lose all my men in limbering up," Bigelow protested. "For God's sake, depress your guns and double shot with canister!" McGilvery shouted. As he retired, Bigelow insisted on doing it by prolonge. But before he could give the command, Pvt. Nelson Lowell, who had refused to remain behind in the battery park with the spare horses and the forage, thundered into the battery. Bigelow immediately ordered him to dismount: "The chief of the sixth piece is wounded; go and take charge of that gun," he shouted at Lowell.[62]

Bullets missed the right pole horse but cut down #6 limber's remaining horses. The drivers quickly cut the dead animals loose and rigged the piece to withdraw by prolonge. Swing rider Pvt. Eleazar Cole grabbed the harness of the remaining horse with one hand and the limber pole with the other and began leading it from the field. Periodically, minié balls struck the open lid of the chest behind him. Corporal Zimri Whitney discovered Private Stowe coming to his senses as the limber trundled past him and tried to get him to safety. Pulling the severely wounded artillerist to his feet, Whitney struggled to drag him away, but Stowe was totally inert. Reluctantly the corporal left him with his full canteen and made good his own escape. Stowe helplessly watched the 21st Mississippi bear down upon him.[63]

In the confusion and the overwhelming smoke, the 21st Mississippi, in line of battle and pursuant to orders, had stayed to the east side of the Emmitsburg Road. Colonel Humphreys pushed his men north in an attempt to link up with the rest of Barksdale's brigade, which had reformed in an east-west line north of the Sherfy farm house, with its right flank on the western side of the road.[64]

At the same time Humphreys spied Bigelow's guns. Recognizing the danger they posed to Barksdale's and Kershaw's troops, he ordered his regiment to right wheel to take it out. Bigelow saw the maneuver and directed Erickson's right section and Whitaker's center section to change front and

61 Ibid., 74.

62 Ibid., 60, 74, 79, quotes on 74 and 79.

63 Ibid., 76-77.

64 Ladd and Ladd, *The Bachelder Papers*, vol. 1, 480; Humphreys to McLaws, January 6, 1878, GNMP.

unload shot on those Rebels, while Milton's left section cut down Kershaw's skirmishers with canister.[65]

Milton unloaded double canister into the South Carolinians from less than 100 yards. In the woods to the battery's left flank, four enlisted men and an officer from the 118th Pennsylvania laid down a harassing cover fire. Sergeant Augustus Luker and Cpl. DeWitt Rodemal (both Company E), Pvt. James J. Donnelly (Company C), Sgt. Joseph Turner (Company F), and Lt. Samuel N. Lewis (Company E) had decided to stay behind to get in a few more shots at the enemy. Headquarters orderly Donnelly used a cavalry carbine he had captured at Aldie, Virginia, to hold down the right of the line behind the stone wall on the western side of the woods. When he had exhausted all his ammunition for that weapon, Lieutenant Lewis told him to strip the weapon and accoutrements from a corpse that lay about 20 paces away. So despite the rifle bullets zipping constantly about him, Donnelly calmly leapt the wall, walked over to the body, gathered the man's musket and equipment, and walked back to the lieutenant. Lying down, he pointed out a Confederate color bearer to the lieutenant before coldly shooting him down.[66]

Sweitzer's Brigade, V Corps, Army of the Potomac
The Wheatfield

The 9th Georgia caught Sweitzer's men on the right flank as the regiment neared the southern face of the field. At the same time scattered remnants of Anderson's and Semmes' Georgians along with the 3rd Arkansas plowed into the marsh between the opposing lines, heading north, northeast, and east toward the Yankees.

Minié balls zinged into the 4th Michigan from the woods on top of the Stony Hill. Colonel Jeffords immediately sent word to Sweitzer that the Rebs had enfiladed his regiment and had gotten behind it. Sweitzer rode to the front of the regiment and yelled at Jeffords to change front to rear to meet the assault.

65 Baker, *9th Massachusetts Battery*, 60, 74; McNeily, "Barksdale's Mississippi Brigade," 249.

66 Bohannon, (ed.), "Wounded and Captured at Gettysburg," *Military Images*, May–June 1988, vol. 9, 14; Survivors' Association, *118th Pennsylvania*, 245-246, 248.

The colonel shouted for the left wing to swing back on a north-south line, then called for the right wing to do the same.[67]

The only commands Private Houghton (Company K) heard were to "right about face" and to "double-quick." With men dropping fast and the Rebels smashing into their formation, the two halves of the regiment managed to stand back-to-back momentarily before flanking north. Houghton figured the regiment was trying to get across the Wheatfield before the Rebels took it on the flank. A handful of Confederates snatched up Sgt. Maj. Edward H. C. Taylor on the northern end of the line and sent him under guard to the rear.[68]

Farther to the left, Colonel Prescott (32nd Massachusetts) saw the 4th Michigan execute the command—double back on its flanks then begin a quick march toward the Millerstown Road—but was too far away to hear it. Rather than get his men slaughtered, he shouted into the din, "About face, forward!" The shock of seven spent rounds hitting him successively sent Prescott sprawling. Two enlisted men picked him up by the arms and dragged him away to Lt. Col. Luther Stephenson, Jr., who assumed command. Stephenson had not seen the Confederates on the right of the brigade, so he sent the regiment forward instead of to the rear. Corporal West (Company H) threw his fistful of wheat to the ground and moved out with his company.[69]

When Lt. Col. James C. Hull (62nd Pennsylvania) got to Stephenson, he advised him to have the 32nd Massachusetts change its front to meet the flank attack. Hull, returning to the regiment, saw the Rebels charging into the ranks of the 4th Michigan. Sweitzer yelled at him that the Rebs had also flanked his men and ordered him to refuse his right toward the Confederates. Sweitzer finally grasped that the Rebs had enveloped his brigade. He dispatched his aide, Lt. John A. M. Seitz, to find Barnes and tell him what was happening, and the lieutenant galloped away.[70]

Seitz bolted toward the northwest corner of the Wheatfield only to find it occupied by Wofford's Georgians. Spurring north, toward the woods, he was

---

67 *Supplement to the OR 5*, pt. 1, 193; Ladd and Ladd, *The Bachelder Papers*, vol. 2, 1,071, vol. 3, 1,867.

68 Houghton, Journal, UMI, 14; Ladd and Ladd, *The Bachelder Papers*, vol. 2, 1,071, vol. 3, 1,867; Sgt. Maj. Edward H. Taylor to his mother, July 4, 1863, Vertical Files, GNMP.

69 Ladd and Ladd, *The Bachelder Papers*, vol. 3, 1,867; Parker, *32nd Massachusetts*, 170; West, "On Little Round Top," *National Tribune*, November 22, 1906.

70 Parker, *32nd Massachusetts*, 170; *Supplement to the OR 5*, pt. 1, 193.

nearly captured by Confederate skirmishers. Still looking for Barnes, he headed southeast toward the left of the brigade. As he crested the knoll behind the 32nd Massachusetts, he saw the Confederates coming in behind it. Without waiting for directives, he reined alongside Stephenson, commanded him to retire from the field and spurred away toward the right of the line. He had not gone far when his horse was killed. Pulling himself free, he staggered over to Sweitzer, near the 4th Michigan and the 62nd Pennsylvania with the bad news. The brigade was surrounded, and they were in damned bad shape, the lieutenant reported.[71]

Sweitzer, however, refused to believe him. To the east he saw the 32nd Massachusetts marching out of the fight in good order. Spurring his horse over to the front of the regiment, he bawled at it to halt, swearing and demanding to know who gave them the order to retreat. Stephenson vehemently replied that it came from Sweitzer's own aide-de-camp then commanded his men to about face. This cost the regiment severely, as men quickly began dropping. Three bullets struck down Sgt. James M. Haskell (Company A). One snapped his left leg, and the other two slammed into his right thigh and right kneecap. Private Barney Clark (Company G) got hit in the spine from behind.[72]

Simultaneously, on the southern end of the 4th Michigan, a bullet smacked into the color bearer, Thomas Tarsney. As he dropped the regimental flag, Cpl. James D. Putnam (Company F, Cobb's Legion) snatched it up and started

---

71 *Supplement to the OR* 5, pt. 1, 193; *OR* 27, pt. 1, 612; Parker, *32nd Massachusetts*, 170; West, "On Little Round Top," *National Tribune*, November 22, 1906. Both accounts from the 32nd Massachusetts assert that the brigade aide-de-camp (Lieutenant Seitz) ordered them to retire and that Sweitzer rushed up to the regiment and demanded that it make a stand. Sweitzer in both OR accounts said that he ordered a retreat after Seitz reported back to him. The OR indicates that Sweitzer had control of the brigade, whereas the accounts of Colonel Prescott (32nd Massachusetts), Private Houghton (Company K, 4th Michigan), and Sgt. John M. Bancroft (4th Michigan) clearly imply or state that the 4th Michigan was quitting the field on its own before the Rebels charged into the regiment. It is clear that Sweitzer did not give the command to retreat and that the events unfolded too quickly for him to react to them.

Seitz's course along the line of battle is my reconstruction of the event. According to Sweitzer's own statement, Seitz had concluded that Confederates had surrounded the brigade before he reached the colonel. As the aide-de-camp, he had an obligation to find Barnes before returning to the colonel. Quite naturally, he would have retraced the line of advance back to the woods.

72 West, "On Little Round Top," *National Tribune*, November 22, 1906; Parker, *32nd Massachusetts*, 170-171.

toward the woods.[73] Colonel Jeffords saw him and reacted immediately. Shouting at Adj. R. Watson Seage and 1st Lt. Michael J. Vreeland (Company I), he dashed after the Rebel. Jeffords seized the flag staff with his left hand while Seage brought his sword down on the back of Putnam's neck, knocking him down. A Yankee bayoneted him as he hit the ground.

But other Rebels swarmed the three officers and made short work of them. A bullet penetrated Jeffords at close range while Sgt. Alonzo C. Adair (Company D, Cobb's Legion) thrust his bayonet into his body, dropping him. First Sergeant James L. Born (Company C, Cobb's Legion) yanked the flag staff from Jeffordsʼs dead hands and carried it from the field.

Two bullets penetrated Adjutant Seage's chest, and Adair bayoneted him in the left leg as he fell. Vreeland took a round in the left breast and the right arm before Adair creased his skull with his musket butt and knocked him unconscious. Nearby, 5th Sgt. Orvey S. Barrett (Company B, 4th Michigan) crashed, helpless, to the ground. Not 15 yards to the south Pvt. James Johnston (Company K), Houghton's messmate, shrieked, "I am killed," as he collapsed several feet in front of Houghton, groaned a little, and died.[74]

From where he stood, Stephenson saw Jeffords disappear into the melee around the regimental colors. Sweitzer, whose horse was killed and whose hat had a bullet through its crown, finally decided retreat preferable to getting wiped out; he directed his battered regiments toward Little Round Top.[75]

The Georgians would not disengage from the 4th Michigan and the 62nd Pennsylvania. The Phillips' Legion tore into the Pennsylvanians with a fury. A private shot Sgt. Jacob B. Funk (Company A, 62nd Pennsylvania) in the shoulder and lunged toward the state colors that he carried. Clubbing down five others, he got to the now bayoneted Funk and reached for the flagstaff when Pvt. Edward J. Smith (Company E) hurled himself in front of him and grabbed the flag. The infuriated Georgian felt like bashing Smith's head in, but he

---

73 Ladd and Ladd, *The Bachelder Papers*, vol. 2, 1,071; Houghton, Journal, UMI, 14. Houghton said the man was wounded and dropped the flag. Seage said he heard that the color bearer got captured or threw down the flag and ran.

74 Ladd and Ladd, *The Bachelder Papers*, vol. 2, 1,071; Barrett, "Reminiscences," 22; Houghton, Journal, UMI, quote, 14; Report of W. T. Wofford, August 14, 1863, Letters to the Adjutant and the Inspector General's Office, NA.

75 Parker, *32nd Massachusetts*, 171; West, "On Little Round Top," *National Tribune*, November 22, 1906; *Supplement to the OR* 5, pt. 1, 194.

relented when Smith explained that he had a family and children he desperately needed to see. The furlough for taking the standard would allow him to do that.

Simultaneously, Pvt. Thomas B. Jolly (Company B, Phillips' Legion) pulled the 62nd Pennsylvania's regimental flag from Company I's Sgt. Thomas H. Budlong, but the color guard shot and bayoneted him as he yanked the colors free. Jolly collapsed with the staff in his hands, and Pvts. Michael McGovern (Company F) and Jacob A. Blanton (Company B) with an enlisted man from Company D leaped to his assistance. McGovern and Blanton each bayoneted the Yankees on either side of Sergeant Budlong, while the third Georgian jerked the color sergeant's revolver from its holster and shot him dead with it. In the melee, Cpl. Johnson C. Gardner (Company E, 62nd Pennsylvania) grappled the flag from the severely wounded Jolly and escaped with it toward the eastern side of the Wheatfield. Private Alford Norris (Company E, Phillips' Legion) came away with a company marker.[76]

Stephenson's regiment, having withstood several minutes of disastrous small arms fire, decided on his own to get his men out of the action. Backing up, the Bay Staters fired as they retired. One of their officers hurled his empty revolver in a rage at the Rebels. Another officer, faint from blood loss, sat down behind a large boulder, where two Rebels stumbled upon him. Summoning up his last reserves of energy, he leaped to his feet and raced around the other side of the boulder with the two Rebels in close pursuit. They chased him around the large rock several times before he took off toward Little Round Top and left them standing, rather dumbfounded, behind him. When the 32nd Massachusetts neared the woods on the eastern side of the Wheatfield, a bullet smashed into Stephenson's face. Striking him behind the nostrils, it bored through his face below his eyes, shattering his cheekbones.[77] His men carried him from the field.

On the Confederate side, Lieutenant Colonel Taylor screamed for the 3rd Arkansas to halt and fall back to the cover of the woods. A number of the men, among them Private Wilkerson and several of his comrades in Company H, did not hear him through the racket. They surged ahead with the men around them,

76 Parker, *32nd Massachusetts*, 171; Jay Jorgensen, *Gettysburg's Bloody Wheatfield* (Shippensburg, 2002), 112; Richard Coffman, "A Vital Unit," *Civil War Times Illustrated*, June, 1982, 44; Richard A. Sauers, *Advance the Colors* (Lebanon, 1987), vol. 1, 174, vol. 2, 577; OR 27, pt. 2, 775; Report of W. T. Wofford, August 14, 1863, NA.

77 Parker, *32nd Massachusetts*, 171-172; West, "On Little Round Top," *National Tribune*, November 22, 1906.

unaware that the regiment had withdrawn from the fight. Dropping to one knee, Wilkerson snapped a shot at what appeared to be two Yankee infantry regiments approaching his position. Standing up to load, he found himself alone, smoke flaring in front, bullets swarming around him. His left leg gave way, and he collapsed hard on his side, before rolling onto his back. Digging his hands into the ground, he pushed himself backwards toward the cover of a large rock, dragging his shattered leg after him. Exhausted, he lay down, hoping to escape further injury. Within a minute or two, Pvt. William S. Cockman of his company found him. "John," he quietly reassured the wounded man, "If I live until it is over, I will come back and get you."[78]

Ayres' Regular Division, V Corps, Army of the Potomac
The Stone Wall on the Eastern Side of the Wheatfield

First Lieutenant William H. Powell (4th U.S.), Ayres' acting aide-de-camp, noticed the scores of men leaving the field to the west. Turning to Ayres, who was conversing with Caldwell, he boldly interrupted: "General, you had better look out, the front line is giving way." An irritated Caldwell thought they were Sweitzer's men and curtly shot back: "That's not so, sir; those are my troops being relieved." The unconvinced lieutenant looked toward the Stony Hill again. After a couple of minutes of observation, he again interrupted the generals. "General Ayres," he warned, "you will have to look out for your command. I don't care what anyone says, those troops in front are running away." This got the generals' attention, and they both quietly studied the field.[79]

By then, 1st Lt. John H. Page (Company I, 3rd U.S.), having observed the commotion on the Stony Hill from the stone wall, reported to Ayres what he had seen. "Those regiments are being driven back!" the general spat, at which someone on his staff brushed his concern aside with a comment that the soldiers in the Wheatfield were moving to a new position. "A regiment does not shut up like a jack-knife and hide its colors without it is retreating," Ayres retorted. At that, Caldwell wheeled his horse to the left and galloped toward the

---

78 Wilkerson, "Experiences of 'Seven Pines' at Gettysburg," GNMP.

79 Powell, *The Fifth Army Corps*, 534-535.

Millerstown Road. Simultaneously, Page raced back toward his company, and Ayres dispatched an aide to Colonel Day.[80]

The Wheatfield

The Confederates charging from the Stony Hill caught Burbank's brigade on the flank and rear. A rifle ball snapped the flagstaff of the 2nd U.S., the colors literally falling into the hands of the color bearer. Major Arthur T. Lee immediately ordered the regiment to back out of the fight. The 7th U.S., to its left, peeled back with it. Command and control now disintegrated. A horrific volley tore into the exposed right flank of the 10th U.S., knocking down a large number of men. Burbank ordered the regiment to retreat then headed to the left of his brigade. In the din and smoke most of the rank and file did not hear it. They stayed put, futilely tussling with the much larger Confederate force.[81]

In the meantime, Lieutenant Page reached his place as file closer behind Company I, where he found Day on horseback. Ayres' staff officer spurred alongside of Day, telling him to pull back to Little Round Top as soon as the 2nd Brigade cleared the stone wall. The colonel nonchalantly called Page over and asked him to strike a match so he could light his pipe. Page struck the match, and Day leaned over in the saddle, sucking on his pipe stem. A bullet tore through the horse's neck. It dropped like a shot onto its side, throwing the colonel into a heap.[82]

Back in the Wheatfield, the 11th U.S. began falling back. The Confederates caught them from the front, flank, and rear, and Regulars fell like corn before the scythe. Half of the regiment never made it to the wall. The withdrawal became a rout. The 17th U.S., having relieved the 5th New Hampshire, bolted northeast. The 5th New Hampshire, rather than die in the hollow, fixed bayonets and charged back into the woods.[83]

The Regulars found themselves flanked and withdrew from the right, heading back toward the protection of Weikert's ridge. Once again, a Confederate ball clipped Lietenant Pratt (11th U.S.), breaking the skin on his

---

80 Reese, *Sykes' Regular Infantry Division*, 248; Powell, *The Fifth Army Corps*, 535.

81 *OR* 27, pt. 1, 646-647, 649.

82 Powell, *Fifth Army Corps*, 535.

83 Child, *5th New Hampshire*, 207; *OR* 27, pt. 1, 650.

leg. He did not stop to check it. Captain Thomas Dunn (12th U.S.) received orders to flank his regiment to the right the distance of his regimental front. The retreating troops to his right front thwarted him. Ayres directed him to face his regiment by the rear rank and return to Weikert's. Captain James J. Patterson (Company G, 148th Pennsylvania), realizing his men would get "gobbled up" if they stayed in the woods any longer, ordered them to skedaddle. Dunn's 12th Regulars got as far as the stone wall along the Millerstown Road east of Weikert's. While the right wing continued to the rear, the left wing about faced and delivered a volley into the confused mass along Plum Run.[84]

Hazlett's Battery, V Corps, Army of the Potomac
Little Round Top

At great risk to their lives, Weed and Lieutenant Hazlett remained mounted to observe the action on the elevated northern plateau. Hazlett stood a little to the general's left; Captain Martin stood on Weed's immediate right. Sykes and his staff had ensconced themselves to the right front among some boulders on the northwestern slope from which they could safely see what was happening to the front.

As the Regulars fell back across Plum Run, Weed leaned down toward Martin, and said, "Martin, I would rather die on this spot than see those rascals gain one inch of ground." The captain paid little heed to the remark and began working his way down the face of the hill toward Sykes and his entourage. While turning north along the western face of the hill, he looked back and saw Weed sway in the saddle and topple from his horse. Wheeling toward Sykes, he cried out, "General Weed has fallen," and he started back to the crest.[85]

Corporal William Taylor, the gunner on Hazlett's #3 gun, shouted, "General Weed is shot!" When Lieutenant Rittenhouse raced to Weed's side, he found him lying alone behind the piece. As he bent over the general, Weed gasped that he was cut in two and needed to see Hazlett. Paralyzed from the chest down by a bullet which had severed his spine, Weed pulled Rittenhouse a

---

84 OR 27, pt. 1, 640-641; *The Soldier of Indiana*, 117, USAHEC; Muffly, *148th Pennsylvania*, 703.

85 Martin, "Little Round Top," *The Gettysburg Compiler*, October 12, 1899.

little closer and asked him to take care of the few small debts he owed fellow officers.[86]

Word instantly reached Hazlett, on horseback to the left rear of the #3 gun. The #1 man on that piece, 17 year-old Pvt. Thomas Scott, watched Hazlett swing his right leg over the crop of his horse, while turning his head to the right. A minié ball crashed into the lieutenant's skull just above and behind his left ear, the impact hurling him to the ground. Throwing his sponge staff down, Scott sprang to the trail of the gun and cradled the officer's bleeding head in his hands. Corporal Taylor came to his assistance. Rittenhouse, hearing the sickening crack of a bullet smashing bone, instinctively wheeled toward the sound to see Taylor holding the lieutenant in his arms. From where he stood, Martin thought he had seen Hazlett dismount to help Weed and continued on to Sykes.

Rittenhouse never heard Weed's further instructions above the deafening noise. He ordered enlisted men to take both officers to cover below the rocks on the eastern side of the hill. The lieutenant saw Hazlett's eyes move and, thinking he might have recognized him, asked if he had any messages for his mother. Hazlett could not answer: his eyes quickly froze, glazed over, and stared blindly into the trees overhead. Rittenhouse told Bugler Welding to stay with Hazlett until he died.[87]

9th Massachusetts Battery, First Volunteer Brigade,
Army of the Potomac
South of the Trostle Farm Lane

Bigelow lost sight of the 21st Mississippi as his four guns recoiled below the brow of the ridge on their right, completely blocking the Confederates from

86 Scott, "On Little Round Top," *National Tribune*, August 2, 1894. Rittenhouse attributed this incident to Weed with Hazlett, then proceeded to say that he heard the bullet strike Hazlett. The lieutenant was behind him to the right, he said. If Hazlett had been over Weed at the time, he would have been immediately by Rittenhouse's side and not behind him. I believe that Weed spoke to Rittenhouse, not to Hazlett, and that Rittenhouse "romanticized" Hazlett's death by having Weed speak his last words to Hazlett rather than to him.

87 Scott, "On Little Round Top," *National Tribune*, August 2, 1894; Rittenhouse, "The Battle of Gettysburg," *Military Essays*, vol. 1, 37-41.

view. The captain mistakenly attributed the Confederates' disappearance to the intense pressure of those two sections[88]

Humphreys' Division, III Army Corps, Army of the Potomac

The Confederate enfilade increased in volume. A solid shot bounced into the 71st New York, killing two men. It also wounded Col. Henry L. Potter and broke the ankle of Sgt. Henry Funk (Company F). With Birney's shattered troops streaming behind Humphreys' line, the "contagion," as Captain Cavada referred to the panic, spread beyond control. Colonel Brewster's Excelsior Brigade in the northern end of the Peach Orchard collapsed, and the 8th Alabama poured into the break in the Yankee line. The Excelsiors backed out of the fight, halting and firing as they withdrew. A bullet cut down Brewster's horse. The retreat herded the dismounted colonel and the mounted Humphreys east along the north side of the Trostle farm lane. Major Thomas Rafferty (71st New York) joined them, quietly walking alongside with the reins of his horse draped casually over his arm. An enlisted man from his old Company H ran up to him clutching in his bloodied hand a superb looking bridle that Rafferty recognized as the one from Brewster's dead horse. "M-m-major," he stuttered, "don't you want a b-b-bridle?" Two minutes later, the soldier lay dead from a case ball.

Two bullets thudded into Col. John S. Austin's arm and side, yet he refused to dismount. A minute or so later, the Rebels shot down his horse. He passed the command of the 72nd New York to Lt. Col. John Leonard and stumbled on foot to the rear.[89]

---

88 Baker, *9th Massachusetts Battery*, 60, 74.

89 Cavada, Diary, July 2, 1863, Vertical Files, FSNMP; Westbrook, "On the Firing Line," *National Tribune*, September 20, 1900; OR 27, pt. 1, 565; Rafferty, "Gettysburg," Personal Recollections, vol. 4, 27, quoted; H. L. Potter, "Seeley's Battery at Gettysburg," *National Tribune*, May 24, 1888.

Chapter 14

July 2, 1863
6:30 p.m.-7:00 p.m.

"Surrender you damned Yankee."

—*Unidentified soldier, 21st Mississippi*

Barksdale's Brigade, Longstreet's Corps,
Army of Northern Virginia
North of the Trostle Farm Lane

Barksdale's three leftmost regiments pushed north, while the 21st Mississippi wheeled east, behind the 8th Alabama and away from the brigade. At the western terminus of Trostle's Lane, the 13th, 17th, and 18th Mississippi regiments stumbled upon the 11th New Jersey from Carr's 1st brigade. Carr, with an opportunity to take part of the Confederate line on the flank ordered Colonel McAllister to refuse the left battalion of the 11th. The Jerseymen quickly swung their left wing at right angles to the rest of the regiment, after which the entire regiment went prone, unseen by the 8th Alabama and the 21st Mississippi.

McAllister commanded the line to fire by ranks, rear rank first, to stall the Confederate advance. Captain Le Grand Benedict, Carr's assistant adjutant general, rode up to the colonel. Pointing in the direction of the house and barn, he cautioned him not to fire on his own men.[1]

Barksdale responded to the volley by right wheeling the three regiments under his immediate command toward the threat, completely unaware of either

---

1   OR 27, pt. 1, 553; Marbaker, *11th New Jersey*, 98-99, 104.

Maj. Philip J. Kearny
11th New Jersey
Library, GNMP

the Federal line in the road farther to the north or Cadmus Wilcox's remaining four regiments charging blindly up the ridge south of Rodgers' farm lane. The 9th Alabama, with the 11th to its right, in cresting the hilltop, abruptly halted to avoid colliding with the rear of Barksdale's line. The brigade's second line, the 14th and the 10th Alabama, could not brake their assault and slammed headlong into their fellow Alabamians, throwing the formation into a tangled mess.

At that instant, a minié ball zipped through Company D, 10th Alabama, striking Private McClelan's right leg and hurling him to the ground. His messmates, Pvts Young A. Brock and John F. Walker, sprang to his assistance. With one on each side, they pulled him upright and tried dragging him away. Several feet behind the regiment Colonel Forney shouted for them to lay the wounded man down and return to the charge. Brock and Walker did so. Forney ordered McClelan to lie flat, and the wounded soldier stayed behind as the brigade dashed right into Barksdale's men.[2]

Near the crest, the Yankee skirmishers at first behaved as if no threat approached from the west or the south. It didn't take long, though, for them to

2 Rourke, *I Saw the Elephant*, 42; Bachelder Map, July 2, 1863; John G. Barrett, (ed.), *Yankee Rebel: The Civil War Journal of Edmund DeWitt Patterson*, 116, Vertical Files, GNMP. Bachelder's map shows the brigade advancing east on the north side of the Spangler Lane, which agrees with Herbert's account of the attack. Bachelder, however, has the 8th Alabama on the right flank of the 9th Alabama. Nor does he indicate that a collision occurred between the 10th and the 11th Alabama. An unexpected halt had to have caused the collision. Bachelder's map is incorrect: it does not show any troops blocking the front of Wilcox's advance. McClelan said his wounding occurred before they could get to the battery in their front. That battery had to have been Seeley's, which would have been directly in front of the 11th Alabama, east of Staub's orchard. Corporal Edmund Dewitt Patterson verifies that he saw the 5th New Jersey form squares around the guns to protect their retreat.

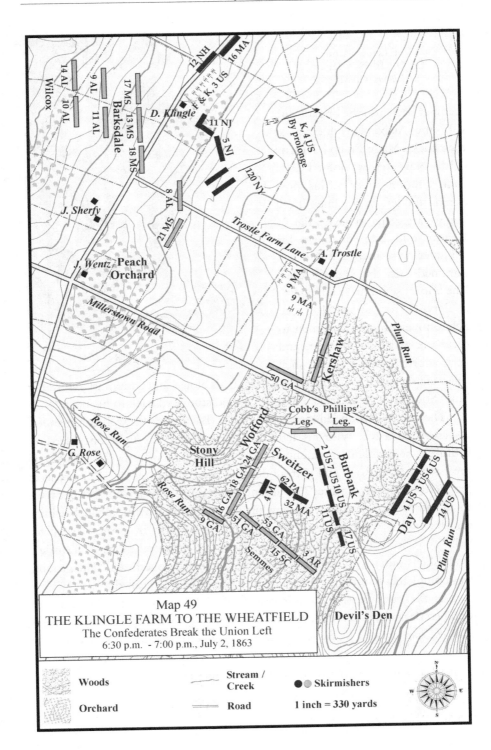

Map 49
THE KLINGLE FARM TO THE WHEATFIELD
The Confederates Break the Union Left
6:30 p.m. - 7:00 p.m., July 2, 1863

Capt. Luther Martin
Co. D, 11th New Jersey
Library, GNMP

scamper back into the brigade line with the Alabamians literally at their backs. Major Philip J. Kearny (11th New Jersey) joined Adj. John Schoon- over at his post behind the left of the line. "I tell you we are going to have a fight!" Kearny told him, hand on his shoulder. Just then a minié ball slammed into the major's knee. The impact sent him spinning like a dervish for about 10 feet. Schoonover ordered two men to carry the major to the rear, and very shortly after a spent shell fragment slammed him in the chest, tearing his blouse and temporarily stunning him.[3] Soon enough he picked himself up and stumbled back to his post.

The severely wounded Lieutenant Seeley (Battery K, 4th U.S) commanded his crews to leave. With his left thigh bruised and his right one bleeding profusely, he could not mount up to escape. The 5th New Jersey fell back out of the Emmitsburg Road and surrounded the battery to provide cover fire as it prepared to escape capture. Two infantrymen yanked Seeley upright between them and dragged him away. Meanwhile his guns retired by prolonge, belching canister as they went. Seeley never expected to get away from the place alive. Solid shot bounded and skipped through the low ground north of Trostle's while shells burst with terrifying frequency in the sky overhead. "The ground was completely scoured by the projectiles," Seeley later recalled.[4]

As the guns passed the left rear of the 11th New Jersey Schoonover watched Barksdale's three Mississippi regiments right wheel, face east, and head into the gap created by Seeley's evacuation. The Jersey men responded with

---

3   *OR* 27, pt. 1, 553; Marbaker, *11th New Jersey*, 98-99, 104, quote on 98.

4   Ladd and Ladd, *The Bachelder Papers*, vol. 1, quote on 608; *OR* 27, vol. 1, 554, 576.

rapid fire "at will" while he raced toward the right of the regiment to inform McAllister of the gap in the line.[5]

Barksdale's men, now thoroughly mixed up with Wilcox's Alabamians, stopped along the western side of the Emmitsburg Road to engage the Yankees. Both generals managed to shake their brigades into some semblance of a battle line. The Rebels crested the open hill top north of Spangler's farm lane in the field southwest of the Rodgers house, across the front of the 5th New Jersey, 12th New Hampshire, and Turnbull's Battery F and K, 3rd U.S. Artillery. Yankee fire decimated Pvt. William Abernathy's mess (Company B, 17th Mississippi). Private Frank Ross, whom Abernathy remembered as "manager of the circus," died in the melee as well as the "polished, cultivated gentleman," Pvt. Billy McRaven, with a mortal chest wound. Private Fleming W. Thompson (Company B, 11th Alabama) watched his comrades drop all around him. Private John C. Ridgeway died near him, while Pvt. John Hatter took a ball through the meat of his one arm, and 1st Lt. Frank H. Mundy went missing.[6]

Corporal Edmund DeWitt Patterson (Company D, 9th Alabama) marveled at the 5th New Jersey's superb discipline. "Under the terrible fire they did not run, but retreated slowly and in good order, and returning our fire, but leaving the ground literally covered with their dead," he recollected. Men from the 5th formed squares around each of Seeley's pieces to protect the crews as they loaded canister while retreating. As each piece got fully charged, the infantrymen parted to the flanks to let the gun fire, and then sealed the opening again with their bodies.[7]

At about the same time, Carr spotted a Confederate officer wearing a fez and mounted on a white horse enthusiastically riding in front of his line, cheering them on. "His example and enthusiasm were equal to a brigade of men," Pvt. Thomas D. Marbaker (Company E, 11th New Jersey) remembered. Carr adjudging the bold Rebel as the heart of the attack, sent his assistant adjutant general, Capt. Le Grand Benedict, to Col. Robert McAllister with orders to kill him.

---

5 OR 27, vol. 1, 554.

6 Abernathy, Our Mess, 34; Sergeant Fleming W. Thompson to [Mother & Sisters], July 17, 1863, USAHEC; George W. Clark, "Wilcox's Alabama Brigade at Gettysburg," in Confederate Veteran, vol. 17, 229; Barrett, Yankee Rebel, 117, GNMP.

7 Barrett, Yankee Rebel, 117, GNMP.

The colonel directed Capt. Ira W. Cory's Company H to bring the man down. When McAllister gave the command, "Fire!" four balls killed Col. James W. Carter (13th Mississippi); Lt. Col. Kennon McElroy, who took over the regiment, was shot in the shoulder. Command devolved to Maj. John M. Bradley, who collapsed in short order with a mangled ankle. As the only uninjured staff officer on his feet, 1st Lt. Edward P. Harman, the adjutant, stepped into the major's place.

Turning to the left to troop the center of the 11th New Jersey, McAllister crumpled to the ground with a minié ball in his left leg and a shell fragment in his right foot. Before Capt. William B. Dunning (Company K) could assist the seriously wounded colonel, the rear rank of the entire regiment volleyed, followed within seconds by the front rank. Smoke temporarily engulfed the line until the southerly breeze carried it away.[8] From there things escalated into a kaleidoscopic frenzy.

Once on the right wing, Schoonover discovered that McAllister had been carried from the field. He automatically informed senior officer Capt. Luther Martin (Company D) to assume command of the 11th and then returned to his position on the left wing.[9]

Amidst all the chaos on the smoky field, no one seemed to have noticed the stray 8th Alabama crossing the worm fence into the field south of Carr's Brigade. Lieutenant Colonel Herbert had no idea that the regiment had separated from the rest of his brigade. When the Excelsiors threw down the fence on their right flank and filed into the field west of the orchard around the Trostle barn, he decided to give chase. Sergeant Luney P. Ragsdale (Company F) stepped out with the regimental flag and began executing a precise left half wheel, and the rest of the regiment aligned upon their fearless color bearer. With the 8th Alabama fronted to face northeast, Herbert screamed out the command to charge. His regiment struck the farm lane at an oblique about 100

8   E. P. Harman to W. S. Decker, August 16, 1886, OCHS; William H. Hill, Diary, July 2, 1863, Mississippi Department of Archives and History, Jackson, MS; Robert McAllister to Samuel Toombs, January 10, 1888, Rutgers University Library, New Brunswick, NJ; Marbaker, *11th New Jersey*, 98. In the regimental history, Marbaker's name appears as "Marbacker" and "Marbecker." In the New Jersey roster, it is "Marbacker." More than likely, Marbaker pronounced his name as it was spelled.

9   Marbaker, *11th New Jersey*, 99; *OR* 27, 1, 554; Robert McAllister to Samuel Toombs, January 10, 1888, Rutgers University Library, New Brunswick, NJ.

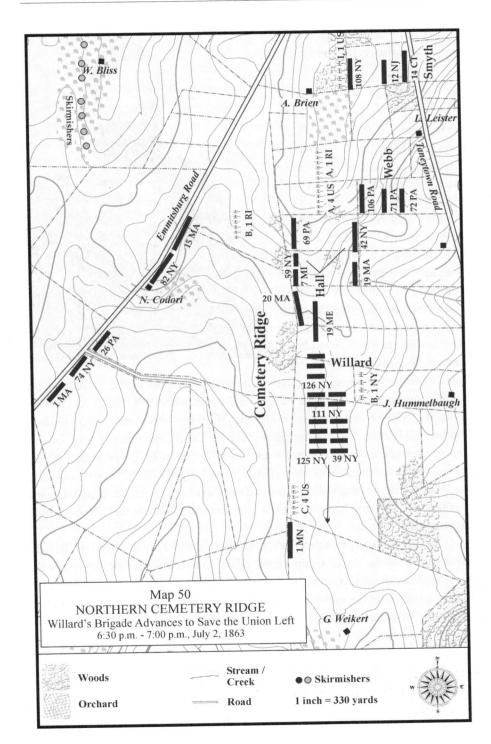

Map 50
NORTHERN CEMETERY RIDGE
Willard's Brigade Advances to Save the Union Left
6:30 p.m. - 7:00 p.m., July 2, 1863

Woods

Orchard

Stream /
Creek

Road

Skirmishers

1 inch = 330 yards

Sgt. Luney P. Ragsdale
Co. F, 8th Alabama
*James Ragsdale Collection
Library, GNMP*

yards west of the barn. Fence rows destroyed whatever formation he had tried to maintain and forced the Alabamians to halt and reform.[10]

To the north, the 120th New York remained hidden on the slope behind the stone wall with Graham's and Brewster's refugees stumbling over and through their ranks. Brewster fell in behind the New Yorkers and paced their line like a file closer. Humphreys turned his mount about and silently trooped the rear, completely absorbed in the peril of the moment. The horrendous cacophony of the raging battle compelled Pvt. Eseck G. Wilber (Company K)—and doubtless thousands of others—to examine his spiritual condition. He mouthed a silent prayer, for his family, for himself, and for the preservation of his life. The regiment stood up from its cover and volleyed point-blank into the Rebels along the Emmitsburg Road. Yelling maniacally, the New Yorkers clamored over the wall in a mad charge, completely unaware that the 8th Alabama had broken through along the Trostle farm lane to their exposed flank.

Company K's Capt. James Barker, on the left of the line, spotted the Rebels through the smoke, raced to the center of the line to inform Col. Cornelius D. Westbrook of the threat, and then rushed back to his company. The order came to refuse the entire regiment to the left. Lifting his sword above his head, Barker shouted, "Take it cool, boys. Listen to the command and every man stand to his

---

10 Herbert, "A Short History of the 8th Ala. Regiment," 10-11, GNMP; Fortin, "History of the Eighth Alabama Volunteer Regiment, C.S.A.," in *Alabama Historical Quarterly*, vol. 39, 116; Ladd and Ladd, *The Bachelder Papers*, vol. 2, 1,057.

post." A minié ball bored through the back of his skull from ear to ear, and he collapsed in a heap without a sound. Wilber shortly stared at his corpse before the New Yorkers loosed a second well-aimed volley.

It caught the fiendishly screaming 8th Alabama as it passed over the 73rd New York's former position and tore the line to ribbons. The disabled Lieutenant Moran (73rd New York) gaped dumbfounded at the huge number of casualties that single blast brought down. The Rebels literally stopped in their tracks, and only the feverish exertions of the officers kept the ranks from panicking. But then the Alabamians returned the fire, and the New Yorkers found themselves trapped. "The way the shells flew wasent [sic] slow and the musket balls was thicker than any hail I ever saw," Wilber later wrote. His comrades fell all about him, and he expected to join them at any time.[11]

Willard's Brigade, II Corps, Army of the Potomac
The Eastern Side of Cemetery Ridge, South of Ziegler's Grove

Hancock, now commanding the III Corps by Meade's authority, clattered onto northern Cemetery Ridge, desperately looking for regiments to shore up the disintegrating III Corps position to the south. He spotted Brigadier General Hays and Colonel Willard, both mounted behind Willard's brigade, and immediately dispatched his adjutant general, Lt. Col. Orson H. Hart, with specific orders to commit them to action. Hart breathlessly interrupted the two officers. "General Hancock sends you his compliments," he said to Hays, pointing south, "and wishes you to send one of your best brigades over there." Abruptly turning toward Willard, Hays snapped, "Take your brigade over there and knock the Hell out of the Rebs."[12]

11 Esesck J. Wilber to Father and Mother, July 10, 1863, Murray J. Smith Collection, USAHEC, quoted; Van Santvoord, *120th New York*, 73-74; *New York at Gettysburg*, vol. 2, 820, 821; Westbrook, "On the Firing Line," *National Tribune*, September 20, 1900; Moran, "What Was Seen by a Captive Federal Officer," *Philadelphia Weekly Times*, April 22, 1882. There is some confusion as to how the regiment behaved in the action. Wilber's account, the most contemporary, indicates that the regiment charged and was quickly broken. The regiment rallied with the rest of its division, but it did not hold the stone wall as long as the colonel and the account in *New York at Gettysburg* implied it did.

12 Ladd and Ladd, *The Bachelder Papers*, vol. 3, 1,984; George W. Sweet to Charles A. Richardson, September 4, 1894, p.4 in Eric Campbell, "Remember Harpers Ferry," *Gettysburg Magazine*, June 1, 1992, 64, n.69, quoted.

Col. Francis E. Heath
19th Maine
*Maine State Archives
Library, GNMP*

Willard spurred over to his regiments and yelled them to their feet. "Fix Bayonets!" Steel clinked coldly on steel. "Shoulder arms! . . . Left face; forward march." Swinging into columns of division, the four New York regiments marched steadily south on two company fronts at the common time. The 125th New York took the right with the 39th to its left. The 126th New York covered the 125th and the 111th fell in behind the Garibaldi Guards.[13]

Galloping south, Hancock ran into Lt. Gulian Weir's Battery C, 5th U.S. Artillery, and hollered at him to wheel his guns into the low ground southeast of the Codori buildings. Weir, suffering from a chronically ulcerated throat, rasped at his men to wheel right over the crest of Cemetery Ridge. Before he could effectively execute the command, the volatile Hancock had ridden to the top of the ridge, about 375 yards due east of the Codori barn, where he found the 19th Maine from Harrow's 1st brigade prone in the tall grass.

Hancock leaped from his horse and charged down upon the front rank of Company F on the left of the line. Grabbing Pvt. George Durgin from the end file, he yanked the short, stocky man to his feet and pushed him to the wooded knoll about 40 feet to the front left of the regiment. Posting the enlisted man exactly where he wanted him, Hancock bellowed, "Will you stay here?" Staring into Hancock's face, Durgin shot back, "I'll stay here, General, until hell freezes

---

13 Hardee, *Infantry Tactics*, vol. 1, 29; Arabella M. Willson, *Disaster, Struggle, Triumph* (Albany, 1870), 168. The regimental history of the 126th said the brigade formed in four columns but did not specify the front. In light of subsequent testimony, I believe the men advanced in a column four companies wide and 10 companies deep.

over." With a grin, Hancock trotted back to the startled Col. Francis E. Heath and emphatically told him to dress the rest of the regiment on Durgin.[14]

Heath immediately snapped the command as Hancock swung into the saddle and began to ride away. The thundering and clanging of Weir's battery approaching from behind attracted Heath's attention. With his right company squarely in the path of the onrushing artillery, he promptly yelled for the files on the end to break to the rear to allow the guns to pass. Hancock, misunderstanding what was going on, stormed to Lieutenant Weir and his officers, swearing up a blue streak. "If I commanded this regiment, I'd be God Damned if I would not charge bayonets on you." As Hancock headed south, the chastened artillerymen rolled down the slope into the hollow and went into battery with their left flank at the northern end of the ravine running from Trostle's. The 19th Maine advanced downhill across a demolished fence onto the low ground southwest of the wooded knoll. With the regiment to the left rear of the battery, Heath ordered the line to lie down to protect them from the incoming rounds from the smoke-covered Emmitsburg Road.[15]

Humphreys' Division, III Corps, Army of the Potomac
The Rodgers Farm, Along the Emmitsburg Road

By the time the 11th New Jersey's Adjutant Schoonover reached the left of the regiment, the situation had spun out of control. Birney ordered Humphreys to refuse Carr's Brigade to thwart the 13th and the 17th Mississippi regiments' advance. Carr sent word to Lieutenant Colonel Baldwin (1st Massachusetts) to hold the skirmish line at the Rodgers house as long as possible until the brigade could maneuvered to meet the attack from the south. Baldwin immediately dispatched two stalwarts to the skirmish line with that directive. Hard pressed from both west and south, Carr directed his brigade to swing the line back to face south. The orders, however, reached the regiments individually, which fragmented the intended reverse right wheel into a series of individual "front to rear on the tenth company" by regiments. The 16th Massachusetts dissolved during the maneuver and quit the field, leaving no Federal infantry between the 11th Massachusetts and the 12th New Hampshire.

14 Smith, *19th Maine*, 70-71, quote on 70.

15 Ladd and Ladd, *The Bachelder Papers*, vol. 2, 1,153, 1,164, vol. 3, 1,651, quote on 1,651; ibid.

Capt. Andrew Ackerman
Co. C, 11th New Jersey
GNMP

Rifle fire killed Capt. Luther Martin (Company D, 11th New Jersey). At about the same time a bullet struck Capt. Dorastus B. Logan (Company H) in the foot. Private Edward J. Kinney (Company E) and a private from Company C immediately tried to carry him from the field, but a bullet killed the soldier. Kinney struggled to get Logan away when a shell fragment knocked him down and a second round killed Logan. Word of the captain's death had just reached Schoonover on the far left of the line when a bullet snuffed out Capt. Andrew Ackerman (Company C) right at the adjutant's side. Schoonover immediately called for the senior captain, William H. Lloyd (Company F), to assume command of the regiment, but Lloyd had just left the field wounded, so Schoonover had to take charge. In direct response to the pressure from his flank, the adjutant yelled for the regiment to back up at right angles to its former line, which faced it south, immediately in the rear of the 120th New York.[16]

The slightly wounded Lieutenant Colonel Westbrook (120th New York) saw the Jerseymen behind him and erroneously assumed they had come to his relief. The moment his men flanked left and right by wings to unmask the regiment to his rear, another shot knocked him down. Privates Alonzo Lewis, John Myers, and Charles Yates (all Company I) hurried to his side. As Yates

---

16 Marbaker, *11th New Jersey*, 99, 103; Bartlett, *12th New Hampshire*, 124; "Where Honor Is Due," *The Sunday Herald*, Boston, July 23, 1899. I have found no accounts of the 16th Massachusetts during this part of the action, unlike the rest of the regiments in the brigade. The dearth of accounts and the fact that the regiment had the lowest casualty return in the brigade lead me to conclude that the regiment did not stay on the field.

stooped to get the colonel to his feet three balls thudded into him, knocking him flat. Lewis and Myers left him there while they hauled the colonel away.

Major John R. Tappen, who took over the regiment, vainly attempted to conduct an orderly retreat, but to no avail. His company-sized regiment got shattered and ran back toward the creek bottom north of the Trostle house. Brewster and Humphreys, unable to stem the human flood, went with them, desperately seeking a favorable point to rally the line. Lieutenant James Everett (Company K) brought the 120th's state flag away with him, but the national colors fell in the tumult. Tappen took them from the downed color bearer and handed them to Sgt. John J. Spoor (Company D). As a minié ball snapped the staff, the intrepid Spoor grasped the pole above the break and bore the colors aloft from the fight.[17]

Schoonover stubbornly held his regiment in the breach, but with his bruised chest he was struggling to breathe. In quick order, the 11th New Jersey lost two color bearers, and began to waver. Fearing a rout, the adjutant loudly ordered Cpl. Thomas Johnson (Company I) to step forward with the flag. Johnson took the colors, walked ahead of the line some 20 yards, and defiantly planted them in front of the Rebels. Personal bravery could not hold the position any longer, however. With an estimated half of the regiment or more already killed or wounded, the adjutant yelled at Johnson to return to the line and ordered a withdrawal.[18]

Lang's and Wilcox's Brigades, A. P. Hill's Corps,
Army of Northern Virginia
The Emmitsburg Road

To the west Lang's Florida brigade, unobserved by the Yankees in the Emmitsburg Road, shifted north to accommodate Wilcox's two left regiments, which had crossed its front and blindly surged toward the hole between the 26th Pennsylvania from Carr's 1st brigade and the 82nd New York from Harrow's 1st brigade. The Floridians swept the stubborn skirmishers from the

---

17 Van Santvoord, *120th New York*, 74-75; *New York at Gettysburg*, vol. 3, 819-821; Westbrook, "On the Firing Line," *National Tribune*, September 20, 1900; "Where Honor Is Due," *The Sunday Herald*, Boston, July 23, 1899.

18 OR 27, pt. 1, 554; Marbaker, *11th New Jersey*, 101-102.

1st Massachusetts back upon their reserves at the Rodgers house and into the confused mob of Federals on the eastern side of the road.[19]

Farther north in the low ground south of the Bliss Orchard, Brig. Gen. "Ranse" Wright's Georgia brigade temporarily halted at the fence in the hollow to pick up part of the 2nd Georgia Battalion. A small portion of the battalion formed on the left of the 48th Georgia. The rest of the regiment had spread out along the entire front of the brigade. Portions of its right wing fell in on the right of the 3rd Georgia.[20]

Humphreys' Division, III Corps,
Army of the Potomac
The Klingle Farm

The smoke from the 12th New Hampshire's first volley into Barksdale's Confederates had hardly cleared when Capt. John F. Langley, acting colonel, received the impossible command to execute a "front to rear on the first company" from Carr. Captain Nathaniel Shackford, the acting major, shouted the command to Lt. Henry A. L. French (Company F) when a minié ball slammed into his skull and sent him crumbling at Langley's feet. Simultaneously, the state color bearer Sgt. William J. Howe (Company E) fell dead with the colors in his hands; Sgt. Luther H. Parker (Company D), with the national flag, also went down. Mortally wounded, he tried to hand the staff off to Cpl. Edwin Brown (Company E), who was killed while reaching for it. Corporal William T. Knight (Company B), another member of the color guard, also died while lunging for the staff. Acting adjutant, Lt. Andrew M. Heath wrested the flags from both dead sergeants' grasps and carried them safely to the rear. The 12th New Hampshire and the 11th Massachusetts simultaneously executed an about face with their backs to the Confederates and right quarter wheeled south, which put them face-to-face with the Alabamians from Wilcox's Brigade, who had just crossed the Emmitsburg Road into the breach between the Rodgers and the Klingle houses.

By then Confederate small arms fire had drastically thinned the ranks of both regiments. Unable to withstand fire to the rear of his exposed line, Langley shouted for the 12th New Hampshire to retreat. Captain Shackford, already hit

---

19 Bachelder Map, "Second Day's Battle" (Boston, 1876).

20 *OR* 27, pt. 2, 627-629.

in the wrist and the thigh, took another shot through the lung, which forced his evacuation from the field. Langley had to quit the field also, wounded by a shell fragment. Command now fell upon 1st Lt. William H. H. Fernel (Company I), who led the regiment to the rear. The Massachusetts men completed the maneuver and returned fire with their buck and ball loads as fast as they could, all the while retiring toward Plum Run. Farther to the north, the completely exposed 26th Pennsylvania broke and streamed rearward.[21]

The Mississippians began fighting in four-man clusters, known as "comrades in battle." The deafening noise forced the officers of the 11th Massachusetts to communicate orders by hand signals. During the withdrawal, 1st Lt. Henry Blake (Company K) happened upon Carr and his brigade color bearer. "Take that flag!" Carr commanded. "Go to the rear with that flag!" The Irish orderly turned about, mumbling, "Faith, an' I was as willin' to run with it to the rear as he was to have me."[22]

The general's staff drew their swords and rushed into the frightened mob, trying to turn Brewster's men back and to restore their ranks, but to no avail. Confusion reigned everywhere. In the smoky field, regimental lines melted into disoriented squads of men from different commands.

The 11th New Jersey backed into part of the 12th New Hampshire's decimated formation and then into Seeley's retiring line of caissons behind them, creating a tangle that no officer could unravel. Seconds before his men reached the artillery line, Schoonover caught a load of buckshot. Completely unaware that he had six bullet holes through his clothes and no further injury,

21 Blake, *Three Years in the Army of the Potomac*, 210; Bartlett, *12th New Hampshire*, 123-126; *Supplement to the OR* 5, pt. 1, 183-184. There is little information about the 26th Pennsylvania other than a small description of the action at Gettysburg. It is my supposition that the 26th broke and ran during this attack. The recorder of the attack clearly states that the regiment held an indefensible position easily susceptible to artillery and small arms fire. Then "late in the day" the regiment changed front to meet the Confederate advance, charged, and drove the Rebels "across" the Emmitsburg Road. The Confederates in their first attack clearly captured the Federal position along the Emmitsburg Road. The Federal counterattack at 7:45 p.m. drove them from that position. The reference to the counterattack and the capturing of Rebel prisoners has to describe that counterattack and not the earlier one. The author simply did not describe the Rebel breakthrough and thereby evaded having to deal with the Pennsylvanians' initial rout.

22 Blake, *Three Years in the Army of the Potomac*, 210, quoted; Bartlett, *12th New Hampshire*, 123-126; *Supplement to the OR* 5, pt. 1, 183-184.

he turned over the remnants of the 11th to Captain Lloyd (Company F) (who, though wounded, had returned to the regiment) and headed toward the rear.[23]

On the right, Lt. John G. Turnbull (Battery F and K, 3rd U.S.) retired his six Napoleons by prolonge, blasting the Rebels with every round of canister he had left. The 17th Mississippi caught the four guns in the open and summarily slaughtered the remaining horses of the two left sections, forcing their abandonment. Mississippians swarmed around the abandoned guns. While Private Abernathy (17th Mississippi) hunkered down, one of his comrades hopped onto one of the pieces and was gunned down by the Yankees. Lieutenant Colonel John C. Fizer boldly raced his horse along the front of the disorganized line urging the men to halt and reform.

In the distance, through the smoke, Abernathy thought he saw the Yankees coming back toward the battery in a solid mass. A bullet plowed through Capt. James O. Ramsaur's mouth, and another smashed into his left hand. Unable to speak, he leaned upon the sword in his right hand, clutched his ragged hat in his wounded hand and pathetically waved at his men. Within seconds, the company lost its two Englishmen—a man named Brown, and the other, Billie Gast.

As Gast, kneeling down behind a bush, propped his rifle in its branches and fired, a ball cracked into his forehead. With a gasp, he settled back on his rear, a dead man, with his head on his knees. While the right section retreated northeast toward Codori's, Abernathy foolishly leaped upon one of the pieces, and a bullet instantly knocked him to the ground. He fell close to where lay two of his friends, Cpl. Scott S. Lynch and Pvt. Charles Connoley.[24]

The 19th Maine, II Corps, Army of the Potomac
The Eastern Side of the Codori Farm

Colonel Heath anxiously paced the front of his prone regiment. Its right flank was southwest of the wooded knoll, and its left flank rested at the head of the overgrown ravine, which ran almost parallel with the creek bottom. Peering toward the smoky ridge along the Emmitsburg Road, Heath spied General Humphreys and his staff emerge some 150 yards ahead of the remnants of the general's shattered division. Passing through Weir's silent battery, the gaggle of

---

23 Cavada, Diary, July 2, 1863, FSNMP; Blake, *Three Years in the Army of the Potomac*, 208-209; OR 27, pt. 1, 554; Marbaker, *11th New Jersey*, 104.

24 Ladd and Ladd, *The Bachelder Papers*, vol. 1, 284; Abernathy, *Our Mess*, 33-35.

officers rode up to Heath, and the general demanded that he call the regiment to its feet with fixed bayonets and stop the rout of his men. Heath defiantly refused to comply: Humphreys' mob would carry away his line, he said.[25]

Noticing that Humphreys' men had about caught up with their general, Heath yelled, "I was placed here by an officer of higher rank for a purpose and I do not intend to go to the rear. Let your troops form in the rear and we will take care of the enemy in front." Humphreys fired an angry salvo of oaths at Heath, which the hot-tempered colonel returned in kind.[26]

Unable to curse Heath into compliance, Humphreys and his staff flanked the 19th Maine and tried getting the New Englanders to their feet. Heath stayed right at his heels, defiantly countermanding the general. All the while, Humphreys' horde of shattered regiments, with the skulkers and walking wounded in the lead, trampled over the prone New Englanders. "They were all of them in a hurry," Sgt. Silas Adams (Company F) wrote. "These men were not particular where they stepped in walking over us, they only seemed intent upon getting to the rear and out of the reach of their relentless pursuers." First Lieutenant David E. Parsons (Company A) counted 13 flags passing over the regiment.[27]

Barksdale's Brigade,
Longstreet's Corps,
Army of Northern Virginia
The Klingle Farm

Longstreet's orderly, Private Youngblood, found Barksdale on horseback behind the brick milk house on the Klingle farm. Upon receiving the orders, Barksdale immediately trotted along the rear of his exhausted brigade stopped a few feet away. Colonels William B. Holder (17th Mississippi) and Thomas M. Griffin (18th Mississippi) both pleaded with him to halt long enough to reform the shot-up brigade. "No," Barksdale said. "Crowd them. We have them on the run. Move on your regiments. Advance! Advance!" Youngblood turned quickly toward the distinctive sound of a bullet hitting flesh and saw Barksdale toppled from his horse. With his mission done and Barksdale apparently dead, the

25 Ladd and Ladd, *The Bachelder Papers*, vol. 3, 1,651-1,652.

26 The Executive Committee, *Maine at Gettysburg*, 292.

27 Ladd and Ladd, *The Bachelder Papers*, vol. 3, 1,651-1,652; Smith, *19th Maine*, 71, quoted.

private spurred his lathered animal toward the Emmitsburg Road and General Longstreet.[28]

Private James M. Crump (Company B, 17th Mississippi) leaped over the wounded Abernathy (Company B), shouting for a bayonet charge with color Cpl. Joseph "Arch" Lee (Company I) right behind him with the flag. Now remnants of 13th, 17th, and 18th Mississippi regiments and Wilcox's Brigade bolted toward the low ground west of Plum Run. Barksdale, struck by a minié ball just above left knee, painfully remounted and chased after his men, but a short distance into the charge, a case shot carried away his left foot at the arch. Though faint and bleeding profusely, the general stayed in the saddle.[29]

Nearby, Lieutenant Colonel Fizer (17th Mississippi) caught two rounds in his leg and one through his cheek. Reacting to a musket ball in the right hip, Pvt. Robert N. Crawford (Company B, 11th Alabama) threw his right hand over his breast and gasped, "Boys, I am ruined." His good friend, Private Thompson, watched him stagger back towards the Klingle house, some 100 yards to the rear, oblivious to the fact that the ball had traversed Crawford's bowels and lodged near his left hip joint.[30]

McGilvery's Batteries, First Volunteer Brigade,
Army of the Potomac
South of the Trostle Farm Lane

Meanwhile, Captain Phillips (Battery E, 5th Massachusetts) withdrew part of his command back through a plowed field. About 200 yards from the Millerstown Road, he directed the #1 gun onto a grassy spot to the right. His

---

28 Youngblood, "Longstreet's Courier," in *SHSP*, vol. 38, 315-316; J. S. McNeily, "Barksdale's Mississippi Brigade at Gettysburg," 243; [Michael] Jacobs, "Later Ramblings Over the Field of Gettysburg," in *United States Service Magazine*, February 1864, vol. 1, 161.

29 Youngblood saw the general knocked from his horse. Barksdale in his deathbed testimony identified the sequence of his wounding as follows: above the knee on his left leg, the left foot by a cannonball, and in the chest which knocked him off his horse. (I have concluded the general was unhorsed twice.) Youngblood, "Longstreet's Courier," in *SHSP*, vol. 38, 315-316.

30 Ladd and Ladd, *The Bachelder Papers*, vol. 1, 231, vol. 3, 1,976; Abernathy, *Our Mess*, 33-35; David Parker to Barksdale, March 22, 1882, Mississippi Department of Archives and History, Jackson; H. T. Squires, (ed.), "The Last of Lee's Battle Line," LOC; Thompson to [Sisters & Mother], July 17, 1863, USAHEC, quoted. One unnamed source in the Bachelder Papers wondered if the 11th, 16th Massachusetts, or the 13th Vermont rescued the guns. The second reference asserts that the 16th Massachusetts saved the guns. The evidence strongly suggests that the 72nd and 73rd New York actually brought them off the field.

command secured, Phillips mounted up and headed toward Trostle's to seek help. He met Sergeant Pattison coming up with a limber and directed him toward the gun, and farther along ran into Lieutenant Lull, whose section had been left at Trostle's as a rendezvous point for the rest of the battery.

Back at the farmhouse, Captain Hart (15th New York Battery), not finding an officer of Phillips' battery present, assumed command and ordered the section to the rear with his guns. By then Pattison had brought up the limber and, meeting the men with the gun in Trostle's Lane, hitched up the left piece. An enraged Phillips managed to put his remaining four guns in battery in the hollow south of the house.[31]

With Hart's guns gone and Phillips' on the way to the rear, Bigelow (9th Massachusetts Battery) found himself in a bad fix. His four guns had backed themselves into a pocket at the gate in the northwest corner of the field, and now large boulders and a formidable stone wall along the eastern side the field obstructed their left and rear. The ridge to their front and right completely blocked their line of sight while the fence along Trostle's Lane forced them to man the guns at dangerously close intervals between each piece. Number 5 and #6 guns went into action 50 yards west of the gate, part way up the slope on the western face of the orchard.

The gate into Trostle's Lane had become the center of a deadly vortex, sucking everyone in the immediate area toward it. With the artillery closing in on the western and southern borders of the apple orchard, the 7th New Jersey was forced to back toward its northeastern corner.[32]

Private Eleazar Cole of Bigelow's battery had almost reached the gate when the Rebels killed his pole horse which partially tipped the limber on its side as it fell. Suddenly a caisson racing toward the gate knocked the limber completely over and careened into the right center of the startled 7th New Jersey, just missing the color company. The terrified horses trampled a couple of enlisted men as well as 2nd Lt. Thomas Clark (Company H). Scattering for cover, the four right companies scampered over the fence into the farm lane, into the field around the barn, and finally into the sparse woods to the north, taking

---

31 Regimental Committee, *5th Massachusetts Battery*, 624-628, 636, 638, 640; Ladd and Ladd, *The Bachelder Papers*, vol. 1, 168.

32 OR 27, pt. 1, 578. Major Cooper did not refer to the retrograde of 200 yards. However, when the Rebels closed in on the left of Bigelow's Battery, the regiment fell back with the battery. This is a clear reference to Bigelow's withdrawal occurring simultaneously with the regiment's retreat.

2nd Lt. Thomas Clark
Co. H, 7th New Jersey
Scott Hann collection
Library, GNMP

Lieutenant Colonel Francis Price with them. The line officers hastily reorganized what they could find of the regiment.

Under a lone tree against the fence row on Trostle's Lane, Capt. William R. Hillyer anchored what remained of the regiment on his Company K, the color company. Unable to return accurate fire against the Confederates, whose slouch hats he discerned through the dense smoke blanketing the field, or to take shelter in the clogged lane, Colonel Francine realized that his men would be slaughtered if they stayed where they were. "Fix bayonets," he commanded. "Forward, double-quick, charge!"[33]

Bolting through the orchard to its exposed southern face, the Jerseymen came upon the left rear of the 2nd New Hampshire rapidly falling back from the Peach Orchard. A wall of rifle fire stopped the regiment cold. Francine dropped with a severely wounded thigh; Adj. Charles R. Dougherty took bullets in the shoulder and the breast but managed to stay on his feet. Bullets hit 1st Lt. Michael Muller (Company K) in the groin and 1st Lt. Mathias Hay (Company I) in both legs. Almost 100 men went down in the fusillade. After a hasty realignment the 7th New Jersey loosed a feeble volley and disintegrated. Sergeant Major Joseph Johnson, Cpl. William Hooper, and Pvt. William Kirby (all Company A) helped the colonel to his feet and started to the rear with him. Kirby was terribly wounded in the leg on the way, but they safely evacuated the colonel.[34]

---

33 Samuel Toombs, *New Jersey Troops in the Gettysburg Campaign* (Orange, NJ, 1888), 223-224, quoted on 224.

34 Toombs, *New Jersey Troops,* 223-224.

In riding over to supervise the mess near Trostle's, Lieutenant Whitaker (9th Massachusetts Battery) took an eventually mortal bullet in the knee. He ordered Private Cole to assist with the remaining guns before he rode away. Bigelow, intending to escape with his guns through the gate, yelled at his men to limber up. McGilvery raced up to him. "Captain Bigelow," he yelled:

> there is not an infantryman back of you along the whole line from which Sickles moved out; you must remain where you are and hold your position at all hazards, and sacrifice your battery, if need be, until at least I can find some batteries to put in position and cover you. The enemy are coming down on you now.

Bigelow immediately countermanded his order to retire. The #5 and #6 crews hurriedly pulled the fixed ammunition from the caissons and laid the canister rounds on the ground next to their respective guns. While they were running the ammunition, the #3 men charged their pieces with double canister.[35]

Through the heavy, suffocating smoke, McGilvery had not seen the right flank of Tilton's right regiment, the 118th Pennsylvania, which was lying behind the stone wall about 200 feet south of the gate. The 1st Michigan lay right behind it, while the rest of Tilton's men struggled through the Army's ammunition wagons.[36]

Major James C. Biddle of Major General Meade's staff careened his horse into the line from behind pleaded with the panicky regiment. He begged the men in God's name to halt and not retreat. This was the only broken part of the line, Biddle told them (though it wasn't). Think about the safety of the ammunition train, he urged. If they left, the entire army would have to retreat. The veterans ignored him, some of them standing and silently walking east, heedless of both Confederate bullets and Biddle's loud entreaties. Most of the 118th Pennsylvania took to its heels and in the process smashed into the 1st Michigan, which had stood up to retire, thereby destroying the regimental line.[37]

---

35 Baker, *9th Massachusetts Battery*, 60-62, 64, 79-81, quote on 60; Toombs, New Jersey Troops, 223; Hayward, *Give It To Them, Jersey Blues!*, 115; Lader, Paul J., "The 7th New Jersey," *Gettysburg Magazine*, January 1, 1997, 60.

36 Lockley, Diary, July 2, 1863, UMI.

37 Aiken, *Inside the Army of the Potomac*, 305; ibid.

As men ran past Captain Donaldson, he noticed his 1st Lieutenant Crocker remaining behind. When Donaldson asked him why he did, Crocker calmly said it was "too bad" the boys had not held out any longer, since he wanted to see how many Rebs were out there and what they were going to do next. To both officers' amazement, the Confederates stood along the wall, cheering and yipping, rather than pursuing the Yankees any further. Crocker suddenly snatched Donaldson's revolver from his right hand, emptied the two remaining chambers at them, and took off running with Donaldson close behind. Behind lay Lts. Berzila J. Inman (Company F) and James B. Wilson (Company B), disabled upon the field.[38]

Tilton's Brigade retreated across the marshy ground along Plum Run toward the woods north of the John T. Weikert farm and reformed its ranks. All of a sudden what appeared to be an entire Georgia regiment, their weapons at the right shoulder shift and colors flying, raced past the 118th Pennsylvania at the double-quick. They were also heading toward the trees—under guard—in the heat of the action, their escort had not taken the time to disarm them. As the Pennsylvanians cleared the stone wall at the Weikert lane, Maj. Charles P. Herring stopped on the hill to the east with the color guard and waved the colors to and fro pleading with the men in his booming voice to rally and to stand fast. They paid him no heed.[39]

On the left of the brigade, along the Millerstown Road, Colonel Sherwin (22nd Massachusetts) fell. Several of his men rushed to his side and quickly checked him over. A bullet had grazed his chest; it knocked him down but did no further damage. Sergeant James Heckman and Pvt. Steven Osborn (both Company G, 145th Pennsylvania) finally stopped running to catch their breath long enough to check Osborn's wound, which seared him like a scalding iron. Heckman stuck his finger through the hole in Osborn's pants and traced the wound: a red welt left by the bullet passing through the pants leg but nothing more. A sheepish Osborn had experienced a "phantom" blood flow triggered by a very active imagination.[40]

About that time, the 21st Mississippi, firing as they advanced, crested the ridge not more than 50-60 yards from the muzzles of Bigelow's 12-pounders.

---

38 Aiken, *Inside the Army of the Potomac*, 305; Survivors Association, *118th Pennsylvania*, 250.

39 Lockley, Diary, July 2, 1863, UMI; Survivors Association, *118th Pennsylvania*, 250-251.

40 Carter, *Four Brothers in Blue*, 312; Calvin, (ed.), "Recollections of Army Life," 93.

On the left of the battery line, six of Kershaw's skirmishers managed to get within point-blank range of Bigelow and first bugler Charles W. Reed, who had not left the captain's side since the fighting began. Bigelow yelled at Reed to sound the "Retreat," which prompted the skirmishers to level their weapons at the two mounted men. Reed instinctively pulled back on the reins, rearing his horse onto its haunches while six minié balls zipped underneath the animal. Two went wild, two struck Bigelow's horse, and two hit him, one through the waist and the other his little finger. Bigelow's frightened mount careened toward the gate at the northeast corner of the field throwing Bigelow from the saddle about 100 feet from his left section. The faithful Reed and orderly John Kelley stayed mounted by their downed captain, ignoring his pleas for them to escape.

Canister punched gaping holes in the Rebel line, but their charge had picked up too much momentum to stop. Private Lowell abandoned the #6 gun to assist gunner William L. Tucker on #2. He gathered the remaining three rounds in the limber and ran to the gun's muzzle. Serving as both the #1 and #3 men on the crew, he stayed by Tucker until they had fired all three rounds. Amidst the chaos, second bugler Orin Reynolds sat on his horse behind the piece, instructing Tucker in his thick brogue, "Pint your gun a little lower, Bill." Sergeant Charles E. Dodge, commanding #2 and out of canister, loaded his last round of shot, while the remaining Federal gunners frantically charged their pieces with double canister again. The four Napoleons seemingly discharged in unison into the Rebels who were virtually in their faces.

The cannoneer on #2, rather than get bayoneted, tried to run away but the Confederates leaped on top of the limber and methodically killed all of the horses. A rifle ball mortally wounded Sergeant Dodge, and Sgt. George Murray (gun #1) staggered away with a wounded foot. While Private Lowell took off at a run for the stone wall on the east side of the field, the Rebs collared gunner William L. Dawes.[41]

Upon riding up to Pvts. John K. Norwood and Ralph C. Blaisdell as they tried to limber up #5, Lieutenant Erickson asked if he could help them. Almost instantly, two bullets slammed into Erickson's forehead while another broke his wrist. Two more rounds hit him in the hip and shattered his leg above the ankle.

---

41 Baker, *9th Massachusetts Battery*, 62-65, 79-81, 200, quote on 81; John Bigelow to the Adjutant General of the U.S.A., June 19, 1895, Supplemental Report, 424, 496-502, NA; "How the Battle Was Won," *The Minneapolis Journal*, August 31, 1895; Campbell, "*A Grand Terrible Dramma*," 115.

As he fell from the saddle, the horse bolted into the ranks of the 21st Mississippi. John Ligal, at the muzzle of the piece, brained a Confederate with his sponge staff. Ligal caught Pvt. David Brett, who was trying to retrieve his lost cap, on the run and carried him away under his arm. Rebels quickly mowed down Sgt. Joseph Hirst and cannoneers Augustus Hessie and Louis Langeleer, while a bullet ripped through Pvt. John K. Norwood's lungs. Ralph C. Blaisdell, uninjured, dropped to the ground next to him under the limber. They lay there trapped as the color bearer of the 21st Mississippi climbed onto the ammunition chest over their heads and waved his flag triumphantly. First Lieutenants George C. Kempton (Company I) and William P. McNeely (Company E) raced for the silent pieces. Colonel Humphreys found Kempton on top of one of the guns jubilantly waving his sword above his head and hollering, "Colonel, I claim this gun for Company I." Meanwhile McNeely "captured" the next cannon for his Company E. The Rebels slaughtered the horse team to immobilize the gun.[42]

The left section limbered up, rather than retire by prolonge. As the guns neared the northeast corner of Trostle's field, Lieutenant Milton unlimbered the section and fired his last two rounds of case shot at the Rebels to the south. Limbering his two guns again, he had his men knock the top rocks off of the stone wall behind them. Whipping the horses into a gallop, they attempted to vault the wall onto the marshy ground west of Plum Run. Number 4, his left piece, tipped on its side getting over, but Private Lowell and volunteers from the other crew righted it. His #3, however, clattered through the gate into the farm lane with no problems. Both pieces had escaped.[43]

Private Cole saw the Rebs to the west mown down like hay before a scythe. He snatched the harnesses of the lead and swing horses on the right side of the #6 caisson while Pvt. Stephen H. Goodwin took hold of the swing horse on the opposite side. Together, they brought the caisson off the field. Once far enough to the rear, Goodwin picked up a discarded musket and tried to lead several of the artillerymen back into the fighting.[44]

---

42 Baker, *9th Massachusetts Battery*, 60-62, 74-77, 80-81, 221; Charles Reed to [Mother & Sister], July 11, 1863, USAHEC; McNeily, "Barksdale's Mississippi Brigade at Gettysburg," 248, quoted; Campbell, *A Grand Terrible Dramma*, 117-118.

43 Baker, *9th Massachusetts Battery*, 62, 76, 80; Deane, "*My Dear Wife*," 70.

44 Baker, *9th Massachusetts Battery*, 60-62, 74-77, 79. Goodwin served on the #6 gun also and therefore probably saved the #6 caisson.

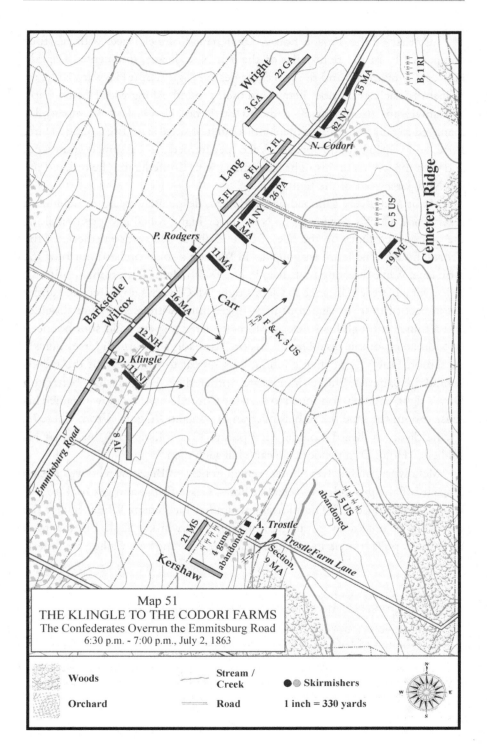

Map 51
THE KLINGLE TO THE CODORI FARMS
The Confederates Overrun the Emmitsburg Road
6:30 p.m. - 7:00 p.m., July 2, 1863

Woods

Orchard

Stream /
Creek

Road

● Skirmishers

1 inch = 330 yards

Just east of the Trostle house, Lieutenant Colonel Price, with his four companies from the right wing of the 7th New Jersey, intercepted Captain Hillyer (Company K) and the two color bearers, Sgt. Aaron Hayward and Cpl. William Kissick, and made them stand their ground. Along with Hillyer, Capt. William Evans (Company B) and 2nd Lt. James H. Onslow (Company D) managed to rally a handful of men until a burst of small arms fire wounded him, Price, and Onslow. Major Frederick Cooper immediately assumed command, and with the woods on his right flank filling with Confederates, he ordered the 7th New Jersey out of the fight.[45]

Major McGilvery galloped up to Phillips, desperately trying to organize a reserve line. Clark's Battery B, 1st New Jersey Light, rolled into position along the demolished fence on the rise of ground about 500 yards northeast of the Trostle house. The leftmost gun was in Weikert's small orchard north of the farm lane. While directing Lt. Edwin P. Dow's 6th Maine Battery into position a little over a battery's distance to Clark's right, McGilvery's horse recoiled under the impact of four simultaneous hits—three in his withers and front shoulder and a fourth through his forelegs. Moments later, a spent solid shot bounced into him, temporarily disabling the major. The badly shot-up 7th Jersey quickly passed on Dow's right then continued its retreat to the safety of the woods behind the batteries. Phillips immediately ordered his four guns into battery on Dow's right, and they continued to shell the Confederates. Bigelow regained his senses about the time the Rebels overran his #5 and #6 guns. From where he lay, he distinctly heard Colonel Humphreys (21st Mississippi) bellow at his soldiers, "Hold! Don't shoot. We can't kill such men."[46]

McGilvery, on his dying horse, reined in next to Bigelow, who was raising himself off the ground, and yelled at him, "Cease firing, and get back to our lines as best you can." The mortally wounded Lieutenant Whitaker met the captain as he unsteadily got up and proffered his whiskey flask. Bigelow took three quick pulls from it, its artificial heat strengthening him. Calling for orderly

---

45 Toombs, *New Jersey Troops*, 224-225; OR 27, pt. 1, 578-579; Hayward, *Give It To Them, Jersey Blues!*, 116-117; Lader, "The 7th New Jersey," *Gettysburg Magazine*, January 1, 1997, 65-67.

46 Regimental Committee, *5th Massachusetts Battery*, 625, 627-628, 636, 638; Ladd and Ladd, *The Bachelder Papers*, vol. 1, 168; Edwin B. Dow to the Adjutant General, U.S.A., August 3, 1895, and Bigelow to same, June 19, 1895, Supplemental Report, R&P, 424, 496, NA, quote in Bigelow letter. I concluded that Clark's battery occupied that position. In the regimental history, Philips and the others said that Hart took three of his guns. The wartime letter in Bachelder said that Hart commanded only one section.

Kelley, the ever-present bugler Reed ordered him to give Bigelow his horse. As the orderly heaved the captain onto the saddle, Reed gathered up the reins of his own horse and the captain's. Striding next to the dazed Bigelow, he supported the captain's back and started walking slowly east, Whitaker by their side. Bigelow told Whitaker to stay with him so they could look after each other. As the Confederates, however, started walking shells down the farm lane, Whitaker worked his horse into a trot and the left the captain behind. Bigelow did not attempt to call him back; Phillips and Dow withheld their fire rather than take a chance on hitting the captain.

Nearly half way between the house and the two batteries, 1st Lt. William H. Rogers from Dow's battery intercepted the two men. Rogers begged Bigelow to increase his pace so they could open fire on the Rebels before they could get enough momentum to charge his position. Bigelow weakly told them to fire because he could not hurry. So Dow commanded his left section to open with shell, and two rounds stopped the advance.[47]

By then the Rebels were swarming all over the Trostle farm. One grabbed Pvt. Samuel Toby (Bigelow's battery) by the shirt and pulled him in through a lower window of the house as the hapless artilleryman tried to make his escape. The plucky Private Lowell (Bigelow's battery), having found his horse, "Old Tom," swung into the saddle near the gate when a Confederate infantryman shoved the muzzle of his rifle under his nose and demanded, "Surrender you damned Yankee." Lowell went for his service revolver just as a minié ball killed "Old Tom." Horse and man went down as one, and pinned to the ground under the dead animal, Lowell lay helpless.[48]

Nearby Cpl. Josiah A. Bosworth (Company B, 141st Pennsylvania) wounded in his right leg below the knee, hobbled across the corpse-strewn field south of the Trostle house and pulled himself into the thick brush on the other side of the stone wall between the gate and the wood lot. He stood there as Confederate infantrymen scrambled over the wall around him. He stopped one of the Rebels and asked him for a drink of water. As he was taking a long drink, the Rebel loaded his rifle and moved forward. But after going about 50 yards, he turned and took a shot at the startled corporal, who hurled himself into the

---

47 Baker, *9th Massachusetts Battery*, 60-62, 74, 200, 226-227; Dow to the Adjutant General of the U.S.A., August 3, 1895, and Bigelow to same, June 19, 1895, Supplemental Report, 424, 496 – 2, NA; "How the Battle Was Won," *The Minneapolis Journal*, August 31, 1895.

48 Baker, *9th Massachusetts Battery*, 80.

tanglefoot and stayed there. Not too far away Sergeant Bloodgood (Company I, 140th Pennsylvania), his face blackened and his mouth dry and parched, stooped over a mud puddle with his tin cup, scooped up a pint of dirty water, and downed it without coming up for air. "Water never tasted better anywhere than that did," he recollected later.[49]

The 15th Massachusetts and 82nd New York, II Corps,
Army of the Potomac
Codori House

Lang's Florida brigade crossed the Emmitsburg Road between the right flank of the 26th Pennsylvania and the left flank of the 82nd New York. Wright's Georgia brigade, on the Floridians' left rear, pushed straight for the Codori farm buildings.

Fleeing pickets were leaping over the small breastworks of the 15th Massachusetts, but the slight rise in ground west of the regiment completely hid the oncoming Georgians from view. Private John "Bob" Marsh (Company B), a man known for his tenacity in battle, leapt to his feet with his rifle cocked. Leveling it at an escaping picket, to his front, he swore he would kill the man right there if he did not stop. For a moment, Private Bowen thought Marsh would do it, but the frightened skirmisher blurted that he had no ammunition and that a Reb battle line was right behind him.

Glancing to the south Bowen watched tremendous numbers of III Corps men fleeing to the rear through the fields. Incredulous, he asked a couple of men nearby if they thought all those men were wounded. They both agreed with him they were not. As the III Corps' retreat flowed closer and closer to the Codori buildings, 1st Sgt. Amable Beaudry (Company B) approached Bowen muttering, "Oh! It's too bad, it's too bad."[50]

The Massachusetts men managed to corral most of the fleeing skirmishers into their ranks before the Confederates came into view. Bowen and his comrades laid handfuls of cartridges on the ground next to them and laid their ramrods alongside. Some men shouted they could see the Rebs, and the Yankees began shooting blindly across the road. Bowen stood up but could only see a few bayonets sticking up above the tall grass to his front. The

49 Craft, *141st Pennsylvania*, 128.

50 Bowen, Journal, GNMP.

Georgians had lay down and were crawling in closer to make a charge. Bowen flattened out, as a hostile volley went high and the Rebel yell rent the air. The inevitable charge began.[51]

From their elevated position on a slight knoll to the rear, Brown's Rhode Island gunners saw the attack beginning before the infantrymen did. As soon as the Rebel volley passed overhead, the artillerymen jumped to their stations and fired spherical case with four-second fuses. The successive explosions rained showers of lethal musket balls upon the Confederates' heads. The Massachusetts men got to their knees and fired a devastating volley into the Georgians, who recoiled but quickly reformed. The New Englanders fired into them again, but by then the Georgians steadied like the professionals they were and returned the fire with a vengeance. The artillerists behind the 15th Massachusetts burst another salvo, this time with three-second fuses over the opposing lines.[52]

51 Ibid.

52 Andrew E. Ford, *The Story of the Fifteenth Regiment Massachusetts Volunteer Infantry* (Clinton, MA, 1898), 267-268; OR 27; John H. Rhodes, "*The Gettysburg Gun,*" (Providence, RI, 1892), 11, in *Personal Narratives of Events in the War of the Rebellion, Being Papers Read Before the Rhode Island Soldiers and Sailors Historical Society*, 10 vols. (Wilmington, 1993), vol. 7, 387.

Chapter 15

July 2, 1863

7:00 p.m.-7:30 p.m.

"I won't die! I won't die!"

—Unidentified private, Company B, 13th Pennsylvania Reserves

Wright's Georgia Brigade,
A. P. Hill's Corps, Army of Northern Virginia
The Codori Farm

Swinging northeast, the intermingled Georgians and Floridians enfiladed the 82nd New York, forcing them to refuse the left of their line. First shot in the leg, Lieutenant Colonel Huston was killed by a second ball in the head. With the Rebs getting way too close, Brown's Rhode Island gunners unloaded another barrage of case shot, with two-second bursts. The rounds knocked men down by the dozen, many of them from the 15th Massachusetts, whose one-legged Colonel Ward collapsed with multiple wounds. The Georgians were closing fast. "Where's the officers?" yelled Private Bowen (Company B) anxiously. Ward, Joslin, the major? He got no answer. The New Yorkers broke and streamed back toward Cemetery Ridge. When the last man of the 82nd New York quit the field, Bowen, raving like a mad man, cursing and swearing, vowed he would not leave. His good friend "Bob" Marsh leaped to his feet, fired off a final round and bolted, yelling, "Never be a prisoner—Never!" But someone else screamed, "Give them hell!" Bowen fired his last round, and throwing his weapon to the ground, he pulled his cap off, raised his hands in the air, and hoped not to be killed in the mayhem.[1]

---

1 Bowen, Journal, GNMP; *OR* 27, pt. 1, 423, 426.

With its left flank of the 15th Massachusetts exposed and with men dropping rapidly from incoming "friendly fire," Joslin shouted for the command to retreat. The Rebels snatched up quite a few of them during the rout. As the Bay Staters ran, the artillerymen loosed case with one-second fuses then rapidly loaded with canister. The thoroughly frightened Private Bowen watched the Rebels stream around him without uttering a sound. Instinctively hurling himself onto the opposite side of his own breastworks, a second later he realized that canister would turn those rails into sawdust. Out of options, he took off running with all his might toward Seminary Ridge. The first artillery blast from the rear cut down Yankees and Confederates in droves. The Rebels directed their riflery upon Brown's exposed Rhode Islanders. Brown screamed the order, "Limber to the rear." The crews of guns #'s 1, 2, 3, 5, and 6 quickly got their guns pintled and started for the low spot in the northwestern corner of the stone wall at the Angle.[2]

Sergeant Albert A. Straight, commanding the already loaded #4, held his crew back. With the Confederates literally on top of him, he gave the command to "Fire," followed immediately by "Limber to the rear." The words had hardly left his mouth when the Georgians shot down his team's two lead horses. Screaming, his artillerymen tried to escape, every man for himself. His remaining four horses went down along with the dying Pvt. David B. King. Meanwhile two of the guns had managed to escape to the Federal side of the ridge. In the rush to escape, two others jammed together trying to get through the gap in the wall, which left gun #6 stranded in the open between the two battle lines. The Rebels killed one of the horses and wounded another on the limber. The three drivers abandoned the piece and skedaddled for safer ground. In the melee, a musket ball plowed into 1st Lieutenant Brown's neck. Bleeding severely, he turned the battery over to 2nd Lt. William S. Perrin.[3]

The 69th Pennsylvania, with the 59th New York and the 7th Michigan to its left, waited behind the stone wall a little more than 100 yards to the east for the guns to clear their line of fire. As the Georgians swarmed over the #4 gun, the three regiments brought the charge to a halt with rifle fire. But one of the Rebel officers dashed upon the gun and brazenly straddled the muzzle. Captain

---

2   OR 27, pt. 1, 423, 426; Raus, *A Generation on the March*, 35, 72; Rhodes, *The Gettysburg Gun*, 12, quoted.

3   Raus, *A Generation on the March*, 147; OR 27, 1, 478; Rhodes, *The Gettysburg Gun*, 12-14, quote on 12.

Michael Duffy (Company I, 69th Pennsylvania) hollered at his men: "Knock that damned officer off the gun." A second volley swept him away. The Pennsylvanians leapt the wall intent upon finishing the Rebels off, but Harrow and Webb shouted them back to their cover.[4]

Lang's Florida Brigade, A. P. Hill's Corps,
Army of Northern Virginia
Southeast of the Codori Farm House

Screaming demonically as they pushed through the smoke engulfing their advance, Lang's Floridians bore down upon Lieutenant Weir's Regular battery. The frightened 25-year-old had barely unlimbered when Humphreys' disorganized Federal troops stampeded through and around his guns. Limber up and leave the field, he commanded. He led the retreat until a bullet cut down his horse and sent him sprawling onto the ground. He tried to gain his feet, but a spent ball dazed him. Simultaneously, a round through the left section cut down Lt. Homer H. Baldwin's mount "Everything seemed to be very much confused," Weir truthfully wrote in his largely imaginative after-action report. With Baldwin down, 1st Sgt. Paul Roemer mounted a horse and managed to get one of Baldwin's guns with its limber and five of the battery's caissons to the safety of Cemetery Ridge.[5]

Weir managed to get three of his guns to safety, but the 2nd Florida overran the remaining three pieces as well as their limbers when the crews cut the traces off the horses and abandoned them. Fortunately all of his men escaped capture. Colonel Francis Heath (19th Maine), having witnessed this less than stellar affair, later recalled, "The battery on my right at this time was deserted, the guns not firing a shot."[6]

Major General Abner Doubleday (commanding the Third Division, I Corps), whose battered division happened to have several regiments in the vicinity, witnessed the debacle as well. He immediately spurred to the north to find a regiment to fill the gap. He found an isolated one in column of divisions

---

4   Ladd and Ladd, *The Bachelder Papers*, vol. 3, 1,407; Gottfried, *Stopping Pickett*, 161.

5   *OR* 27, pt. 1, 881, quoted; Ladd and Ladd, *The Bachelder Papers*, vol. 2, 1,152, vol. 3, 1,652.

6   *OR* 27, pt. 1, 881; Ladd and Ladd, *The Bachelder Papers*, vol. 2 , 1,152, vol. 3, 1,652, quoted; Raus, *A Generation on the March*, 167; Frederick Tilberg to Mrs. Joseph C. Moore, August 12, 1954, Vertical Files, GNMP.

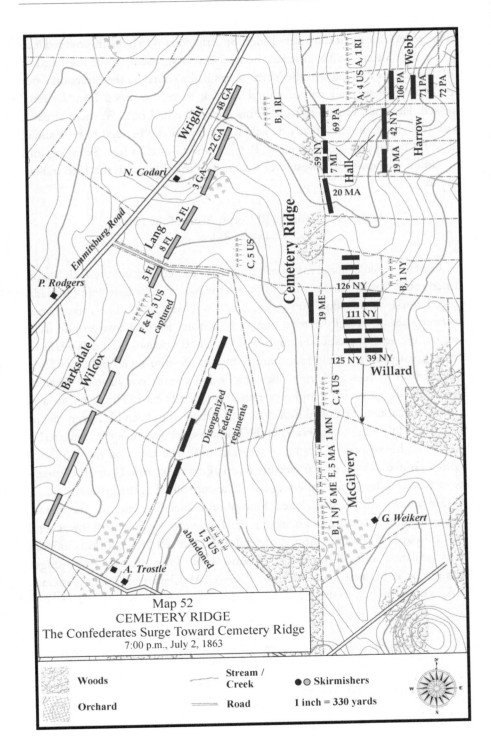

Map 52
CEMETERY RIDGE
The Confederates Surge Toward Cemetery Ridge
7:00 p.m., July 2, 1863

on the reverse slope of Cemetery Ridge. Spurring down to it, he discovered it to be the 13th Vermont. Doubleday shouted encouragement to the men and to Col. Francis V. Randall that the Vermonters had to hurry in the direction from which the general had come. Find Hancock there, he urged Randall: hard pressed, Hancock was going to lose his guns if he had not lost them already. With half the regiment already detached to support the Federal right, Randall called his battalion—Companies A, B, C, E, and G—to its feet. Swinging into the saddle, he raced southwest over the crest of the ridge with the 13th trailing behind.[7]

Humphreys' Division, III Corps, Army of the Potomac
Cemetery Ridge

Captain Cavada, in the midst of a gaggle of refugees behind the 19th Maine, turned south toward the marshy hollow on the New Englanders' left. His badly injured horse "Brick Bat," however, could not run at all. The infantrymen swarming about virtually herded him and his horse into the low ground. Like Cavada, the assault pushed Humphreys, Carr, and one aide, Capt. William H. Chester, toward the creek. Humphreys' mount, despite seven bullet wounds, remained on its feet. Suddenly Chester's body violently convulsed: "General, I'm shot," he gasped. Humphreys reined up beside him. Throwing an arm around the captain, he pulled him close and struggled to keep him from reeling from the saddle. Lieutenant Harry H. Humphreys, the general's son, came to his aid. While he steadied Chester, a sergeant took the reins of the wounded captain's horse. A solid shot hissed in on top of them. It carried away the horse's lower face and decapitated the sergeant. Chester spilled to the ground.[8]

Simultaneously, a shell killed Humphreys' bleeding mount. Its impact threw the animal into the air and sent it crashing onto the field with the general still on board. While the stunned general pried himself loose, a flurry of rifle shots whistled into the officers around him. One struck the younger Humphreys in his arm. Carr and Capt. Carswell McClellan (Adjutant General's Office) both pitched to the ground aboard horses that had been hit. They, like

---

7 Howard Coffin, *Nine Months to Gettysburg* (Woodstock, 1997), 204-205, in George H. Scott, *Vermont at Gettysburgh*, Proceedings of the Vermont Historical Society (Montpelier, 1930), vol. 1; *OR* 27, pt. 1, 351-352.

8 Cavada Diary, July 2, 1863, FSNMP.

the general, were badly jarred but otherwise uninjured. Upon reaching the thinly wooded creek bed, Cavada and several other officers managed to rally a considerable number of the men. As they went to cover behind felled trees and large rocks, Cavada twisted in the saddle and was startled to see three Confederate battle flags just a few yards from him.[9]

Defiant to the end, Colonel Heath called his veteran 19th Maine to its feet. With the Rebels less than 50 yards in front of them, the color bearer of the 8th Florida, energetically semaphored his flag from left to right and caught Heath's attention by bolting several yards ahead of his own regiment. The colonel, standing in front of the Mainers, next to the colors, called over his shoulder to the nearest private in Company C, "Drop him." The fellow instantly brought his weapon to bear and fired. The color bearer collapsed whereupon Heath commanded the regiment to fire by battalions. The volleys halted the Florida regiments, and they immediately returned fire. On the level ground to the left of Company F, Lt. Evan Thomas' six 12-pounders (Battery C, 4th U.S.) thundered, shaking the ground violently. The gunners, in the intense heat, stripped off their shell jackets and rolled up their sleeves as they charged their pieces with canister.[10]

Humphreys' Division, III Corps, Army of the Potomac
The Ravine to the 19th Maine's Left Front

At that moment, a bullet killed Cavada's "Brick Bat." The poor animal fell on top of the startled captain, pinning him to the ground. Caught between two fires, Cavada frantically pulled himself free, snatched his pistol and flask from the saddle, and staggered eastwards, toward the ridge behind him. To avoid "friendly fire" he cut south toward Trostle's, looking for deeper cover. Finally reaching a place of safety behind his own lines, the aide collapsed on a large stone to gather his breath. Not too far away, the 11th Massachusetts rallied what remained of their men around the colors.[11]

9 Ibid.

10 Smith, *19th Maine*, 72; Ladd and Ladd, *The Bachelder Papers*, vol. 3, 1,652, quoted; Heath, "The 19th Maine at Gettysburg," 2, Vertical Files, GNMP.

11 Cavada, Diary, July 2, 1863, FSNMP; Blake, "Personal Reminiscences of Gettysburg," 16-17, USAHEC.

21st Mississippi, Longstreet's Corps,
Army of Northern Virginia
North of the Trostle House

Having overrun Bigelow's battery, Colonel Humphreys halted what he could find of his 21st Mississippi in the smoke and the chaos in the hollow directly east of the house. The rest of the brigade, the regiments all jumbled up in their charge, had stalled on his left. During the momentary halt, an enlisted man brought him 1st Lieutenant Erickson's horse from Bigelow's battery along with the deceased lieutenant's spyglass and personal satchel. Humphreys quickly rifled the pouch and found photographs of two "fine looking boys" whom he presumed to be the dead officer's sons.[12]

Willard's Brigade, II Corps, Army of the Potomac
The Ridge Northwest of George Weikert's House

Under Hancock's personal supervision, Colonel Willard (with the Third Division's adjutant general, Captain Corts by his side) led his brigade into position on the eastern slope of Cemetery Ridge along the front of the woods behind the rallied batteries on the top of the ridge. The regiments arrived amidst a horde of III Corps refugees, wounded and unhurt, who swarmed around their flanks and pushed through their formations to the rear. Even Hancock's prolific swearing could not get them to stand firm. At one point, a stretcher party passed through Captain Thompson's Company F, carrying an officer with a mangled leg. Thompson mistakenly recalled it was Sickles—whom the ambulance had already carted off.

Willard, a professional from the regular army, sent markers forward, onto the ridge in front of McGilvery's guns. The brigade then advanced through the artillery line with parade ground precision, the regiments aligned on the markers. The 39th New York deployed facing southwest to cover the flank overlooking the Trostle farmhouse. Two hundred fifty yards to its right front, the 125th New York, with the 126th to its right, wheeled into line facing west. The 111th New York, which went prone some 200 yards farther east, supported the 126th. Corporal Harrison Clark (Company E, 125th New York), to the left of Color Sgt. Lewis Smith (Company C), recalled, "We were halted amid a heavy

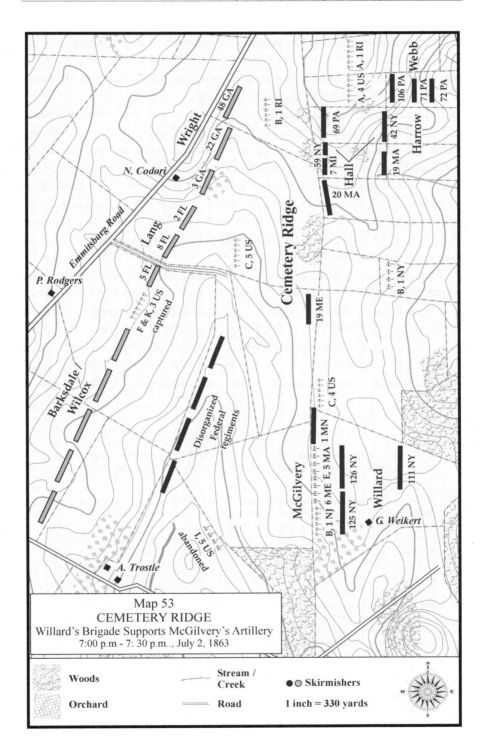

Map 53
CEMETERY RIDGE
Willard's Brigade Supports McGilvery's Artillery
7:00 p.m - 7: 30 p.m.., July 2, 1863

Woods

Stream / Creek

Skirmishers

Orchard

Road

1 inch = 330 yards

cloud of smoke in front of a swale and a new growth of trees." The regiments stood their ground in the face of a rain of rifle and artillery fire. Without orders, men in the two lead regiments returned fire at the muzzle flashes from the swale to their front—to sudden screams of: "Firing on your own men!"[13]

"Cease firing!" Willard yelled above the din, to which the company officers responded immediately, running along the front of their commands shouting the rattled soldiers into silence. Now the Confederates loosed a volley at the confused Yankees. A soldier on the left of the 125th New York pitched forward dead. Color Sergeant Smith collapsed, also killed. Corporal Clark snatched up the flag before it touched the ground. Another bullet mortally wounded Sgt. John E. Lawrence (Company H, 111th New York), who lay near Pvt. Norman Eldred. And one of the shells brutally struck Willard in the face before he could issue another command.[14]

Colonel Eliakim Sherrill (126th New York) assumed command of the brigade and urged the line forward. The 125th New York, the 126th New York to its right, began crossing the small level plain into the rock-strewn valley north of Trostle's. As they moved out, Sherrill spurred to the 111th New York and got it to its feet. Firing erupted from the two center regiments, the men loading and shooting as they advanced. Just at the first gentle decline toward the creek bottom, Sherrill ordered the 125th and the 126th New York to charge.

---

13 Thompson, "This Hell of Destruction," in *CWTI*, vol. 12, 18; R. L. Murray, *Redemption of the "Harper's Ferry Cowards"* (Wolcott, NY, 1994), 74; *York at Gettysburg*, vol. 2, 886-887, quote on 887.

14 Thompson, "This Hell of Destruction," in *CWTI*, vol. 12, 18; Ladd and Ladd, *The Bachelder Papers*, vol. 2, 1,134, vol. 3, 1,357; N. Eldred, "Only a Boy: A first-hand account of the Civil War," 26, Vertical Files, GNMP; Ezra D. Simons, *The One Hundred and Twenty-fifth New York State Volunteers* (New York, 1888), 111-112; *New York at Gettysburg*, vol. 2, 886-887, quote on 887; Beyer and Keydel, 2 vols., *Deeds of Valor*, vol. 1, 225. Some controversy surrounds when Willard died. The traditional accounts are based upon Chaplain Ezra Simons' reminiscences, and the after-action report of Lt. Col. James S. Bull. Hancock wrote in 1885 that "I ordered the brigade to advance into the swale in front. Willard was killed, but his command from that time performed quite important services and met with great losses." His statement implies that the brigade took its heaviest losses after Willard died. Lieutenant Colonel Morgan, Hancock's I.G. and chief of staff, stated, "The brigade had hardly engaged the enemy when a shell struck Colonel Willard in the face, killing him instantly." Both of these, in conjunction with Thompson's eye-witness account have more credence than Simons' story, which seemed embellished and contrary to Corporal Clark's statements. Bull's account is likely secondhand also; he did not say he saw Willard go down, but Thompson clearly recalled the location and the time of the incident.

Someone in the ranks cried out: "Remember Harper's Ferry!" The shout carried along the front like as if electric as man after man picked up the cry.[15]

Barksdale's Brigade, Longstreet's Corps,
Army of Northern Virginia
North of the Trostle House

The Yankees' unexpected rally caught Barksdale's three left regiments helplessly in the open, and Mississippians fell in groups. The Rebel general's prolific swearing had attracted the attention of the two New York regiments, and he naturally drew fire. One bullet found its mark: a minié ball ploughed through the general's back, exiting through his right chest, and jerking him from the saddle. Private Jack Boyd (Company I, 13th Mississippi) and two other enlisted men sprang to his aid. The general regained consciousness when they tried to lift his 240 pounds of deadweight from the ground. Weakened, and in a great deal of pain, he pled with them to leave him lay where he was, and they did. Somehow the general managed to get himself to a standing position, because Pvt. David G. Maggard (Company K, 13th Mississippi) saw him weakly leaning against the side of his horse, literally bleeding to death. "Boys, I am a dead man," he rasped, "but charge 'em, darn 'em, charge 'em, and don't fall back." Colonel Griffin (18th Mississippi) immediately took over the brigade, and shortly thereafter, shot in the leg, he ordered his regiment out of the fight.[16]

17th and 21st Mississippi, Longstreet's Corps,
Army of Northern Virginia
Plum Run North of Trostle's

Colonel Holder (17th Mississippi), the only uninjured field grade officer among the three left regiments, hunted out Humphreys (21st Mississippi) to transfer brigade command to him. From the shelter of the rocky creek bottom, Holder saw what appeared to be a Yankee battery (Battery I, 5th U.S. Artillery) rolling into position several hundred yards to the east, onto a small shelf of land

15 Murray, *The Redemption of the "Harper's Ferry Cowards,"* 77, quoted; Campbell, "Remember Harper's Ferry," in *Gettysburg Magazine,* July 1, 1992, 67.

16 "One of the Veterans of Gettysburg," newspaper clipping, n.d., Vertical Files, GNMP, quoted; E. P. Harman to W. S. Decker, August 16, 1886, and "Willard's Brigade at Gettysburg," both OCHS; Ladd and Ladd, *The Bachelder Papers,* vol. 1, 339, 481.

north of the farm lane before it entered Weikert's Woods. Finding Humphreys, who had also seen the threat, he shouted: "If you will give me Company A of the 17th, I will take that battery before it can fire a gun."[17]

Humphreys agreed and detailed his Company A to go in with Holder's men. The two companies, well below strength, formed ranks, wheeled into line, and charged into a maelstrom of small arms fire. With Holder leading the assault, Humphreys rashly ordered the rest of the 21st Mississippi into the attack.[18]

Second Lieutenant MacConnell (Battery I, 5th U.S.) immediately yelled for his men to grab the implements for the four 3-inch rifles and make off for safer ground. One of the section commanders, Lt. Samuel Peeples, raced east along the face of the woods toward George Weikert's, when he ran into two general officers, whom he did not know, and begged them to help him to save his guns. They said they could do nothing: their hands were full trying to preserve what was left of the III Corps.

Captain John B. Fassett, Birney's senior aide-de-camp, had just finished establishing rallying point for the III Corps on Cemetery Ridge behind McGilvery's small artillery line, when he found Peeples standing on top of a boulder, anxiously watching the Confederates close in on his battery. Why wasn't he with his battery? Fassett asked. "Because it has just been captured," Peeples answered, "And if those Confederates are able to serve my guns, those troops you have just been forming on the ridge, won't stay there a minute."[19]

Fassett wheeled about and headed back to the first regiment he could find. Encountering Major Hildebrandt and the 39th New York, he told him to retake the battery. "By whose orders?" Hildebrandt countered. "By order of General Birney," Fassett yelled back. "I am in General Hancock's Corps," the major insisted. "Then I order you to take those guns, by order of General Hancock."[20]

Hildebrandt commanded his regiment to stand up, faced it about, and moved north. Crossing George Weikert's farm lane, he swung his regiment into line facing west and ordered his New Yorkers to charge; Peeples picked up a

---

17 [untitled article], George J. Leftwich, *The Aberdeen Examiner*, August 22, 1913, Brake Collection, USAHEC.

18 Ibid. It is evident from the witnesses that both Holder and Humphreys participated in the assault.

19 Beyer and Keydel, *Deeds of Valor*, vol. 1, 240-241.

20 Ibid., 241.

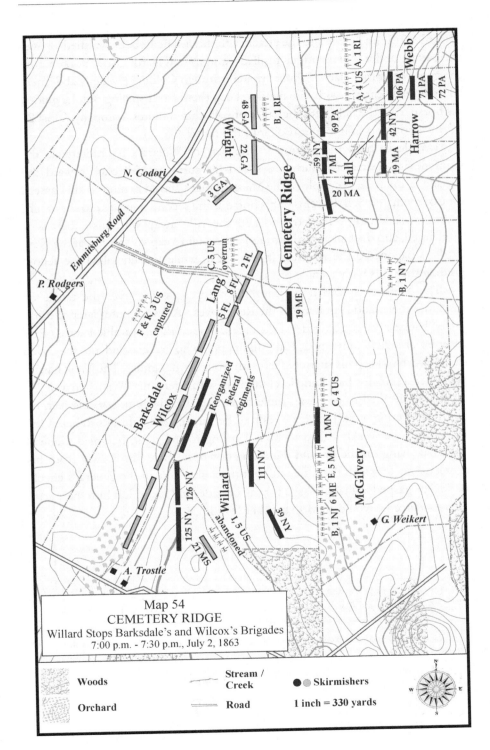

Map 54
CEMETERY RIDGE
Willard Stops Barksdale's and Wilcox's Brigades
7:00 p.m. - 7:30 p.m., July 2, 1863

Woods

Orchard

Stream / Creek

Road

Skirmishers

1 inch = 330 yards

discarded rifle and went into the attack with them. The Rebels swarmed all over the battery under a tremendous fusillade, and now Willard's New Yorkers tore the guts out of the attack. A bullet ripped through Colonel Holder's abdomen. Clutching his entrails with one hand to keep them from spilling out, he guided his horse from the field with the other one. Within minutes Company A lost 22 of the 41 officers and men it took into the fray.[21]

Unable to hold the ground in the face of Willard's counterattack, the Confederates retreated. Humphreys and his survivors fell back toward the Trostle farmhouse. A couple of the Mississippians stayed behind to kill Fassett. One of them grabbed the reins of his horse as the second one went to shoot him at point-blank range. Fassett knocked the rifle away with his saber as it discharged, and the ball passed through the captain's cap visor. One of the New Yorkers bayoneted the rifleman in the chest, while Fassett killed the fellow holding the reins with a single pistol shot.[22]

The Yankees spilled down into Plum Run, passing over the tangle of casualties there, and kept herding the Rebels west. A few minutes later, the line pulled back to the eastern side of the creek. One of them stumbled across Pvt. Joseph C. Lloyd (Company C, 13th Mississippi) who had crawled into the cover of the brush to keep his shattered left arm from further injury. The Yank hastily fashioned a sling for Lloyd and left him there with a genuine, "Wish you well."[23]

Lloyd decided to get away while he could. Weakly getting to his feet, he began staggering west. Just as he realized he was the only upright Rebel in the field, someone weakly called to him. Turning to the right, he spied General Barksdale lying on the ground. Kneeling down, he gave him a swig from his canteen only to watch the water roll out through a hole in the general's cheek. Barksdale gasped a final message for the brigade, and Lloyd left him there with the assurance he would send a stretcher for him.[24]

---

21 Ladd and Ladd, *The Bachelder Papers*, vol. 3, 1,869; Beyer and Keydel, *Deeds of Valor*, vol. 1, 240-241; Bacarella, *Lincoln's Foreign Legion*, 137-138; [untitled article], George J. Leftwich, *The Aberdeen Examiner*, August 22, 1913, USAHEC.

22 Ladd and Ladd, *The Bachelder Papers*, vol. 1, 481; Beyer and Keydel, *Deeds of Valor*, vol. 1, 241-242.

23 McNeily, *"Barksdale's Mississippi Brigade at Gettysburg,"* 239.

24 Ibid.

Walcott's Battery, V Corps Artillery Brigade,
Army of the Potomac
The John T. Weikert Farm

Throughout the entire action in the Wheatfield, 1st Lieutenant Walcott and his men in Battery C, 3rd Massachusetts, had suffered only half a dozen casualties from spent balls coming in from the southwest. And thus far, the Confederates had accidentally killed two horses and wounded four others. Unable to return effective fire through the smoke, Walcott had no real concept of what was happening anywhere around him.[25]

Suddenly, blue uniformed soldiers emerged from the sulfuric veil in front of his guns. He and his officers frantically waved their caps at the men to hurry them forward. First Lieutenant Page (Company I, 3rd U.S.) and his battalion commander, Capt. Henry W. Freedley, saw the artillerymen and broke into a run until they got stuck in the muck of Plum Run. At that moment, a minié ball slammed into Freedley's leg, hurled him into Page, and knocked the lieutenant flat upon his face into the marsh. Raising himself up, Page wiped the mud from his eyes in time to see the crews of Walcott's left section signaling with their caps for the infantry to stay down. As "Canister!" flashed through his mind, the lieutenant clawed with several enlisted men for the cover of a nearby boulder. The guns roared, and cast iron balls whistled around the rock, slaughtering a handful of Rebels who had just passed by it. The Rebs in the open ground near Plum Run broke and ran.[26]

The guns ceased firing and as the smoke cleared, Page limped toward a line of infantry in the distance, which he believed were wearing VI Corps badges. These troops' colonel, whom Page mistook for Col. William H. Penrose (15th New Jersey) intercepted him near the mouth of the farm lane and shook his hand. The lieutenant bolted up the farm lane for the woods. In the distance, he saw the head of the Pennsylvania Reserves running at the double-quick down the lane in column of fours.[27]

25 Parker, *22nd Massachusetts*, 313-314.

26 Powell, *The Fifth Corps*, 536.

27 Ibid., 536-537. Penrose was nowhere in the vicinity. If anything, the men he saw were from Wheaton's brigade of the VI Corps. In the fading light, it would have been difficult to identify them by their Corps badges.

Crawford's Pennsylvania Reserve division had moved to the gentle slope on the western side of the wooded ridge, surrendering the farm lane to the walking wounded and the ambulances. The column halted at the southern edge of the wood line immediately north of the J. Weikert house and shifted from column of fours into column of battalion. The two brigades found themselves standing in reverse order, the rear ranks facing west.[28]

Colonel Joseph W. Fisher's 2nd brigade stood in front with the 12th Reserves at the head of the column, followed respectively by the 5th, 9th, 10th, and 11th Reserves. From his post in front of the 12th Reserves, Col. Martin D. Hardin scanned the rolling ground to the west. The situation did not look good at all. A slow moving herd of retreating infantry blanketed the ground all the way to the ridge along the Emmitsburg Road. Abandoned guns, like rocks in a sluggish stream, occasionally broke the mass, which flowed around them. Every now and then, a stalwart would stand alone in their wake to snap off a defiant shot before running back to the mob.

Panicked troops unexpectedly burst from the woodlot bordering the Millerstown Road to the division's left front. Crawford, realizing he could not hold the low ground, ordered the regiments to turn around and retire to the security of the woods on the top of the ridge. The division marched to the eastern base of the hill, crawled over the rail fence along the face of the woods, right about faced, and lay down.

Hardin now spurred southeast toward Little Round Top to examine the situation there for himself. To the rear of the brigade Col. Adoniram J. Warner (10th Pennsylvania Reserves) remained mounted, painfully adjusting himself to his saddle. The nine-month old bullet wound in his right hip from Antietam, rather than healing, had putrefied and seeped pus incessantly. The pain made it nearly impossible for the colonel to ride, much less walk. He generally could not spur his horse beyond a walk, and he had two hefty canes strapped to his saddle so he could hobble along on the march.[29]

---

28 Nicholson, *Pennsylvania at Gettysburg*, vol. 1, 278.

29 Ibid., 279, 282; Col. Adoniram Warner narrative, "Save the Flags" Collection, USAHEC. First Lieutenant Hannibal K. Sloan (B, 11th Pennsylvania Reserves) said that the 12th led the column, followed by the 5th, 10th, and 11th with no reference to the 9th, which he accidentally omitted in his account. The 9th must have been in the center of the column because the 12th and the 5th deployed together at Little Round Top, and the 9th and the 10th went into battle beside each other at the hill. The 10th being in front of the 11th, and the 5th behind the 12th,

The regiments had hardly settled down when one of Sykes' staff officers galloped up to Colonel Fisher and ordered him to send his brigade to Little Round Top. He told the 12th Reserves to stand up, face right, and countermarch to the right to put it in a proper battle formation. The 5th, 9th, and 10th Reserves quickly followed.

"Shoulder arms, right face," Col. Samuel M. Jackson (11th Reserves) shouted above the din. But before he could execute the march, Maj. James P. Speer, the division inspector general, galloped up to him. "General Crawford directs that you remain in position and hold this hill at all hazards," he told him. Exchanging salutes, Jackson immediately bellowed, "Front; forward march!" The 11th left faced and started toward the crest of the hill. As the left of the regiment came up behind Walcott's right section, the anxious lieutenant—whom Jackson mistook as from Gibbs's Battery L, 1st Ohio—sprinted up to him and blurted something about having to limber his guns to save them. Jackson calmly advised him to "double-shot" his guns, and his boys would protect them from capture. "Stand by your guns, Dutchy!" a nearby enlisted man cried out, "and we will stand by you." And Walcott returned to his battery.[30]

Meanwhile Colonel McCandless deployed his brigade from column of regiments. The 6th Reserves countermarched to the left, fronted, and moved into line on the right rear of the 11th along a stone wall at the base of the hill. The 1st Reserves countermarched to the right and maneuvered into position along the same stone wall on the 11th's left rear. As the 1st Reserves went to cover not 60 feet behind Walcott's center section, the nervous lieutenant approached the men and pleaded, "Dunder and blixen, don't let dem repels took my batteries." Private Henry N. Minnigh (Company K) laughed it off. The 2nd Reserves followed suit to the left of the 1st, leaving the 13th the last to countermarch to the south.[31]

---

the 9th had to have occupied the center of the column. Sloan also said that the brigade marched "back onto the hill close to the artillery on the top of the hill."

30 Nicholson, *Pennsylvania at Gettysburg*, vol. 1, 258-259.

31 Ibid., 279, 301; OR 27, pt. 1, 657; H. N. Minnigh, *History of Company K, 1st (Inft.) Penna. Reserves* (Duncansville, 1891), 26, quoted. Based on Colonel Jackson's account, the First Brigade (McCandless') lay at the base of the hill behind him. First Lieutenant John P. Bard (K, 13th Reserves) said the 13th Reserves countermarched to put it on line in the correct formation. It is safe to assume the other regiments maneuvered likewise.

Col. Samuel M. Jackson
11th Pennsylvania Reserves
*Kavin Coughenour Collection
Library, GNMP*

Wofford's Brigade,
Longstreet's Corps,
Army of Northern Virginia
The Wheatfield

Part way through the Wheatfield, Adjutant Shallenberger's two assistants turned him over to another pair of volunteers from the 140th Pennsylvania. By the time they reached the northwestern side of the Wheatfield, he realized that he slowed them down too much, making capture almost inevitable. Nevertheless, they dragged him through the woods beyond the Millerstown Road to the stone wall on the far side. After passing over the wall, he told them to leave him at the log cabin northwest of the John T. Weikert house. But the two Company H volunteers refused. Presently, Confederates from the Phillips' Legion burst in to "bag" the three Yankees. To Shallenberger's amazement, instead of mistreating them, the Rebs freely expressed their frustration with the war.[32]

First Lieutenant Purman and orderly Sergeant James M. Pipes (both Company A, 140th Pennsylvania) ran as fast as they could to the southeast corner of the Wheatfield. They plopped their butts on a boulder to regain their composure. Shooting a hurried glance into the woods, Purman spied a large body of Rebels crashing through the trees. Turning to the sergeant, he blurted, "We must get out of this or we'll be gobbled up." "Yes," Pipes gasped.[33]

A short distance beyond, they happened upon Pvt. John Buckley (Company B) shot through both legs. "Comrades, carry me off," he pleaded.

32 Stewart, *140th Pennsylvania*, 422-423.

33 Ibid., 425.

The lieutenant, not recognizing Buckley, shouted back, "We can't do that. I doubt if we can get away ourselves, but we'll do the best we can for you." Lifting him, they hauled him in between two large rocks and put him down. Shaking his hand, Purman said, "Good-bye, comrade."[34]

From behind, he heard, "Halt, you damned Yankee, halt!" Purman did not; he took off at a dead run, figuring the Rebs could not hit him. But a minié ball drilled through his left leg, smashing the bones four inches above the ankle. The jolt sent the sword in his right hand flying and brought him down with a thud. "I am struck," he cried. Pipes was a few rods ahead, but before he could respond, a bullet also struck his leg. Pipes tried to keep going using a discarded rifle as a crutch, but the Rebels easily overtook him.

In all of the noise, Pvt. Henry Meyer (Company B, 148th Pennsylvania did not leave with his comrades. As an unexpected silence fell over the ground behind him, he glanced about and found himself alone, facing a Confederate battle line, crashing through the woods. Meyer thought with his feet, running back to the protection of the stone wall on the east side of the Wheatfield, where to his dismay, he found Pvt. Jacob Lanich dead, with a bullet wound through his head from ear to ear. Sergeant George W. Leitzell, nearby with a bullet lodged in his knee, asked Meyer to help him get away. Meyer got the man to his feet only to find himself too exhausted to take him anywhere. He lowered Leitzell to the ground and swapped his full canteen for the sergeant's empty one.

A staff officer from General Crawford intercepted the stray Company G from the 148th Pennsylvania as the men reached the eastern side of Plum Run northwest of the John Weikert house. Leading them to the stone wall on the opposite side of the Weikert Woods north of the Millerstown Road, he marched them south and placed them on the left of his Pennsylvania Reserves. What remained of the Irish Brigade had fallen in to its left rear.[35]

The 24th Georgia trampled over 1st Lieutenant Purman, their colors passing right around him. With the Rebels to his front, Purman sat upright in the destroyed wheat to examine his shattered leg. His sword, the point imbedded in the ground, swayed from side to side a few feet away as he sat there shuddering in pain. Farther northwest, Lieutenant Fuller (4th Company, 61st New York suddenly realized that a Confederate skirmish line led by a mounted

34 Ibid.

35 Muffly, *148th Pennsylvania*, 538.

officer was loping past him. Presently, scattered rifle shots echoed over him from the north, and the Rebels came back. A small one with a powder stained face stopped to pick up Fuller's sword, which lay by his side. "Give me that scabbard," he demanded. "Johnny," Fuller winced, "you will have to excuse me, as my arm is broken and I can't unbuckle my belt." The Reb silently moved off with the sword.[36]

From the crest of the ridge, Colonel Jackson (11th Reserves) peered into the smoke- blanketed hollow in front of him, vainly trying to distinguish fleeing Yankees from pursuing Rebels. His regiment lay among the trees and brush in front of him anxiously waiting for someone to do something. Refugees from the Wheatfield stumbled over his prone line. Stray bullets occasionally took men out of the ranks, and here and there, men dragged the wounded and the dead away. At the base of the hill, Jackson noticed what appeared to be a column of men milling about. Unable to tell friend from foe, he stopped two stragglers before they could brush by him and asked, "How many of our people are down there?" "Not one," they replied. "Those people you see coming up the hill," one said matter-of-factly, "are 'Johnnies'." "Fire!" Jackson bellowed. Flame slashed through the trees, and the acrid smell of burned powder enveloped the Pennsylvanians.[37]

With the roar of the volley barely gone, Crawford, whom Walcott mistook to be Brig. Gen. Charles Griffin, galloped up to him: "Get that battery out of here. You can't live in that place five minutes." Walcott reacted immediately. With Wofford's Georgians springing over the stone wall along the eastern side of the Wheatfield and rushing his position, he screamed for his men to spike the guns. They managed to disable one piece before the Rebs got too close.[38]

Company H, covering the 32nd Massachusetts' retreat only a few paces ahead of the Georgians, ran by Battery C as the gunners frantically dragged off the limbers and caissons to escape capture. On the ridge along the J. Weikert farm lane, Corporal West spied the brigade flag atop the hill, and to the south, the Confederates swarming over the stone wall. "Left face, and every man get

---

36 Stewart, *140th Pennsylvania*, 109, 423; Fuller, *Personal Recollections*, 96, quoted.

37 Nicholson, *Pennsylvania at Gettysburg*, vol. 1, 279, 283.

38 Parker, *22nd Massachusetts*, 313-314, quote on 313. Griffin did not arrive on the field until July 3 and did not assume command of Barnes' Division of the V Corps until July 4. I assume the general officer whom Walcott saw was Samuel Crawford: his division was the closest supporting body of troops near the battery.

out of this the best way he can," came the order from the company commander. As the tallest corporal in Company H and, therefore, on the right of the skirmishers, West became the last man in the regiment to escape. With the Rebels, practically on his heels and bullets zinging past his ears, he bolted across the marshy creek bottom of Plum Run. At the woodlot east of the J. Weikert farm lane, the 13th Pennsylvania Reserves opened ranks to let him rush through.[39]

The Confederates in the vicinity of the Devil's Den, having gained the higher ground to the left of U.S. Regular brigade, turned its flank and broke it. The 14th U.S. Regulars scattered back toward Crawford's prone line. The Confederate fire followed them, and a number of the rounds ploughed into the 13th Pennsylvania Reserves while it countermarched into position along the rail fence at the base of Weikert's ridge. This threw the ranks into some confusion and wounded several men. A minié ball glanced across Capt. Hugh McDonald's skull, laid open his scalp, and knocked him cold. Another struck the color sergeant of the 1st Reserves in the hand. He handed the flag over to a color corporal from Company G and walked away.

Captain Frank J. Bell (Company I, 13th Pennsylvania Reserves) stared intently at the rise of ground to his immediate front and one of Walcott's abandoned Napoleons. A moment after the Wheatfield's refugees had cleared the 13th, a lone Rebel popped into view. Grasping the muzzle of the piece with both hands, he screeched over his shoulder for his comrades to come help him turn the gun on the Yankees. Bell's blood was up: leaping to his feet, he drew his revolver and emptied it at the man. At this point Captain Hillyer, with the color guard of the 9th Georgia, had reached the guns. Private James J. Meade (Company B) used a cannon tube for a bench rest and squeezed a round off at one of Gibbs's battery men on the northern crest of Little Round Top. Hillyer studied the western slope of the hill. The 155th Pennsylvania lying among the rocks below the section caught his attention, as did Hazlett's battery farther to the south. Hastily glancing right and left, he spied lots of Confederate battle flags but only squads of men gathered about them. The veterans around him could also see the situation, and they were quickly melting away back toward the Stony Hill.[40]

39 West, "On Little Round Top," *National Tribune*, November 22, 1906.

40 Bell, "The Bucktails at Gettysburg," GNMP; Hillyer, "Battle of Gettysburg," 9.

To the right, Pvt. Henry C. McCauley (Company B, 1st Pennsylvania Reserves) stared in horror as the Confederates succeeded in turning a section of Walcott's battery upon his regiment. But well-placed rifle fire from the Pennsylvanians cleared the Confederates from the pieces. A portion of the 2nd South Carolina only got as far as the stone wall along the eastern side of the Wheatfield. "Here the bullets literally came down upon us as thick as hailstones." Lieutenant Colonel Gaillard (2nd South Carolina) later wrote home. General Wofford abruptly halted the men around him, and seemingly oblivious to the lead zipping about him, calmly studied the ground in front of him through his field glasses.[41]

Private John Coxe (Company B, 2nd South Carolina) was capping his rifle when a bullet ripped open his right jacket sleeve from the wrist to the elbow: he was jarred but not hurt. Artillery rounds from Hazlett's battery soared harmlessly overhead. "It is scarcely necessary to say we fell back," Gaillard told his family after the battle. Without support and facing tremendous odds, Wofford called off the attack.[42]

At the center of the 11th Reserves, from the top of the ridge north of J. Weikert's, Colonel Jackson stood in the stirrups and hollered, "Fix bayonets!" The men stood up. Steel clanked menacingly against steel through the standing ranks in front of him. "Charge!" Screams rent the air above the din as the Pennsylvanians plunged down the hill. They smashed into the center of the Confederate line before it had a chance to recover from the volley, and Crawford wasted no time exploiting the situation. Waving his hat above his head, he raced his horse from one end of McCandless' 1st brigade to the other, exhorting his steady veterans. "Up, boys, and at them," Col. Charles F. Taylor shouted at his 13th Pennsylvania Reserves. They opened fire with their breech-loading Sharps rifles at the ridge to their front and into the woods and eastern end of the Wheatfield. For several minutes, which to some witnesses seemed like 30, they blanketed the creek bottom with musketry. Soon enough,

41 Henry C. McCauley to Father, July 31, 1863, GNMP; Gaillard, "Franklin Gaillard's Civil War Letters," 36, quoted, GNMP; John Coxe, "The Battle of Gettysburg," in *Confederate Veteran*, vol. 21, 435. The traditional interpretation has the Confederates getting into Battery L, 1st Ohio, at Little Round Top. I found no evidence to support that story.

42 John Coxe, "The Battle of Gettysburg," in *Confederate Veteran*, vol. 21, 435; Gaillard, *Franklin Gaillard's Civil War Letters*, 36.

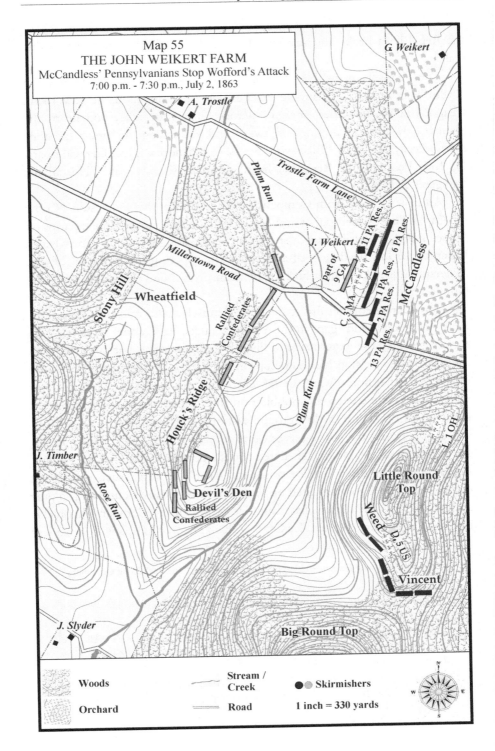

Map 55
THE JOHN WEIKERT FARM
McCandless' Pennsylvanians Stop Wofford's Attack
7:00 p.m. - 7:30 p.m., July 2, 1863

the Rebel lines broke and scattered for the cover of the Wheatfield's stone wall.[43]

The Pennsylvanians' bloodcurdling screams startled Captain Donaldson (118th Pennsylvania). Snapping his head in their direction, he saw them, weapons at the shoulder, charging across Plum Run valley and heard the distinct, rhythmic snapping of twigs and crunching of brush as they methodically advanced. "Black your boots!" Sgt. Andrew J. Deming (Company D, 13th Pennsylvania Reserves) heard his men scream. And "Hurrah for Lanigan's Ball!"[44]

An enlisted man from Company H sprang to Captain Bell's side. "Come on, Cap, I'll beat you into that timber," he said, pointing toward the treetops on Houck's Ridge. Bell bolted over the rail fence along the 13th Pennsylvania Reserves' front heading pell-mell into the open ground south of the Millerstown Road. A bullet hit Lt. Col. Alanson E. Niles in the hip, knocking him down.[45]

Confederate counter fire stymied the Pennsylvanians midway through the field, punching bloody gaps in the Yankees' ranks. As Colonel Jackson's 11th Reserves neared the eastern side of Plum Run, he suddenly became aware that the rest of the division had come up on his flanks. Screams from the south directed his attention toward the far left of the line, where the 13th Reserves with the distinctive deer tails bobbing on their kepis, raced madly across the Millerstown Road into the low ground east of the Wheatfield.[46]

To the north, the 6th Reserves came abreast of the 11th and in so doing, swept past the log cabin that sheltered about a dozen members of the Phillips' Legion and their three Yankee prisoners. Unable to resist such a target of opportunity, the Georgians fired upon the Pennsylvanians' right flank, sniping at the regiment's file closers. Sergeant George W. Mears (Company A) quickly informed right wing commander Capt. William Dixon (Company D) what was

---

43 Vox Populi to the *Daily Evening Express*, July 8, 1863; Bell, "The Bucktails at Gettysburg," both in GNMP.

44 Aiken, *Inside the Army of the Potomac*, 305; A. J. Deming, "Bucktails at Gettysburg," *National Tribune*, February 4, 1886, quoted.

45 Bell, "The Bucktails at Gettysburg," GNMP, quoted; Howard Thompson and William H. Rauch, *History of the "Bucktails," Kane Rifle Regiment of the Pennsylvania Reserve Corps (13th Pennsylvania Reserves), 42nd of the Line* (Dayton, 1988), 267.

46 "Vox Populi" to the *Daily Evening Express*, July 8, 1863, GNMP; Bell, "The Bucktails at Gettysburg," GNMP; Nicholson, *Pennsylvania at Gettysburg*, vol. 1, 279.

happening. Unable to spare a company, he ordered Mears to get a detail together and take care of the problem. Mears called for volunteers from among the file closers. Corporal Chester S. Furman and Sgt. John W. Hart from his own company peeled away from the regiment, as did Sgt. Wallace W. Johnson (Company G), Cpl. J. Levi Roush (Company D), and Cpl. Thaddeus S. Smith (Company E).

Braving pot shots, the little squad charged the door of the cabin. Tearing the barricades out, they burst inside, capturing the startled Confederates and in the process, rescuing adjutant Shallenberger and his two loyal rescuers from the 140th Pennsylvania. When Mears and his stalwarts returned to the regiment, Captain Dixon detached one of the men to the rear with the prisoners and ordered the others back into the ranks.[47]

Crawford, heedless of his own safety, dashed his horse over to the center of the 1st Reserves and tried to snatch the furled colors from the color bearer, Cpl. George K. Swope, who refused to release them. The general curtly reminded the enlisted man of his rank at which Swope released his grip on the staff but latched onto the general's pant leg. Unrolling the banner in the heavy smoke, Crawford spurred his horse to the left, dragging the corporal along. Swope wanted the flag back. All the while, Crawford screamed, "Forward Reserves!" As he cleared their fronts, the 1st and 2nd Reserves volleyed across the open ground. By the time he got to the end of the division, they had loosed another volley and surged forward with a cheer.[48]

Captain Bell (13th Pennsylvania Reserves), on the far left of the division line, having nabbed some disgruntled Rebs and sent them to the rear, suddenly noticed that everyone to his right had stopped at the edge of Plum Run. Glancing north, he saw Crawford, draped in the colors of the 1st Reserves, racing on horseback along the front of the stalled charge, frantically yelling at them to get moving. Believing a handful of the 13th Pennsylvania Reserves "Bucktails" could hold the woods against superior numbers, the captain bolted forward an enlisted man by his side. The regiment broke by squads to the front,

47 Stewart, *140th Pennsylvania*, 423; Arrington, *The Medal of Honor at Gettysburg*, 16-17; William D. Dixon to the Secretary of War, December 22, 1896, Vertical Files, GNMP.

48 William J. Cake to Philip J. Raw, August 30, 1892, Vertical Files, GNMP; Thompson and Rauch, *History of the "Bucktails,"* 266; W. Crawford to Peter F. Rothermel, March 8, 1871, Rothermel Papers, Pennsylvania State Archives; R. Dobson to W. Crawford, June 16, 1882, Crawford Papers, LC. This story comes from several sources. I used Crawford's earliest account that credits Swope with handing him the flag.

with men taking cover in the boulder-strewn valley to return fire against the Rebels at the Devil's Den. Through the dense, asphyxiating sulfuric pall blanketing the valley, the captain spied Smith's abandoned Parrotts among the rocks on the northern end of the Den.

An electric shock seemed to jolt Crawford's division forward. Cheers reverberated along the line into a swelling crescendo as the Yankees plowed through the swamp, heading toward the stone wall on the knoll. As the 1st Reserves neared the crest of the hill, the panting Corporal Swope persuaded Crawford to hand back the colors.[49] The general spurred to the center of the 11th Reserves, whom he found in the trees on the Plum Run side of the Wheatfield. Finding Jackson behind his men, Crawford jubilantly congratulated him. "Colonel Jackson," Crawford cried out, "you have saved the day. Your regiment is worth its weight in gold, worth its weight in gold, sir! Worth its weight in gold! Worth its weight in gold, sir!" The general ordered Jackson to post his line along the wall and dig in.[50]

Private Meyer (Company B, 148th Pennsylvania), hoping to find his own regiment fell in with the 13th and went back into the fight. The Pennsylvanians cleared the wall, and Companies C, I, and D of the 148th Pennsylvania stood up and retired toward Little Round Top.[51]

Walcott's artillerymen returned to their guns with the limbers and retired the pieces by prolonge. Farther to the left, the Pennsylvanians stumbled over the severely wounded Lieutenant Purman (140th Pennsylvania). Sitting up in the wheat, he loudly demanded, "Come and cut my boot off my foot." The enlisted man knelt down, but the dull knife he used to try and cut through the thick leather only heightened Purman's pain; he told the man to stop.[52]

The Pennsylvanians lay down in the thin woodlot immediately west of the stone wall. Sergeant John A. Burns (Company A, 140th Pennsylvania) collapsed from exhaustion several feet in front of the Reserves, too exhausted, he thought, to go any farther. Lying there gasping on the ground, he quickly regained his composure. Spurred on by Confederate shots plowing up the

---

49 "Vox Populi" to the *Daily Evening Express*, July 8, 1863, and Bell, "The Bucktails at Gettysburg" both GNMP; Sauers, *Advance the Colors*, vol. 1, 85-86.

50 Nicholson, *Pennsylvania at Gettysburg*, vol. 1, 279, 283.

51 Muffly, *148th Pennsylvania*, 537-538, 604.

52 Parker, *22nd Massachusetts*, 314; Stewart, *140th Pennsylvania*, 423, quoted.

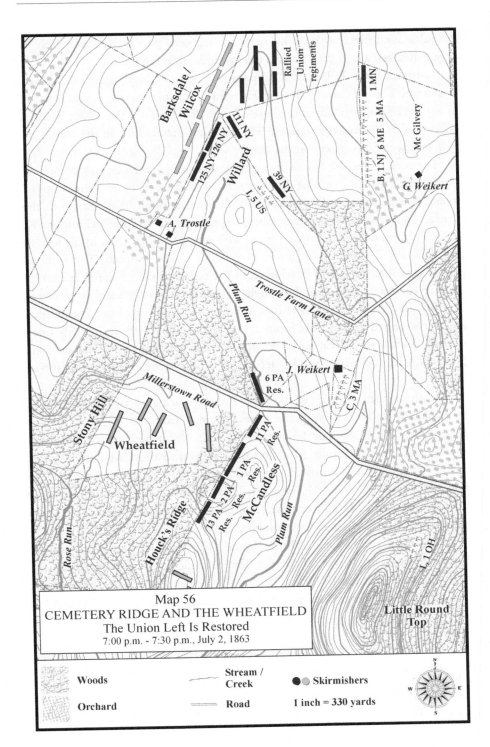

Map 56
CEMETERY RIDGE AND THE WHEATFIELD
The Union Left Is Restored
7:00 p.m. - 7:30 p.m., July 2, 1863

ground around him, he got to his feet and staggered past the Reserves only to drop exhausted again, face first, to the ground behind them.

Corporal Jesse T. Power (Company E, 140th Pennsylvania) had already passed well beyond Crawford's line. He temporarily planted the regimental flag on the left of his regiment at the base of Little Round Top. The 140th had lost 241 out of 515 effectives engaged. The 5th New Hampshire, in the woods on their southern flank, also quit the field.[53]

The men of the 4th Michigan were the last troops in Sweitzer's command to retire, and they had no idea the Pennsylvanians were there until they popped up and blasted the Rebels behind the Wolverines at point-blank range. As the Confederates recoiled from the volley, Capt. James B. McLean (Company K, 4th Michigan), who was limping along with wounds to his chin, in his left leg and heel, asked Private Houghton to get him to the hospital. The stunned private gaped at the blood flowing from the captain's chin wound. It trickled quite freely in a bright red trail through his long beard, completely saturating it. The private promised to assist him any way he could. McLean complained about his sword hurting his injured leg when it clattered against his open wound. Taking all the captain's accoutrements including his sword and belt, Houghton let McLean place his left hand on his right shoulder to support himself.[54]

The rout stunned Caldwell. With the Rebels pouring across the Wheatfield, he could do nothing to stop the retreating men from his brigades. Having returned to the field after hurrying Maj. Gen. John Sedgwick's VI Corps forward, Lieutenant Colonel Morgan found himself surrounded by the flotsam of the fighting in the Wheatfield. Caldwell's soldiers streamed from the place in horrible disarray. Colonel Morris (66th New York) brushed by him, his tunic thrown open and blood streaming from a chest wound. Nearby, he spied Colonel Brooke limping about, searching for his brigade.[55]

Crossing to the east side of Little Round Top, Corporal West (Company H) happened upon what was left of the 32nd Massachusetts. Judging from the sparse line, he estimated its losses at around 50 percent. He rejoined the ranks as Col. Patrick Guiney marched the 9th Massachusetts toward the southern end of

---

53 Stewart, *140th Pennsylvania*, 106, 108-109; Child, *5th New Hampshire*, 207.

54 Houghton Journal, 14, UMI.

55 *OR* 27, pt. 1, 379-80; Ladd and Ladd, *The Bachelder Papers*, vol. 3, 1,355.

the hill. Reining his horse up behind the 32nd Massachusetts, Guiney cut loose with a blasphemous tirade. The brigade had gone in without him, he raged. He said would lead the regiment forward personally but he did nothing, except continue on into the low ground between the two Round Tops.[56]

Captain Bell's Squad, 13th Pennsylvania Reserves,
V Corps, Army of the Potomac
The Woods on Houck's Ridge

Captain Bell and his tired squad from Company H reached the woods a few yards from the southern end of the stone wall without the rest of the regiment, which had gotten widely strung out during the charge. There they halted among the smoke wreathed trees to catch their breaths and wait for reinforcements.[57] To the right Capt. Neri B. Kinsey had his Company C lie down behind the stone wall. Incoming shots from the left rear still buzzed into his position. He refused his line to respond and to keep the Rebs under cover at the Devil's Den.

The 15th Georgia, along the northern crest of the Den, had run dangerously low on ammunition. Every available officer, armed with knives, left their companies to cut cartridge boxes from the dead, dying, and disabled. From his place on the top of the hill overlooking Plum Run, Private Fluker (Company D, 15th Georgia) ruefully noted, "The sun looked bigger and redder to me than I had ever seen it, and I watched to see if it was going down any, but it seemed to be hung up like it did for old General Joshua at the time of his famous battle at Gibeon."[58]

Lieutenant John E. Kratzer (Company K, 13th Pennsylvania Reserves), having hung close to Colonel Taylor, hustled into Kinsey's position from the open field behind him. The colonel, he panted, had sent him over to find out where Kinsey was and what he was doing. The exasperated Kinsey testily yelled back that he was doing the obvious and that if Colonel Taylor would allow Kratzer's Company K to reinforce him, he believed he could roust the Rebels out of the rocks at the base of the hill. Kratzer darted back into the field. A shell screamed low overhead. "Captain, that means us," one of his frightened men

---

56 West, "On Little Round Top," *National Tribune*, November 22, 1906.

57 Bell, "*The Bucktails at Gettysburg,*" GNMP.

58 Willingham, *No Jubilee*, 36.

yelled. "No." Kinsey retorted, "That is one of our own shells, and is meant for those fellows in the rocks."[59]

A second later, a shell crashed into the wall, killing an enlisted man in Company I and hurling deadly rock shards everywhere. The shot wounded at least seven men. It ripped the arm off a boy in Company B who leapt to his feet, screaming hysterically: "I won't die! I won't die!" as he wildly ran in a tight circle. His bleeding stump sprayed blood over everyone around him. Suddenly he fell to ground, stone dead. Kinsey then realized he had also been injured. Stone fragments had wounded his right arm, lacerated his left wrist and mangled the fingers on his left hand. Bleeding profusely, he headed back toward Little Round Top.[60]

Kratzer brought Company K into the line along the stone wall along with a baker's dozen of stragglers from several other companies. They had barely gone to ground when the Rebels peppered their line with musketry from the left. Captain Samuel A. Mack (Company E) "volunteered" a couple of nearby enlisted men from Company G, Cpl. Elijah S. Brookins and Pvt. Abraham S. Davis, to follow him into the woods to the south to investigate. Passing unseen behind Bell and his handful of stalwarts, the three pushed to the left front and stumbled into a much larger Confederate line. Mack and Brookins quickly sheltered behind some trees; Davis dashed behind a large rock. The ever-present Lieutenant Kratzer with Pvt. Ellis J. Hall (Company K) quickly joined them. The five men agreed it would be decidedly insane to take on the much larger Rebel force.[61]

By then the dismounted Colonel Taylor had come up on his right with Bell's squad and a detachment from Company I under 1st Lt. R. Fenton Ward. "Why don't you fire?" the colonel rasped from his parched throat. Kratzer told him they did not have enough men to make an assault. Taylor's mouth was so dry he could not issue a command. Bell climbed up onto the large rock immediately in front of the colonel to get a better look at the terrain. As he did so, the colonel pulled Bell's canteen off his back and took a long, blessed drink.

Rebels were working their way through the woods on their left, not 50 yards away. Kratzer and many of his men yelled at the colonel to take cover, but

---

59 Thompson and Rauch, *"History of the Bucktails,"* 268.

60 Ibid.

61 Ibid., 267-268.

he ignored them. He and Bell spied the Rebels at the same time. "By the left flank, march," the colonel yelled. Bell, standing on the rock to his front repeated the command, "By the left flank, march." Corporal Brookins aimed his rifle and tried to bring down the Reb he saw drawing a bead on Taylor. The cap snapped, but the weapon did not fire.[62]

As Bell jumped to the ground, a bullet zipped past him and cut the colonel down. Taylor collapsed into Kratzer's arms. The lieutenant laid him down as Cpl. Aaron Baker (Company H) came to help. It was a chest wound, Taylor gasped; could he have some water? He swallowed from the corporal's canteen and instantly blood trickled from his mouth. He began muttering. Baker could only make out, "Mum. Mum." He died in the corporal's arms.[63]

Kratzer, Baker, Ward, and Hall, with 1st Lt. George A. Ludlow (Company E), who had just joined the stray squads, picked up Taylor's limp corpse and struggled toward the rear with it. When the colonel's head dropped back, Brookins quickly lifted it parallel with the ground while Private Davis and Captain Mack provided cover fire. They had barely started when the same Reb who killed the colonel shot Davis. He screamed for them to leave him and continue on with the colonel. So they left him there and continued toward the stone wall.[64]

Meanwhile, Bell surged ahead with his screaming men trailing out behind him on both sides. A volley crashed through the trees showering branches, leaves, and twigs down upon the Yankees. Bark flew in their faces. A couple of the Pennsylvanians hit the ground wounded. Common sense soon overtook enthusiasm. Without orders, the enlisted men instinctively snatched up their wounded and lugged them toward the eastern side of the Wheatfield. With their left on the end of the stone wall, their line just inside the wood line, the Pennsylvanians turned about and lay down for a long evening. In the encroaching darkness, Lieutenant Kratzer and his comrades stole back into the woods and retrieved the dying Private Davis without receiving any hostile fire.[65]

62 Bell, "The Bucktails at Gettysburg," GNMP.

63 Ibid.; Aaron Baker to Annie Taylor, July 11, 1863, *The Pennsylvania Magazine of History and Biography,* July 1973, 360-361, Vertical Files, GNMP.

64 Thompson and Rauch, *History of the "Bucktails,"* 269-270.

65 Bell, "The Bucktails at Gettysburg," GNMP; Thompson and Rauch, *History of the "Bucktails,"* 270.

Col. Clinton D. MacDougall
111th New York
*MOLLUS Collection
Library,* GNMP

Willard's Brigade, II Corps, Army
of the Potomac
In the Swale North of the Trostle
House

Willard's two center regiments, the 125th and 126th New
York, advanced firing. The
rock-strewn, marshy creek bottom, however, cost them unit
cohesion. Color Sergeant Erasmus E. Bassett (Company B,
126th New York), revolver in one hand and the regimental colors in the other,
advanced about five yards ahead of the center of the line, waving his flag to urge
the men forward. As he stepped into the creek bottom, a bullet hit him in the
leg. His older brother, Lt. Richard A. Bassett (Company B), in the front rank of
the company on the far right, noticed the flag dip and then continue forward
through the thick veil of smoke in the hollow. A few feet farther on, the colors
went down. Sergeant Byron W. Scott (Company E), immediately aimed his
weapon and fired a round at the Reb he thought had killed Bassett. Sergeant
Ambrose Bedell (Company E), despite a bullet wound through his hand, pulled
the staff from Bassett's death grasp and raised the flag again, leaving the former
school teacher where he lay, a bullet through his heart.[66]

Farther right, the 111th New York ran into a snag. Rather than mess up
their formation by plowing into the creek, Col. Clinton MacDougall
maneuvered the regiment from line into column of fours so the men could
cross the narrow corduroy bridge across the ditch in front of them. The New
Yorkers hurried across the bridge under a murderous fire of canister and case
shot, and a lot of men died in the process. Color Sergeant Judson Hicks
(Company A) died instantly with two bullets through his body and one through

---

66 Wayne Mahood, *Written in Blood* (Highstown, 1997), 131; Murray, *The Redemption of the
"Harper's Ferry Cowards,"* 78.

his skull, but Cpl. Payson Derby (Company G) instantly raised the flag again and continued forward. Lieutenant Augustus Proseus (Company E) shouted at his men, "Stand firm[!] Don't yield an inch!" A minié ball killed him as the last word left his mouth. Once over to the other side, the men deployed into line again only to catch flank fire from Barksdale's and Wilcox's line on their unprotected right. The slightly wounded MacDougall, having pried himself from his dead horse, ordered the regiment into the ditch behind them, where they hunkered down to return fire.[67]

The 19th Maine, II Corps,
Army of the Potomac
Cemetery Ridge, Southeast of the Codori Buildings

The stalled Floridians stood their ground about 50 yards from the 19th Maine and slugged it out, volley for volley, with men on both sides dropping regularly. A minute or two into the volleying, Capt. Isaac Starbird (Company F) dashed to Colonel Heath with news that the Rebs had gotten terribly close to his company. Heath followed Starbird back to his line. Squinting through the smoke, he spotted what appeared to be a Confederate regiment in double column about 25 yards off preparing to maneuver into battle line. Obviously once deployed the Rebels would overlap the 19th Maine's left wing, so he ordered Starbird to refuse his company at right angles to the rest of the regiment to enfilade them.

As the colonel returned to his post behind the colors at the center of the regiment, Starbird yelled at his men to cease fire, and his veterans instinctively went to "shoulder arms." The captain marched it 35 yards to the rear and took up a new firing line. The maneuver temporarily uncovered the right flank of Thomas' Battery C, 4th U.S. Artillery. The lieutenant quickly silenced his pieces, rolled them back to conform to Company F's new line, and opened fire again.[68]

---

67 N. Eldred, "Only a Boy: A first-hand account of the Civil War," Stewart B. Lang Memorial Library, Cato, NY, n.d., quoted; Murray, *The Redemption of the "Harper's Ferry Cowards,"* 79-80.

68 Silas Adams, "The Nineteenth Maine at Gettysburg," in *War Papers, Read Before the Commandery of the State of Maine, Military Order of the Loyal Legion of the United States,* 4 vols. (Portland, 1915), vol. 4, 254; Ladd and Ladd, *The Bachelder Papers,* vol. 3, 1,652; Executive Committee, *Maine at Gettysburg,* 293.

The 1st Minnesota
On Cemetery Ridge
About 350 yards southeast of the 19th Maine

Hancock, riding north with his staff from the George Weikert farm, noticed the same regiment which had attracted Starbird's attention. At first, he dismissed them as a Federal unit, but an unexpected burst of small arms fire from that direction, however, abruptly changed his mind. One of his staffers, Capt. William D. W. Miller, jerked under the impact of two hits. Twisting about in the saddle, Hancock saw the 1st Minnesota drawn up in column of fours. Spotting an officer mounted upon a splendid black horse, he galloped to Lt. Col. Charles P. Adams. "Colonel, do you see that flag?" Adams followed the general's pointing finger toward the overgrown low ground in the distance. "I want you to take it." "Yes, sir," Adams replied.[69]

Adams called the regiment into formation and was about to lead it forward when Col. William Colvill, Jr. unexpectedly rode up to him. Having been under arrest since June 29, for crossing a river on logs rather than fording as ordered, Colvill explained that he had been released from arrest and was assuming command.

"Boys, will you go along with them?" the colonel shouted. A resounding "Yes" from the ranks answered him. The field officers positioned their mounts behind the line: Colonel Colvill 30 paces behind the colors, Lieutenant Colonel Adams 12 paces behind the center of the right wing, and Maj. Mark Downie 12 paces behind the center of the left wing. "Forward, double-quick!" the colonel bellowed.[70]

The veterans automatically stepped off, smartly bringing their weapons to "right shoulder shift" in "one time and two motions corresponding to the steps of the advance," Colvill later recollected. The glint of the musket barrels moving in unison awed the colonel. Thirty yards across the field, they walked into a sheet of lead from the Confederate skirmishers hidden in the dried up creek about 170 yards west of the regiment. Men began dropping, but the

---

69 Ladd and Ladd, *The Bachelder Papers*, vol. 3, 1,358; W. K. Adams to the Editor of the *Journal*, n.d., Charles Powell Adams Papers, Minnesota Historical Society, St. Paul, Minnesota.

70 G. Sydney Smith to C. Powell Adams, November 25, 1887, Charles Powell Adams Papers, Minnesota Historical Society, St. Paul, quoted; Moe, *The Last Full Measure*, 262.

companies surged onward toward the shallow ravine about 100 yards south of the 19th Maine.[71]

13th Vermont, I Corps, Army of the Potomac
About 200 Yards to the Right Rear of the 19th Maine

Colonel Francis V. Randall (13th Vermont) saw Hancock and rode to him. "Colonel, where is your regiment?" Hancock spat, "Close at hand." "Good," Hancock replied, "the enemy are pressing me hard. They have captured that battery yonder and are dragging it from the field. Can you retake it?" (The general pointed into the low ground southeast of Codori's.) "I can, and damn quick too, if you will let me," Randall confidently shot back. He later reported that Hancock warned him it "would be a hazardous job and he would not order it, but, if I thought I could do it, I might try."[72]

Randall returned to his battalion, which had just arrived upon the field. He maneuvered his five companies from column of divisions into line. As the companies came onto front, he instructed each of his five company commanders exactly what he intended them to do. The second Randall called to the regiment to move out, a shell burst over his head. A fragment gouged his gray mount in the neck and brought the animal down on top of him. The impact of another to the temple of Pvt. Albert H. Chase (Company B) hurled him to the ground unconscious and apparently dead.[73]

Sixteen-year-old 2nd Lt. Charles W. Randall (Company A), the younger of the colonel's two sons in the battalion, got Capt. John Lonergan's permission assist his father. Private Henry Sparks and several others from Company E and G reached the downed colonel first. "Damn them," Randall snarled, "They did not get me that time." In trying to roll the heavy animal off of Randall, Sparks felt something pop in his groin. A nasty rupture curled him up in a ball of pain. The infuriated Randall shouted above the noise, "Go on boys, go on, I'll be at

---

71 William Colvill, "The Old First Minnesota at Gettysburg," 7, Goodhue County Historical Society, Red Wing, MN; W. K. Adams to [Editor of the *Journal*], n.d., Charles Powell Adams Papers, Minnesota Historical Society, St. Paul; Charles Muller, "History", Minnesota Historical Society, Robert L. Brake Collection, USAHEC. Colvill's postwar account is a little suspect. He describes the fighting in detail, which he never saw because he was wounded two minutes before the regiment returned fire.

72 Coffin, *Nine Months to Gettysburg*, 204-205.

73 Ibid., 205.

your head as soon as I get out of this damned saddle." Major Joseph J. Boynton ordered the battalion back into formation. And as soon as he had painfully regained his feet, Randall noticed Lang's Brigade extending its line to the left. He took off at a limping run, his sword unsheathed, to the front of the formation. "Come on, boys," he shouted with a flourish, I'm all right."[74]

Webb's Brigade, II Corps, Army of the Potomac
At the Angle

With the 48th Georgia desperately fighting to hold on to Brown's abandoned gun on the knoll in front of the 69th Pennsylvania, General Webb decided to reinforce his line. He sent Lt. Col. William L. Curry with his 106th Pennsylvania to the crest of Cemetery Ridge immediately north of the copse of trees. He also detached the 71st Pennsylvania to the north-south stone wall, which ran to the hog pen on the south side of Brien's barn. Together the two regiments fired two volleys into the weakening Georgians. As the Confederates fell back from the gun, Curry yelled his regiment to its feet and commanded the men to fix bayonets. With a shout, they raced down the slope, bolted the stone wall along their front, and chased after the Rebels. The 71st Pennsylvania followed closely in the 106th's wake. Sweeping past the guns, Curry's men headed directly for the Codori orchard, leaving their 20 prisoners and the 12-Pounder Napoleon in the hands of the 71st.[75]

The 19th Maine

Colonel Heath had no sooner returned to the colors from Company F on the left flank when Lt. Col. Henry W. Cunningham, who—like Colonel Randall (13th Vermont)—also had seen the Confederates flanking to the left, told him that the Rebs had gotten around the regiment's right flank. Unable to see anything in the smoke, Heath decided to march in retreat. He gave the command: "Face to the rear! Battalion about – FACE! Battalion, forward –

---

74 Ibid., 205, quoted; *OR* 27, pt. 1, 351-352.

75 *OR* 27, pt. 1, 432-433.

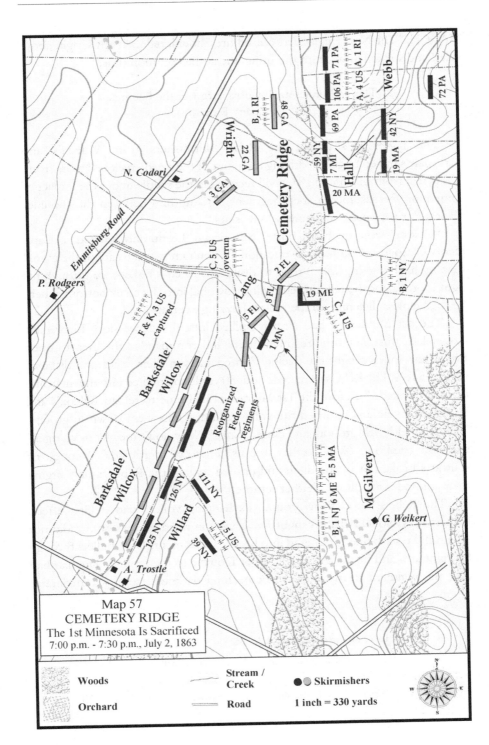

Map 57
CEMETERY RIDGE
The 1st Minnesota Is Sacrificed
7:00 p.m. - 7:30 p.m., July 2, 1863

Woods

Orchard

Stream /
Creek

Road

Skirmishers

1 inch = 330 yards

MARCH!" The New Englanders ceased fire, shouldered their arms, right about faced and walked away from the firing line at the common time.[76]

The 1st Minnesota, II Corps, Army of the Potomac
Cemetery Ridge

The regiment scattered the Rebel skirmishers from Wilcox's and Barksdale's mixed brigades, driving them out of the dried creek bed to its front. A few feet from the "ravine," Colvill recoiled in the saddle under the impact of something (he assumed a shell fragment) striking him between the shoulder blades. For a moment, he literally "saw stars."

"Colonel, you are badly hurt?" Still dazed, he numbly reacted to Capt. Henry C. Coates (Company A) question: "I don't know; take care of the men." Reining his horse in, Colvill tried to dismount when a bullet tore through his right foot. Falling, he felt himself rolling downhill into the creek bottom, where he lay, helpless, listening to the bullets buzzing over his head.[77]

The 1st Minnesota had already spilled into the depression. Lieutenant Colonel Adams halted the regiment there and commanded the men to open fire. Their volley caught the fleeing Confederates in their backs at a distance under 15 feet. The Rebels retreated about 50 yards and melted into the main line of their "brigade." Before the 1st Minnesota had time to reload Wilcox's and Barksdale's veterans returned the volley. Minnesotans went down in groups. The men held their ground, and closed ranks. "Why don't they let us charge?" someone cried out. "Why do they stop us here to be murdered?" A couple of stalwarts broke out of the ditch and dashed toward the Rebs, futilely urging their comrades to follow. Neither returned.[78]

The Rebels stood their ground, exchanging volleys with telling effect. Lieutenant Colonel Adams caught five bullets in rapid succession but did not fall until the sixth one hammered into his chest. Moments later, bullets through his right arm and his foot brought Major Downie to the ground. The halt had cost the regiment dearly. In the encroaching darkness, some Confederates

---

76 Ladd and Ladd, *The Bachelder Papers*, vol. 3, 1,652.

77 Colvill, *"The Old First Minnesota at Gettysburg,"* 7; W. K. Adams to [Editor of the *Journal*], n.d., Minnesota Historical Society, St. Paul.

78 J. W. Sonderman to the Editor of the *Spirit*, February 24, 1901, Vertical Files, GNMP.

managed to get around the right flank and poured a devastating enfilade into the Westerners.

Word now came to the 1st Minnesota to pull back. In the confusion, the right wing had retired halfway back through the open field east of the ditch before the left wing found out about the order to withdraw. Sergeant John W. Plummer (Company D) did not expect to make it back uninjured, much less alive. "It was then I had the first feeling of fear during the fight," he told his brother a short time later. Stumbling across their own dead and wounded, he finally found the colors. Only 25 men remained to rally around them. The rest of the regiment were dead, dying, wounded, or busy bringing in those whom they had a hope of saving.[79]

The 19th Maine, II Corps, Army of the Potomac
Cemetery Ridge Southeast of the Codori Buildings

Thirty-five feet behind its former position, the 19th Maine emerged from the small arms smoke only to discover that the Rebs had not actually flanked it. Colonel Heath immediately ordered the regiment to about face and fire. The men shot at will into the shadows below. In short order, Company F rejoined the regiment on the left. After loosing several rounds, Heath gave the command "Fix Bayonets," followed instantly by "Charge Bayonets." He ran to the front of the colors. "Come on, boys!" he yelled and led them in a wild race down into the low ground.[80]

---

79 Sgt. John W. Plummer to his brother, n.d., Robert L. Brake Collection, USAHEC; Charles Muller, "History," n.p., USAHEC; J. W. Sonderman to the Editor of the Spirit, February 24, 1901, GNMP.

80 Adams, "The Nineteenth Maine at Gettysburg," in *War Papers*, vol. 4, 255-256; Smith, *19th Maine*, 72; Executive Committee, *Maine at Gettysburg*, 293-294; John Lancaster, [unpublished narrative], Robert L. Brake Collection, USAHEC, quoted.

Chapter 16

July 2, 1863
7:30 p.m.-Late Evening

"It makes the hart sick."
—*Private William F. Stilwell, Company F, 53rd Georgia*

Wofford's Brigade, Longstreet's Corps, Army of Northern Virginia
The Emmitsburg Road North of the Millerstown Road[1]
7:30 p.m.-7:45 p.m.

Private Youngblood (15th Alabama), watching Generals Longstreet and Wofford personally ride into the ranks of Wofford's retreating brigade and quell the panic they feared would overwhelm the Georgians, also pitched in to help reform their broken ranks. Shortly thereafter along the wood line on Seminary Ridge, Maj. Thomas J. Walton, Longstreet's volatile commissary of subsistence, unexpectedly popped up alongside of the private, startling him. His mouth blackened from having bitten off cartridges, Walton explained that his horse had died, and he commandeered Youngblood's. Swinging into the saddle, he told the private to hunt up the corps headquarters and to wait for him there.

As the major clattered away, Youngblood glanced about. A nearby Georgian pointed out into field between the lines at an abandoned, fully equipped horse barely visible in the gloaming. It lazily chomped the grass, paying attention to nothing around it. It was too dangerous to get that mount, Youngblood protested. The infantryman laughed. "It is easy," he replied.

---

1 Ladd and Ladd, *The Bachelder Papers*, vol. 1, 481. Colonel Benjamin G. Humphreys (21st Mississippi) said he rallied at the Peach Orchard to the left of Wofford. The steep banks of the Emmitsburg Road at that intersection would have provided good cover to the infantry.

Gritting his teeth, Youngblood lowered himself to his knees and crawled out to the animal. It was too hungry and "blown" to bolt. Climbing quietly aboard, he threw himself low over its neck and dug spurs. The horse lumbered toward the Confederate lines, with minié balls whistling past the private's ears. "He proved to be a good draft horse, but a poor saddle horse," Youngblood later groused.[2]

1st Texas, Longstreet's Corps,
Army of Northern Virginia
The Devil's Den

In the dusk, Private Sims (Company F, 1st Texas) heard the Federal officers across Plum Run preparing their men to make another charge. General Benning heard them too and instructed the Texans and Georgians in the area: "Hold your fire until they come right up. Then pour a volley into them, and if they don't stop, run your bayonets into their bellies." But nothing came of the chatter, and Company F drew picket duty.[3]

III Corps Counterattack,
Army of the Potomac
The Ridge Northeast of Trostle's House

A mounted sergeant from Turnbull's 3rd U.S. Artillery madly galloped to the Excelsior Brigade. Reining his horse to a halt at the center of the line, he pleaded: "Boys! You said you'd stick to us. Is this the way the brigade is going to leave the field? There's the gun!" He pointed toward the two abandoned sections along the Emmitsburg Road. "If you're men, come on!" Spurring his horse about, he madly galloped toward the swarming Rebels, his saber cutting the air above his head.[4]

An awestruck Pvt. Felix Brannigan (Company A, 73rd New York) watched as the artilleryman crashed into the Rebels with his saber slashing. Instantly, individual soldiers from all of the mixed up commands cried out, "Charge!" followed by a shrill banshee "Hi—hi—hi-i-i-i!" Sergeant Mears (Company A,

2   Youngblood, "Unwritten History of the Gettysburg Campaign," in SHSP, vol. 38, 317, quoted; G. Moxley Sorrel, *At the Right Hand of Longstreet* (Lincoln, 1999), 36.

3   P. A. Work to Tom Langley, May 28, 1908, GNMP.

4   Felix Brannigan to his Father, n.d., Vertical Files, GNMP.

6th Pennsylvania Reserves), who was scrounging through an ammunition box at the time, immediately bolted into the fray. The 73rd New York's color guard raced 12 paces ahead of the line. Colonel Brewster spurred his horse to the front, dragging the rest of the brigade, some 150 men, with him.[5]

No one in the confusion knew exactly how it started, but the counterattack spread like a brush fire all along the ridge. "Charge 'em! Take our old ground!" 1st Lieutenant Blake (Company K, 11th Massachusetts) heard men around him shout. Captain William H. Lloyd (Company F, 11th New Jersey) rallied the few men he found and hobbled forward with them into the fight. Shaking his sword at the Rebels, 1st Lt. William H. H. Fernel (Company I, 12th New Hampshire) went berserk. He brandished the blade above his head and screamed "Come on!" And with the handful of men he mustered, he dashed raving into the smoke blanketed field.[6]

"We seemed to be borne on wings," Brannigan (73rd New York) later told his father. Humphreys, whose orders were to hold the ridge, could not stop the attack. "Halt! Halt! Stop those men! Stop those men!" he screamed, but to no avail. The Yankees crashed through the rock-strewn, brush-clogged creek bottom of Plum Run and into the Confederate ranks before they had time to reorganize from their charge. The 126th New York got caught up in the frenzied impetus of the attack. Climbing out of the creek bed, they surged forward with the rest of the soldiers, leaving the 111th and 125th New York where they were.[7]

The 19th Maine and the 13th Vermont
Codori's Farm, South and East of the Buildings

The 19th Maine, with the 13th Vermont trailing behind it to its right rear, swept Lang's Floridians back across the low ground south of Codori's. The 19th Maine headed straight for Turnbull's four abandoned guns 100 yards east of the Rodgers house, while the 13th Vermont made due east toward Weir's

5   Ibid.

6   Blake, "Personal Reminiscences of Gettysburg," 20, 22, quoted on 22, USAHEC; Marbaker, *11th New Jersey*, 99; Bartlett, *12th New Hampshire*, 126.

7   Ladd and Ladd, *The Bachelder Papers*, vol. 1, 340; Felix Brannigan to his Father, n.d., Vertical Files, GNMP; OR 27, pt. 1, 559; Brown, *72nd New York*, 105; Potter, "Seeley's Battery at Gettysburg," *National Tribune*, May 24, 1888, quoted.

guns and the Codori farmhouse. The Mainers picked up part of the rallied 26th Pennsylvania on the way, who actually bolted ahead of the 19th Maine, eager to regain the ground they had lost. Firing point-blank into the backs of the 2nd Florida, they wounded the regiment's color bearer. He immediately handed the flag over to another man in the color guard but Sgt. George Roosevelt (Company K, 26th Pennsylvania) got the drop on him. The sergeant started rearward with the man and his flag when a stray shot snapped his leg, and he fell to the ground, unable to move. His prisoner dropped the flag and took off for safer ground.[8]

Seconds later, the 19th Maine passed over the wounded sergeant. Colonel Heath, on the right wing, vividly recalled tramping on top of the colors. A large number of unwounded Floridians, heading east, made their way through the regiment. On the left, the Rebels skedaddled, leaving the 8th Florida's flag draped over one of Turnbull's field pieces. The 19th Maine brushed past the guns, making for the Emmitsburg Road.[9]

The 13th Vermont and the 106th Pennsylvania
At the Codori Farm

The Confederates, before the 13th Vermont, either hurled themselves to the ground or skedaddled. Hancock, who had followed the untested battalion onto the field, urged Randall to push his men farther and recapture Weir's guns.

8   Arrington, *The Medal of Honor at Gettysburg*, 21; Richard Rollins, *"The Damned Red Flags of the Rebellion": The Confederate Battle Flag at Gettysburg* (Redondo Beach, 1997), 127; Studnicki, Jim, "Perry's Brigade': The Forgotten Floridians at Gettysburg," (accessed May 23, 2014) http://www.2ndflorida.net/perrys.htm. Colonel David Lang said the 2nd Florida lost its flag on July 3 and never recovered it. According to Richard Rollins, 5th Sgt. Charles Brink (Company K, 16th Vermont) picked up the flag on that day and turned it in to the proper authorities. I believe that the 2nd lost its flag on July 2. Studnicki says the wounded color bearer of the 2nd Florida handed the flag over to another man, who carried it a few yards before he surrendered. This had to have happened on July 2, and the man who captured the flag was Sergeant Roosevelt (26th Pennsylvania). Roosevelt fell, wounded, and the prisoner escaped without the flag. Colonel Heath (19th Maine) stepped on those colors shortly after Roosevelt's wounding. That night, according to the *Gettysburg Star and Sentinel*, July 9, 1895, a captain from the 8th Florida returned to the former position of Turnbull's abandoned guns and found the colors of the 8th Florida (actually the 2nd Florida) under the bodies of the color guard but apparently did not return with the flag. It was still there the next day when the 16th Vermont flanked the Florida Brigade.

9   Frederick Tilberg to Mrs. Joseph C. Moore, August 12, 1954; Adams, "The Nineteenth Maine at Gettysburg," vol. 4, 257; Smith, *19th Maine*, 72; Ladd and Ladd, *The Bachelder Papers*, vol. 3, 1,653.

While the regiment tramped over the top of their prostrate "prisoners," Sgt. George H. Scott (Company G,) rushed forward. The Confederates, hauling the four 12-pounders toward the Emmitsburg Road, got caught in the middle of the field between the road and Cemetery Ridge. Tossing the drag ropes aside, they ran toward the Codori orchard, where Maj. George W. Ross (2nd Georgia Battalion) and Capt. Charles R. Redding (Company C) struggled to swing the lead team of one of Weir's limbers toward the road.

Scott reached one of the guns seconds before Captain Lonergan and Company A arrived. Placing his hand upon the bronze tube closest to him, he yelled at the Rebels to surrender. Simultaneously, small arms fire crashed into the orchard from the north. Redding was killed and Major Ross fell mortally wounded. Colonel Randall, with the 13th Vermont's Company G, spotted the fleeing Rebels at the same time. "Halt!" he shouted but they did not slow down. "God damn you, boys," he screamed, "stop that running." To his amazement, about 50 of them turned around and walked into the Vermonters' ranks.[10]

The others ran into the oncoming 106th Pennsylvania. Captain Robert H. Ford (Company I) and his men stumbled upon a large portion of Wright's Brigade sheltering behind the Codori house and barn. An officer bearing a white flag attracted Ford's attention in the fading light. Ford had an enlisted man poke an old newspaper on his bayonet, faced the company by the flank, and marched them up to the house. The Confederate with the flag of truce identified himself as Capt. Claiborne Snead (Company G, 3rd Georgia). Nearby lay a desperately wounded Col. William Gibson (48th Georgia). Snead feared the colonel would die without medical attention. Would the Federal officer consider bringing the colonel within the Union lines to receive treatment? Ford agreed to help the colonel provided the men who had gathered around him also came in and that the officers surrender their swords. Snead protested: the men should be allowed to return to their own lines. No, insisted Ford, the colonel and the men had to surrender. Snead reluctantly agreed. So Company I rounded up the colonel, five captains, 15 lieutenants, and about 100 dejected Georgians, wounded and uninjured alike, and started toward the Copse of Trees with them.[11]

---

10 Coffin, *Nine Months to Gettysburg,* 205-206.

11 OR 27, pt. 2, 433; Robert H. Shirkey, ["William Gibson,"] unpublished draft, December 5, 1988, Vertical Files, GNMP; Ward, *106th Pennsylvania,* 161-162. The106th Pennsylvania credited itself with capturing three guns and 250 Confederates, which, including the men the

With his arms curled around a bundle of swords, Captain Ford headed back toward Cemetery Ridge, while the rest of the regiment merged with the 13th Vermont on the eastern side of the orchard. With the Vermonters' prisoners under the charge of Company C, the rest of the regiment about faced and started to the rear with Company A's "boys" and a number of the 106th Pennsylvania's rolling the guns away.

As soon as the Vermonters turned their backs upon the Codori buildings, they came under fire from behind. Within earshot of Cpl. Eli T. Marsh (Company C), Colonel Randall barked at Company A's Captain Lonergan: "That house is full of sharpshooters; take your company and capture them." "Boys," the captain screamed, "those fellows are firing at us. We will drive those damned Rebels out of those buildings or kill them—about face charge."[12]

Picking up their weapons, the Yankees countercharged and surrounded the house covering all of the windows and doors to prevent anyone's escaping. Lonergan kicked the front door in. "Surrender!" he shouted at an officer with a rifle standing close by. "Fall out here, every damned one of you!" The officer handed over his sword on the way out of the door; 82 enlisted men followed him out, tossing aside their weapons as they exited the house. Greatly outnumbered, Company A escorted its catch back to the rest of the battalion. Wright's Brigade had taken a horrific beating. Only 577 officers and men of the 1,450 which had gone into the fight returned to Seminary Ridge unhurt. The killed and captured comprised 83 percent of the casualties. Both the 2nd Battalion and the 48th Georgia had to leave their colors upon the field.[13]

13th Vermont bagged, would make the after-action report correct. Snead did not belong to the 48th Georgia. The prisoners came from Wright's entire brigade and not just the 48th Georgia.

12 Coffin, *Nine Months to Gettysburg*, 206; Ward, *106th Pennsylvania*, 161-162.

13 OR 27, pt. 1, 352, pt. 2, 630; Beyer and Keydel, *Deeds of Valor*, vol. 1, 226, quoted; Coffin, *Nine Months to Gettysburg*, 206-207; Rollins, *"The Damned Red Flags of the Rebellion,"* 127. According to Sergeant George H. Scott (Company G), "Our Colonel was not the most modest man in the world." This is evident in Randall's after-action report which would lead one to believe that the regiment got as far as the Emmitsburg road and that a pair of guns to the south flanked them. The accounts of others in the regiment indicate that the battalion got as far as the Codori orchard and no farther. The 106th Pennsylvania claimed some of those prisoners also.

The III Corps Counterattack
East of the Emmitsburg Road

Lieutenant Colonel John Leonard with Sgt. Henri LeFevre Brown and Pvt. M. Luther Howard (both Company B, 72nd New York) reached Turnbull's captured guns ahead of the rest of the III Corps. They quickly cut the disabled horses free of one limber, wheeled the gun around without any assistance, and dragged it away, leaving the three remaining pieces upon the field.

Sergeant Thomas Horan (Company E, 72nd New York) snatched up the colors of the 8th Florida. In the meantime, about 100 yards from the Emmitsburg Road, the right companies of the 19th Maine bagged 30 Floridians and their severely wounded Maj. Walter R. Moore (2nd Florida) as they were attempting to drag off one of Turnbull's pieces. As they forced the captured Rebels to wheel the gun about to haul it back to the Federal lines, the New Englanders heard some loud cheering. In the distance, through the smoky, fading light, they saw the New Yorkers jubilantly waving about the colors from the 8th Florida and heading back to Cemetery Ridge with them. While the 71st New York hauled away one of Turnbull's 12-pounders, the 19th Maine recovered what remained of the battery. With their prisoners dragging off one piece by ropes, the New Englanders hauled off the last two guns and the battery's four abandoned caissons.[14]

After the 11th Massachusetts had driven the Rebels across the Emmitsburg Road, it abruptly halted to the amazing sight of apparently lifeless Federal bodies in the field rising from the dead unscathed. "This resurrection was greeted with laughter," Lieutenant Blake (11th Massachusetts) recalled. Scouring the field, the Yankees rounded up prisoners and sorted the dead from the wounded. Blake found men too frightened to move. One wounded Floridian, a boy of about 16, complained that "General Lee always puts the Fifth Florida in front." A little further on, he came across about 30 Confederates crammed in a little gully. Using his sword to direct them to the Federal lines, Blake commanded, "Get up, boys. Get up and go to the rear." Suddenly a musket shot cracked by his head. Whirling around he saw Cpl. William H. Brown (Company B, 11th Massachusetts) still holding his smoking weapon at the ready. "What on earth are you doing?" the lieutenant demanded.

---

14 Brown, *72nd New York*, 105; Felix Brannigan to his Father, n.d., GNMP; Blake, *"Personal Reminiscences of Gettysburg,"* 20, 22, USAHEC.

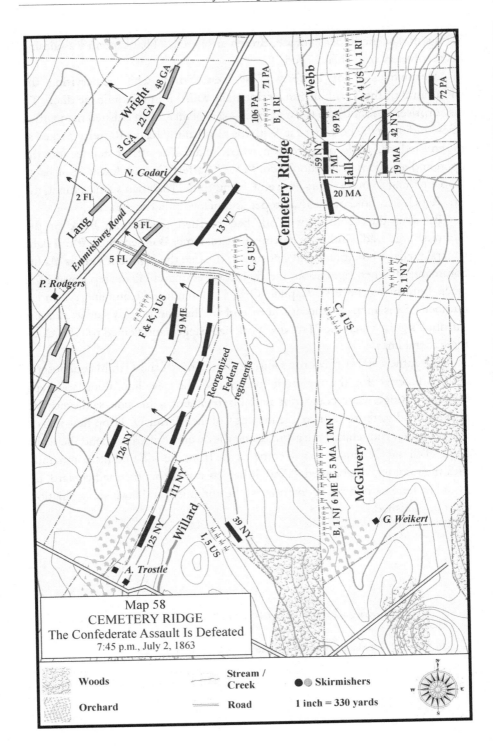

Map 58
CEMETERY RIDGE
The Confederate Assault Is Defeated
7:45 p.m., July 2, 1863

Woods

Orchard

Stream / Creek

Road

Skirmishers

1 inch = 330 yards

With a nod at the Rebel's corpse, Brown answered, "That captain was aiming his revolver at you when I fired."[15]

Meanwhile, Major Rafferty (71st New York), while supervising the withdrawal of the Turnbull gun, accidentally rolled it into a drainage ditch. To his surprise, he found two Confederates—a captain and an enlisted man with a rifle—hiding in the bottom of it. With his pistol at the ready, Rafferty barked at the enlisted man to drop his weapon, which he did. The officer stepped into the open and asked what he should do. "Do?" Rafferty incredulously shot back. "Do anything to make yourself useful." And to the Irishman's amazement, the two Rebels laid hold of the drag ropes and helped pull the gun free.[16]

By then the 126th New York had reached the eastern bank of the Emmitsburg Road. Finding no enemy, Lt. Col. James Bull sent the left and right general guides to their respective posts and dressed the regiment's ranks. At his command, the men right about faced and started marching in step toward the creek bottom to the east. Captain Orin J. Herendeen (Company A) and a number of his men on the northern end of the line quickly laid hands on Turnbull's gun, which the 71st New York had bagged and helped roll it back to the Federal lines.

Presently, a staff officer rode into the remnants of the 11th Massachusetts with a directive for the regiment to retire to the new line along southern Cemetery Ridge. Carr could not find his regiments, the aide said, and the regiment had to retire at once. Lieutenant Colonel Porter D. Tripp flew in to a rage. His men had retaken the ground, and they were entitled to spend the night on it. "Tell the General if he will come to the front, he will find his commands with their colors," he bristled. "And, if he was not such a damned coward, he would be here with them." Nevertheless, he complied, and his insubordination went unpunished.[17]

---

15 Felix Brannigan to his Father, n.d., GNMP; Blake, *"Personal Reminiscences of Gettysburg,"* 22, quoted, USAHEC.

16 Rafferty, "Gettysburg," *Personal Recollections*, vol. 4, 28-29, quoted on 29.

17 Blake, *"Personal Reminiscences of Gettysburg,"* 23-27, quoted on 27, USAHEC; Rafferty, "Gettysburg," *Personal Recollections*, vol. 4, 28-29; Ladd and Ladd, *The Bachelder Papers*, vol. 1, 340, 342.

Humphreys' Staff, III Corps, Army of the Potomac
Cemetery Ridge near the G. Weikert Farm
Dark—After 8:00 p.m.

As the fighting died out, Captain Cavada's orderly approached him on horseback. When the captain noticed the fellow had a severe foot wound, he told him to go to the hospital and send his mount forward from there. Cavada decided to search out the division headquarters in the dark. After an hour of stumbling over casualties, quite by accident he found the staff huddled on the ground. They eagerly shook his hand, glad to see him alive, then gave him a full report of the losses among their officers' mess. To his dismay, he learned that Captain Chester lay on the field among the mortally wounded. And Lieutenant Humphreys, the general's son, showed Cavada his bandaged arm where a bullet had passed through without striking bone. The rest of the staff reported that they had lost their mounts.[18]

McGilvery's Artillery Line, Army of the Potomac
Cemetery Ridge, East of Trostle's
After 8:00 p.m.

The Rebels rolled a couple batteries onto the high ground east of the Peach Orchard and returned fire on Dow's two left guns, which were still responding to Confederate artillery. Captain Bigelow and bugler Charles Reed quietly walked their two mounts in between the guns. As soon as the two had cleared the trails, Captain Dow (6th Maine Artillery) had his battery charged with canister. The bugler's devotion to his captain left a lasting impression upon Dow.[19]

Phillips and Dow maintained their counter battery fire until dark. When a staff officer and his horse went down not 10 feet away from Phillips, 17-year-old Pvt. William Purbeck, unable to bear hearing the horse scream and the officer pleading for help, hurried to their assistance—and gave his life: a shell fragment mortally wounded him in the back. Having shot away his remaining 70 rounds of ammunition, Philips left the battery hunting for

---

18 Cavada, Diary, July 2, 1863, FSNMP.

19 Dow to the Adjutant General of the U.S.A., August 3, 1895, NA; John Bigelow to the Adjutant General of the U.S.A., June 19, 1895, NA.

assistance and returned with Battery K, 4th U.S. Artillery, under Lt. Robert James. He then took his three guns to the rear. In the fading light, he saw the colors of the VI Corps coming onto the field. "Thank God, there's the Sixth Corps!" Cpl. Jonas Shackley heard Phillips exclaim.[20]

Meanwhile, Colonel Humphreys and his "boys" from the 21st Mississippi assembled around Bigelow's four abandoned Napoleons. Ordering one gun spiked, Humphreys pulled the rest of the guns back with his command to the northern leg of Millerstown-Emmitsburg Roads intersection.[21]

Ward's Brigade, II Corps, Army of the Potomac
Plum Run Gorge

As the bloodied 124th New York retreated toward the northeast, Adj. Henry P. Ramsdell and his party, carrying the colonel's and the major's bodies, stumbled into a VI Corps regiment, which marched onto the field on battalion front. The regiment's colonel, riding in front, impressed the lieutenant with his massive red beard, and he was equally struck by the precision of the regiment's marching. Nearby, he spied a near heat-stricken Capt. William C. Silliman (Company C) limply riding the adjutant's horse toward the rear.

With the VI Corps troops retaking the ground between Little Round Top and Houck's Ridge, Color Sergeant Munsell (Company A) leaped from his shell hole, the colors clutched to his chest, and raced back to his 99th Pennsylvania. His comrades, believing him dead, filled the air with shouts of joy as he calmly took his place in the line and unfurled the national colors.[22]

The 13th Vermont, I Corps, Army of the Potomac
The Codori Farm

The unexpected artillery barrage caught Colonel Randall (13th Vermont) by surprise. Wheeling toward the firing, he noticed in the hazy twilight what appeared to be two guns in the Emmitsburg Road. Believing the Rebs had deliberately singled out his battalion, he detached Capt. Lewis L. Coburn with

---

20 Regimental Committee, *5th Massachusetts Battery*, 625, 627-628, 636, 638, 640-646, quoted on 638.

21 Ladd and Ladd, *The Bachelder Papers*, vol. 1, 481.

22 Ramsdell, Account, GNMP; Rodenbough, *Uncle Sam's Medal of Honor*, 189.

his Company C to capture the noisome pieces. The company veered southwest, brushing past the right flank of the 19th Maine en route, and upon reaching the Emmitsburg Road, discovered two destroyed caissons, nothing more. They returned empty handed to the battalion.[23]

II, V, and VI Corps, Army of the Potomac
The Wheatfield

Private Meyer (Company B, 148th Pennsylvania), after refreshing himself at a small stream, headed back to Little Round Top to find Manasses Gilbert (Company A). He peered at the sun setting behind the distant ridges, swathed in a veil of smoke. Unable to find his regiment, Meyer cut into the woods where he had last seen his own men. Doubling back along the southeastern edge of the Wheatfield, he happened across Gilbert, who was painfully meandering back with a shoulder wound. He helped his friend to a tree on the northern side of Little Round Top and left him there, for he was too weak to continue any farther.[24]

Not too far away, near the Millerstown Road, Col. Frederick H. Collier (139th Pennsylvania) rode up to the center of a regiment lying behind the stone wall on the eastern side of the Wheatfield and asked: "What command is this?" Colonel Jackson (11th Pennsylvania Reserves) told him. "Pennsylvania will support you," Collier quietly answered. He told Jackson that his regiment was immediately behind him and would relieve him if he desired it. Jackson glanced over his shoulder and in the dim light saw the surrounding ground covered with new troops. Those men were a division of the VI Corps which had just arrived, Collier told him.[25]

20th Maine, V Corps, Army of the Potomac
Little Round Top

With dusk came a respite from the musketry with the exception of the sporadic shots from Confederate sharpshooters who still lingered in the woods south of Little Round Top. Colonel Chamberlain (20th Maine) walked over to

23 Coffin, *Nine Months to Gettysburg*, 207.

24 Muffly, *148th Pennsylvania*, 538.

25 Nicholson, *Pennsylvania at Gettysburg*, vol. 1, 279.

the colors of his regiment around which the diminished guard stood. Only Color Sergeant Tozier, Cpl. William T. Livermore (Company B), and Private Coan (Company D) remained of the original five enlisted men in its ranks. "Boys," Chamberlain began, "I am asked if I can carry that hill in front," referring to Big Round Top. Those within hearing replied, "Yes."[26]

Forming the bloodied regiment in line, they advanced across the hollow between the two hills and began their ascent up the rocky slope. Reaching the top without incident, Chamberlain sent out skirmishers who spread out in extended formation and headed down the hill's western face. They got so close to the 4th Texas they could see the Rebels in the lights of their coffee fires and distinctly hear their conversations. Rather than get "gobbled up," the New Englanders headed up the slope.

The Texans sent out a detachment to investigate the crackling in the brush. Company E, on the right of the line, called out for them to identify themselves. A Southerner answered, "Fourth Texas," to which the Mainer responded, "All right. Come on. We're Fourth Texas." And just like that, they duped 30 men under Lt. Thomas L. Christian, Brigadier General Law's acting assistant adjutant and inspector general, into surrendering without firing a shot. Privates John Bradford and Eugene Kelleran (Company I) headed rearward with the disgruntled prisoners. Losing their way in the darkness, the two Yankees bedded their captives down in a clearing on the mountainside to await the morning.[27]

In the darkness, Chamberlain detected a large body of men crashing through the woods on the right of his line. The pickets challenged them and discovered they were the 5th and the 12th Pennsylvania Reserves, their long delayed supports, which had gotten lost on the way. Chamberlain led them to their assigned position. The Pennsylvanians, however, marching by the right flank, were facing away from the Confederate position when they fronted. As their officers tried to right the situation by having them face by the rear rank, the inept Reserves created an awful racket. It in turn attracted fire from the Rebel pickets, so the Pennsylvanians marched down the hill away from the shooting.

Rather than risk getting overrun in the darkness, Chamberlain posted a strong picket to the front and right and pulled the rest of the regiment down the

---

26 Styple, *With a Flash of His Sword*, 78.

27 Ibid., 129-130, quoted on 129; Spear, *Recollections*, 37; William C. Oates to Joshua L. Chamberlain, March 8, 1897, BCL.

northern slope of the hill to the base of the first climb. He sent a runner to Colonel Rice, then commanding the brigade, for the 83rd Pennsylvania. Shortly thereafter, he had the 44th New York brought up on his right rear. With his flanks secured, Chamberlain advanced to the crest and beyond its original position, where the men spent the rest of the night, lying on their arms.[28]

61st New York, II Corps, Army of the Potomac
The Wheatfield

With the field growing quiet, Lieutenant Fuller (4th Company, 61st New York) lay as still as he could to suppress the horrendous pain, which bolted through him whenever he moved. He was not particularly thirsty, and it worried him because wounded men tended to get dry. Nor did he want to groan with so many seriously injured men lying about him. That also worried him: he wondered if he were really as badly hurt as he thought. The more he contemplated it, the more he needed to determine the extent of his plight. He decided to groan. Sucking in a deep breath, he let out a genuinely "manly" moan. The volume pleased him so much that he felt no need to utter another.[29]

13th Pennsylvania Reserves, V Corps,
Army of the Potomac
The Woods on Houck's Ridge

A lieutenant with a picket detail materialized out of the darkness and reported to Captain Bell (Company I, 13th Pennsylvania Reserves), who immediately told the lieutenant to deploy across Plum Run Valley and make contact with the Federal troops, whom they could hear hacking away at the timber in the direction of Little Round Top.

The night dragged into an eternity for the bone-tired Pennsylvanians. Bell would not allow himself to sit down, knowing full well that if he did, he would pass out. He continually trooped the line in the woods, braving pot shots, to shake his men awake.

At one point, his men encountered a severely wounded soldier from the 20th Georgia, who had fallen in the open ground north of the Devil's Den. His

---

28 Styple, *With a Flash of His Sword*, 128-129.

29 Fuller, *Personal Recollections*, 96-97.

continual rasping for water prompted one of Bell's veterans to call out to him, "I would bring you a drink but your men will shoot me." "Go ahead, Yank," the Rebel hoarsely replied, "we won't shoot." The compassionate Pennsylvanian loped over to the Confederate's side. Kneeling down, he raised the fellow's head to give him a drink from his canteen when a flash illuminated the dark, and the Good Samaritan keeled over with a bullet through his skull. Picket fire from both sides instantly cracked and popped in the darkness, continued for several minutes, and then abruptly died away. "There was no more truce that night," Bell lamented.[30]

140th New York, V Corps, Army of the Potomac
The Bushman Farm, East of Little Round Top

When the fighting ended at Little Round Top, the 140th New York's Adjutant Farley detailed Sgt. John H. Wright and three other men from Company A to take Colonel O'Rorke's corpse back to the division at the Louis A. Bushman farm. Farley, who accompanied them, stood over the colonel, too grief stricken to say anything. O'Rorke, in death, seemed unnaturally pale and eerily restful. The captain loved him like a brother. Kneeling down, he removed the colonel's watch and several "trifles" before pulling the gauntlets from his cold hands. The captain folded the gloves and tucked them under the colonel's waist belt. Next, he crossed O'Rorke's hands near his waist and then straightened his still pliant body. Calling in the enlisted men, Farley started with them back to the regiment.[31]

4th Michigan, V Corps, Army of the Potomac
The Millerstown Road, North of Little Round Top

While the Pennsylvania Reserves held their own on the eastern side of the Wheatfield, Private Houghton (Company K, 4th Michigan) patiently helped the crippled Captain McLean limp toward the rear. All along the roadside, he stared at ghastly puddles of blood from the hundreds of terribly wounded. Here and there, injured men, too exhausted to go farther, sat under the shade of the intermittent trees along the road to get some respite from pain and weariness,

---

30 Bell, "The Bucktails at Gettysburg," GNMP.

31 Farley, "Bloody Round Top," *National Tribune*, May 3, 1883.

and, in some cases, to bleed to death. The ambulance drivers, who continually trundled along the route, refused to take on anyone whom they adjudged not severely injured enough to ride. McLean had to stop and rest several times. And with every step he took, Houghton heard the blood sloshing and squishing in his left boot.

Half a mile east of Little Round Top, they found a III Corps Hospital in a barnyard. The guard at the gate told them they had no more room, but McLean insisted upon lying down. He would stay there until the attendants could get to him. Houghton limped into the yard, totally unprepared for the rows upon rows of mangled and dying men he found there. The incessant groans of the wounded drove him from the crammed barn. He returned to McLean who told him to give his sword and belt to his first lieutenant.

Houghton left McLean to locate the regiment when he accidentally ran into his lieutenant. At the officer's insistence, they went back to the hospital where they acquired a stretcher and hauled the captain away to another hospital, where he got prompt medical attention.[32]

Around 8 p.m., the ammunition wagons found the demoralized 118th Pennsylvania and unloaded enough ammunition to supply a division. Captain Donaldson (Company K), well aware that the men would take about 30 rounds each and leave the rest on the field, hated to see the ammunition wasted when it could have been distributed to regiments that really needed it. As darkness fell over the battlefield, he noticed how a heavy sulfuric cloud crept into the hollows like a baleful fog. To Houghton (4th Michigan) the heavy, suffocating, and pungent air reminded him of "the infernal regions."[33]

The 139th Pennsylvania from the 3rd brigade, 3rd Division, VI Corps, established a picket line along the northern side of the Wheatfield. Hearing them close by, Lieutenant Fuller (61st New York) managed to get the attention of a sergeant. Fuller told him he wanted to be removed from between the lines, and the man said he would get his officer. Presently, he showed up with his lieutenant, who asked what they could do for him. Fuller asked to be taken to the rear of the skirmish line. He asked the two to make a chair with their hands to carry him off. They did, but his mangled leg got caught in the wheat, and they had to put him down. The lieutenant who reeked of alcohol, said he could carry Fuller and got down on his haunches with his back to the wounded New

32 Houghton, Journal, 14, UMI.

33 Aiken, *Inside the Army of the Potomac*, 306-307; Houghton, Journal, 15, UMI.

Yorker. The sergeant wrapped Fuller's good arm around his lieutenant's neck. His attempt to lift Fuller up from a full squat sent both of them tumbling into the wheat with Fuller on the bottom. Gasping for breath, Fuller told them to cover him with a blanket and to leave him where he lay. So his would-be rescuers abandoned him in the wheat, surrounded by the dead and dying, alone in the darkness. The groans of the wounded swelled and swirled around him.[34]

Private Meyer (Company B, 148th Pennsylvania) reached Little Round Top by dark. Manasses Gilbert (Company A) was not where he had left him. Exhausted and dejected, Meyer nestled up against a large boulder and fell asleep, not caring whether he saw another day or not.[35]

Captain Phillips spent the night looking for his other artillery pieces. He left three corpses upon the field along with 30 dead horses, his #1 limber, and one harness. Private Charles Stiles and another enlisted man found Lieutenant Scott near Trostle's. They carried him to the battery's bivouac on the bank of Rock Creek and left him there to fend for himself. Nearby, Corporal Chase found his gun's caisson. There, he finally got his wounded left arm bandaged.[36]

Later that night, Chase exchanged buttons with two captured Confederates from the 8th Georgia. First Lieutenant Peleg W. Blake (Battery E, 5th Massachusetts) returned to the field with Sergeant Pattison and Corporals Graham and Shackley to recover their abandoned limber, but they returned without it because the Rebels were too close to their lines.[37]

Battery B, 1st New Jersey Light, bivouacked at the W. Patterson farm. Before the driver could dismount, Captain Clark gathered the remaining men of his battery together. "Boys, those of you who survive this war will have reason to be proud of this day's work. I ask you all to return thanks to God that he brought you safely out of this day's battle." With that, the veterans turned out to

---

34 Fuller, *Personal Recollections*, 97-98.

35 Muffly, *148th Pennsylvania*, 538.

36 Regimental Committee, *5th Massachusetts Battery*, 625, 627-628, 632, 636-637, 645.

37 Ibid., 639. After the war, Corporal Graham asserted that he and three enlisted men hauled the gun away after he crawled out between the lines alone and got the dead horses out of their harnesses. Unfortunately, this does not agree with Phillips' official report of July 6, 1863, which says the gun was not brought back until July 4. The act that Graham describes was too noteworthy to be left out of the official records, and the captain probably would have sent such a party back under a lieutenant, rather than a sergeant. Graham's exciting account is too self-serving to strike the same note of authenticity as Shackley's matter-of-fact account of the failure to retrieve the piece.

smoke their pipes and to boil their coffee, which they readily shared with a few of the Berdans.[38]

Nearby in the Patterson's stone barn, the surgeons were busy at their grisly work. Ambulances and stretcher parties hauled in the mangled and the dying all through the night. A large portion of the wounded ended up in the apple orchard south of the farm buildings. There, lying on freshly strewn straw, they received coffee and whatever medical assistance was available.

Rather than stay near the area, some of the artillerymen filled their canteens and walked back toward the front to succor the wounded, who remained upon the field under a full moon. Private Hanifen stumbled across a severely injured man from the 82nd New York, who refused aid until his wounded colonel, James Huston, who lay nearby, received treatment. When he learned his colonel was dying, he wept uncontrollably.[39]

The severely wounded from Collis' Zouaves who had taken shelter in Sherfy's barn never got to the hospitals. Instead they died horrible deaths when the barn caught fire from artillery shelling during the Federal retreat.[40]

Major Dunne and the survivors of the 115th Pennsylvania found their missing brigade commander, Colonel Burling, after dark. "I thought you were captured," he told the exhausted Dunne, "as you remained so long after the 8th New Jersey." De Trobriand happened across what was left of the 5th Michigan. "How have you fared?" he asked with genuine concern. Through the darkness came the low reply, "These only are left, General." Tears streamed down his powder stained cheeks. With an emotional choked voice, he exclaimed, "Oh! My little 5th; I had rather command you than command a division."[41]

Not too long after dark, an aide from Major General Sykes told Sweitzer that Barnes was missing and that he was to assume division command. By then Colonel Prescott had returned to the 32nd Massachusetts. The seven bullets, which had struck him in the Wheatfield, had ripped holes through his clothing and thoroughly stunned him, but inflicted no lasting harm. At 10 p.m., the rest

---

38 Hanifen, *Battery B*, 80.

39 Ibid.

40 Bowen, "Collis' Zouaves," *Philadelphia Weekly Times*, June 22, 1887.

41 Ladd and Ladd, *The Bachelder Papers*, vol. 2, 1,050; Monument Commission, *Michigan at Gettysburg*, 102, quoted.

of the Sweitzer's Brigade tramped down to Plum Run. Crossing the creek, they went into line along the stone wall on the eastern side of the Wheatfield.[42]

At about the same time, Sgt. David A. White, along with Pvts. William S. Cockman, Dan Ford, Isom Burns, and Thomas W. Hagood (Company H, 3rd Arkansas), stole into the Wheatfield to where they thought they had left the badly wounded John A. Wilkerson. Cockman softly called for his friend only to have scores of desperately hurt men reply. "Let me call to him again," Wilkerson heard Cockman stage whisper. "Seven Pines," Cockman called, and Wilkerson, who lay close by, feebly replied. His comrades found him, worked him onto a stretcher, and sneaked away with him in the darkness to the Rose barn.[43]

The picket line of the 139th Pennsylvania crossed into the no-man's-land in the vicinity of Trostle's and found Lt. Barzilla J. Inman (Company F, 118th Pennsylvania) lying alone in the field. The sergeant in charge of the party, after reporting his "find" within the Rebel lines to his colonel, immediately ordered his men to return to the regiment. Soon after this a number of hogs wandered into Inman's ghoulish bivouac and began rooting and tearing at the dead. With a loud grunt, one of them, soon joined by others, began poking the lieutenant with his snout. The petrified Inman eventually jabbed the beast with his sword, and his nemesis squealed and ran away. After this incident, Inman found it quite impossible to sleep.[44]

The officer in charge of the picket permitted Corporal West (Company H), with three other volunteers from the 32nd Massachusetts, to venture into the trampled wheat to search for fallen comrades. Bodies lay everywhere, and the moans and cries of the wounded piercing the darkness lent the area the unmistakable aura of hellish horror. The corporal and his party found the desperately wounded Sgt. James M. Haskell (Company A), and West, tormented by his inability to offer even the least succor to the injured remained by his side while the others continued on into the darkness. When his comrades returned, they said they were little inclined to stay with a dying man, so the four of them rolled Haskell, with his wounded legs, onto a blanket, carried him to the skirmish line, and placed him in a waiting ambulance. Returning to the field,

---

42 *Supplement to the OR 5*, pt. 1, 191; Parker, *32nd Massachusetts*, 171; West, "On Little Round Top," *National Tribune*, November 22, 1906.

43 Wilkerson, *"Experiences of 'Seven Pines' at Gettysburg,"* GNMP.

44 Survivors' Association, *118th Pennsylvania*, 250.

they brought in Pvt. Barney Clark (Company G), whose spine had been severed by a bullet. Since it was after midnight, the ambulances had already returned to the hospital, so they carried him across Plum Run to the reverse slope of Little Round Top where they turned him over to another stretcher party.[45]

Little Round Top

At about the same time, Pvt. John A. Goldsticker (Company A, 4th Texas foolheartedly darted into the no-man's-land between the wood line and the southwestern end of Little Round Top. A Yankee rifleman loosed a round into the shadows and dropped him. Unable to crawl back, Goldsticker repeatedly pleaded, "Water! Water! Great God, bring me some water!" Private West (Company E)—along with many others in the shelter of the woods—tried to shut out Goldsticker's entreaties, because no one dared go to his aid. West later rationalized that despite the fact his unfortunate comrade was a gambler and a German Jew to boot, "he died at the front!"[46]

140th Pennsylvania, II Corps, Army of the Potomac
The Wheatfield

Out in the Wheatfield, Lieutenant Purman (Company A, 140th Pennsylvania) glanced up at the full moon and the moving clouds. Nervous and wracked with intense pain, he could not sleep. Periodically the clouds immersed the field in total darkness, and it seemed he might be alone there, until the clouds and drifting smoke unmasked the brilliant, cold moonlight and the hundreds of dead, dying, and wounded around him. The faces of the dead glowed in a ghostly white until the moon disappeared again. Off in the distance, he heard a man repeatedly groan: "Oh, Seventh Michigan." Purman longed for sunrise. Farther to the northwest, the severely wounded Private Cole (Company A, 57th New York) tried to block out the woeful sounds of the injured and dying by covering his head, but it did no good. He finally succumbed to exhaustion and blacked out into a merciful sleep.[47]

---

45 West, "On Little Round Top," *National Tribune*, November 22, 1906.

46 Polley, *Hood's Texas Brigade*, 178.

47 Stewart, *140th Pennsylvania*, 426; Cole, *Under Five Commanders*, 203.

A slight breeze cleared the smoke away and revealed a night sky bristling with twinkling stars and an intense, unnerving silence. The exhausted, anxious soldiers of the 118th Pennsylvania curled up where they sat and tried to get their sorely-needed sleep. Captain Plumb (3rd Company, 61st New York), unbuckling his sword belt before bedding down, felt a queer knot in his vest pocket. Fishing his fingers into it, he pulled out the ring of small keys he kept there. A minié ball had struck his belt plate, passed under his belt and through his vest. It ended up lodged in the key heads. Obviously, Plumb's time had not yet come.

In the field east of the Stony Hill Pvts. James Brice and Clem Humphreys (Company K, 50th Georgia) stumbled upon Sgt. William Jones who lay on his back, crippled with a shattered ankle. Placing him on a litter, they trundled him down the hill to the Rose's stone barn where they laid him on a pile of straw and handed the parched sergeant a canteen. He guzzled it while they cut the boots off his feet. After washing off his right ankle, they gave him a second canteen of water and left him on his own.[48]

In the dark, Captain Weygant (124th New York) fell in with four stretcher crews, who said they belonged to the III Corps. They carried their burdens single file through the woods towards the hospital. The captain slipped alongside the first litter and asked to which regiment he belonged. "3rd Michigan," came the reply. He repeated his question to the next man. "Sergeant, 63rd New York," he heard. The third man said he was from Pennsylvania. The fourth, despite the fact he stared right into Weygant's eyes, made no reply. The captain felt his forehead. It was cold and clammy—a corpse.[49]

Weygant found the grove surrounding the hospital blanketed with casualties—so thick it seemed that he could not walk without stepping on a body. Threading through the brush to the edge of the woods, he came upon the operating theater. He tried working his way toward the center, hoping to find his own men. Instead, he got himself immersed in an infernal world of unearthly shrieks, moans, and howls. Delirious men, mistaking him for a surgeon, clutched at him, begging him to attend to their wounds. While trying to step over one such man, the fellow unexpectedly leaped to his feet in front of him. Ripping the bloody bandage from his chest and shoving it at Weygant, he

---

48 Survivors' Association, *118th Pennsylvania*, 253; Fuller, *Personal Recollections*, 99; Bohannon, (ed.), "Wounded and Captured at Gettysburg," *Military Images*, vol. IX, 14.

49 *New York at Gettysburg*, vol. 2, 873.

loosed a terrifying howl. As he did so, a sudden spurt of blood shot from the wound into the captain's face. Flinging his arms open, the man collapsed, face first, across another wounded man, who screamed. Unable to endure any more such horrors, Weygant ran from the place as fast as he could go.[50]

73rd New York, III Corps, Army of the Potomac
Cemetery Ridge in the Vicinity of the G. Weikert Farm

The ambulances went out as soon as the firing subsided. Private Brannigan (Company A, 73rd New York) mused about the red lanterns of the stretcher-bearers from both armies that flickered like hundreds of fireflies in the dark. The Yankees, at least, were out there against orders. When men from the 11th Massachusetts asked permission to relieve the wounded, General Humphreys refused, saying he had no authority to allow it. Despite the prohibition, a number of them stole canteens from their sleeping comrades and disappeared into the darkness on their errands of mercy. At one point, a Rebel strayed into the 11th Massachusetts' picket line. "I am your prisoner, if you say so, but I am giving water to all who ask for it." They let him go with their blessings and encouragement. "In every house or barn, in every shady nook, under every wide spreading tree were established hospitals, and by the flickering of watch fires limbs were lopped off and wounds bound," Brannigan grimly informed his father.[51]

In accordance with the dictates of "rank has its privileges," Humphreys allowed his staff, under Captain Cavada's guidance, to slip into the darkness to find Captain Chester's body. The whole time Cavada kept thinking about the fate of his brother, the lieutenant colonel of the 114th Pennsylvania. As the party gingerly picked its way toward Plum Run, they encountered a large number of twisted Yankee bodies. Many lay by themselves, others in clusters of three or more. Cavada noted how they lay in "most unnatural attitudes." An occasional injured man pleaded for help, and they would give him water and the false promise that the ambulance would follow in a few minutes. Here and there, they found a Rebel casualty. Crossing to the west side of the creek, they discovered many more Rebel dead. Then they proceeded to scour the area where they last saw Chester alive.

50 Ibid., 874

51 Felix Brannigan to his Father, GNMP.

Presently they came upon his lifeless white horse, its lower face blown away. And next to him, they discovered the headless corpse of the sergeant in charge of the orderlies and nearby the outstretched body of a Rebel with his brains oozing out from a pistol shot in his forehead. Unable to find Chester, the officers returned sadly to their bivouac only to discover that someone else had brought him in earlier and he now lay dying in the III Corps Hospital.[52]

Around 10 p.m., a completely spent 1st Lieutenant Blake (Company K, 11th Massachusetts) draped his gum blanket over a cradle of two fence rails. Placing his spectacles in his kepi, he nestled between the rails, pulled his great coat over himself, and fell asleep.[53]

1st Texas, Longstreet's Corps,
Army of Northern Virginia
The Devil's Den

Private Sims (Company F, 1st Texas) walked his post, trying not to hear the anguished pleas of the wounded and dying for help. "Oh, pardner, bring me a drink of water," came a plaintive cry not too far away. "I'll assure you that no one will hurt you. My leg is shot off or I would come to you. I'll give you a dollar for a drink of water. I'll give you all the money I have for a drink of water." Sims shut out the man's entreaties and continued on his beat. Having no water himself and unable to leave his post, he did everything he could to fight off overwhelming exhaustion, including rubbing tobacco in his eyes to keep them open.[54]

14th Vermont, I Corps, Army of the Potomac
Near the Creek Bottom, North of Trostle's

Under Col. William T. Nichols' direct orders, Pvt. David Parker (Company C, 14th Vermont) and three of his comrades had searched the field for a couple of hours to bring in Brigadier General Barksdale, dead or alive. Bone weary of stooping over and inspecting the dead, dying, and wounded, the search party finally found the general around 11 p.m. Parker kneeled down beside the

---

52 Cavada, Diary, July 2, 1863, FSNMP.

53 Blake, *"Personal Reminiscences of Gettysburg,"* 27, USAHEC.

54 Sims, *Recollections*, 2, GNMP.

general, Parker cradled his head in his lap and began spoon feeding him coffee from his canteen.

Barksdale readily identified himself and asked the Yankees to procure a stretcher because he weighed too much to carry on a blanket. As two of the party took off to get assistance, the general painfully told Parker he was dying and related as much as he could of his last will and testament. His wife and two sons preoccupied him. "To leave them is the hardest struggle I ever knew," he whispered. "But tell them all that I died like a brave man, that I led my men fearlessly in the fight." Barksdale described his wounding in detail and continued to ramble on, "Tell them all, all my friends at home that I have never regretted the steps I have taken and, although dying, I do not regret my steps now." He began drifting away, lapsing in and out of consciousness. "May God ever watch over and care for my dear wife and, oh, my boys, may God be a father to them. Tell them to be good men and brave, always defend the right."

His voice trailed off as he drifted off into labored restiveness. The stretcher crew under 1st Sgt. Henry Vaughan (Company B) lifted him onto the litter and carried him back to the Hummelbaugh farm on Cemetery Ridge. Barksdale gave the sergeant his hat and gloves and left him with the message, "Tell my wife I fought like a man and will die like one."[55]

148th Pennsylvania, II Corps, Army of the Potomac
The Hummelbaugh Farm

The 148th Pennsylvania slept on its arms several hundred feet west of the farmhouse. In the dark, Pvt. William C. Meyer (Company A) noticed the dark silhouettes of the stretcher party laboring across the field with Barksdale's stretcher. He followed them up to the house and watched as they laid him down in the shadows of the light from the windows. When the stretcher-bearers left, he quickly slipped up to Barksdale and cut a patch of gold lace from his collar then hurried back to the "boys" to show them his trophy.[56]

The 148th Pennsylvania's Assistant Surgeon Alfred T. Hamilton saw a staff orderly and litter party bring in the bald Confederate general. The Confederate

---

55 David Parker to Mrs. Barksdale, March 22, 1882, Mississippi Department of Archives and History, Jackson, quoted; Benedict, *Vermont at Gettysburg*, 9; Eric Ward, (ed.), *Army Life in Virginia, The Civil War Letters of George G. Benedict* (Mechanicsburg, PA, 2002), 201-202.

56 Muffly, *148th Pennsylvania*, 543.

officer wore what the doctor referred to as "jean" pants, with double gold stripes down the outer seams, and a short "roundabout" jacket with braided sleeves and a white collar with three gold stars on each side. His jacket had a Mississippi button with a star in the center and three Masonic studs fastened his shirt. The orderly identified the patient as General Barksdale.

Hamilton examined the former U.S. Congressman. He had a bullet exit wound through his left breast, and a broken left leg, which had apparently been hit by two rifle balls. The doctor administered opiates to Barksdale to relieve his pain. Several times, the general asked him whether the wounds were fatal, and each time, Hamilton bluntly assured him they were. Barksdale asked the doctor about the Union army's strength to which Hamilton replied there were heavy reinforcements on the way. "Militiamen under McClellan?" Barksdale surmised, evidently aware of the rumor that Lincoln had reinstated McClellan to army command. The doctor administered what succor and assistance he could and had him placed outside under the care of a company drummer.[57]

Not too far to the west of the house, the wounded Adjutant Muffly (148th Pennsylvania) stepped on something that felt strange. Bending over in the darkness, he picked up the obstruction and quickly hurled it aside: it was a severed arm. He turned around and saw a light shining through the window on the west side of the Jacob Hummelbaugh house. In the moonlight, he could see a grisly pile of amputated arms, feet, hands, and legs, which the doctors had chucked out of the window until they had "topped out" at the sill. Stumbling around to the front of the house, he happened upon a drummer boy who was spoon-feeding water to a badly wounded Confederate general. The officer had a hole in his breast and a shattered leg. In between spoons, Barksdale, clearly out of his head, rasped, "Bring me water, cold water. When I am well I am a great lover of water, and now when I am shot all to pieces and burning with fever, I must have cold water." Then he unexpectedly blurted: "Yes, you think you have whipped us, but wait till morning and you will hear Ewell thundering in your rear." Muffly limped away, distraught over the general's fevered ravings.[58]

57 Ibid., 245.

58 Ibid.

17th Mississippi, Longstreet's Corps,
Army of Northern Virginia
The Field West of the Sherfy Farm

Private James W. Duke (Company C, 17th Mississippi), exhausted from the afternoon's battle, began searching for his brother, Archibald, whom he had lost contact with when the shooting started. The adjutant, having seen Arch go down, told Jim where he could find him. Alone, in the dark, the worried soldier scoured the casualty-strewn field for his brother. As he stooped over one wounded man, he heard: "Thank God! My prayers are answered. I have asked Him to take me in place of you, as I am prepared and you are not."

Jim burst into tears as he lowered himself next to his brother. He promised to live a better life. (The doctors later amputated Arch's leg, but he died from gangrene two weeks later. In 1906, Jim confessed it took many years for him to turn his life around. "I am trying to meet him over the river," he conceded.) Not too far away Surgeon William F. Shine (Phillips' Legion) rode over the hard fought ground around the Rose farm, trying to hunt out injured men of his own brigade. The groans and pleas of the wounded inundated the fields. The contrasts the field presented struck Shine: "The moon is shining beautifully," he observed, "and the ground in front is almost black with Yankees." But Pvt. William F. Stilwell (Company F, 53rd Georgia) was more profound: "War is like the infidels," he wrote, "faith it will do well until you come to test it and then it makes the hart sick."[59]

59 Duke, "Mississippians at Gettysburg," in *Confederate Veteran*, vol. 14, 216; William F. Shine, Diary, July 2, 1863, copy in Vertical Files, GNMP; William R. Stilwell to Mollie, July 10, 1863, C. Denise Peters Collection, Vertical Files, GNMP.

Appendix
Order of Battle for the Troops on Cemetery and Seminary Ridges, July 2, 1863

Army of the Potomac—Maj. Gen. George G. Meade
I Army Corps—Maj. Gen. John Newton
3rd Division—Maj. Gen. Abner Doubleday

3rd Brigade—Brig. Gen. George J. Stannard (Codori)

Regiment	Engaged	KIA	WIA	CIA	Total	%
13th VT[1]	350 est.	2[2]		2	4	1

II Army Corps—Maj. Gen. Winfield S. Hancock
1st Division—Brig. John C. Caldwell

1st Brigade—Col. Edward C. Cross[3] (Wheatfield)

Regiment	Engaged	KIA	WIA	CIA	Total	%
F & S	3		1[4]		1	33%
5th NH	179	27	53		80	45%
61st NY	104	6	56		62	60%
81st PA	175	5	49	8	62	35%
Brigade	*461*	*38*	*159*	*8*	*205*	*45%*
Total %		8%	35%	2%	45%	

2nd Brigade—Col. Patrick Kelly (Stony Hill)[5]

F & S	2				0	0%
28th MA	224	8	57	35	100	45%
63rd NY	75	5	10	8	23	42%
69th NY	75	5	14	6	25	33%
88th NY	90	7	17	4	28	31%
116th PA	66	2	11	9	22	33%
Brigade	*532*	*27*	*109*	*62*	*198*	*37%*
Total %		5%	21%	12%	37%	

3rd Brigade—Brig. Gen. Samuel Zook (Stony Hill)[6]

F & S	4		1[7]		1	25%
52nd NY	134	2	26	10	38	28%
57th NY	175	4	28	2	34	19%
66th NY	147	5	29	10	44	30%
140th PA	515	37	144	60	241	47%
Brigade	*975*	*48*	*228*	*82*	*358*	*37%*
Total %		5%	23%	8%	37%	

(Note: the 'notes' for this Appendix are located at the end of the Appendix.)

4th Brigade—Col. John R. Brooke (Wheatfield, The Loop)[8]

Regiment	Engaged	KIA	WIA	CIA	Total	%
F & S	1				0	0
27th CT	75	10	23	4	37	49%
2nd DE	234	11	61	12	84	36%
64th NY	204	15	64	19	98	48%
53rd PA	135	7	67	6	80	59%
145th PA	202	11	69	10	90	45%
Brigade	*851*	*54*	*284*	*51*	*389*	*46%*
Total %		6%	34%	6%	46%	

2nd Division—Brig. Gen. John Gibbon[9]

1st Brigade—Brig. Gen. William Harrow (Cemetery Ridge, the Angle)[10]

F & S	3		1		1	33%
19th ME[11]	439	23	155	3	181	41%
15th MA[12]	239	10	94	28	132	55%
1st MN[13]	262	27	141	1	169	65%
82nd NY[14]	335	19	51	8	78	23%
Brigade	*1278*	*79*	*442*	*40*	*561*	*44%*
Total %		6%	35%	3%	44%	

2nd Brigade—Brig. Gen. Alexander Webb (the Angle)[15]

F & S	3				0	0%
Band	16				0	0%
69th PA[16]	284	11	17		28	10%
71st PA[17]	261			1	1	0%
72nd PA[18]	380	3	1		4	1%
106th PA[19]	280	9	54	1	64	23%
Brigade	*1224*	*23*	*72*	*2*	*97*	*8%*
Total %		2%	6%	0%	8%	

3rd Brigade—Col. Norman J. Hall (Cemetery Ridge, the Angle)

F & S	2				0	0%
19th MA[20]	163	2	2		4	3%
20th MA[21]	243		3	1	4	2%
7th MI[22]	165	3	12		15	9%
42nd NY[23]	197	1	7		8	4%
59th NY[24]	152	2	13		15	10%
Brigade	*922*	*8*	*37*	*1*	*46*	*5%*
Total %		1%	4%	0%	5%	

3rd Division—Brig. Gen. Alexander Hays

1st Brigade—Col. Samuel S. Carroll (Ziegler's Grove, Emmitsburg Road)[25]

Regiment	Engaged	KIA	WIA	CIA	Total	%
8th OH[26]	209	3	29		32	15%
Total %		1%	14%		15%	

2nd Brigade—Col. Thomas A. Smyth (Ziegler's Grove, Bliss Farm)

F & S	2				0	0%
14th CT[27]	172		1		1	1%
1st DE[28]	251	5	16	11	32	13%
12th NJ[29]	150	4	37	1	42	28%
108th NY[30]	200	1	24		25	13%
Brigade	*775[31]*	*10*	*78*	*12*	*100*	*13%*
Total %		1%	10%	2%	13%	

3rd Brigade—Col. George L. Willard
(Ziegler's Orchard, Bliss Farm, George Weikert Farm)

F & S	2	1			1	50%
39th NY[32]	269	12	38		50	19%
111th NY[33]	390	28	103	3	134	34%
125th NY[34]	392	14	21	2	37	9%
126th NY[35]	455	18	84	2	104	23%
Brigade	*1508*	*72*	*246*	*7*	*325*	*22%*
Total %		5%	16%	1%	22%	

II Corps Artillery—Capt. John G. Hazard (Ziegler's Grove, The Angle)

F & S	4				0	0%
1st NY, Btty. B[36]	117	1	8		9	8%
1st RI, Btty. A[37]	117		3		3	3%
1st RI, Btty. B[38]	129	1	7	1	9	7%
1st US, Btty. I[39]	112	1	24		25	22%
4th US, Btty. A[40]	126	2	6	2	10	8%
Battalion	*605*	*5*	*48*	*3*	*56*	*9%*
Total %		1%	8%	0%	9%	

III Army Corps—Maj. Gen. Daniel E. Sickles; Maj. Gen. David B. Birney

1st Division—Maj. Gen. David B. Birney; Brig. Gen. J. H. Hobart Ward

1st Brigade—Brig. Gen. Charles K. Graham (Peach Orchard, Sherfy Farm)[41]

Regiment	Engaged	KIA	WIA	CIA	Total	%
F & S	3		2	1	3	100%
57th PA	207	11	46	58	115	56%
63rd PA	246	1	29	4	34	14%
68th PA	320	13	126	13	152	48%
105th PA	274	8	115	9	132	48%
114th PA	259	9	86	60	155	60%
141st PA	209	25	103	21	149	71%
Brigade	*1518*	*67*	*507*	*166*	*740*	*49%*
Total %		5%	33%	11%	49%	

2nd Brigade—Brig. Gen. J. H. Hobart Ward; Col. Hiram Berdan (Pitzer's Woods, Houck's Ridge, Devil's Den, Slyder Farm)[42]

F & S	6		1		1	17%
20th IN	400	32	114	10	156	39%
3rd ME	210	18	59	45	122	58%
4th ME	287	11	59	74	144	50%
86th NY	287	11	51	4	66	23%
124th NY	238	28	57	5	90	38%
99th PA	277	18	81	11	110	40%
1st USSS	312	6	37	6	49	16%
2nd USSS	169	5	23	15	43	25%
Brigade	*2186*	*129*	*482*	*170*	*781*	*36%*
Total %		6%	22%	8%	36%	

3rd Brigade—Col. P. Regis De Trobriand (Rose Farm, Plum Run, Wheatfield)[43]

F & S	1				0	0%
17th ME	350	18	112	3	133	38%
3rd MI	238	7	31	7	45	19%
5th MI	216	19	86	4	109	50%
40th NY	431	23	120	7	150	35%
110th PA	152	8	45		53	35%
Brigade	*1388*	*75*	*394*	*21*	*490*	*35%*
Total %		5%	28%	2%	35%	

Second Division—Brig. Andrew A. Humphreys

1st Brigade—Brig. Gen. Joseph B. Carr
(Klingle Farm, Rogers Farm, Codori Farm)[44]

Regiment	Engaged	KIA	WIA	CIA	Total	%
F & S	2		2		2	100%
1st MA	321	16	83	21	120	37%
11th MA	286	23	96	10	129	45%
16th MA	245	15	53	13	81	33%
12th NH	224	20	70	2	92	41%
11th NJ	275	17	124	12	153	56%
26th PA	365	30	176	7	213	58%
Brigade	*1718*	*121*	*604*	*65*	*790*	*46%*
Total %		7%	35%	4%	46%	

2nd Brigade—Excelsior Brigade—Col. William R. Brewster
(Peach Orchard, Klingle Farm)[45]

F & S	3		2		2	67%
70th NY	288	20	93	4	117	41%
71st NY	243	10	68	13	91	38%
72nd NY	305	7	79	28	114	37%
73rd NY	349	51	103	8	162	46%
74th NY	266	12	74	3	89	34%
120th NY	383	32	154	17	203	53%
Brigade	*1837*	*132*	*573*	*73*	*778*	*42%*
Total %		7%	31%	4%	42%	

3rd Brigade—Col. George Burling (Peach Orchard, Sherfy Farm,
Trostle Farm, Stony Hill, Wheatfield)[46]

F & S	2				0	0%
2nd NH	354	20	137	36	193	55%
5th NJ	206	13	65	16	94	46%
6th NJ	207	1	32	8	41	20%
7th NJ	275	15	86	13	114	42%
8th NJ	170	7	38	2	47	28%
115th PA	151	3	18	3	24	16%
Brigade	*1365*	*59*	*376*	*78*	*513*	*38%*
Total %		4%	28%	6%	38%	

III Corps Artillery—Capt. George E. Randolph
(Peach Orchard, Klingle Farm, Devil's Den)[47]

Regiment	Engaged	KIA	WIA	CIA	Total	%
F & S	2				0	0%
1st NJ, Btty. B	131	1	16	3	20	15%
1st NY, Btty. D	116		10	8	18	16%
4th NY, Indpt.	126		13		13	10%
1st RI, Btty. E	108	3	26	1	30	28%
4th US, Btty. K	113	2	19	4	25	22%
Battalion	*596*	*8*	*81*	*17*	*106*	*18%*
Total %		1%	14%	3%	18%	

V Army Corps—Maj. Gen. George Sykes

1st Division—Brig. Gen. James Barnes

1st Brigade—Col. William S. Tilton (Stony Hill)[48]

F & S	4				0	0%
18th MA	139	1	23	3	27	19%
22nd MA	137	3	27	1	31	23%
1st MI	145	5	33	4	42	29%
118th PA	233	3	19	3	25	11%
Brigade	*655*	*12*	*102*	*11*	*125*	*19%*
Total %		2%	16%	2%	19%	

2nd Brigade—Col. Jacob B. Sweitzer (Stony Hill, Wheatfield)[49]

F & S	1				0	0%
32nd MA	242	13	62	5	80	33%
4th MI	342	25	64	76	165	48%
62nd PA	426	28	107	40	175	41%
Brigade	*1011*	*67*	*232*	*121*	*420*	*42%*
Total %		7%	23%	12%	42%	

3rd Brigade—Col. Strong Vincent (Little Round Top)[50]

F & S	1		1		1	100%
20th ME	386	21	91	5	125	32%
16th MI	263	23	34	3	60	23%
44th NY	391	26	82	3	111	28%
83rd PA	295	10	45		55	19%
Brigade	*1336*	*88*	*253*	*11*	*352*	*26%*
Total %		7%	19%	1%	26%	

2nd Division—Brig. Gen. Romeyn B. Ayres

1st Brigade—Col. Hannibal Day (Plum Run, Wheatfield)[51]

Regiment	Engaged	KIA	WIA	CIA	Total	%
F & S	2		1		1	50%
3rd US	300	6	66	1	73	24%
4th US	173	10	30		40	23%
6th US	150	4	40		44	29%
12th US	419	8	71	13	92	22%
14th US	513	18	110	4	132	26%
Brigade	*1557*	*46*	*318*	*18*	*382*	*25%*
Total %		3%	20%	1%	25%	

2nd Brigade—Col. Sidney Burbank (Plum Run, Wheatfield)[52]

Regiment	Engaged	KIA	WIA	CIA	Total	%
F & S	2				0	0%
2nd US	197	6	55	6	67	34%
7th US	116	12	45	2	59	51%
10th US	93	16	32	3	51	55%
11th US	286	19	92	9	120	42%
17th US	260	25	118	7	150	58%
Brigade	*954*	*78*	*342*	*27*	*447*	*47%*
Total %		8%	36%	3%	47%	

3rd Brigade—Brig. Gen. Stephen H. Weed (Little Round Top)[53]

Regiment	Engaged	KIA	WIA	CIA	Total	%
F & S	4		1		1	25%
140th NY	453	26	89	18	133	29%
146th NY	460	4	24		28	6%
91st PA	222	3	16		19	9%
155th PA	365	6	13		19	5%
Brigade	*1504*	*40*	*142*	*18*	*200*	*13%*
Total %		3%	9%	1%	13%	

3rd Division—Brig. Gen. Samuel W. Crawford

1st Brigade—Col. William McCandless (J. Weikert Farm, Plum Run, Wheatfield)[54]

Regiment	Engaged	KIA	WIA	CIA	Total	%
F & S	1				0	0%
1st PA Res.	382	8	38		46	12%
2nd PA Res.	235	3	33	1	37	16%
6th PA Res.	327	2	22		24	7%
13th PA Res.	301	7	39	2	48	16%
Brigade	*1259*	*20*	*132*	*3*	*155*	*12%*
Total %		2%	11%	0%	12%	

2nd Brigade—Col. Joseph W. Fisher
(Little Round Top, J. Weikert Farm, Plum Run)[55]

Regiment	Engaged	KIA	WIA	CIA	Total	%
F & S	1				0	0%
5th PA Res.	288		2		2	1%
9th PA Res.	325		5		5	2%
10th PA Res.	401	2	3		5	1%
11th PA Res.	327	3	38		41	13%
12th PA Res.	276	1	1		2	1%
Brigade	*1618*	*6*	*49*		*55*	*3%*
Total %		0%	3%		3%	3%

V Corps Artillery—Capt. Augustus P. Martin
(Peach Orchard, Little Round Top, J. Weikert Farm)[56]

	Engaged	KIA	WIA	CIA	Total	%
F & S	3				0	0%
3rd MA, Btty.	115		6		6	5%
1st OH, Btty.	113		2		2	2%
5th US, Btty. D	68	7	6		13	19%
5th US, Btty. I	71	1	19	2	22	31%
Battalion	*432*	*8*	*33*	*2*	*43*	*10%*
Total %		2%	8%	0%	10%	

VI Army Corps—Maj. Gen. John Sedgwick
3rd Division—Brig. Gen. Frank Wheaton
3rd Brigade—Col. David J. Nevin (Little Round Top, Wheatfield)[57]

	Engaged	KIA	WIA	CIA	Total	%
F & S	1				0	0%
62nd NY	237	1	11		12	5%
93rd PA	245		10		10	4%
98th PA	368		11		11	3%
102nd PA	103				0	0%
139th PA	464	1	19		20	4%
Brigade	*1418*	*2*	*51*		*53*	*4%*
Total %		0%	4%		4%	

Cavalry Corps—Maj. Gen. Alfred Pleasonton

1st Division—Brig. Gen. John Buford

2nd Brigade—Col. Thomas C. Devin
(Emmitsburg Road, Peach Orchard, Sherfy Farm)[58]

Regiment	Engaged	KIA	WIA	CIA	Total	%
F & S	5				0	0%
6th NY[59]	218	2	1	6	9	4%
9th NY[60]	367			1	1	0%
17th PA	464			4	4	1%
3rd WVA	59			4	4	7%
Brigade	*1138*	*2*	*1*	*15*	*18*	*2%*
Total %		0%	0%	1%	2%	

Horse Artillery—Capt. James M. Robertson

2nd Brigade—Capt. John C. Tidball (Peach Orchard, Sherfy Farm)

Regiment	Engaged	KIA	WIA	CIA	Total	%
2nd US, Btty. A[61]	75				0	0%

Army Artillery Reserve—Brig. Gen. Robert O. Tyler, Capt. James M. Robertson

1st Regular Brigade—Captain Dunbar R. Ransom
(Cemetery Ridge, Codori Farm)[62]

Regiment	Engaged	KIA	WIA	CIA	Total	%
F & S	2				0	0%
3rd US, Btty. F&K	115	9	14	1	24	21%
4th US, Btty. C	95	1	18		19	20%
5th US, Btty. C	104	2	14		16	15%
Battalion	*316*	*12*	*46*	*1*	*59*	*19%*
		4%	15%	0%	19%	

1st Volunteer Brigade—Maj. Freeman McGilvery (Millerstown Road)[63]

Regiment	Engaged	KIA	WIA	CIA	Total	%
F & S	2				0	0%
5th MA, Btty. E	104	4	17		21	20%
9th MA	104	4	18	2	24	23%
15th NY Indpt.	70	3	13		16	23%
PA Indpt., C & F	105	2	23	3	28	27%
Battalion	*385*	*17*	*71*	*5*	*93*	*24%*
Total %		4%	18%	17%	24%	24%

4th Volunteer Brigade—Capt. Robert H. Fitzhugh
(Peach Orchard, George Weikert Farm)[64]

Regiment	Engaged	KIA	WIA	CIA	Total	%
F & S	2				0	0%
6th ME	87		13		13	15%
1st NY, Btty. G	84		7		7	8%
Battalion	*171*		*20*		*20*	*12%*
Total %			12%		12%	

Summary
Army of the Potomac—Maj. Gen. George G. Meade

	Engaged	KIA	WIA	CIA	Total
I Army Corps—Newton	350	2		2	4
3rd Div.—Doubleday	350	2		2	4
II Army Corps—Hancock	9340	367	1732	268	2367
1st Div.—Caldwell	2819	167	780	203	1150
2nd Div.—Gibbon	3424	110	551	43	704
3rd Div.—Hays	2492	85	353	19	457
II Corps Art.—Hazard	605	5	48	3	56
III Army Corps—Sickles; Birney	10608	591	3018	589	4198
1st Div.—Birney; Ward	5092	271	1383	357	2011
2nd Div.—Humphreys	4920	312	1553	216	2081
III Army Corps Art.—Randolph	596	8	81	17	106
V Army Corps—Sykes	10326	365	1603	211	2179
1st Div.—Barnes	3002	167	587	143	897
2nd Div.—Ayres	4015	164	802	63	1029
3rd Div.—Crawford	2877	26	181	3	210
V Army Corps Art.—Martin	432	8	33	2	43
VI Army Corps—Sedgwick	1418	2	51		53
3rd Div.—Wheaton	1418	2	51		53
Cav. Corps—Pleasonton	1138	2	1	15	18
1st Division—Buford	1138	2	1	15	18
Horse Art.—Robertson	75				0
2nd Bde.—Tidball	75				0
Army Art. Reserve—Tyler, Robertson	872	29	91	5	125
1st Reg. Bde.—Ransom	316	12	46	1	59
1st Vol. Bde.—McGilvery	385	17	71	5	93
4th Vol. Bde. Fitzhugh	171		20		20

Army of the Potomac—Meade

	Engaged	KIA	WIA	CIA	Total
I Corps	350	2		2	4
II Corps	9340	367	1732	268	2367
III Corps	10608	591	3018	589	4198
V Corps	10326	365	1603	211	2179
VI Corps	1418	2	51		53
Cav. Corps	1138	2	1	15	18
Horse Artillery	75				0
Artillery Reserve	872	29	91	5	125
Total	34127	1358	6496	1090	8944
Total %		4%	19%	3%	26%

Army of Northern Virginia—Gen. Robert E. Lee
First Army Corps—Lt. Gen. James Longstreet

McLaws's Division—Maj. Gen. Lafayette McLaws

Kershaw's Brigade—Brig. Gen. Joseph B. Kershaw
(Rose Farm, Peach Orchard, Stony Hill)[65]

Regiment	Engaged	KIA	WIA	CIA	Total	%
F & S	6				0	0%
2nd SC	412	27	125	4	156	38%
3rd SC	407	18	63	2	83	20%
7th SC	408	18	85	7	110	27%
8th SC	300	21	79		100	33%
15th SC	449	21	98	18	137	31%
3rd SC Bttn.	203	10	33	3	46	23%
Brigade	*2185*	*115*	*483*	*34*	*632*	*29%*
Total %		5%	22%	2%	29%	

Semmes's Brigade Brig. Gen. Paul J. Semmes (Rose Farm)[66]

F & S	4	1			1	25%
10th GA	303	17	73	11	101	33%
50th GA	303	17	65	14	96	32%
51st GA	303	15	40	40	95	31%
53rd GA	422	30	61	8	99	24%
Brigade	*1335*	*80*	*239*	*73*	*391*	*29%*
Total %		6%	18%	6%	29%	

Barksdale's Brigade—Brig. Gen. William Barksdale
(Peach Orchard, Rogers Farm, Trostle Farm)[67]

F & S	4		1		1	25%
13th MS	481	39	171	33	243	51%
17th MS	468	64	108	98	270	58%
18th MS	242	20	81	36	137	57%
21st MS	424	18	110	11	139	33%
Brigade	*1619*	*156*	*470*	*178*	*804*	*50%*
Total %		10%	29%	11%	50%	

Wofford's Brigade—Brig. Gen. William T. Wofford
(Wheatfield, J. Weikert Farm)[68]

Regiment	Engaged	KIA	WIA	CIA	Total	%
F & S	4				0	0%
16th GA	303	20	41	43	104	34%
18th GA	303	13	16	17	36	12%
24th GA	303	10	29	46	85	28%
Cobb's Leg.	213	6	16		22	10%
Phillips Leg.	271	6	41	19	66	24%
3rd GA Bn.	233	3	3	7	13	6%
Brigade	*1632*	48	*184*	*138*	*370*	*23%*
		3%	11%	9%	23%	

Division Artillery—Col. Henry C. Cabell (Warfield Ridge)

Regiment	Engaged	KIA	WIA	CIA	Total	%
F & S	4				0	0%
1st NC, Co. A (Manly) [69]	131	4	15		19	15%
Troup GA Art., (Carlton)[70]	90	1	1	4	6	7%
Pulaski GA Arty., (Fraser) [71]	63	3	12		15	24%
Richmond How. 1st Co. (McCarthy) [72]	90		7		7	8%
Battalion	*378*	*8*	*35*	*4*	*47*	*12%*
Total %		2%	9%	1%	12%	

Hood's Division—Maj. Gen. John B. Hood, Brig. Gen. Evander M. Law

Law's Brigade—Brig. Gen. Evander M. Law, Col. James L. Sheffield
(Big Round Top, Little Round Top, Slyder Farm, Devil's Den)[73]

Regiment	Engaged	KIA	WIA	CIA	Total	%
F & S	4				2	2	50%
4th AL	346	18	55	19	92	27%
15th AL[74]	499	17	54	90	161	32%
44th AL[75]	363	27	130	32	189	52%
47th AL	347	10	46	13	69	20%
48th AL	374	8	81	17	106	28%
Brigade	*1933*	*80*	*366*	*173*	*619*	*32%*
Total %		4%	19%	9%	32%	

Anderson's Brigade—Brig. Gen. George T. Anderson, Col. William White, Lt. Col. William W. White (Rose Farm, Wheatfield)[76]

Regiment	Engaged	KIA	WIA	CIA	Total	%
F & S	10		1		1	10%
8th GA	311	36	103	29	168	54%
9th GA[77]	340	27	130	32	189	56%
11th GA[78]	309	23	171	5	199	64%
58th GA	525	37	75	30	142	27%
Brigade	*1495*	*123*	*480*	*96*	*699*	*47%*
Total %		8%	32%	6%	47%	

Robertson's Brigade—Brig. Gen. Jerome B. Robertson, Lt. Col. Phillip A. Work (Rose Farm, Slyder Farm, Devil's Den, Little Round Top)[79]

F & S	5		1		1	20%
3rd AR	479	41	101	40	182	38%
1st TX[80]	426	25	48	20	93	22%
4th TX	415	28	53	31	112	27%
5th TX	409	54	112	45	211	52%
Brigade	*1734*	*148*	*315*	*136*	*599*	*35%*
Total %		9%	18%	8%	35%	

Benning's Brigade—Brig. Gen. Henry L. Benning (Devil's Den)[81]

F & S	4		1		1	25%
2nd GA	348	25	66	11	102	29%
15th GA[82]	368	17	43	10	70	19%
17th GA	350	31	66	11	108	31%
20th GA[83]	350	23	77	4	104	30%
Brigade	*1420*	*96*	*253*	*36*	*385*	*27%*
Total %		7%	18%	3%	27%	

Division Artillery—Maj. Mathias Henry, Maj. John C. Haskell (Southern Warfield Ridge)[84]

F & S	9		1		1	11%
40th NC, Co. H (Latham)	112	1	2		3	3%
10th NC, Co. D (Reilly)	148	2	4		6	4%
Battalion	*269*	*3*	*7*		*10*	*4%*
Total %		1%	3%		4%	

First Corps Reserve Artillery—Col. James B. Walton

Alexander's Artillery Battalion—Col. E, Porter Alexander (Northern Warfield Ridge)[85]

Regiment	Engaged	KIA	WIA	CIA	Total	%
F & S (Moody)	9				0	0%
Madison (LA) Lt. (Fickling)	135	4	29		33	24%
Brooks Art. (SC)	71	7	29		36	51%
Co. C, 12th (VA) Bttn. (Taylor)[86]	90	2	7		9	10%
Ashland (VA) Art. (Woolfolk)	103	3	24	1	28	27%
Bedford (VA) Art. (Jordan)	78	1	7	1	9	12%
Parker (VA) Lt. (Parker)	90	3	14	1	18	20%
Battalion	*576*	*20*	*110*	*3*	*133*	*23%*
Total %		4%	19%	1%	23%	

Third Corps—Lt. Gen. Ambrose Powell Hill

Anderson's Division—Maj. Gen. Richard H. Anderson

Wilcox's Brigade—Brig. Gen. Cadmus Wilcox (Trostle Farm)[87]

	Engaged	KIA	WIA	CIA	Total	%
F & S	5		1		1	20%
8th AL	477	40	146	80	266	56%
9th AL	306	8	32	76	116	38%
10th AL	311	15	89		104	33%
11th AL	311	7	68		75	24%
14th AL	316	8	40		48	15%
Brigade	*1726*	*78*	*376*	*156*	*610*	*35%*
Total %		5%	22%	9%	35%	

Wright's Brigade—Brig. Gen. Ambrose R. Wright, Col. William Gibson (Codori Farm)[88]

	Engaged	KIA	WIA	CIA	Total	%
F & S	4	4			0	0%
3rd GA	441	49	139	31	219	50%
22nd GA	400	41	70	60	171	43%
48th GA	395	70	97	57	224	57%
2nd GA Bn.	173	24	37	21	82	47%
Brigade	*1413*	*184*	*343*	*169*	*696*	*49%*
Total %		13%	24%	12%	49%	

Perry's Brigade—Col. David Lang (Klingle Farm, Codori Farm)[89]

Regiment	Engaged	KIA	WIA	CIA	Total	%
F & S	7				0	0%
2nd FL	242	11	70	16	97	40%
5th FL	321	12	63	16	91	28%
8th FL	176	10	84	16	110	63%
Brigade	*742*	*33*	*217*	*48*	*298*	*40%*

Summary
Army of Northern Virginia—Gen. Robert E. Lee

	Engaged	KIA	WIA	CIA	Total
First Corps—Longstreet	14,576	877	2942	874	5023
McLaws's Div.—McLaws	7149	407	1411	427	2245
Hood's Div.—Hood	6851	450	1421	441	2312
Artillery Res.—Alexander	576	20	110	3	133
Third Corps—Hill	3881	295	936	373	1604
Anderson's Div.—Anderson		295	936	373	1604

Army of Northern Virginia—Lee

	Engaged	KIA	WIA	CIA	Total
First Corps—Longstreet	14576	877	2942	871	4690
Third Corps—Hill	3881	295	936	373	1604
Total	18457	1172	3878	1244	6294
Total%		6%	21%	7%	34%

Chapter Endnotes

1. The 13th Vermont had 700 men and engaged a battalion or about 50% of them.

2. The roster does not record any casualties for those companies on July 2. The two recorded here come from recollections.

3. John W. Busey and David G. Martin, *Regimental Strengths and Losses at Gettysburg*, 4th Ed. (Hightstown, NJ, 2005), 128. Subsequent references, Busey and Martin, *Regimental Strengths and Losses at Gettysburg*. Strengths and losses, unless otherwise noted, come from this source. Many thanks to Dr. David A. Martin for his permission to cite extensively from their invaluable work.

4. Cross was mortally wounded.

5. Busey and Martin, *Regimental Strengths and Losses at Gettysburg*, 128.

6. Ibid.

7. Zook, mortally wounded. For details on Zook's wound, see John Michael Priest *One Surgeon's Private War* (Shippensburg, PA, 1996), 73-74.

8. Busey and Martin, *Regimental Strengths and Losses at Gettysburg*, 128.

9. This division did not divide its casualties by day. The casualties for July 2 and 3 are recorded as one number.

10. Busey and Martin, *Regimental Strengths and Losses at Gettysburg*, 129.

11. This amount represents the deduction of 22 confirmed casualties from the nominal list in Smith's regimental history. Smith, *19th Maine*, 86-88.

12. Adjutant General, *Massachusetts Soldiers, Sailors, and Marines*, Vol. II (Norwood, MA, 1931), 140, 145, 150, 152, 161, 170, 177, 182, 184-185, 195-196, 198, 200. This reflects the confirmed dead and wounded on July 3, 1863. Most of the wounded and missing are recorded for July 2-3, 1863.

13. Joseph N. Searles, *History of the First Regiment Minnesota Volunteer Infantry, 1861–1864* (Stillwater, MN, 1916), 346, 369-370. The 1st Minnesota had 262 men engaged on July 2, 1863. The resulting casualties do not include the 59 casualties incurred on July 3, 1863.

14. http://dmna.ny.gov/historic/reghist/civil/rosters/Infantry/82nd_ Infantry_CW_Roster.pdf This tally from the Adjutant General's Office of New York includes only casualties, and 1 deserter, listed on July 2, 1863. It does not include 11 men listed as wounded July 2-3, 1863, nor 3 men listed as wounded during July 1863 at Gettysburg.

15. Busey and Martin, *Regimental Strengths and Losses at Gettysburg*, 129. Unless otherwise noted, the casualties shown reflect those of July 2 and 3, 1863.

16. *OR* 27, pt. 1, 431. Report 106 of Capt. William Davis, 69th PA.

17. Bates, Samuel P., (comp.), *History of Pennsylvania Volunteers, 1861-5*, vol. 2, (Harrisburg, 1869-71), 824

18. Ibid., 850, 852, 858-859.

19. The 106th Pennsylvania took no part in the repulse of Longstreet's July 3, charge. These casualties reflect those incurred on July 2.

20. Adjutant General, *Massachusetts Soldiers, Sailors, and Marines*, vol. 2, 413, 447, 452, 471.

21. Richard F. Miller, *Harvard's Civil War: A History of the 20th Massachusetts Volunteer Infantry* (Lebanon, NH: U. Of New England Press, 2005), 259-260. The one man listed as captured, actually deserted.

22. *OR* 27, pt. 1, 451. Report #113 of Col. James E. Mallon.

23. http://dmna.ny.gov/historic/reghist/civil/rosters/Infantry/42nd_Infantry_CW_Roster.pdf

24. *OR* 27, pt. 1, 452. Report #114 of Col. William McFadden.

25. Only the 8th Ohio participated in the late afternoon action.

26. Franklin Sawyer, *A Military History of the 8th Regiment Ohio Vol. Inf'y: Its Battles, Marches and Army Movements* (Cleveland, OH, 1881), 127-128.

27. *OR* 27, pt. 1, 466. Report #124 of Maj. Theodore Ellis. The regiment reported a captain seriously injured by a runaway horse.

28. Ibid., 469. Report #125 of Lt. John T. Dent.

29. Ibid., 470. Report #126 of Maj. John T. Hill; Haines, *History of the Men of Company F,* 38-39; Thompson, "A Scrap of Gettysburg," Papers, vol. 3, 98-99; Christopher Mead to his wife, July 6, 1863, USAMHI; Albert Stokes Emmell to his aunt, July 16, 1863, Manuscript, Now is the time for Buck & Ball, n.p., GNMP; *OR* 27, pt. 1, 470; Nicholson, *Pennsylvania at Gettysburg*, vol. 1, 552; Gerry Harder Porriss and Ralph G. Porriss, (eds.), *While My Country is in Danger* (Hamilton, NY, 1994), 76; Edward G. Longacre, *To Gettysburg and Beyond* (Highstown, NJ, 1988), 127, The regiment had 444 present but only 150 men between Companies B, E, H, and G, took part in the action on July2, 1863.

30. http://dmna.ny.gov/historic/reghist/civil/rosters/Infantry/108th_Infantry_CW_Roster.pdf. The following information came from the roster: 6 wounded on July 2, 1 killed at Gettysburg, 9 wounded at Gettysburg, 1 wounded on July 1; 8 wounded between July 1-3, 1863. The remaining casualties are dated July 3, 1863. The regimental history said about 50 were wounded on July 2. I have, therefore, counted the casualties with non-specific dates or July 1 as July 2 casualties.

31. The number of killed and wounded is not precise. Brigade strength reflects only men engaged that day and not the entire 12th New Jersey.

32. http://dmna.ny.gov/historic/reghist/civil/rosters/Infantry/39th_Infantry_CW_Roster.pdf. This tally from the AGO rosters included 6 men wounded on July 1 (clerical error) and 4 wounded in July 1863.

33. http://dmna.ny.gov/historic/reghist/civil/rosters/Infantry/111th_Infantry_CW_Roster.pdf. This total includes 1- killed in action July 2-3; 21 wounded July 2-3; 1 desertion.

34. http://dmna.ny.gov/historic/reghist/civil/rosters/Infantry/111th_Infantry_CW_Roster.pdf. The two CIA include 1 deserter and 1 man wounded ad Gettysburg, no date.

35. http://dmna.ny.gov/historic/reghist/civil/rosters/Infantry/111th_Infantry_CW_Roster.pdf. The CIA reflects 1 man reported as deserting on July 1.

36. *OR* 27, pt. 1, 477. Report #132 of Capt. John G. Hazard.

37. Aldrich, History of Battery A, 389, 392, 404. This total includes 1 wounded enlisted man found in the roster for wounded at Gettysburg with no date attached.

38. *OR* 27, pt. 1, 477. Report #132 of Capt. John G. Hazard.

39. Busey and Martin, *Regimental Strengths and Losses at Gettysburg*, 130. This battery's casualties for July 2 could not be positively identified. These numbers reflect the total number of casualties for July 2 and July 3.

40. Kent Masterson Brown, *Cushing of Gettysburg: The Story of a Union Artillery Commander* (The University of Kentucky Press, 1993), 264-67.

41. Busey and Martin, *Regimental Strengths and Losses at Gettysburg,*131.

42. Ibid.

43. Ibid., 132.

44. Ibid.

45. Ibid.

46. Ibid., 133.

47. Ibid.

48. Ibid.

49. Ibid. 134. The 9th MA was detached from the brigade and not engaged on the field with it.

50. Ibid.

51. Ibid.

52. Ibid., 135.

53. Ibid.

54. Ibid.

55. Ibid., 136.

56. Ibid. Battery C, 1st New York did not participate in the battle on July 2.

57. Ibid., 138. Wheaton's was the only VI Corps brigade actively engaged on July 2.

58. Ibid., 144. The casualties for the 17th PA and the 3rd WV on July 1 and 2 cannot be separated. Considering that they lost missing in action only, they probably occurred on July 2.

59. Committee of the Regimental History, *History of the Sixth New York Cavalry (Second Ira Harris Guard)* Worcester, MA, 1908), 292, 332, 336, 341, 347-348.

60. Newel Cheney, *History of the Ninth Regiment, New York Volunteer Cavalry, War of 1861 to 1865* (Poland, NY, 1901), 405. The records show 1 man captured on July 2.

61. Busey and Martin, *Regimental Strengths and Losses at Gettysburg*, 146; OR 27, pt. 1, 1029. Report #375 of Lt. John H. Calef.

62. Busey and Martin, *Regimental Strengths and Losses at Gettysburg*, 146.

63. Ibid.

64. Ibid., 147.

65. OR 27, pt. 2, p.370. Report #432 of Brig. Gen Joseph B. Kershaw.

66. Busey and Martin, *Regimental Strengths and Losses at Gettysburg*, 268.

67. Ibid., 267.

68. Ibid., 269.

69. OR 27, pt. 2, 381. Report #437 of Capt. Basil C. Manly.

70. Ibid., 385. Report #440 of Lt. C. W. Motes.

71. Ibid., pt. 2, 382. Report #438 of Lt. W. J. Furlong.

72. Ibid., pt. 2, 379. Report #436 of Capt. Edward S. McCarthy.

73. Busey and Martin, *Regimental Strengths and Losses at Gettysburg*, 262.

74. OR 27, pt. 2, p.393. Report #444 of Col William C. Oates.

75. Ibid., 394. Report #445 of Col. William F. Perry.

76. Ibid. 264. Anderson detached the 7th GA to the Currens Farm, therefore it did not participate in the attack. Unless otherwise noted, these returns are from Busey and Martin's work.

77. OR 27, pt. 2, 400. Report #449 of Capt. George Hillyer.

78. Ibid., 402. Report #450 of Maj. H. D. McDaniel.

79. Busey and Martin, *Regimental Strengths and Losses at Gettysburg*, 260.

80. *OR* 27, pt. 2, 410. Report #454 of Lt. Col. Phillip A. Work.

81. Unless noted differently, these numbers come from the source listed below. Busey and Martin, *Regimental Strengths and Losses at Gettysburg*, 263.

82. Colonel DuBose said he lost 70 casualties on July 2 and 101 on July 3. The numbers of casualties are estimates based upon the brigade ratio of 23% KIA, 62% WIA, and 14% CIA

OR 27, pt. 2, 424. Report #460 of Col. D. M. DuBose.

83. Ibid., 426. Report #462 of Col. J. D. Waddell.

84. Busey and Martin, *Regimental Strengths and Losses at Gettysburg*, 265. Bachman's and Garden's South Carolina Batteries did not participate in the action.

85. Ibid., 277. Unless otherwise noted, these numbers come from Busey and Martin.

86. *OR* 27, pt. 2, 432. Report #465 of Capt. O. B. Taylor.

87. Busey and Martin, *Regimental Strengths and Losses at Gettysburg*, 308.

88. Ibid., 311.

89. Ibid., 307; *OR* 27, pt. 2, Report of Col. David Lang. Lang said he lost about 300 men on July 2. The number from the Army of Northern Virginia returns shows a loss for killed and wounded only which comes to 250. By dividing a balance of 48 by 3, I estimated that the regiments lost about 16 men each overall as prisoners, which brings the casualties to 298 for the brigade.

Bibliography

Manuscripts

Andrew J. DeCusati Collection [Private Holding]
Affidavits from Pension file of Major James H. Coburn
Bentley Historical Library, University of Michigan, Ann Arbor, MI
   George Lockley Diary
   James Houghton Journal
Bowdoin College Library, Bowdoin College, Brunswick, ME
   William C. Oates Account
Brown University Library, Providence, RI
William H. Brown Papers, 1861-1865
Clarke Historical Library, Central Michigan University, Mount Pleasant, MI
   Isaac Plumb Letter
Confederate Research Center, Hill Junior College, Hillsboro, TX
   Rufus K. Folder Letter
Detroit Public Library, Detroit, MI
   Burton Historical Collection
   Charles H. Salter Letter
Fredericksburg and Spotsylvania National Military Park (FSNMP), Vertical Files
   Adolfo Fernandez Cavada Diary
Gettysburg National Military Park (GNMP), Vertical Files
   "116th Pennsylvania Vs. 140th Pennsylvania." Affidavit, July 12, 1895
   Aaron Baker Letter, copy
   John B. Bachelder Letter
   Frank J. Bell, "The Bucktails at Gettysburg" Manuscript
   Roland Edwin Bowen Journal
   James D. Brady Letter
   Felix Brannigan Letter
   W. H. Bullard Letter, copy
   Emil A. Burger Official Report
   Minnesota Company, U.S. Sharpshooters, July 5, 1863"
   William J. Cake Letter
   Francis E. Heath's Account
   Andrew B. Cross, The War. Battle of Gettysburg and the Christian Commission, 1865
   William D. Dixon Letter
   John P. Dunne Report
   Norman Eldred, "Only a Boy: A first-hand account of the Civil War," Manuscript, copy
   Albert Stokes Emmell. "Now is the time for Buck & Ball," Manuscript.
   George W. Ervay Civil War Letters
   L. E. Estilow, "Doing My Duty, The Wartime Experiences of John S. Hard"

Fred E. Gaillard Civil War Letters, copy
Henry Hartford, "At Gettysburg: My Most Vivid Recollection," Newspaper clipping
G. Humphreys Letter
Hilary A. Herbert, "A Short History of the 8th AL Regiment" Manuscript
George Hillyer, "Battle of Gettysburg," Newspaper clipping
Rufus Jacklin Folder
William A. Johnson, "The Battle of Gettysburg, July 2, 1863," Newspaper clipping
Thaddeus Kenderdine, "A California Tramp." Typed Transcript
Zack Landrum Letters
Henry C. McCauley Letter
Freeman McGilvery, "Part taken by the 1st Brigade Vol. Div. Arty. Res., et al." Manuscript,
   copy
Benton H. Miller Account
B. P. Mimmack Letter
Tom and John Mounger Letter
New Jersey State Archives, Records Subgroup: Military Records, Series, Civil War,
   Miscellaneous, copy
Wesley Nichols Autobiography
Oliver W. Norton Letter
"One of the Veterans of Gettysburg," Newspaper clipping
Jedediah C. Paine Letter
Henry P. Ramsdell War Record
John C. Reid Diary, copy
"Reminiscences of the Boys in Gray, 1861-1865" Manuscript
Gilbert V. Riddle, "Gettysburg and the 8th New Jersey Volunteer Infantry," Manuscript
N. A. Roberts Letter
R. Rodgers Letter
Shine, William F., "Philips's Legion," Typed Transcript, copy
Robert H. Shirkey Manuscript
J. W. Sonderman Letter
Charles E. Sprague Letter
William R. Stilwell Letter, copy
Edward H. Taylor Letter, copy
Texas Troop Folder
Frederick Tilberg Letter
Henry E. Tremain Letter
R. Turrill Letter
Allen A. Young Letter
John P. Vincent Letter
George Whipple "Father's own story of his army life in the civil war of 60's," Manuscript, copy
John A. Wilkerson Diary
James A. Woods, "The Second Day at Gettysburg," Manuscript
P. A. Work Letter
G. W. W. Letter, copy
Goodhue County Historical Society, Red Wing, MN.
   Colvill, William, "The Old First Minnesota at Gettysburg"

Lilly Library, Indiana University, Bloomington, IN
    Manuscripts Department
        "Account of an Unidentified Soldier of the 64th New York Infantry"
        Martin Sigman Diary, 1861-1864
Indiana State Library, Indianapolis, IN
    Erasmus Gilbreath Manuscript
    Francis A. Osbourn Collection
        Osbourn, Francis A., "The 20th Indiana Infantry"
Library of Congress, Manuscript Division, Washington, DC
    Crawford Papers
    Squires, W. H. T., (ed.), "The Last of Lee's Battle Line"
Military Order of the Loyal Legion of the United States (MOLLUS) Library, Philadelphia, PA
    Hamilton, J. C., "Recollections"
Minnesota Historical Society, St. Paul, MN
    Charles Powell Adams Papers
National Archives, Washington, DC
    Edwin B. Dow to US Army Adj. Gen., August 3, 1895, Supplemental Report,
        [Reports & Papers]
    John Bigelow to US Army Adj. Gen., June 19, 1895, Supplemental Report,
        [Reports & Papers]
    Microfilm Letters to the Adjutant and the Inspector General's Office
    RG 94, War Records Office, Union Battle Reports
New York State Library, Albany, NY
    Gouverneur K. Warren Papers
Ontario County Historical Society, Canandaigua, NY
    Charles A. Richardson Papers
Pennsylvania Historical Society, Philadelphia, PA
    John Rutter Brooke Papers
    Rothermel Papers
Pennsylvania State Archives, Harrisburg, PA
    Hale, Charles A., "With Col. Cross in the Gettysburg Campaign" Manuscript
Queen's University at Kingston, Archives, Douglas Library, Kingston, Ontario, Canada
    Wafer, Francis Moses, Diary
Rutgers University Library, Rutgers University, New Brunswick, NJ
    Robert McAllister Letter
Southern Historical Collection, University of North Carolina Library, Chapel Hill, NC
    J. F. H. Claiborne Papers
State of Mississippi Department of Archives and History, Jackson, MS
    David Parker Letter
    William H. Hill, Diary
U.S. Army Heritage and Education Center (USAHEC), Carlisle, PA
    CWTI Collection
        John Berry Diary
    Greg Coco Collection
        J. W. Ames Files
    Massachusetts MOLLUS Collection
        Blake, Henry N., "Personal Reminiscences of Gettysburg"

Murray J. Smith Collection
Robert L. Brake Collection
   A.C. Sims Article
   Charles E. Nash Account
   Charles Muller "History"
   Charles W. Reed Letter
   Christopher Mead Letter
   E. D. McSwain Article
   Fleming W. Thompson Letter
   H. W. Berryman Letter
   George J. Leftwich Clipping
   James M. Goggin Letter
   John Lancaster Account
   John W. Plummer Letter
   St. Louis *Globe-Democrat*, March 19, 1913, Clipping
   The Sunday Herald, July 23, 1899, Clipping
  "Save the Flags" Collection
   Adoniram J. Warner Account
Vermont Historical Society, Montpelier, VT
  Clarke, Albert, "The Thirteenth Regiment"
Virginia Historical Society, Richmond, VA
S. R. Johnston Letters
Fairfax Papers
  John Fairfax Letter
William Clements Library, University of Michigan, Ann Arbor, MI
  Schoff Civil War Collection
   William C. Oates Letter
Yale University, Manuscript Department, New Haven, CT
  Joseph H. Twitchell Letter

Internet

"Col. Troop's Action Report of the First Michigan Infantry at the Battle of Gettysburg," Accessed May 28, 12014. http://www.esthersscrapbook.com/HHawkinsGettysburg.htm

Hamilton, J. C. M., "The 110th Regiment in the Gettysburg Campaign" Accessed May 28, 2014. http://www.gdg.org/Research/Other%20Documents/Newspaper%20Clippings/v6pt2k.html

Studnicki, Jim, "'Perry's Brigade'": The Forgotten Floridians at Gettysburg" Accessed May 28, 2014. http://www.2ndflorida.net/perrys.htm

Newspapers

Anniston Star (Anniston, Alabama)
Daily Enquirer (Richmond, Virginia)
Daily Evening Express (Lancaster, Pennsylvania)
Daily Huntsville Confederate (Huntsville, Alabama)
Gettysburg Compiler (Gettysburg, Pennsylvania)

Gettysburg Star and Sentinel (Gettysburg, Pennsylvania)
Maine Bugle (Rockland, Maine)
Middletown Whig Press (Middletown, New York)
Minneapolis Journal (Minneapolis, Minnesota)
Montgomery Mail (Montgomery, Alabama)
New York Sunday Mercury (New York, New York)
Philadelphia Public Ledger (Philadelphia, Pennsylvania)
Shenango Valley News (Greenville, Pennsylvania)
Sherman Register (Sherman, Texas)
South Western Baptist (Texas)
The Irish American (New York, New York)
The Press (Jesup, Georgia)
Waco Daily Times-Herald (Waco, Texas)

Published Primary Sources

Articles

Adams, Aurelius J., "The Fight in the Peach Orchard," *National Tribune*, April 23, 1883.

[Alexander, Edward P.]. Report, *Southern Historical Society Papers*, vol. 4, 1877, 235-239.

"A Man of Pluck Pluck. Sergeant Mears, Who Won a Medal of Honor at Gettysburg," *National Tribune*, June 24, 1897.

Ayars, Peter B., "The 99th Pennsylvania," *National Tribune*, February 4, 1886.

Bennett, Edward, "Fighting Them Over," *National Tribune*, May 6, 1886.

[Benning, Henry L.], Report, *Southern Historical Society Papers*, vol. 4, 1877, 167-175.

Bohannon, Keith, (ed.), "Wounded and Captured at Gettysburg, Reminiscences by Sgt. William Jones, 50th Georgia Infantry," *Military Images*, May-June 1988, 14-15.

Bowen, Edward R., "Collis' Zouaves: The 114th Pennsylvania Infantry at Gettysburg," *Philadelphia Weekly Times*, June 22, 1887.

Bradfield, J. O., "At Gettysburg, July 3," *Confederate Veteran*, vol. 30, 1922, 225-236.

Bradley, Thomas W., "At Gettysburg: The Splendid Work Done by Smith's Battery," *National Tribune*, February 4, 1886.

Brown, William H., "A View From Little Round Top During the Progress of the Battle," *Philadelphia Weekly Times*, March 17, 1882.

Campbell, Eric, "Caldwell Clears the Wheatfield," *Gettysburg Magazine*, July 1, 1990, No. 3, 27-50.

————."Remember Harpers Ferry," *Gettysburg Magazine*, July 1, 1992, No. 7, 51-76.

Carr, Ira, "A Sharpshooter at Gettysburg," *National Tribune*, November 25, 1886.

Clark, Almond E., "The Stand Made by the Remnant of the 27th Connecticut," *National Tribune*, October 10, 1918.

Clark, George W., "Wilcox's Alabama Brigade at Gettysburg," *Confederate Veteran*, vol. 17, 1909, 229-230.

Coffman, Richard, "A Vital Unit," *Civil War Times Illustrated*, June 1982, vol. 20, 40-45.

Colestock, W. W., "The 16th Michigan at Little Round Top," *National Tribune*, March 26, 1914.

Coxe, John, "The Battle of Gettysburg," *Confederate Veteran*, vol. 21, 1913, 433-436.

Deming, A. J., "Bucktails at Gettysburg," *National Tribune*, February 4, 1886.

Duke, J. W., "Mississippians at Gettysburg," *Confederate Veteran*, vol. 14, 1906, 216.

Farley, Porter, "Bloody Round Top," *National Tribune*, May 3, 1883.

Fortin, Marian S., (ed.), "History of the Eighth Alabama Volunteer Regiment, C.S.A.," by Col. Hilary A. Herbert, *The Alabama Historical Quarterly*, vol. 39, 1977.

Gerrish, Theodore, "The Battle of Gettysburg," *National Tribune*, November 23, 1882.

Hanford, J. Harvey, "The Experience of a Private in the 124th New York in the Battle," *National Tribune*, September 21, 1885.

Hazen, Samuel R., "The 140th New York and Its Work on Little Round Top," *National Tribune*, September 13, 1894.

Jacobs, [Michael]"Later Ramblings Over the Field of Gettysburg," *United States Service Magazine*, February 1864, vol. 1, 66-76.

Jones, A. C., "Longstreet at Gettysburg," *Confederate Veteran*, vol. 23, 1879, 551-552.

L. Long to Jubal A. Early, April 5, 1876, *Southern Historical Society Papers*, vol. 4, 1877, 66-69.

Lader, Paul J., "The 7th New Jersey in the Gettysburg Campaign," *Gettysburg Magazine*, January 1, 1997, No. 16, 46-67.

Libby, Elias D., "The 6th Maine in the Peach Orchard," *National Tribune*, May 28, 1885.

Lindsay Walker to Fitzhugh Lee, January 1, 1878, *Southern Historical Society Papers*, vol. 5, 1878, 180-182.

Lokey, John W., "Wounded at Gettysburg," *Confederate Veteran*, vol. 22, 1914, 400.

Loring, William E., "Gettysburg," *National Tribune*, July 9, 1885.

McLaws, Lafayette, "Gettysburg," *Southern Historical Society Papers*, vol. 7, 1879, 64-85.

Moran, Frank M., "What Was Seen by a Captive Federal Officer from Seminary Ridge," *National Tribune*, February 4, 1886.

Perry, W. F., "The Devil's Den," *Confederate Veteran*, vol. 19, 1911, date 161-163.

"Pickett and Hood at Gettysburg," *Southern Bivouac*, vol. 3, 1888, 75-78.

Potter, H. L., "Seeley's Battery at Gettysburg," *National Tribune*, May 24, 1888.

Purifoy, John, "Longstreet's Attack at Gettysburg, July 2, 1863," *Confederate Veteran*, vol. 31, 1923, 292-294.

———."The Horror of War," *Confederate Veteran*, vol. 33, 1924, 252-253.

Purman, J. J., "Recitals and Reminiscences," *National Tribune*, March 25, 1909.

Quay, W. H., "Still in Error," *National Tribune*, April 30, 1891.

Robbins, Richard, "The Regular Troops at Gettysburg," *Philadelphia Weekly Times*, January 4, 1879.

[Robertson, Jerome B.]. Report. *Southern Historical Society Papers*, vol. 4, 1877, 161-165.

Sanderson, W. H., "Sykes' Regulars," *National Tribune*, April 2, 1891.

Scott, Thomas, "On Little Round Top," *National Tribune*, August 2, 1894.

Shepherd, William S., Report. *Southern Historical Society Papers*, vol. 13, 1885, 198-199.,

Shively, David, "A Blighted Career. The Work of Two Bullets at Gettysburg—A Sad Story," *National Tribune*, July 3, 1884.

Smith, J. E., "The Devil's Den—In Defense of It at Gettysburg by Smith's Battery and Its Supports," *National Tribune*, March 4, 1886.

Taylor, Osmond B., Report, *Southern Historical Society Papers*, vol. 13, 1885, 213-216.

Thompson, Benjamin W. "This Hell of Destruction," *Civil War Times Illustrated*, October 1973, vol. 12, 12-23.

Tucker, Albert A. "From Comrade Tucker," *National Tribune*, February 4, 1886.

Tucker, Albert [W]. "Orange Blossoms: Services of the 124th New York at Gettysburg," *National Tribune*, January 21, 1886.

Walker, Elijah. "The 4th Maine at Gettysburg," *National Tribune*, April 8, 1886.

Ward, W. C. "Incidents and Personal Experiences on the Battlefield at Gettysburg," *Confederate Veteran*, vol. 8, 1900, 344-349.

West, Oscar W. "On Little Round Top," *National Tribune*, November 22, 1906.

Westbrook, Cornelius D. "On the Firing Line," *National Tribune*, September 20, 1900.

Wilson, E. A. "An Incident at Gettysburg," *National Tribune*, June 10, 1886.

Winslow, George B. "Battery D at Gettysburg," *Philadelphia Weekly Times*, July 26, 1879.

Youngblood, William, "Unwritten History of the Gettysburg Campaign," *Southern Historical Society Papers*, vol. 38, 313-318.

Books

Abernathy, William M. *Our Mess: Southern Gallantry and Privations*. McKinney, TX: McKintex Press, 1977.

Adams, Silas, "The Nineteenth Maine at Gettysburg," in *War Papers. Read Before the Commandery of the State of Maine, Military Order of the Loyal Legion of the United States*, 4 Vols. 1915. Reprint, Broadfoot Publishing Co., Wilmington, NC, 1992.

Adjutant General, Soldiers, Sailors, and Marines, vol. II. Norwood, MA: Norwood Press, 1931.

Aiken, J. Gregory. (ed.). *Inside the Army of the Potomac, The Civil War Experience of Captain Francis Adams Donaldson*. Mechanicsburg, PA: Stackpole Books, 1998.

Aldrich, Thomas M. *The History of Battery A, First Regiment Rhode Island Light Artillery*. Providence, RI: Snow & Farnham, Printers, 1904.

Ames, Nelson. *History of Battery G, First Regiment New York Light Artillery*. Marshalltown, IN: Marshall Printing Co., 1900.

Baker, Levi W. *History of the Ninth Massachusetts Battery*. Lancaster, Ohio: Vanberg Publishing, 1996.

Bartlett, A. W., *History of the Twelfth Regiment New Hampshire Volunteers in the War of the Rebellion*. Concord, NH: Ira C. Evans, 1897.

Barrett, John G., (ed.), *Yankee Rebel: The Civil War Journal of Edmund DeWitt Patterson*, Chapel Hill, NC, University of NC, 1966.

Barrett, Orvey S. *Reminiscences, Incidents, Battles, Marches and Camp Life in the Old 4th Michigan Infantry in the War of the Rebellion, 1861-1864*. Detroit, MI: W. S. Ostler, 1888.

Benedict , George G. *Vermont at Gettysburgh*. Burlington, VT: The Free Press Association, 1870.

Beyer, W. F. and O. F. Keydel, (eds.). *Deeds of Valor*. Detroit, MI: Perrien-Keydel, 1901.

Blake, Henry N. *Three Years in the Army of the Potomac*. Boston, MA: Lee and Shepard, 1865.

Bloodgood, John D. *Reminiscences of the Civil War*. New York: Hunt and Eaton, 1893.

Brown, Henri LeFevre. *History of the Third Regiment, Excelsior Brigade, 72nd New York Volunteer Infantry, 1861-1865*. Jamestown, NY, 1902.

Brown, J. Willard. *The Signal Corps, U.S.A. in the War of the Rebellion*. Boston, MA: U.S. Veteran Signal Corps Association, 1896.

Campbell, Eric A.*"A Grand Terrible Dramma" From Gettysburg to Petersburg: The Civil War Letters of Charles Wellington Reed*. New York: Fordham University Press, 2000.

Carter, Robert G. *Four Brothers in Blue*. Austin, TX: University of Texas Press, 1978.

Carter, Robert G., "Reminiscences of the Campaign and Battle of Gettysburg," in *War Papers Read Before the Commandery of the State of Maine, Military Order of the Loyal Legion of the United States*, 4 Vols.Lefavor-Tower Co., Portland, 1902.

Cheney, Newel. *History of the Ninth Regiment, New York Volunteer Cavalry, War of 1861 to 1865.* Poland, New York: Martin Merz & Son, 1901.

Child, William. *A History of the Fifth New Hampshire Volunteers, in the American Civil War, 1861-1865.* 1893. Reprint, Ron Van Sickle Military Books, Gaithersburg, MD, 1988.

Clark, George. *A Glance Backward; or Some Events in the Past History of My Life.* Houston, TX: Rein & Sons, Co., 1914.

Coffin, Charles Carleton. *Eyewitness to Gettysburg.* Shippensburg, PA: Burd Street Press, 1997.

Cole, Jacob H. *Under Five Commanders.* Patterson, NJ: News Printing Co., 1906.

Committee of the Regimental History. *History of the Sixth New York Cavalry (Second Ira Harris Guard).* Worcester, MA: Blanchard Press, 1908.

Craft, David. *History of the One Hundred Forty-first Regiment, Pennsylvania Volunteers, 1862-1865.* 1885. Reprint, Butternut and Blue, Baltimore, MD, 1991.

Cross, Andrew B., *The War and the Christian Commission*, 1865.

Deane, Frank Putnam, (ed.). *"My Dear Wife. . . : The Civil War Letters of David Brett, 9th Massachusetts Battery, Union Cannoneer.* Little Rock, AR: Pioneer Press,1964.

Dickert, D. Augustus. *History of Kershaw's Brigade.* 1899. Reprint, Morningside Press, Dayton, OH, 1976.

Engert, Roderick M., (ed.). *Maine to the Wilderness: The Civil War Letters of Pvt. William Lamson, 20th Maine Infantry.* Orange, VA: Publisher's Press, Inc., 1993.

The Executive Committee, *Maine at Gettysburg.* 1898. Reprint, Stan Clark Military Books, Gettysburg, PA, 1994.

Favill, Josiah Marshall. *Diary of a Young Officer*, Chicago, IL: Donnelley & Sons, 1909.

Fletcher, William Andrew. *Rebel Private Front and Rear.* Washington, DC: Zenger Publishing Co., Inc., 1985.

Ford, Andrew E. *The Story of the Fifteenth Regiment Massachusetts Volunteer Infantry.* Clinton, MA: Press of W. J. Coulter, 1898.

Frederick, Gilbert. *The Story of a Regiment Being a Record of the Military Services of the Fifty-Seventh New York State Volunteer Infantry in the War of the Rebellion 1861—1864.* Chicago, IL: The Fifty-Seventh Veteran Association, 1895.

Fuller, Charles A. *Personal Recollections of the War of 1861.* 1906. Reprint, Edmontson Publishing Co., Hamilton, NY, 1990.

Fremantle, Arthur J. L. *Three Months in the Southern States.* 1863. Reprint, New York: Time-Life Books, 1984.

Gallagher, Gary W., (ed.). *Fighting for the Confederacy, The Personal Recollections of General Edward Porter Alexander.* Chapel Hill: University of North Carolina Press, 1989.

Gerrish, Theodore. *Army Life: A Private's Reminiscences of the Civil War.*1882. Reprint, Butternut and Blue: Baltimore, MD, 1995.

Graham, Ziba B. "On to Gettysburg, Ten Days from My Diary," in *War Papers. Read Before the Commandery of the State of Michigan Military Order of the Loyal Legion of the United States*, 4 Vols. Detroit, MI: Wine and Hammong, 1893-1898.

Haines, William P. *History of the Men of Company F with the Description and Marches of the 12th New Jersey.* Vols. Camden, NJ: C. F. McGrath, Printer, 1897.

Hanifen, Michael. *History of Battery B, 1st New Jersey Artillery.* Ottowa, IL: Republican Times, 1905.

Hardee, W. J. *Rifle and Light Infantry Tactics*, 2 vols. Philadelphia, PA: J. B. Lippincott & Co., 1861.

Hardeen, Charles W. *A Little Fifer's War Diary*. Syracuse, NY: C. W. Hardeen, 1910.

Hardin, Martin D. *History of the Twelfth Regiment Pennsylvania Reserve Volunteer Corps*. New York: Martin D. Hardin, 1890.

Martin A. Haynes. *A History of the Second Regiment New Hampshire Volunteers: Its Camps, Marches And Battles*. Manchester, NH: Charles F. Livingston, 1865.

Haynes, Martin A. *A History of the Second Regiment, New Hampshire Volunteer Infantry in the War of the Rebellion*. Lakeport, NH:1896.

————. *A Minor Raw History, Compiled From a Soldier Boy's Letters to "The Girl I Left Behind Me,"* Lakeport, NH, 1916.

Hewett, Janet B., et al., *Supplement to the Official Records of the Union and Confederate Armies*. vol. 5, Wilmington, NC: Broadfoot Publishing, 1995.

Houghton, Edwin B. *The Campaigns of the 17th Maine*. Portland, ME: Short and Loring, 1866.

Johnson, Hannibal A. *The Sword of Honor: A Story of the Civil War*. Hollowell, ME: Register Printing House, 1906.

Johnson, Robert Underwood and Clarence Clough Buel, (eds.), *Battles and Leaders of the Civil War*, 4 Vols., 1884. Reprint, Castle Books: Atlantic City, NJ, 1956

Jordan, William C. *Incidents During the Civil War*. Montgomery, AL: The Paragon Press, 1909.

Judson, Amos M. *History of the Eighty-Third Pennsylvania Volunteers*. Reprint Morningside Bookshop, Dayton, OH, 1986.

Ladd, David L. and Audrey J., *The Bachelder Papers*, 3 Vols. Dayton, OH: Morningside Press, 1994.

Large, George R., (comp.). *Battle of Gettysburg*. Shippensburg, PA: Burd Street Press, 1999.

Lochren, William, "The First Minnesota at Gettysburg," in *Glimpses of the Nation's Struggle. A Series of Papers Read Before the Minnesota Commandery of the Military Order of the Loyal Legion of the United States*. 1903-1908, 6 Vols. Wilmington, NC: Broadfoot Publishing, 1992.

Longstreet, James. *From Manassas to Appomattox*. 1895. Reprint, New York: Da Capo Press, 1992.

McNeily, J. S. "Barksdale's Mississippi Brigade at Gettysburg," in Franklin L. Riley, (ed.) *Publications of the Mississippi Historical Society* (University, MS, 1914), vol. 14, 231- 265.

Marbaker, Thomas D. *History of the Eleventh New Jersey Volunteers*. 1898. Reprint, Longstreet House, Highstown, NJ, 1990.

Martin, James L. *History of the 57th Regiment Pennsylvania Veteran Volunteer Infantry*. Meadville, PA: McCoy & Calvin, 1904.

Minnigh, H. N. *History of Company K 1st (Inft.) Penna. Reserves*. Duncansville, PA: "Home Print," 1891.

Monument Commission. *Michigan at Gettysburg*. 1889. Reprint, Longstreet House, Highstown, NJ, 1998.

Muffly, J. W., (ed.). *The Story of Our Regiment, A History of the 148th Pennsylvania Vols*. Des Moines, IA: Kenyon Printing and Mfg. Co., 1904.

Mulholland, St. Clair A. *The Story of the 116th Regiment, Pennsylvania Infantry*. 1903. Reprint, Olde Soldier Books, Gaithersburg, MD, 1993.

Nelson, Alanson H. *The Battles of Chancellorsville and Gettysburg*. Minneapolis, MN, 1899.

New York Monuments Commission for the Battlefields of Gettysburg and Chattanooga. *New York at Gettysburg*. 3 Vols. Albany, NY: J. B. Lyon Co., 1900.

Nicholson, John, (ed.), *Pennsylvania at Gettysburg*, 3 Vols., Harrisburg, PA: William Stanley Ray, State Printer, 1904.

Norton, Oliver W. *The Attack and Defense of Little Round Top*. 1913. Reprint, Morningside Press, Dayton, OH, 1978.

Oates, William C. *The War Between the Union and the Confederacy and Its Lost Opportunities*. (New York: Neale Publishing Co., 1905).

Page, Charles D. *History of the Fourteenth Regiment, Connecticut Vol. Infantry*. Meriden, CN: The Horton Printing Co., 1906.

Parker, Francis J. *The Story of the Thirty-second Regiment Massachusetts Infantry*. Boston: C. W. Calkins & Co., 1886.

Polley, J. B. *Hood's Texas Brigade: Its Marches, Its Battles, Its Achievements*. 1910. Reprint, Morningside Press, Dayton, OH, 1976.

Porriss, Gerry Harder, and Ralph G., (eds.). *While My Country Is in Danger*. Hamilton, NY: Edmontson Publishing, 1994.

Priest, John Michael, (ed.), *One Surgeon's Private War*. Shippensburg, PA: White Mane Publishing, 1996.

Rafferty, Thomas, "Gettysburg," in *Personal Recollections of the War of the Rebellion, Addresses Delivered Before the Commandery of the State of New York, Military Order of the Loyal Legion of the United States*, vol. 1. Astor Place, NY: J. J. Little & Sons, 1891.

Regimental Committee. *History of the 5th Massachusetts Battery*. Boston, MA: Luther E. Cowles, Publisher, 1902.

Rhodes, John H. *The Gettysburg Gun*. Providence, RI: Snow & Farnham, 1892.

Ripley, William Y. W. *Vermont Riflemen in the War for the Union, 1861-1865, A History of Company F, First United States Sharpshooters*. Rutland, VT: Tuttle & Co., Printers, 1883.

Rittenhouse, B. F. "The Battle of Gettysburg as Seen from Little Round Top," in *War Papers Read Before the Commandery of the District of Columbia, Military Order of the Loyal Legion of the United States*, 4 Vols., 1887. Reprint, Broadfoot Publishing, Wilmington, NC, 1993.

Rodenbough, Theodore F., (ed.). *Uncle Sam's Medal of Honor*. New York: G. P. Putnam's Sons, 1886.

Rourke, Norman E., (ed.). *I Saw the Elephant*. Shippensburg, PA: Burd Street Press, 1995.

Sawyer, Franklin. *A Military History of the 8th Regiment Ohio Vol. Inf'y: Its Battles, Marches and Army Movements*. Cleveland, OH: Fairbanks & Co., 1881.

Scott, Kate M. *History of the One Hundred Fifth Regiment, Pennsylvania Volunteers*. 1877. Reprint, Butternut and Blue, Baltimore, MD, 1993.

Searles, Joseph N. *History of the First Regiment Minnesota Volunteer Infantry, 1861-1864*, Stillwater, MN: Easton and Masterson, 1916.

Seventh Annual Re-Union of the 120th NYV. Regimental Union. "Lt.-Col. J. J. Rudolph Tappen," February 22d, 1875. Kingston, NY: The Daily Freeman Steam Printing House, 1875.

Silliker, Ruth L., (ed.). *The Rebel Yell & the Yankee Hurrah: The Civil War Journal of a Maine Volunteer*. Camden, ME: Down East Books, 1985.

Simons, Ezra D. *The One Hundred and Twenty-fifth New York State Volunteers*, New York: Ezra D. Simons, 1888.

Smith, James E. *A Famous Battery and Its Campaigns, 1861-1864*. Washington, DC: W. H. Lowdermilk & Co., 1892.

Smith, John Day. *The History of the Nineteenth Regiment of Maine Volunteer Infantry 1862-1865*. 1909, Ron Van Sickle Military Books, Gaithersburg, MD, 1988.

Sorrel, G. Moxley. *At the Right Hand of Longstreet.* 1905. Reprint, University of Nebraska Press, Lincoln, NE,1999.

Spear, Abbott, et al., (comp.). *The Civil War Recollections of General Ellis Spear.* Orono, ME: The University of Maine Press, 1997.

Stevens, C. A. *United States Sharpshooters in the Army of the Potomac, 1861-1865.* 1892. Reprint, Morningside Press, Dayton, OH, 1984.

Stevens, John W. *Reminiscences of the Civil War.* Hillsboro, TX: Hillsboro Mirror Print, 1902.

Stewart, Robert L. *History of the One Hundred Fortieth Regiment Pennsylvania Volunteers.* Regimental Association, 1912.

Stocker, Jeffrey D.m (ed.). *From Huntsville to Appomattox.* Knoxville, TN: University of Tennessee Press, 1996.

Survivors Association, *History of the Corn Exchange Regiment, 118th Pennsylvania Volunteers.* Philadelphia, PA: J. L. Smith, 1888.

Taylor, John Dykes. *History of the 48th Alabama Volunteer Regiment, C.S.A.* 1902. Reprint, Morningside Press, Dayton, OH, 1985.

Thompson, O. R. Howard and William H. Rauch. *History of the "Bucktails," Kane Rifle Regiment of the Pennsylvania Reserve Corps (13th Pennsylvania Reserves), 42nd of the Line.* 1906. Reprint, Morningside Bookshop, Dayton, OH, 1988.

Thompson, Richard S. "A Scrap at Gettysburg," in *Papers Read before the Commandery of the State of Illinois, Military Order of the Loyal Legion of the United States*, vol. 3. Chicago, IL: Dial Press, 1894.

Toombs, Samuel. *New Jersey Troops in the Gettysburg Campaign.* Orange, NJ: The Evening Mail, 1888.

Tremain, Henry E. *Two Days of War: A Gettysburg Narrative and Other Experiences.* New York: Bonnell, Silver and Bowers, 1905.

United States War Department. *The War of the Rebellion: A Compilation of the Official Records of the Union and the Confederate Armies*, 128 vols. Washington, D.C.: U.S. Government Printing Office, 1880-1901.

Van Santvoord, Corneilus. *The 120th Regiment New York State Volunteers, A Narrative of Its Services in the War for the Union.* Roundout, NY: Kingston Freeman Press, 1894.

Vermont at Gettysburgh. Proceedings of the Vermont Historical Society, Vol. 1, No. 2, Montpelier, VT, 1930.

Ward, Eric, (ed.). *Army Life in Virginia, The Civil War Letters of George G. Benedict.* Mechanicsburg, PA: Stackpole Books, 2002.

Ward, Joseph R. C. *History of the One Hundred And Sixth Regiment Pennsylvania Volunteers*, Philadelphia, PA: F. McManus, Jr. and Co., 1906.

West, John C. West. *A Texan in Search of a Fight.* Waco: J. S. Hill & Co., 1901.

White, Russell C., (ed.). *The Civil War Diary of Wyman S. White, First Sergeant of Company F, 2nd United States Sharpshooter Regiment, 1861-1865.* Baltimore, MD: Butternut and Blue, 1991.

Willingham, Robert M., Jr. *No Jubilee: The Story of Confederate Wilkes.* Washington, GA: Wilkes Publishing Co., 1976.

Published Secondary Sources

Arrington, Benjamin T. *The Medal of Honor at Gettysburg*, Gettysburg, PA: Thomas Publications, 1996.

Bacarella, Michael. *Lincoln's Foreign Legion*. Shippensburg, PA: White Mane Publishing Co., 1996.

Brown, Kent Masterson. *Cushing of Gettysburg: The Story of a Union Artillery Commander*. Frankfort: The University of Kentucky Press, 1993.

Busey, John W. and David G. Martin, *Regimental Strengths and Losses at Gettysburg*, 4th ed. Highstown, NJ: Longstreet House, 2005.

Chapman, Laura K. *Descendants of John Messer Lowell, Revolutionary Soldier Who Changed His Name to John Reed*. North Syracuse, NY, 1992.

Coffin, Howard. *Nine Months to Gettysburg*. Woodstock, VT: The Countryman Press, 1997.

Dunn, Craig L. *Harvestfields of Death*. Carmel, IN: Guild Press of Indiana, Inc., 1999.

Editors of Time-Life Books. *Echoes of Glory: Civil War Battle Atlas*. Alexandria, VA: Time-Life Books, 1996.

Gottfried, Bradley M. *Stopping Pickett: The History of the Philadelphia Brigade*. Shippensburg, PA: White Mane Publishing Co., 1999.

Hagerty, Edward J. *Collis' Zouaves: The 114th Pennsylvania Volunteers in the Civil War*. Baton Rouge: Louisiana State University Press, 1997.

Hayward, John. *Give It to Then, Jersey Blues!* Highstown, NJ: Longstreet House, 1998.

Jorgensen, Jay. *Gettysburg's Bloody Wheatfield*. Shippensburg, PA: White Mane Publishing, 2002.

Longacre, Edward G. *To Gettysburg and Beyond*. Highstown, NJ: Longstreet House, 1988.

Mahood, Wayne. *Written in Blood*. Highstown, NJ: Longstreet House, 1997.

Martin, David G. *Confederate Monuments at Gettysburg*, vol. 1. Highstown, NJ: Longstreet House, 1986.

Miller, Richard F. *Harvard's Civil War: A History of the 20th Massachusetts Volunteer Infantry*. Lebanon, NH: University of New England Press, 2005.

Moe, Richard. *The Last Full Measure*. St. Paul, MN: Minnesota Historical Society Press, 1993.

Murray, R. L, *Redemption of the "Harpers Ferry Cowards,"* Wolcott, NY: Benedum Books, 1994.

Pendleton, Constance, (ed.). *Confederate Memoirs*. Bryn Athen, PA: n.p., 1958.

Penny, Morris M. and J. Gary Laine. *Law's Alabama Brigade in the War Between the Union and The Confederacy*. Shippensburg, PA: White Mane, 1996.

Raus, Edmund J., Jr. *A Generation on the March—The Union Army at Gettysburg*, Lynchburg, VA: H. E. Howard, Inc., 1987.

Reese, Timothy J. *Sykes' Regular Infantry Division 1861-1864*, Jefferson, NC: McFarland & Co., 1990.

Rollins, Richard. *"The Damned Red Flags of the Rebellion,"* The Confederate Battle Flag at Gettysburg, Redondo Beach, CA: Rank and File Publications, 1997.

Sauers, Richard A. *Advance the Colors*, 2 vols. Lebanon, PA: Sowers Printing Co., 1987 and 1991.

Wert, Jeffrey D. *General James Longstreet: The Confederacy's Most Controversial Soldier*. New York: Simon & Schuster, 1993.

Wycoff, Mac. *A History of the Second South Carolina Infantry 1861-65*. Fredericksburg, VA: Sergeant Kirkland's Museum and Historical Society, 1994.

Index